D0866959

MORDECAI

Also by Charles Foran

Sketches in Winter
Kitchen Music
The Last House of Ulster
Butterfly Lovers
The Story of My Life (So Far)
House on Fire
Carolan's Farewell
Join the Revolution, Comrade

MORDECAI

THE LIFE & TIMES

CHARLES FORAN

ALFRED A. KNOPF CANADA

PUBLISHED BY ALFRED A. KNOPF CANADA

www.randomhouse.ca

Pages 724 to 727 constitute a continuation of the copyright page.

Library and Archives Canada Cataloguing in Publication

Foran, Charles, 1960–
Mordecai : the life & times / Charles Foran.

Also available in electronic format.
Includes bibliographical references and index.

ISBN 978-0-676-97963-3

1. Richler, Mordecai, 1931–2001. 2. Novelists, Canadian (English)—20th century—
Biography. 3. Authors, Canadian (English)—20th century—Biography. 4. Jewish
authors—Canada—Biography. I. Title.

PS8535.I38Z67 2010   C813'.54   C2010-901854-0

Text design: Andrew Roberts

First Edition

Printed and bound in the United States of America

2 4 6 8 9 7 5 3 1

CONTENTS

PREFACE

In February 1973, Mordecai Richler was on the "touring Can. Lit. writer's circuit," as he dubbed it. He had agreed to speak at a Jewish student conference in Niagara Falls, Ontario. Then forty-two, and twice winner of the country's top literary prize, he stood at the vanguard of a literature fiercely aligned at the time with the wider phenomenon of cultural nationalism. His status was indisputable; no Canadian literary figure could claim such a high local profile and international reputation alike. It was also problematic for Richler. He did not care for nationalisms, cultural or otherwise. Nor was he interested in being bannered a "Canadian author," having gone to some trouble to establish himself first in England. He wasn't disputing the stamp on his passport, or on his character, courtesy of a Montreal childhood. He knew that his fiction was at its best when he wrote about his homeland. But Mordecai Richler, in addition to being the sort of artist who, like Groucho Marx, wouldn't join any club that would have him as a member, didn't fit any recognizable mould of how a Canadian author should behave, think or write. More to the point, a single-category mould would soon have shattered under his outsized sensibility. As a writer and public figure, he was singular—his own club, in effect.

He was also Jewish. Here, too, his profile was high, and his reputation, at least among many Jews—the self-hating Jew, the anti-Semitic Semite—likewise established. In Niagara Falls, the fact that he was the grandson of a prominent Montreal rabbi was well enough known for someone to have mentioned it at a reception the night before. "I am writing this in my hotel room at seven a.m.," Richler began his speech. "It is a drummers' hotel. A dirty weekenders' haven. Overheated. With a toilet that stinks of dampness. Outside, the town is shoddy. Choked with cheap souvenir shops. Squalid wax museums. . . . I've been on the road a week and, for the second night running, I haven't had much sleep. I tell you all this because in spite of my fatigue, and last night's boorishness, I am flattering you with a special effort. I'm really trying to get through." Later, in a write-up of the tour, he admitted to having been "ensconced in a gloomy, dimly lit bar watching a roller-skating derby on TV with four other early-afternoon drinkers." That rather dismal interlude occurred, presumably, between banging out his early morning remarks on his portable typewriter and delivering them towards the end of the afternoon. Here is part of what he told the students:

> There was somebody here last night with sufficient curiosity— or decency—to ask whether or not I was enjoying myself. To him I would answer my first thought on leaving here last night was, my God, what was I doing in this seedy hotel, in a garish provincial town, locked in with a company of boors. And I seriously considered hiring a taxi, escaping to Toronto airport, and returning home. To civility.
>
> This is not my prepared speech. I left that in my hotel room. Because it would be a waste to deliver it here to such moral and intellectual primitives.
>
> My prepared speech . . . dealt with present literary confusions, modish philosophies, brutalized sex, and rampaging Canadian nationalism, cultural nationalism, which I consider unfortunate. In a word, it dealt with non-Jewish themes, and I don't think such matters interest you. You are altogether too narrow. But let it pass. What I've really come here to question is the nature of your Jewishness . . . about which you seem so confident.
>
> To return to last night.

Once I decided to stay on, my second thought was to buy a bucket of paint, and dab the outside wall of this hotel with swastikas . . . because, above all, I am a considerate guest . . . and I can think of nothing that would have given you more pleasure, a larger thrill, certifying your ghetto-paranoia, as it were.

What I'm trying to say is your Jewishness, unlike mine, is distorted, mean-minded, self-pitying, and licensed not by Hillel or Rabbi Akiba, but by urban ignorance. Bigotry born of know-nothingness.

You feel your survival is contingent on the continuing anti-Semitic pressures of the larger community outside, and where they do not exist, you invent them.

Put another way, I heard more anti-Gentile remarks here last night than I have anti-Semitic remarks in years passed in Gentile company. Something else. I have, in years of speaking in public, in Canada, England, and the United States, never stumbled among such yahoos before.

There was a girl here last night, somebody genuinely troubled, a girl who [seemed] to me bright, who put in a good word for Jewish education. I said I agreed with her, and I agree with her now, with this proviso.

You, my dears, are not only in need of a Jewish education, but a general education. There is hardly one of you, and I include your leaders, who can speak English coherently, let alone grammatically. You are prolix and inchoate. You are unable to postulate intellectual ideas. You confuse name-calling with invective and mistake abuse for wit. Given your mean intellectual equipment, your grasp of real moral dilemmas, I should have thought you would . . . of necessity . . . be overcome with modesty. Instead you are aggressive, ignorance your shield, arrogance your armour. You are also sadly mistaken if you think you represent what is best in our long Jewish tradition.

What had set him off was the group's agitation, voiced to him the night before, over whether they should pressure their

university to alter the date of a dance so it would not conflict
with the Sabbath.

MiGod, MiGod, until last week babies were being fried in
napalm in Vietnam; as I speak, other babies are dying in Latin
America, dying for lack of nourishment. Black men are being
beaten in South Africa. They are deprived of the most basic
human rights. The world is charged with injustice, insult, and
depravity, and you are worried about next week's Friday night
dance. I thought I was coming here to address a group of young
Jewish intellectuals, idealistic students, not a motley bunch of
self-centred adolescents, obsessed with trivia. So foolish, so ill-
informed, as to think grace . . . Yiddishkeit . . . if you like . . .
revolves round the Friday night dance, and whether or not one
attends.

What is more distressing, is you even seem to think that you
have a special hold, a privileged grip, on the Jewish tradition,
and that by observing the Sabbath, eschewing the Friday night
dance, you are doing more to perpetuate it than such infamous
shabbas goys as Leon Trotsky, Franz Kafka, Albert Einstein,
Saul Bellow or Isaac Babel. Or Isaac Bashevis Singer. To make
a random selection. More fools you, because the torch, the tradition, is in their hands, not yours. There is more to Jewishness
than observance. There is invention, imagination, a cherishing
of the book, reverence for scholarship, appetite for life, sensual
appreciation, and, above all, humanity, tolerance. . . .

It would also help to be a mensh, a gentleman, and I found
more grobbers here last night than menshin.

He held them for maybe a declamatory half-hour. Imagine
being a teenager on the receiving end of this demanding, moral
harangue. But March 1973 was not only Vietnam, Latin America
and South Africa; it was less than a year after the massacre of
Israeli athletes at the Olympics and a few months before the Yom
Kippur War. This was no time for youthful complacency about
equating the ideals of Judaism with holding a dance—or

not—on the Sabbath. "Beware of those that don't upset you," Richler warned the students. Upset them he surely did. Crack jokes, he did not; any humour stayed back in the grubby hotel, along with the original speech. That afternoon in Niagara Falls, an event of no consequence to his tour, let alone to his career— these remarks were never published or used again—he must have seemed more a cross of Old Testament prophet with drill sergeant than anything so effete as novelist mixed with cultural commentator. What a public voice he possessed, too—learned and authoritative, blunt and blistering. Decades later, the furious words still read like a combination by a heavyweight at the peak of his form.

He wouldn't have minded the boxing analogy. A kid from the streets of Montreal, Richler never could be, and never wished to be, anything other than a strong, slightly intimidating presence. The highest praise he could accord an individual was to declare him or her an "original." The highest attribute an "original" could possess was "appetite." Appetite meant lust, longing, drive, and ambition. Appetite meant unashamed fullness of character. It also tended to disavow tidiness as being for the meek, the small. A devotee of shaded characters in his novels—the lively scoundrel over the boring nice guy—he transferred this preference into life, seeking, for the most part, the company of the strong, the interesting, the intriguing. No surprise, much of this reflected his sense of himself. Detractors of Mordecai Richler, familiar only with the public figure, tended to affix terms such as abrasive, aggressive and bullying to his manner, in print and flesh equally. Admirers preferred courageous and honest, a man of moral constancy and integrity. Friends employed a whole other vocabulary. For them, he was generous and loyal, reserved and sentimental, kind and even elegant, the mensch he told those students they should aspire to be. To his children, meanwhile, he was tender and loving; to his wife he was passionate, devoted and, above all else, deeply sensitive.

Could everyone be, to some degree, right? Lucky the biographer presented with such complexity in his subject. Luckier still if that character reveals itself with equal force in the work and in the life. Once he found his voice as a novelist, the force that was Mordecai Richler the man began to course through his fiction, quickening it with the same complex, attractive qualities. In a sense, his genius was to compress the two, to become himself on the page, to let Richler be Richler—funny, profane and defiant.

Which isn't to say he wrote about himself. He didn't. He wrote novels, as well as essays and journalism. A pleasure, and a danger, of undertaking a biography about a writer is the apparent overlap of life and art. To draw from the fiction thematic or narrative unity for the life itself might be fun, and appear at first blush a nifty congruence—reading Richler's life into his books and his books into his life—but it's reductive and, in my opinion, incorrect.

There are several attributes a biography can't claim. One is absolute authority or insight. Another is an exhaustive accounting. Given that we scarcely understand our own lives, and either can't recall large swaths of them or do so poorly, this should hardly be a surprise. More interesting, and possibly more surprising, is what a literary biography can manage. It can allow empathetic strangers—that is, readers—an experience of a person whose work has given them pleasure. The biography can "put you there," fleetingly, at the moment of a bris in a Montreal apartment in February 1931 and a Ste. Agathe boarding house in summer 1947, a bachelor's pad on the Spanish island of Ibiza in May 1951 and a London bottle party *circa* 1954. It can then surround those private moments with the public times that inflected them with their specific meaning. And so on, from childhood to adolescence, marriage to parenthood, middle years to advanced, robustness to illness to, finally, death; from juvenilia to gawky first efforts, breakout novel to major works, final statement to last fragments. Tracking and thinking about how the artist and the art grow up and old together, intersect and mutually enrich—or deplete—each other, is what solid biographical craft attempts, offering, at its best, some insights and authority.

In the case of Mordecai Richler's bustling life and long, productive career, there is scarcely any end to the private moments
and public times to consider. Given that he was a novelist who,
though he debuted at twenty-two and published *The
Apprenticeship of Duddy Kravitz* at twenty-eight, may not have
produced his finest works of fiction for another three decades,
the rhythms of that literary career are unusual and intriguing.
That is good material as well.

Finally, the title. Once beyond a rendering of his childhood,
Mordecai: The Life and Times will refer to its subject mostly by
his family name. It may seem odd to then title the biography
so informally. An irony of Richler's profile in Canada was that
this inward man, whose lifelong character and principles precluded role playing, became a celebrity, recognized in the
streets. For a writer possessing limited social graces and less
small talk, casual encounters could be difficult. He wasn't comfortable in public and had trouble negotiating approaches by
strangers. Things didn't always go well. A few outright disasters
are on record.

Regardless, from about midway in his life onwards, Canadians
who had never had any personal encounter with Mordecai
Richler, including those routinely offended by his novels and
journalism, still felt comfortable referring to him by his first
name. Something about severe, judgmental "Mordecai" actually
disclaimed the Olympian. Something about his manner suggested to Canadians that he was, if not quite regular folk, then
a person who fought on their side, who knew their interests and
concerns. They understood that for all his perceived grumpi-
ness and actual reserve he was about challenging nonsense and
asserting real values; that his work was dedicated to what, in
his view, constituted the humane, the real, the civilized. People
rarely "read" public figures wrong for long. If they are shown a
mask, they soon see who lurks behind it. With Richler there
was no mask—no one but him, like it or leave it—and by
bestowing upon his public self the title of "Mordecai," people
were showing their recognition of that truth. The national

outpouring on his death in 2001, closer to the responses to the passing of Prime Minister Pierre Trudeau or hockey icon Maurice Richard than of even the most admired literary figures from his generation, demonstrated the same unmistakable affection and respect. The highest of praise, surely.

PART I

MUTTLE,
MUTTY,
MORDY

I

THE REBBE AND THE *SHAMMAS*

Of course Rabbi Rosenberg would perform the bris. Who better to welcome the newborn son of Moses and Lily Richler into the covenant? Yudel Rosenberg wasn't only the family patriarch, who happened to be both a rabbi and a mohel, qualified to do circumcisions; he was the rebbe, as much guru as leader of Montreal's Hasidic community. They called him the Skaryszewer Illuy, the Genius of Skaryszew. He was a Ba'al Shem, a Master of the Holy Name. Scholar and author, teacher and mystic, Rabbi Rosenberg couldn't walk down a street in the neighbourhood without people seeking a blessing for their child or a word of comfort for themselves. He couldn't enter a synagogue without all present standing up out of respect. Nor could the seventy-year-old walk those streets wearing his long beard and fur hat, black coat and white stockings, without also being called a *maudit Juif,* a damn Jew—or *muzhi Zhwiff,* to his Yiddish-tuned ears—usually from a passing vehicle. Now semi-retired, the rabbi had suffered a stroke a year before. The illness hadn't diminished his intellect at all or his stamina by much, but it had left him with muscle tremors.

Still, as far as his daughter Lily was concerned, no other mohel need be approached. Five years earlier the rabbi had had a dream in which an old teacher from Poland appeared and declared that Rosenberg's daughter would bear a son, a child to be named after him. Lily had dutifully called her firstborn Avrum. The same thing happened during the latest pregnancy. Again, the rabbi's dream prophesied a boy. Again, he should be called after the teacher who had visited Rosenberg in his sleep. This time the name would be Mordecai, known to all Jews from the holiday of Purim and the Book of Esther. Once more Lily agreed without hesitation. Her father was her instructor and idol; he and he alone held full claim to her heart. In effect, he was more than a rabbi and she was more than a respectful daughter. He was the rebbe and she the *shammas*, caretaker of her illustrious parent.

This despite his forcing her to marry a man she did not love, and now held in contempt. The code of Jewish law declares "an ignorant man should not marry the daughter of a priest." Yudel Rosenberg had made a mistake and Lily Richler, née Rosenberg, was paying for his error.

But the bris was hardly the occasion to revisit old sorrows. It took place on Tuesday February 3, 1931, in the north end of the Jewish neighbourhood and in the hollow of the Great Depression. More than two-thirds of Montreal's 58,000 Jews lived within half a dozen blocks of the Richlers' second-floor walk-up at 5300 Esplanade. Approximately two miles long by a mile wide, the rectangular "ghetto," as it was then called, ran from the eastern slope of Mount Royal to a few streets beyond St. Lawrence, a.k.a. "The Main," and from Sherbrooke Street north to Bernard. A city unto itself, it was entirely immigrant and mostly poor. Sounds and smells, languages spoken and foods cooked, situated the district in some corner of Mitteleuropa, mysteriously transported four thousand miles. Even its appearance—the turrets and spires on its commercial buildings, the Byzantine arches of its synagogues, the citizens in black fur hats and ankle-length coats, curled locks and kerchiefed heads—was more likely to evoke Cracow or Kiev. East of it sprawled an enormous French city, also largely poor, with its own smells and sounds and its own priests and churches. To the west, over the wooded mountain, lived a group who happened to be the wealthiest, most powerful people not only in Montreal or the province of Quebec but also in the country known as Canada. Those people spoke English.

In west-of-the-mountain Westmount—as in behind-the-mountain Outremont, the enclave exception of French-speaking affluence just west of the ghetto—residents lived in brick and stone houses. Often these were grand edifices, with finished basements and backyards. Frequently they were mansions, complete with fairytale towers and Corinthian columns. Everyone else, especially in the tableland called "The Plateau," lived in apartments. Singular to Montreal were block upon block of uninterrupted residential buildings, two or three storeys high. Each floor constituted a unit, similar in size and design. Outside staircases ran from the upper or middle floor down to the sidewalk; balconies, however small, overlooked the street, with smaller ones facing the back alleys. Shops clung to corners or clustered along commercial avenues. In the French streets, churches and convents of imposingly greater dimensions dwarfed the residences, sometimes consuming entire blocks with their rectories and gardens. In the ghetto, synagogues, mostly modest brick buildings, nestled amidst the apartments.

Fitting snugly into the duplexes and triplexes in both French and Jewish districts were families of half a dozen children or more. Decorations may have been sparse, but Plateau apartments were extravagant with people. "Be fruitful and multiply," admonished the mitzvah. For Catholics, there were similar priestly commands, along with the undeclared turf politics of the province, played out using procreation as a tool. *La revanche du berceau*, it was called. The revenge of the cradle.

At 5300 Esplanade, the furnishings were modest. For Orthodox Jews, a circumcision is equal parts commandment and celebration. The ceremony, often conducted in the home, is simple. Candles are lit and prayer shawls donned. The baby is passed from adult to adult before being held by the *sandek*, the godparent usually chosen from among the elders. The mohel, not necessarily a rabbi, recites blessings in Hebrew and then performs the brief procedure. Now officially named and blessed, the child is declared brought into the covenant in order to live a life of Torah, full of good deeds, including a worthy marriage. The

parents sip wine on behalf of their offspring to commemorate
the rite of passage. A meal is laid out.

Moses and Lily Richler were the hosts. She was a petite woman,
the second-youngest of seven full siblings, and had the Rosenberg
family forehead and nose, the dark eyes and thin lips more naturally pursed than smiling. Glasses, thick-lensed and heavy-
rimmed, obscured her eyes, which were dark and angry—her
most striking, if unsettling, feature. Though she had kept her
black hair shoulder-length as a child, she now wore it short,
parted on the side and often tucked behind the ears. There was
no nonsense to her face or hair, or her plain dress. There was no
nonsense to her person.

Moses Richler, age twenty-nine, was slim and narrow-
shouldered, slightly below average height for his time. His complexion was swarthier than his wife's, and his sharp, hawklike
features were distinctly of the Richler clan, who tended to have
small noses and mouths and burning black eyes. In his father, and
in many of his siblings, it was a fierce countenance, as though the
bearer was always paying close, skeptical attention, always alert.
But in Moses, despite his being the eldest of fourteen, the features
transmitted nearly the opposite impression. He was meek and
mild and had trouble holding gazes. He had little to say.

Unable to make the rent on their previous apartment, Moses
and Lily Richler had fled it during the night, their belongings
piled in the back of a Model T Ford. The sitting room at 5300 was
furnished as befitted a family that might relocate again in haste.
Relatives occupied any chairs left over once the four grandparents had been seated, or else stood in the doorway watching.
Cakes and lemon tea were served. Conversation was in Yiddish.

If Lily's mood was sombre that day, she had cause. She had
borne a second son after a near-fatal miscarriage in 1929. Money,
as much as health, had kept her awake with worry during this
latest pregnancy. The fee for the obstetrician had been $50,
which she had borrowed from an older sister, and she had no
idea how they'd settle the bill with Dr. Burgess and the Montreal
Maternity Hospital, where Mordecai was born. Moses was being

paid irregularly for his work in the family business, and was taking odd jobs to supplement his income, including delivering 50-lb bags of coal up flights of stairs. Now she had two sons to look after, and a father who required her care. For his part, amiable "Moe" Richler may have tried countering his wife's intensity with a few jokes, his sense of humour lively but odd. Then he would have retreated to where the children gathered around their *zeyda*. Rabbi Rosenberg loved his grandchildren as much as they loved him. He dangled his white beard over their faces. He made drawings of men with long beards to give as gifts. His own offspring, eleven in total, were grown up and gone—gone from their parents' home, aside from the youngest, Abraham-Isaac, a rabbinical student receiving instruction from his own father, and gone, for the most part, from Montreal. Only Lily and her older sister Rifka, or Ruth, were still in the city.

Among the children surrounding the old man that afternoon would have been Lily and Moses' older son, Avrum, and Moses' youngest brother, David. Avrum was five, David three. The other grandfather, Shmarya Richler, far less warm-hearted or cuddly, was still more prodigious. Moses and David served as bookends to his fourteen, most of whom still lived at home.

The marriage of the eldest Richler boy and the youngest Rosenberg daughter had been arranged by their parents back in 1924. From the start the barter had been money for status, security for *yiches*, the connection with Talmudic lineage prized by Orthodox Jews. Shmarya Richler was a prosperous businessman. He and his younger brother Jacob had formerly co-owned a scrapyard in Griffintown, near the port, and had done with some of their profits what good Jews were supposed to do—support charities and Hebrew schools, and help fund the building and maintenance of synagogues. Jacob Richler in particular revered Rabbi Rosenberg, visiting him at home and quietly helping out with expenses. Believing it would benefit both sides, Jacob had suggested the match. The entire Richler family would gain *yiches*. In turn, the rabbi, who had migrated from Poland to Toronto and, more recently, to Montreal, lured by a congregation with promises of the income supplement gained by controlling the kosher meat certification process, could rest easy knowing he had secured stability for Lily. Shmarya Richler offered him verbal assurances that Moses, then employed as a driver at Metal Smelting and Refining, would soon be made a partner. He took his prospective daughter-in-law to a jeweller and purchased her a ring and pendant. He furnished an apartment for the couple in advance of the wedding, which he paid for.

In private, the bride had doubts. It wasn't only that Lily was barely nineteen and believed herself in love with a law student who had given Hebrew lessons to one of her brothers. (Her father had sent the boy away.) It was Moses himself. He certainly wasn't a likely soulmate for a bright teenager with a self-described tendency to chatter and a hunger for knowledge. She expressed her misgivings to her parents without threatening to disobey them. Her mother was certain that Moses would grow on her. The rabbi told his daughter that she could mould her husband into the man she wanted. Nothing about the wedding thrilled Lily more than her dance with her sixty-two-year-old father. People stood on chairs to watch the lucky girl waltz with the rebbe.

For families like the Richlers and Rosenbergs, the perceived options were limited. Orthodox Jews did not marry secular or Reform Jews and were reluctant to trust even Conservative Jews to live the faith, beginning with an embrace of the Torah as the literal word of God, handed down to Moses. The Decalogue—the first ten commandments, given to Moses on Mount Sinai—was only the foundation for the other mitzvoth, the codified rules for Jewish living. These numbered 613 in all, as found throughout the Torah, and while a couple of hundred of them were obsolete, an Orthodox Jew was expected to abide by the rest. That meant keeping kosher and observing the holidays. On Sabbath it meant abstaining from any labour, including riding in a car or bus, lighting a stove or turning on a light. Men dressed each morning for prayer: tefillin on the forehead and a *kippah* or yarmulke over the skull, the tallith around their shoulders. In public they wore black on black, to show mourning for the destruction of the Second Temple in Jerusalem in A.D. 100. Hasidic men grew beards, long ones, and some of the wives shaved their heads and donned wigs, to ensure they would not be attractive to other men. (Lily's mother, Sarah-Gittel, was one such wife.) There were rules about these matters, and rules about many of the rules. No compromises were allowed. There was only the covenant and those who honoured their faith, and their fathers, by keeping it. Orthodox Jews married other Orthodox Jews.

And so, following one uncompromising custom, the morning after the wedding Shmarya Richler barged into the nuptial chamber, intent on checking the bedsheets for blood. Lily was aghast. If he said anything, Moses probably tried swallowing his embarrassment with a quip. He was, and would remain, a gentle, passive man, fond of movies and cabarets and playing pinochle in the backrooms of local shops for a quarter-cent a point. His young bride was, and would remain, intense and difficult, a loner excited by music and paintings, a rabbi trapped in a woman's body. Maybe the union brought happiness to their families and communities. For each other, it produced mostly the opposite.

The early years were at least secure. Lily had been wed into, if not actual prosperity, then an approximation of it. "Best Rosh Hashonah Greetings to our Jewish clientele!" read an advertisement in the *Canadian Jewish Review* from the distributor of the high-end Paige and Jewett sedan car. The date was September 1926, and among the clientele was "S. Richler, 55 Prince St (Metal Smelters Ref. Ltd)." Moses, resolving to strike out on his own, opened "Richler Auto Parts," the East Coast distributor for Sieberling Tires, at 4226 St. Lawrence Boulevard, in the heart of the neighbourhood's commercial district. It was a good business at a good address.

Overdue with Avrum earlier that same year, Lily and Moses had moved back in with her parents at 9 Esplanade, at the foot of the street. This was also a good address. An elegant brick

mansion on the same block housed a social club and later the
Jewish Public Library. The first proper retirement home for the
community had opened up near Fairmount. Across the street
sprawled Fletcher's Field and the wooded east slope of Mount
Royal, where Jews strolled along the promenade on Saturdays.
With the red-brick Grenadier Guards Armoury at the corner of
Rachel, the fields were filled with soldiers executing manoeuvres.
Once Moses started earning money selling tires, they moved to
another building on Esplanade, adjacent to the armoury. Avrum's
earliest memories were of parades, and martial music drifting
through the open windows.

But the modest good fortune did not last. The Richler family
finances experienced their own crash a few months in advance
of October 1929. An investment involving cement blocks failed,
leaving Shmarya cash-strapped, at risk of losing business and
property alike. October 29, 1929, Black Tuesday, put an end to
easy purchases of nearly everything for nearly everyone. Richler
Auto Parts soon became one of the many empty storefronts
along The Main, and Moses returned to doing odd jobs for
irregular pay at the scrapyard on Prince Street. The family abandoned the lower blocks of Esplanade, with their views of the
fields and mountain, their elegant buildings and respectable
Jews, for the stretch of the street north of Mount Royal, where
flats had less cachet and lower rents. Even with Moses bringing
home car batteries to empty the acid and salvage the lead at the
kitchen table, the couple could not manage. Collectors threatened to shut off the water and gas. Paying grocery bills meant
not paying for the coal.

Lily's parents, whose own survival was dependent on the
grace of benefactors, sent them food packages. At her behest,
the rabbi spoke with her father-in-law about the earlier promise
of a partnership in the company for Moses. Shmarya Richler
seemed to consider his eldest boy a natural menial; his younger
son Joe was already showing more of a head for business. Lily's
distress at her marriage went from chronic to acute. How could
her parents have done this to her? She vented anger and assigned

blame. The elderly couple absorbed her disappointment. Though dismayed by the idea—the life of Torah precluded failure in marriage—Yudel Rosenberg began to be receptive to a divorce. But then Lily got pregnant again. Her mother tried cheering her up. "When a child is born, he brings with him his own destiny, his own ability and his own luck," Sarah-Gittel Rosenberg said.

On this note was born the second child of Moses and Lily Richler; born to a mother who prayed at once that he would become a rabbi and a father who did not even wait at the hospital to learn the gender of his child, removing himself instead to the movies. Eight days later, at his bris, the baby was named Mordecai—no middle name, like his brother—and he was soon being called Muttle, a diminutive that would stick until supplanted, especially among friends, by Mutty. As a teenager he would answer to Mordy or Mort.

Ten days after the bris, the cover of the *Canadian Jewish Chronicle* featured a photograph of a distinguished gentleman in yarmulke and black robe, his side curls still dark but his beard, nearly down to his belly, the salt-pepper of a raccoon's tail. The subject was shown at work, poised over the page of a book, quill in hand and ink pot on table. "Seventieth Anniversary of Rabbi Jehudah Rosenberg," ran the caption. "Local Talmudist and Scholar." The weekly Anglo-Jewish journal also ran a photo of the Rosenberg clan gathered in a hall on Hutchison Street to fete the patriarch on his seventieth birthday. In one corner stands Moses in a tuxedo, his son Avrum next to him, with Lily in the front row beside her sisters, her eyes pins behind those thick glasses. Absent is the newborn Mordecai, likely in the care of his other grandmother.

The coverage of Yudel Rosenberg's birthday was especially meaningful for his daughter Lily. Despite her hapless husband and domineering father-in-law, and her entrapment in a poverty whose very avoidance had been the trigger for her union with the son of a scrap dealer, she now had two boys to mould. Both sons bore the names of her father's teachers. Both were Rosenbergs at least as much as they were Richlers. With Yudel Rosenberg still alive, she could expose Avrum and Mordecai to his wisdom and culture; expose them to his Judaism, sophisticated and rich with the mysteries of the Talmud and tales of the Golem.

II

THE SIMCHAT TORAH

As the *Canadian Jewish Chronicle* noted, Rabbi Rosenberg was a Talmudist, author of twenty volumes on Jewish law and legend, including a translation of sections of the Zohar, the essential Kabbala text. But he was also a populist storyteller. The best stories, especially for his grandchildren, concerned the Golem. They told how Jews in sixteenth-century Prague had lived in fear of persecution. The dreaded "blood-libel"—an urban legend concocted by the majority Catholics—accused them of the ritual murder of Gentiles, for their own obscure reasons. The accusation made it easy to scapegoat Jews for any crimes being committed and to take righteous revenge. The one hope was for Jewish residents of the city to solve the murders themselves and so prove they were blameless. Enter the Maharal—a.k.a. the Chief Rabbi of Prague, Judah Loew ben Bezalel—master of both human relations and supernatural feats, along with his magical creature.

How the Golem came into existence was one of Yudel Rosenberg's most popular tales. His story went like this: By the banks of the Moldau River, in the dead of night, the Maharal and his two rabbi assistants moulded the form of a man out of clay and loam. Seven times one assistant, and then the other, circled the lifeless shape, reciting the words that had come to Judah Loew in a dream. Finally the chief rabbi himself enacted the ritual, and then all three incanted a line from the *Book of Creation* invoking fire, water and air. The creature opened its eyes. Ordering it to its feet, they dressed it in clothes and, with dawn approaching, marched through a sleeping Prague to the Jewish Quarter. There, the Maharal assigned it a name taken from a term in the Talmud for unshaped matter, and issued it instructions to safeguard Jews from harm. Only a select few needed to be aware of the Golem's true identity and purpose. To others he was a simpleton on whom the Maharal had taken pity. Yossele the Mute, he was dubbed, and he could be found seated in the corner of the room most days and nights, head resting in hands. His master's command alone would cause him to come to life and go about the tasks for which he had been created.

Most people in Jewish Montreal knew the Golem stories. They were as much a part of their heritage as the taste of *lokshen kugel* and the sound of klezmer music. As refugees from Galicia, Russia, Lithuania, Romania and Russian Poland, they understood the wishful thinking that underlay tales of Jews being saved from catastrophe by superheroes. Though most could trace the legend to the Talmud, fewer would have been aware that the "modern" Golem, the creature who could speak, read and write, and who fought against the blood libel that had been the scourge of Jewish lives in Eastern Europe in the late nineteenth and early twentieth century, was the creation of their own Rabbi Yudel Rosenberg.

Born in Russian Poland in 1859 to a family with deep rabbinical roots, Rosenberg emerged from a yeshiva education with a reputation for brilliance. Talent could not spare him the poverty of the itinerant rabbi's life. To supplement his meagre income in Tarlow, Lublin, Warsaw—where his tenth child, Leah, or Lily, was born in 1905—and finally Lodz, he began publishing books in rabbinical Hebrew of classic tales either loosely retold or out-and-out fabricated. A degree of fame came his way in 1909 with *The Golem and the Wondrous Deeds of the Maharal of Prague*. It claimed to be an edition of a manuscript belonging to the "Royal Library of Metz" and the handiwork of the Maharal's son-in-law. As no such library existed, and as the folkloric tales of the sixteenth-century Prague rabbi and his creature were so brash and innovative, putting forth the duo as community saviours, authorship was widely understood to belong to Rosenberg himself. More fanciful books followed, several of them maintaining the ruse of being manuscripts "found" by the rabbi, including a lifting of an Arthur Conan Doyle story that takes the Maharal to London to solve a theft. Even when simply collecting legends about Elijah the Prophet and King Solomon, he couldn't resist tossing in stories of his own invention. Yudel Rosenberg was a maker of fictions.

Once in Canada, however—the family emigrated in 1913, leaving several grown-up children behind—his creative energies ebbed. He lost contact with his publishers in Europe. He may have lost his sense of the audience, or even the landscape, for his imaginings. Whatever the reason, Rosenberg's final books were less inspiration and more scholarship and stern instruction.

But with his grandsons, the rabbi relaxed back into the deeds of the Maharal and his Golem.

Avrum and Mordecai saw as much of their *zeyda* as their mother could arrange. With the arrival of her second son, Lily Richler had made a private vow to raise them in "Jewish isolation." Skullcaps were forever on their heads, indoors and out. At night she dressed them in tallith katan, the sleeveless undershirts worn by men, as ordained in Deuteronomy 22:12. On Friday afternoons the boys would be instructed to tear off sheets of toilet paper in preparation for Sabbath, then would watch on Saturdays as a Shabbas goy, a French kid from a few blocks over, earned a few pennies turning the lights on and off so the family would not break any rules. She described the festivals and helped Avrum and Mordecai memorize the prayers and blessings. By the age of three each could recite the four questions at the Passover table in Hebrew. At the festival celebrating the year's reading of the laws, the Simchat Torah, they waved tiny flags as elders paraded up the synagogue aisle with the Torah scroll on display. Lily sent Avrum to Hebrew studies at the Young Israel synagogue on Park Avenue, and began putting aside money for the extra instruction Mordecai too would receive once he started school.

Her father remained a blessing. She translated his thoughts and stories for her sons. Sometimes seven-year-old Avrum, already fluent in Yiddish, also tried explaining to his kid brother what was being said. Mordecai's grandparents spoke Yiddish, Hebrew and Russian. His parents—both born in Poland, though Moses was brought to Canada as a baby—retained Yiddish inflections in the English they had learned in local elementary schools. But Avrum—Voomy (or Vroomie, as nicknamed by his mother)— and Muttle were from Montreal: North American English was their native tongue.

At first, the isolation Lily desired for her sons was easily maintained. Moses, his upbringing also observant, supported the regimen. Residing in the belly of an urban shtetl ensured security from any breach, especially with the rebbe a regular sight on the streets. "Do you know who you are?" a cousin recalled being asked by one of Rosenberg's admirers. With their grandfather the Richler boys walked either to the Young Israel synagogue at Park and St. Viateur or, less often, to the smaller synagogue on Jeanne Mance where the rabbi liked to pray—both within a few blocks of the house. Being well under bar mitzvah age, and so allowed to carry things on the Sabbath, Mordecai gripped the purple velvet bag containing the prayer shawls. Moe's barbershop, where the brothers got their first haircuts, was on the corner of Park and Laurier. For bagels there was the St. Viateur bagelry or its rival on Fairmount. Steinberg's grocery was over on The Main, near Mount Royal. Vegetables and fish could also be bought at the boisterous outdoor market at the corner of Pine.

Things didn't get any easier for the Richlers after the birth of their second son. Moses found only intermittent work, usually at the junkyard, up at dawn driving the company truck to Griffintown for a shift. Lily continued to elude the bill collectors who came knocking. Around the same time that Avrum saved his toddler brother from choking on a nail—"What did you do?" his mother shouted at him, when Mordecai began to cry—he contracted scarlet fever. For two months he languished in an isolation ward in the fever hospital. A sickly child, Avrum went on to suffer bouts of diphtheria, appendicitis and a mild case of polio. Medical bills kept Lily Richler's mood black and her anxiety high. By her own admission, she was an impatient mother, her discontent infecting her relationships. Physical contact with her children—kissing and hugging, even touching—was infrequent, and her antipathy towards her husband made their sex life fraught. No sooner was Avrum released from hospital than she slapped him across the face for complaining. Moses could slip away to the movies or a cabaret to escape her ire. The boys had no such option.

Being with her father seemed about the only thing that brought Lily contentment. So in 1934, when another midnight flight from another cold-water rental landed the family back with Yudel and Sarah-Gittel, the humiliation carried a blessing. The elderly Rosenbergs were now living at 4587 Jeanne Mance, in the block between Mount Royal and Villeneuve. Only Abraham-Isaac remained at home. Actor and playwright Israel was a New Yorker, manager of a popular Yiddish theatre. Daughter Ruth, married to a prosperous tire merchant, lived across the "tracks" on Davaar Avenue in Outremont, where wealthier Jews were colonizing the eastern fringes beyond the social divide of Park Avenue. Two other daughters had settled in Ontario.

With only three occupants for six rooms, the Rosenberg apartment was scandalously under-occupied. More the norm in the Jewish ghetto was six rooms filled with double that number of residents, among them children and grandchildren, grandparents and great-grandparents, spinster aunts from Minsk and second cousins, once removed, from Bratz, sponsored and now ensconced at the back, near the furnace. That, or boarders were taken in, obliging kids, already grouped three to a cramped room with a single bed, to move over for a surly fourth sibling, his own chamber now rented to a stranger. On Jeanne Mance there was ample space for Moses, Lily and the boys, and if Moses had any objections to being put up by a retired rabbi, the body count over at his parents' house—fourteen or so in Shmarya Richler's two-storey dwelling; eleven at his brother Jacob's next door—can hardly have been more attractive.

His wife's contentment was likely worth the mild humiliation of not having his own house. Finally, Lily was back among learned Jews. Finally, she could resume her duties as *shammas*, last performed with the intensity she craved during the halcyon days before her arranged marriage. Yudel Rosenberg, who still sat on the Council of Montreal Orthodox Rabbis, welcomed a daily procession of visitors. Escorted by Lily into his study with its floor-to-ceiling bookshelves and desk piled with manuscripts, supplicants would air their complaints and seek his advice. The rabbi would take down the relevant volume from the Code of Jewish Law while pondering how to resolve sexual difficulties between aging couples or the duty of children to pay for their parents' dentures. Gershon the shoemaker with bad teeth and Getzel the frustrated husband would bring their concerns to Rosenberg. An herbalist as well, he would provide homemade remedies for various ailments—tonics and poultices mixed in the kitchen from rows of jars.

Avrum was now at school every day—Bancroft Public, on St. Urbain—but Mordecai sat at the kitchen table or on the floor in the sitting room while cantors and scholars paid their respects. Among the more unusual guests was a Catholic priest who, aware of Rosenberg's reputation for openness, came to discuss theology, Lily serving as translator. Men raising funds for old-age homes and yeshivas, unemployed rabbis looking for a reference, also came knocking. A woman appeared on the landing one day with a chicken. She asked the rabbi to declare the bird kosher. Suspecting she could not afford another one, he gave the chicken his blessing.

Yudel Rosenberg wasn't beyond needing the extra cash brought in by performing weddings and circumcisions. If the wedding ceremony was held in the Rosenberg dining room, it meant the couple were too poor for a synagogue. Lily would hold up one of the rods of the *chuppah*, the canopy under which the vows were exchanged, and bang out the wedding tune on the family's upright piano: *"Chusn, Kaleh, Mazel Tov"*—"Good luck, bride and groom!"

There was a further reason for Lily to be grateful for being with her parents. Hard times abounded in the neighbourhood. Many of the shmatte factories off St. Lawrence had shut down, or were constantly reducing staff. Men stood idle on the street corners while their women competed for piecework jobs as seamstresses, sewing by candlelight in kitchens. The sight of families being evicted by landlords, their belongings piled at the curb or onto the backs of flatbed trucks, was disheartening, as was the opening up of a soup kitchen at Esplanade and Mount Royal. Diets were reduced to eggs, flour and potatoes. Unable to afford coal, men offered to sweep the wood shavings at lumberyards, packed them into potato bags and hauled them home. Paying for medicine for your sick child or yourself—Lily suffered from inflamed eyelids and, unable to afford an ophthalmologist, had to resort to free outdoor clinics—constituted one stress. The prospect of a hospital stay in those pre–public health care days was another.

Nor could she count on Moses, ostensibly employed by his father, even to return with the money he earned. Her father-in-law, she believed, was playing his own son—and her entire family, by extension—for fools. Shmarya had already humiliated her once before by forcing Moses to bring her in on a cheque-cashing scam involving local grocers. Moses had also acted twice as witless middleman in schemes perpetrated by the elder Richler upon his own in-laws. Years earlier, when the rabbi lent Moses a thousand dollars to start a brick-making business, the work to be done in the yard of the Richler compound, the money went missing, the result, he was told, of the cheque being stolen and cashed. More recently Lily's sister Ruth, encouraged to act as silent partner in a business scheme with Moses as front man, had felt similarly duped. According to Rosenberg family lore, her money wound up in Shmarya's pockets as well.

Lily dissected Moses' failings as husband and man with her father. She complained that Shmarya Richler directed his children's lives and did their thinking for them; he made the rules and they obeyed. For a while, she and her rabbi parent plotted to wean her husband from his clan. He should forsake the scrap business and, regardless of the failure of Richler Auto Parts, start again on his own. Though he lacked education—Shmarya had seen no reason for him to attend high school—Moses had a natural facility for bookkeeping. An accountancy firm, perhaps, using start-up funds that the Rosenbergs would help raise. Yudel Rosenberg even wrote to a son-in-law in Hamilton asking if he could find work for Moses. But, Shmarya warned his oldest boy, now in his mid-thirties, leave Montreal and his family would disown him. Once more the Richler patriarch promised Moses that long-delayed real position, with a real salary, at the yard. Once more it did not materialize.

In truth, Lily was none too keen to renounce everything and everyone she knew for a job in Ontario. Hamilton was hardly the Promised Land. As well, in early 1935 Yudel Rosenberg made a stunning announcement; he and Sarah-Gittel were going to relocate to Jerusalem. The rabbi had bought four plots of land in Palestine from a salesman plying the diasporic trade some years earlier, and would build a house. Word had reached him that the Chief Rabbi of Palestine was set to retire, and his name had come up as a possible replacement. At seventy-five, his stroke six years in the past, he felt he could still do the work, and his eyes lit at the prospect of finally seeing the Western Wall and Temple Mount. Lily, he decided, should accompany them, bringing along her boys, who could grow into their Jewish identities in the place— if not yet the state—that was Eretz Yisrael.

So this time it was the rabbi himself who began musing aloud about the inevitability, even the rightness, of his daughter divorcing the junk dealer's son. When Lily told Moses as much—she did so regularly, and with little tact—he shrugged off her threats, disbelieving, she sensed, that anyone could be so decisive. Her mother, too, remained opposed. God's order of events could not be altered, Sarah-Gittel declared, however mysterious they were.

All these things the Richler boys took in, to the extent, and in the ways, that children absorb the adult activities that are in the process of shaping them. Avrum would retain vivid memories of his maternal grandfather: being taught to draw and play chess in his bedroom; walking into synagogue clutching his hand as everyone stood up out of respect; pleading and occasionally winning the privilege of sharing the old man's bed, thus allowing the boy to have a burning question answered—did the rebbe sleep with his long beard inside or outside the blankets?

Little Muttle, the lively child with the fine dark hair and wincing smile, the tall forehead and Dumbo ears, would later recall his illustrious grandparent only faintly and unreliably. How the feather of his beard passed over the faces of both his *yingelech*. How he smoked in bed and kept a canary in the house. The time he called his youngest grandchild into his study, sat him on his lap and made a drawing of first a horse, then a rider, then a rider with a beard and black satin coat, a saucer-shaped fur hat called a shtreimel—exactly as the rabbi wore.

In the summer and fall of 1935 the Richler boys witnessed huge changes within the Rosenberg home. First their bubbe suffered a stroke that left her an invalid, needing months of nursing to recover partial health. Her husband concocted ointments for her bedsores. Every Friday Lily stripped Sarah-Gittel and washed her. Then Yudel Rosenberg himself had a heart attack. That doubled Lily's nursing duties, leaving little time or energy for the boys. With Moses either at the junkyard or playing cards with friends, Avrum and Mordecai were shunted to the Richler compound up on De la Roche Street. Lily spent hours at the bedsides of her parents. She listened to the old woman's anxieties about the future; once Yudel was gone, who would look after her? With her father she sat enraptured while he foresaw the spiritual journeys yet to be taken by all his children and grandchildren. There would be no actual journeys for him, though; Jerusalem and the Holy Land receded once more to dream and yearning.

During the Simchat Torah festival that October, Avrum and Mordecai attended synagogue with their parents at the Young Israel. Lily had agreed, against her nursing instincts, to spend the holiday with the Richlers. The festival, which literally means "rejoicing in the Torah," was a joyful day for the congregation. Celebrating the end of the yearly reading cycle of the Torah, with the death of Moses and his burial in an unmarked grave, the festival expresses the most fundamental principle of life—the cycle of birth to death to birth again. First came the reading from Deuteronomy. Then came the fun: the Torah dance on Simchat Torah night. Kids paraded around the synagogue seven times carrying the twin scrolls of the Sefer Torah, bells jingling, while the adults clapped and sang. Later followed the kiddush, the party where grown-ups sipped schnapps and children ate squares of honeycake and kugel with raisins.

Lily tried calling her parents that Saturday evening. Getting no reply, she dialled a neighbour. Her father, having decided to host a kiddush, had collapsed and been taken to the Jewish General Hospital. Three days later he died. Many Jewish businesses shut down for the funeral, and a police escort was required to move the body through the crowd from Paperman's Funeral Home on St. Urbain Street to 4587 Jeanne Mance, where it lay, coffin closed, for visitors. "A Light Has Gone Out in Israel," ran the headline in a Yiddish paper.

III

RICHLER ARTIFICIAL STONE WORKS
(NO SUCCESS)

On the day his grandfather died, Avrum Richler was pulled out of school by his Uncle Israel. Instead of bringing him to the apartment on Jeanne Mance, Israel Richler drove him up to 6911 De la Roche. Mordecai had already been transferred to the care of his Richler bubbe. For years the boys had been spending weekends and holidays running between the houses of their second *zeyda*, Shmarya Richler, and, until recently, their great-uncle Jacob next door, eating the *lokshen* made by the twin grandmas at 6911—Esther, their actual grandmother, along with *her* mother, Molly, then in her late eighties—and the chocolate cakes baked by their Great-aunt Mirel at 6897. Their cousins— sixteen-year-old Louie, a big brother to Avrum, and eighteen-year-old Anne, who had been babysitting Mordecai since he was an infant—acted as minders, and their Uncle David, nicknamed Duddy, was a playmate. But Jacob Richler had recently suffered a bankruptcy, relocating his household back to the old neighbourhood. Even without the Jacob Richler clan around, Shmarya Richler's house must have been a bewildering home for a four-year-old, who surely could not tell an uncle from a cousin or one grandmother from another. Being so young, and cut off by language from his Yiddish-speaking elders, Mordecai knew little of what was unfolding.

But his brother was old enough to register, and feel, the change. Entering the dining room at 6911 De la Roche that day, Avrum was confronted by his grandfather, seated at the head of the table surrounded by his brood. "When is your grandfather getting home?" Avrum recalled Shmarya Richler barking at him. "When he gets better," the nine-year-old replied. "He's dead!" his grandfather said in his clipped English. The boy broke down in front of his cousins.

Shmarya Richler tended to spare words but not feelings. He was a wiry, sharp-eyed man, a Jehovah's enforcer who ruled house and business with a firm hand and devout Orthodoxy. The firm hand was applied to his own children and, later, his grandsons. The Orthodoxy took forms both benign and tyrannical. Evenings, he expected his progeny to join him at prayers. Saturday afternoons, he demanded family gatherings in the dining room, yarmulkes on all heads, for recitations of passages from *Ethics of the Fathers*, a collection of parables extolling the observant way. The recitations were in Hebrew; Shmarya criticized and rebuked the performances of his children and grandchildren in Yiddish. Discussions of a sort would follow, mostly clarifications of the many rules, none of which could be questioned. The women were largely silent figures, moving from room to room like discreet servants. Children and grandchildren kept what distance they could from their hot-tempered patriarch.

Born in August 1877 near the family village of Rava-Ruska, in a corner of Galicia where three nations overlapped, Shmeryahu Reichler had served as a young man in the Austrian army. Jews in Europe's various imperial armies were not welcomed by their fellow countrymen, and Shmarya told stories of routine beatings by Cossacks. Anti-Semitism within the military only matched broader prejudices. Jews were then absorbing the implications of the pogrom in Kishinev, a programme of persecution initiated by an editor at the newspaper that would shortly become the first to publish the notorious *Protocols of the Elders of Zion* in Russian. Going AWOL in 1903, Shmarya made his way to Liverpool, boarding a ship, the *Lake Ontario*, in late February, with a train ticket to Chicago tacked on to the price. In steerage he met a man from a neighbouring village whose train ticket was for Montreal but who had relations in the American city. Not minding where he settled, Mordecai's grandfather swapped destinations sometime between February 25 and March 12, when the manifest showed "S. Reichler" disembarking at the port in Saint John, New Brunswick. Once in Montreal, Shmarya quickly raised enough money, most likely working for the railway, to send for his kid brother Jacob.

Jacob Reichler had joined the Austrian army as well, and his older sibling believed he might not survive it. He arrived in Canada in the fall of 1903 and found a job in a clothing store, and then in a silent-movie theatre. Soon, a third brother, Shmuel Wolfe, turned up, while a fourth opted for the States. Back in Poland it had been arranged for Wolfe to marry a niece named Mirel Deutscher. When he backed out, Jacob married her instead. They emigrated to Canada together.

Shmarya had left his own young wife, Esther Druker, in Galicia. Just nineteen, she had given birth the previous December to their first child. Already, he had an heir: Moses Isaac, born on December 25, 1902. Mother and infant crossed the Atlantic in the summer of 1903.

Richler family lore about the early years emphasized brothers Shmarya and Jacob coming into their own as observant business and family men. Both quit working for Gentiles over the issue of breaking Sabbath laws, joining together to rent property in Griffintown and open a scrapyard and smelter. The business wasn't hereditary—back in Galicia the family had been peddlers and farmers—but they were good at it, tough and resilient. Metal Smelting and Refining at 55 Prince Street thrived until the Depression, when it subdivided once for Jacob and his boys to branch out as lead merchants, and then again for several of Shmarya's sons to venture into scrap. "Reichler" may have drifted into "Richler" around 1910 when a sign for a business venture came back with the name newly spelled. Much later, a family story claimed, the brothers, who did well during the First World War by recycling rubber, wholesaled the product to Sam Bronfman, for use in lining boxes for smuggled bottles of liquor.

Other tales centred on Shmuel Wolfe Richler. The youngest of the three Canadian brothers, he was also the wildest. Though he worked for Shmarya and Jacob, Wolfe may have robbed his own family business one year, on Yom Kippur. The Richlers constructed a foundry in their yard, and he managed the furnace until contracting lead poisoning. During the war Wolfe Richler bought stolen sheets of copper, the fault lying, perhaps, in his lack of English. The theft brought ignominy to the family and sent him into exile. He drifted around the United States until settling in the northern Ontario city of Fort William, his pursuits ranging from prospecting to Prohibition activities of a less defined nature. Wolfe only showed up in Montreal again after the Second World War, broken and sick, his family scattered. He died in 1952, though not before an eleventh-hour marriage—his third—to his own niece, a woman who had stayed in his house as a girl.

But Shmarya and Jacob were upstanding Jews. They married once and for good, bought homes for their expanding broods and supported their local synagogues. They sponsored a half-brother from Poland, bringing him into the business. Purchasing houses side by side in a largely French neighbourhood allowed Shmarya to excuse any activity on the Sabbath as the behaviour of Gentiles. The large yard also meant they could keep sheep and goats and grow corn. Regardless, the lingering stigma of Wolfe's stolen copper sheets may have partially impelled the patriarch, through Jacob's friendship with Yudel Rosenberg, to push for the marriage of his oldest boy, Moses, to Lily.

The other spur could well have been the emerging character of Moses himself. Wolfe Richler's status as prodigal son wasn't the only Bible story resonating within the family. In 1922 Shmarya had encouraged his twenty-year-old son in a scheme to bake bricks in the yard between the houses. Richler Artificial Stone Works, it would be called. Moses dutifully tried mixing mud with straw and then firing and chiselling the bricks, exactly as his namesake's people had done. On his foot-long chisel he wrote an inscription in orange chalk. *Used by M.I. Richler*, it read.

Richler Artificial Stone Works. 1922. De La Roche Street. NO SUCCESS. As predicted by its maker, the venture failed.

On the day more than a decade later that Avrum and Mordecai were brought to De la Roche Street for minding, Lily Richler's plan to raise them for the rabbinate also met its demise. That the Richlers were a business family, at risk of luring the boys into scrap metal, would never be the issue. Nor would the family's limited interest in any culture beyond that approved of by their Orthodoxy—at least, not for a few years. Ironically, despite the Hasidic conservatism of the Rosenbergs, it was the Richlers' brand of "Jewish isolation" that wound up killing any rabbinical impulses in the brothers. After the death of Rabbi Rosenberg, the oppressiveness of the Judaism practised by the Richler family became the tone that religion itself took in the emerging think-ing, and sense of identity, of the boys. Grim piety, often masking hypocrisy, was no advertisement for a life of Torah.

Once Yudel Rosenberg was buried in the Baron de Hirsch Jewish cemetery, Moses, Lily and the boys moved in permanently at 4587 Jeanne Mance. Someone had to look after the ailing Widow Rosenberg. When not carrying on conversations with her dead husband, she was scolding her grandsons, one of whom, five-year-old Mordecai, was a handful.

Sarah-Gittel's subsequent medical crisis—a massive stroke in March 1936 that resulted in partial paralysis and permanent loss of speech—proved irreversible. Doctors informed Lily that stroke victims who did not die immediately often lingered for years. From here on, her mother would be confined to a wheelchair and require assistance with everything, including bodily functions. By Lily's account, her siblings were bent on placing their mother in a nursing home. Ruth, married to a prosperous tire merchant named Ben Albert, began making arrangements to install her in a new nursing facility downtown. But mindful that Sarah-Gittel's mental capacities were likely undiminished, and recalling, per-haps, her mother's favourite prayer from the *Tseno Ureno* about not forsaking the elderly, Lily insisted on becoming her surviv-ing parent's keeper as well.

On April 3, 1936, the *Canadian Jewish Review* ran a memoir "I Pay a Visit to the Beloved Rabbi," by Lily Rosenberg Richler. The tale, the second of several she would publish over the next three years, mixed soft nostalgia for her eternally blameless father with undercurrents of fantasy and revenge about her own fate. Retelling tales of Yudel Rosenberg's career as counsellor to his Orthodox congregants, Lily rehashed alleged Richler scams, hinted at her loveless marriage to a boor, and even mused on other directions her life might have taken. The "Beloved Rabbi" tales were both psychologically acute and untidy. A forceful, complex character lay beneath their bland surfaces.

Had Mordecai seen a copy of the magazine around the apartment, he would have gazed at an appealing image of his mother. Lily addressed the camera frankly, unsmiling but agreeable, her eyes cloaked behind glasses. A serious person, grave and dignified.

A thousand dollars was all the cash the rabbi left in his will. Lily demanded, and received, help from her siblings with the costs of looking after Sarah-Gittel. She also requested an audience with the Jewish Community Council. In a room of senior rabbis she argued for a small pension for Yudel Rosenberg's widow, as repayment for his lifelong services. The request was granted. Lily then hired an attendant to massage her mother's limbs, dedicating herself to most of the nursing duties, including the lifting and cleaning of the ravaged body. Avrum and Mordecai, unaccustomed to physical affection from their mother, were nonetheless instructed by her to embrace their bubbe each day and devote a few minutes to talking to her. The only reply their grandmother could make was a vocable, described by those who heard it as either "avoy-you, avoy-you" or "buoyo-buoyo." It was the one sound Sarah-Gittel Rosenberg would make during the final seven years of her life.

Lily's state of mind must have been more distressed than usual. Plans to flee Canada for the Promised Land with her esteemed father and beloved mother, her boys by her side, her marriage left behind and happily forgotten, had come to nothing. Less than nothing, really, with the rabbi dead and her mother diminished, and Moses Richler still her lawfully wedded. A cruel blow, never mind how vague and unlikely the Eretz Yisrael dream had been. She had been destined for a life more commensurate with her family prestige and her self-regard. Again, she'd been thwarted.

Yet another apartment change followed in spring 1937. This time, the relocation was just a few doors down, to 4599 Jeanne Mance, though with wheelchair-bound Sarah-Gittel in tow the move was arduous. But it saved a little money, and Moses accepted his wife's arguments that the cash was better spent on Avrum's afternoon Torah classes. Lily may also have warned her husband that she intended to have Mordecai receive the same after-class instruction at the synagogue *and* properly educate him during the day at Talmud Torah. The parochial school for more affluent neighbourhood Jews, Talmud Torah combined regular classes with extra Hebrew language instruction. It charged tuition fees that, while affordable to Jews across Park Avenue in leafy Outremont, posed hardships for the vast majority still crowding the streets running up from Fletcher's Field. Lily was adamant and Moses, no doubt, quiescent—proud, too, of studious Avrum, a good boy, mild and smart, and of Muttle, now of school age. His youngest may well have been as intelligent as his brother; for sure, he was already more mouthy and fearless. A double dose of Jewish education would straighten him out.

That boy, newly turned six, doesn't seem to have registered the event of January 28, 1937, that soon brought much of the city to grief. Hockey player Howie Morenz of the Montreal Canadiens crashed into the boards at the Forum, fracturing his leg in several places. In early March, he died of complications from the injury. Within a few years Mordecai would bleed Habs *bleu, blanc et rouge*, and the team cheered on by French factory workers and railroad men would be his team as well.

Moses Richler, who avoided trouble, would say and agree to almost anything to get his grim wife to stop berating him, stop telling him, often in front of his sons, that he was no good, and she had deserved better. Ill-advised efforts at cooling her ire with pranks—an ink pot on her chenille bedspread, a knish filled with absorbent cotton—ended badly. Jokes went over no better. "Hey," he might ask, hoping to earn a laugh from the boys and a reprieve from her, "do you know why we eat hard-boiled eggs dipped in salt water just before the Passover meal?" To which he'd deliver the punch line: "To remind us that when the Jews crossed the Red Sea they certainly got their balls soaked."

No success there, either.

IV

<hr>

5257 ST. URBAIN STREET

On moving day in the spring of 1938, seven-year-old Mordecai, now called Mutty, sat on the front staircase of still another apartment building watching his father unload furniture from a truck with some uncles. The truck, a slightly less decrepit Model T—the previous vehicle had been abandoned by Moses in the street after a wheel fell off—belonged to the scrapyard; much of the furniture, including the upright piano formerly used to serenade brides and grooms, had until recently been part of the Rosenberg household. Besides the piano, the most difficult haul up the staircase was Sarah-Gittel Rosenberg herself. His grandmother wasn't heavy—her wheelchair may have outweighed her—but the stairs were steep.

The Richler uncles had driven over to help, and his Aunt Ruth as well. Ruth Albert, an attractive, high-spirited woman who reminded men of the actress Jean Harlow, would have had no trouble finding a parking spot for her rumble-seated Hudson. A car, even a jalopy, cost four to six months' salary—residents of this street didn't own many.

St. Urbain wasn't poor like east of The Main, with its rats and cockroaches and single coal stoves for heat. Boasting an alleyway running behind the block, for garbage collection and peddlers, it was one rung up the ladder from neighbouring Clark, whose occupants had to haul their refuse back through apartments to the sidewalk. But neither had St. Urbain the elegance

of Esplanade or Jeanne Mance in the blocks below St. Joseph.
Their flat was the middle floor of a triplex. Surrounding Moses
and Lily Richler now were Montrealers with names like Falcon
and Blatner. Moving to the block of St. Urbain between Fairmount
and St. Viateur meant an extra five-minute walk for Mutty to
Talmud Torah and, starting that fall, an extra ten minutes for
Avrum to Baron Byng High School. For their parents it meant a
separate room for Sarah-Gittel, as well as a small saving in rent.

Seated on the stairs that morning, the boy would have gazed
out at a street much like every other one he had lived on. The
apartment at the top of the outdoor landing would have struck
him as equally familiar. Of standard Plateau design, 5257 had
seven rooms and two balconies. A tiny room off the front hallway, large enough for a desk and chair, would soon belong to
Moses. The desk had nooks, in one of which he kept his diary, a
daily record of events and, it seemed, reflections on everything
from business transactions to the quarrels, insults, injuries and
betrayals he endured. No need for Moses to lock the drawer to
keep the diary from prying eyes; he composed the entries in a
code of his own devising. That room opened onto the balcony
that Mordecai later, returning to a locked house, would climb
onto to gain access through the window. The double parlour next
to it had a chesterfield and two sofa chairs. The piano filled one
wall, until Lily had to sell it for $25 to make the rent. The RCA
radio took up another corner, and on Sunday mornings would
be tuned to WEVD New York for the plays written and performed
by Israel Rosenberg and his wife, Vera Rozanka, a.k.a. the Yiddish
shiksa. It was rare to hear Lily and Moses laugh together.

At the back of the living room, incongruously, was a single
bed. Moses slept here. On the floor beside it were the kind of
magazines—*Popular Mechanics* and *Reader's Digest*—that he
encouraged his sons to read, for educational purposes, along
with issues of *Doc Savage* and *Black Mask*, comics preferred by
adults and children alike. Their father's domain extended a few
feet down the hallway to an angled closet beneath the interior
staircase. Moses kept a bottle of whisky in the closet, along with

stacks of the science and pulp fictions he read. A year later he bequeathed the chamber to Avrum, for use as a darkroom—his eldest had been given a Kodak bellows camera for his bar mitzvah.

Beyond the stairwell chamber, the apartment became Lily's space. Down the hallway was the dining room, including a table and buffet, with two small bedrooms off it, one for her, another for the boys. Their room could hold two beds, each covered in a checkered blanket, and little else. The kitchen, farther back, had a sink, a coal-fired stove and an icebox, a table covered in a flower-patterned cloth. Though the vegetable seller was able to negotiate the winding interior staircase at the rear, sacks of coal and blocks of ice had to be hauled through the apartment from the front. At the back was a chamber housing the furnace and coin-operated water heater. The heater earned such homes the designation "cold-water flat," though the presence of any kind of furnace distinguished the building from its poorer cousins east of St. Lawrence. The heater also dictated the economy of a once weekly bath for most families, including the Richlers. There was a separate water closet and, finally, the small room where Sarah-Gittel Rosenberg stayed. From the kitchen Lily could keep an eye on her mother and respond to her calls of *avoy-avoy*. Often she asked one of the boys to go see what their grandmother wanted. They could scarcely tell, but would report guesses, based on her gestures and eyes. Avrum was expected to empty her commode.

St. Urbain served as an artery into the downtown from the north island and beyond. Refrigeration trucks and travelling salesmen stopped for a bite at Wilensky's, then located at the corner of Fairmount, a hundred feet away. Wilensky's sold "specials" and sour pickles at the front, along with cigars, used books and magazines. Moe Wilensky cooked and his brother Archie retailed the cigars. Both were Communists, and their cheap prices were a reflection of their political beliefs. Their phone booth was popular with locals who had no home lines, and the counter stools were often occupied by men waiting to place calls with bookies. The bagelry around the corner on Fairmount was also familiar—twelve bagels sold on a string—and a block north loomed the enormous St. Michael the Archangel, built for the Irish community in 1916. If Mordecai got lost, he could find his way back using the church's green dome as a beacon.

Horse-drawn wagons delivering coal and ice, dairy products and produce moved along the inside lanes of St. Urbain, a clip-clop in summer and a jingling of bells in winter, when runners replaced wheels. "Vadermelon!" the fruit man called out on hot days. Housewives addressed the milkman and iceman by family name; they were in and out of their apartments, sometimes daily, the latter obliged to make repeated trips up and down those staircases, pinching the heavy blocks with tongs. The ragmen who plied the alleys, their decrepit wagons pulled by scrawny horses, informing occupants in Yiddish of their interest in buying rags and bottles, generally remained nameless. Some also bought old tin pots, making them bottom-rung scrap dealers.

The tram along The Main, two blocks east—the #55 running from the Craig terminus up to Cremazie Boulevard—rattled on its tracks, the ding-ding audible from 5257. Balcony-to-balcony and staircase-to-staircase communication between housewives during the day and husbands out for a smoke in the evenings was now mostly in English. Ragmen aside, the majority of the deliv-erymen were French-Canadian, their wagons boasting names like Dion and Brunelle. English with some French was the mon-grel lingua franca for exchanges, though Yiddish crept in as well. "So *fiel*, monsieur," a woman bargained with a merchant, "for this chicken? *Vous* crazy?"

Like immigrant streets in New York and Chicago, St. Urbain teemed with the progeny of Old World optimism about New World prospects. With its wide sidewalks and block-length alley-ways and deficit of cars to interrupt ball games, and with Fletcher's Field a long enough walk to make it worthwhile only for an afternoon outing, the road was as much playground as traf-fic artery. On the day Mordecai Richler became a resident of St. Urbain, two or three hundred kids around his age were pouring out, or being tossed out, of those crowded apartments, told to occupy themselves until dinner. They might stuff socks with rags to serve as footballs or whack them with sticks of wood doubling as bats. They might construct scooters from the orange crates left behind the shops, along with abandoned or stolen roller-skate wheels.

They could also smoke. Seven years old was a bit young to be scavenging with the older boys for things to stuff onto the end of discarded butts or into clay bubble pipes bought for a penny, but not by much. Corn husks and orange rinds worked. So did banana leaves and bamboo sticks, once they'd been shredded. When not in the alleys, up to no good, St. Urbain boys could be found out-side Wilensky's, sharing a cherry Coke and showing off their yo-yo tricks. A bona fide champion in a red jacket stopped by one day to shame them with his versions of "walking the dog" and "racing around the moon."

For a child, Anglo Montreal, where kids had names like John, James, Melinda and Vanessa, was a rumour of fairytale mansions and preposterous wealth on the far side of Mount Royal. Pea-soupers—a.k.a. working-class French—still kept to themselves over to the east, though the more Mutty wandered, the more he came into contact with boys and girls called Jacques, Pierre, Marie and Francine. Affluent French Canadians, it was true, pros-pered a scant few blocks from the ghetto, in tree-lined Outremont, and within shouting distance of better-off Jews who lived across Park Avenue, including the Alberts and, later, Uncle Bernard Richler and his family. But for now, the children he knew went by names like Hershl, Yankel, Malke and Zippora.

Local newsstands did little to clarify any sense of his status as a "Montrealer." At the stand where St. Lawrence and Fairmount met, he might have noticed a dozen or more news-papers competing for trade. Because of the neighbourhood, the city's English dailies, the *Gazette*, *Star* and *Herald*, dominated, alongside the *New York Daily News* and *News of the World*. Copies of the largest newspaper, *La Presse*, would be kept for French speakers with business along the street (often with pawnshops and moneylenders), along with smaller piles of *Le Canada, La Patrie, Montréal-Matin* and the high-brow *Le Devoir*. Yiddish newspapers were displayed, including, from Montreal, *Der Keneder Odler,* and those brought up on the train from New York. Moses bought the *Herald*, along with one of the New York English dailies. *"Daily Mirror!"* Avrum and Mordecai would shout as they entered the apartment, eager to read Dick Tracy, Alley Oop, Red Ryder and Li'l Abner. Moses himself went straight for the track results, before proceeding to the celebrity gossip and quirky news items, repeating salacious stories of misdeeds to his sons, despite Lily's scowls.

Farther down on St. Lawrence, students from the Université de Montréal had menaced local Jews a couple of years before, claiming to be hunting for Communists. Police rarely interfered with such outbursts, especially after the 1936 victory of Maurice Duplessis's Union Nationale in the provincial election. Most Jewish Montrealers believed the new premier denigrated Jews: "Members need not listen to the only Jew in the room," he once declared, interrupting Joseph Cohen, the member for the St. Lawrence district, in the National Assembly. The complex Duplessis had Jewish friends, but nevertheless selected Adrien Arcand, leader of the Quebec fascist party, to be part of his first cabinet. "Now more than ever we have to fight against the Jews," Arcand had written three years before being made labour minister. He spoke of their "subversive ideas and despicable methods."

As St. Lawrence was the nerve centre of the ghetto's commerce and radical politics, St. Urbain over the next decade achieved standing as its working-class soul and criminal heart, a view crystallized by a *Time* magazine article after the war calling the street "the Hell's Kitchen of Montreal." Jewish mobsters had controlled much of the gambling and narcotics business for a decade. Only a few years earlier, in 1934, a hood named Charlie Feigenbaum had been gunned down on the block of Esplanade between St. Joseph and Fairmount. Starting in the mid-1920s, the district was watched over by one of the city's few Jewish cops, Detective Inspector Ben Greenberg.

The apartment at 5257 St. Urbain would remain Mordecai's home for the next ten years. His formative memories began on the street. On any given block an adult could exchange words with a rabbi dressed in medieval garb or consult a matchmaker, buy Superman and Batman comics and newspapers in four languages, shoot a game of snooker or bet on a horse, inhale the scent of smoked meat and the tang of working men lined up outside the public baths. By late spring, 1938, the Richler with the thick head of black hair, watchful eyes and sombre features might be off on an errand atop his brother's hand-me-down bike to find his father. He would start by riding along St. Viateur to the Young Israel synagogue on Park, hoping to meet up with Avrum, who would be emerging from his after-school cheder with Mr. Feinberg in the back room (where he himself would be starting extra religious instruction soon enough). If Avrum didn't know where Moses was, the boy might continue along Park the two long blocks to Laurier. Farther up, at Bernard, across from Pascal's hardware, stood the cavernous Rialto cinema. Near the corner of Laurier was the Regent. Though his father might well be at the movies there, more likely he would be hiding away in a downtown cinema. With any luck Mutty would come across him chatting with the men in the barbershop at Laurier and Park. He was tall enough now to sit on the black leather seat, no longer needing to perch up on a board slipped between the arms of the silver chair for his monthly 25-cent haircut—a passage, of sorts.

If Moses wasn't there either, he might find him playing gin rummy and eating chocolate cookies in Schacter's Cigar & Soda on Laurier. Schacter's was across the street from the Stuart Biscuit Company, where kids could buy broken biscuits and cupcakes for pennies. Talmud Torah, his day school, was a block farther down Jeanne Mance, at the corner of St. Joseph; beyond that was the imposing YMHA, built through the generosity of Mortimer Davis, a fabled wealthy Jew. He was too young then to know of the divide between his kind and the "uptown Jews" of Westmount, though if any class distinctions registered in his imagination, they were within his twin Galician clans. There was

Uncle Bernard's hot-water shower in his apartment in Outremont. There was also Aunt Ruth's cigarette holder and perfume. And during rare visits to the Albert house on Davaar, the boy observed the finished basement, the set of encyclopaedias, the suit of armour in the front hall.

For a kid, even a brash one, Mount Royal was intimidating, an urban demesne where people rode horses and skied in winter. Fletcher's Field, adjacent to it, was over a thousand yards long and a quarter as wide, and stories were told and retold about the battles between French and Jewish kids at the south end of the park, or whispered about the carryings on in the woods. By the time the boy reached the southeast corner he would be eight blocks below his house, near Paperman's Funeral Home and Baron Byng High School. Two blocks farther east and he'd be at the corner of St. Lawrence and Duluth. Here was the epicentre of the ghetto, and of Jewish Canada: the offices of Wolofsky's newspaper, with Horn's cafeteria, gathering place for the intelligentsia, on the ground floor below it; the Balfour building, heart of the shmatte trade, plus the commercial block that housed Schwartz's Hebrew Deli, Moishe's steakhouse, the Schubert and the Colonial Baths. A few years later, when Mordecai was attending school at Baron Byng, he would grow intimate with this geography, declare it, too, part of his backyard.

Many of the institutions barely predated his birth. Though Montreal was an old city, where a tiny number of mostly Sephardic Jews had exercised quiet influence for nearly two centuries before the arrival of the Eastern Europeans, Jewish Montreal belonged to the twentieth century. Schwartz's had opened its doors in 1927, the Colonial Baths in 1914. Steinberg's grocery dated from 1917, Schreter's department store from 1920. The brick fortress of Baron Byng had begun teaching the children of those shtetl immigrants in 1921. Farther north, past the Mont Royal Arena where both the Maroons and the Canadiens had once played, things were even newer: 1929 for Fairmount Bagel and 1932 for the St. Viateur bakery. Only a year before Jewish immigration to Canada was formally shut down, the ghetto was nearing its apogee. Mordecai Richler was coming of age in time to witness the growth, and the beginning of the decline.

———

On May 18, 1939, King George VI and Queen Elizabeth arrived in Montreal on the first royal tour of Canada by a reigning monarch. A stop in the dominion's largest city was mandatory. Still, officials in Ottawa had concerns about including Montreal. Three months earlier Mayor Camillien Houde had declared that if England went to war with Italy, Quebec might side with Mussolini. How would Houde behave before "his" king and queen? Or Premier Duplessis, who the previous year had stopped by a private club favoured by provincial Liberals and urinated into the fireplace? Would *le chef*, as Duplessis liked to be called, also misbehave before the royals? Then there was the small matter of the million French-speaking residents. A motorcade was planned, twenty-three urban miles in all, with the expectation of large crowds lining the sidewalks, waving the country's flag, the Union Jack, and singing "God Save the King." The itinerary couldn't avoid the swaths of Montreal that "belonged" to its majority solitude.

More problematic still was the undeclared reason for the tour: to ready the Dominion of Canada to once more take up arms in support of the motherland. Escaping a war with Nazi Germany was now unlikely. French Canada had shown scant interest in England's conflicts in the past, and the carnage of World War One had hardened the indifference. Mandarin foreheads broke into a sweat at the possibility of a lukewarm, even hostile response to the royals in certain city neighbourhoods.

They needn't have worried. Cardinal Villeneuve, head of the province's Catholic Church, told his flock that he expected the king and queen to be accorded a warm welcome. Predictably, English Westmount and the downtown were picture-perfect: adoring crowds and beaming monarchs, all beneath a sunny spring sky. The French cheered as well, first in Outremont, along

Côte St. Catherine, below the hillside residences of the aristoc-
racy—including the teenaged Pierre Elliott Trudeau—and then
later along St. Hubert Street and Mount Royal. Though this crowd,
too, waved the Union Jack, flags showing the tricolours of France
and the yellow and white of the Vatican could also be spotted.

Only on Park Avenue might the king and queen have noted
a slight chill. The route had skipped the ethnic sights of St.
Lawrence Boulevard. It had, in fact, forgone the neighbourhood
where Jews lived. But Fletcher's Field marked one ghetto
boundary, and with the sweatshops along The Main allowing
workers the afternoon off, and schools closed for the occasion,
both sides of the avenue filled with seamstresses and cutters,
peddlers and scrap merchants, schoolchildren and their teachers. Many did cheer and wave the flag but others, among them
Communists and Labour Zionists who disapproved of the
British position on Palestine, simply watched the motorcade,
polite but silent. In the crowd was eight-year-old Mutty Richler,
for whom the day was a holiday with a parade.

V

BATTLES

He had a *pisk*, the boy. A mouth. At Talmud Torah, where Mordecai studied Hebrew in the mornings, math, French and English in the afternoons, he had a reputation. Fellow students admired his boldness while fearing his tongue. He was among the fifteen or so children studying together from grades one through seven, but also apart; a ringleader who was simultaneously aloof. Teachers were baffled. The child was smart—hardly a surprise, being the grandson of Yudel Rosenberg; real *k'vod*, or distinction—and gifted, in particular as an artist, forever doodling in his notebooks. He liked to challenge them, especially the old, underpaid men who taught Hebrew and, by the by, twisted ears and rapped knuckles. "Obviously, Adam and Eve's sons had to marry their own sisters," he might say. "Was that allowed in those days?" For his trouble he would be told to wash the blackboards, or be sent down to the office of the school principal, Mr. Magid, for discipline. Suspension would be threatened. A call placed to his home.

Along with Lily Shatsky, also of St. Urbain Street, Mutty Richler was one of a handful of kids from the ghetto side of Park Avenue. His classmates from Outremont had better clothes and more pocket money; they were driven to school in cars. Their homes were houses too, located on elegant streets named Davaar and Querbes. He was also one of the rare students with an Orthodox lifestyle. Talmud Torah may have been a parochial school for Jews wishing their children to be educated within a religious framework, but the majority still came from families that were either secular or Reform. For those kids, the Torah wasn't the literal word of God and the 613 rules not a chokehold. They didn't have a grandfather who took a belt to his grandchildren for minor infractions of religious laws. They didn't have a mother who made her son wear his tallith katan, marker of a Hasid—though the boy was careful to stuff the tassels, *tzitzis*, inside his trousers to avoid mockery.

It was Lily Richler who walked down to Talmud Torah in the middle of the day to answer complaints about him. In her no less sharp manner and her verbal quickness, Mr. Magid glimpsed one source of Mordecai's emerging character. Rumours abounded concerning his parents' marriage; even his classmates recognized that the household on St. Urbain wasn't happy. Lily did nothing to quell such rumours, chastising her husband in public and telling all who would listen about her thwarted hopes. Among Moses' failings was his role as breadwinner; he found the annual fees for Talmud Torah a burden. The father who couldn't provide and the mother who couldn't stop telling everyone.

The case of smart, scrappy Mordecai Richler required special handling.

Leibel Yalofsky, long-time Torah instructor in the cheder at the Young Israel synagogue, shared the principal's pain. Any fond memories of studious Avrum Richler dissipated in the presence of his brother. No amount of knuckle rapping or ear twisting would stop the boy from sneaking peaks at the *Herald* comics folded in his lap, or reading one of his father's Ellery Queen mysteries, during the twice-weekly class. For this, Lily and Moses paid an extra $8 a month. Walks home from the cheder, especially after dark, brought the Richlers into contact with the French kids who trolled neighbourhood boundary lines. Being scrawny helped; they dashed along St. Viateur, dodging the Hasidim men in black coats and the women pushing triple-carriage prams, until they lost their enemies in the maze.

Conflicts, battles, loomed. On St. Urbain Street, Mordecai seemed in perpetual dispute with his mother. After one scolding from Lily, the nine-year-old announced that he was leaving home. "Fine," she said. "I'll make a sandwich for you." When Avrum, then a freshman at Baron Byng, realized they were both determined, he tried talking sense into them. Off went Muttleke, as she called him, in a downpour. Hours later the doorbell rang and there he stood, shivering. "I forgot my rubbers," he said. Lily dried him with a towel, saying not a word.

Moses Richler, busier than ever at the scrapyard—the looming war, and the hasty buildup of the Canadian air force in factories around Montreal, were benefiting the family business—sat at the kitchen table at the end of long days in his underwear. Stout and fleshy, his bald head shiny in the light, he scrubbed his callused hands to get out the grit and grease. He also belched and farted and clipped his toenails in full view. True, he didn't appear to enjoy the company of his own family, especially his wife. "You're nothing!" was one of her favourite taunts. "And I don't want my children to be nothings!" Slipping off to the Gaiety Theatre on Saturday nights, he would roar with pleasure at the jugglers and comedians. Nothing could compare, however, with the show's climax: the striptease by Peaches or Anne Curie or the legendary Lili St. Cyr (her specialty involved simulating being ravaged by a swan). On Sundays as well, Moses would depart early and return late, bleary-eyed from marathon movie viewings at the Princess, then the Capitol, then the Palace or Loew's. About the movies themselves, he had little to say, though he liked catching production inconsistencies—clocks on walls left unchanged from scene to scene, tanks with their fuel gauges showing empty.

For her part, did Lily consider how her behaviour affected others? Mutty's cousin Lionel, sometimes in the house while his mother, Ruth, was helping with Sarah-Gittel, decided that his aunt had two personalities. One second she was friendly and sweet, the next vicious and unhinged. Always, she carried herself like a fallen queen and saw her boys, especially Mordecai, as princes. Still, that didn't stop her from chiding him. "Why can't you be more like Lionel?" she would say. Away from his mother, he would shove his cousin and throw wild punches in revenge.

The same thing happened with his uncle and playmate, Duddy. In 1938, the boys started spending more time together after Shmarya Richler, giving up on the idea of raising his family outside the ghetto, rented a two-storey house at 5444 St. Urbain, directly across from Moses and Lily. But after his grandfather, citing Sabbath laws, destroyed some chemistry set test tubes they were playing with by smashing them against the wall, Mordecai blackened Duddy's eye out of frustration. For this, he got a thrashing from his grandfather. His relationship with his playmate cooled as well.

One day he found himself in the office of Richler Smelting and Refining, as Shmarya's side of the business was now called, in LaSalle, possibly after a drive out to St. Hubert airfield or Dorval with Avrum and his Uncle Joe, who let the boys wait in the truck while he negotiated the purchase of scrap from planes being dismantled by Canadair. There he witnessed his grandfather giving short weight on his scales to an Irish peddler. When he informed his father, seeking vengeance for the beating, he was rebuffed. "What do you know?" Moses scolded, a common refrain, adding that Gentiles, being anti-Semites, got what they deserved. That was hardly the point, especially for a boy desperate for a sense that his parent would stand up for him—or for anything. It also wasn't a denial. A few years later Moses explained a standard Richler scrapyard scam to Avrum: weighing the truck before picking up a load, collecting it, then sliding heavy stones under the carriage to falsely increase the total.

Mordecai was beginning to chafe. When he visited the house across the street, passing through the kitchen to the yard out back, he could be sure of a smile from his bubbe Esther. (Molly, his great-grandmother, made no effort.) But his *zeyda* was becoming a nemesis. Saturday afternoon "lessons" in the living room, after a week at Talmud Torah, extra cheder instruction from Mr. Yalofsky, plus Shabbas observance, was too much. To then be expected to sit with his cousins and recite passages from a book about respecting elders? Nevertheless, he often stayed for the Havdalah ceremony after sunset, marking the end of Sabbath.

Once Shmarya Richler had made a blessing over the spice box, shaking it and passing it around for all to inhale the fragrance, he would hand out quarters, pinching cheeks as he did. "Shabbas graft," Moses Richler called the cash.

Twenty-five cents bought two comic books from Wilensky's or Schacter's, with change back. Avrum Richler and his friends had had to content themselves with newspaper comic strips, which were plentiful but left them at the mercy of the adults who controlled the paper. By the time Mutty came of reading age, slim ten-cent Tip Top Comics were promoting the adventures of Tarzan and The Batman (the article was soon dropped), Wonder Woman and Captain Marvel. Stories were action-packed and violent, with sex a giddy undercurrent. The early Batman shot the bad guys, while Wonder Woman tied them up in S&M gear. Kids across North America loved reading the comics under bedsheets or in backyard sheds; to trade them, resell them, collect them in secret or, if their parents were tolerant (or, like Moses Richler, a fan as well), in the open. They loved the unruly, disrespectful tone of the pulp stories and superhero fantasies.

Jewish kids had special reason to identify. Many of the cartoonists, scarcely older than their readers, were first-generation Jewish North Americans. They were crafting strident visions of right and wrong, good and evil, born of their own childhoods smoking orange rinds and watching their fathers lose their jobs in Depression-era America. Superman emerged in 1938 from the nineteen-year-old imaginations of Jerry Siegel and Joe Shuster of Cleveland. (Shuster was originally from Toronto.) Though the Superman of these children of the European diaspora wasn't the first comic hero to battle evil, he soon came to embody the idea, and the look. It was the look—the capes and masks, leotard pants and tight shirts over bodybuilder torsos—that excited kids. But the idea, or perhaps the wish, behind the cape was still more potent. Evil was evil indeed in the universe of comic villains. Good needed to be no less strident or powerful. "Now listen to me, Clark," says Superman's foster father in the very first edition, "this great strength of yours—you've got to hide it from people or they'll be scared of you." To which his foster mother adds, "But when the proper time comes, you must use it to assist humanity."

Why would humanity need assisting, even at the level of ten-cent escapism, in 1930s North America? Many adults and teens alike may not have had a clue. But in certain places, certain neighbourhoods, the anxiety, the foreboding, was real, and had been for years. Among the magazines in the Richler apartment were the issues of the *Canadian Jewish Review* featuring Lily's arti-cles. Each issue offered an editorial. On September 18, 1936, the editorial "Deepening Shadows" spoke of how holding the Olympics in Berlin meant "the last star of hope was extinguished for the German Jew, as for any of the myriad others who are being brutally badgered by the present regime." A year later the editor-ialist lamented the "harrowing picture [out of Europe] of tidal wave upon tidal wave sweeping down and seeking to destroy the children of Israel." Twelve months later again, in the issue for September 23, 1938, the review wondered: "Shall we then con-clude that Nazism and Fascism will continue indefinitely? That, indeed, would mean hopelessness and doom and endless misery for mankind." As if to arc back gently to the local situation, the editorial denounced as "the lie of the century" the assumption that all Jews were communists—a theme promoted by the Quebec fascists who were tolerated by the government of Duplessis.

Within months of the start of the Second World War, with Mutty Richler and millions of other adolescents and teens fol-lowing along, Superman, at least, began combatting Hitler and the Germans in monthly instalments. So did stalwart Captain America, portrayed in similar skin-tight apparel and outrageous musculature—in this instance, chest and shield bearing the stars and stripes. The overture to a 1941 edition explained: "As ruthless war-mongers of Europe focus their eyes on a peace-loving America . . . the youth of our country heed the call to arm for defense." A box on the same page showed Nazi fifth-columnists joining the U.S. army to "carry out the führer's plans." "Yah," a fellow truncheon-wielding thug says. "Everything is in readiness!"

When American comics were banned in Canada in 1942 to save on paper, black-market prices climbed as high as 25 cents per issue. The Richler brothers wrote and produced their own book instead. Called *Catman*, the comic was eight pages long and, with no photocopying available, existed in a limited edition of one, shown carefully to friends and select family. Story by A. Richler, drawings by M. Richler, declared the cover.

The "phony war" of the fall and winter of 1939–40, after Germany conquered Poland, was an eerie eight-month waiting period that ended with the *blitzkrieg* of the spring. The invasions of Belgium and the Netherlands, and the stunningly swift capitulation of France in June, announced the world war so many had feared. Adrien Arcand, who had welcomed the Nazi sweep across Europe, was arrested at his party offices in Montreal in July 1940. The RCMP found swastika banners and fanciful plots for a Canadian Nazi army of seventy thousand fifth-columnists ready to carry out the Führer's plans. Immigrant Italians with similar sympathies for Mussolini, especially those expressed after June 10, 1940, when Italy declared war on the Allies, were also rounded up. Internment camps in Ontario and New Brunswick were quickly bursting with suspect Germans, Italians, Hungarians and Finns—a wide, indiscriminate cull. One camp in New Brunswick became home to a high-profile enemy within: Camillien Houde, the popular mayor of Montreal. Houde earned his time behind the fence for encouraging fellow Montrealers to refuse the federal government's request, issued that summer, that all males over the age of sixteen register for possible service. The *National Resources Mobilization Act*, claimed authorities, wasn't conscription in disguise. But the mayor disagreed, and said so once too often.

One-fifth of all eligible Jewish Canadian males eventually enlisted to fight, some 16,880 in total, along with 279 women. A third of these were Montrealers, some of whom responded to the sandwich-board sign outside a recruiting office on St. Lawrence that proclaimed, "Canada Needs You" and "Enlist Here Now!" in English, Yiddish and French. Old men at the Young Israel wept at the sight of a youngster in a first lieutenant's uniform.

Different tears were shed when the Kugelmass boy died crashing his Harvard Trainer near Montreal. Another young man from the synagogue who signed up, to the shock of his father, was Israel Richler, the second of four Richler boys then of military age. Mordecai's uncle was a self-taught mechanic who enlisted in the Army Ordnance Corps, in part to avoid being conscripted into the so-called Zombies, regiments eligible only for service within Canada. Shmarya Richler's great fear was that his boy would end up desecrating the Sabbath and being forced to eat non-kosher food. Another son, Max, would also join, and strike a similarly glamorous pose in his brown uniform, though he was stationed in Montreal for the duration. "The Jewish Commandos," they were called by envious kids.

And Mutty Richler was already a combat veteran. Waiting until his older brother and parents were out of the apartment—he was in no danger of being caught by his bedridden grandmother—he would crawl on his belly from the kitchen to the front door, Red Ryder air rifle in his good arm, Arab bullets whizzing past. It was 1920 in the village of Tel Hai in the Galilee. Arabs, unsettled by increased Jewish immigration, had begun attacking settlements. The boy was pretend-playing the one-armed Zionist hero Yosef Trumpeldor, part of a group of Russian Jews who had made early aliyah to Palestine, who carried on fighting with a mortal stomach wound, expiring with the words "It is good to die for our country" on his lips.

The feats of Trumpeldor were the street talk of neighbourhood kids. The same was true of Mordecai's emerging passion for sports, in particular the wartime Montreal Canadiens, *nos glorieux*, featuring the soon-immortal "Punch Line" of Maurice "The Rocket" Richard, Elmer Lach and Hector "Toe" Blake. Baseball excited him as well. Hank Greenberg, the Jewish first-baseman for the Detroit Tigers, was a hero, along with local boxer Maxie Berger. Who said Jews were too small to excel at sports? In February 1942 he sat by the radio in the living room with his father and brother listening to Berger take on Sugar Ray Robinson at Madison Square Garden in New York, the main event of that week's fight night. For the great Sugar Ray, the bout was routine, and he dropped Berger to the mat three times. But for the Richler males, and thousands of other Montrealers, those forty-five minutes, many spent throwing air punches on Maxie's behalf, were legend-forming.

Before the ghetto birthed its first war hero—RCAF flyer Sydney Simon Shulemson, recipient of the Distinguished Service Order and Distinguished Flying Cross—adolescents and teens were dramatizing the exploits of Richard and Blake, Berger and Greenberg. All belonged to the city of Montreal and the continent of North America, not to any vanished Galicia, with its guttural language and retrograde religion. Mutty was growing up into a wider, secular world.

He was also growing up, and into, the Second World War. The nine-year-old who heard CBC newsreader Lorne Greene, a.k.a. "The Voice of Doom," detail the disastrous Allied withdrawal at Dunkirk in early June 1940 may have registered little more than Greene's grave intonations. But a year later, the boy who stared at THE WALLS HAVE EARS and THE ENEMY IS EVERYWHERE signs posted in the local shops understood the message differently. By the time of Pearl Harbor, the early battles in the Pacific, then the Canadian advances into Sicily and Italy, he would be cheering the Allied cause like an adult while still pretending to fight the war like a child. He and his friends re-enacted the Guadalcanal campaign of summer, fall and winter 1942–43 in the snowbanks along St. Urbain, shouting, "Take that, you yellow devil!" and "Schweinhund!" With so many men away at war, snow removal suffered, making for mounds as high as fifteen feet from which to launch those epithets, along with snowballs passing for grenades. Gas rationing also aided their warfare; fewer cars than usual were parked along the curbs.

Avrum and Mordecai still talked most nights in their bedroom. They whispered about their mother's cruelty towards their father, and his meekness with her and everyone else. He was Mr. Milquetoast, or Mr. Hot-Milk-and-Matzos, his preferred bedtime snack. They talked about their Richler grandfather,

hypocrite and tyrant, and certain of their uncles who, newly prosperous, were moving their families across Park Avenue to
Outremont, fleeing the old neighbourhood. Mutty had questions.
He wanted to know about Baron Byng, the high school where
Avrum was an A student, member of the all-Jewish choir that
sang *Messiah* in St. Paul's at Christmas and one of the cadets who
marched across Fletcher's Field. He wanted to know about girls.

The age difference suddenly yawned between the brothers.
Gone were the days when Avrum smoked cigarettes in the alley
with Mordecai and Duddy, or played ball hockey alongside them
in the streets. Gone as well were the magic shows the Richler
boys had put on together, a passion born out of the evening their
father took them to see "Blackstone the Magician" at the Palace,
an extravaganza featuring a woman sawn in half. Their own act,
cleverly titled "White Rock the Magician" and performed in the
living room at 5257, was less flashy. An enthused Moses bought
some routines from a magic shop: the disappearing coin trick,
the fake thumb, the Chinese rings. He also sawed a hole in a table
for the climactic trick. It involved Mordecai, stuffed underneath
the table for ten long minutes, handing things up to White Rock
through the hole. They charged five cents and did two shows to
solid reviews.

Until the fall before his bar mitzvah, Mutty continued to play
the role of an obliging, if already skeptical, adherent. In October,
time of both the Sukkot festival and the Simchat Torah, Moses
erected the *sukkah* on the apartment's front balcony, hanging
grapes and bananas from the roof slats despite frigid temperatures and early snow squalls. Dressed in an overcoat, his younger
son swallowed his dinner of meat and potato, or knishes, as fast
as he could, listening to Lily needle Moses, comparing his meagre
hut to the superior one her father had constructed on Esplanade,
where the likes of Sholem Asch, the great Yiddish novelist and
playwright, had visited during the festival. The boy also still took
his turn parading the Sefer Torahs around the synagogue at the
end of the month. One year he found himself carrying a double
burden: an unusually heavy set of scrolls that were the

penmanship of his illustrious grandfather. He was warned not to stumble. "Remember who you are," he was cautioned. Pious Hasidim were making pilgrimages to Yudel Rosenberg's mausoleum on Côte-des-Neiges during the Ten Days of Awe, lighting memorial candles and leaving petitions—for a blessing of fertility or remission from cancer—for his spirit to consider.

But Avrum, now fifteen or sixteen, was done with the religion his grandfather and parents pushed on him so ardently. He rode the streetcar on Saturdays and put away his prayer phylacteries, unless Lily was watching. For Moses, perfunctory about his own morning prayers and inclined to disappear after lunch on Shabbas to play cards and listen to baseball—both infringements of Sabbath law, along with those *trayf*, non-kosher biscuits, and Cokes—this was a disappointment. Lily, though, realizing her eldest would not be pursuing the rabbinate, shifted her attention to her other child. No longer willing to endure the arguments between his parents, or their scolding for his drift from the faith, Avrum began spending as much time as he could away from 5257, where there was a new smell in the house—gangrene—from Sarah-Gittel's failing body.

Movies were the neighbourhood escape on a Saturday or Sunday night. Avrum might run into his brother at the Rialto, where kids would be watching newsreels about the war and applauding every time King George VI or Winston Churchill appeared on screen. The older boy would be perched in the balcony, where there was greater privacy, before settling into a double feature starring Mickey Rooney as Andy Hardy and a comedy with Bob Hope and Bing Crosby. In 1941 one of the English war-propaganda features advertised on the marquee was *Forty-Ninth Parallel*, starring Laurence Olivier as a French-Canadian trapper who stymies Nazi submarines trolling the St. Lawrence. Avrum, hoping to impress girls with his neckties and hair goop, might or might not acknowledge his sibling down below.

Back on St. Urbain, he wasn't too old to sit with Mutty and fiddle with the shortwave band of the radio, hoping to catch a speech by the evil Adolf Hitler. More likely they'd fall upon

Edward R. Murrow or J.B. Priestley broadcasting from London, England, where people were toughing out the Blitz and Churchill was vowing to fight on land and sea and never surrender. Or else intrepid CBC correspondent Matthew Halton, reporting vividly on the Canadian army's assault on the German bastion of Ortona in December 1943. "Soaking wet, in a morass of mud," Halton told listeners in his strong, familiar voice, "against an enemy fighting harder than he's fought before, the Canadians attack, attack, attack." Months earlier another reporter, Ross Munro, had informed a gathering of ten thousand in the Montreal Forum about the bravery of the Fusiliers Mont-Royal at the tragic Dieppe landing. While under-reporting the overall disaster, Munro was careful to honour local soldiers, singling out their commander, Lieutenant-Colonel Dollard Ménard. Ménard, a French Canadian willing to fight, took five bullets in his attempt to neutralize a concrete pillbox on top of a parapet above the beach.

Although the likes of Dollard Ménard were abundant, and Camillien Houde's insurrection far from represented the dominant view, a vocal number of French Canadians had no wish to fight in a war they believed to be still another defence of an empire of which they were only marginally, and reluctantly, part. For Jews, this apparent indifference to a world in tumult was hard to swallow. They were already dealing with the shock of the official shutdown of immigration of European Jews to Canada—the notorious "None is too many" policy voiced by the director of the Immigration Branch, Frederick Blair, in Mackenzie King's government, and rendered visceral in 1939 when a boatload of nine hundred Jewish refugees vainly appealed to land in Canada and were turned back to Europe. By late 1942 they were also beginning to hear rumours of the mass murders of their kind by Nazis, tales in equal parts credible and unthinkable. Cousins in Poland failed to reply to letters. Transatlantic phone lines rang dead.

Mutty wasn't with Avrum on March 27, 1942, at the YMHA, when the Montreal Jewish ghetto came under brief assault. Though the government still hadn't introduced conscription, it did call for a plebiscite asking Canadians to release the Prime Minister from his earlier promise never to conscript. Even this contingency found support among just one in four Quebecers (64 percent of English Canadians supported Mackenzie King). On that late winter day a protest moved down Park Avenue shouting, "*À bas la conscription!*" ("Down with conscription!") and smashing streetcars and shop windows. In the course of a few blocks the rally transformed itself into a mob. "*À bas les Juifs!*" ("Down with Jews!"), they now cried. The crowd also began focusing their fury on businesses they believed, often incorrectly, to be Jewish-owned. Teenagers inside the Y, Avrum Richler among them, found their own weapons and returned the favour.

Skirmishes weren't occurring only in Plateau Montreal. The geography of 5257 St. Urbain, and the neighbourhood surrounding it, had a rival in Mutty's imagination. Since he was a baby his parents had been relocating him and his brother in the countryside north of the city for July and August. By pooling funds, all but the poorest Jews could afford the $30–40 charged by French-Canadian farmers for the use of wooden shacks they had built for such purposes. Moses and Lily had managed to scrape the money together, first going to Piedmont, an hour beyond Montreal's second island, Laval. A Mr. Hammond rented to them then, and Avrum remembered the farmer allowing him and his toddler brother to keep him company while he hayed the fields. Subsequent summers involved the village of St. Basile and, eventually, the routine of renting rooms either in a house in Shawbridge, where Muttle and his cousin Lionel watched Mr. Blondin, the blacksmith, shoe horses in his yard, or in a shack down the hill in the adjoining village of Prévost. Boys in shorts and knee socks had their picture taken in fields and by the muddy rivers where they swam. Even their mother, pleased to be away from the city and from her husband—fathers generally came up only for weekends—was caught smiling in photos.

Hostility between the French and the Jews was approaching its nadir. During the Depression, local government, Church and media had ganged up to practise lazy bigotry. Whether it was

Arcand's bullies concocting street riots or *Le Devoir* remarking on the body odour and crooked noses of this disloyal minority, or the 1936 bestseller *La Réponse de la race*, which had postulated a Jewish conspiracy to inject venereal disease into the tampons sold to French-Canadian women, the hardships of the era, in conjunction with the rise of "legitimate" discourse rooted in race and ethnic nationalism, congealed into a gleeful anti-Semitism. Arcand may now have been interned, and Duplessis's Union Nationale temporarily out of power, but the ugliness, typified by the occasional *À bas les Juifs* signs on the shoulders of Highway 15, remained visible and unashamed.

Among city Jews, in turn, there was little admiration or respect for their French neighbours, whom they took to be the natural servant class. (Shmarya Richler disliked goys in general, and counselled his grandsons to feel the same.) And yet, as was the case on the crowded Plateau, it was among the rural French, equally rough-hewn and English-challenged, that Jews like the Richlers wound up spending July and August. The Eastern Townships south of Montreal, prettier and more proximate to the American border, were virtually *Judenfrei*. Affluent Quebec Anglos employed a strategy of Olympian indifference, a cover for their own bigotry. Like colonial masters sent to dwell in the Empire, they were adept at remaining so aloof from the "locals" that they could scarcely be accused of disliking or disfavouring them—aside, of course, from discriminatory hiring polices inside their businesses and institutions. The French, less insulated by wealth and less aloof by temperament, time and again rubbed up against these similarly noisy, gregarious immigrants.

Starting in 1938, the Richlers rented in Prévost for six straight summers. A farmer named Morin had put up nine shacks on his property. They were primitive, without indoor plumbing or electricity. Oil stoves were run on kerosene. Lamps provided reading light after dark. Each shack could shelter two or three adults plus gaggles of kids, including plenty of babies. The Richler shack, the cost split between Lily and her sister Ruth, included mute, paralyzed Sarah-Gittel. Lily had no choice—there was no one to look after her on St. Urbain Street, least of all Moses, who worked full days at the yard—but she also wanted her mother to enjoy, as much as her condition allowed, the countryside where she and the rabbi had spent happier times. Her bed was positioned by the front window, obliging kids from neighbouring houses to keep their voices down as they raced past. Or else she sat in her wheelchair in the lane, a cap over her nearly bald skull and a shawl across her shoulders.

When not minding her mother, Lily relaxed on the front steps or took herself down to dangle her legs in the river. In either place she could usually be found reading a book. A serious one, too: Jane Austen or George Eliot. With her cropped hair and thick glasses, her worn dresses and frayed aprons, she struck onlookers as a solitary figure.

The summer settlement, a more authentic Galician shtetl, had shops selling soft drinks and candies, a post office and a synagogue, and a temporary market run by local French farmers. Except for the post office, all the buildings were seasonal; after September, the stretch along the river lay empty. But in July and August it offered up faces and voices, sounds and even smells, akin to those on St. Urbain Street. A bakery truck dropped off fresh bread and matzos each morning. One of the shops, Bishinsky's, featured a jukebox and a balcony, for impromptu evening dances. Down at the "beach," a stretch of sand a hundred feet before the bridge, men in shorts and undershirts set up card tables for marathon games of gin rummy and poker. Women sat at separate tables in bras and bloomers, their pale skin crisped pink, or else they waded into the Richelieu River, keeping an eye on their kids, shirtless and cap-free, farther downstream or climbing the mud "cliff" directly across. Nothing fancy, and certainly nothing as elegant as the lake at Ste. Agathe, with its sailboats and speedboats, and its raked beaches in front of full-service resorts, some twenty of which were then owned by Jews. But still, Prévost was easy summer living: the days long and golden; troubles in the city—or out in the world, with the war entering via the newspapers, or radios in the shops—at a remove.

Mutty Richler slipped into the country idyll. He fished and played floating deadman in the river, even in August, when authorities condemned the waters as breeding grounds for polio. With Lionel and Duddy he stole apples from orchards and snuck into the Boys' Farm above the town to watch baseball games between teams of juvenile delinquents. To the north, west and east of Shawbridge were wooded hills of cedar and pine, the slopes latticed with trails. Up behind the Boys' Farm was the hill they called Flag Mountain, and the cliffs where Avrum and friends went hiking, followed by "the squirts." A hut stood at the top, a good spot for smoking cigarettes and taking girls.

One afternoon the soft clay ledge suddenly gave way beneath the younger boys. Lionel rolled forty feet down the cliff face. Mordecai tumbled farther, splitting open his forehead on a rock. To everyone's astonishment, he didn't cry or even complain. It was important that the injury be looked after without Lily finding out. Dr. Lightstone agreed to stitch him up, and in a manner that couldn't be detected. Mutty sat there being sewn, his features set. Sure enough, his distracted mother noticed nothing that evening.

In Prévost, it was easier being from an Orthodox clan. He was still expected to wear a cap, except in the water. Food still had to be kosher, though the candies in the shops were unregulated and the chickens in the market unsanctified. Nor were his parents less observant on the Sabbath—Lionel was present when Mordecai started absently ripping up a leaf, for which his father, deciding the action violated a rule, stung him with the epithet Shabbas goy. But away from the adults, a kid in shorts and a T-shirt fishing a river or wandering orchards, climbing up hills to play at war, was just a kid. Cap in pocket. Picking and eating raspberries.

VI

WARS

One afternoon in September 1942, Avrum Richler returned home from his part-time job at the Grover Knitting Mills on de Lorimier to find Sarah-Gittel Rosenberg laid out on the living room floor, her body covered by a mourning blanket. His brother, banished from the apartment, sat on a stoop a few doors down, telling the neighbourhood kids about his dead grandmother. Allowed to stay while psalms were recited, Avrum noticed that the smell had dissipated. He also thought, not unreasonably, that he would finally be getting his own bedroom. His grandmother was eighty-two, and had been an invalid for seven years; he was sixteen, busy with high school and multiple jobs.

But his parents had other plans. Specifically, Lily did. With the death of her mother, she was losing both the pension she had arranged from the Jewish Community Council and the monthly help from her siblings. She was also once more contemplating divorce. Anxious to generate her own income, she decided to rent out the "spare" room and cook evening meals for pay. The war had boosted such business. German and Austrian Jews, interned as enemy aliens in England since 1939, were being transported to Canada, where they were scarcely more welcome. Eventually released from detention, most headed for the comfort of the Montreal ghetto. Moses liked the idea of a boarder, figuring he'd be welcoming a hayseed from a Polish village whom he could mentor and befriend.

Instead, the Richlers eventually invited Julius Frankel into their house. Tall and lanky, fluent in French, German and English, as well as Yiddish and Hebrew, Frankel sang opera in the bathtub and quoted Goethe in the original. He was bright and funny and had seen the world. Soon it seemed *he* was condescending to his landlord, a junk dealer who'd never been anywhere. He was also enchanting Lily.

Kosher dinners brought a second outsider into 5257. Evelyn Sacks was twenty-three in September 1943, with a science and teaching degree from McGill and a husband away in the war. Unable to work in the Protestant school system, which didn't allow married women in the classroom, the petite, attractive Sacks was hired at Talmud Torah, where she was relieved to discover the school wasn't as religious as she had feared. More to worry about than an Orthodox teaching environment, apparently, was a grade five student named Mordecai Richler. For two years she had listened to complaints about the difficult boy. Now she was his homeroom instructor for grade seven, and was actually impressed. A paragraph by him contained more style and insight than entire essays by others. His drawings were so good, and Sacks so unsure as an art teacher, that she allowed the thirteen-year-old to co-teach the classes. She also let him write topic sentences for discussions, startled by the clarity of his thinking. There were lots of smart kids at Talmud Torah, and plenty who were easier to teach, but Mordecai Richler was unique.

During the winter of 1943–44, Evelyn Sacks began paying for occasional meals from Lily. Her doctor advised this remedy for fatigue and depression, and on learning that Mutty's mother was providing partial board, she walked up St. Urbain after classes.

Starting in September as well, Avrum was no longer at the table. Blocked from studying medicine at McGill—Jews were even more disfavoured in the professional schools—Avrum enrolled at Queen's University in Kingston, Ontario, for what he hoped would be only a single year's absence from Montreal. As a result, he missed the defining months of his brother's adolescence.

Shmarya Richler had relocated his household again not long before. Diminished by marriages and army service, the remaining Richler clan rented the upper floor of a duplex on Jeanne Mance between St. Viateur and Fairmount. If the move from St. Urbain Street was not undertaken to put three blocks between himself and his grandson, it might soon have been. Mordecai was skirmishing openly with his *zeyda*. Expelled from the Saturday afternoon *Ethics of the Fathers* lessons for not wearing a skullcap—"Come back when you have a hat," Shmarya told him—the adolescent took to walking past the house hatless, a cigarette between his lips, while his grandfather sat glaring from the porch.

Moses was no help. He pleaded with his son to observe decorum in front of his elder, even feeding him the chapter of the Torah that had been read in *shul*, in case Shmarya quizzed him for details. But when his grandfather also denounced Mordecai as a Shabbas goy, evicting him with a beating, the boy vowed never to speak to the old man again.

This time, revenge upon two generations of Richlers had him stopping by Wilensky's for a baloney and salami "special." He had already partaken of a bacon and tomato sandwich at Horn's cafeteria and not been laid low by a thunderbolt. To eat *trayf*—non-kosher food—right under his father's and grandfather's noses was still more insolent. Following Avrum's example, he could be seen eating a Wilensky's sandwich on St. Urbain on the Sabbath. Shabbas goy, indeed.

Shoplifting was another activity spurred by rebellion. An early effort, carried out in the Kresge's department store on Park Avenue after a pre–bar mitzvah cheder with Mr. Yalofsky, earned him a scolding from the store manager, a Scots Presbyterian who lamented that a Hebrew would resort to petty crimes more the domain of the hard-luck youth who wound up at the Boys' Farm. In response, Mutty and friends wandered downtown to the anonymity of Eaton's department store on St. Catherine Street. Back at Schacter's to look for Moses, he might steal candy and bother the men playing chess or cards. It was in that shop that he was reported to have taunted a mentally retarded boy, a regular on one of the stools, whose father sold rags. That cruelty would be shameful to him later.

A by-election in the neighbourhood was as urgent news in Wilensky's as the war on the Russian front and the march of Canadian troops up the boot of Italy. Though the Communist Party of Canada had been outlawed since 1931, it had created a front in 1943 called the Labour Progressive Party. When Cartier, the riding that included the Jewish ghetto, went to the polls in May 1943, it elected Fred Rose, a Labour Progressive activist who had already been jailed twice for subversive activities. Rose won with thirty percent of the vote in a four-way race.

Among the candidates he defeated was the young lawyer David Lewis of the social democratic Co-operative Commonwealth Federation, or CCF. Born in 1907, Lewis had come to Canada from Russia at age thirteen, teaching himself English by reading Charles Dickens. His career had included working in an uncle's clothing factory and a Rhodes Scholarship to Oxford. Had Mutty Richler found himself near the offices of *Der Keneder Odler* on St. Lawrence, he might have noticed David Lewis in one of the booths at Horn's, drinking coffee and debating with a fellow lawyer, the poet A.M. Klein. Lewis would eventually shift his fortunes to a winnable riding in suburban Toronto. Klein, a blazing orator, would also fail to convince the voters of Cartier. High school teacher Irving Layton, who had once dated Mordecai's relation Suzanne Rosenberg, might be in another booth in the restaurant, arguing with more revolutionary-minded and self-consciously poetic sorts.

Fred Rose's victory shocked the city and country equally. Reasons for a Communist procuring one in three votes in the riding included the recent victory of the "new" Soviet allies at Stalingrad and, locally, anger at anti-Semitism. Not so incidentally, the Communists mounted a smart, well-organized campaign in 1943 and again in 1945, when Rose was re-elected. Was the Montreal ghetto so radical? The flight from Europe brought nearly as many traditions and ideas to North America as it did immigrants. Once settled into city neighbourhoods, Jews from Poland

and Russia found themselves presented with an embarrassment of intellectual riches, especially if they were willing to cast off hereditary affiliations. Secular traditions as various as anti-Czarist republicanism and Communism of every faction—Leninist, Trotskyist, Stalinist—along with German socialists and Zionists with anti-capitalist ambitions for Eretz Yisrael, competed in the Montreal ghetto from 1900 to 1939. For those who kept the faith, emerging sub-categories within Orthodox and Reform Judaism allowed for new degrees of political committment and social activism, with only the extremes still rubbing up against the inconvenience of secular life in Canada. Views mostly ranged across the political spectrum from Left to far Left and back again.

The Richler house was much less engaged. As Orthodox Jews, with Lily's Hasidic roots still strong, the family were committed to their own closed affairs. But the parents read the same anti-Semitic signs posted along Highway 15 and outside certain resorts in Ste. Agathe. They heard the stories of relations in Poland and Ukraine who had gone missing, and were privy to the whispers in synagogue that something appalling was happening in Europe. Terrible rumours were escaping the Soviet Union as well: of campaigns and purges, of camps constituting a gulag. Lily's letters to a sister-in-law and niece in Russia went undelivered, eventually making their way back to St. Urbain Street, frayed from their brief experience inside Stalin's nightmare.

Add to these narratives the everyday accounts and activities of the war: Lorne Greene and Matthew Halton on the CBC; headlines in the newspapers, either local or out of New York; the rationing of gas and food, the knitting of sweaters by various Richler sisters and spouses for servicemen overseas; and the ubiquitous signs warning of fifth columnists and even women who might bring soldiers to grief. ("IF SHE'S GAME, SHE'S GOT IT!" warned one about venereal disease.) No house could remain aloof, even if it wanted to.

For Mordecai, the war blew a window out of the musty room of his Orthodox childhood. With the glass shattered, the window would never be closed again. He couldn't have been happier.

A Boy Scout, if not a Jewish commando, he and his friends canvassed the neighbourhood in their uniforms collecting aluminum bottles for redeployment in fighter planes. They would turn the bottles in at the depot or sell their haul to a junkyard, splitting the take. Regardless, the profiteers sang: "Hitler has only got one ball / Goering has two, but they are small / Himmler is somewhat similar / But poor old Goebbels has no balls at all." Taunting Nazis from across the ocean demonstrated adolescent spirit, if not the fortitude needed by adults. Around the city were nine thousand workers producing ammunition alone. Thousands more made canvas for tents and fabric for uniforms, cloth for gas masks and surgical dressings. Aircraft production also continued to boom. Twelve thousand workers in five factories throughout the south-shore suburb of Longueuil built Harvard trainers and Mosquito fighter bombers for the Noorduyn Aircraft company. Seven thousand others at Fairchild Aircraft put together Helldivers for the American forces and Bristol bombers and Cornells for the RAF.

Such activity, it was believed, left the city a target for intrepid German bombers travelling via Norway and Greenland. Air-raid preparations in Montreal included staged blackouts such as the one on the evening of June 9, 1941, when sirens sounded the alert. Streetcars joined regular vehicles in dimming their lights, and the few remaining horse-drawn carts pulled over. Fifteen thousand volunteer wardens patrolled the city in civilian clothes, on the lookout for spies and saboteurs, hushing giggling teens and writing up $10 fines for anyone who failed to turn off lights. Bombers from the new Royal Canadian Air Force dropped leaflets urging citizens to buy War Savings Bonds.

It was a serious time, and a time for serious people to step up. But kids and adolescents could only whoop in cinemas at the sight of General Montgomery and shout rude rhymes about Nazis, stifling their complaints about the rationing that carefully allotted tea and coffee, butter and meat, and sugar.

On January 27, 1944, Mutty Richler turned thirteen. The first Saturday after his birthday, two dozen Richlers gathered in the

Young Israel to witness the bar mitzvah of their most vexing progeny. Among the non-family present was Evelyn Sacks. His grade seven teacher wasn't the only one to be astonished that the bar mitzvah boy insisted on performing the entire morning service himself. No rabbi was sought for any of the seven sections. (Often, the boy reads only the final section, the *maftir*.) He recited the portion allotted him from the Books of the Prophets—the *Haftarah*—using the proper chant, and then delivered his own commentary on the day's Torah reading, called the *d'var torah*. The commentary could be done in English, but the rest had to be in Hebrew. Though a cantor was present to lead the prayers, Mordecai made his way through the ceremony in the language he had been learning, in between glances at the sports page, at cheder and at Talmud Torah.

Afterwards, there were cakes and schnapps for guests and a scattering of gifts for the bar mitzvah boy, including paints and an easel from Mrs. Sacks and a signet ring from his classmates. It was a perfunctory event, Orthodox and restrained. No doubt his own hostility—presumably he did not exchange words with Shmarya Richler—dampened the mood. Lost in the dourness was an assertion, conscious or not; by insisting on performing the ceremony himself, the thirteen-year-old was making a declaration. He did know "who he was," both as a grandson of Rabbi Rosenberg and as a learned young Jew, and he could undertake to fulfill the formal requirements of his family's religion without being beholden to it. If the rite of passage was about declaring his readiness to be counted an adult, fine. If others thought the bar mitzvah represented, as the term suggested in Hebrew, an acceptance that the initiated would henceforth perform God's commandments and enter deeper into the Jewish faith, well, that was their problem.

For Lily, the performance must have been bittersweet. In effect, her son demonstrated the excellence and aptitude she had been hoping he would show for the religion and, by extension, the life he was in the process of renouncing.

Moses, too, was likely a proud parent on that Saturday in late January, with his oldest boy at university and his youngest reciting the Pentateuch, the Torah scroll, in Hebrew. In front of all those Richlers, no less, including Shmarya. They had to be impressed by Mordecai—for once. And though she could be a difficult wife, Lily was well liked by her in-laws. She had remained devoted to her own parents, looking after her ailing mother all those years. Any Richler who fell ill went to Lily for care. She *was* family, despite her self-importance and need to be set apart.

But the bar mitzvah, it turned out, was all that had been holding the marriage together. Lily had made it known months before that she would be seeking a divorce once their second son was ordained a man. Moses had tried placating her with flowers and gifts, to no avail. For months rabbis in black gabardine coats had been knocking on the door of 5257 St. Urbain, hoping to dissuade her. Divorce was more than a scandal in the Orthodox community. It marked a kind of breach, a gash in the social fabric. While Mordecai looked on, the rabbis, playing eleventh-hour marriage counsellors, asked Moses to name his biggest grievance against his wife. Rocking on his heels and snapping his suspenders, he replied that, on waking from his nap on Saturday afternoon, would it be too much to expect a cup of hot tea with lemon? The day came, and Moses Richler packed his bags and moved into a room to let in a house on Esplanade.

Avrum learned about the separation in a letter from his mother. He returned to Montreal and made the rounds. "Do something!" his grandfather demanded, concerned about the family's good name. Visiting his father in his room on Esplanade, Avrum found him stunned and humiliated, and also heard that the boarder, Julius Frankel, had taken a larger role in his mother's life. "St. Urbain's cuckold," Moses would soon be labelled. Finally, at 5257, Avrum Richler was met by Frankel himself, who insisted they retreat to a restaurant on Laurier for a chat, man to man. There he announced: "Your mother and I are in love."

The teenager could do little. His father was out; this younger man from Europe, who sometimes screamed a woman's name in his sleep—a woman, likely a Jew, left behind in Germany—was in. Frankel was in the apartment and, it seemed, in their mother's bed. Avrum made his peace with an unpleasant and upsetting situation; then he went back to Kingston to finish the school year.

For Mordecai, there was no escape. He was no longer welcome at his grandparents', even though his grandmother remained fond of him. Uncles, aunts, even cousins, viewed him as trouble best avoided. Worse, he was asked to take sides within his own family, and did, agreeing with his mother that she deserved her happiness. He turned on his father—summoning, perhaps, his own list of grievances—and shortly thereafter, in an argument officially over his newly proclaimed atheism, a position arrived at by reading about Charles Darwin, exchanged awkward blows with him. Father and son did not talk again for nearly two years.

Now he found himself alone in the apartment with his mother and her lover, witnessing some things, overhearing others. He was certainly hearing about the legal manoeuvres. A civil divorce in Quebec required parliamentary approval, a long and costly process. The other route involved a Jewish divorce, called a *get*, whereby the marriage was legally and in religious terms deemed to have never happened. Lily hired a lawyer who made the case that, because she had been only seventeen when she married, and had done so without her father's permission, the union had been illegal under Jewish law. Given the widespread knowledge that Rabbi Rosenberg had arranged the match, and the still-vivid memory of the dance between the rebbe and his nineteen-year-old *shammas* at the wedding, these were evident misrepresentations. Even so, they worked. As solutions went, a *get* was practical and, in theory, face-saving. It took a thirteen-year-old to point out the absurdity of claiming to undo the past with the stroke of a pen. Referring to himself and Avrum, and using the Hebrew word for bastard, Mordecai asked his parents: "What does that make us, *mamzerim*?"

Other people thought so. Soon enough Mutty was being punished for the sins of Moses and Lily. He was not invited to a classmate's party on account of the scandal. He felt the burn of gazes and heard the buzz in the synagogue. For someone born with an innate sensitivity to hypocrisy and nonsense, the injustice was palpable. With Avrum in Kingston, he had no one to talk to about the turmoil around him and within his own heart. Small wonder that he was being pronounced moody and abrasive, or was trying to pass for older than his birthdate allowed. A different war had broken out on St. Urbain Street, and even a boy who could recite the bar mitzvah ceremony and spar with a Jehovah's-enforcer grandparent could not negotiate this battlefield, never mind sort out his true allies.

Evelyn Sacks volunteered as a friend. She had noticed Julius Frankel's sophistication and charm. She also noted that Lily and her lover allowed no outward expressions of affection in front of Mordecai, and how, on the evenings she came to supper, the charade extended to the meal itself. At 5:30 Mutty would sit at the dining table, laid with cloth napkins and a checkered cloth, for a dinner of plain, hearty food and dessert, in the company of his mother, their boarder, and his grade seven teacher. No wine would be served. Nor would there be conversation across the table. Mordecai would turn to Evelyn Sacks and talk to her and her only. Young female teachers at Talmud Torah were progressive, none more so than Mrs. Sacks, and the two together revisited schoolroom topics of the day—the radical Bartolomei Vanzetti's proud speech to the U.S. court before his execution; John Steinbeck's exposés of class injustice in America; the exploits of El Campesino, the Republican commander during the Spanish Civil War, who later fled to the Soviet Union once the fascists took control. Or he might talk about the thrilling playoff run of the Montreal Canadiens, then in pursuit of their first Stanley Cup in fourteen years. At no point would he address Julius Frankel.

His anger, and mouth, nearly got him thrown out of Talmud Torah before graduation. When his Hebrew teacher's habit of spraying spittle on students became too much, Mordecai asked that he quit doing it. Offended, the teacher demanded he be expelled. Evelyn Sacks pleaded his case with the principal, emphasizing the situation at home. He served a suspension and was allowed to graduate.

His *annus horribilis* ended, at least, with two happy auguries. The Habs did win their first Stanley Cup since 1931—the birth year, it so happened, of one of their biggest fans in the Jewish ghetto. The victory was spectacular, an overtime win in the fifth and final game. The opponents were the Chicago Black Hawks and the date was April 13, a night Mutty would have spent next to the radio. He may have jumped up when goaltender Bill Durnan stopped the first-ever penalty shot in finals' overtime. He may have roared when Toe Blake scored the winning goal shortly thereafter. If every living room along St. Urbain Street didn't echo his delight, streets a few blocks to the east were undoubtedly celebrating Maurice Richard and *nos glorieux.*

What were celebrated on St. Urbain Street, as all over Canada, were the June 6 CBC reports of the D-Day invasion of Normandy. "They sailed under cover of darkness to smash down the walls of Fortress Europe," announced a newsreader. The landing of Canadian troops at Juno Beach was bannered across the newspapers of the country. On June 8 Matthew Halton—famed now as the "voice" of the war—told listeners: "A few hours ago I was in France. I have come back [to London] for a day to try and describe the liberation of France." Noting how Hitler's "West Wall" had turned out to be a myth, Halton had travelled inland with the with troops. French villagers, he said, were showing their gratitude to Canadians by honouring fallen soldiers with flowers.

VII

COMRADES

Down at 4251 St. Urbain, in a cavernous building named after a British soldier who became governor general of Canada, Mordecai Richler was starting fresh. His brother had graduated from Baron Byng High two years before, leaving, once again, memories of a studious and respectful Richler boy. A couple of his Talmud Torah classmates, still from the wrong side of Park, were destined as well for this public school of one thousand. But otherwise the Richler with the home address three-quarters of a mile up the same street was just another name on the class sheet assigned to a ground-floor room. He was also just another member of the ninety-five per cent majority student population. *Strive hard and work /With your heart in the doing* was the school motto. *Up play the game /As you learnt it at Byng.* To which the males of Baron Byng would gleefully add: *Issey, Ikey, Mikey, Sam /we're the boys that eat no ham.*

By September 1944 Baron Byng had already transitioned two generations of Jewish youth from mid-Atlantic childhoods into mainstream North American adult lives. Neither its success at assimilation nor its academic excellence was exactly by design. But year after year, teenagers whose parents worked as shopkeepers and seamstresses, as hawkers in newspaper stands, graduated not only with passages of Keats and Shelley committed to memory and songs like "God Save the King" and "The British Grenadiers" on their lips, but also with the best matriculation results in

Quebec. Soon-to-be doctors and dentists, lawyers and accountants emerged from the twin doorways: males onto Clark Street,
females onto St. Urbain. Boys occupied the east wing, thirty-six
to a class, and girls the west, meeting at lunch in the side yard
off Rachel or in a central courtyard. Students rose up from the
ground level in grades eight and nine to the upper floors in
grades ten and eleven. Then they burst through the ceiling into
universities across Canada and the United States, often on schol-
arships. Graduates included David Lewis and A.M. Klein, actor
William Shatner and Supreme Court Justice Morris Fish. The
prominent gangster Harry Ship was also an alumnus, as were
ruthless business tycoons, nervy boxers and fighters for Israel.
It was a mostly distinguished roll call, without match in any other
Montreal school—except, arguably, Collège Brébeuf, where the
future political ruling classes, among them Pierre Trudeau, were
being educated.

"I suppose most of you expect to go on to McGill University four
years from now," the principal, Dr. A.K. Astbury, told the rows of
grade eight boys in their freshly pressed trousers in the gym one
morning in September. "Well, you will have to work hard," he
added, citing the ten percent gap between entrance marks for
Jews and Gentiles. He needn't have bothered with the pep talk.
Those same fathers and mothers, relegated by fate to menial jobs,
had their children's futures as carefully plotted as the unfolding
Allied assault on Germany. Well aware of the double standard at
McGill, they had been subjecting their sons to "Word Power" columns in *Reader's Digest* and biographies of famous doctors. They
already viewed fellow Jews as competition for the few scholar-
ships and slots in the professional schools. In this regard, Lily
Richler was no exception. The day Mordecai came home with a
rank two Talmud Torah report card, his mother made a single
comment: "Who came rank one?"

As for the students themselves, they were Depression-trained
in alertness and hustle. Nobody was giving anything to anyone
on St. Urbain Street; chance was what you made of it. For all
their attitude and mischief, these teenagers were eager to learn,

to achieve success as upwardly mobile Montrealers, which, being
native-born and English-speaking, they felt more entitled to than
their parents.

The school faculty played a role in moulding these new
Canadians. Dr. Astbury, a legend for both his insistence on academic excellence and the crack of his strap across palms, oversaw a staff that was ninety percent Gentile, with names like
Hoover, Stewart, Dunn and Patterson. Many were either veterans
of the First World War or, in later years, young men just back
from the latest one. Students whispered that the Protestant
School Division, which oversaw Baron Byng by default (any non-
Catholic school came under its auspices), had resolved to concentrate those teachers returning from the trenches with injuries
or shell shock in a single institution. Among the older staff was
the English teacher Mr. McCletchie. A United Empire Loyalist,
McCletchie told students he had survived a rat-infested trench at
the Somme by reading Milton and Donne using a candle attached
to his helmet. Then there was the deaf physics teacher, O.J.
Lummus. He sported a hearing aid on his chest the size of a box
of chocolates. Boys would lower their voices, obliging him to turn
up a dial, and then would shout, ringing his shell-damaged ears.
These men were quirky but decent; they were mensches. For
their decency many were awarded Yiddish diminutives: "Yossel"
for Lummus and "Mechel" for McCletchie.

There were also a few women on staff, including Frances Katz,
one of the handful of Jewish teachers. She taught grade nine
drama. Also the art teacher, Miss Savage, who had once dated
the painter A.Y. Jackson and was a talented artist. She oversaw
a massive mural designed and painted by the students in the
locker area, Mordy Richler—as he had begun introducing himself—among them.

Other faculty members were less commendable. An industrial
arts instructor made snide comments about the family back-
grounds of the boys, predicting they would turn out no better.
Another, asking his class if they knew how Jews made an "s,"
scrawled an "s" on the blackboard and ran two strokes through

it—the $ sign. Still others could be cruel with words and punishment alike. The notorious Mr. Shaw strapped twelve kids in a single afternoon, ten strokes per hand, for the crime of refusing to divulge who had farted in his class. Another strap-happy teacher had his Austin disappear. Seniors had picked it up and relocated it a block away.

In his early high school days, Mordecai and his friends gravitated towards the less scholarly environments in the streets around Baron Byng. His initial forays into the pool halls along St. Lawrence and over on Park dated to the final autumn of the Second World War. So did his visits to the backroom of Beauty's Deli, where card games were for higher stakes. Shoplifting sprees downtown, peaking at age fourteen with the pilfering of bats and balls at Eaton's, were more engaging activities than any on offer in the classroom. The same held true for fisticuffs and shoving matches with classmates, including a brawl with Jack Wolofsky, grandson of the founder of the Yiddish daily—a fight initiating a friendship, as is so often the case with boys. The angry, smart loner who almost got expelled from Talmud Torah had shown up at Baron Byng with the same edge, and from the outset he was someone to be wary of.

Mordy tried poses. First up was the adolescent sophisticate. Terrified of girls, but desperate to meet them, he sat in the stands at basketball games, chewing on an unlit pipe and feigning to turn the pages of tomes as daunting as *The Outline of History* by H.G. Wells, borrowed for three cents a week from the local Jewish library. The pipe, let alone the book, did nothing to gain him any of those sweetly scented girls of his dreams—they were, not unreasonably, more interested in the basketball players—but did earn the friendship of one of the team's stars. Jack Rabinovitch was the son of Ukrainian Jewish immigrants who had fled the 1926 pogroms. His father was a "newsie," selling papers from a stand at the corner of Ontario and St. Lawrence, and Jack delivered the dailies after school each day. Tall for his age, and gifted athletically, the grade nine student befriended the undersized smart aleck with the pipe and book, admiring his chutzpah and

dry sense of humour. Since neither went home for lunch, they
were soon eating hot dogs at a stand on Clark or walking the two
blocks down The Main to splurge on smoked meat sandwiches,
two for twenty-five cents, with fries for a nickel, at Schwartz's.
The Rachel Pool Hall wasn't far away, or the Royal, where hot
dogs cost five cents. Jack liked pool as well.

Back at 5257 St. Urbain, Mordecai was once more sharing the
cramped bedroom with his brother. To pay the tuition at the
Université de Montréal, where he was now enrolled in optometry, Avrum tutored students and drove a taxi on weekends.
Sunday mornings he made collections, at three percent of the
gross, for a local butcher. Studying was best done at a library.
As a result, he kept irregular hours and rarely ate at home. But
he and his kid brother would talk at night, as in the old days,
the subjects more evolved versions of the familiar complaints.
The theme of hypocrisy continued to dominate, the cast of the
guilty larger than ever: their mother with her secret lover and
sham Jewish divorce; their brash Uncle Joe, vaunting his sen-
iority at the scrapyard, and their pompous Uncle Bernard, now
a resident of Outremont, his house filled with the baubles of the
nouveau riche; their hapless father, striving to please the family
that disrespected him. There was the incident, even before the
divorce, when Mordecai was in the scrapyard offices with his
father and Uncle Joe. When the phone rang he picked it up and,
on learning the call was for "Mr. Richler," passed it to Moses. For
this he was chewed out by Joe, who informed him that if the
caller wanted his father they'd ask for "Moe." "Mr. Richler" was
his exclusive preserve. When Mordy, indignant on behalf of his
parent, swore at him, he got cuffed. Again.

But the brothers didn't talk much about Julius Frankel.
Mordecai had something enormous to tell Avrum about Frankel
and their mother—an incident that had scalded him—but didn't
say it. Either he wasn't sure of what he had seen, or he couldn't
find the words. Or else, the reality of their mother's romantic
involvement with the boarder was impossible for the boys to
broach.

Shmarya Richler, retired to the balcony porch on Jeanne Mance, was no longer cuffing his grandson. He couldn't get close enough to him; confrontations had now been reduced to stare-downs as Mordy deliberately walked past his apartment yarmulke-free and puffing on a cigarette. If the elder Richler shared any quality with his daughter-in-law, it was a capacity for sustained enmity. But Mordecai, combining the bloodlines of both sides of his family, was already their near match at holding a grudge.

What Avrum Richler was detecting in his brother was the emergence of a strident moral character. Even at thirteen, he had a strong sense of right and wrong. Certain realities, ranging from Nazis to lying mothers, disgusted him, and he could not feign otherwise. Avrum, thinking of his own reluctant acceptance of Frankel—he had agreed to give him driving lessons, despite neither trusting nor liking the man—observed that Mordecai could not, would not, make any similar peace. Nor would he accord the German Jew the respect children were supposed to extend automatically to adults. To Avrum, his younger sibling *was* a Jewish commando in embryo, fearless and fierce, occasionally to be seen, in fact, in the uniform of the Baron Byng cadets, which he joined on reaching the rank of high school student, albeit as a lowly grade-eighter.

Still, there was some space for being a teenager. Girls were a sudden preoccupation. How do you touch them? he asked. How do you undo a bra? Avrum was no expert—he would remain a virgin until his marriage at age twenty-four—but he tried to caution his kid brother. Masturbate too much, he warned, and you'll go blind. Mordecai had been born with an undescended second testicle, about which Avrum commiserated; he also claimed he would be unable to produce semen. Mordy already knew him to be wrong, thanks to drawings of lingerie models in the *Herald* and even the chaste *Canadian Jewish Review*. Of course, he still had much to learn. Baron Byng held "tea dances" in the gym on Friday afternoons, when the sexes could mingle. When a boastful classmate claimed to have "gone the limit" with a girl, one who had, he reported, self-gratified herself after seeing movies involving hunky stars like Tyrone Power, young Mordecai knew better. "How could she?" he asked. "She's a girl, for Christ's sake."

Mostly, though, he was in a war at 5257 St. Urbain, and fighting it solo. Each evening he would spar, largely in silence, with his mother and her lover, then retreat to his room to resume cheering on the withering of the Third Reich. Rome had been liberated in June 1944, and Paris was freed of Nazis on August 25. U.S. troops reached the Siegfried Line in mid-September. By October Holland had been retaken, Athens likewise liberated, and the great General Rommel had been forced to commit suicide. Along the Belgian-German border perched the medieval town of Aachen, one of the first cities inside the Reich to surrender. In mid-December Hitler launched his final, desperate counter-assault in the Ardennes region—the brutal month-long Battle of the Bulge.

Unnoted on Mordecai's bedroom map of Europe was the surrender of the Polish Home Army to the Germans on October 2, marking the end of the Warsaw Uprising and, later that month, the final use of gas chambers in Auschwitz. (Other concentration camps, including Dachau and Buchenwald, continued exterminating Jews until the spring.) It would be another half-year before he became familiar with those places and incidents, when they would be not only pinpointed on a map, but lodged forever in his moral imagination.

That same autumn, the fourteen-year-old made his first efforts at writing fiction. Classmates already stole glances at the drawings that crowded the margins of his notebooks. Now Mordy reprised his role from Talmud Torah by being the first to read out his Current Events essays, writings whose grasp of the news and clarity of expression came as a fresh surprise to everyone. But his early stories, had he shared them, would have had less impact. School readers at the time favoured tales such as "The Face on the Wall," where two Englishmen scare each other at their club with yarns of supernatural dread. He used these as models. "Sir Marmaduke Tingley Winterbottom," ran one Mordecai Richler story, set in a London private club, "remembering to pass the port to the left, says to Lord Beauchamp, pronounced Beecham, 'I say, did I ever tell you about the time our thin red line confronted the Fuzzy Wuzzies on the African plain.'" Or, from a fragment called "The Story That Marvin Told": "Marvin was hardly an intimate acquaintance, but rather, we were school cronies and more or less chips off the same block."

Parodying what little literature he had read—G.A. Henty and Rudyard Kipling—marked the extent of his early reach. Novels, Mordecai explained once, were of little utility to the active teen. Sports and the war were real; stories weren't. But a novel he did manage to get through, John Buchan's popular *The Thirty-Nine Steps*, constituted his first formative reading experience, mostly for its thrilling plot. The book had a curious local connection, especially for a kid attending Baron Byng High: until his death in 1940, Buchan had been, like Byng, the governor general of Canada. Every Saturday morning at synagogue the congregation had dutifully wished a long life to Lord Tweedsmuir, as Buchan was otherwise known. The matter-of-fact redaction of the toxic *Protocols of Zion* conspiracy for world Jewish domination, outlined by a character in Buchan's opening pages, did not register with him until much later.

Poetry had even less purchase, especially given its frequent use as punishment for swearing or tardiness. ("*A thing of beauty is a joy forever.* Explain," would be a typical task.) But sixteen lines of memorized Tennyson stayed with him: "Break, break, break / On thy cold grey stones, O sea! / And I would that my tongue could utter / The thoughts that arise in me." But while John Buchan, or even Sir Marmaduke, could arouse strong emotions, most of the boys of Baron Byng found such poetic sentiments sissy and unreal.

Hockey, in contrast, had everything to do with the lives of Jewish boys, who, while less likely to join outdoor leagues with the skilled French players, were skaters on the frozen ponds and street-hockey fanatics in the alleys, using coal-stuffed socks for pucks and department store catalogues for pads. Many Baron

Byng students lived and died with the Habs. The team was the
nightly sports lead in the *Herald* and on CJAD radio, the talk of
barbershop conversations and back-of-synagogue chatter. In particular, Maurice Richard's assault on history preoccupied the city
during the winter of 1944–45. Richard, who had scored all five
goals for the Canadiens in a 5–1 victory over the hated Toronto
Maple Leafs the previous spring, was now on pace to achieve the
impossible: fifty goals in the same number of games. Richard's
intensity, his flair for the dramatic gesture, had won over all
Montrealers with hot blood in their veins. For the more engaged,
especially with the outbreak of anti-conscription riots—a
response, for once, to an actual imposition: conscription to compensate for the loss of troops in the battles of spring and
summer—the Rocket's well-known attempts to enlist in the
Canadian army added to his stature. For Jews, especially, the fact
that the French city's biggest sports figure had been aware of the
stakes was consoling.

A year later, another sports icon made a brief but no less
significant appearance in Montreal. Mordecai and his grade eight
friends played hooky to watch baseball at Delorimier Downs,
where on weekday afternoons kids were admitted free to the left-
field bleachers. That fall, with the Royals in the pennant race,
games were sold out, fans perching on the roof of the Grover
Knit-to-Fit building across the street. With the 1945 squad including its first-ever Jewish player, Kermit Kitman, the loyalty of the
Baron Byng truants was assured. But it was the 1946 team, featuring a young African-American second baseman named Jackie
Robinson, that sounded a noise heard far beyond Montreal. He
batted .349 with the Royals that season, stole forty bases and had
a near-perfect fielding record. Montreal fans gave him a standing
ovation for every bold play. On the road in America, Robinson
endured vicious taunting, most of it racial; in the Canadian city,
he was embraced. When the Royals won the Triple-A
Championships, Robinson was paraded around the infield on the
shoulders of fans and mobbed outside the stadium. The next
season he was called up by the Brooklyn Dodgers, where he

broke the colour barrier in major-league baseball. Kermit Kitman, a decent fielder with a weak bat, didn't make the Royals squad.

In his freshman year Mordecai Richler met the three friends who would, along with Jack Rabinovitch, remain his comrades throughout high school. The most exciting was Murray Greenberg. Only a few months older than the others, Greenberg already shaved daily and dressed in pegged trousers. At the many games at which Mordy wanted to excel, Greenberg naturally shone: snooker and basketball, baseball and boxing, where he fought in the Golden Gloves for the YMHA. That, plus girls. Greenberg stopped by Wilensky's to show off the condom he kept in his wallet—"just in case." He also invited his new friend to catch for him in the alleyway behind St. Urbain while he perfected the fastball that would, he boasted, eventually attract the interest of a local scout. Greenberg claimed he had a stepbrother flying for the U.S. 5th Air Force in the Pacific. They had already made plans to settle in Palestine once the Nazis, and the Japanese, were sorted out.

Earl Kruger and Eli Weinstein couldn't match Greenberg's charisma. Still, the tall, serious-minded Kruger admired the works of John Gunther and preferred movies of social import, while Weinstein, son of a barber, had an easy laugh and warm personality. One night Greenberg shared his plans for Palestine with Mordy at dinner, not in a neighbourhood deli, but in the popular Dinty Moore's on St. Catherine Street, where hockey players and mobsters dined. Over corned beef and cabbage, paid for with the American dollars sent by his stepbrother, he invited Richler to a meeting of Habonim, the socialist Zionist youth group. If he liked what he saw, maybe he would join.

Soon enough all four boys were proper *chaverim*, card-carrying members of Habonim and regulars in its clubhouse on Jeanne Mance. For teenage boys with impulses raging in all directions, it was the perfect club. Their political awakening as secular Jews destined to help build a socialist state in Palestine was underway. Their social calendars, too, were happily filled.

Mordecai joined Habonim just in time to celebrate Montreal's VE Day. The news reached Canada at 9:36 p.m. Eastern Daylight

Time on May 7, 1945: "Germany has surrendered unconditionally." People were in the streets within minutes, looking to express their relief. May 8 saw the city transformed into an outdoor party. Soldiers were raised up on shoulders and kissed by girls. Papers streamed from office windows. But for many, the joy was almost immediately muted. On May 11, in the *Canadian Jewish Chronicle*, A.M. Klein contextualized the victory. "Every Jew felt the Nazi tentacle stretch out to reach him, personally," he wrote. "Until the last Jew was cremated, Hitler, we knew, would feel that his task had not been done." Klein then summarized what was already known by a few about the dimensions of what would shortly be called the Holocaust. "Conservative estimates place the number of our martyred at five million; only the months to come will reveal the actual figure. Yes, we have survived; but as we take count of our numbers, and take stock of our condition, we discover that we have survived bleeding and maimed."

Klein's estimate of five million, with the real total yet to come, was staggering. It was also sober and clear-eyed, both in its calculation and about the implications of such a genocide. The U.S. 7th Army had liberated Dachau on April 29, the day before Adolf Hitler swallowed cyanide in his Berlin bunker. For the rest of the spring, and into early summer, the movies Mordy and his friends watched at the Rialto—Errol Flynn in *Objective Burma!*, and *Back to Bataan*, with John Wayne sticking it to the Japanese—were bookended by newsreels that induced no cheers. Pits covered in lime. Mounds of corpses. Living skeletons staring blankly at the camera. Camp gates opened to liberate the already dead.

Even with his uncle soon to return from overseas, for Mordecai the battle for civilization had consisted of jumpy newsreels and crackling radio reports. Superman and Captain America, General Montgomery and General Patton, might have defeated Adolf Hitler in the end, but no superhero had been able to rescue those five million Jews. They had gone unsaved, the Golem failing to come to life.

VIII

MAKING ALIYAH

In the spring of 1944, Lily Richler had hit upon a new scheme for extra income: a rooming house in the Laurentians that would cater to the Orthodox holiday crowd. Ste. Agathe, principal destination for Jews and Gentiles equally, was the right setting. Though she wanted a place of her own, for her first two seasons she rented rooms in a house on Préfontaine Street, a few blocks up from the waterfront. As always, Mordecai spent July and August with her, helping out. So did Avrum, who, though in his second year in optometry, obligingly gave much of his summer to serving as sous-chef for the kosher meals Lily prepared. News of Hiroshima and Nagasaki, and the Japanese surrender, reached them via the daily papers from the city. The *Herald*, priced at five cents, was still Mordy's favourite, the appeal of the tabloid now beyond the comics and sports pages.

The alternative was to sweat out the summer on St. Urbain Street with Julius Frankel. Whether she was aware of it or not, Lily was right to keep her youngest son away from her paramour. She was in love with Frankel, and with the scandal of the divorce receding, a proposal of marriage seemed imminent. A protracted illness had recently led to a hysterectomy, an operation of some delicacy. Happiness, still hard to come by, might finally be her reward.

An unexpected guest in the Laurentians in the summer of 1945 was Evelyn Sacks. The return of her husband from the war had ended her suppertime appearances at 5257, but she had found other ways to keep close to her protégé. Starting in the fall, she became a sounding board for Mordecai from her position in the newly opened Herzliya High School, a private institution operating first out of the YMHA and then from a house at the corner of Esplanade and Pine—a block from Baron Byng. He would visit her at lunch or after school, and she would listen to his complaints about his family, assure him that he was gifted and one day would be an artist or—in her mind perhaps even before his own—a writer.

She was, in short, infatuated with the boy, and in Ste. Agathe, where Mordy didn't have much to do, they spent the days together, at the town beach or, better still, in private spots along Lac des Sables, going for canoe rides and swims. There, the twenty-six-year-old appears to have either initiated or been receptive to sexual contact with the fourteen-year-old. Groping, kissing, almost certainly occurred; intercourse, probably not.

Rosenberg's Lakeside Inn opened the following summer. Determined to be her own proprietor, Lily demanded that Avrum approach Moses for a loan. He did so, and Moses, though already sending $25 monthly cheques for Mordecai's care and helping out with Avrum's tuition, obliged. Lily purchased a plot of land near the town from a local farmer. Another aspiring developer named Otto Kahn came along and offered more, and the farmer reneged on the deal. Showing her own toughness, Lily Richler sued, bringing her sons to the trial in nearby St. Jérôme. She won, and with the additional money bought a small house off the lake. Kahn himself came to a bad end. When his hotel caught fire he ran into the building to save the cashbox, and was burned to death—or so the story went.

Lily's business was across the street from the Laurentide Inn and within a few feet of its sign. STRICTLY FOR RESTRICTED CLIENTELE, it read, both during and after the war. Her own establishment was small and poky, stripped of frills. Entire families shared one of the small rooms running off a long, narrow hallway; the living room had been divided into two units by a flimsy wall. Eating was done in shifts in the crowded dining room, with families expected to spend the days in town or at the beach. Evenings were for card games, the stakes penny-ante, either at the table or on the porch. There were sodas and cigarettes, but no alcohol. Rates were kept low, along with expectations.

Avrum was the kitchen help, buying meats and produce from the market in the early morning, washing and chopping, and then waiting on tables. Mordecai cleaned rooms during the day and did odd jobs for guests in the evening, including fetching cigarettes and Cokes, bought for a nickel and resold for a dime. One guest who booked into the inn for an extended stay presented him with half of a $10 bill. "Treat me right," the man said, "and you'll get the other half." With Lily offering no wages, markups and tips were all her boys could expect. Though dutiful, and happy to be in the Laurentians, they both began to resent the arrangement. Rosenberg's Lakeside Inn was a joyless place to work. Over the years their mother had not improved much as a hostess. Though needing to establish a clientele base, she was still inclined to hang up on callers and scold guests. Cutting remarks didn't help, either. "What happened to your face?" she asked a boy suffering the ravages of acne.

In early 1946 Mordecai was reconciled with his father. He found Moses modestly reborn. With his straw hat and sports jacket, and the aftershave lotion he sprinkled liberally, the elder Richler was a mid-life Orthodox bachelor. When his son discovered a bottle of rye in the glove compartment of his Chevy, he explained that the liquor was for the "femmes." "It makes them want it," he said, wiggling his eyebrows. Soon there was a new woman, a widow named Sarah Werb. A mother of two boys, she was willing to look after Moses as well.

Postwar fortunes shone upon the various Richler businesses, and if Moses Richler remained the eternal underachieving, bullied son of Shmarya, his income was finally decent. With the extra cash, and perhaps the newfound confidence, he treated his boys on Saturday nights, waiting until dark and the end of Sabbath. They might go to a movie or a burlesque at the Gaiety, where

Moses would insist on the front row. He beat the comedians to their punchlines and went slack-jawed at the striptease acts. "That was something, wasn't it?" he'd ask Mordy afterwards. Or they would head over to Joslin's bowling alley on Park Avenue. By letting their dad win, Mordy and Avrum could be sure he'd slip them $5 each for pocket money—"Daddy graft," they called it. The night would end with smoked meat on The Main. Moses was in good spirits, affable and funny, if still the same odd and oddly incomplete individual. Later he would marry Sarah Werb, blushing when he informed his youngest that he was "getting hitched again."

Moses wasn't the only Richler with a burgeoning sartorial sense. Down St. Lawrence Mordecai would stroll on Friday nights, dressed first in the cheap zoot suit he bought after Avrum bequeathed him the job of collecting for Stillman the butcher, and then in the all-black apparel he favoured as a Zionist revolutionary. Sweet Caps were the cigarette of choice and sodas still the beverage. (Except for beer, alcohol would have to wait until college.) The look was brash and arrogant, and if the persona was half bluff, it was also half-true to his emerging character. Mordecai Richler at fifteen and sixteen *was* intimidating, and could be tough. He could even be a tough, once slashing the seat in a streetcar with a penknife after the conductor told his friends to quit singing. Girls were finding him mopey, awkward on the dance floor and aggressive. The following summer, Avrum got a paying job at a Jewish camp in Michigan. When his kid brother rode the bus from Montreal to visit, they double-dated with some local girls. Mordy's date had to keep slapping his wandering hands.

The incident in the streetcar occurred on the way home from a Habonim event. The group was now the anchor of his high-school social life. Involvement in the cause marked his first, and last, impulse to find a substitute for the religious Orthodoxy he had rejected. To be in Habonim was to belong to a cause and embrace an ideology. Three youth groups committed to an independent Jewish state competed for Montreal's ardent teens.

The Hashomer Hatzair (Young Guard), with their blue shirts and neckerchiefs, Marxist group analysis and show trials, were for aspiring zealots only. The Young Judaea, in contrast, thriving in posh Outremont, had the air of a social club. Habonim, or The Builders, fell somewhere in between. Founded in Eastern Europe in 1899, the group had from the outset been socialist and Zionist. Its purpose was to train diasporic Jews for "self-fulfillment through aliyah"—literally, by "ascending" to what was still offi-cially Palestine. Immigration to the Promised Land by age twenty was the ideal, though an unwillingness to physically move there didn't lead to expulsion. Homebodies could still serve the strug-gle of the working classes against "capitalism, fascism and oppression" out in the North American diaspora.

Plus, there was the clubhouse on Jeanne Mance. Habonim tended to attract smart boys and girls. Lily Shatsky, his neighbour from St. Urbain, joined, and the group's reputation for serious-ness was likely the reason Murray Greenberg thought Mordy Richler might be interested. Members sprawled on the clubhouse floor during Friday-night meetings listening to their group leader, Ezra Lifshitz, lecture on Zionist foundation stories. They heard about Theodor Herzl, Viennese assimilationist until he witnessed Colonel Alfred Dreyfus being stripped of his badges while Parisian crowds chanted, "Death to Dreyfus! Death to the Jews!" Herzl had chaired the first Zionist Congress, demanding that delegates wear black tie and tails if only to show the goyim that not all Jews were shtetl peasants. (Dress shirts and ties were mandatory at Habonim meetings.) Lifshitz, then an engineering student at McGill and son of one of Mordy's Hebrew teachers from Talmud Torah, was yet another model youth: bright and idealistic, a nat-ural athlete.

Though he would graduate to a Habonim training camp in Ontario, and then to a kibbutz in Israel, Ezra Lifshitz was not the primary proselytizer. That was left to the *shaliach*, the recruiter, who visited the clubhouse to address the group. A grim, bespec-tacled European Jew with a thick accent, he told of displaced Jews, many of them Dachau and Treblinka survivors, drowning in the Aegean Sea, thanks to the blockade keeping the refugee ships from reaching Palestine. To concerns that militant Zionist groups, including the Irgun, were bombing Arab villages, he remarked that he understood coffee had been rationed in Montreal during the war, and fathers forced to go without new tires for their cars. On the other hand, to the excited youth who stood up to volunteer to make aliyah on the spot, the recruiter mentioned that he knew boys their age rotting in prisons. "They hang resistance fighters," he said.

His verbal assaults on the troops sent by the British government—"imperialism's bully boys," he called them—met with mild resistance. These young builders, after all, had been raised on "God Save the King" and "Gunga Din," John Buchan and the operettas of Gilbert and Sullivan. The more progressive, Mordy Richler among them, had even cheered the victory of the Labour Party in postwar elections in England. Wasn't new prime minister Clement Attlee their socialist brother?

By the end, Habonim heads were spinning. Allegiances and duties weren't obvious or clear-cut. Jews, yes, but also Canadians; Canadians, yes, but also members of the British dominion. "God Save the King" or "Am Yisrael Hai" ("The People of Israel Live")? Did it have to be one or the other?

At Kvutza, the group's camp in the Laurentians, to which Mordecai hitchhiked from Ste. Agathe on Friday afternoons, things were simpler for these New World *chaverim*. They fished and swam and canoed. They courted in the woods. Boys and girls sang songs written by Hebrew poets in praise of physical toil, linking arms to spin into one ecstatic hora after another. "Oh, who can save us hunger's dread?" they sang in the Hebrew of poet Chaim Nachman Bialik. "Who always gave us ample bread / And milk to drink when we are fed?"

Gitel Kravitz may have been among those dancers. One of two sisters—Avrum Richler was sweet on her older sister, Fayge— Gitel was a beauty, and Mordy wasn't alone in worshipping her. For a teenager, proximity to girls, at the camp and in the clubhouse, was reason enough to take aliyah to heart. Girls who joined Habonim weren't necessarily more liberated. (Rumours of communal showering at *kibbutzim* in Palestine run by the radical Hashomer Hatzair caused excitement and envy.) But they were permitted to stay out after ten at night, and were known for their sophisticated selections at The Hut or other local restaurants: toasted bacon and tomato sandwiches and shrimp cocktails. Being around girls, even if the dream still outshone the reality, was a thrill.

So was the now-urgent Zionism of the immediate postwar, with its mandate to populate Eretz Yisrael with Holocaust survivors and to press, by whatever means, for the creation of a Jewish state. Not to be overlooked was the transgression his involvement in Habonim represented for a boy from an Orthodox clan. Mordecai still made sure to march by Shmarya's balcony en route to the clubhouse, to let him know that not every Richler declined progressive politics—or, perhaps, that uncles Israel and Max weren't the only boys willing to fight for a cause.

Neighbourhood politics could also fulfill any youthful yearning for political engagement, or at least strife. The Cartier riding had now twice elected Communist Fred Rose to Ottawa. Within months of his re-election, however, a young cipher clerk at the Soviet embassy in Ottawa, Igor Gouzenko, defected with confidential documents outlining a Soviet espionage ring active inside Canada. Amidst a flurry of press releases about the "Red Menace," scores of people were arrested, held without legal counsel and pressured to incriminate each other. Among those implicated was the member for Cartier; Rose was tried and convicted in the spring of 1946 of "communicating official secrets to foreign officials." He denied any guilt, but his sentence of six years in prison stunned and shamed the many Jews who had voted for him. In the ensuing by-election another Jew won for the Liberal Party.

Earl Kruger lived across the street from the clubhouse with his mother. After the meetings the boys would sit in his living room listening to boxing matches and talking. Kruger would read them stories, including some he had written. Mordy was still scribbling tales of English fops and, when not editing the Baron Byng

newspaper, trying to sneak into the Forum to interview hockey
players for the *Herald*. But he was allowing fiction and poetry to
slowly awaken him. At Habonim his fellow *chaverim* had read and
denounced Arthur Koestler's novel *Thieves in the Night*, taking
umbrage at the fact that the protagonist, a half-Jew raised as a
Gentile in Oxfordshire, wound up making aliyah mostly because
he had been dumped by his shiksa lover, his circumcised penis
found a horror. At the deli afterwards the boys carried on the
debate, wondering how the girl had managed not to notice earlier. Simultaneously, his mother, resigned to the sorrow that
Mordecai was even less likely material for the rabbinate than
Avrum, was pressing Shelley and Shakespeare on him.

Lily was more alone and isolated than ever. At some point in
1946 Julius Frankel, the unusual boarder at 5257 St. Urbain, ended
his relationship with her, leaving the city for Toronto. The
decampment was cause for cheer between the Richler boys, but
it meant their mother had to generate fresh income to support
herself and her younger son. Renewing her efforts at providing
partial board—Mordecai, at least, would be spared any more live-
in lodgers—she placed a small ad in a paper offering "delicious,
strictly kosher meals at a reasonable price in a warm, family
atmosphere." Bachelors with names like Hoppenheim and Stein
were soon paying for her cooking. But one applicant was a dapper
older gentleman named Sullivan. Though she tried putting him
off, explaining that, being kosher, they served no alcohol, Sullivan
insisted, agreeing to the terms of 80 cents per fish meal, $1.05 for
meat. He was soon a regular, dining each evening in a pressed
suit and spats, his fork turned demurely down. If his rising when
the hostess joined them for dessert didn't unnerve the other
men, his elegant speech did. They stopped removing jackets and
ties and grabbing at bowls of food.

Mordy, now his mother's server, warmed to Mr. Sullivan, and
not only because of the tip he left beneath his tea saucer each
evening. A bank employee, Sullivan arrived with small gifts,
including tickets to a Royals game. These were likely the teenager's first conversations with a non-Jew, aside from his high

school teachers. And Mr. Sullivan, a widower who had lost a son
in the war, appeared interested in him. On learning that the fervent Zionist might get called up to serve in "our army in Palestine"
any time after his eighteenth birthday, he recommended that
Mordecai finish his studies before volunteering. He also brought
him a book—George Eliot's *Daniel Deronda*. Sullivan recommended the novel for two reasons: its portrait of a diasporic Jew
in nineteenth-century England who takes his bride to Eretz
Yisrael to restore "a political existence to my people," and the
character of Ezra Mordecai Cohen, saintly mentor to the slowly
awakening Deronda.

Soon he would widen his own reading discoveries beyond
Zionist concerns, seeking and embracing his generation's inter-
nationalist voices and moral consciences, as well as the heroes of
literary style and fashion. W.H. Auden, e.e. cummings, Ernest
Hemingway and André Malraux were not far off. But he paid little
attention to the writing that was beginning to emerge from authors who lived only a couple of miles from St. Urbain Street.
Montreal had lately asserted itself as the literary capital of English
Canada. Those writing for a poetry audience—P.K. Page and
A.J.M. Smith, F.R. Scott, A.M. Klein and Irving Layton—were
admirable local sources of inspiration. But bestselling literary
novelists were on a whole other level. Gwethalyn Graham's 1944
novel *Earth and High Heaven*, Hugh MacLennan's *Two Solitudes* in
1945 and Gabrielle Roy's *The Tin Flute*, a 1947 translation of *Bonheur
d'occasion*, were all published out of New York, which was hardly
surprising; there were no Canadian publishing houses of note.
Taken together, they offered a comprehensive portrait of
Montreal's various classes and divides, from Roy's working-class
St. Henri residents to the affluent Westmount denizens of Graham.
MacLennan, meanwhile, shifted from rural Quebec to Anglo
Montreal, thus building, for the first time in print, a group por-
trait of French/English tensions—the city as it was, and had been,
almost from its inception.

Out of such material had sprung three critical and commercial
successes. Gwethalyn Graham's version of the *Daniel Deronda*

story—an interracial marriage between a Westmount girl and a Jewish lawyer undermined by the anti-Semitism of the pre-war years—sold more than a million copies across North America. MacLennan's novel, also broaching the dark waters of a "mixed" marriage, in his instance between a Protestant and Catholic, was no less a sensation, selling out its printing on the first day. But it was *The Tin Flute*, guaranteed an initial printing of 500,000 after being made a Literary Guild Book Club selection, that carried the biggest literary news. The story of the Lacasse family of St. Henri, Roy's novel contained characters that one could actually spot around the city—living, breathing Montrealers, rendered on the page. The novel affected many, including a bright, attractive bilingual journalist named Mavis Gallant. Then a reporter for the weekly *Standard*, the forceful twenty-five-year-old convinced her editors to set up a photo recreation of scenes from the book even before it appeared in English.

In her short career as a features writer in Montreal, Gallant would also persuade her bosses to let her write on everything from local hoodlums to "What Is This Thing Called Jazz?" One 1946 piece, "Why Are Canadians So Dull?" would surely have appealed to a restless teenager living near The Main. But Mordy Richler scarcely noted the emergence of Roy, MacLennan or even Graham. Nor did he know about A.M. Klein's *The Rocking Chair*, a collection of poems designed to bridge the gap between Montreal Jews and French Canadians. Even Klein's outsized presence in the neighbourhood since the war—calling it the "Jewish ghetto" was starting to sound a tinny note—did not register, except perhaps during the month preceding the spring 1949 election, when the productive poet, journalist and lawyer, also a speech writer for liquor tycoon Sam Bronfman, ran for Parliament with the CCF party. For his trouble he was mocked by his Liberal rival as a man "wallowing in filth, vituperation and dirt" because of his party's position on Zionism.

Klein was, in effect, too close by for the teenager to notice. So were MacLennan and Roy. Everything from Canadian self-abnegation and Anglo-Montreal colonialism to the English literature texts at

Baron Byng and the Zionism of Habonim directed his gaze and imagination outwards—south of the border and across the ocean—his allegiances and interests already conflicted and complex.

The nature of those allegiances close to home had become clear the spring before his senior year at Baron Byng. Shmarya Richler died at the age of seventy-two, and when Mordecai showed up to pay his grudging respects—the body, as was the custom, had been laid out in the living room—he was met in the front hallway by his Uncle Joe. Accusing the sixteen-year-old of hastening the death by refusing to visit during the months of his grandfather's decline, Joe told him Shmarya's will had forbidden him even to touch his coffin. The boy was furious and humiliated. Richlers, it was now apparent, not only nursed grudges for years and decades; they took them into the grave for safekeeping.

IX

ROOM 41

Class president Mordecai Richler—granted, he had been acclaimed; no one else wanted the job—enjoyed a good argument. Most mornings at Baron Byng he waited at his desk at the back of row four, one row in from the window, while Mr. McCletchie, poetry lover and survivor of Verdun, unpacked his briefcase at the front of the room. The routine was established. Arriving ten or fifteen minutes before class, Mordy would read a newspaper until his teacher was settled in. Then, ignoring whatever pranks his classmates were up to, he would rise and, driving his hands into his pockets, launch a fresh shell. In these instances, the shell would be a remark about politics or books, calculated to provoke if not explode. At the very least, the boy wanted a debate, and he wanted it man to man, in a meeting of equals. If declaring incarcerated Fred Rose a victim of government hostility to socialism or announcing the moral imperative of creating a state of Israel didn't work, he could always fall back on a classic stance: denouncing the perfidy of the British Empire. He knew his stuff, facts and figures, and would cite articles out of the *Herald* or *Gazette*. With the bell about to sound, the older contestant would plead no contest. "That's enough," his teacher would say. "Let's go on."

Mr. McCletchie tolerated his star pugilist's need to exercise his burgeoning verbal and analytical intelligence. As he had with Evelyn Sacks at Talmud Torah, Mordy won over the Baron Byng

teachers he wanted to impress, because he either liked the subject or was fond of the instructor. Mr. McCletchie was one example.
So was Mr. Dunn in history, and the art teacher, Anne Savage.
English and history in particular excited him, and he responded
by dominating discussions and displaying the same facility at
prose. For an annual essay contest, students were asked to choose
one of four topics. When he combined all four into a single essay,
he was disqualified, despite having written a superior piece.

The sixteen-year-old, it was becoming apparent, responded to
his own rules and measures. It wasn't only about declining to
sing "God Save the King" along with his Zionist comrades the day
Baron Byng hosted a British official in its gymnasium. That was
a group agitation. More characteristic was ignoring thirty-five
classmates while engaging with Mr. McCletchie every morning.
Likewise his willingness to barely scrape by in classes—maths
and chemistry mostly—that didn't hold his interest. Certain
classmates, including his vice-president, Jerry Brown, found him
intimidating but powerful, a natural leader. Others cautiously
believed themselves to be friends, laughing at his jokes while
remaining wary of his temper. Still others thought Mordy a bully,
prickly and mean-spirited. He slapped a boy who had failed to
produce a gift purchased by the class for Mr. McCletchie on the
appointed day. He scrapped with classmates twice his size over
slights, real or perceived. And while some teachers too noted his
sensitivity, his quiet desire for approval—if, again, on his terms—
a vocal minority decided he was bad news.

Ironically, the aspect of his character that both classmates and
staff at Baron Byng should have been wary of went largely
undetected. At some stage Mordecai began passing the time in
class by taking notes. He wasn't jotting down anything to do with
the lesson. He was observing and listening, and then describing
the appearance of teachers and the mannerisms of classmates.
Though he continued to sketch faces and figures in the margins,
and accepted his mother's offer of a summer course in drawing
at the Montreal Art Gallery, more and more he cared how words
were arranged and sentences created. "What are you writing?" a

classmate once asked. He first answered that he didn't know. Then he admitted that he might write a book one day.

But he was mostly taken up with attending demonstrations for Israel, and mimeographing and handing out sheets of propaganda at goyish intersections around town. Now a real warrior, he badgered his family into boycotting British goods. The Richlers mostly infuriated him, especially once they threw their financial support behind the Lubavitcher Rebbe, an ultra-Orthodox Hasidic group based in Crown Heights, Brooklyn. When their aunts and uncles spoke only of the foolishness of fighting British rule in Palestine and the certainty of defeat, Avrum and Mordy whispered bitterly of their cowardice, their unwillingness to support a Jewish homeland even in the wake of the Holocaust.

Meetings at the Habonim clubhouse, attended feverishly through the summer and fall of 1947, brooked no such defeatism. Would the United Nations opt to divide Palestine into two states or allow for a binational Palestinian-Jewish entity? A single state would be a disaster; Jews would end up a minority within it, as vulnerable as before. While U.S. president Harry Truman was said to favour partition, many within the U.N. pressured for a single Palestine. Finally, at the end of November, the U.N. General Assembly voted to end the British Mandate in Palestine no later than the following August, with the territory to be divided into Palestinian and Jewish states. In the neighbourhood there was hugging and horn-honking, and bottles of schnapps and apricot brandy were brought out for toasting. Photos of Chaim Weizmann and David Ben-Gurion were taped to front windows. Stars of David flapped from balconies. On Jeanne Mance, meanwhile, the *chaverim* gathered forces to march downtown singing "Am Yisrael Hai." Bold Habonim, Mordy Richler among them, danced a hora outside the Forum, blocking traffic. To be a proud Jew, a proud Zionist, was the best of things that day.

The singing of earnest Zionist anthems stopped well short of the doors of the Royal Billiard Room or the Rachel Pool Hall. Jack Rabinovitch had already graduated to McGill, where he was both playing on the varsity basketball team and hustling

Westmount kids at a dollar per game in the pool halls down-town. Never having his friend's talent with a cue, Mordecai thrilled nonetheless to the smoky, masculine culture of such rooms. His final class of the school day was math. Rather than endure it, he would often slip out of Baron Byng and round the corner to the Rachel, counting on the Serbian owner to stand on guard by the front window and watch for any teachers scavenging for truants. Apprentice players, likely to rip the baize with a clumsy cue strike, were relegated to the back four tables, the ones with the Coca-Cola stains and black tape patching existing rips. A game cost twenty cents, the loser paying the rate. The owners kept a live goat, and the animal sometimes nipped at the teenager's heels while he was taking a shot.

No less watchful in the Rachel than in Room 41, Mordy studied the habitués to learn how to select the best cue and acknowledge a difficult pot. (Bang three times on the floor with your cue.) Though the Rachel didn't attract sharks, the "pros" who trolled the pool halls in fedora hats and suits and ties fascinated him. In the likes of Mendy Perlman, "Atomic" Eddy Agha and the unbeatable Izzy Halprin, whose day job as a sailor had shipped him out to the British blockade of Palestine, Mordecai glimpsed versions of manhood at intriguing odds with his father and his extended family. These were tough hombres, clipped of word and unapologetic of behaviour. Once he actually met them, through Rabinovitch or by hanging around, he often found them shifty. But that, too, was okay. Nice people, he observed early, weren't nearly as interesting.

Men like Eddy Agha and Izzy Halprin knew about life. They told stories about the roaring, outsized Montreal of the postwar era, the city whose own character blazed across the *Herald* headlines every morning: "Cop Killed in Verdun!" "Raid on Gambling Dens!" With Camillien Houde back as mayor, the city was once again open for business. Like all neighbourhood kids, Mordy had been weaned on tales of Baron Byng's Harry Ship, a.k.a. the Boy Wonder, a world-class Jewish mobster. Ship, who had earned his nickname by making it so young in a tough business, operated two illegal casinos, one in a shabby industrial building in Côte-de-Liesse and the other in a mansion in Greenfield Park. Drivers picked up customers at a hotel for delivery to these unmarked sites. Liquor and food were free; at his barbotte and blackjack tables, bets soared into the thousand-dollar range. Harry Feldman ran a betting parlour right on St. Catherine Street, near the corner of Bleury, and if police had to raid it to prove they were combatting vice, they made sure to call first. The same held true for the brothels along de Bullion Street for working-class clients, and the fancier establishments over on Milton, where government ministers were discreetly serviced. The celebrated Mme Beauchamp owned some twenty-five *lupanars*, catering to all incomes and preferences. During her visits to the courthouse, and prior to her release, she would consult with officers over which houses of ill repute would be raided next.

Venues for legal fun were scarcely less lively. Newspaper ads shouted out the range of clubs and bars—the Baronet Room and El Morocco, Clover Café and Normandie Roof—and out-of-town musical talent competed with another local boy wonder, this one legitimate. By the age of seventeen, pianist Oscar Peterson— born and raised in Little Burgundy, an equally poor neighbour- hood adjacent to St. Henri—was being called the Brown Bomber of Boogie-Woogie. The prestigious Johnny Holmes Orchestra signed him in 1942, only to be informed by the Ritz hotel man- ager that no "coloured pianist" would be allowed to play the ball- room. It took the threat of a boycott to put the dazzlingly gifted pianist on the Ritz stage. Within a few years he would be head- lining his own trio at the Alberta Lounge, across from the Windsor Hotel. Shortly thereafter, his talent too huge for Montreal, Oscar Peterson would debut at Carnegie Hall in New York.

But until he had both his knees smashed because of his own outstanding debts, Harry Ship was the big man around town, his sightings at Ruby Foo's Chinese restaurant on Decarie, across from the Blue Bonnets Racetrack, recorded by Al Palmer. Palmer's *Herald* column, "Cabaret Circuit," was a must-read. And prize fighters like Maxie Berger were among those who slugged it out to get their picture in the *Star* or *Herald*, preferably with a moll draped on their arm. No longer could Jews be reduced to the stereotype of the black-clothed, Yiddish-speaking ghost from the Old World, or the disloyal socialist with the rolled-up sleeves and radical views. Neither could they be seen, by themselves or by others, as simply postwar middle-class newbies, aspirants to the emerging suburbs over in Snowdon or up in Côte-St-Luc via an expansion of their parents' shmatte factories or a coveted place in law or medicine at McGill. Jews were now decent middleweights and starters on university basketball teams. They owned night-clubs as well as gambling dens.

Mordy learned a lesson in the shading of human nature in the winter of 1947–48. His Habonim chum Murray Greenberg had been raised in a single-parent household, with a father capable of blowing a week's wage as a plumber on a horse at Blue Bonnets. Boxer Greenberg was himself developing into a tough guy. Feverish fundraising for the soon-to-be-declared state of Israel earned their chapter $200. Of those who banged on doors and charmed housewives into making donations, none was more effective than handsome Murray Greenberg. But when he arrived at the clubhouse with the news that the money had been stolen from his bedroom, his comrades were skeptical. He threw a chair against a wall and resigned from the group. Later, having quit school to drive a cab and run scams, he laid the blame for the money's disappearance on his father.

Murray Greenberg was no longer a candidate for making aliyah. But for the others, the time was both momentous and right. On May 14, 1948, David Ben-Gurion proclaimed the state of Israel, promising it would be a "beacon to the nations." Five Arab states declared war on it the next day, with Egypt bombing Tel Aviv. Mordecai's age had robbed him of the chance to fight either the fascists in Spain or the Nazis throughout Europe, and so to be defined by what he had done rather than what had been done around him. In seven months, he would turn eighteen: old enough to serve in the army, as he had explained to the kindly Mr. Sullivan, his mother's elderly paying supper guest; old enough to define the times. For once, age was about to become his ally.

But before that January 1949 date, he had to survive more mundane life passages. While he scored 81 percent in history and 78 percent in English literature, his overall average on graduation from Baron Byng was 64.6 percent. Frantic studying the night before his matriculation exams netted just 36 percent in algebra, and French, at 58 percent oral and 50 percent written, also dragged him down. Even had he been a Gentile, the class president of Room 41 was still .4 of a percent short of McGill admission. With those marks, it had to be the local college, Sir George Williams, or a job. He enrolled in Sir George for September.

There was another summer to get through working for his mother in Ste. Agathe. Lily now had income enough to pay two of his friends, Jack Basuk and Dave Gursky, to help. The teens had fun together after hours, swimming and fishing, slipping into the fancier resorts like Castle des Monts and the Manor House to chat up girls and watch the floor shows. Comedians were the mainstay, and Jackie Kahane, resident comic at the Manor House in the late 1940s, was the funniest. A Baron Byng graduate himself, Kahane worked as a pharmacist in the neighbourhood while honing his stand-up skills in the Laurentians. His shtik delighted Mordecai, as did his forbearance in performing long nights in front of tough, noisy rooms. Soon to graduate to the Borscht Belt in the Catskills and the big Montreal clubs off-season, Kahane wasn't above clowning with balloons and eggs, and kept his act, replete with jokes about bad luck and physical ailments, annoying relations and nagging wives, near lily-white. A "blue" bit might only go this far: One Jewish wife whispers to her friend that she's having an affair. "Oh, who's the caterer?" her friend replies. "My doctor said I was in terrible shape," ran a more typical gag. "I told him, 'I want a second opinion.' 'All right,' he said, 'you're ugly too.'"

His friend Dave Gursky, happy to tag along to the better-class hotels, was none too pleased the night Mordy borrowed his pants to take a guest at Rosenberg's Inn on a date, and returned them

with semen stains. When not serving clients or attempting to
seduce their daughters, Mordecai was sitting at a table in a small
side room hammering on a typewriter. He was smoking one
Lucky Seven after another. Now he was drinking bottles of Molson
beer as well, purchased for him by sympathetic adults. He was
smoking and drinking and typing, and the stories he was peeling
out, still about English fops with funny names, were being read
by his friend Jack Basuk, whose opinion he respected. When
Avrum, shortly to open his own optometry business, visited Ste.
Agathe that summer, his brother told him he was setting aside
his plans to become a professional visual artist. He was going to
be a writer instead.

"Yeah, right," his sibling responded.

X

CUT/CUTTING LOOSE

The fall of 1948 had to be unsettling. In the space of a month
Mordy Richler was twice banished from St. Urbain Street.
Graduating to Sir George Williams College, a half-college,
half-university operating downtown out of the YMCA on
Drummond Street, marked one internal exile. Baron Byng High,
with its ninety-five percent of boys (and girls) who didn't eat ham,
its crowd of kids named Rifka, Yossel, Yankel and Sam, had
allowed him to come of age among his own, where his idiosyn-
cratic character was recognized if not always appreciated. At Sir
George, he was abruptly part of a minority among the mixed-bag
majority of either Anglo-Saxons who had graduated with similar
lack of distinction from city schools or adult learners, including
many veterans, who filled the evening classes that were the mainstay of the schedule. Either way, dark-haired, dark-eyed Mordecai
Richler was suddenly adrift in a sea of blue-eyed, pale-skinned
classmates named Terry, Florrie, Kay and Bob. Goy culture, formerly gleaned by reading newspapers and listening to the CBC,
and the mysterious Anglo "other"—a group far more elusive than
the French, who, again, had been around him since he could
remember—could now be observed up close. Including, of course,
those pretty shiksas.

The second, possibly starker exile followed Lily Rosenberg's
decision to give up 5257 St. Urbain. That autumn she rented a
small apartment for herself and Mordecai across the street from

Avrum's new business, in the Winchester Apartments, at 5715 Sherbrooke Street West. Freshly graduated, twenty-three-year-old Avrum decided to open an optometry practice in Notre Dame de Grace, a near-suburb adjacent to Westmount. Its French name notwithstanding, the neighbourhood was a fortress of middle-class Presbyterianism. Shops closed at six and sidewalks rolled up at ten; there were no noisy delis or bustling outdoor markets, communal baths or Communists arguing with Zionists on park benches. Even the signature blocks of three-storey dwellings, so characteristic of the Plateau, lost a floor in N.D.G., although the apartments remained spacious.

Living in N.D.G., where Mordy Richler had possibly never set foot before his mother's decision to uproot, and where he seems to have done little more than lay his head at night, may have had less impact than the commute from Sir George to the Winchester Apartments. There was only one route: the bus along Sherbrooke Street, out the west corner of the downtown and through lower Westmount. Barely a half-century earlier, residents of the Golden Square Mile, as the downtown residential area was called, were said to have possessed better than three-quarters of the country's wealth. These included the Molsons and Holts, Strathconas and McGills, and they had amassed fortunes running banks, railways, timber companies and steamship lines. The scions of the various financial empires had then shifted into Westmount, leaving the family mansions along Sherbrooke and up the slope to be converted into private clubs and university buildings. The vast neighbourhood across Atwater Street absorbed the riches, and the exclusivity. No sign was posted declaring Westmount to be gated or segregated by race. Zoned off, as it was, by wealth it was clear to Montrealers who belonged there—and who did not. Mordecai Richler had likely never strolled, collar turned up and hands shoved in pockets, along any street above Murray Hill Park, let alone been inside a Westmount residence.

But he was well aware that at least one Jewish clan had climbed to the summit—the Bronfman brothers, former bootleggers turned "legit" owners of the Seagram Company, then the largest distiller of alcoholic beverages in the world. Mr. Sam Bronfman owned a mansion up at the top.

The intersection of Sherbrooke and Atwater did offer a familiar dynamic to the boy as he headed each evening to a flat pokier than 5257 St. Urbain: the Mother House of the Congregation of Notre Dame, a typically imposing Catholic edifice, and the Temple Emanu-El synagogue, the temple where rich Reform Jews worshipped, stood almost side by side on Sherbrooke, their proximity a reminder of how Jews and French lived back over the mountain. But once past the synagogue, Mordy gazed out of the bus window at the ivy-covered private schools, demure shops, manicured parks and stone library of the Anglo elite. Soon enough the bus crossed Décarie Boulevard into N.D.G., where the men who worked for the men who lived in Westmount resided.

Lily had fled the setting of her marriage and adulthood. Officially, she did so to be near Avrum. Shame over Julius Frankel may have played a part, along with an anticipatory sense that she was about to slip further down the economic and social ladder, a plunge best made away from judging gazes. Within a year she would be employed first in a plumber's shop and then, remarkable for an Orthodox Jewish woman, as a coat-check girl at a strip club. While her accounting skills soon earned her a promotion to bookkeeper at the Esquire Show Club on St. Lawrence— her Jewish-mafia bosses suggested she learn how to use a handgun—the fact was that by 1949 the rabbi's daughter, his *shammas* and errand runner, worked in a nightclub, including on the Sabbath. She also lived on a busy goy street a long five miles from the neighbourhood, the tribe and faith that she had once assumed would hold her in its embrace forever.

A mother's humiliation proved to be her son's opportunity. Busy since his adolescence trying to flee the airless house built around him by that tribe and faith, Mordecai was suddenly being given a push out the door. The push wasn't violent and, at first, he didn't travel far. But at age seventeen, he was out.

His first actual flight took him to New York. Montreal Jews

often had more direct family and business links with New York and Chicago than with Toronto or Winnipeg. Though there were Rosenbergs in Ontario, a result of the rabbi's years there during the First World War, and Mordecai had stayed with an aunt in Toronto when he was a boy, the family still looked southward. Uncle Israel and Aunt Vera lived in Brighton Beach in south Brooklyn, and since the war Lily had been rewarding her sons for their summer labours with a fall trip to visit them. They loved the outing. The train ride was an adventure, passing through Customs and then settling into the glorious Adirondacks before descending the spine of New York State onto Manhattan. But the company of the Rosenbergs themselves, especially Israel, was a bigger thrill.

Mordy's playwright uncle, written off by some family members as a Communist, cut a dashing figure—handsome and dapper in fedora and cravat, funny and extroverted in manner. Lily may have been reserved, like her mother, but at least two of her siblings—flamboyant sister Ruth and brother Israel—showed traces of other Rosenberg qualities, along with the residue, possibly, of the rabbi's semi-secret life as a fabricator of tales and actor of parts. Then in his fifties, Israel was a generous host, slipping his nephews "stipends" and taking them to the delis and cafés he frequented—Katz's on East Houston and the Royal Café on Second Avenue. Yiddish theatre was winding down in New York, choked by the suspension of Jewish emigration to America during the war, but Israel Rosenberg still managed his small theatre on Clinton Street, writing and performing plays with Vera and their daughter Betty. He also did radio shows for the handful of surviving Yiddish stations. A beloved figure in entertainment circles—during one of Avrum's visits, singer Eddie Cantor took him aside to say that if his uncle could write in English, his plays would be on Broadway—he lived his modestly bohemian life with relish. That energy must have been infectious.

Mordecai's weekend visit in September 1948 coincided with the staging of one of Israel Rosenberg's final successes. *Men Without Eyes* was a stage play adapted from his popular radio melodrama of the same name. Aware that his nephew had limited

Yiddish, Israel didn't insist that he stay to watch Vera and Betty perform. Instead, he funded days and evenings of Mordy wandering museums and seeing movies, forays aided by the gift of a new suit and coat—courtesy of the sponsors of his radio show, who paid out in product instead of cash.

Registered at Sir George to study English, social science, history, commerce and economics, he gave over his early months at college to establishing himself as a journalist. On October 14, 1948, the (poorly edited) school newspaper, the *Georgian*, featured two articles signed "Mordecai Richler." (He would also sign "Mordy Richler" and, once voted onto the masthead, the more serious "M. Richler.") One piece—coverage of the freshman gala in Victoria Hall in the heart of lower Westmount, halfway along that bus ride out to N.D.G—was likely assigned by an editor. "Over 100 couples had a riotously good time at the gala Emancipation Dance," the cub reporter began. The other article was of his own making. "On the Jump from High School to College" offered a wry meditation on his first days at Sir George. Claiming his high-school teachers had agreed that, upon graduation "like old Polonius, I showed a 'plentiful lack of wit,'" he quotes an uncle who, taking him aside, had predicted: "Mordy, I always knew you were to be a bum some day. I'm glad you're going about it the right way."

In subsequent months he would report on school elections, the winter ski carnival and a lecture by a visiting Chinese scholar, and produce a passionate defence of "one of the new miracles of modern times"—the state of Israel. Putting those Friday evenings at the Habonim clubhouse to use, Mordecai opened "A People Come Home!: Israel Today" with a Zionist foundation narrative: "Towards the end of the century, a tall man with a magnificent black beard, sat at the trial of one Captain Dreyfuss." The man was Theodor Herzl, and this paean to the "great work of an inspired and fearless people" in developing the "desert lands of Palestine" must have seemed exotic stuff to readers encountering names like Herzl and Chaim Weizmann for the first time. Scarcely less exotic was the author of this call to arms, a journalist-militant

who insisted on contextualizing the recent assassination of a diplomat: "the shameful murder of over six million Jews, and present
megare existence of the remainder of European Jewry is much
mor significant than the activities of the recently squelched Stern
Gang." By then, still early into his first semester, he had been
appointed as the Sir George representative on the executive of
the U.J.S.A (United Jewish Student Association), run by the Hillel
Foundation at McGill University, a long three blocks and a flight
or two up in the social and educational ladder from his institution. The November 1948 issue of the *Hillel McGillah*, the group's
monthly newspaper, featured in its lead "'Mr Hillel' Entries Pouring
In," by Mordecai Richler. On page 2 was a photo of the student
executive, all 75-per-cent-average Jews who had presumably
gained lawful entry into McGill along with the interloper from
down the road—a young man attired in suit and tie. Of the ten
united Jewish students, he is the only one not attempting a smile.
He had also not yet turned eighteen.

If his first year as a student-journalist witnessed the birth of
an ethos of hustle, as well as a knack for getting to know the
right people quickly, his second, and final, year in the academy
revealed still more bedrock instincts. M. Richler was elected "day
editor" at the *Georgian*, alongside McFarland, Ellison, Robertson
and Philips, and led the muckraking charge on several contro-
versies. He helped report a series of unsigned articles detailing
the goings-on at a known underworld bar and brothel located
next to the campus on Stanley Street. In January 1950, when the
college decided to hold its carnival at a hotel in the Eastern
Townships that welcomed only a "restricted clientele," the
Georgian spearheaded a campaign to have it cancelled.

A few weeks after this victory, and a week after leaving its
editorial page empty in protest that "for the past three issues
there have been no letters to the editor," the *Georgian* published
an inflammatory editorial. It advised against recognizing the
Hillel Society at Sir George, declaring that "the recognition of
this group would not only mean toleration—*but active endorsement*—of religious segregation on our campus." Like the many

restrictive fraternities and sororities over at McGill, Hillel, the
editorialist argued, was simply a "pretentious fraternity" that
had no place in an open environment. As was the custom, the
editorial was signed only with initials: "MR."

The letter page of the *Georgian* was quickly crowded with complaints. Offended students denounced the assault on the Jewish
society and, by extension, Jews everywhere endeavouring to
make their way in the post-Holocaust world, hurling epithets at
"MR" ranging from "the cantankerous embryo, boy genius" to
"lowly Mordecai" to "the notorious Mordecai Richler." "Richler
rides again," asserted a letter writer who had earlier taken offence
at another article by the already heat-seeking teenage journalist.
Accusations included slander, the production of "worthless trash"
in the guise of truth, and the "flagrant misuse of editorial privilege invested in destructive individuals." In the dynamics of the
exchange could be found a blueprint for the future: Richler adopt-
ing a stance calculated to both outrage and set himself apart;
responses of predictable anger and resentment, all leading to the
creation of a battling, argumentative persona known to many
solely by his first name. In his attack on the very same group
whose executive he had joined a year before were similar early
warnings of a creed of independence, of being beholden, out-
wardly at least, to no one.

Richler filed reviews as well, of Sholem Aleichem's *It's Hard to
Be a Jew* and S. Ansky's folk drama *The Dybbuk*. The latter, performed by the Little Theatre of the YM-YWHA on Mount Royal
Street, starred David Lewis's older brother Charles and a young
actor named Stanley Mann. He also wrote a piece about refugees
in his classes, including a Belsen survivor who bore a concentration camp number on her arm. (He preferred evening classes,
filled largely with adult learners. They had seen and done things;
they knew a little about life.) When the YMCA board of governors blocked an invitation issued by student union radicals,
Mordecai Richler among them, to an English clergyman with
leftist views, he used his *Georgian* pulpit to denounce the decision in the loftiest of terms. His grandiloquence extended to

support for Progressive Party candidate Henry Wallace as U.S. president and for nuclear disarmament via the Stockholm Peace Appeal. When not penning his socialist politics he was demonstrating them, joining protests against McCarthyism.

In his busy first year his class attendance, no surprise, suffered. Having dropped commerce and history, he squeezed out four C grades and, rather surprisingly, an A in economics. The next year, his grades would climb to the mid-B level, the only A being in the English course taught by a professor named Neil Compton, whom he liked. Telling a classmate he would need better French to be a reporter in Montreal, he added to his workload by enrolling in a continuing education course at McGill in the evening. He prepared and read essays to the class.

Specifically, he aspired to report for the *Herald*, the tabloid he had been reading since he was a boy. A friend of Avrum's from the old neighbourhood had graduated from McGill to a desk job at the paper. Percy Tannenbaum, who knew him as Mutty, spoke to the night editor, who offered the teenager a part-time job as copy boy at the paper's head offices on Craig Street. That didn't last long, but Mordecai did meet enough people to finagle some freelance assignments. Five cents a word was the *Herald*'s going rate—less than he earned spotting pins at Joslin's bowling alley back on Park Avenue, a job he still had—and the assignments were, for the most part, unglamorous and unsigned. He filed on social and sporting events in and around Sir George, and one time he was asked to cover a concert by the great pianist Artur Rubinstein. And on February 25, 1948, a day when the *Herald* reported on the violent asbestos strike in Asbestos, Quebec, and noted with bemusement that of the 248 divorces granted in Canada the previous year, 233 had involved Montrealers, page 11 featured the impressionistic confessions of a "smuggler" of oleo. Oleo, a newfangled butter substitute widely available across the country, was then still banned by the government of Maurice Duplessis, and had been front-page news for several years. The eighteen-year-old cub reporter duly identified as Mordecai Richler recast the controversy as absurd. "Earlier today," he

wrote, "the Herald met a veteran trespasser of Canada's margar-
ine curtain." Among the smuggler's comments were a denial that
he was the mastermind behind an "oleo smuggling band" and an
expression of worry that the law, in the form of "Mr. Butterfat
Legrue," had devised a radar machine that could detect the
banned substance. As satire went, the piece was lame, but satire
it was, and duly signed with his full name.

Getting a *Herald* byline was a minor breakthrough. It was not
so much the money as the status it conferred: this was real journalism in a real newspaper. The lively tabloid, with its lurid headlines and isn't-life-strange stories, its dozen pages of movie and
club listings and dozen more of sports, represented the city he
was coming to know and adore. Page 11 was close by the regular
columnists he read for their attitude and gossip, and only a dozen
pages from where the syndicated American journalist Walter
Winchell appeared. Moses Richler loved Winchell. Moses may
even have picked up the *Herald* that winter morning and read his
son's oleo exposé—this time without needing to be told which
article he was responsible for.

Mordy was still seeing his father on weekends. But even Moses
Richler, soon to marry Sarah Werb, had left the neighbourhood
and rented an apartment in Côte-des-Neiges. Other uncles and
aunts were likewise drifting over to Snowdon and Côte-St-Luc,
where bungalows came with shower faucets and refrigerators.
Reasons to be back on Jeanne Mance, either at 4846, still home
to his widowed Richler grandmother, or a block farther north, at
the Habonim clubhouse, were fewer and fewer. The world that
had been so defining was suddenly removed, literally and figura-
tively, from the here and now.

As if to mark the distance, for his new downtown life Mordecai
was seeking new friends. Besides the newspaper and student
union, he joined the college literature club. He was reading more
widely now than even Mr. McCletchie might have predicted.
Malraux's *Man's Fate*, destined to hold sway over generations of
young men with its tale of heroism and betrayal among 1920s
Shanghai Communists, enthralled him. So did Ernest Hemingway,

then arguably the most celebrated living writer. Both the early stories and the novels *A Farewell to Arms* and *For Whom the Bell Tolls* were magnetic. George Orwell had lately emerged as a cultural hero, only to die at the age of forty-six on January 27, 1950, shortly after *Nineteen Eighty-Four* appeared. Orwell passed away on Mordecai's nineteenth birthday. Norman Mailer's *The Naked and the Dead* and Truman Capote's *Other Voices, Other Rooms* were literary sensations by authors around his own age: Mailer was twenty-five, Capote just nineteen. Here was proof that the postwar world needed fresh voices, with Jews and homosexuals welcome (if not in the pages of the Montreal *Star*, whose book critic had called Mailer "obscene.") Among the Canadians, only the short stories of Toronto writer Morley Callaghan, gritty and urban in tone, spoke to him the way Hemingway or Malraux did. "What? You're going to be a *Canadian* writer?" he was being taunted. The successes of Gabrielle Roy and Hugh MacLennan notwithstanding, there appeared to be two categories: "real" writers, and Canadians who wrote books. From the start, Mordy knew which one he wanted to be.

Serious books and no-less-serious magazines—the *Partisan Review* and *Horizon*, the *New Statesman* and the *New Yorker*—were only part of his early self-education as an author. With his new friends he listened to opera and watched art films, including Roberto Rossellini's landmark *Rome, Open City*, and attended his debut ballet: the famed Sadler's Wells troupe, visiting Montreal on a North American tour. In truth, he attended half the ballet, having waited outside and then strolled in for free with the smokers after intermission.

Books and urgent political discussions were enhanced by alcohol at parties or in bars. Neither an Orthodox childhood nor teenage years among fellow Jews had taught him much about drinking. College with Anglo-Saxons soon changed that. Not yet legal—twenty-one was then the age of majority—Mordy Richler was abruptly a drinker. Tolerant of wine and beer, he was almost from the start attracted more to gin, whisky and cognac. From the start, too, he could hold hard liquor while keeping syntax and

face intact. At the Shrine, a bar off Sherbrooke popular with journalists and literary types, he sat at the table with the *Herald* editor
Percy Tannenbaum and a lively, personable *Standard* staff writer
named Jackie Sirois. Like Tannenbaum, Jackie Sirois was a few
years his senior, already once married and divorced. Mordy
Richler loved the company of these older, more accomplished
adults. He didn't seek permission to push his way in with them,
but he would if need be, and then prove that he belonged.

At the "Orange Crate," a student apartment in N.D.G so dubbed
for its citrus façade and Salvation Army furnishings, the eighteen-
year-old was shown up a little. Third-year McGill students Joan
Cassidy and Kina Mitchell threw quality parties there. Mordecai
got himself invited to one, and sat listening as Joan Cassidy
recited Dylan Thomas's sexually purple mock-epic "Ballad of the
Long-Legged Bait." Puzzled by a phrase, he interrupted the reci-
tation to ask its meaning. Her explanation that the phrase was a
reference to fellatio did not, unfortunately, clear the matter up—
Mordy didn't know that term either. Undaunted, he asked several
follow-up questions, as if he were back in Room 41 of Baron Byng,
sparring with his homeroom teacher. For at least one sophisticate at the party, war veteran and bookshop owner Jack Lieber,
the incident showed the kid had guts. Another gaffe, in which
Mordecai demonstrated for Gentile bemusement how he had
held a live rooster over his head during Passover as a boy, showed
the kid was still a kid. But he liked the literary crowd, even if they
didn't know quite what to make of him. He had already befriended
John Sutherland, who also hosted parties attended by the likes
of the elderly Stephen Leacock and the lawyer-poet F.R. Scott.
Sutherland's journal, the *Northern Review,* was one of a handful
of publications providing a venue for local writers to get published. Half-brother to the actor Donald Sutherland, he produced
a "real" magazine that paid up to $25 for a story—often, it was
assumed, out of his own pocket. One day, on being told by
Mordecai that he was bound for Europe, Sutherland offered to
set up a lunch with a friend of Jackie Sirois's, another writer
determined to make an Atlantic crossing: Mavis Gallant. When

she asked about this Mordy Richler, Sutherland replied that he was talented but brash, as well as a bit of a know-it-all. "He'll come up and say something outrageous," Sutherland warned her. A veteran of interviews with gangsters, Gallant figured she could handle him.

They met in an Italian restaurant downtown. Sutherland soon fell silent while the youngsters—at thirty, he was two years Gallant's senior, a dozen the elder of the boy—chatted. Actually, Mavis Gallant scarcely got a word in either, so garrulous and opinionated was the skinny kid with the thick head of curly hair. For someone who couldn't vote yet, he had a lot to say, especially about politics. She didn't find him aggressive or offensive. She found him chatty. In turn, Mordecai, who had studied Gallant's photograph at the top of her column in the *Standard*—face attractive and intelligent, hair cut short beneath a beret—thought her a glamorous figure. She was both a journalist of repute and a published short-fiction writer in the *Northern Review*; she was the real literary deal.

His own identity was far less clear. He was still a poser, with his all-black uniform and dangling cigarette, his glasses of hard liquor. His journalism was notorious in certain small circles, but those stories and sketches he sent out to magazines—they came right back. If anything, his manner remained closer to pool hall hustler than young man of letters. When Avrum Richler became engaged in spring 1950, he asked his brother to be his best man. At a wedding shower in a Snowdon apartment the sister of the bride-to-be "caught" a hoodlum using a bedroom phone. "Don't worry," Mordecai said, reading her alarm. "I won't steal anything." The incident led Avrum's fiancée to object to his choice of best man, but he surprised everyone by dressing properly on the day and executing his duties as master of ceremonies with composure.

John Sutherland's lunch companions were both another half-year away from Paris. The date for Mordy Richler's flight was determined by three events. In March 1950 he put his name forward to be editor of the *Georgian*, a position that carried a two-thirds reduction in tuition fees. A fellow senior editor named

Trevor Phillips formed the opposition. Mordy requested a meeting over Cokes in a café, where he asked Phillips to withdraw on the grounds that he couldn't continue at school without the fee waiver. Phillips, a recent immigrant from England who was paying his own way through Sir George, declined. He also got the job. Rumours around the college claimed that school officials didn't want Mordecai Richler editing the paper. Further, they didn't want him there at all. Failing to win the job, and uncertain that academic learning was for him, he considered dropping out.

Chatty though he may have been, Mordecai talked about his intimate self with only one person: Evelyn Sacks. His erstwhile teacher and, perhaps, first lover remained his confidante, convinced of his gift and his sensitivity. He would visit her at her school, despite her concern about her husband's jealousy over their "friendship," and would confess his boredom with Sir George and his hunger for direct experience. Girls provided experiences, in particular wild, fallen girls, although the double date he arranged with a stripper he met on assignment for the *Herald*— Mordy and a friend, the stripper and a friend—ended with the young men downing a bottle of Scotch alone, their lust cooled. Once, invited to a professor's country house for a weekend, he returned disappointed that the man hadn't made a pass at him. A pass would have been an experience; a pass, Evelyn Sacks noted to herself, could have become material for a story.

Sensing that he needed a push in one direction or the other, she suggested he visit her cousin Elie Abel on his annual trip to New York to see his uncle. Abel, a Montrealer who had graduated from McGill and served in the Royal Canadian Air Force, and whose career had already included a spell as court reporter at the Nuremberg war-crimes trials, was a journalist for the *New York Times*. That spring he took Mordecai to lunch and offered advice of helpful directness and simplicity: if he wanted to become a journalist, stay in school; if he wanted to write, get started.

He wanted to get started.

The summer of 1950, spent partly in Montreal, partly in Ste. Agathe, marked the transition. He worked for Lily at the Rosenberg

Inn, smoking and drinking beer openly around her. He also waited on tables at the Castle des Monts in the evenings, where he could listen to Jackie Kahane and other comedians and troll the dance floors for girls. In August, with no classes to return to and no college newspaper to write for, he accepted a job offer from his Uncle Max. Max Richler, twenty-eight and newly married, was his favourite relation. Serving in the army until the summer of 1945, he had missed much of the domestic warfare between Mordecai and his grandfather (and Max's father) Shmarya. Max had also declared himself an exception by *not* making a career with one of the family firms, starting a business called Atlas Hoist and Body. It manufactured heavy equipment, including a hydraulic machine of his own design, for the mining industry.

By temperament as well Max was different: more gentle and introspective than his father and certain of his siblings. (His older brother Jacob worked along with him.) When he decided the firm needed someone to write and design advertising, he thought of his nephew, good at both, who had, he'd been told, decided to forgo his final years of college. Some family members wondered if he could handle the smoking, drinking, Sabbath-breaking, grandfather-killing Mordecai, but he had no such concerns. He liked the boy's spiritedness.

For his part, every morning Mordecai put on a collared shirt and tie and made his way to a small office building on Wellington Street. Max Richler, who paid himself $30 a week, gave him $35 to be his advertising manager. His nephew proved adept at designing brochures and composing copy for trade publications, as well as handling office correspondence. At work, he was diligent and serious, suggesting to no one, a certain slouching body language aside, that he was slumming it. Even so, after a few weeks he informed his uncle that, while he was grateful for the job, he was off to Europe to write a novel. Why there? Max asked. Because he could live more cheaply, he answered.

To others, he was more strident: Montreal was a mediocrity, a provincial backwater, suffocating and boring; Canada a nothingness. Who could write—write like Hemingway and Malraux—in

such a place? He had to go where writers weren't freaks and culture wasn't alien. He had to go where there was action.

Somewhat surprisingly, Moses Richler voiced support for his
plans to become a writer. Doctors, dentists, even barbers, his
father reasoned, needed to rent offices and purchase equipment.
But an author required only a typewriter and paper. As start-up
expenses went, it was a bargain. Moses had bought him one half
of the package for his birthday a couple of years earlier: a Royal
Portable typewriter. About going to England or France, he was
less certain. Europe was a graveyard for the Jews, he said, a continent where everything was old and broken. Then there were
European women. Did Mordy know about safes? he asked. "If
you have to do it—*and I know you*—use 'em," he advised. "Don't
get married over there," he added. "They'd do anything for a pair
of nylon stockings or a Canadian passport." The father had
already taken his son to Bond Clothes on St. Lawrence and out-
fitted him with a new coat. He had also lent him his old blue
steamer trunk and promised $50 a month in support. Avrum,
with a new business and wife, had no cash to help fund his brother's flight. He told him he'd last six weeks in Europe, tops.

In the end, it was Lily, consulted neither about his decision to
quit college nor his intentions to go abroad, who really came
through. She had taken out an insurance policy when her youngest was born, contributing a small amount each week. On being
told of his plans, she cashed the policy in—$800 for his
adventure.

What did Mordecai Richler tell himself about his reasons for
boarding the *Franconia* in late September, destination Liverpool?
To get started as a writer. To experience Europe and find women
who would do things for nylons. To escape his family. To escape
his own anger and unhappiness. The latter, a largely unconscious
impulse, may have been the most forceful. Furious, restless,
nervy and sexually wound up pretty much all the time, he was a
bundle of energy—and, he hoped, of talent. He had to get out, or
else he would explode. He was nineteen years old.

Mordecai Richler was born into the two large Montreal clans of Rosenbergs and Richlers. Above: his Rosenberg rabbi grandfather's seventieth birthday, one week after the *bris* of the absent newborn; Mordecai's father, Moses, is in a tuxedo on the left with his brother, Avrum, 5; his mother, Lily, is seated in front of them.
Below: the Richlers gather to celebrate the return of Israel Richler from war in 1945; Mordy, 14, is on the far left, his father behind and Avrum behind him. No Lily: she had dissolved the marriage a year earlier.

"I have one imperishable memory of my grandfather. Once he called me into his study, set me down on his lap, and made a drawing of a horse for me. On the horse he drew a rider. While I watched and giggled he gave the rider a beard and the fur-trimmed round hat of a rabbi, a *straimel*, just like he wore."
From *The Street*.
Rabbi Rosenberg with his wife, Sarah, and his daughter Lily in 1934.

"My grandmother had been a beautiful girl [and] a shrewd, resourceful, and patient wife. . . . Bright afternoons my mother would lift the old lady into a wheelchair and put her out in the sun and once a week she gave her a manicure." From *The Street*.
Sarah Gittel Rosenberg, circa 1940, after her stroke, with Lily, her caretaker, and her glamorous older daughter, Ruth Albert.

Mordecai in a typical studio portrait photograph of the time, 1932.
"My mother was fond of reminding me that the night I was born my father had not waited at the hospital to find out how she was, or whether it was a boy or a girl, but had gone to the movies instead." From "My Father's Life," *Home Sweet Home*.

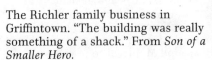

The Richler family business in Griffintown. "The building was really something of a shack." From *Son of a Smaller Hero*.

Easy summers in the Laurentians for city Jews. Avrum, Lily and Mordecai in a field near Shawbridge, circa 1933. Mordecai pulls on his left earlobe, which friends noted later was a lifelong habit.

Avrum and Mordecai on the front steps of their apartment, at 5257 St. Urbain Street, circa 1938.
"On each corner a cigar store, a grocery, and a fruit man. Outside staircases everywhere. Winding ones, wooden ones, rusty and risky ones. Here a prized plot of grass splendidly barbered, there a spitefully weedy patch. An endless repetition of precious peeling balconies and waste lots." From *The Apprenticeship of Duddy Kravitz*.

Business, boys and airplanes . . . "Mutty" and "Voomy" were sometimes taken along by their Uncle Joe on his trips to airfields around Montreal to purchase scrap metal.

1943. Mordecai, Lily and Avrum in Prévost, their next Laurentian summer holiday village, the year before "my unhappy mother . . . arranged to have their marriage annulled." From "My Father's Life," *Home Sweet Home*.

"We were a rude, aggressive bunch around The Main. Cocky, too. . . . We used to race down to The Main to play snooker at the Rachel or the Mount Royal." From *The Street*.

Nattily dressed, a cigarette-smoking teenage Mordecai with his father on a neighbourhood street.
"After his marriage to my mother blew apart, he moved into a rented room. . . . He bought a natty . . . hat. A sports jacket. He began to use aftershave lotion." From "My Father's Life," *Home Sweet Home*.

Class president (acclaimed) Mordecai Richler, centre, and the Class of '48, Baron Byng High School.
"Bad news. They're closing Baron Byng High School. Our Baron Byng. I speak of a legendary Montreal school, founded in 1921, that resembles nothing so much as a Victorian workhouse. Architecturally, the loss will be minimal (the building's a blight), but emotionally . . . ah, that's something else." From "St. Urbain Street Then and Now," *Home Sweet Home*.

ST. VIATEUR

ST. VIATEUR
BAGEL SHOP
263 ST. VIATEUR W.
1932

5618 ESPLANADE
IRVING LAYTON
LIVED HERE

SATMAR CHASSIDS

FAIRMOUNT

ICE

1929
FAIRMOUNT
BAGEL
74 FAIRMOUNT W.

FIRST YM-YWHA
365 MOUNT ROYAL W
1929

MT. ROYAL

THE LOUIS RUBINSTEIN (1862-1913)
FOUNTAIN HONOURING THE
WORLD FIGURE-SKATING CHAMPION
AND LONGTIME ALDERMAN

1914

ORIGINAL JEWISH
PUBLIC LIBRARY
4499 ESPLANADE

HEBREW OLD
PEOPLES' HOME
4373 ESPLANADE

1926

MARIE-ANNE

RACHEL

FRUIT

BAGG

DES PINS

SHERBROOKE

S. Berne

HUTCHISON

TO THE GOLDEN
SQUARE-MILE

PARK

ESPLANADE

ST. URBAIN

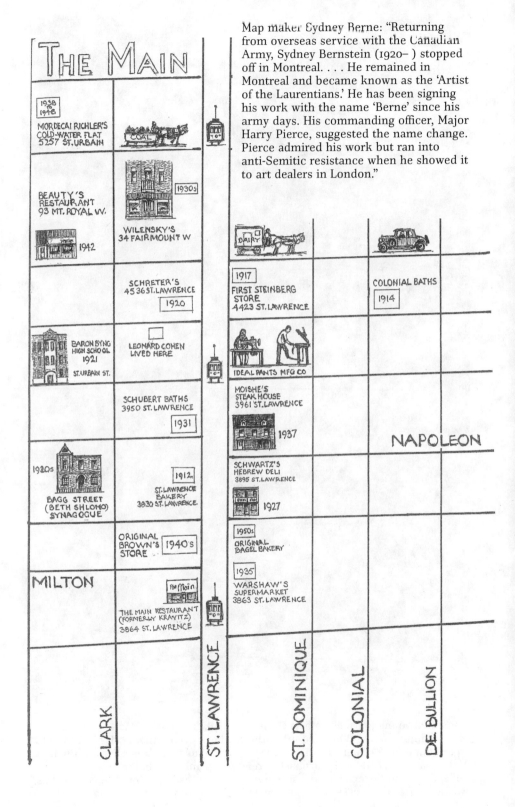

THE MAIN

MORDECAI RICHLER'S COLD-WATER FLAT 5257 ST. URBAIN — 1938 to 1948

COAL

BEAUTY'S RESTAURANT 93 MT. ROYAL W.

1942

WILENSKY'S 34 FAIRMOUNT W — 1930s

SCHRETER'S 4536 ST. LAWRENCE — 1920

BARON BYNG HIGH SCHOOL 1921 ST. URBAIN ST.

LEONARD COHEN LIVED HERE

SCHUBERT BATHS 3950 ST. LAWRENCE — 1931

1920s — **BAGG STREET (BETH SHLOMO) SYNAGOGUE**

ST. LAWRENCE BAKERY 3830 ST. LAWRENCE — 1912

ORIGINAL BROWN'S STORE — 1940's

MILTON

THE MAIN RESTAURANT (FORMERLY KRAVITZ) 3864 ST. LAWRENCE

DAIRY

1917 — **FIRST STEINBERG STORE** 4423 ST. LAWRENCE

IDEAL PANTS MFG CO

MOISHE'S STEAK HOUSE 3961 ST. LAWRENCE — 1937

SCHWARTZ'S HEBREW DELI 3895 ST. LAWRENCE — 1927

1950s — **ORIGINAL BAGEL BAKERY**

1935 — **WARSHAW'S SUPERMARKET** 3863 ST. LAWRENCE

COLONIAL BATHS 1914

NAPOLEON

CLARK

ST. LAWRENCE

ST. DOMINIQUE

COLONIAL

DE BULLION

Map maker Sydney Berne: "Returning from overseas service with the Canadian Army, Sydney Bernstein (1920–) stopped off in Montreal. . . . He remained in Montreal and became known as the 'Artist of the Laurentians.' He has been signing his work with the name 'Berne' since his army days. His commanding officer, Major Harry Pierce, suggested the name change. Pierce admired his work but ran into anti-Semitic resistance when he showed it to art dealers in London."

The gifted young journalist Mavis Gallant in 1948. "I first met Mavis Gallant in Montreal in 1950. . . . When [John] Sutherland discovered that both Mavis and I were bound for Paris, he arranged for the three of us to get together for lunch. Mavis was already a local journalist of repute, a glamorous figure, and I was still a college student, ostensibly cocksure but actually awash in printed rejection slips." Richler's afterword to *The Moslem Wife and Other Stories* by Mavis Gallant.

PART II

APPRENTICE

I

THE RIGHT AGE

They were all the right age. Papa Hemingway had said as much about an earlier crowd of North Americans in Paris. His generation, disillusioned by Verdun and Ypres, but still young and spirited: Henry Miller and Ezra Pound, F. Scott Fitzgerald and Ford Madox Ford, Canadians Morley Callaghan and John Glassco. Plus Gertrude Stein, poet and mentor in Montparnasse, who coined the expression "the lost generation." Besides these New Worlders, Irishman James Joyce had lived there for a period, along with D.H. Lawrence and Walter Benjamin. Not to mention the painters and sculptors, musicians and composers, choreographers and dancers and outlandish cabaret stars. Paris in the 1920s had indeed been a moveable feast, punch-ups and all. Between the Depression and the subsequent Nazi occupation, the city—or, rather, the corner of it given over to outsiders for their dramas and rites of passage, with the larger population amused, indifferent or simply unaware—had been frozen in literary time. Hemingway had even felt obliged to personally "liberate" Sylvia Beach's bookshop, Shakespeare and Company, with the Allies in 1944. She had published Joyce's *Ulysses* when no one else would touch the modernist classic.

Postwar Paris recovered its standing, the allure stronger than ever. The city hadn't been levelled, hadn't even been particularly scarred. Existentialists Jean-Paul Sartre and Albert Camus were seen in the streets and cafés once more, as was the noble André

Malraux, his writing an earlier model of engagement and honour. The scandalous Louis-Ferdinand Céline, tried *in absentia* for wartime collaboration, would soon return from Denmark, to be visited by adoring American beat writers, including Allen Ginsberg and William Burroughs, who cared more for his inventiveness than his morals—or his virulent anti-Semitism. French literary passions were volatile and exciting, while French literary feuds, as much about politics as literature, mattered. Even French ennui had cachet.

More Americans than ever came this time. The G.I. Bill put cash in the pockets of veterans to travel overseas to study and write, or not study and not write. They weren't lost or disillusioned, and were feeling modestly chuffed about the rebuilding of Europe under the Marshall Plan using American money and optimism. But mostly they just wanted to be in the City of Light. American jazz was embraced by Parisians, as were its musicians, black men and women who felt little such warmth back home, outside of a few neighbourhoods in a few cities. Homosexuals and lesbians found attitudes in Paris more sophisticated about human sexuality than they could expect elsewhere.

Richard Wright, author of *Native Son*, arrived in 1946, fleeing the book's fame. James Baldwin was finishing *Go Tell It on the Mountain* in a hotel in Saint-Germain-des-Prés. Young turks Norman Mailer, Truman Capote and Gore Vidal had all been through Paris, manuscripts in hand, and in 1950 another emerging titan, Saul Bellow, returned to Chicago after two years in Montmartre, a partial draft of *The Adventures of Augie March* in his suitcase. Irwin Shaw would arrive soon, his name already on U.S. blacklists on account of his novel *The Troubled Air*, which depicted the rise of McCarthyism. Within a couple of years George Plimpton, Peter Matthiessen and William Styron would be in town, launching the *Paris Review* and hanging out at the Café Tournon. The cheap hotels and grotty apartments of the Latin Quarter and Saint-Germain-des-Prés afforded Americans a chance to write more daringly and live more freely, to discover Europe a little, and each other a little more.

At thirty-four and with two novels, Bellow was almost too old to be the right age. Baldwin, twenty-six and a year away from his own remarkable debut, was closer to the norm. Twenty-eight-year-old Mavis Gallant was six months short of her first *New Yorker* credit, while Styron, though just twenty-six, arrived in Paris with *Lie Down in Darkness* already a stateside sensation. Matthiessen and Plimpton, both twenty-four, had yet to publish much at all. Being very young was fine. So was being published well, or marginally, or not at all. The point was being there.

A bohemian's delight, the city attracted those in pursuit of stimulation, if not liberation, of the senses. Boulevardiers filled the terraces of Le Sélect and Le Dôme in the early evenings, the Bar Vert and Rose Rouge later into the night. Americans Terry Southern and Mason Hoffenberg, who met in Paris, were equally serious about their writing and their pleasures. They ran with a fast crowd that included Alexander Trocchi and Christopher Logue, Herbert Gold and David Burnett. Some expats liked hash and even heroin. Sinbad Vail, son of Peggy Guggenheim, published them in his magazine *Points*, a publication with the subtitle "Fiction by Young Writers." Trocchi did the same in *Merlin* and Burnett in *New Story*. No magazine paid much, and copies were mostly read by fellow seekers. Real money for fiction meant committing pornography for Maurice Girodias at Olympia Press. He paid upwards of $1,000 for book-length smut, and if writing good porn wasn't as easy as it sounded, talking and joking about writing it was good café fun.

The smallest expatriate group involved those who arrived in Paris determined to interact with the French-speaking city of six million. Novelist and playwright Samuel Beckett, a Dubliner by birth, was one such expatriate. Another would be his newly made acquaintance Mavis Gallant, lately of Montreal. Beckett, married to a French woman, began writing in his adopted language; the bilingual Gallant was soon exploring the inner lives of Parisians in the elegant, neutral English of her Canadian childhood. These writers tended to avoid the transient and rowdy.

Mort Richler, as he now introduced himself, arrived in the first days of October 1950. He had boarded the *Franconia* in Quebec

City in the company of fellow *Georgian* journalist Terry McEwan, a young man no less determined to make a mark outside Canada—in the music business. Also on board was Douglas Cohen, whose Westmount breeding didn't prevent him from co-sharking poker games with Richler. They won a hundred dollars from fellow passengers over the eight days, a few pennies at a pot. Liverpool, where the three disembarked, was grimy and cramped, and after a week in a still-blitzed London, Richler got back on a boat, this time for Calais.

Once in Paris, he checked into a cheap hotel on rue Cujas, off the Boulevard Saint-Michel in Saint-Germain-des-Prés. A block to the west sprawled the magnificent gardens where Louis XIV had once strolled. To the north stood the university that had graduated Diderot and Voltaire. The Luxembourg Gardens! The Sorbonne! There was nothing to do but buy a pack of Gauloises and a blue beret and sit that same evening in the Café de Flore, notebook open and pen poised.

Expatriate attire favoured wispy beards and sandals, trousers with buttons instead of zippers. Richler wore those clothes for a while. He wore them for too long, earning a reputation as a bohemian who did not bathe—though he was far from alone in that. His accommodations didn't help. Hotels of the no-star variety often came unheated, unclean and busy with scampering mice. Laundry, hand-washed and hung on lines in rooms, ended up neither clean nor dry. A bathroom was shared by an entire floor, the hot water irregular. Hot-plate cooking was limited in scope, and frowned upon by hoteliers worried about fires. For a teenager who had been looked after by his mother, cooking must have been a vexing concept. "i'm going to prepare my own breakfast and suppers right here in my room," he reported to his father, his lower-case lettering in homage to the poet e.e. cummings. But "it's certainly a relief to eat French food after the crap they serve you in London restaurants." For 200 francs, or 70 cents, he could eat a *choucroute garnie* or *croque-monsieur* in a student restaurant, complete with grey vegetable soup to start and a "pint of Bordeaux" to wash it down.

Walking the city cost nothing. "i think there are more whores on the monmartre than there are in all of canada," he told his father. "you cant walk more than ten feet before a girl grabs you by the arm and makes an offer." Knowing that Moses would enjoy such details, he followed up with an account of a "nudie girl show" in Pigalle. "They begin here where lili st. cyr leaves off in montreal," he wrote, citing his parent's favourite exotic dancer. "Love, Mutty," he signed letters.

He was mostly alone those first weeks, and lonely, scared by the leap he had taken. A girl he spotted in a café reading Faulkner's *Sanctuary* spurned his overture. At the U.S. embassy he lingered long enough to drink three cups of American coffee, finding the French equivalent too strong. His French remained stubbornly poor, limiting his contact with locals. But the doubts, the mice, the aloof girls, scarcely mattered. He was in Paris, wandering the cathedrals and gardens, devouring the writings of Camus, Céline, Malraux and Sartre—he attempted *La Nausée* in the original— within a few blocks of where those men (and Simone de Beauvoir, Sartre's companion and equal) could be espied and approached. Céline's *Voyage to the End of the Night*, in English, was another early revelation.

"Shades of Darkness," by Mordecai Richler, was accepted for publication by *Points* in late October. "The waters of Lac des Sables were high, and restless, in the middle of August," his first published story began, "but they rose higher still, and became still more restless as the night grew older." These three "mood pieces," taking up five pages of the magazine, had been written back in Montreal and polished in Saint-Germain-des-Prés. The first told of overweight David Israeli Wallman, a Laurentians summer resort comedian whose self-directed fat jokes go over badly. His woeful tale—of drowning in water and misery alike— is followed by a sketch of a New Yorker named Sammy Callabro, son of an emigrant Italian father and the daughter of a Jewish sweatshop owner. "Maw, I want to be a Jew," Sammy tells his mother after one too many beatings by "dago" and "kike" gangs. "I want to be like you." Finally, there is Armand Cloutier, a

Quebecer who resets pins in a bowling alley. "He hated the Jews who came there at night in loud suits and always in the company of fat girls with deep red lipstick and big noses, but they tipped well and he smiled at them." He helps keep Jews out of the Montreal suburb of Laval with the aid of a rusty lead pipe, "a happy Canadien" doing his racial duty.

Quality aside—and editor Sinbad Vail had published worse than this earnest effort—"Shades of Darkness" was an advance on his flippant Baron Byng tales of Sir Marmaduke and the chums at the club. Here, at least, was Montreal, and here, in some form, were two of the city's solitudes, as understood by a young man— Jews and French Canadians in uneasy relation.

The amiable Vail, appreciated by many for using Guggenheim Trust funds to pay contributors and settle bar bills, was one of his first literary acquaintances. Others invited him to a mid-November weekend in Normandy. Stuffed into a battered Renault, Richler and his party had a "swell time" imitating the bark of movie Nazis as they read off the commands—*VERBOTEN! ACHTUNG!*—scrawled on crumbling walls. But he also told Moses, "the coast is still studded with german fortifications, gun-emplacements, cement pillars." He strolled along one of the D-Day beaches amidst the shattered pillboxes in meditative silence, watching the receding tide lay bare the concrete teeth buried in the sand to impede incoming landing craft.

More defining experiences, along with real friendships, would emerge from his second, longer spell in Paris the following autumn and winter. The central encounters during this first pass were with fellow Montrealers. Mavis Gallant didn't reach France until a month after her chatty lunch mate from the previous spring. She found him in a café, and was right away impressed by the number of expats he already knew—or knew how to drink with.

From the start, Gallant, an independent, slightly intimidating woman who lived for her work, saw through his beret and Gauloises. She could overlook the afternoon that Richler, catching her with Elizabeth Bowen's *The House in Paris* on a café terrace, said, "Look, Mavis, you are never going to get anywhere if you keep on reading this crap." She could even ignore the fact that he was a card-carrying member of the Sartre cult, mouthing platitudes about wise Joseph Stalin and the bold Soviet Union. Reminding herself of his youth, and aware, to some extent, of how St. Urbain Street must have contributed, Gallant found him simultaneously irksome and endearing.

When Bill Weintraub, one of the friends Gallant had left behind in Montreal, came to Paris in November, she asked if he wanted to meet this aspiring young writer. Five years his senior, Weintraub had grown up in a non-observant household in Verdun, where few Jews resided. Laconic and self-deprecating, and lately fired from the *Gazette* for a flippant, and drunken, remark about an editor, he was up for any adventure. They talked about their respective Montreals, and argued about books and movies. They also engaged in the café blood sport of the era: dissecting the pretenses and pufferies of others, character assassinations by wit, with no pause for fairness. It was how young men auditioned for each other's respect.

"Did I tell you about this Richler?" Weintraub wrote to his friend Brian Moore, still on staff at the *Gazette.* "He's from Montreal, has a peculiar first name—Mordecai—and wants to be a writer. Very young and rather cheeky, without proper deference when dealing with older citizens like myself." These remarks, too, were in code. The kid is okay, he was reporting. You'll like him as much as I do.

The *canadiens errants* gloried in Paris. Along with Alex Cherney, yet another Montrealer, Weintraub and Richler sampled the bistros and boîtes of the Left Bank. For late afternoon there were Pernods at the Deux Magots or the Mabillon. Dinner was mostly dispensed with, although the arrival of a cheque or money order from home would allow a feed at the Procope, where Hugo and Balzac had dined. Early evenings belonged to the Bar Vert, with Francis Lemarque installed as house *chanteur*—his 1948 song "À Paris" was becoming a second national anthem—or to L'Échelle de Jacob, to marvel at Cora Vaucaire, the renowned Dame Blanche de Saint-Germain-des-Prés. All that culture for the price of a drink. The unfolding jazz revolution that was *le be-bop* at the Club

Saint-Germain-des-Prés wasn't quite so cheap—the club charged a cover—but worth it once in a while.

In one of his first letters home, Richler requested a care package containing tins of beans and soup, a jar of Nescafé and a box of tea bags, powdered eggs and a salami. Fruit being expensive in postwar Paris, he also asked for oranges, pineapples and grapefruits, which he needed "badly for the citrus content." In late November Gallant heard tell of a flu-ridden Canadian living in a fleabag hotel on Île de la Cité. Figuring it had to be him, Gallant paid for some oranges and climbed his dark stairs. She found Richler reading in bed, muffled in a wool hat and scarf. A woeful sight, especially when he confessed his worry, based on the spots covering his elbows, that he had contracted venereal disease— proof, apparently, that not every girl in Paris had rebuffed him. Gallant suspected scurvy brought on by a vitamin C deficiency, and left the fruit.

Despite the fun—or because of it; money had run low—he removed himself from Paris after just two months. Cheaper, less gloomy living, he had been told, was available in Franco's Spain. Ibiza, an island off the coast from Barcelona, was a gem: unspoilt, authentic, nearly empty. Since his arrival in Europe he had been planning to go to Berlin. Instead, he first flew to England in early December for a week, ostensibly to visit "editors, publishers, writers, etc," that is, "some important people I had to see there"— though Gallant had a suspicion he'd fled back across the Channel to find an English-speaking doctor who could reassure him he hadn't contracted VD. Then he boarded a night train from Paris, his pockets lined with the extra funds that his father and brother had both wired, *Don Quixote* and *Spanish Self-Taught* in his knapsack.

II

C/O BAR ESCANDELL, SAN ANTONIO, IBIZA, SPAIN

Blame Hemingway again. He had written Spain so passionately and lived it so bravely; he'd even sold his vision of the nation's civil war to Hollywood, staring Gary Cooper and Ingrid Bergman. Who could resist the climactic Pamplona scenes in *The Sun Also Rises* and the metaphysics of bullfighting in *Death in the Afternoon*? Or the dispatches he filed during the heroic first stand against Fascism, a few hinting at his personal involvement with the republicans, and then transposed into the mythopoeic assertions of *For Whom the Bell Tolls*. Mordecai Richler, who had been hearing about Spain, and dreaming about it, ever since Evelyn Sacks's rousing classroom lectures and dining table conversations on St. Urbain Street, certainly couldn't. Riding down the centre of France, through the Pyrenees, and pulling into Barcelona epitomized the freedom that was suddenly his. He had no one to explain himself to, no apologies to make. No one quite knew where he was.

An overnight stop on Mallorca, and the ferry reached Ibiza the next evening towards sunset. The tiny capital, also called Ibiza, clung to a rocky hillside, its upper town protected from erstwhile Barbary pirates by a fort above a sixteenth-century wall. The buildings, balconies facing the sea breezes, were bleached white. Even before he stepped off the gangplank, Richler would have noticed the waterside café advertising *tapas*, *vinos* and *licores*, with the Hotel Marina nearby. Fishermen may have been bringing in their catch, creatures like *bonitos* and the enormous *meros* with their gaping red mouths. With so few visitors, the arrival of the Barcelona ferry was an event. The boardwalk bustled, and eyes fell on him.

For reasons he could not fathom, he was accosted immediately by a local fisherman named Juanito Tur-Guerra. Having decided the newcomer was a wealthy American fleeing the Korean War, Tur-Guerra, known locally as "Juanito Pus," insisted that Mordecai tell him about his experiences over drinks. Guided to a dockside bar by the leathery forty-year-old, Mort Richler got his first taste of Fundador, the sweet local brandy. Hours of drinking with Juanito and his fishermen friends, their congeniality overlooking his lack of Spanish and emerging identity as a mere *canadiense* henceforth to be called "Mauricio," were followed by a midnight climb up through the narrow streets to a brothel, the men gone silent for fear of their wives overhearing them. At Casa Rosita the girls took their clients by the hand, bringing along a bucket of water and soap for washing off the salt and grime. One client, possibly cleaner than the others, stumbled into the Hotel Marina towards sunrise, the initiation complete.

For Richler, the night was the beginning of many prowls with Juanito Tur-Guerra and the fishermen of Ibiza town. Soon he was friends with a local doctor as well, an anarchist named Juanito Villan-Gomez, and buzzing around the island on the back of his motorcycle. Content to stay in the hotel near the port, to drink until he teetered and then climb up to Rosita's, he embraced the freedom and licence that his intrepidness had won him. He genuinely liked these men, their gruff humour and lustiness and hard-drinking, hard-smoking ways. They, in turn, liked the curious Canadian kid, so young and full of appetite, who could drink and whore all night and still, apparently, do his own mysterious "work"—the clack-clack-clack of his typewriter audible on the docks during the temperate winter days.

He could not explain this life to his family back in Montreal. Richler's summary of his first night on Ibiza—"Querido Padre," he wrote to Moses—left out most details. "i arrived here last night at six-thirty and its everything they said it would be. my room cost me a $1 a day with everything & there's even the balcony overlooking the port—I'm right on the quai." But shortly, in letters requesting a camera and Kodak film, typewriter ribbons ("black, royal portable") and food, along with "two clip on bowties," "one softball," and "a summer dress for a kid of nine"— all gifts for his new friends, or their children—he did divulge a little. "the people here are exceedingly nice to me," he wrote on February 8, 1951, "especially a local fish ship owner—juanito. He brings the hotel cook fresh fish for me every day, and threatens to kill him if he doesn't cook it for me."

In his one-dollar room he set out to prove what he had suspected in Paris, if not since his early teens. He mapped and drafted a novel from beginning to middle to end. He did so by sitting down each morning, regardless of his state of mind or head, and working until lunch, resting, and then working another couple of hours in the afternoon. He did so by discovering within himself the equal-sized reservoirs of discipline and compulsion that are, along with talent, the raw materials required to be a novelist. About the talent, he could not yet be sure. But the discipline came almost naturally.

Richler had arrived in Spain with a few story fragments, some dating back to Montreal. He had also brought along a blue and white notepad. It contained entries scribbled in Paris, with more added on Ibiza, concerning the story he wanted to tell. Already, he had a working title—*The Rotten People*—and a cast of characters. Notepad by his side, he banged out some three hundred pages in the hotel. Then he started the manuscript all over, at the end of March, while also drafting new short stories to send to the *New Yorker*, *Harper's* and *Atlantic Monthly*, providing a return address—with international postage coupons enclosed—c/o a fisherman's bar. "I work regularly every day here," he assured his father, "which is more than I did in paris. The novel is finally beginning to take on shape and substance but please don't ask me about it in every letter it makes me nervous."

Besides the novel, the notepad showed him making lists of letters to write, including one to "Evelyn"; tasks requiring attention,
among them "shave," "bath" and "dentist"; and towards the end
of February, with a trip to Valencia and Madrid in the works,
"address for money Madrid" and "see house for Mavis." The "dentist" entry involved a filling, patient and doctor both sipping
brandy as anaesthetic. The ferry ride over to Valencia, and then
the train to Madrid, occurred in early March, and it was from the
latter that he wired a telegram to his father. IMPERATIVE. CHECK
PRONTO MADRID C/O COOKS WAGON LITS ALCALA NR 23
MADRID. BROKE. MORDECAI.

The cheque was duly sent—a loan, not a gift; Moses kept tally
in his own notepad, just as he kept all the letters from his boy,
with a date received and a date replied to in a corner—and Richler
strolled out into Madrid. Experiencing the city during Semana
Santa, Holy Week, with a bloodied Christ on the Cross being
marched down a simulated Via Dolorosa followed by soldiers
blowing on trumpets and barefoot penitents in red robes, the
twenty-year-old, who knew a thing or two about zealotry, allowed
his thoughts to brood. He summoned a poem by Garcia Lorca—
"What is it you feel / in your red, thirsty mouth? / The taste of
the bones / of my big skull"—and decided it was unfair to bring
children into the post-Hiroshima world. The novel, he mused
while busily writing his own, was a dead art form.

Heading next to Las Fallas, the Festival of Fire, he travelled to
the great port city of Valencia, eternal battleground for Moorish-
Christian conflicts and capital of the republic until the generalis-
simo laid siege. He wandered the old town, many of the buildings
still bombed out, and attended a bullfight in the Plaza de Toros,
his copy of *Death in the Afternoon* tucked out of sight. Starved for
movies, he watched Joel McCrea sidle up to a saloon bar and ask
in dubbed Spanish, "*Un cognac, por favor.*"

Rooted in the middle ages, when carpenters made bonfires of
their old wood shavings, called *fallas*, the fiesta culminated every
March 19 with fireworks and bonfires rendering Valencia a phantasmagoria. He had never seen or felt anything like it. Amidst

the noise and colour, which he took to be kind of willed aban-
donment of the senses, Richler declared his Orthodox childhood
gone up in the ecstatic flames. Las Fallas preached flight from
reason and moderation, from studying medicine or law, saving
up for a house in the suburbs, suffering Canadian rectitude or
even winters. He was free of all that and was, now and forever,
his own man.

Back on Ibiza, dealing with "my troubles here—teeth had to
be fixed, general ennui, change of house, etc," Richler thanked
his father for the offer of a Passover parcel with a similar declaration delivered in free-form prose. "i'm afraid i'm no longer
the orthodox boy i was brought up to be," he wrote. "you'll have
to be tolerant, that's all—everyone is entitled to their own way
of looking at things—and as for me I'm afraid I can no longer
accept the ritualistic dogma of orthodoxy—Judaism has other,
more significant i think, connotations for me—nevertheless
you'll be pleased to hear i have ordered many books for England—
translations (selected) of the zohar, Talmud, midrsh, etc, also
maimonides, Spinoza, etc in order to begin a comprehensive
study for a book i'm planning to do next year." Moses Richler
responded sharply, initiating an exchange about the son's views
on religion that was surprising for the mutual respect it displayed. A key pattern in the relationship between father and son
was established during these months; despite all that had happened on St. Urbain Street, and despite Moses' narrow experiences and views, they could and did discuss subjects of import.
"you accuse me of being selfish and insincere," Mordecai wrote
during the height of the exchange. "God daddy if I was selfish I
could have remained in Canada, taken a degree, amassed money,
and lived a comfortable life." Then, in upper-case lettering: "BUT
I BELIEVE IN WHAT I AM DOING—AND I'M DOING WHAT I AM
DOING BECAUSE I HAVE A FAITH IN THE GENERAL GOOD
AND WANT TO CREATE AND ADD TO LIFE, TRUTH, BEAUTY,
AND SO TO THE GENERAL GOOD. IS IT UNFAIR THEN THAT
I SHOULD ASK FOR HELP, ENCOURAGEMENT, AND SUPPORT
FROM MY FATHER?"

Moses Richler served as a sounding board for his boy, allowing him to think through in words what kind of adult he wanted to be.

"you have your faults daddy," he wrote in that same passionate letter of May 1951. "we all have—but unkindness has never been one of them. You are perhaps quick, hot-tempered, a trifle prejudiced, and sometimes too inclined to believe the worst of me." But his father didn't think of his son as a "tramp, libertine, satyr, and God knows what else." That was the general view of the larger Richler clan—a truth Moses needed to acknowledge. "Even your father, daddy, didn't so much as congratulate me at my bar-mitzvah, not that many of the others so much as came over to shake my hand." As far as the "family en masse" were concerned, "I don't like them and they don't like me."

In Paris the previous autumn, he had discussed sharing a place on Ibiza with Mavis Gallant. His island friends had helped him find a "house for Mavis" for the end of March, but his latest letter to her went unanswered. On April 1 he tried reaching her through Bill Weintraub, himself lately returned to the city. Weintraub had hosted a party for some Canadian visitors the week before, including Mavis and his friend Brian Moore, who was honeymooning with his new wife, Jackie Sirois, the young *Standard* reporter Mordy Richler had smoked and drunk with in the Shrine off Sherbrooke St. He was treated to a cheeky letter from his friend. "I'm broke and not broke," his note began, explaining that his traveller's cheques, representing the $300 remaining from Lily's insurance policy, were not being honoured by Spanish banks. After confessing that he owed small amounts "all over Spain" and requesting a loan of "$25 or $50 until Sept, or Oct," he asked Weintraub to try persuading Gallant of the charms of the house. These included "three large bedrooms, a living room with fireplace, kitchen, bath, ETC," along with a patio shaded by palm, fig, orange and almond trees, with grapevines and generic "flowers" festooning the garden. All this, he boasted, for one thousand pesetas, or $20–25, per month. Then, hoping to lure Weintraub as well, he alluded to available pleasures "best not enlarged upon thru the mails."

Bill Weintraub was sold on visiting "your little haven of luxuri-ance and lechery," as he put it. Richler met him at the pier in Ibiza later that month. Breakfast on the terrace at the Hotel Marina—the dapper Weintraub well groomed, his hair slicked and combed, in contrast to his unshaven, louche host—preceded a ten-mile cab ride across the island to the house in the village of San Antonio Abad. A litre of wine, delivered to the front door each morning, caught the guest's attention at once. So did the mention of the maid/cook, who raised the monthly expense to $30, and the pristine beach three minutes away. A letter from Brian Moore awaited Weintraub at the Bar Escandell, Richler's poste restante, on the beach. After a morning of writing and a lunch prepared by the maid, the men walked down to the Escandell to play chess and sip Fundador. "It's expensive here *not* to drink," Weintraub reported to Brian Moore, crediting the wit-ticism to his "friend and host Mordecai Richler."

Life was good. "Mordy knows everybody on the island and is considered both a character and a respected citizen," Weintraub told Gallant. Hosting "fiestas" at the house, often impromptu, with his fishermen and anarchist buddies showing up at all hours, bringing booze, women and flamenco, had helped cement his standing. At one party, Pepe the Gypsy tried seducing a couple of French ladies while Mariano the bus driver and Vincente the mechanic emptied the available bottles. When rambunctious Juliano joined in, the night took off. "Great fun," Bill Weintraub said afterwards.

Fun was everywhere that spring. A dark-haired American named Helen disembarked from the ferry one day and stepped almost directly into Richler's arms. She was lively, uninhibited, and soon his first proper lover. "*Venga!*" ("Come here!") she would bark imperiously at waiters. Though her mother's arrival com-plicated matters, youth, lust and the callousness that accompan-ies both kept them entwined, even to the extent of an unwise tryst on a public beach. Amiable Bill Weintraub's battle with envy—skinny Mort Richler gets the pretty American shiksa?—was assuaged by the timely appearance of a girl named Mercedes, on holiday by herself, from Barcelona. The two gentlemen of San Antonio, via Montreal, did all right.

Meanwhile, Richler was redrafting his novel. Every morning, Weintraub observed, no matter if Helen had been by or Pepe the flamenco dancer hadn't dragged himself home until dawn, the incessant tapping of the typewriter would invade hungover dreams. If the nature of the material could have affected the typing, the sound should have been more akin to a hammer on coffin nails. The good people he was meeting in Ibiza were in no way dampening his urge to pillory the rotten people of Montreal in his manuscript. Real people, it seemed, served as early models for his characters. Notebook scribbles often aligned a fictional character with an actual person; names were used, to be changed later. These include a tricky refugee from Vienna called Frankel who beds the protagonist's mother; an Orthodox grandfather who can tolerate the boy no more than the boy can tolerate him; and a paralyzed dying grandmother who smells of gangrene. There is even a teacher, nearly twice the hero's age, whom he fondles on a rock in the Laurentians. He asks her to sleep with him, but she is too guilt-ridden to go that far.

While sharing the house in San Antonio, the aspiring novelists—Weintraub spent his mornings crafting a mystery about the theft of the *Mona Lisa*—got to chew on a friend's startling news. A letter from Mavis Gallant in the French Riviera town of Menton reached them. She was proofing her first story in the *New Yorker*, and had already submitted another. Professional writers could publish a dozen novels and a hundred stories over the course of a career without managing a byline in the pages of the regal magazine. It was a summit for North American authors, and Gallant, not yet thirty and with only a couple of publishing credits, was already at the peak. "Mavisian" would be Brian Moore's jokey name for her literary voice, already in evidence in that debut: detached and observant, thoughtful and reserved. Never a love interest for Richler, and a very different kind of writer, Gallant would shortly, and permanently, become a touchstone of seriousness and dedication for him.

Offered a job in Montreal, Bill Weintraub took reluctant leave of paradise at the end of May. His own fling had returned to Barcelona and Helen's mother had dragged her to the safety of the Côte d'Azur, after apparently confronting Mort and accusing him of being both a bad influence and a carrier of VD. On June 8 Richler, just back from another trip to Valencia, wrote to his friend. "Bill, you Sweet Shit," it began. Literary news—his "world shattering novel," he claimed, "should be ready in about six to eight weeks"—was offset by reports of further carousing, most notably a midnight run to Rosita's brothel with Villan-Gomez. The doctor had collected him in San Antonio astride his motorcycle. Richler also reported that "rene and his fascist outfit" had been spreading rumours about him while he was off-island.

"Rene and his fascists" refers to an intrigue that lent his final month on Ibiza an abrupt gravity. The rumours suggesting "Mauricio" was an anarchist and ne'er-do-well grew during the month of June into accusations that he was some kind of foreign spy, meriting police investigation. He was ordered to drop by headquarters for "friendly" talks. His friendships with local men, many known republicans, had been unusual for a foreigner. Now those contacts were under suspicion, especially after he and Weintraub had tried bailing an acquaintance out of jail. And since Weintraub had a notion to write an article about Ibiza and spoke very little Spanish, Richler had been spotted in several places querying locals on his behalf. That could also have been construed as suspect.

Then there was the matter of a Swiss-German resident of Ibiza named Mueller, a former SS colonel with whom he sparred verbally in bars and who later filed a complaint about him. Mueller accused Richler of breaking into his villa, and of being a Communist and a spy. He also hinted that the cash the Canadian was receiving from abroad—monthly cheques from his parents—was for the finance of covert operations. "I'd hate to be thrown out of Spain at this point, as I'm broke and can't think of any place else to go," Richler wrote to Bill Weintraub. " I'm not dramatizing. Something is definitely in the wind."

By July 5 the blackening of his reputation on Ibiza was complete. Given forty-eight hours by the police to quit the island, he expressed his defiance as a young man might: a "whopping party in Ibiza last night," complete with a chicken dinner at the brothel in the company of Madame Rosita herself, followed by "fuckey-fuckey" and a morning after of feeling "woozy and generally rotten." He was off to Barcelona and then to Nice, where he would be hooking up once more with Helen. "Not exactly a sad thought," he told Weintraub. But in an earlier letter he had worried aloud about her "monthlies"—a fair concern, it would soon prove.

"Without even a fig-leaf," Weintraub cracked, "this is no time to get kicked out of the Garden of Eden."

But he was kicked out—a perfect ending to the adventure.

III

GIRLS, GIRLS, GIRLS

In August 1951 a Canadian painter named Jori Smith met a fellow Montrealer in a café in Tourrettes-sur-Loup, a walled, medieval village in the Alpes-Maritimes, so picturesque it had long been favoured by artists, including Matisse and Picasso. He was much younger than she was—twenty to her forty-four—and wore raggedy clothing and a scruffy beard. But he had rented a two-room apartment and was looking for someone to share expenses. After chatting with chain-smoking, cognac-swilling Mort Richler over a two-day period, Smith, until then renting a room in a *pension*, took him up on the offer. She got the couch for a bed and the kitchen for a studio, and he kept the bedroom—necessary, he explained, on account of his all-night writing binges. Her diary entry records her dissatisfaction with her roommate. He worked ten hours a day, often until 4 a.m., during which he routinely did not address a single word to her, unless it was to ask how to spell "perspiration" or "conical." "Breathing the same air but not communicating" was her summary of the silence. An egoist and opportunist who had taken advantage of her patriotism, he had no consideration for others, she wrote; his "ambition" overrode everything. "He bores me so much."

Curiously, she continued taking evening meals with the opportunist in the nearby Café Cresp, run by the Cresp brothers, where two hundred francs, or about a dollar, procured food and wine—and cheerful conversation. Perhaps Richler spared a few words for her then.

Much had happened in the month since he had been escorted off Ibiza, some of it enough to take the talk out of a young man. Making straight from Barcelona to Cannes, where Helen awaited, he had learned that she had become pregnant and gone ahead with an abortion. He wasn't unhappy with the news. "she knew about it for two months and never wrote a word," he wrote Bill Weintraub. "a brave kid. Does that sound lousy?" Her mother seemed to think so. Undaunted, the young lovers resumed their affair, hitchhiking in the foothills of the Alpes-Maritimes north of the city. There, almost ten miles inland, he first set eyes on the village of Tourrettes, perched on a craggy outcrop above the bony ravine of the Loup River. Together they explored its old streets. Richler was smitten with the American, if also possibly feeling guilty at the calamity he had triggered. She appeared in love with him. Smith, who found Helen sweet, got her to pose nude, painting in the kitchen while the boyfriend typed away.

Whatever the reasons, Richler informed Weintraub that he might just marry her and bring her back to Canada that fall. "I'm going to pop the question next week." At a meet-and-greet dinner with Lily Rosenberg in late August, Weintraub delivered on his promise to his friend to "perjure on your behalf." "He doesn't drink much, does he?" Lily asked of her son, on learning about the parties they had co-hosted on Ibiza. Absolutely not, Weintraub replied. About Mordy's girl, he was effusive. "I gave Helen a big build-up and was very sincere when I said I regretted your getting there first." Weintraub was no less sincere in his admiration for Lily. "I found her très sympathique and a damn good cook," he said, before signing off with "How's Helen? Are you married? Do give her my love."

"Bang, bang, bang," was how Jori Smith described the racket of Richler's ten-hour work days and nights. He raced to finish the second draft of *The Rotten People*, completing it in the third week and affixing "August, 1951, Tourrettes-sur-Loup" on the title page. The haste was both typical and telling. The novel was a screed, cross-eyed with self-absorption and judgmental to the point of being hateful; its young protagonist's capacity to see through the hypocrisy around him was almost plaintive in its wishful thinking. External anti-Semitism found its match in expressive self-loathing as a Jew. Flirtations with madness, including a talking rat that taunted "Jewsi-woosie," ended with an affirmation of sanity based on "real" rats climbing the walls of a Paris hotel, confirming the troubled young hero as "happy and free as he had never been before." Such a "tale" had been building inside Mort Richler for years. It only needed the occasion—months of isolation on Ibiza—and the necessary strut, acquired by starting to mingle with writers in Paris, to tumble out. (The story even managed to include an ex-Nazi colonel.) The manuscript cribbed freely from Céline's stylized shock tactics and Hemingway's bullet prose—and any and every other modernist he happened to be reading that week.

Less expected was how quickly he himself came to understand *The Rotten People*. A week after putting a completion date on the manuscript, he had relocated six miles back towards the Mediterranean, to an apartment with a sea view in Haut-de-Cagnes. Here he was visited by Eric Protter, Parisian boulevardier and co-editor of *New Story*, along with "various other inscrutable intellectual types." They read parts of *The Rotten People* and pronounced its author "stupendous . . . and brilliant," and the material at once tremendous and unpublishable. Nevertheless, after sending the manuscript out a few times, including to the avant-garde New York publisher Creative Age Press, Richler abandoned it. He did so ostensibly on the advice of those same intellectual types, Protter in particular, that he needed to write a second novel "a bit more digestible for the tender bourgeois stomachs." That second book, he joked with Weintraub, "will be my first great novel." He also asked his friend for a loan of $25, and pined for a smoked meat sandwich from Ben's deli on Maisonneuve—a first hint of homesickness.

He was no quitter even then, and the ease with which he moved on from the project suggested two things. First, the exercise had served its purpose. He could write a novel. As well as the almost-too-burning need to express himself, and the haste, he did have the discipline to complete the job. He could do it again and, being a quick learner, would do so next time with surer craft. Second, he was not ready to burn the bridge back to his family and community to the degree evident in *The Rotten People*. With its slander, group character assassination and exposure of dark secrets, the book was a scorched-earth policy enacted in print. At this stage, Richler, who would sketch, re-sketch and re-sketch again the canvas of his own childhood, may well not have known why he didn't want to burn those bridges in that manner. But he didn't.

Cagnes, another French village with an artistic pedigree—Renoir had called it "the place where I want to paint until the last day of my life"—lasted him about a month. Helen, who cooked him an *arroz a la valenciana* in her apartment in Cannes, was still officially his girl. But he also made sly reference to an impending trip to Italy with a "beautiful Swedish girl" he had met. He told Weintraub he was both "revising my book completely" and not "doing much work lately," and worried that he had annoyed his friend by asking for the $25. He mentioned reading Gallant's debut story in the *New Yorker* and not being impressed, and that, though he was living in a nice flat, he was surviving on pâté sandwiches and fresh figs. Through an ex-GI living in Nice who got a job as casting director for a film called *Twenty-Four Hours in a Woman's Life*, he was hired as an extra, receiving $10 a day to pretend to be a gambler in a casino.

After a two-week tour of Italy he did indeed appear in Paris with a Swede on his arm. Her name was Ulla. Helen, a potential wife just a month earlier, seemed over and done with. "So I'm back in Paris," Richler wrote on October 29, "and it's wonderful."

In town he stayed with his Sir George friend Terry McEwan, with whom he had crossed the Atlantic. "My friend Terry has struck it rich and is coming through like a great pal," he wrote Weintraub on the same date. By "rich" he meant that the witty, creative McEwan, in contrast to most people he knew in Paris, had a job. Employed by Decca Records, McEwan was renting an apartment on rue Brémontier, a few blocks from the Arc de Triomphe, on the establishment Right Bank. He had already sent Richler the remaining train fare and, even more generously, was granting his desire to make room for Ulla as well. Soon enough the apartment was crossing bourgeois with bohemian, with the latter in the ascendancy. McEwan, who was gay, was seeing a young French tenor who made a pass at Richler, disregarding the girl in his bed.

It was the autumn and early winter of "barefoot existential sex." There was a farce involving a countess looking for a new boy toy that earned him a fresh suit of clothes (McEwan said he had to look the part), a ride in a Jaguar to a party where Jean Cocteau was granting audiences, and the brief notoriety of being her "little Canadian." Nothing happened, except much drinking. More seriously, a not-quite-resigned Helen showed up in Paris about the time that Richler's cousin Lionel Albert paid a visit. Lionel, lately a student radical at McGill, found Muttle in a *ménage à trois*, if not *à quatre*, with another girl named Sanki also in the mix. He met a petite, attractive woman in a trench coat and beret one evening, and took her to be Helen … or Sanki, who may have been Sephardic. Definitely not the curvaceous Ulla, who had a brother in Paris meant to protect her from young men like Mort Richler. "running into all kinds of snags in my work and love life," he confessed to Weintraub.

Leaving Ulla and/or Helen in McEwan's apartment, the Montrealers rode the Métro back across the Seine. On the Left Bank, Lionel Albert saw the cafés where "fellow bohemian degenerates" went "crawling from one den of st. germain sexual perversion to another." He came away impressed by his cousin's swagger and the banter at tables in the Dôme and the Sélect. About the company itself, he wasn't convinced.

The assemblies included Scotsman David Burnett and Fulbright-winner Herbert Gold, *New Story* editor Eric Protter and poet Alexander Trocchi, along with fun-loving Joe Dughi, another ex-GI, who had access to a nearby U.S. army canteen, with its cheap cigarettes and beer and wine. Richler also met Terry Southern, a tall, dashing Texan, and the wiry New York Jew Mason Hoffenberg. Among the men—and men they mostly were—the books of others, and certainly their own, were "sissy" topics. They preferred rigorous debates about Duke Snider's pitching and the real age of boxer Jersey Joe Walcott. How far Joe McCarthy would take things was fair game, as was the question of whether suspected spy Alger Hiss had been lying.

Afternoons and evenings among expatriates on the Left Bank involved more than hand-rolled cigarettes and shots of Johnnie Walker. Pot smoke frequently hung over the tables, and at one café Mort Richler tried hash for the first time. There was also the far darker dare of heroin. Paris was a good place to get hooked. Mason Hoffenberg was a proselytizing addict, and Trocchi and Burnett were on "horse" as well.

He was especially pleased to be in the company of the brash Hoffenberg, son of a shoe factory owner, and patrician Terry Southern, a native of Houston. Both traded in black humour and sarcasm; both could also be gentle and tender. Hoffenberg, described by one observer as having eyes "full of false promise," was a poet, and seemed to know lots of hip people back in America, including Henry Miller and William Burroughs. Southern, likewise in Paris on the GI Bill to, theoretically, attend the Sorbonne, was writing the hipster stories that would soon be central to the American literary avant-garde. He was also taking café existentialism to heart, especially its creed of living the moment. That meant viewing Paris, and Europe, as one long wild night of experience. The much younger Richler—as so often the case, he was their junior by half a dozen years—set off to explore the extremes with him. Booze and hash, carousing and jazz, he was game for; heroin, he was not. Neither was Southern. Both, however, wound up helping Hoffenberg shoot up.

Southern was friends with James Baldwin, then so poor that Southern was sneaking him into the Sorbonne student cafeteria for free meals. Richler went drinking with Baldwin, and occasionally ran into the loner Richard Wright playing the pinball machines at the Café Tournon. Clever ex-GI Art Buchwald, meanwhile, had struck it big by selling the *Herald Tribune* on the idea of a Paris restaurant column. Such a gig made him Right Bank, not Left.

Amidst the wild loud nights at café tables, at least one voice of dissent was reaching Richler's ears. Mavis Gallant, now removed from the Latin Quarter, rarely saw him on his own that winter. But when she did, and he showed her a fragment of a manuscript, possibly from *The Rotten People*, she declared the writing neither stupendous nor unpublishable. Instead, she called it a juvenile and pointless exercise in revenge, suggesting that he was still trying to prove to his mother that he had done the right thing in leaving home.

Christmas found him broke once more and living in a hotel that had once served as a brothel. His own sex life bore certain similarities. "a big problem is that I have fallen out with Helen," he reported to Bill Weintraub. "(she drops around almost every day.) there is also ulla, who likes to get it every day. And sanki. (I hope this doesn't sound rude but I feel depressed and I might as well take it out on someone who cant hit back for a week.)" Weintraub expressed only mild condolences about the demise of Helen. But he did take him to task for his dismissal of Mavis Gallant's debut in the *New Yorker*. "The writing was a beautiful piece of craftsmanship," he argued. "She has a terrific understanding of the language and a definite talent." Though the older man conceded that he hoped Gallant would one day "get around to territory that isn't so Elizabeth Bowenish," the rebuke was clear.

"i'm pretty damn broke, Bill," Richler wrote in January 1952. "can you lend me 50 bucks?" He'd already shaken his tin in various letters, including one to his Uncle Louie. Anxious to show his street laurels, he quoted "Auden to Maimonides" in his appeal to his uncle for love and understanding, plus cash. Louie sent back an injunction that he cut the crap, and a cheque for $100. A trip to Toulouse that same month, with Ulla and Kina Mitchell, the ex-McGill student and co-renter of the "Orange Crate" apartment in N.D.G. to whom he had directed his gauche query about Dylan Thomas's phallic poem, ended when their Renault was rear-ended. No one was hurt but the car was totalled, and after two days of drinking in Limoges, they returned to Paris by train. In February he travelled more successfully to England. Lionel Albert was in London, and Montrealers Sidney Lamb and John Harrison were enrolled at Cambridge. He went up to visit them, and promised, in exchange for the hospitality of Harrison and his wife, to smuggle steaks and pounds of butter into ration-dreary England. Ulla did not accompany him on this trip, and in a letter written from Cambridge on February 9, Richler confessed further girl troubles to Weintraub. "i got into a bit of a jam before i left. a woman again. sloppy again. but we were lucky."

Or not. A letter from Ulla dated the day before, February 8, and sent from the Hôtel de Nesles in Paris, reached Richler in Cambridge, where he was now renting a room in the Harrison flat. "Mordy dear," it began in uneven English, "I didn't get your letter before Wednesday night, and have been wondering so long how you have been. For three days after you left I was so sick and didn't dare to tell you that I was carrying that big trunk," she continued, referring to the trunk that Moses had lent his son for his travels, "and felt a horrible pain in my stomach and was many days bleeding like a mother who borned her children to the world." She didn't like, she wrote, "any idea of killing any thing" and added that her time, when not spent alone, involved the company of Mason Hoffenberg. "Mason is trying to make me more thin even," she remarked, a possible reference to heroin. The letter ended on a plaintiff note: "Write me soon Mordy, please. Don't you wish to kiss me anymore? Why not? My lips are warm and soft. All the birds are sending their love, Ulla."

By the time he returned to Paris four months later, she was gone—only to turn up again in the summer. But his trunk, where he stored his manuscripts, awaited him.

Through an acquaintance in Cambridge, Richler received an audience with E.M. Forster. The iconic, semi-retired novelist had been made an Honorary Fellow at King's College, Cambridge, a few years before, and at age seventy-three, still the Edwardian figure, welcomed authors to his rooms for sherry. His last great novels—*Howards End, A Passage to India*—were almost thirty years behind him, although he had recently released his *Collected Short Stories*. Richler overcame his fear—Forster was a couple of degrees of separation from any writer he had met—to manage a few minutes of desultory conversation with the great author, even leaving him his copy of Nelson Algren's *The Man with the Golden Arm*. His only real faux pas was downing the sherry like synagogue schnapps. But after the visit, he despaired at his self-delusion and that of his Paris friends. Weren't they just a bunch of kibitzers and wastrels, complaining of their awful Yiddish mommas and writing bad prose? A form-letter rejection of *The Rotten People* from John Lehmann Ltd. deepened his dark mood. They published Sartre in English. Why would they publish him? Even his gift failed the mark; the Algren novel was returned a few days later with a note from Forster saying he had given up after a hundred pages.

Regardless, he had less reason to suffer "dos arty blues," as he dubbed them, than he imagined. It was true that his stories, doggedly sent out to magazines as grand as *Harper's* and *Atlantic Monthly* or as modest as *New Story* in Paris and *New Writing* in London, came back rejected. "gee yre a great kid!" he paraphrased the rejections. "you really shd. be published. like yr. stuff swell, BUT. . . ." His new novel, though, begun before Christmas, was already several hundred pages long, the beneficiary of eight-hour workdays in Cambridge. *Only God Never Dies*, the original working title, would be a "clarion call to retreating liberals." In England he renamed it *The Jew of Valencia,* and by summer, when he started showing the manuscript to friends, *The Edge of Time*. "I'm glad to hear you're working hard," Weintraub wrote in mid-March. Once again, his friend proffered advice in the form of a joke. "Hope you're including a few Good People in the cast, not just those sybaritic, syphilitic, nymphomaniacal, alcoholic, venal, schizophrenic, unchristian boys and girls."

That winter, Weintraub offered a home-grown reading recommendation. "Have you read A.M. Klein's book *The Second Scroll*? It's really magnificent." Without saying so, he was alerting Richler to the fact that the poet and aspiring politician, also a Jew from the old neighbourhood, had just published a novel with the prestigious firm of Alfred A. Knopf in New York. In his reply, where he outlined a pleasant weekend up in London, attending *The Sleeping Beauty* at Sadler's Wells in Covent Garden and a Japanese film, Richler in turn remarked on the forthcoming British publication of a Hugh MacLennan novel. While he had no plans to pick up *Each Man's Son*—"I can do without reading it, thank you very much"—he was taking note of how other Canadians were faring in the metropolis.

Girls, girls, girls, was a constant subject of the letters crossing the Atlantic that year. In the same March exchanges, he admitted that while he and Helen continued to correspond, that relationship was "more palsy than passion." But then he added about the American: "we shall still sleep together, etc, we're planning a fortnight's orgy before i leave, but marriage off." Then there was Ulla, "the lovely Swede." "Should I get married?" he asked Weintraub rhetorically. "i don't think so," he concluded. For several months he had been talking about winding up his European adventure, and he was looking ahead to jobs in Montreal, starting in September, perhaps working as a proofreader at *Weekend Magazine*, launched by the Montreal *Star* just the previous year, or driving a cab, as his brother Avrum had done. "i'd appreciate it if you tell everyone what a great guy I am." But his feelings were still raw about his hometown. Mentioning that he was now an uncle, he added: "god when I think of the ignorance and darkness in which that poor kid will be raised, i honestly shudder. If I'm for sterilization of 90 percent of the population, does that make me a fascist?"

Back in Paris in May, he worked hard on the new novel. The playwright Michael Sayers, a former editor at the publishing house of Faber & Faber in London and "pal of Eliot and Pound," was living in the same hotel. He read his manuscript and made helpful suggestions. Richler's plan now was to spend the summer months rewriting it. Cash kept running out, and though he could be resourceful, borrowing from friends and parents, he tried pitching a piece to *Weekend*, to be co-written with his American friend Joe Dughi, using Weintraub as a conduit. He also entered a story competition run by *Maclean's* in Toronto. He didn't get the commission and the story didn't win. "SO MUCH OF IT IS CONNECTIONS, BILL. AND IT MAKES ME WANT TO PUKE," he concluded bitterly.

Though Mavis Gallant was "in Italia"—"she has sold the Nyorker again," he reported—he did make new Canadian friends. The wry young diplomat Geoff Pearson, son of the future prime minister and Nobel Peace Prize winner, was a rare native English-speaker at the embassy, posted to Paris only the previous year. Richler began dropping by for chats, and to bum cigarettes, and later Pearson and his intelligent wife, Landon, took him to a show by the "wild" Quebec painter Jean-Paul Riopelle, then the highest-profile Canadian artist in Paris—one of his large abstractions had been chosen for the Venice Biennale.

"QUARTIER GOSSIP," he alerted Weintraub: "a guy named dave is gunning for me in montparnasse . . . waving around a .45 and asking for this sonofabitch richler." The cause? "i laid his woman, or something. (dramatic, eh wot?)" Back in Tourrettes in July, he was rewriting *The Acrobats*, as the novel was now called—"see Rilke's fifth elegy," he explained. There, his romantic entanglements became the stuff of French bedroom farce. "ulla is here with me," he summarized for Weintraub, "and Helen is in cannes, all of which complicates things. . . . Helen by the way may be coming back to Canada with me. Wouldn't that be funny as hell?" But then, with the work completed by August 15, he acknowledged the presence of a new girl. "i've been fornicating somewhat earnestly since I finished my book, about a wk ago. kina and others have been around to lend a helping hand." Naïve, Mort Richler was no longer; gauche and reckless, a walking cliché of the callow young man, he could sometimes be.

"Christ, it's hot!" he wrote as his second summer in the south of France proved even more magical than the first, dramatic women adding to the effect. Tourrettes remained a small colony of foreign artists, still largely undiscovered by the rest of the world, where he could write all day and carouse into the night

with an Australian potter and Viennese abstract painter, a would-
be novelist from Texas and an aspiring French playwright. One
day, meandering through the narrow cobbled streets in the
nearby town of Vence, which for centuries had seduced writers
and artists with its beauty, and where D.H. Lawrence had died
and been buried and exhumed again a quarter-century before,
he and a friend came upon a gregarious eighty-year-old who
spoke intimately of "Isadora"—Isadora Duncan—and W.B. Yeats,
as well as of his own early days on stage with the legendary
Shakespearean actor Henry Irving. The elderly raconteur was the
theatre legend Gordon Craig, and he began riding the bus up to
Tourrettes to enjoy the company of the young artists in Café
Cresp. He would bring along a folio of cartoons by Max Beerbohm,
copies of his own books, most notably the one on Irving that
Russian filmmaker Sergei Eisenstein claimed he had studied like
a Bible, and photos of himself, which he graciously signed as
gifts. The energy and camaraderie of the titan impressed the
twenty-one-year-old. Richler's apprenticeship that summer
wasn't only in restructuring a manuscript and juggling several
girls at a time without getting shot.

Maimonides' *The Guide for the Perplexed* had kept him company
during his two years abroad. Though the massive book, written
in the twelfth century by the great Hispanic Jewish philosopher
Moses Maimonides, may possibly have been "employed" on occasion in cafés to evidence less the seriousness of his intellect than
the singularity of his perspective as a Jew and the product of an
Orthodox upbringing, it seemed to be a genuine pillar of the kind
of self-education he had been explaining to his father in letters.
He had moved through the three books of the *Guide* slowly,
absorbing their meditations on the nature of God and their evalu-
ations of the great traditions—Jewish, Islamic and ancient Greek.
For a boy raised on the laws as intractable "rules," Maimonides'
generous considerations of the 613 laws of the Pentateuch must
have been a challenge. It was one he could both accept and
meet—still another reminder, perhaps, of the thirteen-year-old
who had performed his bar mitzvah by himself. That *The Guide*

for the Perplexed had been treasured by his grandfather Yudel Rosenberg may have exempted it from the disdain he then displayed for so much else about the religion of his family. The rabbi, whom he remembered only slightly, had been, by most accounts, a different sort of Orthodox Jew.

His exchanges with his father continued to veer into the theological, often explosively. Both sides were making an effort across a vast divide. Though he didn't write the book he had mentioned in Spain, he continued to read widely about Judaism, and smugly encouraged Moses to be better informed. "kafka was the only modern Hebrew writer—and a great one—in the cabbalistic tradition," he wrote of the Czech novelist. "He was so jewish it came out of his ears." His request that his father mail him a copy of a history of Jewish mysticism available in a shop in the old neighbourhood, and inquire how much a complete English translation of the Zohar would cost, served to remind Moses once again that his son remained a thoughtful Jew. In making his father drive back across Montreal to a store located a few blocks from where Rabbi Rosenberg had once worked on his own translations of the Zohar, he may likewise have been suggesting that, while he had no patience for punitive Richler Orthodoxy, he was connected to aspects of his legacy as a Rosenberg. That and being a pain, demanding and exasperating. Moses struggled to contain his anger at how his outspoken boy was asserting his individuality. "Speaking of religions, while we are on the subject, they all believe in honouring and respecting their parents. Do you?"

His father, too, could summon grievances from the dark days of the grandson-grandfather wars. "Whenever you come to Babas or Zeidas place you are expected to do as they do," Moses wrote. "Religiously, or otherwise, when you go to a church you show respect by not wearing a hat, and vice versa in a Synagogue, or a Jewish religious home, you do not do just the opposite to antagonize them, and thats what you have been doing, and would not want to understand." He believed that Mordecai could still "admit where you were, and return to a respectable life." But he also threatened, not for the first time, to sever relations. "I will not create another Frankenstein," he vowed.

The magical summer was nearing its end. Richler would be in Paris for two days, saying goodbyes to friends and buying gifts, including some flamenco records requested by Bill Weintraub, and then would leave for England to catch the boat to Canada. The scene in Paris had begun to sour. Reality had set in: book contracts for a few of the café bohemians, often followed by repatriation to the States to launch careers; or more disappointment, and heroin, for the rest. He himself had one abandoned novel, one ongoing manuscript of five hundred pages, and a pile of rejection letters. He was penniless and in debt to various family and friends, and had no skills as such. Existential sex and anti-bourgeois fiction writing, caustic café banter and European cultural worldliness, didn't translate into a job. "i have absolutely no prospects," he admitted to Weintraub. "my father will pay me $25 a week to answer the phone in his office and tease me about becoming a writer." Weintraub did, however, have a lead on a position for him at the CBC. "i promise to be a good boy—especially politically," Richler wrote of it. (The beard, he assured him, was gone.) "in some ways it will be nice to see Montreal again. i wonder, tho, how long the charm will hold out."

So it might have ended: wild oats sown, to be aggrandized later as anecdotes about the good old days; much typing to be consigned forever to desk drawers, along with fond memories of the time when he was young and wild in the graveyard for Jews; and with an "adult" career involving salary and benefits ahead of him. By 1952, CBC radio and the new television network were already the destination of choice for those with talent and culture who dared not risk seeing if they could really make a go of it as artists—especially on the dry cultural rock that was their nation.

Then it happened. Michael Sayers, who had promised to recommend him to Norman Mailer's U.K. literary agent, did give his name to Joyce Weiner, a leading London agent known for her advocacy of younger writers. While in the city, awaiting passage out of Liverpool, Richler called her up. She agreed to give him a few minutes. Shoving the manuscript of *The Acrobats* into a record sleeve, he appeared at her office in Eyre Court, a "farouche" young man by her account, "strange, wild-eyed, diffident," with a massive manuscript under his arm. She was prepared to escort him back out when he offered a thank you of such sincerity that it softened her. But she warned him it could be months before she had a chance to read his book, which was, she was already fairly certain, "no bloody good."

Weiner, thirty-five, unmarried and Jewish, then did the farouche young man an extraordinary turn. She read enough of the novel that same night to decide that its author possessed a talent worth cultivating. She called Mort Richler the next morning to say as much, cautiously—she was amazed that he was only twenty-one—and to agree to serve as the book's agent. She even sent it out to a friend, a publisher whose opinion she trusted. He would be hearing back from her, and the publisher, shortly.

Suddenly he had a novel worth being published and an agent who was committed to selling it. Suddenly, he *was* a novelist, albeit still in infancy, one who could hold his head high in the company of not only Mason Hoffenberg and Terry Southern but Mavis Gallant. He wasn't on his way home to Canada as a washed-out boulevardier; he was on his way home as a writer.

IV

MONTREAL, DULL AND ANAESTHETIC

In a letter to Europe, Bill Weintraub had warned about the state of their hometown. "Duplessis has closed the gaming houses," he wrote, "and insists that pubs close at 2 a.m. (10 p.m. on New Year's Eve)." The city Richler saw again for the first time in two years in September 1952 wasn't quite the 1950 town of gangsters and gamblers, casinos and nightclubs. But Avrum Richler, who drove to Quebec City to collect his brother at the port, could attest that not all the gaming houses had been shut down. Now a husband, father and optometrist, Avrum was frequenting Harry Ship's gambling emporiums in Greenfield Park and Côte-St-Luc. And the "Boy Wonder" himself, who had done six months in jail back in 1946 during a brief police crackdown, was also going "legit" with his latest venture—the Chez Paree nightclub on Stanley Street. The amiable gangster was soon hosting jazz musicians Charlie Parker and Brew Moore and, after much deliberation over his $10,000 fee, Frank Sinatra.

Richler didn't follow his sibling into mild vice. But he did trail Bill Weintraub into the Montreal Men's Press Club, recently moved to the basement of the Mount Royal Hotel. Weintraub was doing some work for CBC TV, which began broadcasting the same month Richler docked in Quebec. He was also putting together movie nights at the club, where exotic European films could find local audiences. There Weintraub finally had an opportunity to introduce the "very young, very cheeky" Mordecai, as he had described him the previous year, to his good friend Brian Moore.

A product of Catholic Belfast, the stout Moore had immigrated to Canada a few years earlier. He had witnessed the devastation of the war first-hand, having worked for the United Nations in Poland in 1946, and was hard-drinking and hard-headed, competitive and observant, a gifted raconteur with a deep sensitivity to women and a sharp, occasionally cruel disposition towards men. Besides writing for the *Gazette*, he was publishing pulp thrillers under two pseudonyms while struggling with his own literary fiction. He was now living on St. Catherine Street in Westmount with his new wife, Jackie Sirois—Mavis Gallant's closest friend—and he welcomed Richler into a fun-loving circle that included Bill Weintraub, Paris alumni Alex Cherney and his wife, Gloria, and Moore's younger brother Sean, then studying medicine at McGill. The centre of the group, Gallant, remained in Paris, but her friends back in Canada counted themselves cosmopolitans in a sea of provinciality. Weintraub and Gallant were already Richler's friends and mentors. Soon Brian Moore would become important to him, despite—or perhaps because of—the decade gap in their ages.

Drinks at the Press Club and dinners at the Moores' could not disguise the reality that, being broke, he had only one real option for accommodation: his mother. In this instance, it was literally a boarding arrangement, albeit free of charge. Besides doing the accounts for the Esquire show club, Lily was now back in the rooming-house business. Hallowell Avenue in lower Westmount, while perfectly nice, occupied a pocket of non-affluence in the Anglo fortress, and she rented three rooms to the predictable sorts of men, few of them Jews. In electing to stay over on the "Anglo" side of the mountain once her boys had moved on, she was further cutting herself off from her past, and her people. Her behaviour remained unusual for the daughter of an Orthodox rabbi, an attribute that her youngest son might have admired had he recognized in it the seeds of his own spirited independence. But Mordecai, while aware of her shortcomings, was blind to any brand of courage or intrepidness implicit in Lily's life decisions. Some basic respect for her had gone missing.

For her part, Lily Rosenberg was delighted to have her golden son back under her roof. And he, while no doubt weary at once more having to share the bathroom with strangers, was content with her cooking and, in truth, her smothering affection. Visiting Moses again in his Côte-St-Luc apartment was less of a mixed experience, although his father did not fail to remind him of the debts he had incurred in Europe. When told the definitive title of his novel-in-progress, he barked, "What the hell do you know about the circus?" But he finally decided that *The Acrobats* worked for its alphabetical qualities, figuring it could be the start of a series—the next book titled with a B, then a C.

A letter from London awaited Richler at 61 Hallowell Avenue. Daniel George of Jonathan Cape Publishers, the editor friend on whom Joyce Weiner had imposed to read *The Acrobats*, encouraged him to redraft the manuscript with an eye to the less-is-more principle. George offered to read the new version as well. Weiner likewise counselled him to "save the vigour while pruning the extravagances." She had recently read Hemingway's new novel, and noted in passing that he remained "a master of atmosphere, dialogue, character and economy." Her specific requests included tempering a lengthy brothel scene, making a few of the characters agreeable and displaying less evident anger. "If you rage less, for instance on the racial question, you can be a lot more effective." Joyce Weiner saved her most important suggestion to the end. "Take it easy with the revisions," she said. "These should not be rushed."

But taking it easy, in life and in his art, was not his mode of being. In his reply to Daniel George, he admitted, "It's not the revising that bothers me but the other books that aren't being written! I've got at least three novels buzzing around in my head." He also took the opportunity to announce himself a de facto American novelist, one of those "ill-behaved, raucous yahoos" British critics liked to indulge. Norman Mailer was one, along with Nelson Algren. And surely the energy of these writers more than compensated for their manners, especially compared with the sedate British novelists tending their suburban literary gardens? As pitches went, it was sly in its distancing of himself from, say, the newest Hugh MacLennan published in London, and smart in aligning Mordecai Richler, ostensibly of Montreal, with the energy of those fresh American voices, mostly Jewish, and many fellow graduates of the Left Bank finishing school.

————

Ted Allan was a name Richler likely recognized even before Michael Sayers, the friend in Paris who made the connection to Joyce Weiner, mentioned him as someone he should meet. Born Alan Herman in Montreal in 1916, Ted Allan had spent part of his childhood on St. Urbain Street in modest circumstances. As a youth he had served in the International Brigade in Spain alongside the pioneering Canadian medic Norman Bethune, an experience he wrote up first as a script for Hollywood, and much later as the co-authored bestseller *The Scalpel, the Sword: The Story of Doctor Norman Bethune.* He had been asked to leave the United States not long before as a suspected Communist, and cut a dashing, attractive figure. Though he was not tall, his big smile and bigger laugh made him appear outsized, as did his skills as a storyteller. Funny and warm, Ted Allan was forever writing the next great play, the next great novel; he was always out to charm men and seduce women. His current employer was CBC Radio in Toronto, where his politics were again causing a stir. He was married with two small children, including a son called Norman—after the great Bethune.

Richler's decision not to wait until chance brought him into contact with Allan was typical. He wrote a letter and then called, citing the Sayers link. On receiving an invitation to visit, he got on an overnight bus for his first adult visit to the Ontario city eight hours to the west along the still-unfinished 401 highway.

Ted Allan welcomed the acolyte into his midtown house, offering a couch for the night. A couple of weeks later he replied to Richler's thank-you note. "I am still very interested in seeing your book," he wrote on December 18, 1952, "and when you send it, please write me as to who has seen it up to now in the publishing world. Do you want me to show it to my publishers? Please send it to me—NOW IS THAT CLEAR?" In a PS, the older man—Allan was eleven years his senior—sought to be clearer still: "Your letter evoked in me something you probably evoked in Mike [Sayers]. We see and hear ghosts of our youth and we're excited to see how it will develop in this particular case. So hurry and send your book along and I shall do my utmost to help you along in your career."

Unknowingly, Ted Allan would soon do Richler's life and career a favour that landing him the best publisher in New York couldn't have matched. The manuscript of *The Acrobats* arrived in Toronto, and Allan read it. He then asked a friend's wife if she'd like to take a look as well. He knew Florence Mann—a stunning, sophisticated twenty-two-year-old married to his CBC Toronto colleague Stanley—to be an unusually serious reader. She read *The Acrobats*, pronouncing it the work of an intelligent, and indeed interesting, author.

After doing odd jobs for a few months, including as a night watchman for an uncle and, apparently, brief employment selling diapers, Richler landed one of those coveted positions at CBC Montreal, writing radio copy in the evening for on-air use the next day. A typical news segment ran to twelve hundred words, obliging him to learn how to craft tight, vivid stories to his deadline. He wrote about fellow Baron Byng graduate, Reuben Ship, a Hollywood screenwriter in the process of fighting deportation from the United States, like Ted Allan. He reported on the bitter final months of Julius and Ethel Rosenberg, the American Jews awaiting execution for having divulged information about the atomic bomb to the Soviet Union. He was now sharing a basement apartment on Tupper Street with his cousin Lionel Albert, near the border of Westmount and the downtown and only a few minutes' walk from Lily Rosenberg's house. He brought along a recording of Franz Lehar's *The Merry Widow*, borrowed from Lily's collection, as well as the dozen jazz records Terry McEwan had given him back in Paris. Soon he was playing the Lehar and the jazz not only for Lionel but for his new lover.

In Paris Lionel had mentioned two sisters who lived a door away from him on Crescent Street. Tess and Cathy Boudreau, from a working-class French-Canadian family in the southern Ontario town of St. Catharines, had been drawn to the energy of Montreal. In 1953 Tess, soon to be married to a renowned Dutch photojournalist named Kryn Taconis, was thirty-two, her sister thirty. Tess, too, was friends with Mavis Gallant and Jackie Moore. Jack Lieber, the bookstore owner who had also witnessed Richler's awkward interactions at the "Orange Crate" apartment a couple of years before, made the introduction. Kiev-born Lieber, Baron Byng graduate and war veteran, ran a Sunday afternoon salon out of his small shop on St. Catherine Street, where discussions of Stalin and Marx were accompanied by smoked meat and liquor. Already feared for his scathing wit, Richler sat in a corner to smoke, drink, and say very little. Still, Lieber surmised that the taciturn aspiring novelist would be just right for the gregarious Cathy, then working as a secretary.

Surprisingly, he was right. Mordecai took an immediate liking to Cathy, an attraction she returned. She was tall and thin, with black hair and dark features, especially flashing brown eyes. Known for her own biting, often cruel wit—she made him laugh, and vice versa—Cathy wasn't only a decade older; she was also a divorcee. Her spiritedness, even her temper, may have reminded him of the Helens and Ullas of Europe. So, possibly, did her experience with sex.

In the apartment on Tupper Street, Lionel witnessed first-hand the energy and decisiveness of his cousin. There were the daytime rewrites of *The Acrobats,* and work on new short stories, all before heading off to the CBC. In early March, Lionel and Cathy stood in the kitchen as Richler learned in a call from Joyce Weiner that the London publisher André Deutsch was making a conditional offer on the novel. "You're only twenty-two!" his cousin exclaimed in astonishment.

"We were very impressed by the book," André Deutsch himself wrote on March 13. "We are even more impressed by your potentialities as a writer." The Budapest-born publisher—the word

"potentialities" spoke to his formal English—had already founded
two firms, the most recent, eponymous one only a few months
old. Deutsch, thirty-five, was a dapper man, individualistic, and
charming. He and Diana Athill, a founding editor of his year-old
publishing house and sometime lover, were considered more
receptive to new writers than the larger, older London firms. He
included a four-page critique of the manuscript, a document that
would have been devastating had it not been delivered in the context of a conditional acceptance. In fact, Deutsch had first rejected
The Acrobats, as the more established and influential Jonathan
Cape had done. But when he had requested the right of first
refusal of Richler's next novel for a small fee, Weiner had gambled
and insisted he take the current one as well. The advance offered
was £50 immediately and £50 more on acceptance. If Deutsch
declined the revised manuscript, Richler kept the advance.

One hundred pounds, or $250 Canadian, for two years of work?
"I don't get you," his Uncle Louie said. "You could have earned
more than that cutting my lawn."

With the good news from London, Richler could begin con-
ceptualizing how his professional career would unfold. Dragging
on a cigarette and furrowing his brow, he would explain to any
who asked that he planned to be a "serious" author. His sole
ambition was to write a great novel, one that would last. All other
things would have to come second. Such convictions would
shortly be transformed into a lifestyle, and a living, in England,
where such talk sounded neither pretentious nor vaguely demented. In Montreal, outside that small circle of friends, it came
across as both.

In a long letter back to André Deutsch, he seemed to be talking as much to himself as to his publisher. "For the past two
years," he wrote, "my great fear has been that I might end up an
intellectual hobo." He sketched the type: "a guy who could yak
just endlessly about Kafka and cabalism, contributed blank prose
to an All Directions Annual, swore like Hemingway in bourgeois
salons, just-missed-making-it, misunderstood and a devil, and
lectures in Creative Writing at Black Valley U." Instead, he

promised to become a player, by dint of effort and a disavowal of illusions about the stakes, or odds. "There are too many anonymous writers, men who never write anything really bad or anything really good. . . . I believe that if you are going to write and ask people to read you—and that is asking a helluva lot— then you shd make it original, like Mr. Pound said. Original, like Hemingway, like Faulkner, like Sartre, like Céline . . . . I am not yet truly original but I am trying," he said, analyzing his own intentions and skill with remarkable honesty for one so young. "I am going to write many books and someday I am going to be original. I will not write like these great men have written because they have already written that way. I will try to absorb what they done [sic] and come out like myself. . . . I will try hard. I should improve as I go along."

Especially telling was the "intellectual hobo" remark. In Europe Mort Richler had played the part of the decadent, self-stylized artiste. Looking back on the experience from Montreal, he acknowledged that it had been a kind of act, and he recognized in it the fallback persona of the untalented. A real author knew his talent and his worth; he comported himself with confidence and humility, and took the work very seriously. That, he wanted his publisher to know, was the author he would be. "I don't thk I am great," he told Deutsch, "but if I work hard might be very good. . . . What I am trying to say is that I think (sometimes) that I have the 'things'—or talents, if you like—that are essential." A month later, while making the requested revisions, he offered a further self-insight. "The bk is hard," he confessed to Diana Athill, already renowned for nurturing writers, "and I am truly exhausted. Often I thk I don't like or dislike writing, it's just something I've got to do."

One other thing he had to do: draw or doodle. "Mr. Deutsch," he added, "may I submit a layout and drawing for the bk jacket?? Once, when I was pretty young, I won an art scholarship (without revising one goddam drawing so help me!) I have done commercial art work professionally, the odd painting or mural, and I draw all the time. In fact," he said, "when I refused to become a rabbi I was supposed to study commercial art." His offer wasn't taken up, but its hopeful sweetness likely struck the same receptive chord in Deutsch as had the fateful thank you the "farouche young man" had extended to Joyce Weiner in her London office the previous autumn. People who might not have taken to "Mauricio" of Ibiza or the "sonofabitch Richler" of Left Bank Paris liked this kid.

"Don't rush the revision," Diana Athill advised as well. But of course his pace that spring—rushing the revision and drafting stories, writing news copy and sharing a bed with Cathy—was relentless. He saw his parents, always separately, and socialized with the Moore-Weintraub crowd. Matters took a serious turn there when Brian Moore, swimming alone in a lake near his cabin in the Laurentians, was hit by a motorboat, suffering six skull fractures and losing the power of speech for a worrying period. Richler also visited Evelyn Sacks, despite her husband's jealousy. At one meeting his still-infatuated teacher made a pass, becoming irate when he refused her.

Parties were the way Montreal's literati and journalists widened connections and made friends and enemies. The Moores were good hosts, as was Bill Weintraub, and the nights were long, boozy and smoky, with the men in suits and the women in dresses and jewellery. At one soiree, hosted by Neil Compton, the popular Sir George Williams English professor, Richler met Bernard and Sylvia Ostry. She was a lecturer at McGill and he was researching a book on Mackenzie King. Both were in their mid-twenties, intellectual and ambitious and likewise anxious to define themselves outside Canada. Bernard already held a research position in Birmingham; Sylvia was off to Cambridge to complete her doctorate. They had to bend over to meet the would-be novelist: Richler lay on the floor, a glass of whisky balanced on his chest. When he issued a string of witty put-downs about the other guests, the Ostrys decided on the spot that he was not politely, dully Canadian and was worth getting to know. A long friendship was born.

To another literary party he brought Flora Rosenberg, cousin of the disgraced politician Fred Rose. Rose had been released from prison a few months before, after serving nearly five years. Broken and unemployed, he was being trailed by RCMP officers to job interviews, where his past would be pointed out to potential employers. Richler had known Flora from Baron Byng High, and on his return he called her, despite her family's status as pariahs due to the perceived shame Rose had brought upon the city's Jews. On noticing Flora Rosenberg in tears at the party from a grilling by two men, he threatened to punch her interrogators. He then escorted her home.

"It'll be nice to be out of a job again!" he had quipped to André Deutsch back in May. On August 26 he booked passage to England, trusting he now had enough money to "live and work for a year as I please." Joyce Weiner tried dampening his enthusiasm. "You cannot expect to live by your writing for a very long time," she warned. But he was already thinking practically, willing to hustle, do what was required. The only "real jobs" he would hold thereafter—as visiting professor, Book-of-the-Month Club judge, and columnist—would be offshoots of his profession as a writer. Henceforth, he would be freelance, his own master and servant. Without security. Without nets.

He did have Weiner working on his behalf. The relationship between "Mr. Richler" and "Ms. Weiner" was proving key. In her stern admonitions ("rather revolting" she described one passage in *The Acrobats*) and chidings (a genius "you are definitely not"), her displays of impatience ("You <u>are</u> touchy, aren't you") and patience alike ("keep this letter with you for many years if need be and you'll come to agree with me"), she showed a quiet determination to direct her client wisely. She wanted to lead him away from Vandyke beards and sandals, Céline-worship and café credos of shocking the bourgeois, and towards "taste and refinement and perspective"—that is, literary craft of a somewhat middlebrow variety. These, she summarized, were the qualities he would need if he was to be "a permanent and not a passing factor in the literary scene."

More often than not, Richler took her advice. In a letter in which he transcribed a rejection of a story from *Harper's* magazine he apologized to her: "I feel I've meddled enough, and that you know best, so send it where you please." The issue was his seeking separate representation for North America, where he desperately wanted a New York publisher. Weiner offered assurances: "I do not really think you will find me letting the grass grow under my feet or regret the presence of an agent in New York." He was now sending her short stories, hoping she could place them with magazines. Weiner liked one, called "MacPherson's Cloud," about a teacher attempting to control an unruly class. But a story titled "Beyond All Blessings and Hymns" she found "old, time-worn, almost trite." Several more also concerned a Jewish ghetto and a Jewish boy. Weiner criticized these as "still clinging to the background." "Get some new experiences, young man," she wrote, "and leave the world of childhood and adolescence behind." And again, she pleaded with him to take his writing more slowly. "I beg you not to send out stories that are not absolutely tops. You have a reputation to consider, and I have mine."

Joyce Weiner was the perfect agent for Mordecai Richler at twenty-two. "I hope your Mama will think 'that agent woman' of some use now," she said after placing *The Acrobats*. Curiously, all business letters continued to be sent c/o Lily Rosenberg on Hallowell, not to his apartment on Tupper.

The early stories deserved her dismissive criticisms. She did get the commercial appeal of the slight "The Secret of the Kugel," a folksy tale about a boy discovering that his unmarried aunt's beloved kugel is actually bakery-bought; and she recognized the potential of "MacPherson's Cloud." It dated back to his first sojourn in Europe—an early draft bears Terry McEwan's Parisian address—and opened simply: "With his wife so ill these past weeks, and the prospect of three more full days of teaching before the weekend break, MacPherson felt old and gloomy this morning on his way to classes. . . ." Richler would keep working on the story for years.

Shortly before he left for Europe again, aboard the *Samaria*, he arranged for his first publicity photo. The shot, by photographer David Bier, could almost have been taken with Joyce Weiner's stipulations in mind. He wore a tie and dress shirt, the cuffs folded in lieu of cufflinks. Cheeks were clean-shaven and thick hair combed into a cresting wave. Ears were large and nose was significant. The forehead was tall. If an expression was readable in the downward gaze—since the eyes were not for viewing—it was reflective. If the cigarette pinched between thumb and fore-finger suggested an attitude, it was mitigated by the starched shirt. Here was a lean, clean young man, handsome in an irregu-lar way, taking himself seriously. A London man of letters, ready to find and assume his place in literary society.

V

M, THE BOY WRITER

[To Bill Weintraub and Brian Moore]
Sept 6, 53

'iya Maties:

The trip was godawful. Don't, by any means, travel Cunard. Cathy still suffering from a cold. I arrived with a fever, and my ass shot full of penicillin but I'm okay now. . . .

Spoke to Deutsch about you, and he wd like to see the story. Mr D, bytheway, seems to be a damn fine fellow. Had lunch and drinks with him yesterday. There wasn't enough he could do for me, etc. He will get me odd jobs reading mss., ghost-writing and revising, BBC, and will see abt a fulltime job for me when and if I need one. . . . He wants me in Eng for drinks when the bk comes out. W Allan, Mr D., thk my bk is definitely a "first novel" BUT also that Im just abt the best and most "natural" boy since Mailer. . . .

Had lunch with Joyce Weiner on the 4th. She was also damn encouraging abt U.S. Market. She is having lunch with Mr & Mrs Knopf next wk, and the editor of Viking the following wk. . . .

Got a flat in Chelsea with Cathy and another girl. 4pds 10 a wk or 30 bob each—not bad, eh??

Mort

[To Brian Moore]
Mordecai Richler
509 Kings Road
Chelsea
London S.W.10
September 7, 1953

Brian,

. . . christ, man, you must come over soon with Jackie. There were many new-born babies on board the samaria. A few of them were stepped on and squished but most of them made the trip okay.

prospects seem excellent. will write in greater length and detail abt lit life here as soon as I have seen more of it. Dining with Mr & Mrs D next wk. D is flying to Canada–New York in abt 6 mos., will ask him to look you up in Montreal. I know youll both like him.

oh, for Bill, will Dave B crop that pic of me smoking and send me 4 copies airmail. . . .

Mordecai

Deutsch says I'll get a rough going-over from the "conservative" critics but that LISTENER, NEW STATESMAN, ETC, shd give me good reviews.

———

[To Bill Weintraub]
Friday, Sept 11, 1953

Bill, My Old:
We, three of us, live in a flat on Kings Road, in Chelsea. There is Cathy, Florrie Macdonald and myself. Our bus stop is called "The World's End" after the pub two blocks down the street. Two blocks, northwards [sic], is the Thames.

Cathy is going out to look for a job today. I have been working on a long short story for two days and I feel pretty good abt it— not abt the story but abt working.

I saw Joyce Weiner again a couple of days ago. She told me that a big man, I forget his name, from 20th Cent. Fox was in to see her and asked if she had any Canadian scripts—which are apparently in a big demand. I immediately told her abt you, and abt the script you outlined to me one night in the press club— remember? . . . Look, man, wd you take 2 days off from drinking & lovemaking & ideamaking and outline that script? . . . I told her I wd ask you for it.

Deutsch, and Joyce W, have both been extraordinarily kind and encouraging. . . . There will be several informal luncheons and drink sessions within the next 3 wks and Im to meet almost everybody. The bk goes into production within 2 weeks, proofs out early in Dec. (will send you one). I met the guy who'll do my jacket. . . .

I sipped a few glasses of sherry with E.M. Forster last wk and he'll look at the proofs—voluntarily. . . .

Hope the oor-mays got my letters alright???

Ov-lay to Bernice, all the est-bay,

Mort

———

Bill Weintraub
Weekend Weekly
231 St James St
Montreal
Canada
Tuesday, Sept 15

Dear Mort—

Copy boy left at noon for Bier's. It is now 4 o'clock and he's not back yet. The lad has no sense of mission. So I'll write now and send the pix tomorrow. . . .

Next on the agenda, the script for J. Weiner. I appreciate your intentions, but don't think anything could come of it except make Miss W. look foolish and waste 20th Century Fox's time. . . . If they want Canadian scripts I would have to put in some Mounties and fur traders. . . . I hope you didn't promise J.W. anything. . . . It isn't that I don't want to interrupt my stagnation to write it down. . . .

Moore was up to see Dr. Cone today for the big checkup. He had his head tapped and Cone said the case was closed. Nothing to worry about. But he advised little or no alcohol, which there is reason to believe is the good doctor's own private temperance crusade.

All your news sounds good and heartening. About Deutsch, new mags, job possibilities, etc. Great. Who's this Florrie McDonald? La vie en trios, eh? Ho ho ho. And how's Cathy? Has she a job?

Montreal is dull and anaesthetic. Will write later about my hopes, ambitions. Have none today.

Bill

————

Bill,

We've got a new boarder at 509. He wears *pince-nez* glasses, speaks a pretty good Russian, calls himself Larry, and last night he ate up Florrie. . . .

I have finished another anti-semitic story, 70pps, and Joyce W has suggested that I've got a half-bk of Jew stories, and suggested further that Mr D might/would be interested in putting out a bk of them—which wd be damn nice. . . . Mrs Knopf has turned down the bk, and this wk it goes to viking. Cathy and myself are dining with Joyce W tomorrow night. . . .

We went down to Petticoat Lane last Sunday am and although we didn't buy anything we did discover Bloom's (Londons—or Whitechapels, Bens) and stuffed ourselves on salted beefs. Afterwards, we went to Hyde Park. We heard a man named 'arry

(so help me) talk abt HOW THE GOVERNMENT CHEATS
INVENTORS.

'arry: The Laboh gov'ment gets in and the worker thinks it's a bit
    of oll right. So what 'appens. Ole Attlee says work 'arder.
    WORK 'ARDER! We want the conditions here that they've
    got in Russia.

heckler: 'ow many full stops in a bottle of ink, 'arry?

'arry: We want Stalin back!

heckler: How long 'ave you been a shareholder in the daily
    worker, 'arry?

'arry: Two 'undred bleeding years!

2nd heckler (very short man): I got a question.

'arry: I don't accept questions from 'arf-wits.

1st heckler: 'Oo's a 'arf-wit?

'arry: You are, you bleeding thief!

2nd heckler: 'Well, 'arry, can I ask 'arf a question?

'arry: 'arf a question! You're so short you're not tall enough to go
    to the gents. If you even went to the lav you'd bloody drown!

3rd heckler (pointing to first heckler): Eh, 'arry, 'e's a reporter!

'arry: 'Oo 'im?? The only place 'e could make a report is in the lav.

And so on, into the night. . . .

Mort

————

Sept 21, 1953

Dear Daddy,

I meant to write to you last week but it has taken me some
time to get settled, down to work, adjusted, and so on. I've got a
flat in Chelsea, which I'm sharing with some friends. This is a
nice, central, part of London—only two blocks from the Thames
and about 20 minutes away from the West End.

Please send my best to the boys, Freda, and Moe Atlas, and
say that I will write to them soon.

Are you going to build the siding before winter sets in?

Write to me, I will write regularly and let you know of any developments here.

Regards to Sarah, the boys, love,

Mutty

———————

[typed onto back of playbill for Granville Theatre "Nudes of the Night" review of October 5, 1953. Featured acts include "The Riviera Lovelies" and "The One and Only Jezebel."]

509 the kings rd school of writing 509
London SW10
England
Oct9/53

BILL, MY OLD:
never mind the 86 bob you owe me. Forget abt it. Pay no mind. It's okay. But I have to type this note on a playbill because I can't afford typing paper—I'm using my mss [manuscripts] to build fires because you cant buy coal in quantities of less than one lb and that's too much of an investment—o well, tomorrow is Saturday EATING DAY (we eat on alternative days now) but never mind, it's okay abt the money, always glad to do a favor for a friend. . . .

He also tells (he meaning Andre or Andy) me that he will publish a bk of ghetto tales—now half-written—after novel no 2. have written a wkend story and a macl story but Joyce says I will have to revise them both. She also says that one Compton-Mackenzie wd read my bk and salut it but he is blind. . . . I expect to start my own [second] bk in abt 3 wks. Meanwhile I am happy working on stories, etc, and have sufficient funds to hold out until Jan or Fev when I shall slap an ms down on Andre's desk and try to make a touch. . . .

Mort

———

[To Diana Athill, late October]
sat pm

DEAR DIANA
Enclosed is
a. one short story, THE SHAPE OF THE GHETTO
b. several photos of THE YOUNG AUTHOR

Re short story—
I wd like, ultimately, to put 4 of these stories
    THE SHAPE OF THE GHETTO
    MR MACPHERSON
    BEYOND ALL THE BLESSINGS AND HYMNS
    THE FIRE
into a collection of stories abt Montreal, entitled BEYOND ALL
BLESSINGS AND HYMNS. (That, altogether, wd be abt 90,000
words.) BUT I fully intend giving you a second novel first.
    (I thk I discussed this with Mr D and yourself in a pub abt two
weeks ago. . . .)
    Re photographs—
    Please note that THE YOUNG AUTHOR is shown in various
moods. . . .
    Young Author Having a Think
    Young Author Having a Smoke (Player's Mild)
    Young Author Looking at Reader
    Young Author Having a Wait in front of Gameland on Saint
Lawrence Boulevard, Montreal
    Young Author in front of Shooting Gallery, same st.
    Young Author Having a Type

All the best,

Mordecai

———

[From Joyce Weiner]
127, Eyre Court
London, N.W.8
Primrose 0749
16th November, 1953

Dear Mordecai,

Many thanks for your characteristic note of November 14th. I think you really are on the wrong wicket with regards to MACLEAN'S. I cannot see your stories ever being suitable for this magazine, nor indeed, do I think you have quite the knack of writing slick stories, which is by no means to your detriment, and I would forget about short stories for the moment . . . and I am so glad that you are concentrating now on the new novel with its excellent and significant title.

Thank you so much for your suggestion that I should go away soon. I feel the same—if only my legs would carry me. . . . The reason I have not allowed you to come and see me is that I have been far from sociable, and it is no fun for any visitor to see me writhing. Nevertheless, I greatly appreciate your solicitude and I hope very soon to be able to see you in normal circumstances.

All the best to you both,

Joyce

PS: Extract from letter received from G.P. Putnam's Sons:
We have finally received the Mordecai Richler manuscript, and Bob Amussen and others have read it. We all agree that there is lots of promise here and would like to make an offer for THE ACROBATS, subject to the author's willingness to revise it a bit for America. . . . Meanwhile, as to terms, we would suggest an advance of $750, payable $500 on signature and $250 on receipt and acceptance of the finally revised manuscript. . . .

———

Nov19, 53

WILLIAM, MY OLD:
I guess (or gather) that you have heard the news by now. . . .
Putnams has accepted THE ACROBATS, definitely. . . . BUT, look
man, I wont get the 1st of this money for one month . . . so, please,
please, (i'm down to my last 10 quid) cd you send me the 50 bucks
right away! so soon as I get the 500 (not that youve asked) I will
send you the fifty I owe you. . . .
 Elsewhere, in the litry world. . . . Item: George's book [George
Lamming, the Barbadian novelist] will be Bk Find selection for Jan.
 Item: George and me going up to John Davenport's tomorrow
night.
 Item: Have seen the jacket for ACRO. Will send you a gross in
3 wks.
 Item: LOSERS, nw bk, is at last coming along. . . .
 Cathy going out for a job Monday. . . .
 How did Jackie [Moore] make out—boy, girl, 2, . . . ???
 Going to see Antony and Cleo next wk with Mike Redgrave and
Others—damn good reviews. Also, Citizen Kane sun night.
 Salud!

 Mordecai

———

Nov 21,53

DEAR DIANA:
(I'll take this point by point)
 1. Would you like to go out for drinks Tuesday night???
 2. We, Cathy and I, are moving tomorrow morning. New address
and Phone No.
 13 Effra Rd
 Brixton
 London
 BRI 7217

3. There has been a change in plans. . . . I won't need yr bed, but thks a lot. . . . Joyce advises that I wont be getting the first money from Putnam for a month anyway—as contracts, so on, must be exchanged first. Life will be hard until then, but Cathy is going jobhunting on Monday, and the new place is cheaper, so I guess we'll manage okay until then. . . .

Mordecai

———

127, Eyre Court
London, N.W. 8
Primrose 0749
23rd November, 1953

Dear Mordecai,
A thousand thanks for your kindness in rounding up that travel literature for me. At least I will have some fun and some vicarious sunshine in reading and studying it. . . .
I hope that the new abode proves comfortable. Brixton is a district full of atmosphere and if you say you don't know the English, then that is more of a reproach to you than to them. You really did something to me when you said that they were "difficult" to know. I hope Cathy finds a good job and will enjoy it.
Good luck to you with the book.

Joyce

———

Nov 26, 53

QUERIDO GUILLERMO:
How is Jackie? Cathy is anxious for news (So am I). . . .
Brixton is a rough, tough district, where (as General Ike said recently eulogizing Abilene) men are men, and good guys shoot

straight. . . . Is Pearson [Lester B. Pearson] really a Red???
You may be next???

Mordecai

———

November 26

Mordecai, lad:
Now for our six o'clock news bulletin: As Moore has probably
written you, it's a boy—almost eight pounds of solid ugliness.
One head, no birthmarks, little chin. To be called Michael. . . .
Did you get my cheque? Don't worry abut the 50 you owe me.
Anytime. Although at the rate you're going I expect you to send
a Jaguar. . . .
Write immediately and at great length.

Bill

———

the society of friends
13 Effra rd
Brixton
london
dec21,1953

DEAR WILLIAM:
Am seated here on Brixton Rd after a weary day puffing on an
export (gawd bless yuh), having just reread jackie's letter to
Cathy, and, of course, wearing my spiffy rodeo tie. . . .
Yr cabled money arrived—thk the lord—but no cheque has
come thru the mail. . . . We're moving again. On Jan 2/ To 23
Belsize Ave, Hampstead. George is also moving out to
Hampstead. (between us, niggers and yids, we'll bring down the
price of real estate as well as the standards of literature.) Phone

PRI 2452 any time after 9 am. Drop in.

Sorry to have to miss xmas dinner at Moores altho I haven't even been invited in any case. Which course is Michael??

Tell Moore (I like sending Moore letters saying "tell Weintraub" and you letters saying "Moore." It makes everything so buddy-ish.) Tell Moore, I said if he and the missus are really coming over April 30 I can probably meet him in Paris—bk scheduled for mid-April here. BUT if he's gonna have a hot ms on him or in the mails he may as well come to London publisher-crawling. (Get it, PUBlisher-crawling. ho ho ho.) Tell Moore, I said that he must come to Pampalona with me in July for the great fiesta. . . .

George and us going to a West Indian dance Christmas eve, and to a drunk out in Surrey the day after Christmas. No plans for New Years but the Mandrake stays open until 3 am—hot dog! Cathy has a new job starting dec 29 working as a typist in the city.

Smogs are getting worse. You get to feel London in yr chest.

Mort

––––––––

December 27, 1953

Dear Mom,

...Everything is fine here, We are moved into better quarters in a nicer district. New address—23 Belsize Ave, Hampstead, London....

Cathy starting on a new job Monday.

Heaven forbid that anybody shd marry a Christian girl. I hope to marry a Moslem myself—preferably two. Right now, however, Im in love with a Negress. She's crippled, a drunkard, and she hates Jews. Im sure the 2 of you will get along fine. . . .

Love

M

––––––––

richler
23 Belsize Ave
Hampstead
london
Dec28or9th,53

DEAR WEINTRAUB:

Am sending, airmail, tomorrow am a proof of THE ACROBATS
to my mother, which I have instructed her to pass on to you as
soon as she has read it. And here's what I want you to do—

Jackie hasn't finished the bk, Bernice (I guess) wd like to read
it, ditto Surrey and Ruddick and Comptons—afterwards, hold on
to it. I will need it for my fellowship application. (I have written
to Moore to ask Surrey whether F.R. Scott might read it and give
me a recommendation. Perhaps, Surrey better read it first.) . . .

I grow old. I shall be three and twenty come Jan 27th.

Lammings, Cathy, myself went to a West Indian dance on
Xmas—ended on a two day drunk. George and myself tried to
bust up the dance. . . . BUT Nina and Cathy inhibited us from
committing further outrages.

MORT

just received Moores Christmas card . . . mine on way.

———

Dec. 28th. 1953
23 Belsize Ave
Hampstead
London Eng.

Dear Billie and Bernice,

Many many thanks to you both for the lovely gifts. Not, mind
you that I was able to get my hands on the cigarettes. M. has
bought me English ones to replace them because he wants to
savour every drag of every Can. cigarette he can get his hands

on. The scarf is just right for several of my ensembles and I am going to enjoy wearing it. The tie looks nice on the wall over Mordecai's collection of western pocket books and he has taken to wearing jeans and brandishing his wooden pistol to the tune of "The Streets of Lorado."

M, the boy writer is working hard on proofs these days and thinking of future days in Spain or thereabouts and also looking forward to seeing Brian and Jackie in April and so am I. Jackie wrote a wonderful letter about her confinement and I am convinced once and for all that a baby is the last thing in the world I want. M. is agitating to go out for a beer.

I start work tomorrow—bye for now—love to you both—keep writing

Cathy

VI

HAMPSTEAD PARTIES

Bolstering their meagre savings by frantic pleas to friends and family and the odd job Cathy could find, while Mordecai attempted to flog the occasional story and waited for those great reviews he dreamt of; moving from one cold-water flat to another, sometimes just before the rent was due, each one a little more down at heel; shamelessly dropping names of admired and upcoming writers as he sought out his literary niche—this was being young and hopeful in London. On February 13, 1954, the couple hosted a Saturday night bottle party in their basement flat on Belsize Avenue in Hampstead. West Indian punch was on offer, along with a bottle of sherry nicked from an art opening the week before. If any food was served, it may have been courtesy of a Lily Rosenberg care package. "The big parcel came earlier this week," her son wrote. "For which much thanks. But no more herring though. Or powdered eggs." Any hosting duties fell to Cathy, more naturally out-going than her boyfriend.

They made a slightly odd couple. The notably older Cathy Boudreau—nine years separated them—had either surprised her lover on board the *Samaria* the previous autumn, having bought a ticket in secret, or else been invited with minimal enthusiasm to join him in Europe. Either way, she was now his companion and, if one of her earliest letters to Lily Rosenberg was an indication—a letter of notable self-assurance, if equal politeness—had taken on a range of roles with regard to "M, the boy writer." Of a night at the movies for Mordecai and George and Nina Lamming, Cathy wrote, "I didn't go I was just too tired out and I refuse to try and keep up with the young ones." Of his struggle with migraines and too many late evenings: "I like to keep M in check to a certain extent. It is very important to him that he does some work every day on his new book and he is really unhappy if he doesn't." In love, insecure about whether his friends liked her, worried that she had only found a few typing jobs so far, and grateful to Lily for the gift of stockings—"This really is a bloody awful country," she wrote of the damp and cold—Richler's lover was concerned with doing her domestic duty. "I would like to have dinner started before M. gets in," she signed off. "Bye and love," she added to "Mrs. Rosenberg."

Bottle parties were 1950s bohemian London and so, to an extent, was Hampstead, a neighbourhood long associated with artists, intellectuals and, more recently, outsiders. William Blake and John Keats, Samuel Taylor Coleridge and Charles Dickens had resided in the tangle of roads and passages running off the 690-acre hilly parkland generally known as the Heath. Earlier in the century Sigmund Freud and Isaiah Berlin, Piet Mondrian and T.S. Eliot had lived there. By the time Richler moved into the first of three flats he would rent in the area—Belsize Park, like Swiss Cottage and Primrose Hill, marked the western end of the district—writers Kingsley Amis and Alan Ayckbourn, actors Dirk Bogarde and Richard Burton, would be neighbours. Though within a few years he would know some of these people, his expanding circle tended for the most part towards émigrés like himself, artistic refugees from the colonies come to the Metropolis seeking interesting lives and careers. "A lot of yids around," he assured his mother.

Six months, and three addresses, into their stay in London, the couple could fill the two rooms with friends, a few illustrious, a few more on their way up. The handsome Barbadian poet and novelist George Lamming, the BBC West Indian Service broadcaster and author of the novel *In the Castle of My Skin*, was responsible for the punch, and Diana Athill, resident of Primrose Hill, who had liked her new young writer "at once," remembered the parties as much for their diversity as for their beverages. André Deutsch was a regular but Mordecai's retiring agent, Joyce Weiner, didn't stop by. He chatted with her most days, however, either on the phone or in the letters that were still so frequent that she soon asked him to label certain ones "personal," to allow her to file them separately.

Such encounters were exhilarating. He had returned to Cambridge to sip sherry again with E.M Forster, an unlikely friendship developing between the repressed elderly Englishman and the St. Urbain ghetto kid, and had asked him to look at the proofs of *The Acrobats* with an eye to obtaining a blurb. Soon too he would be winning praise from the established novelist C.P. Snow, and spending enough time with Graham Greene, whose literary acclaim was high following publication of *The Power and the Glory*, *The Heart of the Matter*, and his intense novel of adulterous love, *The End of the Affair*, to consider asking him for a letter of reference and report in a letter that "Greene's gone to Indochina." John Davenport, the literary critic famous in the pubs of Chelsea for both his wit and his generosity to budding writers, and Julian Maclaren-Ross, equally famed as a raconteur, whose love of hard living in bohemian London was beginning to overwhelm his reputation as a novelist, were drinking companions; the week before the party he had done the "the west end pubs" in the company of the debonair Irish poet Louis MacNeice and Kathleen Thomas, whose wild husband, the brilliant poet Dylan, had died in New York the previous November. When Richler wished her good-night using her first name, the widow snapped: "Mrs. Thomas to you!" "Come, come," MacNeice soothed.

Brushes with literary greatness and exuberant letters home notwithstanding, that first English winter was a shock: the perpetual cold and damp, especially in unheated flats; the miserable food available in shops; nagging concerns about money. Long workdays on *Losers,* as the manuscript was being called, didn't translate into ready income. It was also hard going. "Idling abt impotently on a cold night feeling damn depressed," Richler wrote "the book has slowed down on me." Then there were those "Montreal" stories. Joyce Weiner couldn't sell them, and he was already cannibalizing the material for the novel. Evenings at the theatre or movies cost money; nights by the fire did not. Richler had yet to meet the literary editors at the English newspapers who would pay him to review new releases. For the moment, he read for pleasure, and self-education rather than for cash—books by "Joe Conrad," Orwell's *Homage to Catalonia* ("A man of commendable rages"), and Fyodor Dostoevsky's *The Brothers Karamazov*. About Dostoevsky he wrote to Weintraub, "I thk (William, aka Willy) Faulkner was a better man than Freddy ever was. Insights being equal, Willy has more discipline and a better sense of construction."

Days at the typewriter were followed by overtures, through letters, phone calls or drinks, to literary figures who might either jump-start his career, or simply hire him. He proposed by letter doing a column from London for the Montreal *Star*. "I have had some newspaper training," he told editor Walter O'Hearn. "When I was at college I worked part-time for The Herald. Jackie Moore, Bill Weintraub, Brian Moore, all know me and my work." He didn't get the job. Early mentors like the critic Walter Allen and André Deutsch agreed to supply letters of support for a grant application to the Royal Society of Canada, precursor of the Canada Council. He didn't get the grant either.

Those food packages from his mother helped. Canned goods, including tins of sardines and salmon, were welcome, as were, naturally, cartons of cigarettes and all—or nearly all—Montreal cured meats. "Those Exports were lovely—always the first thing I look for in a parcel," he told her in February. "Sausages are fine too but don't send any more tongue." To his dismay, Lily insisted on being equally generous with Cathy. "I don't want you to send Cathy any parcels—clothes, stockings, or food. You work hard enough for your money. I don't want you sending her anything. I don't like it." He was as ambivalent about the small sums of money she sent. Sometimes he accepted the cheque with gratitude. Other times he balked. "You won't have to send me any others," he said. "Putnam's contract has arrived and money will follow shortly." His father, too, had resumed financing his apprenticeship, sending $10 or $20 with most letters. In a rare mention of Moses to Lily, Richler wrote, "My father writes. Apparently he isn't doing too well. He wants to know when I will make money and be able to send him some. ho ho." In that same note he promised to write to his brother Avrum "when I have the time."

It was a fine line the twenty-three-year-old was seeking to walk. Asking for, and taking, all he could from family and friends, but then guiltily disallowing support for his lover; asserting his independence from his parents, especially his clingy mother, while behaving like an entitled son. Other attributes, including a consuming self-interest and absorption, a drive that cancelled out most proprieties, belonged more to the young artist mould. His reflective comments in Montreal notwithstanding, Mort Richler was still capable of acting the cliché.

And Lily Rosenberg was deeply engaged with her boy's life. She was determined to be involved, and Mordecai, given his ambivalences and needs, expressed no strong—or perhaps consistent—objections. But he did draw the line at his business affairs. When his editor at Putnam's in New York, Bob Amussen, mentioned that he was planning a trip to Montreal, Richler was emphatic about two things. First, Bill Weintraub and Brian Moore should meet him. Second, Lily should not. "Look," he told Weintraub, "if Amussen comes to Montreal next weekend. Keep my mother away from him. . . . I don't care what you or Moore tell her but I don't want this to become a family affair." He was no less blunt with Lily herself. "The Putnams editor will only be in Montreal for a weekend," he wrote. "You will not be able to see him and even if you could I wouldn't want you to." But two months later *The Acrobats* was published with a dedication: FOR MY MOTHER.

His efforts to connect his friends to his American editor were typical of him. That was the real stuff of friendship, beyond the jokes and drinking. Already evident was a fierce loyalty to the people he really cared about. He asked Bill Weintraub when he wanted him to show his novel to "Andy D"—"Sure hope and do expect he'll take it"—and attempted to convince Deutsch to issue a British edition of Ted Allan's book on Norman Bethune. He agitated on behalf of Moore and Gallant. "When we had lunch together, some time ago," he wrote his publisher, "I told you about Brian Moore—a friend of mine who was writing a serious novel. Moore is a highly intelligent and sympathetic man and a pretty good writer as well." "Pretty good" was plain speech between pros; to overpraise was unmanly. He did the same for Mavis Gallant in March, pitching her to Diana Athill: "Next week I'll send you a recent New Yorker with a short story in it by Mavis Gallant. . . . She's pretty good." The prospect of getting friends published was pleasing. "What a list we'll have then!" he told Weintraub.

Many of his emerging friendships were with fellow writers. Hence there could be no avoiding the complexities between adults—most of them competitive men, to boot—vying, in effect, for the same prizes: publishing contracts and movie deals, fellowships and awards. Jealousy and resentment would creep in, and even a friend as true as Bill Weintraub would simultaneously admire and struggle with Richer's often raw ambition. With Brian Moore a certain tension, based in no small part on the eleven-year age difference and the fact that Richler published first, was present from the start. Moore himself had been telling people in Montreal that he was spurred to finish his own novel by a friend's getting his very bad manuscript accepted—that was *The Acrobats*.

January 1954 saw Richler grappling with the rigid British censors. "Talking abt obscenities," he wrote to Weintraub, "there was a big fuss here. Printers refused to print [*The Acrobats*]. They got a lawyer. André got a lawyer. Richler was called in, charged with obscenity, blasphemy, and worse. Bang bang bang. Several minor changes have been made; e.g. tits to breasts, kick you in the balls to kick you where it hurts, bloody christ to christ. Nothing important really. All most amusing." Though the issue was resolved, it caused a stir inside André Deutsch. Five years earlier, Athill and her boss, then at Allan Wingate, had faced a court injunction against publishing another first novel: *The Naked and the Dead*, by Norman Mailer. The problem with Mailer's debut had been simpler: the word "fuck" and "fucking," sprinkled throughout the war tale of American GIs fighting in the Pacific. A wholesale shift to "fug" and "fugging" had allowed the house to publish the book to acclaim.

That same letter to Bill Weintraub was also full of despair and whimsy and rage. The sensitivity of the young writer, hidden behind a tough exterior, is clear in these private correspondences, often written in the dead of a cold English night. His youthful convictions may have found a name—existentialism—and a trendy vocabulary in Paris, but they were as deeply ingrained in his character as his reticence. "It seems to me there is but one thing serious writers can write about today—Man without God. Approaches may vary tremendously, but this is the hard core. Chaos. No values. Embarrassment. Relative values no longer related to anything."

————

On April 10 it was Diana Athill's turn to host a party in her flat overlooking Primrose Hill. She was a vivacious thirty-four-year-old with clear English features and an accent reflecting her upper-class background. Single and sexually independent, she brought a curiosity and openness to experiences, along with an anti-establishment bias to her choices in writers. She enjoyed the company, and occasionally the physical affections, of her authors, and showed a preference for outsiders, ultimately building a list heavy with West Indians, Canadians and Irish. She liked these writers and they liked her in return, none more so than the young Mordecai Richler, who she decided nearly on first meeting was generous, kind, honest and very funny—despite his awkward reserve and general reluctance to speak at all.

The occasion was the publication of "the remarkable first novel by a young Canadian," as the André Deutsch advertisement in the *New Statesman* called *The Acrobats*. By Richler's own count, two bottles of gin and one each of Dubonnet and Cinzano were consumed by a crowd of well wishers that included Louis MacNeice and John Davenport. Everybody got drunk, and at midnight carried on to the Mandrake club in Soho. Bohemian poets favoured the Mandrake—Dylan Thomas had drunk there; George Baker and Julian Maclaren-Ross still did—along with George Lamming and his friend Sam Selvon from Trinidad. Over more drinks Cathy accused MacNeice of writing obscure poetry. When the Irishman called her simple, Richler intervened with a question for his girl about her preferences. She gave an answer, and then defended it. "What's wrong with John Donne?" she demanded. Davenport observed that the wife of another guest had breasts like small eggs. "Cathy kissed Louie and I kissed Diana," he summarized for Weintraub. "Everybody thinks I wrote a good bk."

Reviews were actually mixed. The *Spectator* weighed in first, calling him a "distinguished talent" and the novel "astonishing," if only as a "guide to intelligent, contemporary pastiche." Dubbing him both a spokesman for the generation that had "missed the opportunity (their term) of taking physical part in the good-evil struggle," and a "worried, whirling, over-read young man," the reviewer concluded that his debut "should be looked at, and looked at by a lot of people." A BBC radio review described the author of *The Acrobats* as a "young American Jew of 22 . . . incredibly crude and brash and mistakes violence for strength. He's impatient with words and also extremely excited by them." The *Glasgow Herald* praised "the maturity in some of the writing," while the *Liverpool Jewish Gazette* declined to cover *The Acrobats*, explaining in a note to André Deutsch that their reviewer would only be able to treat it "in the most scathing terms."

In Canada the Toronto *Telegram* called it a "good book" by someone whose next one "will be better and the one after that— perhaps great." Adjacent to the author photograph—the "Young Author Looking at Reader" from the portfolio—was a bracing opening sentence: "Arrogant, opinionated, rebellious, scornful, resentful and refreshingly angry, 23-year-old Mordecai Richler announces in his first novel that his writings will never be infected by what he belligerently terms 'mediocrity wrapped in the Maple Leaf." As in the letters his Hillel editorial in the *Georgian* had provoked four years earlier, the list of adjectives used to describe him and the temperament lurking behind them foreshadowed a gap in sensibility between the writer and the majority of Canadians. A complex, invigorating engagement between artist and society would be forged and sustained out of this discord— possibly the country's first real such tussle.

The Acrobats tells the story of André Bennett, a young Canadian painter drinking himself to death in Franco's Spain. The city of Valencia during Las Fallas is Dionysian, and the cast, who careen from brothel to bar in long scenes heavy on crisp dialogue, tend towards caricature. Prominent are a Nazi named Kraus, still convinced of his racial superiority, a hot-blooded Spanish mistress called Toni, a wandering Jew of philosophical disposition called Chaim, a roster of vacuous American tourists, most notably a Jew named Barney with a bored wife, idealistic communists, crass rich people, and hookers with hearts of gold. André himself, a man without "hope or reason or direction," cannot follow Toni's advice and escape the "sadness of Europe" by taking her back to Canada. Characters drink too much and, ruled by either loathsome values or wayward sexual needs, treat each other miserably. Any respite from the anxiety and hopelessness tends to be furtive. Bennett, who attempts to live by a code of honour, including an insistence on trying to understand human frailty, achieves a kind of peace only in the moments preceding his fatal plunge, courtesy of Kraus, off a bridge while explosions fill the night sky. "I am a bigger man now, he thought. My feelings are more than anger. His laugh began slowly then swelled up and broke out happily. But he was not yet certain what was happening to him. It will take time, he thought."

Brian Moore showed up in London in late March. Nights of pub-crawling with his host to venues like the Mandrake, full of "bearded Britishers, black Little Englanders, all sorts of—to me—phoney lit people," brought out the Gael in the quietly fierce Belfast native. "A pity I cannot like the British," Moore admitted to Weintraub. About Mort Richler, he was scarcely less critical. "Many points in Mordecai's vocabulary have been revealed to me as jargon," he wrote. "All unliked artists are 'a trick.' Anything unliked is 'a trick.' People who dance or play bingo are 'hilarious.' People who drink heavily in the bar are 'tourists.'" Neither was Moore buying his anti-bourgeois creed. "He talks a lot about money, sales, ways and means," he said. But Moore was also dismayed by his young friend's circumstances in Hampstead: the dank rooms, the pauper's budget. At thirty-three, with his manuscript of *Judith Hearne* complete, Brian Moore was past his own bohemian days. A month later Richler would greet Jackie Moore at the Waterloo Terminal and put her up in those same dank rooms. She was en route to Spain, where her husband had preceded her to write a new book.

Other Montreal business took the form of awkward letters from Evelyn Sacks, still anxious to be part of his life. In one lengthy note she apologized for her behaviour the previous summer, analyzing herself as a frustrated older woman who cannot abide the fact that the younger man she desires sees her only as a mother figure and friend. In another, written after he must have told her that he and Cathy were considering marriage, Evelyn advised him not to go through with it, saying that Cathy wasn't the only woman who loved him. She used the word "revolting" to describe her own feelings, and the effect, she imagined, her words were having, and said she would take whatever he had to offer. For his part, Richler, while not giving her any hope, still kept up a correspondence with his former teacher. Writing to Bill Weintraub, with a separate envelope enclosed, he instructed: "The R Sacks letter is for Mrs R Sacks of St Ignatius St—and her husband is *not* your worry. Please forward the letter."

Marry Cathy Boudreau he did, on August 28, 1954, in a civil ceremony in Hampstead. In a photo of the event the groom looks elegant in bow tie and tuxedo while the bride, in a dress suit, silk scarf and stylish hat, projects a more mature profile. Both are smoking. The group shot of the wedding party squeezes twenty-five guests into its frame. Among them are Joyce Weiner and her sister Marjorie, Ted and Kate Allan, Tess and Kryn Taconis, George and Nina Lamming, civil rights campaigner David Pitt, later to become the first black West Indian parliamentary candidate, record executive Terry McEwan, André Deutsch, and E.M. Forster down from Cambridge, as well as Brian Moore, who had earlier advised Richler not to marry Cathy on grounds of incompatibility. Its mix of young and middle-aged (with Forster the elder), colonials with English, white with black with Jew, makes it a typical émigré Hampstead artistic circle of the era. At its centre, in his tux, squats the boy writer. Joyce Weiner hosted a luncheon afterwards, and Ted Allan entertained guests for drinks later in the afternoon.

The wedding marked the culmination of three typically restless, eventful months and a tumultuous ten-minute encounter the night before. Mordecai and Cathy had left London for the continent after *The Acrobats* appeared, spending a month in Paris and two more in Germany. Being back in France for the first time in two years should have excited and pleased him. Staying in a small hotel in Saint-Germain-des-Prés, they visited his old haunts together, going to the play of one acquaintance and to the races with another, running into Richard Wright and "Jimmy Baldwin a few times," including once in the company of George Lamming. "He's been trying to make George," Richler gossiped to Weintraub. He also had drinks with an editor at a publishing house and swallowed a rejection from another. Alcohol formed a large part of their spring days on the Left Bank, including downing "marshall aid scotch." "Drinking too much here," he admitted to Diana Athill.

But he was disenchanted. "Honest," he complained to Bill Weintraub, "Paris is shit. I've had this city, but GOOD." He ripped into the "American one-yr crap-artists," complaining that everyone was "an editor, a writer, and conforming non-conformist."

Weintraub's reply, from dull anaesthetic Montreal, was under-standable. "God, man, what do you mean? . . . I don't see how you can judge a city on the strength of the fact that the homo writers you've met are cruds and the Americans are revolting." His conclusion provided a subtle instruction: "You probably don't agree with me, but I think the people writers should avoid are other writers." The Canadian Authors' Association, he added jok-ingly, recommend that "one mingle with Real People, even Workers, and keep the Writer's Storage Batteries filled with MATERIAL." Normally an astute reader of his friend's nature, Bill Weintraub missed the larger point of this act of ill temper. Distancing himself from the sorts of people he used to hang out with in Paris was one developmental step. Distancing himself from the sort of person *he* had been, or feared he was on the way to becoming, required longer, more strident steps. Once those strides were taken, Richler's subsequent visits to the City of Light would provide pure pleasure, much of it nostalgic.

He and Cathy had moved on to Germany for June and July. The Munich publisher Kindler Verlag had been the first non-English house to accept *The Acrobats*, and was planning to release a translation the following spring. "卐? Heil!" Richler kidded at the close of a letter about the upcoming trip. On arrival he reported on the black Citroën and the publishing representatives waiting for him at the Munich train station—"Ze car is vaiting"—and that their long drive through a wooded area made him wonder what plans they had for him. Though he was flattered by inter-views with media and nights out with the Kindlers, he couldn't quite forget that he was fraternizing with former Hitler Youth, or that his host had been unable to travel to the United States on account of having once been a member of the Nazi party (though later he assured Weintraub that the Kindlers had been "active anti-nazis during war. A postwar firm"). Nor did those army camp signs he kept noting—BUS TO DACHAU EVERY SAT AT 1400. VISIT THE CASTLE AND CREMATORIUM—sit easily.

He and Cathy ended up spending their time in a U.S. army base housing unit in the suburb of Harlaching, paying $14 a month for a room with kitchen. Socializing with Americans was easier and less psychologically fraught. "Richler, Mordecai," he wrote in third person in July, "has been adopted by the Special Service Girls of the U.S. Army, Karlsplatz, Munich." The girls not only procured him paper and food, but also American cigarettes and Gordon's gin. Good times on the base involved serious drinking. "AFTERWARDS," he narrated, "drunken Richler staggers into flat station wagon and is whisked off by two Georgia gals to Officers Club for gallons of scotch, etc, where I made one of my best anti-u.s. speeches."

But amidst the frivolity, he worked away on a new novel. To help convince *Weekend* in Montreal to commission a cooked-up author profile to help sales of *The Acrobats*—Brian Moore would write the text—he offered, via Bill Weintraub, what he hoped would be provocative remarks about the new project, which planned to trace the development of Montreal's Jewish ghetto. "Im not interested in passing judgement or shouting," he said of his story. "I'm simply observing. The only people who cd consider this bk anti-semitic—there are, of course, good and bad people in it—are those Jews who are very afraid. . . I'm not interested in the fact that Jews cant get into certain hotels or golf courses— and Im not writing a 'Jewish Problem' bk. . . . I thk that those who were murdered at Dachau shd not be mourned as Jews but as other men."

Such certainty from a twenty-three-year-old Jew living thirty minutes from Dachau less than a decade after the camp was liberated? "I don't believe that there is any such thing as a Jewish outlook or Jewish problem or Jewish Spokesman," he concluded. "Each man has his own problem (part of that, of course, might be his being a Jew.)" Already sensing the heat that *Son of a Smaller Hero* would attract, he was preparing an aggressive defence of his moral stance. It was one certain to give him a public identity that would be noticed. To make such assertions in Munich, and while simultaneously endeavouring to extract a $1,000 grant from the Jewish Congress—"I'm not yet blacklisted by B'nai B'rith, and I have an excellent in with Yids," he noted—showed chutzpah. Brian Moore savoured the irony. "Moore says an anti-semite like me has no business begging from the jews," he told Athill.

The remarks to Bill Weintraub were part conviction, part dare to his apostate identity. They may also have been a cover-up for the deep anxieties he was experiencing in the literal graveyard of European Jews. Blithely declaring the sojourn interesting and fun, he would only later admit to having grappled every day he was in Germany with feelings of horror and hatred. Nor would he ever write about his visit to the crematoria at Dachau—and not because those who died there should be mourned only as people.

His decision to marry Cathy may have been a consequence of being unnerved by the surroundings. In mid-July, they announced their engagement to friends and family; she did the actual proposing. Knowing his family, Mordecai cannot have been surprised by the July 30 registered letter from his father. "Having had shocking news before," it began, "yr letter of the 18th of July, was not as effective as you thought it would be. I knew the way you are living, and always dreaded the outcome. . . . Hoping you would listen, and not allow this disgraceful act to be"—the "disgraceful act" being marriage outside the faith. Moses Richler continued:

In your letter you state that you are not marrying a Jewess or a Gentile, but a woman, THE WOMAN YOU LOVE. Now tell me did you ever see young couples marry for Hate, No its always for love, or even better love at first sight, that LAFS (lafs is the first letters of love at first sight) because in all marriages for love there is always dreams of escape. . . . She too does not know what she is doing, and what abt her family if any, do they want to accept a Jew in their midst? . . . What happens when you have a bad report, a refusal of story, or anything that might happen in a persons life. And there is no money to pay the bills. You get mad and go to the bottle. Words, arguments, your fault, no its your fault, and so forth, and perhaps a third party mixes in, then what, the first thing youll be told off in these words, the dirty jew, the good for nothing, the boozer, and youll come back with words said in anger, and I am sure they wont be nice words, your book is full of nasty words, and you are saturated with them.

His ire rose to a pitch:

LIVE spelled backwards, spells EVIL, and the way you are starting out I can see only a doomed and disastrous marriage, without a happy ending. . . . THINK THINK THINK THINK THINK hard, before you take this drastic step. For After August 20, your fatal day, my door and all that goes with it will be closed to you. The doors of the Richler family will not welcome you. . . . So now you see that where I was a soft touch when it came to money matters, or any other favours you asked me to do for you, I have to be stern and very hard, when it comes to honour, and respect. . . . With the utmost regrets, I close this letter, which might be the last. IT IS ALL UP TO YOU NOW.

As hurtful as these words were, Richler typed out long passages for Bill Weintraub, as if to remind his friend of the kind of Orthodoxy he had emerged from and to drive their meaning deeper into his own memory. He also called the tirade "the strangest and most human letter" he'd received from his father. "I haven't been able to do a thing all day," he admitted. "Sometimes, reading thru it Im convulsed with laughter. Other times, I feel terribly sad."

And Lily? Her son was concerned enough to ask Weintraub to call her. "She asked me what I thought," he reported, "and I told her all the right things." Lily, who had been receiving letters from Cathy for a year, in fact voiced no objection. This should have been astonishing to Mordecai, another reminder that beneath her odd, irritating exterior lay a surprising soul. Avrum, for his part, did not concur with his mother's laissez-faire attitude, giving long odds on his kid brother's success in interfaith marriage. His Uncle Bernard joined a chorus of family disapproval, cutting him off for two years for the transgression.

The day after reading the letter, Richler received a note from the CBC Radio producer Bob Weaver offering him $75 for the broadcast rights to his story "The Secret of the Kugel." On the basis of a single previous encounter with the shy, amiable CBC producer and anthologist, he felt comfortable enough to pitch another story and recommend Brian Moore's first novel. He also added some personal news: "Im going to get married in London . . . Aug. 20, or so. The girl is French-Canadian, and my family—a sternly orthodox bunch—are taking it pretty hard. I've been cut off, in fact. Right off." If the remarks were meant to sound tough, the older Weaver, renowned for his literary empathy, may well have detected the hurt young man beneath the bravado.

But if any event set Mordecai Richler's head really spinning, it was a chance encounter in London on August 27, the eve of his wedding, which had been delayed a week. He and Cathy were having drinks with Ted and Kate Allan at 18 Kent Terrace, off Baker Street. Encouraged to emigrate from Canada by the head of drama at the BBC, Allan had crossed the Atlantic with his family a couple of weeks before, in the company of their Toronto friends and fellow émigrés, Stanley and Florence Mann. They were all staying in a friend's apartment while hunting for places of their own. It was there that Florence Mann was introduced to the writer whose first novel she had read in manuscript eighteen months before.

The meeting, which lasted only a few minutes, made an impression on her. It wasn't on account of his appearance, though she took note that he stood to be introduced to her— sign of a gentleman. Dressed in a sleeveless yellow vest beneath a corduroy jacket, he had poor posture and wild hair. He was scrawny and seemed undernourished. Florence Mann, shapely and slender in a fitted navy-blue dress and Dior scarf, remembered that first encounter: "I knew I had never met anyone like him. There was a hyper-sensitivity about him; he was almost like someone unfinished. There was something very raw, and it was unnerving, but it was also compelling. He stayed for just a few minutes. It was a very strange meeting, and really quite powerful."

The following evening, Florence and Stanley Mann joined the drinks party for the newlyweds in the same borrowed flat. Still wearing his tuxedo from the ceremony, he trailed around after her, clearly interested, offering to get her drinks and watching her closely. Others noticed, including how his attention to another woman was affecting his new wife. The beautiful Florence Mann, while still taken aback by his unsettling presence and his determined silence, had been approached by enough men to know how to strike at the knees. When Richler, who later granted that on seeing her at the party he realized his mistake in marrying Cathy, finally decided to speak to her, his words were cocksure. Had she by any chance read a first novel by a young Canadian called *The Acrobats*? he asked, already knowing the answer. And had she liked it?

"Yes," Florence replied, "only not enough to want to meet its author."

VII

GENERAL PROGRESS REPORT

In the summer of 1954, Joyce Weiner exchanged a series of long letters with her Canadian client. Shifting from agent to friend to parent, she pinpointed a core problem with Richler's early fiction, while offering him excellent advice. "I have been thinking a lot about you too lately, and thinking that it is a great pity you are moving around so much, collecting superficial impressions, moving into areas of conflict like Munich, being over-stimulated perhaps by new ideas, and taking so little time to assimilate what you have learned." Reversing her earlier position, she counselled writerly routine. "What you needed to do—as far as the new book and, perhaps several new books are concerned—was to sit down in some quiet, dull spot and think clearly and deeply, not merely in febrile style to collect still more surface reactions." In another letter she warned him he was cursed with "too much imagination": "you don't need any more fuel for that flame of yours." Worried that her remarks were wounding, she reminded him of the quality in his nature that had made her hopeful from the start: "you had none of the beginner's arrogance which one knows will be a stumbling block to even the most talented writer."

On a more pragmatic note, she warned that he would have to "clean up those love scenes" in the new manuscript. The British climate of censorship was hard to avoid; the bookseller W.H. Smith, having received complaints about *The Acrobats*, had put the novel on its restricted list.

Her astute letters revealed a beyond-duty engagement with a client. His sensitivity and emotional intensity were attractive to women, in particular to older ones. Weiner, Evelyn Sacks and Cathy Boudreau were all drawn to, and drawn to looking after, the dark-eyed young artist; at twenty-four, Florence would soon be the only significant woman in his life of his own age. For his part, at this early stage Richler clearly didn't mind being mothered a little, and was comfortable with older people of both sexes, which may have been the result, in part, of being raised within a large extended family as much as his restless intelligence.

Personal relationships aside, the attention and counsel he was receiving in London was justifying his decision to launch his career there. The timing of his arrival in the city couldn't have been better, despite its bedraggled state. The depleted and dingy postwar economy was still in wide evidence in 1954. The country, which finally went off rations that year, knew only one colour, grey, and one mood, austerity, mingled with quiet pride at having survived the Germans with character and dignity intact. Postwar financial restraint and a Labour government attempting to hurry a welfare state into being had resulted in deprivations as bad as, or worse than, those suffered during the war.

Parts of London still lay in near ruins. Three-quarters of a million homes had been damaged or destroyed, with rebuilding efforts only just beginning. Bomb sites remained unexcavated, and war-damaged neighbourhoods were marked by dilapidated houses occupied by squatters—including Mordecai and Cathy, during their brief sojourn in Brixton. The city landscape was often dominated by Dickensian fogs and coal-generated smog. Few flats had central heating. Shops were half-empty, and food, served in restaurants or bought from grocers, was bland. Winter greens and root vegetables, hamburger made mostly of oatmeal and grated potato, were typical fare. To taste French cheeses or a real pastry, one had to travel to Soho, with its Continental delis and Indian restaurants, and pay extravagantly.

Once Putnam's accepted *The Acrobats*, Richler might have packed his bags and sailed to New York, a city with which he felt a greater kinship, and where he could have found equal or greater opportunities. In 1957, in his first major interview, he would admit that he had been more influenced by American novelists than English or European ones, and felt closer in temperament to American writers; in fact, he believed himself a kind of proxy American. As a Montreal Jew, he had strong ties with the States. His Uncle Israel lived in New York's Brighton Beach. Relations and former classmates could be found in the various boroughs.

Still, the pull of London was at least threefold. Though he had not meant to be in the vanguard, he was among the first of a Canadian invasion in the television and film business, drawn to England by the rapid birth and expansion of the BBC and the rival commercial network ITV. He was soon poker-playing pals with most of his fellow expats in these industries, a rowdy "Canadian Club" rooted in North London. He was also finding more work that he'd ever imagined back in Montreal. Many new friends would emerge, among them half a dozen essential, lifelong relationships, and he would finance two houses on the proceeds from writing for TV and the movies.

And London had its own artistic appeal to him. He was far from the first young writer who wanted to wrap his arms around the world, and the city in the early 1950s was serving as base camp for artists from countries deeply engaged in the decolonization process. While England recovered and rebuilt from the war, her remaining empire was quickly winding down. The brightest young people were finding their way from the former colonies to the mother country. Publishers, in particular newcomers like André Deutsch, were drawn to the fresh energy (later to be called "post-colonial") of these neophyte authors, and nurtured them into print: West Indians George Lamming and the still-unknown V.S. Naipaul, Indians R.K. Narayan and Anita Desai. Mordecai Richler of Canada didn't fit this mould exactly, but he arrived in England with a similar sense of his own country's character as undeveloped and of its literature as largely unwritten. His circumstances were closer to those of the novelist Doris Lessing, who had moved to London to get away from her mother and family, and from "that dreadful provincial country Southern Rhodesia." She was soon a friend and honorary member of the Hampstead Canadian Club.

The capital tolerated these interlopers, challenging them to integrate with the mainstream or else find a strong enough voice to substantially change the conversation. Unlike Paris, London spoke their tongue. Or rather, the interlopers understood the tongue of Shakespeare and Milton, Dickens and Waugh. The shared language meant that the doors of England's vigorous, competitive culture were open—if you had the stuff, and weren't to be denied.

That culture, finally, was the strongest lure. Writers and journalists in London were expected to be funny and sharp rather than kind or fair. Cruelty wasn't such a bad trait, at least compared to blandness, as long as it was witty. Being a "nice person" was the purview of the vicar class. Creative people had egos and wills and went about sporting them like outrageous hats. The game—a career, fame, writing a book that would last—was full contact, and those preferring a gentler version had best keep to the sidelines. The game was also largely masculine, with the men jousting and their women supporting. The enemies of artistic success were numerous, as Cyril Connolly had outlined, but none more insidious than the pram parked in the hallway. *Enemies of Promise*, Connolly's 1938 apologia for a Nietzschean model for high artistic endeavour, was a near Bible for the postwar crowd. Already anachronistic, it preached pregnant wives and children seen but not heard while the hard-typing, whisky-swilling husbands and fathers pursued literary greatness.

As for vices, they were there to be ignored. Not drinking was more of a problem than drinking, and the bar for excess was set so high few could see it, especially through the cigarette smoke. Most everyone drank and smoked and smoked and drank and, on occasion, went to bed with someone they shouldn't have. Those same people attempted to write a novel a year, along with as many reviews and essays, radio and TV plays, as they could manage without collapsing. Collapse some did, and postwar wives, who had shared the burdens of the war, were frequently readying to walk away from their boozy, reckless spouses. Out of this stew emerged a vigour, often crude and pretentious but also robust; it was a milieu that suited Mordecai Richler just fine. He was big-shouldered enough, talented and brazen enough, for literary London.

———

Son of a Smaller Hero, typed out by Cathy to music on the record player Bill Weintraub had sent as a wedding present, was submitted to Diana Athill in October 1954. "Joyce [Weiner] is delighted with the bk," Richler told Bill, newly married to Bernice Grafstein, a Ph.D. student at McGill, "and I feel as happy as can be after that long and often difficult grind." Athill, he would soon report, "loved the bk," and the critic Walter Allen, who read manuscripts for the publisher, wrote to André Deutsch that while the theme of "the revolt of the second-generation New World Jew against his Ghetto family" was a staple of American fiction, Richler's treatment was unique. Allen called the novel a "real achievement," predicting that it would put its author on the map. He was specific about that map: with *Son of a Smaller Hero*, a book as much about the city of Montreal as anything else, "the Canadian novel emerges for the first time." Allen's decision to highlight the Jewish dimensions may have been for André Deutsch's benefit. The Hungarian was a rarity in British publishing, a Jewish publisher, and like his fellow émigré George Weidenfeld, whose own imprint of Weidenfeld and Nicolson was just five years old, naturally welcoming of those writers who were also outsiders and also looked beyond the old English class-bound themes.

Deutsch offered a £150 advance, up a third from *The Acrobats,* which had lately been retitled *Wicked We Love* for its lurid American paperback edition. Richler, luckily for him and for his creditors—"Will arrange to pay you yr $75 within few wks," he promised Bill Weintraub—was discovering supplemental sources of income, almost all of them better paying than novel writing.

His debut as a Grub Street hack was underway. In September he had remarked to Weintraub, "Ted Allan lives in London, and makes a fortune here," and "yr pal Stanley Mann has just sold rights to a $\frac{1}{2}$ hour TV play to Doug Fairbanks for 1000 bucks." Not long after, he too was writing a radio script for one of Allan's BBC contacts, and co-authoring a TV script with Mann, a silly piece about two blind men. This, in turn, was promising to open doors for him in the especially lucrative movie business. ("May re-write a film script for a producer next month. . . . Two wk job. Well paid.") He was also scheming with Brian Moore by post to generate a thriller that the Irishman would outline, for 25 percent of the advance, and he would write. "Have read yr outline and thk we've got a deal . . . 25% is fine with me. . . . Of this, and movie rights—if any," he told Moore.

Letters to friends from the period, often written as hurried news summaries, every inch of the aerogram covered in type or in his elegant handwriting, were spiked with the usual requests for money and offers to help out in return. Featured as well was gossip ("Kingsley Amis got 5000 quid for film rights to Lucky Jim but the bk sold around 600 copies in U.S. edition") and name-dropping ("Norman Mailer writes from Mexico City that his new novel is with his publishers"), breaking news both international and Canadian ("Fred Rose is living in Warsaw with family"), along with plenty of industry numbers: advances, sales, who was being paid what, new deals in the works. Plans for future books—a third novel, maybe a non-fiction work about Israel—were almost as various as unfolding travel itineraries. ("Thinking of Mexico for '56. That, or North Africa. A trip home, Israel, first tho.") His energy for work, now and always, was boundless. On certain days Weintraub and Moore might have pleaded insufficient energy to read about what Mort Richler was up to in London.

Evident between the lines was a facility for the "business" of being a writer, and a determination to improve at it. So too was the vitality—entrepreneurial, nervy and exuberant—still mostly absent from his published prose. GENERAL PROGRESS REPORT was how he subtitled a November letter to Weintraub. "Come over here, you fool," he wrote. "You cd do great things." Such hustle, after full days of work on *Son of a Smaller Hero*, was enough to lay the sturdiest twenty-three-year-old low, especially a Canadian dwelling in a basement flat in a coal-grimy town. "Cathy has been in bed all wk and I'm fighting off a bad cold and working damn hard too," he admitted. Back problems, exacerbated by hours hunched over a typewriter—he was a two-fingered typist, fast and accurate—had already sent him to hospital twice for minor procedures.

Fred Rose's niece, Flora Rosenberg, whose honour he had defended in Montreal, had settled in a flat down the road. She helped cook matzo balls for parties and taught Cathy Jewish cuisine. (Doris Lessing recalled Cathy boasting that she cooked better than most Jewish mothers.) Cathy's sister, Tess Taconis, who had been living in Geneva with her husband, was bound for Paris, and she encouraged her younger sibling to join them, offering to help find her work with one of the international organizations. The extra income would "take a real load off M's shoulders," Cathy admitted, hinting at her ongoing difficulty generating income. He would meet her in Paris at the end of the month. He anticipated another ramble, heading for Munich— the translation of *The Acrobats* was due out there—a Mediterranean island, onward to Israel, back to London before Christmas, then home to Montreal. "Figure on settling there eventually," he confessed to Brian Moore. "It's the place I know and can write abt best. I have no choice."

Business that January included swallowing the rejection of *Son of a Smaller Hero* in a first-novel contest run by *Maclean's*. "One of our reasons for not using it is the difficulty of publishing it," an apologetic editor wrote to him, citing how many "sharp corners" required rounding off for Canadian readers. Among the worries were the allegedly libellous portraits of several individuals, including Moses Richler and a college teacher who bore a striking resemblance to his Sir George Williams professor and supporter, Neil Compton. "I hope there has been no more trouble," he wrote to Diana Athill later that month from Paris about similar British libel worries, while encouraging her to visit them in the flat that Cathy had rented in Montparnasse. "It's on the sixth floor, but it's got central heating and hot water and costs 17000 a month." A rent of 17,000 francs ($50), plus a $100 down payment, translated into enough expenses to oblige him to seek fresh loans from Brian Moore and his mother. To have the experiences he wanted, Richler was prepared to spend money he often didn't have. But "I'm working feverishly on all sorts of money-making—I hope—projects," he wrote to Athill. Among them were two short stories, one for the CBC and the other for *Maclean's*, a final draft of a radio play, and some writing about Canada for a magazine published by UNESCO. Remembering the lucrative business that was book-length pornography for Girodias's Olympia Press, he contemplated finally having a go at smut, with Cathy helping out.

Odd-jobbing claimed much of his time, while his outline for a new novel, and his attempts to generate interest in a film version of *The Acrobats*, simmered in the background. He managed to meet the "Columbia pictures big cheese" in Paris but had no success. The porn aside, many of these projects did come to pass, and if the results weren't distinguished they were commissioned tasks effectively completed by the professional he now believed himself to be.

"Rain, rain, rain, here every day," he reported shortly before wrapping up his stay in France, "but Ive always preferred a gray Paris to a bright one." There were fewer references to old friends and haunts this time round—the Paris of his earlier youth was already receding—and the rest of the Continental ramble was postponed as he and Cathy returned for the publication of *Son of a Smaller Hero*, renting a flat in Hillside Gardens and awaiting reviews. But before the British or Canadian media could weigh in, he had to weather a private assault. In separate letters dating June 4 and June 9, Bill Weintraub and Jackie and Brian Moore each ripped into the book. At seven lengthy pages, Weintraub's critique was the most substantial. "This is a difficult letter to write," he began, before decrying everything from the inaccuracies to the digressions to the sloppy, often clichéd writing. The characters did not impress—the protagonist, Noah Adler, bored Weintraub with his "eternal philosophizing, his peculiar jokes, his fortuitous vulgarities"—and he took exception to the depiction of Montreal Jews ("certain of your descriptions of people and places in Montreal just don't ring true to me") and wondered, without saying as much, if his friend was distorting reality to pick a fight. "You know Montreal Jewry is going to be highly offended," he said. He reserved his greatest censure for the end. After noting that Richler's letters of late had been more concerned with career than craft, he laid it out: "You ought to be paying more attention to the mechanics and craftsmanship of prose construction." In a PS added four days later, Weintraub admitted, "I was going to tear it up but no, I'll send it. . . . Please don't take offense, okay?"

The Moores made less apology. They had both read Weintraub's agonized missive, and concurred. Firing first, Jackie Moore moved quickly through specific objections, including "stretches of sloppy writing" and "carelessness," to her main point. Unlike Brian, she did think the book was anti-Semitic, if only because "you have failed to put across the emotional life of your characters," all of whom were so unpleasant and shifty—that is, conforming to prejudices. "I think the real reason for the book's weakness is your own hatred and contempt," she said. "In effect, you say, 'the Jews stink, the Gentiles stink; Montreal stinks; Canada stinks.' The end result is an all-pervasive stink." Her husband, while admitting he had read only half the manuscript so far, spoke of "pretty embarrassing" passages and "a careless attitude towards detail." Brian Moore noted that the main character resembled Richler himself, "although I think you are a much better man than he," and that the depiction of Neil Compton had done their mutual friend an injustice.

The criticisms were fair, and to Moore's complaint about the treatment of Neil Compton would soon be added a long list of relations who felt abused in the book. The force of the Weintraub-Moore attacks, however, betrayed other resentments. That they were all writing from Montreal on the eve of the city's excoriation in the novel may have contributed; that, however flawed, it touched several raw nerves and then pinched them as hard as it could didn't help. Moore and Weintraub had both been on the receiving end of two years of occasionally boastful and strutting—if also generous and big-hearted—letters from their younger, more successful colleague. Grievances had been percolating for a while. But tough love of this sort was also rooted in faith in the value of candour, and the durability of the bond between them. What's more, the two friends felt sure not only that Mort Richler needed to hear the truth, but could and would take it. On both counts, they were right: in his reply he more or less thanked them for their honesty. With people he trusted he expected to get as good as, or better than, he gave.

Son of a Smaller Hero, published in June 1955 and dedicated "For Cathy," opens with a combative disclaimer. "Any reader approaching this book in a search for 'real people' is completely on the wrong track and, what's more, has misunderstood my whole purpose." This is a novel, he asserts, "not an autobiography." Noah Adler, aged twenty, drives a cab and lives in a rooming house away from the "ghetto" where he was raised. His scrap-dealing family are a fright, in particular the patriarch, Melech Adler, first seen at a clan meeting he has called to insist that Shabbas rules be observed to the letter. Melech's sons, including Wolf Adler, Noah's ineffectual father, voice support for the bully's dictums without intending to abide by them. This Noah can no longer accept, particularly when he witnesses his family cheat a customer at the scrapyard. His flight takes a turn when, enrolled in a local college, he befriends a decent but simpering Anglo professor named Theo Hall. Invited to move into Hall's apartment, the heavy-drinking, hypocrisy-hating artist soon wins the affections of Miriam Hall. She is his senior by a decade but is dissatisfied with her bland husband. She is also drawn to the brooding Jew. Intoxicated, Mrs. Professor Hall abandons her security and standing to go live with her passionate lover, who, in turn, is dismayed to find himself suddenly attached to a needy, near middleaged woman. Noah's mother, named Leah, pines for her dead rabbi father, who she is convinced was a true *zaddick*, or holy man. In the end Noah leaves Miriam to return to Leah's house—a bitter retreat in his march towards personal freedom. "The ghetto of Montreal has no real walls and no true dimensions," declares the novel's first page. "The walls are the habit of atavism and the dimensions are an illusion."

Scarcely a single childhood experience or grievance remained unaired in *Son of a Smaller Hero*. The wounds were still open, and Richler, riding his talent, nerve and anger, was heedless of fairness or accuracy, never mind literary craft. The novel wasn't looking to critique his family and Jewish Montreal; it was calling them out to a brawl, an Apostate taking on Everybody. Typical of the lack of distance was the clichéd fantasy of Noah Adler's dark countenance proving irresistible to a sexually unsatisfied shiksa. Typical as well was the emotional understanding implicit in the way Noah and Miriam's relationship ends. Nearly every page of *Son of a Smaller Hero* sang of both its author's gift and his virulent disaffections. Every page was likewise marred by haste and impatience. His friends saw it—and saw him—clearly.

Reviewers in Great Britain, finding its setting exotic, praised the novel's candour and intensity. Richler sent Brian Moore a letter at the end of July the same morning the *Times Literary Supplement* deemed *Son of a Smaller Hero* "admirable." The book "recreates the teeming streets, the frustrated passions, the furious inbred life of Montreal's Jewish quarter." "Phone ringing all morning," he wrote of the influential review; "people calling to say they'd seen it." While happily informing Moore of the healthy London sales of his novel *Judith Hearne*—Richler had been clipping and mailing reviews to Montreal for his friend—he also included three typed-out pages ("I had to prepare this for my agent") of additional reviews of *his* book in the provincial papers. "It is a book stained with the blood of violent death and wounded hearts, crisp and sometimes almost brutal," the *Manchester Dispatch* reported. From the *Birmingham Post*: "Mr Richler takes for his theme racial loyalty and solidarity among Jews living in the ghetto of Montreal."

In Canada reviewers were less forgiving. The Montreal *Star* called the novel a "distasteful story" about a "blindly selfish" young man of "limited intelligence" who "succeeds in reducing all those around him to rubble." Had the author not been so evidently working off his resentments, *Son of a Smaller Hero* might have been "an interesting, if morbid novel." The Toronto *Telegram* dubbed the book "tawdry and completely unimportant," while a Jewish paper in that city declared that if all Montreal Jews were as horrible as Mordecai Richler, pity the poor town. The *Globe and Mail* dismissed it as "violent" and noted that it would hardly "do anything to further the interests of the Jewish race." His Jews were a "grasping and frequently dishonest bunch for whom nobody could feel much sympathy." A rare positive notice appeared in the magazine the *Montrealer*.

More widely and positively reviewed in England than *The Acrobats*, the book did put its author on the literary map—at least, a corner of it. He had achieved that goal, and he had worked hard for it. In the same triumphant letter to Brian Moore he defended his emerging reputation as an operator. His critic in this instance seemed to be his friend Mavis Gallant, as relayed, with silent approval, by Moore. "Yes, I do know a lot of the 'right people,'" he wrote. "I meet them at Diana's. Joyce's. Etc. Davenports. Or, like in the case of Peter Green, Telegraph, they write asking to meet me for drinks <u>after</u> they've read my work." Then, his exasperation overtaking his desire to explain the self-evident—why, after all, wouldn't someone take steps to advance his career?—he signed off on the subject. "Oh fuck it!"

VIII

CANADIAN CLUB

In his spare time during the summer of 1955, Richler and his friend Norman Levine put together an outline for an anthology of Canadian literature, hoping André Deutsch would take it on. Thirty-one-year-old Levine, a Royal Canadian Air Force veteran with an M. Lit. from the University of London, had preceded him to England by several years, settling quietly in Cornwall and publishing his first novel, *The Angled Road*, in 1952. But it was the younger man who had the London contacts and knew how to make things happen. "We are particularly interested in *avoiding* the perennial anthology contributors," they said, listing Hugh MacLennan, F.R. Scott and Morley Callaghan as examples of over-exposed Canadians. Their selection would highlight new fiction voices instead, including Brian Moore, Mavis Gallant, Ted Allan, and themselves, along with poets A.M. Klein, P.K. Page and Irving Layton, and essayists like Robert Weaver. Translations of Quebec writers would also be featured: Gabrielle Roy, Roger Lemelin, and Anne Hébert. While this early effort at taste-making failed, Richler continued to press himself and his mostly Canadian writer pals on everyone in London and New York, Paris and Munich, who would listen.

Bill Weintraub finally heeded his command to come to London. He showed up in the early autumn, soon sending back witty eye-witness accounts of Richler in action. There was the Monday noon call from his friend, arguing for knocking off work to see a matinee. Or a glimpse of the "lit factory" that was Mordecai and Cathy's flat, especially during the period when George Lamming, back in town again, stayed with them: "Lamming batting out a novel in guest room, Mort polishing novel in front room, and Cathy doing script-typing job for Reuben Ship in kitchen." Best of all, Weintraub convinced the National Film Board of Canada to make a documentary about Canadians living in London and Paris, landing himself the job of scriptwriter.

Released in 1956, *Canadians Abroad* opens on Trafalgar Square on a soupy day. After an interview with a long-time Canadian resident and member of the British Parliament, the scene shifts to the Troubadour Coffee Shop on Old Brompton Road. The café is run by a Montreal couple and features folk music sessions in the basement. The camera pans from the musicians, most in suits and beatnik beards, to the audience, where in the back corner sits a young man, clean-shaven chin in hand. Next, the documentary cuts to an exchange with that music lover, described as the author of two novels. Richler's voice is high and slightly nasal and his vertical hair accentuates his forehead and ears. He wears his one suit well, tie tightly knotted. To make his points, a cigarette between fingers, he cocks his head and winces, his right eye nearly closing. Otherwise, he is a composed and well-spoken intellectual.

What he has to say, however, would prove less pleasing. "Canada's a very provincial country," he tells the camera—and, by extension, the countrymen laying eyes on him for the first time. Asked if novelists are respected in Canada, his speech turns hipster. "I don't want to be respected, man, I just want to be accepted. Novelists, I'm afraid, are regarded as something of freaks in Canada." But he also makes clear his overall career plans. "I fully intend going back," he replies to a question about his future. "I'm a Canadian writer. I write about Canadians."

Bill and Bernice Weintraub rented in Notting Hill, a little west of the Canadian contingent, but still close enough to get to the Friday night "High Poker Soirees." These were generally hosted by Mordecai and Cathy in their latest flat, a three-room unit minus private toilet or fridge, on the third floor of a decrepit house in Swiss Cottage. Hearing reports of the poker nights, which included Ted Allan and Reuben Ship, Brian Moore ribbed Weintraub about his card-playing prowess: "It seems Weintraub always loses. Mort always wins. True to form?" Weintraub retorted, "It's Weintraub who wins, Richler who loses." Then, it being the day after "Friday's Mortoparty"—a twenty-fifth-birthday celebration for Richler—he summarized the event. "A gay fiesta, on the whole, with the presence of some 30 souls, representing the Canadian colony, various Bolshevist factions and certain indigenous intelligentsia. One guest was a culture lady on a mission from the People's Democratic Republic of Poland, who spoke of the sweetness and light prevailing in that land. Made jokes about Stalin and generally spoke in a way that indicates that the party girdle is loosening. As you know, the Red Menace, at this distance, is neither as Red nor as menacing as at home. However, it was startling to hear somebody say, 'When I was in the agit-prop school with Tito's son. . . .'" Weintraub signed off his mocking survey of Lefty London with: "Yours for world peace, Trotsky."

Thanks to his friendships with Ted Allan and Reuben Ship, Richler was now moving in circles where there was no menace in being Red. Quite the opposite: belief, if no longer in the "dream" of global socialism, then in the inherent values of the Left, remained almost obligatory. Allan had the highest profile, thanks to his Spanish Civil War bona fides and success as author and playwright. His first London-produced play, *The Ghost Writer*, was running, and he was writing scripts for the TV series *Robin Hood*. Allan was soon joined by the same Reuben Ship that Richler had written news copy about for the CBC in Montreal. After being expelled from the United States, Ship had scripted and produced *The Investigator*, a daring radio-satire on Joseph McCarthy's methods of rooting out subversives that had threatened to cause a cross-border scandal. Ship's personal experiences of McCarthyism therefore made him the blacklisted exile of the moment. In 1951 the expatriate radio writer, raised on the same streets as Richler and Ted Allan, had joined the long roster of Hollywood types to

be called before the House Un-American Activities Committee.
An avowed Communist, he had decried his accusers as witch-
hunters. American officials had in turn escorted the ill, hand-
cuffed Ship, deported as an enemy alien, across the bridge to
Windsor, Ontario, and ten months later he had taken his revenge
by writing *The Investigator*. A subsequent vinyl record of the
broadcast sold 100,000 copies, despite being widely denounced
as Communist propaganda. The *New York Times* wondered if it
might cause a breach between the nations.

Richler liked and admired both men, with Allan serving as a
kind of wayward father figure, and through their professional
contacts they helped and encouraged him to write for other
media. At the same time, the apprentice had doubts from the
start about the orthodoxies of these older artists, and challenged
them for betting their lives on politics. Americans of similar col-
oration, including director and actor Sam Wanamaker, were wid-
ening his social network out into exactly those spheres where
Joseph Stalin and Marshal Tito were invoked glowingly at birthday parties. But even at age twenty-five, his own instinctive empathy for the poor notwithstanding, he could never give himself
over to the de facto ideology of 1950s Left politics. That was the
Single Idea with the Single Set of Truths.

Most of Richler's Canadian London friends were Jewish: Allan,
Weintraub, Ship, Mann, Levine, Alvin Rakoff (the youngest pro-
ducer/director at the BBC) and the soon-to-arrive TV maven
Sydney Newman. The fierce passions and arguments of the old
neighbourhood in Montreal—politics brought across the Atlantic
on board those ships of Jews fleeing the Old Country—were now
being played out back on European soil by a new generation. As
touchstones of political belief and artistic sensibility, their parents had had the pogroms and the *Protocols of the Elders of Zion*,
the Ba'al Shem Tov and Maimonides. For their children there
were the Holocaust, the creation of Israel, the stories of Isaac
Babel and, soon, the genius of Saul Bellow. "Jewish writers are
always in danger of becoming fascinated by the problems of
Jewry," the *Times Literary Supplement* review remarked of *Son of*

a Smaller Hero, "to the exclusion of all else." The reviewer, dismissing "Jewry," even in the wake of six million dead and the miracle of Israel, as insufficient material for a novel, confessed that Richler's next book would be "awaited with anxiety."

Jewish artists and intellectuals, most of them children of the diaspora, were popping up everywhere, and by 1956, these young transgressors were beginning to introduce, or perhaps inject British cultural life with an authentic and authentically unsettling sensibility—one functioning independently of those "problems of Jewry." The Canadian Club in London was birthing one such literary Jew.

———————

Richler told told Bill Weintraub, "Ive got very fond of Ted Allan and Kate, theyre really fine people, both, with excellent spirits." Then, disregarding the fact that Stanley Mann was a pal of Bill's, he sniped, "but the Manns, man and wife, give me a pain in the ass." He was not acknowledging that the pain that Florence Mann, whose blend of beauty and intelligence seemed to flummox many men, caused in him was already located elsewhere—in his heart.

Florence Mann was present at many of the same London parties and dinners. She often witnessed Mort Richler, cigarette fuming and glass in hand, knocking over ashtrays in his haste, managing to assert his own broad allegiances while challenging, often with a single clipped remark, his friends' assumptions. She noted how effortlessly he could darken the mood of a dinner or cast a shadow over an evening. He enjoyed parties and was very social, but he also intimidated, often silencing a room without so much as a censorious word. Cathy's sister, Tess Taconis, described him as a "social zombie," in reference to his tendency to wear a scowl in public. When he did speak, his specialty was mocking the champagne socialism of this increasingly affluent community, his bite underscored, Florence sometimes sensed, by his envy of their larger paydays and better apartments. Once, on learning that he had gone to France for a period, an acquaintance wondered to

Florence what they would do without Mordecai. "Yes, we've lost our moral conscience," another agreed. That manner, often difficult if also endearingly awkward and even clumsy, continued to attract her, though not romantically. Her own marriage, meanwhile, was far from easy; Stanley Mann's reputation as a womanizer, including an ill-advised pass at Diana Athill, was no secret. Nor was the fact that Florence was now pregnant.

Another adjunct club member, Doris Lessing, recalled Richler as "the baby of the group." Lessing, already the author of *The Grass Is Singing*, would in a few years publish *The Golden Notebook*, her massive and influential depiction of Left artistic circles in London, containing a sharp portrait of Ted Allan, with whom she had an affair, and a cogent anti-Stalinist argument. The brilliant and sensual Rhodesian, then raising two children on her own, observed a very different side to the Mort Richler of the period, at Canadian Club parties "with his back to a wall, a glass in his hand, inarticulate or almost stammering, lovably modest, genuinely so." His serious nature, in particular his queries about the compatibility of making great art with having a family, struck her as sweetly earnest. Lessing liked Cathy as well, finding her forthright and clever. She socialized with both, once keeping him company at a party thrown for the visiting Irish-Canadian journalist Kildare Dobbs.

Richler had reason to be nice to the respected Dobbs. In late spring 1956 he had borrowed money for a plane ticket to return home and hustle work from the CBC. That meant London to Toronto, where the broadcast corporation was headquartered. Always willing to help a young author out, Bob Weaver asked his friend Kildare Dobbs if he could provide Richler with a bed. Then an editor at the publishing house Macmillan, Dobbs had once profiled Ted Allan, and worked with Cathy's brother-in-law, Kryn Taconis. He had heard of the boy writer, and with his own marriage recently ended, he was living with his sons in a roomy midtown apartment. With Arthur Hammond, an editor at the film board, also in residence, the apartment was a good place for Mort Richler to meet Toronto media and arts people.

Dobbs put him on a cot in the sunroom off the kitchen, and didn't object when he hung linked sausages on the doorknob. The three men, plus Dobbs's sons, shared the space for longer than their host had expected, arguing about the Suez Crisis, drinking plenty. Hammond was great with the boys; Richler mostly ignored them. But neither Dobbs nor Hammond could ignore the cracks in the younger man's relationship with his wife. They overheard transatlantic phone battles between Mordecai and Cathy, exchanges so raw they left him with a racing heart. So Dobbs wasn't especially surprised to be told about a single scriptwriter named Jacqueline Rosenfeld, with whom Richler became involved during his extended stay. Blonde and attractive, the older Rosenfeld was then writing a series about an affluent Toronto neighbourhood, based on Forest Hill. She served mostly as a shoulder for him to cry on, and assumed he was separated from his wife. Richler returned one evening with a story: he and Rosenfeld had been talking in her car when the police knocked on the window to interrogate the presumed lovers. "It was ugly," he said, his negative view of Toronto the Good, as the city was mockingly dubbed, reinforced.

Those shouting matches on the phone to London may have concerned the news that Cathy had become pregnant. She lost the baby in September. "Just back from the hospital," he wrote on the sixteenth, "where Cathy is doing reasonably well after her miscarriage." Later, he confessed to Diana Athill that if she had had a child he would have felt obliged to stay with her. The miscarriage must have come as a relief.

He liked Cathy Boudreau for her wit and liveliness, and the way she looked after him. For a period he believed he loved her, and told her so. Florence Mann, who was almost as wary as he of Cathy's bite, said they made a good couple, temperamentally similar, and more bohemian than she wished to be. But another secret Richler kept to himself was that Cathy, while not necessarily the nearly middle-aged woman that Noah Adler in *Son of a Smaller Hero* comes to regret becoming involved with, was not the one he thought of when he conceptualized either a wife and companion, or a mother to the children he wanted to have. He had realized that he had another, very specific person in mind for those roles and relationships.

The Suez Crisis preoccupied cocktail party conversation on both sides of the Atlantic for much of 1956. Between April, when the Egyptian colonel Gamal Abdel Nasser nationalized the Suez Canal, and late October, when Israel in a tripartite agreement with England and France attacked his army, taking the Gaza Strip and Sinai, London intellectuals denounced Israeli aggression. Fervour was heightened by the participation of British forces, who entered the Suez a week later, mandated by the Conservative government of Anthony Eden under the banner of helping referee the confrontation. For the Left, Britain's involvement amounted to a revival of its imperialist impulse to interfere in other nations. Brian Moore viewed with "total horror and abhorrence" the attempt of "old-line capitalist powers" to undermine the liberator Nasser's nationalization of the canal, notwithstanding the fact that Egypt's actions represented an abrogation of a 1936 treaty that granted Britain a lease. "And don't tell me Eden went to protect Israel," he added in a furious letter to Bill Weintraub. For Richler, it was more complicated. Arab commando raids across the Israeli border had become routine and lethal. The need for Israel, now eight years old and engulfed in Arab hostility, to protect itself and its interests left him unable to declare one side right and the other wrong.

Regardless, on November 4 he and Weintraub joined ten thousand protestors in Trafalgar Square—the same day that Soviet tanks rolled into Budapest to crush the Hungarian uprising. "Eden must go!" the crowd shouted as Labour leader Aneurin Bevan made a passionate speech against British participation in Israel's actions. "Then the mob decided to march on Downing Street to express its sentiments," Weintraub reported to Moore. "We went along, and it is strictly a page for the Memory Album." Scuffles broke out. "We were right up front, with the horses plunging around, and for a minute it was quite dicey." British restraint triumphed and the protest ended peacefully. Prime Minister Anthony Eden's subsequent decision to accede to a U.N. peace-keeping force in the Suez—a strategy suggested and created by Canada's Lester B. Pearson and imposed on Britain, France and Israel by the Eisenhower administration—was widely viewed as evidence of the strength of the new, youthful Left.

Though seven months pregnant, Florence Mann attended the rally on her own. At some point during the day she and Mordecai met up, unbeknownst to the Weintraubs. They used the anonymity to speak intimately for the first time, mutually acknowledging their attraction. Though they separated without touching, something had happened. Richler certainly thought so; having finally received a sign from the woman he already loved and badly wanted to make his life with, he went about winning her. When Daniel Mann was born on December 22 it was his father, Stanley, who suggested their mutual friend Mordecai Richler as godfather. Florence supported the choice.

Ted Allan, finally allowing the "truth" of Khrushchev's denunciation of Joseph Stalin at the party congress earlier that year to penetrate his believer's heart, was suffering a nervous breakdown that winter of 1956–57, but his more cynical friend was making a push to a new level of professional success. First reading and synopsizing novels for possible movie treatment, Richler soon graduated to crafting scripts for TV serials, making a hasty study using a collection of Graham Greene's screenplays. From Greene he learned to insert "action" into dialogue, often by means as simple as adding directions like "He lights a cigarette," to satisfy producers afraid of too much "yak-yak-yak." Co-scripting a potential half-hour comedy series for Peter Sellers, he found himself serving mostly as company for his co-writer, brewing tea and complimenting gags.

Richler opted to use a pseudonym for the Sellers scripts, although he did keep his own name for a project co-written with Bill Weintraub—a short film called *First Novel* about the anxieties of the debut novelist—and both a radio and TV adaptation of *The Acrobats*, the latter performed live on CBC in January 1957.

The CBC story editor Nathan Cohen, whom he had met in Toronto the year before, described his efforts as "pretty good for a first script." Two further TV plays from this period—"Harry Like the Player Piano" and "A Friend of the People"—were also signed "Mordecai Richler." The former, using the same character as *First Novel*, had a Montreal novelist, obsessed with the Spanish Civil War, being interviewed about his Leftist political views. It went unproduced. Echoes of Ted Allan's experiences in Spain, and of his lately collapsed belief system, sounded more forcefully in "A Friend of the People," which aired on the CBC that same January. A Canadian doctor, Max Price, whose womanizing and drinking are reminiscent of Norman Bethune's, is in an unnamed country riven by civil war, tending those fighting the good fight. He winds up disillusioned with his colleagues, especially after they murder a general who has crossed over from the fascist side. Ted Allan had told Richler such tales of betrayal, including one of him spying on his own idol, Bethune, also briefly thought to be a traitor.

East End Thriller was yet another side-project. In September he outlined a mystery film to be shot in London's working-class district. He was encouraged by the British director Jack Clayton, whom he had met not long before. Clayton, thirty-five, tall and slender with striking blue eyes, was a veteran of the Royal Air Force who had progressed from serving as a producer for the great Alexander Korda to directing an adaptation of Gogol's *The Bespoke Overcoat*. The short film won an Oscar, and while Clayton had yet to oversee a full-length feature, he was a notable new talent, especially after the untimely death of Korda earlier in 1956. In a letter to Richler, Clayton offered to shepherd his thriller outline to the next stage, a full treatment. "Let me know immediately what sum of money you have in mind," Clayton wrote. Though Richler went on to draft a forty-page outline, *East End Thriller* stalled. But he had impressed the director. "Jack—who is no bullshitter—seems very pleased with my screen potentials," he reported in December. Clayton had also promised to send him a book—"and if he gets the bk, i.e. the film to do, I will do the script." By then, a scant three months after their first meeting, the two men, united by whisky and wit and a love of stern judgments of others, had become fast friends.

Produced or not, credited or pseudonymous, such jobs paid more than any book reviews could, or indeed a novel that took years to complete. Richler's timing couldn't have been better: television drama in Toronto and London was an emerging industry; scripts were needed, and he was both fast and efficient at writing them. Television money was decent but movie money was often huge, with regular payouts at various stages from pitch to screen, even for the vast majority of projects that never got made. Still, the list of major novelists who struggled vainly to write for TV and film is long. Feature-length movies, with their demanding visual vocabularies, can flummox the fiction writer, accustomed to creating images out of language. But Graham Greene wasn't only a novelist Richler greatly respected; he was a prolific screenwriter whose *The Third Man*, released seven years earlier, had been a critical and popular success. Richler, studying his scripts, was a quick learner. But he was also clear-eyed and pragmatic. "Screenwriting," he would later declare, "is not a writer's medium."

For some, supplementing novels with film treatments and scripts and tossing off book reviews of westerns and Harold Robbins blockbusters would be a full day's work. Richler was also honing a new skill—recycling pieces, a trick learned from Ted Allan—that would soon be a trademark of his freelance practice. The trick was admired by colleagues, though occasionally resented by editors unaware they were purchasing already published, or lightly reworked, material. He had lately recycled an article about his days in Left Bank Paris for use on Weaver's Anthology CBC programme, reading the text himself. But the fall of 1956 marked his adult debut as a journalist as well. In October the *Montrealer* published both an inaugural "London Letter" from him and the short story "Benny, the War in Europe, and Myerson's Daughter Bella," recently aired on CBC Radio. The story, about a St. Urbain Street boy who returns from the war shell-shocked and marries the daughter of the owner of the local cigar shop and soda fountain, was cursory but charming. The letter, titled "Sailors, Suez, and the Stage," shifted from glancing but vivid descriptions of the London visit of playwright Arthur Miller and his new wife, Marilyn Monroe, to the unfolding Suez crisis. For each contribution the *Montrealer* paid him $50, a fee negotiated by Bill Weintraub.

His other credit paid less—12 guineas, or $40—but featured a golden signature on the cheque: Kingsley Martin, editor of the *New Statesman.* The weekly, founded in 1913 with the support of George Bernard Shaw, remained the benchmark for Left intellectual and literary excellence. While the 1930s hadn't been a great decade for the magazine—it ran a glowing interview by H.G. Wells with Stalin and refused to print Orwell's dispatches from the Spanish Civil War on account of their criticism of the Communists— by the end of the 1940s it had become a key player in Labour Party politics. Its eighty thousand readers mattered, and a publishing credit there represented an entry pass into certain circles. His debut, the kitschy "The Secret of the Kugel," wasn't auspicious, but it was a *New Statesman* credit.

He was also redrafting his new novel. *A Choice of Enemies,* originally titled *Till Break of Day,* marked the high point—or low point—of his impulse to draw directly from his own recent experiences. His self-styled "London novel," about the Left-leaning expatriate movie and television crowd, felt lifted from the previous night's Hampstead party. Joyce Weiner appreciated the book's lean storytelling and less impressionistic language but must have been disturbed by his dogged refusal to heed her advice about allowing events to settle in his imagination. FOR JOYCE WEINER, the dedication read.

Certain friends, noticing versions of themselves in *A Choice of Enemies,* were no more pleased. "You say Ted Allan is cool after CHOICE?" Weintraub wrote of the too-obvious model for the protagonist. "Are you really surprised?" Norman Price, thirty-eight and Jewish, has lost his university job in the United States due to McCarthy-era politics. (His father is Max Price from Richler's play "A Friend of the People.") In London he writes scripts for producers like the blacklisted expatriate Sonny Winkleman, who tells him that "in this world you've got to make a choice of enemies or you just can't live." Price has been forcing a mysterious young German named Ernst Haupt on his social circle, even though Haupt has bedded the young woman he had planned to marry. "All marriages ended the same," he decides. "After five years—bickering, little affairs on the side, a resentful tolerance, no more desire." Increasingly frustrated by the hypocrisy of his crowd, he banishes himself from this clique. Norman Price, on learning that the mysterious Haupt murdered his brother turns in a rage on the "little Nazi." But then a bout of amnesia leaves him at large in a grotesque London nightscape. "All alliances," he thinks at his own wedding to a near-stranger, "have been discredited." Even Ernst Haupt is no longer his chosen enemy.

While less hasty than its predecessors, its prose more measured and calm, *A Choice of Enemies* shares their earnest dismay at human venality and self-aggrandizement. People are uniformly tense and unhappy, at each other's throats, having no fun. Nobody—including, apparently, the author—was finding any of this funny.

But that wasn't right; Richler's letters, like his manner around close friends, showed another temperament: generous, loving, delighting in people and wildness and, most of all, hilariously funny. The anger, while undoubtedly part of his makeup, had a currency particular to the age. The lengthy run of John Osborne's *Look Back in Anger* at the Royal Court Theatre the previous autumn had exploded the "Angry Young Man" into British culture. That same fall, Colin Wilson's dark study of alienation, *The Outsider*, was published to acclaim. Osborne was twenty-six, Wilson twenty-four, and both were hailed for their working-class roots and quasi-beatnik lifestyles. They had come to bury Noël Coward and his foppish ilk; the critic Philip Toynbee called the group, soon to include John Braine, Arnold Wesker, Alan Sillitoe and Kingsley Amis, "the most exciting literary movement since the Romantics." *The Acrobats* had beaten both Osborne and Wilson to the zeitgeist punch, even if it lagged in quality. And Richler, now all of twenty-six, certainly had the qualifications, from proletarian roots to bohemian streak. As far as the fuel of anger went, Mort Richler of St. Urbain Street could flare as high as the young English turks.

A Choice of Enemies was published in September 1957 to little fanfare. He'd had months to brace for the disappointment. "Am in a depressed state abt Choice," he had written to Brian Moore before Christmas. "It ought to be good." By June 29, still eight weeks before publication, he was using the same language. "News from here small and depressing," he told Weintraub. "Bob Weaver, I understand, thinks *Choice* is a stinker. Viking thumbs down, after most careful thought, etc, etc." Deutsch was on board, although Athill was secretly still waiting for her boy writer to find his real voice. But Viking set the tone for American dissatisfaction in the manuscript, in no small part on account of the country's fatigue with subjects related even tangentially to Joe McCarthy, along with its indifference to Europe's engagement with Left politics. The political conflicts so alive in Richler's circle were dead elsewhere, and though he offered to rewrite the book for the American market, he found no takers. Unappeased by the dedication, Joyce Weiner ripped into him for his impulse to throw his energies, as both writer and self-promoter, into a fix-it job for yet another novel birthed before it was ready. "Mordy, oh, Mordy," she wrote, "I would say—no lobbying, no reviewing, no extraneous publicity anymore for you until you have turned out the kind of book you yourself can be proud of."

His June letter to Weintraub was postmarked Tourrettes-sur-Loup. In March he and Cathy had abandoned London for the familiar terrain of the Alpes-Maritimes. Their departure for the south coincided with the decision of Stanley and Florence Mann to return to North America with baby Daniel for a period—a convenient coincidental vacating of England. The Richlers journeyed south ahead of a phalanx of publishers and film industry types, willing a kind of mini-émigré colony into existence to make their extended stay more enjoyable, and to provide players for his afternoon poker games. "I've rented 3 houses here," he wrote, "more or less, for Brian, Reuben, and Mason Hoffenberg, and am rather panicky nobody will like their pads, and all complaints will be heard here." Stopping in Paris on the way down to collect Terry Southern and his wife, Carol, they settled into a rented house atop the dramatic *falaise* of Tourrettes. The American couple carried on to Spain and returned in July. Terry Southern had lately had two books accepted by André Deutsch, thanks, in part, to Richler's advocacy. Back in January he had written to Southern saying that Diana Athill was seriously considering Southern's first novel, *Flash and Filigree*, and that being published in the U.K. by them was prestigious, if not well-paying. Even better, in March Deutsch bought Southern's *The Magic Christian*, based solely on an outline for the satiric novel. "YOU ARE NOW ENTITLED TO KNOW THE SECRET HANDSHAKE," he wrote. Then "THE STABLE CHEERS AND—SOON ENOUGH— YOU WILL GET YR DEUTSCH SWEATSHIRT TO WEAR."

Southern was now attempting to finish a project with Mason Hoffenberg. Richler had convinced them both that the Riviera sun would be good for the job, and arranged for the collaborators to resume their work in the village. Hoffenberg's heroin addiction limited his ability to function, but he did sit with the others in the square reviving the café banter of the old days, including a group effort to construct the perfect *Reader's Digest* story, albeit with excessive scatology. Southern and Hoffenberg managed to produce a few pages of what eventually became *Candy*, a novel of satiric hipster erotica based on Voltaire's *Candide*, before returning to Paris. Girodias had promised them a flat fee of $1,000 for their artful porn.

On days when Hoffenberg couldn't write, Richler and Southern worked together on a TV play titled *The Panthers*. Southern had done the original draft, motivated by his assurances of the good money to be made in "telly plays," and now they rewrote it as a team. Despite his own efforts, some successes, Richler too still needed the money. If nothing broke for him by the end of summer, he warned Bill Weintraub, he and Cathy would be back in Canada for good. *The Panthers* told a *West Side Story*–ish tale of street gangs and violence, and featured juvenile delinquents with names like Ritchie and Vince. But the script did nothing to ease the financial burden of either writer; efforts to sell it in Canada and the U.K. failed.

Still, it was summer on the Riviera, and the living, even for anxious and cash-strapped expats, was charmed. Affable, appetite-driven Reuben Ship and his new companion, Winnipeg-born Elaine Grand, herself a well-known broadcaster, arrived in Tourrettes. They liked the villa Richler had arranged for them, but the Moores, appearing in June, and Diana Athill, did not. F.R. Scott's son, Peter Dale, and his wife, Maylie, two more Canadian neighbours in London, came down for a vacation as well. Finding Mordecai and Cathy's place overcrowded with the Southerns and the Canadian TV producer Sylvio Narizzano and his wife, Bea, the Scotts retreated to a hotel. Jackie and Brian Moore wound up in the Welcome Hotel in nearby Villefranche, along with their editor. Diana Athill had her pick of André Deutsch Canadian authors that summer; Mavis Gallant, whose *The Other Paris* had appeared to glowing reviews, was once more in Menton, an hour farther up the coast.

According to a report by Jackie Moore, an even more prominent Canadian was also in the neighbourhood: British press baron Lord Beaverbrook, spotted escorting actress Greta Garbo onto his yacht, its New Brunswick home port label visible. But for Jackie Moore it was Tourrettes, "where the boys play poker all day," that was the centre of their idyll. "In case you'd like to know," Richler taunted Weintraub, "I'm off in half an hour to Juan les Pins for a swim, then with Reuben & Co. to Cannes for a langouste dinner, and from there to the Crazy Horse Saloon for a night of striptease."

It took an outsider, the ever-alert Diana Athill, to perceive the shadow of feuding couples dulling the Riviera sunlight. For all the lovely weather and frolic, everyone seemed so unhappy, she later recalled.

Richler's now five-year-old relationship with Cathy, one lately characterized, as his protagonist Norman Price observed in the

novel, by "bickering, little affairs on the side, a resentful tolerance, no more desire," was at least momentarily eased in
Tourrettes by a new encounter. CBC producer Nathan Cohen,
who had overseen the teleplay of *The Acrobats* and lately interviewed him for the *Tamarack Review*, had told yet another
Canadian film director heading for London that he would find a
good friend in Mordecai Richler. Ted Kotcheff, son of Bulgarian
immigrants to Toronto's Cabbagetown, had a B.A. in literature
and enough of a resumé directing live TV for the CBC to be head-
hunted by Sydney Newman for his newly established drama division at ABC. The lanky, mop-haired twenty-seven-year-old,
veteran of his own sojourn as an existential poet in Spain, made
his way to Tourrettes in late summer. He found Richler in the village square café and introduced himself. The two sat drinking for
two hours, during which time Kotcheff spoke incessantly and the
man with whom he was supposed to have so much in common
managed a dozen words. Richler, absorbed in the final rewrites
of *A Choice of Enemies*—when deeply involved in a novel, he continued his writing day in his mind, remaining largely lost to the
"outside" world—seemed taciturn and rabbinical, uninterested in
company. "Who's your favourite author?" he finally asked the
Torontonian. When Kotcheff answered Henry James, he cracked,
"Then you'll be right at home with my novels, won't you?"

But another essential friendship was born. Over the next few
months, Ted Kotcheff became the only person with whom Richler
shared his feelings about the state of his marriage with Cathy,
and his obsession with Florence Mann—an obsession about to
turn into a pursuit.

IX

ROQUEBRUNE

"Last night we went to visit Stanley and drank vodka with him until one a.m.," Richler told Bill Weintraub from London on December 14, 1957. "He's most depressed, drinking a good deal, and full of film gossip, jokes, tales." The reason for Stanley Mann's depression was not his career—he was scripting a "Lana Turner soap-opera"—but his personal life. Namely, his separation from his wife. "He and Florence hardly see each other," he reported, "the baby looks fine, and Stanley owes and is spending pots of money." This mention of the Manns came well into a letter rich with gossip, little of it happy, and none of it relating to either his situation with Cathy or his desire for Florence. Aside from Reuben Ship and Elaine Grand, who were doing "swimmingly," and the recent romance between director Jack Clayton and Flora Rosenberg, most friends were in crisis. "Ted Allan was here one night," he continued of his mentor, lately separated from Kate, "and is now supporting four people and three analysts. He seems in bad shape."

The letter was occasioned by Weintraub's own troubles: bouts of depression fuelled by professional disappointments and struggles with alcohol. "You are certainly one of my most valued and intelligent friends," Richler told him, "and it grieves me to thk of you sitting up there looking out of the window all day and possibly not sleeping at night." His words were to some avail, but Bill Weintraub's marriage would not survive either.

In October Richler had made another professional trip back to Canada, where he first stopped in Montreal for a "big drinking session with Brian, Jackie, Bill, Bernice" and then moved on to business in Toronto. If the 1956 trip had opened doors for him to write scripts for the CBC, this one began his relationship with a dynamic group of young editors then clustering at the weekly national magazine *Maclean's*. Peter Gzowski, Peter C. Newman and Mckenzie Porter were already on staff when Ken Lefolii began his swift rise up the editorial ranks. All were young, smart and ambitious, frustrated with somnambulant Canada and Toronto the Good. *Maclean's* sent Richler back to London with an assignment. "How I Became an Unknown with My First Novel," published in February 1958, netted a $400 cheque—nearly the same amount he had received for *The Acrobats*. He also got his picture in print, a rare grin on his face as he glanced through the book, pretending to find his own words amusing.

Nathan Cohen's *Tamarack Review* interview with him, published earlier in the year, continued to resonate inside the tiny world of English-Canadian letters. Featured on the cover, alongside a story by a new writer named Alice Munro, the interview sprawled to nearly twenty pages, a de facto announcement of his stature. Nathan Cohen's benign first question—about whether or not he was an expatriate—met with a flinty reply, establishing the tone: "I think words like 'generation,' 'expatriate,' and on another level 'honour' and 'love,' have become almost advertising executive words," the twenty-five-year-old novelist answered, "and those labels when attached to writers are very inhibiting and unfortunate." He ruminated on his earliest days shoplifting at Eaton's and writing bad stories at Baron Byng, his brief career "in advertising" (working for his Uncle Max) and his formative experiences in Paris. "No, I don't think it's a good book," he observed of *The Acrobats*. He was equally frank about his sales figures (two hundred copies of that first novel sold in Canada; around eight hundred of *Son of a Smaller Hero*) and his unsteady income (about $2,000 in total for all the editions of *The Acrobats*, though it may have sold into various markets because "there was

a big scene in a brothel"). He did not have a high opinion of literature in Canada, was skeptical of the modest excitement in the
country surrounding the emergence of younger writers, including himself, Brian Moore, and another Jewish voice, Winnipegger
Adele Wiseman, and felt greater affinity with American authors
than English ones, citing Mailer, Nelson Algren, William Styron
and Herbert Gold. Nevertheless, "All my attitudes are Canadian.
I'm a Canadian; there's nothing to be done about it."

Cohen asked about the effects of being raised deep inside an
Orthodox tradition. "I'm sure it has a hell of a lot of effect," Richler
replied, noting that his family had expected him to become a
rabbi. But he denounced the tendency to portray the Jew in fiction as someone who is "sympathetic, downtrodden, he speaks
in parables, and he has a hard time." The colourful Jewish character was no more legitimate. "It's a form of anti-semitism" he
said of any impulse to pull punches when writing, for example,
about a corrupt Jewish businessman. If an actual anti-Semite
picks up a novel about a corrupt Jew and says, "This is the way
Jews are," that is simply "one of the dangers you run into." In his
view the "class loyalties in Montreal were much stronger than so-
called Jewish loyalties and traditions." Of the reaction to *Son of
a Smaller Hero* in Canada: "I expected people to be hurt, but what
I didn't expect was abuse."

Early in the interview, Cohen wondered if he had come from
a literary background. Many young writers, anxious to establish
their independence and, given the era, working-class affiliations,
might have emphasized the scrapyard and regressive Orthodoxy.
But Richler answered that he could boast two literary family
members: his uncle in New York, manager of a Yiddish vaudeville theatre—"He used to be a journalist in Toronto and
Montreal"—who wrote plays and operettas, and his own *zeyda*.
"He was a Hassid and a scholar," he explained with pride of Yudel
Rosenberg, "and . . . I understand he did the first modern Hebrew
translation of the Zohar."

The corpulent, erudite Cohen, drama critic and story editor at
the CBC, soon to be entertainment editor at the Toronto *Star*, had

to dominate any room he entered. He styled himself an arts maven, and was determined to jump-start a Canadian literary and theatrical scene. He recognized Mordecai Richler as a major figure in embryo and wished to support him—in his own manner. Having granted him the platform of a serious interview, Cohen followed up with a damning article about his work in a subsequent *Tamarack Review*. "Heroes of the Richler View" declared Richler's themes of "the Marxist mirage and the Jewish middle-class family unit" to be outdated, and that the "blasting instruments" of his bullying style refuted his contention that he was honestly engaging with his age. His characters were, for the most part, "empty, trivial, disgusting," and his novels marked by, among other failings, "contrived violence and abundant bedwetting." For good measure, the thirty-five-year-old Cohen, a Jew from small-town Nova Scotia, wondered why all his female characters had tiny breasts.

"Nathan Cohen has butchered me in TAMARACK," Richler wrote to Weintraub, "and—by God—only in Canada wd somebody attempt such a long and definitive piece about a yg punk who has published a mere 3 bks. Makes me feel like I'm dead, or something." But when Cohen was next in London, he wrote ahead asking to be collected at Heathrow airport. Richler played right along with this literary gamesmanship. He calmly picked up the critic who had accused him of bedwetting and showed him the town.

If the ability to attract attention and controversy was any measure, Mordecai Richler was a shoo-in for the literary firmament. And yet: three published works to that name, and he had not yet defined his voice. With *Lucky Jim,* Kingsley Amis sounded like himself from the start. *The Naked and the Dead* was already recognizably Norman Mailer. The Saul Bellow of *Dangling Man* wasn't yet the Bellow of *The Adventures of Augie March*, but James Baldwin's *Go Tell It on the Mountain,* Doris Lessing's *The Grass Is Singing* and Brian Moore's *Judith Hearne* (reprinted as *The Lonely Passion of Judith Hearne*) were early books by contemporaries or friends whose mature styles were on immediate display. For all his raw talent, Richler hadn't yet found his voice as a writer. Financial and critical success, attention and even notoriety notwithstanding, he might not.

Several occurrences around the pivotal year of 1958 changed the direction of his life. In July 1957 he received a rejection letter from the American magazine *Commentary*. For the "socialist writer" of the period, *Commentary* was the U.S. equivalent of the *New Statesman*. As always, he aspired to conquer both sides of the Atlantic, and had sent them the story "Mr. MacPherson and the Boys of Room Forty-One." Now in its sixth year of gestation, the story had grown to twenty pages. The length of the tale of the sad-sack Montreal high school teacher, harassed to the point of using the strap on a gang of mouthy Jewish students, was a problem for *Commentary*—so was the reaction of an editor that the material was anti-Semitic. Theodore Frankel, then an associate editor, disagreed with that assessment, and praised the "vividness of your style and the sharpness of your vision." His criticism focused on the excess of digressions, which weakened the story's impact. But he hoped Richler wouldn't be so upset that he would not drop by the office when he visited New York that autumn, as planned.

One reason "Mr. MacPherson and the Boys of Room Forty-One" was ill-fated as a short story was that it better belonged in a longer narrative. It would become the opening chapter of the book, as yet untitled, that he was struggling that winter to find time to write.

Then there was his new friendship, begun in the summer in Tourrettes. It grew quickly: "Ted Kotcheff—he's new in these parts—is going to produce my first TV play in April," Richler wrote to Bill Weintraub. Not long after their return from France, he had written to the young director, now working on a weekly live show called Armchair Theatre, asking to meet again. Kotcheff brought him in to complete the Canadian trifecta of producer (Sydney Newman), director and writer on three Armchair productions to be aired over the next eighteen months. *Paid in Full* premiered on British television in May. It told of a doctor who, having saved a working-class boy fallen down a well, finds himself conflicted about whether or not to use the child's "celebrity" to fund his clinic for the poor. At the time, the "problem-play" was the rage of live TV drama, and Armchair Theatre's Leftist tendencies demanded work that reflected the Angry Young Men's radical aesthetic. "My first TV play . . . went off rather well here," he told Weintraub. "Ratings, tops, and a phonecall of congratulations for Richler-Kotcheff from Howard Thomas, director of ABC. There will be more by Mort next season." As well, Kotcheff was cultivating another novelist as screenwriter: Terry Southern, whom he had also met in Tourrettes. Southern adapted Eugene O'Neill's *The Emperor Jones*, which Kotcheff directed, complete with ballet sequences. *Candy*, meanwhile, so cheerfully crafted as pornography by Southern and Hoffenberg, was published in October 1958, and though the Paris vice squad banned it, editor Girodias simply reissued the book under a new name. It was soon a cult hit, first in Paris, then in London and New York.

Richler's friendship with Jack Clayton bore similar dividends. Clayton was on the eve of his debut as a feature-film director. His choice of material, an adaptation of John Braine's 1957 novel *Room at the Top*, reflected the times. The story of cunning Joe Lampton, escapee from a nineteenth-century upbringing in industrial squalor, who steadily rises in provincial postwar society, rang all the Angry Young Men bells. A weak initial script had forced Clayton to seek help. "Script doctors" were usually established writers brought in to breathe wit or plot or character, or sometimes all three, into existing material. Pressures were great but fees were large. Work generally went uncredited. Somewhat surprisingly, Clayton, who had liked *A Choice of Enemies*, thought of his young Canadian friend as doctor for *Room at the Top*, despite the book having been written in a kind of English class code. "Jack brought me the original screenplay by Neil Patterson some 3 wks ago, asked me to read it, and I told him what I thought of it," Richler explained to Weintraub. Clayton guaranteed him a smaller sum if he tinkered, a larger one if he fully revised; he would end up making substantial changes to the story and dialogue. "Well, my script's the one they're using," he said, leaving the question of a co-credit to be resolved by the screen-writers' guild. He was happy with the money—£1,400 sterling for three weeks' work—but "better still is that Jack is so pleased with what I've done." He didn't get a writing credit, which proved a shame; Patterson won the 1959 Oscar for Best Adapted Screenplay. Clayton compensated by telling everyone that the script of *Room at the Top* owed much to Mordecai Richler.

All of a sudden, he was making real money, aided by a $2,000 junior fellowship from the newly formed Canada Council. "Am very financially solid now," he admitted, "embarrassingly so, and I can dilly and dally with my novel for months and months, which was the general idea." The dilly, he noted, could be done on the French Riviera. Tess Taconis had found them "an enormous villa on the sea," some twenty minutes towards Italy from Monte Carlo, the rent to be shared by two couples. By early June, Cathy had already flown down to Villa Beatrice in the village of Roquebrune. He would follow shortly.

In recent months he had been wandering up from Winchester Road most afternoons to the flat in Cumberland Place where the Manns lived. Florence and Stanley had recently gotten back together again. Even during the year they were separated, Mordecai and Cathy had gone to dinner at Florence's—on one occasion Sean Connery, a quality raconteur, had told stories late into the night. Now he went there alone, officially as the friend who would take her for walks around the Heath. "The news from here will knock you flatter than piss on a platter," he had told Bill Weintraub in March, efforts at imitating a southern cracker failing to hide his ire. "Take that Stanley Mann critter, remember him? Well I'll be gol'darned if he isn't back with the missus. It's the way she makes those flapjacks, I reckon." Until Ted Kotcheff came on the scene, the only person aware of his ardour had been Florence herself. For almost two years, since the Suez protest in Trafalgar Square, he had been reminding her of his feelings in circumstances that simultaneously amused, annoyed and thrilled her. "I can't bear to be this close to you," he whispered in her ear while she sat at her kitchen table one evening studying a Latin textbook. Or on those walks, kissing her on the cheek and professing his love.

During her separation from Stanley, Florence, once more a mannequin for Dior, had dated a married doctor, a mistake. Unhappy, her feelings in turmoil, she had lately joined Ted Allan and Bill Weintraub in seeking answers through psychoanalysis. Inattentive, philandering Stanley, whose talent and intelligence she continued to appreciate, was not the solution to her problems; she had agreed to the reconciliation only out of guilt at failing as a spouse. When her analyst asked if there wasn't one man she completely respected and trusted, a name did come to mind. But he was "someone with a very difficult personality" who "has a great deal of trouble with most of the people he meets or they with him." No better a choice, surely.

Ted Kotcheff was witness to his friend's lovesick rages. At parties of the Canadian Club crowd, with Florence across the room, Richler would risk scandal by shouting in his ear, "I love her. I want her. She's mine!" He declined to apologize for his feelings, or blunt his determination. "I don't care," he would say of her (and his) married status. "I want her and I'm going to have her."

So Kotcheff was especially surprised to learn that the other couple co-renting the villa in Roquebrune wasn't Kryn and Tess Taconis. Instead, Stanley and Florence had agreed to share Villa Beatrice with Mordecai and Cathy.

Had Richler gone to an analyst in 1958 and offered potted summaries of his parents' marriage, the character of Lily Rosenberg and pathologies of the extended Richler and Rosenberg clans, and then offered descriptions of his own romantic relationships, from Helen to Ulla to Cathy to Jacqueline in Toronto, the therapist might have come up with a sobering psychological portrait. Here was a certain kind of diasporic Jewish intellect, charged with conflicts and contradictions, informed in equal parts by the Talmud and the Holocaust. Here too was a difficult man, reared on dogma and intransigence, trained in judgment and grievance collecting, scarcely capable of a calm or healthy relationship with anyone. Not the kind to marry the right woman or, perhaps, stay married for very long. Not the kind of father most women wished for their children.

Stanley Mann displayed aspects of this character. So did Ted Allan. Why would Mordecai Richler, the most explosive and gifted of the bunch, be any different? The risk, in a sense, was all Florence's, no matter how unhappy she was or how much she admired his intelligence and integrity. The risk was all hers and the luck, if he won her heart, would be all his.

———————

Florence was born on October 19, 1929. Her maiden name, Wood, was not her own. Neither was she first christened Florence. Ethel and Albert Wood adopted her as a baby from a foundling home, and gave a new name to their second daughter and third child. A working-class couple living in Point St. Charles, a Montreal neighbourhood near the Lachine Canal, the Woods had already adopted a boy in 1914 and a girl in 1926. "The Point" housed a mongrel blend of English, Scottish, Irish and French-Canadian. Both Ethel and Albert were born in England. A veteran of the First World War, who had been gassed, he retained traces of a cockney accent. A quiet but kindly man, devoted to his family, Albert Wood worked as a manual labourer for the Canadian National Railway. Ethel Wood, disappointed with her lot in life, battled depression, often spending days in bed in a darkened room, her ailments possibly more imagined than real. Florence was raised in a third-floor apartment on Chateauguay Street in an environment hushed by her mother's condition and her father's nature. The condition only lifted when her maternal grandfather visited, a man of liberal views who, once overruling an objection to a marriage between a Wood family member and a Frenchman, said he hoped someone would marry a Jew. Both parents emphasized politeness, and by the age of seven the girl was known to teachers and neighbours for her pretty features and excellent breeding. She also spoke proper English, thanks to a grade two teacher with clear, elegant enunciation.

The Wood house was certainly quiet by comparison to the five-and-dime store at the corner of Centre Street where Florence went looking for a job at age ten. The Stoplands, a rare Jewish family in the Point, owned the store, and she began babysitting their two sons in the apartment overhead. She saw her first pressure cooker in their kitchen. She met her first Orthodox Jews, complete with black hats and sidecurls, who came in to sell wholesale. By twelve, Florence was helping Mr. Stopland with his ledgers; by fourteen—with her perfect posture and emerging curves, she looked older—she was working behind the counter on evenings and weekends. By now she was also thinking of the Stoplands' store and apartment as a second home. They certainly thought of her as one of their own, encouraging her dreams of a career in the arts, offering to pay for acting or modelling school in New York.

On Saturdays the Stoplands would gather with their clan, many of whom lived on the other side of the city, in the Jewish ghetto and Outremont, for extended lunches in the Laurentians. She remembered these outings. "They would meet at country restaurants, all seated at a long table, with the children and myself at another table. Ostensibly I was there to handle the boys, teach them to draw, read to them. But really the family considered me a part. It was the laughter at the table that so impressed. The laughter, and the wit, the drollery. There was little laughter in my adopted house. These people knew how to enjoy each other. They knew how to enjoy their lives."

During those trips to the countryside, especially in the summer, Florence Wood was likely within a few miles of where Mordy Richler could be found, working in his mother's inn or waiting on tables at a resort in Ste. Agathe. Surrounded by the Stoplands, with her black hair, if not her porcelain skin, helping her blend in, she generally went unnoticed in a crowd of city Jews.

Though the Woods were Anglican, from a young age Florence felt a natural affinity with the Catholic Church. She was also

drawn early on to England. To be a real Cockney, her father liked
to say, you must be born within earshot of the Bow bells. Starting
at ten, she began saving pennies to hear the famous bells of
St. Mary-le-Bow church in Cheapside. At eighteen, as soon as she
completed high school, she set off for London, where she soon
found work as a store mannequin. Even in its devastated condition, the city enthralled her. For the museums and galleries
alone, she was ready to declare it her lifelong home.

On her return to Montreal she became casually involved in the
Mountaintop Theatre group, where she met two up-and-coming
actors: Christopher Plummer and Stanley Mann. Both were handsome leading-men sorts, the blazing and witty Plummer especially. The tall, soulful-eyed Mann, who was Jewish, was more
grave and cerebral, and at the age of twenty-two she became
Florence Mann. The couple moved to Toronto, where he found
work writing scripts and acting for the CBC. They attended a
party at the Allans' house shortly after Ted had hosted Mort
Richler for a night, and soon travelled with their friends to London
in pursuit of greater professional opportunities, a destination that
pleased her at least as much as him. She could resume her self-
education in museums and galleries, stopping in the city's abundant parks to sit and read. With her fine bone structure and
flawless complexion, her graceful manners and speech, she continued to obtain work in the fashion industry. Dior employed her
to model dresses. Vidal Sassoon did her hair in his original salon
on New Bond Road. David Bailey photographed her for *Vogue*.

Once people got past her beauty, they found Florence—Doris
Lessing called her Flo, though she preferred her full name—
quietly smart and thoughtful, a voracious reader and a lover of
classical music. She had an old-fashioned femininity about her,
a sense of decorum and an apparent fragility that hid a strong
backbone. She wasn't combative like Cathy Boudreau, but neither was she meek. Possessed of a high emotional intelligence,
she already preferred the company of artists, and witty conversation, and sought a full, rich life, not an easy one. Now twenty-
seven, a mother, and nearly divorced, she hoped to raise a large,

happy family such as she had not experienced as a child. To her own surprise, she had lately come to the conclusion that she wanted these things with Mordecai Richler.

At Roquebrune the two couples, plus baby Daniel, spent the afternoons together at the beach and evenings in restaurants. Stanley Mann was unusually self-absorbed, even by his own measure, and hadn't given much thought to dishevelled Mort Richler as a rival. His reconciliation with Florence, moreover, wasn't working out—arguments were frequent, and unpleasant. Cathy Boudreau, who had apparently paid little heed to her husband's long visits to Florence Mann during the winter and spring, finally noticed their mutual attraction while dining at a nightclub in Monte Carlo. Richler broke the news to her soon afterwards. "It's over," he said. "I don't love you any more. It's time to end it." Stunned, Cathy fled to Villefranche, though not before travelling with him to the airport in Nice to meet Ted Kotcheff. "We're getting a divorce," she told him. For a while she taught swimming lessons at a nearby children's camp for Americans, where, by her account, she had a nervous breakdown.

Stanley Mann took the news better, and returned to London on his own. Alone now with Ted Kotcheff in the villa for a few days, Mordecai and Florence began their love affair. Discretion remained the rule—Kotcheff heard his friend cross the hallway at night and slip into her room. It was during this heightened time that Florence and then Kotcheff read a rough draft of the new novel. Kotcheff declared on the spot that it was the best book ever written by a Canadian, vowing that he would make it into a film. Florence also expressed her delight. But she had suggestions, marking the beginning of her role as his first and most trusted editor.

Friends and lovers say such things about each other's work, of course, and the three of them must have been high from the drama, the vivid sense that their adult lives were about to take unforeseen shapes. But clearly there was something different about this manuscript. Once Kotcheff had left for a holiday in Spain and Florence had flown back to England with Daniel,

Richler wrote to Bill Weintraub with the "largely depressing and
painfully personal news" of the separation and impending divorce,
along with assurances that he was supporting Cathy financially.
"There was no real incident, so to speak," he said. "Probably it's
simply that we've both been unhappy for a long time. . . . God
knows she's a fine girl, and I wish her well (I hope that doesn't
sound fatuous), but we could no longer make it honestly together."
Only at summer's end would he provide the other news. "Florence
and Stanley are getting a divorce, I thk," he wrote.

The July 25 letter about the separation itemized what was so
unique about the new book. "I'm alone in the villa now and working very hard indeed on my new novel. Its tentative title is THE
APPRENTICESHIP OF DUDDY KRAVITZ and I hope it turns out
well." Notably subdued, compared to the braggadocio expressed
about earlier novels-in-progress, this first mention of the book
that would establish his standing was followed a month later by
an equally tentative remark. "It's not a comic novel," he wrote of
the now completed draft, "tho—I hope—there are 'comic' sections in it and it is a lot funnier than anything I've attempted
before. Am very worried abt it, anyway." The worry was revealing. Earlier in the year Richler had written to Weintraub about
his *Maclean's* piece on the travails of the first-time novelist. The
piece had opened with the quip, familiar to his friends, about his
father assuming *The Acrobats* to be about a circus. Such whimsy
had compelled the new head of Putnam's in New York to ask him
to write a funny novel. "I had no idea," the editor apparently said,
"that you had a sense of humour." Diana Athill had already made
a similar request. Richler was no teller of jokes, then or ever, but
he had more than a very good sense of humour. His letters over
the years had indicated a satirist's eye for excesses and outrages
and an absurdist's taste for silly human behaviour. Happily, he
followed the advice for once and wrote about Montreal—about a
rough-hewn kid from the Jewish neighbourhood, a real *macher*,
doing whatever he needed to make his way.

So much changed so abruptly and permanently for him, starting that spring and summer of 1958. He was finally earning real

money practising his craft. He had ended a marriage he probably shouldn't have agreed to in the first instance, and won the
heart of the woman he not only loved—loved in a way he could
not conceive of loving Cathy Boudreau—but wished to start a
family with. Above all else, by allowing funny into his new book,
by acknowledging, at long last, that he could be a serious novelist and still express the sardonic, wry, tender, savage sensibility
that had lain dormant, he found his voice. At twenty-seven, he
had found the love of his life and his literary voice more or less
simultaneously. This was more than luck, talent and timing
mixed together. This was dogged persistence, never saying quit.
The apprenticeship of Mordecai Richler, in print and in life, was
complete.

Ibiza, ". . . the Upper Town and its surrounding wall, built in the sixteenth century, soaring above the natural harbour. . . . Stepping down the gangplank of the *Jaime II* early one evening in 1952, an exhilarated twenty-one-year-old Joshua Shapiro was immediately hailed by a man who was to become his mentor on the island. . . . He booked him into the small, flaking hotel on the quay and propelled him into the bar for a glass of Fundador." From *Joshua Then and Now*.

A time of sunshine and girls on the French Riviera. Photograph taken by Helen—or Ulla—and proudly sent to his older brother.

"Mordy knows everybody on the island and is considered both a character and a respected citizen." Letter from William Weintraub who had joined his friend in his "little haven of luxuriance and lechery" in Ibiza, 1951.

Mordecai writing in a favourite café, Le Mabillon, St. Germain des Prés.
"I was only a callow kid of nineteen when I arrived in Paris in 1951, and so it was,
in the truest sense, my university. St. Germain des Prés was my campus,
Montparnasse my frat house, and my two years there are a sweetness I retain, as
others do wistful memories of McGill or Oxford." From "A Sense of the Ridiculous,"
Shovelling Trouble.

On the eve of returning to Canada after
nearly two years in Europe, Richler wrote:
"I have absolutely no prospects. . . . My
father will pay me $25 a week to answer
the phone in his office and tease me
about becoming a writer." Letter to
William Weintraub from Cambridge,
where he was visiting E.M. Forster,
August 1952.

The Young Author: in 1953, just before leaving England, Richler was asked to provide publicity shots for his forthcoming book. He sent several choices to his editor, Diana Athill, at the publishing house of André Deutsch: "Please note that THE YOUNG AUTHOR is shown in various moods. . . ." Here we have "Young Author Having a Smoke (Player's Mild)."

Diana Athill: "I liked him at once. . . . He was a rather louche young man. One felt that when he talked, it was because he had something to say—he was very intelligent. What he said about writing, other people's writing, you took seriously. But [he had] absolutely no small talk, and he didn't see why he should. If he had something to say, he said it, and if not he sat quietly. . . . I don't think I ever did much editing of Mordecai, certainly not later on. It would be very minor stuff. He was a born writer. He was finding his way to doing it, but that's what he was. He was very observant and very, very funny. And he has never changed. This was the really great thing about Mordecai. Mordecai was Mordecai, and he went on being that way all his life. He became more able to make small talk if he had to, he relaxed in that way, but his attitudes were the same, his honesty was the same, his ribaldry was the same, his seriousness was the same. . . . The fact that he became really a famous figure made no difference at all."

Richler in the flat he and Cathy shared at 509 King's Road, in the area known as World's End, the "wrong end of the Kings Road," forty years before he and Florence bought a flat off Sloane's Square, the "right end."

"I'm using my mss [manuscripts] to build fires because you can't buy coal in quantities of less than 1 lb and that's too much of an investment—o well, tomorrow is Saturday EATING DAY." Letter to William Weintraub, October 1953.

"We were all, as Hemingway once said, at the right age. Everybody was talented. Special. Nobody had money." From "A Sense of the Ridiculous," *Shovelling Trouble*.

"I'm going to get married in London . . . Aug. 20, or so. The girl is French-Canadian, and my family—a sternly orthodox bunch—are taking it pretty hard. I've been cut off, in fact. Right off." Letter to Robert Weaver, July 1954.

Richler's unusual wedding crowd. Among them, front row: Cathy and Mordecai, centre left; beside Mordecai, in a flowered dress, his agent Joyce Weiner. Kneeling: writers Brian Moore on the left and George Lamming on the far right, next to his wife, Nina. Back row: literary lion E.M. Forster, far left; nearby, at the back, David Pitt, the civil rights activist and first black English MP; playwright Ted Allan, centre right, to the left of his wife, Kate, in a patterned dress.

APRIL 1953 20 CENTS

Chatelaine

FOR THE CANADIAN WOMAN

The Queen looks West
—by Hector Bolitho

How to tell love
from springtime

There ought to be
a school for Frances

Your own

SCHOOL OF BEAUTY

Pages 27 to 31

Florence Mann, 23, on the cover of *Chatelaine*, April 1953, the year before she met Mordecai on the eve of his wedding to Cathy Boudreau.
"There stood the most enchanting woman I had ever seen. Long hair black as a raven's wing, striking blue eyes, ivory skin, slender, wearing a layered blue chiffon cocktail dress, and moving about with the most astonishing grace. Oh, that face of incomparable beauty. Those bare shoulders. My heart ached at the sight of her."
Barney Panofsky on meeting Miriam at his wedding to the Second Mrs. Panofsky, *Barney's Version.*

"Mordecai's social presence was laconic, a bit savage and absolutely, in terms that he wanted you to recognize, realistic. . . . What struck me was that he was my own neighbourhood version of the expatriate, powerful transatlantic writer, and his youthful appearance, which resembled that of James Dean, was all in favour of this." Tim O'Brien, the set designer for *The Trouble with Benny*.

Good friends in Montreal, Brian Moore (left) with William Weintraub, over Christmas 1958. Belfast-born Moore was then writing his Montreal novel, *The Luck of Ginger Coffey*, while Richler finished his Montreal novel, *The Apprenticeship of Duddy Kravitz*, in London.

PART III

HORSEMAN

I

I'LL SHOW YOU THE WORLD

St. Urbain Street, 1947. Mr. MacPherson, history teacher at FFHS (Fletcher's Field High School), is trundling through snow towards another day with the boys of classroom 41. It is "the toughest class in the school," not least because of its president and chief provocateur, Duddy Kravitz. Twenty years on the job have left MacPherson a heavy drinker, disappointed with his life and burdened by a chronically ill wife. His one consolation is that he has yet to strap a student. But a scant few weeks, and ten pages later, the drunken, grief-stricken teacher is strapping fifteen-year-old Duddy ten times on each hand and accusing him of having killed his wife with a late-night prank phone call. Lately he has also joined with fellow Anglo-Saxon faculty in lashing out at the student population in racial terms. For this, he gets taunted as a "nazi fascist!"

When not harassing Mr. MacPherson, Duddy is pulling pranks like dropping by the mission on St. Joseph Boulevard, the one with the neon sign proclaiming JESUS SAVES in English and Yiddish, and assuring the attendant that he and his friends are interested in finding out how they can become "*goyim,* Christians like." Or he is overseeing an assault on the rabbinical college students at the Lubovitcher Yeshiva. Once, they pin a yeshiva student and offer him the choice of a face washing in snow or licking the grille of the school fence.

But Duddy Kravitz, is also returning home to a dinner of

frankfurters and beans in the cold-water flat he shares with his older brother and father, his mother having died when he was a boy. His father, a taxi driver, can be found holding court most evenings at Eddy's Cigar and Soda, regaling the assembled with a familiar tale about underworld boss Jerry Dingleman, a.k.a. The Boy Wonder, who he claims is a friend. "He's only a St. Urbain Street boy, you know."

The months of frenzied work on *The Apprenticeship of Duddy Kravitz* in Roquebrune and Hampstead were exhilarating and strange, especially since Richler felt the book was almost writing itself. Back in London in the fall, he confessed his nervousness to Bill Weintraub. "The news from here is mostly (on my part) hard work on the novel," he said. "reaching end of 2nd draft, getting longer and longer, and me feeling lousy about it." The reason for his anxiety was the way it was coming into being. "This is the 'easiest' novel I've written (so far). I'm doing far less rewriting, practically no re-arranging, and I'm feeling creepy. Is it good or, more likely, have my critical faculties (for what they're worth) just gone haywire? Well, we'll see soon enough, dammit." And two weeks later: "I bunged in my novel a few days ago," he wrote on November 8, "and, bejesus, the reactions are dandy. 'I laughed out loud. Remarkable, head and shoulder above anything you've done before,' Joyce W. 'Clearly the best thg youve ever done,' Diana Athill. And other fulsome remarks." But he couldn't help wondering if he had taken a wrong turn. "Still feel most uneasy, however, because this is the 'quickest' novel I've ever done, also the longest, 130,000 words. Creepy."

He was typing out his worry and excitement from 5 Winchester Road. Returning from France in late summer, Richler, having agreed to let Cathy take their old flat, stayed with their friends Reuben Ship and Elaine Grand for three weeks. When Cathy relinquished control, he moved back in. He also found a roommate. Ted Kotcheff wasn't only his closest confidant, privy to the great secret about Florence Mann; he was also set to direct his latest TV play, *The Trouble with Benny*. Kotcheff got the bedroom while Richler, since he stayed most nights with Florence, slept on a couch in the living room, also his office. Both rooms had mice and fleas and tarpaper on the ceiling and floor. The apartment had no private toilet. But they revelled in their single male artist lifestyle and bachelor pad. Canadian Club poker buddies, the other players now Ted Allan, Reuben Ship, Alvin Rakoff and, for a brief period, Lorne Greene, in London awaiting his breakout role as Pa Cartwright in the American TV series *Bonanza*, were served the same quality liquor offered to movie executives who dropped by. "Ted Kotcheff and I pride ourselves in keeping the best-stocked bar in Swiss Cottage," he reported to Weintraub in December. "We had a big party here Sat night," he continued, explaining some modest renovations, "and by gum you wouldn't know old No. 5 Winch Rd. There's a nifty partition up in the hall, shutting the flat off, a char comes daily, and two men are putting in a john, my very own john." Along with the toilet came a fridge and television.

Such affluence obliged a new wardrobe as well. Mordecai Richler, formerly of blue jeans only, had lately bought a tux. "Need it for the TV ball," he wrote of an industry gala at the Dorchester Hotel. "Am now wearing it to work. A swell outfit, sir."

Work, in tuxedo or jeans, began at 9 a.m. sharp, every morning, regardless of the previous night's activities. Kotcheff was soon another awed witness to his regime. Over a breakfast of salami and eggs or an omelette, Richler read the *Times* and *Daily Express* for an hour, sipping coffee. Then he brewed a pot of black tea with lemon. Clack, clack, clack, Kotcheff heard on his way out to a day of rehearsals or meetings, a sound that did not cease until noon. For lunch Richler walked to a nearby deli for a sandwich and the *International Herald Tribune*, the only newspaper that printed hockey and baseball scores. Next, he napped. At around two o'clock, he resumed typing, quitting at five. Now he was ready for a gin and tonic, or two, or drinks at a pub. "Rumour is circulating," he told Weintraub, "that Ted Kotch and I are . . . well, buggers. Am doing my best to encourage this one. . . ." When he received his paycheque for *Room at the Top*—the film was newly out, and a success—he cashed it into five-pound notes which he and Kotcheff tossed into the air. He then hid the money in books around the flat, promptly forgetting the locations. A slipped disc in January 1959—"damn painful," he admitted—left him walking with a cane for a while, furthering the image of the odd couple on the third floor. Artists, naturally, and foreigners. Greater Hampstead was thick with them.

A slipped disc could not dampen his high spirits. *The Apprenticeship of Duddy Kravitz* was on its way to Weintraub by registered mail; even with the praise of his London editor and agent, and the near-instantaneous acceptance of the manuscript by Atlantic Press in New York, his first book sale in the United States since *The Acrobats,* he still sought feedback from his oldest critic. He had also lately contributed a second piece to *Maclean's,* a funny memoir about his experiences among the communists and socialists of Montreal, Ibiza, Paris and England. "Confessions of a Fellow Traveller" included early retellings of his entanglements with the Nazi colonel on Ibiza and with Left Bank radicals. Tone and texture, and in particular the rendering of voices, were straight out of *Duddy Kravitz.* Accordingly, the piece marked the print birth of the "real" Mordecai Richler for Canadian readers, an announcement authenticated by still another photo of the author, this time with a raffish air and dangling cigarette. He dropped his monthly column for the *Montrealer,* but made his mother proud with a radio adaptation of the story "Benny, the War in Europe, and Myerson's Daughter Bella."

His second Armchair Theatre collaboration with Kotcheff, *The Trouble with Benny,* now due to be shot in April, was another version of the slim story about the shell-shocked boy returning to St. Urbain Street. He asked Weintraub to take some photos to help the set designer visualize the scenes, requesting shots of a garage, the inside of a cigar and soda store, and the city's outdoor staircases. "Area I had in mind is St. Urbain Street corner Fairmount, Laurier Street from St. Urbain to Jeanne Mance, anything ard [around] there." Weintraub complied, and the sets were duly built in Manchester, where Armchair Theatre was filmed on Sunday evenings, the entire cast and crew taking the train up on

Friday for final rewrites and rehearsals. It was a heavily Canadian crowd, from producer Sydney Newman to director Ted Kotcheff and writer Mordecai Richler, narrator Ted Allan and actress Kate Reid, along with, as he put it in a letter, "many London Jew-boys who will pretend to live on St. Urbain Street."

One member of the cast stood out. Though Florence Mann had only a few lines at the end, written by her lover expressly to involve her in the production, her face featured prominently in advertisements. The *Liverpool Echo*, describing her as a "tall, raven-haired beauty with enormous blue-black eyes fringed with thick black lashes," mentioned that she modelled for Christian Dior in London. "Being an actress would be much more stimulating than being a mannequin," Florence was quoted in what the interviewer heard as a "soft Canadian burr." These weekends were theatrical bliss, with meals in French restaurants and rooms in nice hotels.

Tim O'Brien designed the sets for *The Trouble with Benny*. Along with Verity Lambert, Ted Kotcheff's assistant and girlfriend, O'Brien was soon welcomed into the Canadian Club at Winchester Road. (Lambert was a rare female invited to the poker table.) He was struck equally by the on-set professionalism of the director and writer—the volcanic Kotcheff once chewed Richler out in public for a poorly written scene, without hurt feelings—and by their off-set manners. Richler, who seemed to live on tomatoes and gin, had a James Dean aura and laconic, if occasionally savage, social graces. He and Kotcheff cultivated an air of doing exactly as they pleased. Reviews for his teleplays and radio plays weren't always positive—the *Daily Mail* had called *A Friend of the People* "hackneyed" and "overwritten"—but *The Trouble with Benny* won high praise. "As you know," a producer from the network wrote to him, "we really do want another play from you and the sooner the better." Kotcheff too, no less active in the theatre, would shortly be entertaining offers to direct four films and two plays, more or less at once. It was good to be young, talented and Canadian in London in the late 1950s.

Florence's TV debut had led to a call from an agent who told her
she was a natural comedian. He requested a CV with photos, which
Richler and Kotcheff "helped" assemble with inane captions.
Richler had already asked her to marry him once, in Roquebrune;
now she was about to be more widely known—and admired.
A theatre director who had attended a reading of a Ted Allan play
where Florence had substituted for an ill actor contacted her about
auditioning for his project, set to star the handsome, up-and-coming Alan Bates. When she demurred, citing looking after Daniel as
an impediment, he offered to audition her in her flat. Sensing competition, Richler insisted on being present, ostensibly to babysit
his godson. As he feared, the director offered her a role on the
spot, on condition that she bleach her hair. On emerging from the
bedroom, the potential rival now departed, Richler made his
counter-offer. "I'll show you the world," he said. In his mind, she
could choose a career in acting, which he believed she was too
sensitive to survive, or she could choose him. Once again she
laughed at his audacity—he had no real money, and spent what
he earned almost immediately—and remarked to herself on his
possessiveness and the patriarchal side to his character that
already had him issuing her a kind of ultimatum. But she was in
love, and knew he would respect and cherish her. She accepted.

A few days later they sealed their commitment by volunteering past mistakes, things they were not proud of having done.
One of her tales brought a gleam to his eye. Recognizing the
look from dinners and parties they had both attended, and well
aware of how *A Choice of Enemies* had lifted from real people and
conversations, it occurred to Florence that her lover had just
been transformed into a different creature, watchful and dispas-
sionate. "If I was on a branch and it was breaking," she said to
him, "you'd rather observe me fall, wouldn't you?" He denied it
at first, then conceded. The admission obliged her to spend a
little more time thinking about the consequences of marrying
Mordecai Richler. His wrecking-ball social manners she could
accept; secretly, she admired his willingness to disturb the sed-
entary. Likewise his silences, so like her own father's. She didn't

really know his family yet—he had invited her to tea when his mother was visiting London, and Lily Rosenberg, perhaps playing her own hunch, later mailed a teddy bear for Daniel—but had been told enough to suspect that they too would be a source of greater anxiety than pleasure. But an ongoing scrutiny of her character, possibly for use in future novels, by her own husband? It would not be easy living with this man. But the reflection took only one more night; living with him would also be the opposite of dull.

While not a secret among London friends, the love affair had remained discreet. Even Bill Weintraub had to wait until June to be officially informed. "It's Florence Mann that's keeping me here," Richler finally admitted. "I'm waiting for her divorce to come through so that we can return to Canada together. I don't know whether this surprises you—whether you've heard rumours from returning travellers—but, anyway, that's the way things are. We are in love. And we are going to get married when we can." He broke the news in the same letter in which he commiserated with Weintraub about the dissolution of his marriage to Bernice. Ruminating on marriage in general, he added, "Brian and Jackie [Moore] are about the only couple I know who seem to have a happy marriage. . . . Still, I do not believe all marriages are doomed. . . . And speaking for myself I want and intend to have children."

He wished one thing made clear. "My marriage was finished before I got involved with Florence—she's no 'home-breaker,' as they say—in fact both our marriages were done. In fact I can go further and say I never wanted to marry Cathy in the first place but gradually succumbed." He mentioned this because he didn't want Weintraub or the Moores to "start off with any prejudices against Florence," especially as "we hope to be seeing much of you once we're in America." Unmentioned were the reasons he had pursued Florence for almost four years and won her. Sexual attraction and compatibility played a large part. So did her beauty and refinement, which Richler was not, and never would be, above delighting in and pointing out to others. Highly competitive, aware of the status granted by an attractive companion, in dark-blue-eyed Florence Mann he had a glittering prize. But the deeper reasons were born of her character. Her poise and demeanour, which would lead many to assume she was both British and of a certain class, hid from view an adopted child from Point St. Charles, raised in a working-class home cloistered by a parent's depression. No need for him to explain anything to her about 1930s and '40s Montreal, or growing up poor, or wishing and needing to get out, to establish yourself. No need either to apologize for wanting things from life, including security and success but, above all, the happiness that was apparently bestowed on certain households. Years of watching and wooing Florence had impressed several qualities upon her suitor, and nearly everyone else who met her. Her intellect was more coolly analytical than immediately evident, and her wit sharper. She was strong and independent, if also prone to insecurities, and was attracted to intense emotional friendships. Above all, she was naturally kind-hearted, a person the perceptive Diana Athill called "the most beloved woman" of her acquaintance. No fool, he knew to make straight for kindness, and in his oddly modest way would be forever and genuinely grateful to her for loving him.

Their discretion during those eleven months after Roquebrune had been a legal precaution. "All this is highly confidential—not to go past Brian & Jackie—tho it's probably obvious to many people here for Florence and I are together every night and have been seen together almost everywhere. Still, nothing's been said. Certainly not by us. . . . Nothing must be said because the custody of Daniel must be settled first—and naturally Florence wants the boy." His own divorce was two-thirds complete, with the final court hearing scheduled for the fall, when Cathy promised to be in town. "But my divorce is not nearly as crucial at the moment as Florence's, ie, as soon as she's clear we can start living together."

Getting a divorce in 1950s England was no easy matter. Without a spouse's consent—and Cathy Boudreau was declining to part amicably—seven years had to pass before desertion could be evoked as grounds for dissolving a union. The alternative was to commit adultery, or at least simulate it, and be caught in the act. With a director and writer involved, staging such a farce wasn't hard. Sure enough, in March a detective, previously employed to help Reuben Ship exit his marriage, happened to appear at 5 Winchester Road at the precise moment that one Mordecai Richler, age twenty-eight, lay in bed with a woman in a negligee, not his wife. She was actually Verity Lambert, and her boyfriend, Ted Kotcheff, hid in the new "john," flushing the toilet to cover his laughter, while the private eye grilled the sinners. Richler scripted the scene in hard-boiled dialogue for Weintraub's amusement.

Private Eye arrives to discover me with dame here. I say, sez he, have you been cohabiting regularly?
You bet.
Will you sign this voluntary statement, please?
Damn right.

Still more farcical was the route Florence had to take, even with Stanley Mann's co-operation. A wife divorcing her husband had to forswear physical intimacy for six months. If she was discovered with a man—a squad of sex police, the Queen's Proctors, reserved the right to knock on doors at midnight—the entire proceeding could be cancelled. Unwilling for them to be apart for twenty-four hours, let alone for half a year, Richler engaged Ted Kotcheff as his occasional lookout. When a stranger entered Florence's building one evening, Ted, waiting in his Austin Healey by the curb, issued three honks. Luckily, her flat was on the ground floor, aiding her lover's escape through a window.

The matter of Florence *vs* Stanley Mann was considered in late June in London's legendary Old Bailey courthouse, near St. Paul's Cathedral. She and Stanley nearly scuttled the process by being too friendly with each other at the outset. A clerk scolded them for showing affection, and the Queen's Counsel, a young lawyer named John Mortimer, began asking questions. Again she risked the judge's ire, by declining to pronounce her marriage intolerable. Mortimer frowned at this and thereafter made Florence answer only yes or no to his queries. Afterwards, Richler took her to a restaurant to celebrate the interim decree of divorce. Mortimer, QC, soon to be writer for the popular *Rumpole of the Old Bailey* television show, didn't join them, but he could have; he was, it turned out, already a friend to both.

Richler also found time that spring and summer to buy his first car, importing a Renault Dauphine from Canada for its left-side steering wheel. A nervous Ted Kotcheff gave him driving lessons. "Can drive with some skill now, tho not much," the student reported. While no Austin Healey, a Renault was a vehicle befitting a writer for the big screen. A rewrite under the pseudonym Ephraim Kogan on the thriller *Faces in the Dark* netted £1,500— about six months' wages for an office clerk. That work, for producer Betty Box, led to his being offered the chance to script a movie that Jack Clayton might direct. As promised, Clayton had spread word around London about the job he had done on *Room at the Top*. The fee for *No Love for Johnnie*, which would star Peter Finch, was a staggering £3,500, with an extra £350 per week if the job took longer than ten weeks.

This after accepting £500 from André Deutsch for *Duddy Kravitz*. Already, Richler wanted to pull back from film work, citing the drain on his time; already, he was finding the business too lucrative to dismiss. "The truth is," he wrote of the script, "I do want to knock off after this job—rest—and then get back to my new bk." He was trying to establish a career as a literary novelist while orchestrating and advancing an almost parallel career in TV and film. It was a precarious balance, one that would soon begin tipping, especially once he became a father and homeowner. Unsurprisingly, the imbalance would not favour the fiction.

But during this manic, happy period he could do it all. The rest of the novel had told itself with the same ease as those first chapters. Duddy progresses from St. Urbain Street kid to waiter at a resort in Ste. Agathe, where he befriends the in-house comedian, the chubby Cuckoo Kaplan, and suffers the ridicule of elite college Jews. There, in the Laurentians landscape of Richler's childhood, he discovers a forbidden lake he resolves to secretly buy and develop. His adult apprenticeship as bar mitzvah movie producer and land developer, among other schemes, is rendered with narrative energy and bare-knuckled prose, and his capacity to hustle and rudely charm is vividly drawn. Though Duddy is edgy and angry, he is no existential anti-hero, no André Bennett of *The Acrobats* or Noah Adler of *Son of a Smaller Hero.* Evidence of the old haste lingers in awkward phrasings and word repetitions, and the early focus on the plight of Mr. MacPherson, who disappears for good after his collapse, betrays the novel's origins as a short story. But otherwise *Duddy Kravitz* announced in uppercase lettering a writer who had found his subject and knew it.

"I DO intend to make St. Urbain my Yokaappppp . . . County," he informed Weintraub. Citing the fictional Mississippi county, Yoknapatawpha, where William Faulkner set his major novels, amounted to a declaration that a single landscape and group of characters would be a life's project. Faulkner had situated a dozen books so far in his county. Richler planned at least three in his urban village. "The next one," he had already explained to Brian Moore, "tentatively titled DUDDY KANE'S FIRST MARRIAGE I hope is only a few years off. . . . DUDDY, too, is the springboard for a whole clutch of novels, big and small, about St. Urbain Street alumni." His overall plan was Faulknerian. "I'm staking out a claim on Montreal Jew-ville in the tradition of H. de Balzac and Big Bill Faulkner." The final volume, he blithely figured in 1959, would be in about ten or fifteen years.

Duddy Kravitz is his first great character, and the boy's unresolved personality, in particular his disarming mix of ruthlessness and cunning—qualities of the *pusherke,* or "pushy Jew" figure—with tenderness and decency, provided a template for a dozen roaring creations to come. Richler's refusal to smooth out Duddy's jagged edges was in keeping with his maturing understanding of the human beings he found most engaging and worthy of attention. "The moral idea behind Duddy," he wrote to Brian Moore, "was to get inside, and show how sympathetic in

many ways, the go-getter, the guy nobody has time for . . . really
is." Duddy's personality was also in keeping with his own complex self, and the high value he accorded energy and exuberance.
Gone was his earnest belief that to examine values—how a man
might live with dignity—obliged sombre direct engagement with
"important" issues, worldly and freighted. Now he was willing to
allow a Jewish kid's efforts to make his mark in provincial
Montreal to shoulder his thematic interests. He stopped worrying about being relevant and started allowing the story, along
with the language that came so naturally to him, to relay his
preoccupations.

The nine-page script "Happy Bar-Mitzvah, Bernie!" embedded
in the novel was more than a sly nod to his recent adventures in
the movie trade. The avant-garde movie produced by Duddy and
directed by the alcoholic Englishman Peter John Friar was also
the funniest set piece he had written, a phantasmagoria containing something to offend everyone. Montages of African tribal
dancers, including the "circumcision rite of the Zulus," give way
to diving Stuka fighter planes and VD warnings in public urinals.
Panning shots of tables laden with garish gifts for the bar mitzvah boy dissolve into references to Al Jolson singing "Eli, Eli"
and Shylock asking if a Jew hath not eyes. Alongside mentions
of Abraham, Isaac, Jacob and Leon Trotsky is a promotion for
Rabbi Goldstone's book *Why I'm Glad to Be a Jew*, signed by the
author. Wild, outrageous satire, done to both skewer and provoke, would soon be the staple of Richler's arsenal. "Happy Bar-
Mitzvah, Bernie!" brims with gleeful disrespect.

The bar mitzvah scene was one of several additions made at
the suggestion of the manuscript's first reader, back in the villa
in Roquebrune. Florence Mann, knowing both the world where
Duddy Kravitz lived and how vividly her new lover could render
it, recommended that he flesh out the story with the people and
city surrounding his characters. Some of the best writing in the
book resulted from his heeding her advice.

"For Florence," reads the dedication page of *The Apprenticeship
of Duddy Kravitz*. She was flattered and pleased; Cathy Boudreau

was not. Tipped off by a mutual friend, Cathy turned up at the Winchester Road flat one day in September, shortly after copies of the American edition of the novel arrived. Richler wasn't home, leaving Ted Kotcheff to negotiate her rage. Cathy began ripping pages and then, more eloquently, pitched his Olivetti Studio 44 typewriter out a window. (It landed in a bush, and survived.) Kotcheff begged her to stop—she was aiming to destroy all the books—before finally slapping her on the cheek. Cathy collapsed to the floor, sobbing. While the fuller dedication that Richler handwrote in the copy he gave to Florence would not have assuaged Cathy's sense of having been wronged—had she seen it—it might have explained, in part, why he was about to marry and raise a family with this new partner.

From Mordecai with all my love, all the descriptive passages in this book, the march, the bar-mitzvah film, commencement, etc, all of these because you asked for them after you read the part about Mr MacPherson, and the book is certainly better for it.

Mordecai.

II

MONTREAL METEOR

The reviews couldn't have been better. "I don't think there is a false line," said the Toronto *Telegram*, "a blurred image or a contrived motivation in the whole book." Hedging his bets a little, the reviewer predicted, "When Mr. Richler has rubbed off the rough edges of his prose he is probably going to be the best writer in Canada." The *Globe and Mail* saw no need to wait: "It is time to shake the moth balls from the red carpet and roll it out for a young Canadian author who, after three false starts, has now proved himself a mature and brilliant writer." In Montreal, the Toronto *Star* declared with satisfaction that Richler was "the first of Canada's Angry Young Men," while the *New York Times* said it was "sometimes hilariously funny, sometimes brutally pathetic and often unnecessarily vulgar." But for its "revved-up" story and "brash and blatant" effect, *The Apprenticeship of Duddy Kravitz* merited its creator a headline more the preserve of hockey players—the "Montreal Meteor."

Media attention in Canada was heightened by two excerpts in *Maclean's* magazine. Back in January the editor, Leslie Hannon, had offered a striking $1,000 per excerpt, each one to run at a no-less-impressive 10,000 words. Thanking Hannon for deciding to include the bar mitzvah movie script intact, Richler wrote, "I am really very grateful indeed that you have left in so much that to a large audience might seem objectionable, too strong, or what have you." Not to be outdone as a suitor, Robert Weaver contracted him to write a new story for CBC radio, also at a $1,000 rate. That led Kildare Dobbs to remark on the injustices of pay scales: "As for good old Weaver . . . he bought a story from me for $150—yrs fetches $1000." Between *Maclean's* and the CBC, Armchair Theatre and Box Productions—Betty Box's company, behind the *No Love for Johnnie* script—Richler was beginning to appreciate the extent to which his own worth could be self-determined: demand a high fee for your services and your services become more valued. He explained the economic principle of setting the bar high to Bill Weintraub: "Why not?"

In Britain, the reception for *Duddy Kravitz* was equally enthusiastic. Penelope Mortimer strongly recommended it in an early review. The wife of barrister John, she was herself a novelist of repute—her upcoming book, *The Pumpkin Eater,* would set her among the best of British writers. In tandem, the Mortimers belonged to a club that even someone as talented as Mordecai Richler might never be invited to join: the country's literary elite, often of Oxbridge pedigree. For her to call the novel "quite masterly" and of "great originality and considerable stature" was to open, if only partially, the door to that club. "It looks like DUDDY will, well, 'establish' me here—if not in the States," he noted to Weintraub in early November.

The U.S. market was the greater challenge. He knew this, but also believed he had the right book, and was the right author, for the times. To this end he had been encouraging his American editor, Sam Lawrence, to send out advance copies of *Duddy Kravitz* to what he called "all JEW-BOY litmen." These were the east coast critics and intellectuals then doing as much to define the direction of American literature as the novelists, many likewise Jewish, they were championing. The rise of lit crit, as the largely New York movement was being dubbed, with its bestselling books and media-savvy exponents, reflected the centrality of literature in mid-century American cultural life. The literary novel in particular was ascendant. What Irving Howe, Philip Rahv, Norman Podhoretz, Leslie Fiedler and Dwight Macdonald said about a novel or writer in magazines like *Commentary* and

Partisan Review, or on the regular radio and television slots available for such discussions, made a difference. Any positive thoughts from Lionel Trilling, Edmund Wilson or Alfred Kazin, authors, respectively, of *The Liberal Imagination*, *Axel's Castle* and *On Native Grounds,* could ignite a career.

Alfred Kazin, as it happened, was a reader for Atlantic Press, and his high praise of the manuscript had encouraged Sam Lawrence to buy it. In the maverick Kazin, Richler had a natural ally. Kazin himself had been just twenty-seven when he published *On Native Grounds*, and was a four-time Guggenheim award recipient whose apostate Judaism was to remain his lifelong preoccupation. In a note to its author, Kazin praised *Duddy Kravitz* as strong and true. The critic was moved by the novel and empathized with Richler's complaint—expressed in his own covering letter—about having to swallow accusations of being an anti-Semitic Jew. "It's tough, really tough," Kazin wrote, "when you have a subject like yours," and invited him to visit him in his Riverside Drive apartment next time he was in New York.

Richler wasn't seeking contacts of Kazin's stature for such career advancements alone. The near-simultaneous publication of *The Apprenticeship of Duddy Kravitz* in Canada, the United States and the U.K. raised the question for him of *his* literary native ground. With a novel set in distant Canada but indebted, stylistically, to the kitchen-sink realism of books like *Room at the Top*, he had, by his admission, staked himself on English soil. *Duddy Kravitz* was turning him into something of a prodigy back in Canada. And yet, as he had told *Tamarack Review*, as a writer he felt himself to be of the American earth. Though he would make similar efforts to connect with English Jewish novelists, it was to the United States that he looked for fellow travellers. The size and prestige of the American market, while of enormous importance to him, wasn't the issue.

Like many diaspora Jews, he knew that the smallest of actions had made him the citizen of one country rather than another. In his case, the trade his grandfather had made en route from Poland to North America more than a half-century earlier, a train ticket to Chicago for a train ticket to Montreal, had been the difference. That ticket alone separated Richler from the literary sons of Jewish immigrants raised in Chicago, like Saul Bellow, or in New Jersey, like Philip Roth. Certainly the stories they wished to tell— not the standard immigrant tale, but rather a new narrative of striving and self-defining, pushing for space and stature in the New World—were closer to his instincts than anything published in Canada or England. Just as important, their sensibilities were akin to his own. And yet he was simultaneously thriving in literary England and deliberately laying claim to a patch of Montreal. Could he really function as a spiritually Jewish-American Canadian novelist working out of London? Could his work fit within three different traditions? He needed to sort out the complex business of where he belonged.

But America resisted the charms of *Duddy Kravitz*. "In America, I take it, the book has fallen flat," he told Brian Moore. "That's bloody disappointing. I do thk it's a good book—and that it deserved better, and I hope this doesn't sour Atlantic on me."

The U.S. reception aside, the excellent year of 1959 continued. "I've got one lousy hangover," he confessed to Moore. "Last night Ted Kotch did an Angus Wilson play and Angus, his lad, Florence, me, Jack Clayton, Flora, all gathered to watch at Florence's flat. And then Ted arrived with the players and we had a huge and drunken midnight dinner." More celebrations followed a month later when he and Florence celebrated her final decree of divorce—his own would be granted in January—with a five-day holiday in Paris. "Our watering spots—a very far cry from pre-film days—included Laperouse, Maxim's, le Berkeley, la Méditerranée, and other four-star restaurants," he noted proudly. The trip initiated a tradition: regular short visits to the city they both loved, no expenses spared—showing her a little of the world.

Taking time out from London seemed a smart move. "Cathy arrives from Madrid in a few days to check in at the divorce courts," Richler told Weintraub. "May she do well. Haven't seen her in months and months." Several letters hinted at the disapproval, emanating from both his ex-partner and certain mutual friends, which had positioned a small cloud over the otherwise sunny new couple. So a period in Italy—"away from film-land, by God"—suited the fugitive lovers. "We're off to Rome on Nov 25, in our salmon-red Dauphine, and stopping at all the four-star inns en route, for a three-month stay." He invited the now single Weintraub to join them for Christmas. "Seats on the forty-yard line at St. Pete's," he promised, of Mass at St. Peter's Basilica. "Assignations with Wop starlets in the Coliseum. . . . Come on over, man." Even if his friend couldn't get there, Richler would be seeing him soon enough. In Rome he would be completing "a first draft of my new short novel. . . . AFTERWARDS, we will definitely go Canada-wards. Writing-wise it's wise." Promises of repatriating to Canada were already semi-annual occurrences, and Weintraub likely paid them little heed. But the fact that Florence Mann, soon to be Florence Richler—by the new year they would telling friends of their intention to get married in the summer—was herself a Montrealer fuelled his optimism.

Daniel Mann, now a lively two-year-old, stayed with his au pair for the Paris holiday, but he joined them in the Renault for the ride to Italy while the girl went on to Rome directly. The drive along the Rhine and through the Alps was an adventure in itself, with snowstorms and mechanical failures to contend with, as well as an inn filled with former soldiers singing Nazi songs in a private room. "Stalling, skidding, in a blizzard at 5,000 ft in the Brenner Pass" partially described the ordeal, all done with a small child in his mother's lap. They stopped briefly in Germany to visit his publisher, but having translated *The Acrobats* and *A Choice of Enemies*, Kindler Verlag declined to publish *Duddy Kravitz*, worried it might fuel German anti-Semitism.

Their Italian address, 3 Via Biferno, was spacious and comfortable, with a garden and an orange tree. Only two blocks from Rome's largest park, the Villa Ada, and less than two miles from St. Peter's Square, the neighbourhood was handy for walking, and for looking after a toddler. Ted Kotcheff, forced to take a break from his own manic schedule after spending a week in hospital—he had driven his Austin Healey into an oil truck in the fog, injuring himself and a passenger—flew down to convalesce. A trained musician, Ted brought along his violin, playing for hours in the extra bedroom while the au pair swooned over him outside the door. His presence, along with his deepening friendship with Florence, absolved Richler of having to shorten his ritual work-days to sightsee with her. From the start, her appetite for reading, art and music would be the match of his for work. From the start, too, it was understood that the best solution would be a compan-ion for Florence, to spare his routine any disruptions. Evenings could then be spent together, enjoying the mild winter.

Richler wasn't especially taken with the Eternal City. "Rome, at first glance, is not the most," he informed Weintraub in early January, complaining of a surfeit of pasta and veal in restaurants and grocery shops. But work was going fine. "Am working on 2nd draft of the SHALINSKY novel," he told Diana Athill, "and it's fun." He was also writing the TV play of *Duddy Kravitz* and making over-tures to New York agents, capitalizing on the great reviews—if not sales—of the novel in the United States. Sterling Lord, head of the Sterling Lord Agency, expressed interest, but wondered if Richler had spoken yet to Joyce Weiner about cutting her out of America. Richler would be sending both Weiner and Diana Athill a draft of "the Shalinsky novel" in early March. It was short: 35,000 words only, a quarter the length of its predecessor.

Barely a week later, however, he was already plotting another relocation, this time a long, possibly permanent return to Canada. Florence's pregnancy had helped them make the deci-sion. They wanted to get married, and have their child, in Montreal. "We're definitely coming to Canada on March 15," he told Weintraub, "probably flying, as there are no ships to Montreal until late April, and nothing from a Mediterranean port until May." Luckily, he had the capacity to write anywhere, anytime—and he had allies. Jackie Moore made inquiries regarding doc-tors and hospitals for Florence's delivery. In Bill Weintraub, he had the other key to his success: a loyal Montreal-side lieuten-ant. "I have lots of favours to ask," he warned his friend, a now familiar refrain. Closer to their arrival date—March 18 on BOAC,

after a three-day stopover back in London—with Weintraub putting the new arrivals up their first week in Montreal, those
favours became quite detailed: "Have some milk in the house for
Daniel" and "some booze for yours truly."

The letter touched on another regular theme: Weintraub helping "manage" Lily Rosenberg for her son. "Mummy doesn't know
we are expecting a child," Richler wrote. "In fact, nobody knows
but you and the Moores. We will NOT stay with Mummy on
arrival—altogether too trying."

Withholding information about the pregnancy, avoiding staying with her, spoke to his complicated and largely unexamined
relationship with his mother. Lily remained a voluminous correspondent, her letters finding him wherever he wandered, full
of minutiae about her evenings as a rooming-house owner and
days behind the counter of a children's toy store in West End
Montreal, along with details about Rosenberg family goings-on.
Usually fraught, the letters arrived several times weekly. Typical
of their tone was the way she shared her latest medical news.

> Muttkele lechtigs . . . yesterday I was to see Dr. Ballon for a
> check up on my breasts, I did not want to write you that the
> left breast was giving me some pain, I was not worried, but I
> hated the thought of the hospital, still, I knew not to go for a
> check up was ridiculous, all is well thank God, Dr. Ballon says
> there are certain changes in both breasts, but not the kind to
> worry about.

Getting her son to worry about her more, not less, seemed the
underlying purpose of the anecdote.

Though he replied to most of her letters, his own chatty and
full of news, the volume was so overwhelming that a few of her
envelopes, quickly supplanted by others, stayed forever unopened.
She remained a singular woman, her passion for music and literature genuine and her intelligence unmistakable. She was also
joyless, irascible and sharp, unable to get along with people,
appearing curiously disconnected. Now in her fifties, estranged

from most of her siblings and extended family and at odds with her older son, Lily was alone and lonely.

Her one claim to eminence was her younger boy. In Jewish Montreal the name "Lily Richler" still summoned memories of the legendary rabbi whose daughter had married into the junk-dealing clan and then threw her husband out to have an affair with a boarder. It also now meant the mother of the notorious writer. She heard from customers and acquaintances when Mordecai slighted Jews or published something dirty. She heard as well when a radio drama about St. Urbain Street, or a funny magazine piece about a high school that had to be Baron Byng, pleased and flattered those very same Montrealers. One way or another, Lily Rosenberg's younger son was a big deal, and she was finding pleasure in living in his reflected light. In April 1959 Avrum Richler described her response to Mordecai's delay in returning to Canada. "Mother is very disappointed, and for a while I thought she would be ill for the disappointment." He kept his observations about Lily's fixation on his brother general. "You don't know how difficult it is with her," he said. "Or maybe you DO know."

By then a fresh portrait of Lily Rosenberg, not sketched by her son, was in print. In December 1957 Norman Levine was far along on the journey that would produce *Canada Made Me*, his striking, dyspeptic portrait of a somnambulant nation. Levine was passing through Montreal to Ottawa, and Richler had written ahead to Lily to introduce his writerly friend. Late on a snowy November night he showed up at a "narrow wooden house, high, undecorated," on a secluded dead-end street that served as a "no man's land" between the wealth of Westmount and the slums of St. Henri south of the railway tracks. "Mrs R," Norman Levine wrote, "was a small Jewish woman with a harsh nasal voice. She reminded me of a small bright bird: a sparrow." When talking, which she did at length, she appeared confident. "It was only when she was a listener that one noticed the vulnerability: the melancholy look in the eyes, the clumsiness of her generous gesture." A strange scene unfolded, with tenants stopping by the kitchen to chat, including a grumpy Latvian who had lived there for ten years and

whom she called, jokingly, "my boy friend." Another occupant
was a German girl, resident for two years, described by her land-
lady as unemployed, broken, anti-Semitic and recently the
mother of an illegitimate child. Mrs. R "told me of her operations," Levine wrote, "showed me the gallstones kept in a small
glass jar; that she used to work in a nightclub but was now
working in a respectable store 'for a couple of gangsters.'" Once
Lily had reserved four rooms for her own private space; now
she lived in the front room only. She kept it locked.

The letters of Moses Richler, in contrast, reveal a genial, somewhat simpering man. The volatility of the father-son exchanges
throughout the 1950s had been tempered of late. The elder Richler
wrote weekly letters about scrapyard business and family affairs,
his wife, Sarah, his stepsons, his own increasingly precarious
health. His son, never complaining of having to repeat information, replied note for note, often line by line. "Yes, I noticed all
your notations in magazines," he wrote from Rome of the package of Canadian magazines that Moses had sent. "That's just swell
abt you winning the turkey, thank God it was a kosher one." He
commiserated with his parent about his upcoming birthday.
"Hell, how old are you anyway? I guess I'll always go thking of
you as in your early forties . . . but you must be 55 now easy. God,
you've got a son who's 33, and I'll be 29 in a couple of weeks.
Goddamit, it goes quickly, doesn't it?" He also broached a concern he had revisited with his mother too. "What, exactly, is ailing
Av?" he asked. "Has he really got ulcers? Is he very unhappy?"

He had seen his brother only a few times since returning to
Europe in 1953, and exchanged infrequent letters. Avrum had a
busy Montreal optometry practice and a wife and two sons. He
also continued to struggle with a gambling addiction and an
equal, if not actually greater, estrangement from his Richler/
Rosenberg clans. As far as Mordecai knew, courtesy of Lily's
vehement letters on the subject, Avrum's difficulties had caused
him to borrow money from his parents to settle his debts. Not
seeking to confirm the allegations with him, Richler accepted her
version of events, never suspecting she might be exaggerating

Avrum's behaviour. But that is what Lily appeared to do, starting in the late 1950s, in a campaign, its rationale obscure, to drive a wedge between the brothers, predicated on her confidence that they wouldn't sit down together and sort out fact from fiction, and that her younger son, especially, built from the same solid brick of quick judgment and lasting enmity as herself, would hold his grudge. Sadly, her dark instincts were sound. "I would like to say I'm pleased Avrum is buying a house," Richler wrote to his father in 1961, "but, actually, I think it's scandalous. He owes you, my mother, uncles, cousins, and God knows how many others. . . . I have three children. I don't drive a big car. Neither can I afford a house. Yet I send money both to my mother and yourself. I'd be lying if I said I wasn't resentful."

Rome had been a pre-wedding honeymoon for Mordecai and Florence. After their arrival in Montreal, the rest of the spring and into the summer of 1960 had the same air of an extended holiday—albeit of the usual seven-day workweek variety. They stayed first with Bill Weintraub before settling into a furnished sublet in Snowdon, "over the mountain" from Westmount and "where all my rich uncles live . . . and are they impressed," he joked to Diana Athill. In late April they drove down to New York, where Richler connected with various magazine editors and literary mentors, including Alfred Kazin, who was smitten by Florence. "Best to your exhilaratingly beautiful wife," he would write afterwards. Richler took her to meet the Moores as well, first in their apartment in Manhattan and then to their rented beach house in Amagansett on Long Island. Brian Moore had received a Guggenheim, then valued at $5,500, and was happily relocated to the United States. Richler had similar hopes. "Alfred Kazin, Granville Hicks, Walter Allen, Hugh MacLennan, B. Moore, the Pres. of U. of Toronto, etc, have all agreed to recommend me for a Guggenheim," he reported in June. "Am applying under the Canadian quota, and so my chances are not bad, I think." Penelope Mortimer would later be added to his list.

In New York, introducing Florence to his beloved Uncle Israel and Aunt Vera was a priority, and the four of them went to dinner at Moskowitz & Lupowitz, a Romanian-Jewish restaurant on 2nd Avenue that had hosted Milton Berle, Sid Caesar and Eddie Cantor in its heyday. "How did you manage to catch him?" Uncle Israel asked Florence, chewing on a cigar. He and Vera had lost their Clinton Street theatre a few years before, a victim of the slow extinction of Yiddish culture in America, and now were reduced to performing at banquets. Richler also met the agent Monica McCall. "My American agent, Monica McCall, seems very good," he reported afterwards to his British editor, Diana Athill. His British agent, no surprise, wasn't pleased. "I do not for one moment agree with your reasoning," Joyce Weiner wrote of his decision to seek separate American representation, "and I reserve my judgement about its validity."

By the time Richler wrote to Diana Athill on June 29, he was in Montreal awaiting the arrival of "a little visitor, as they say, come Aug 1st." The couple were now settled into the city. "I do miss you and so many of our other London friends," he said "but, on the other hand, it is a damn good thing I finally returned here." The stay, he granted, was going to be longer than first envisioned, for the right reasons. His next article for *Maclean's*— "just returned from a wrestling trip with Tiger Tomasso and Hans Schmidt," he reported—wasn't likely of great interest to her. It would, however, contribute to the "amusing, colourful non-fiction book about this cold bland country" he was piecing together. Richler also assured her he was "working on the short stories." To which Diana Athill eventually replied, "We are agog for the Canada book and the St. Urbain Street stories, and are terrified you may feel we don't deserve them." If so, she pleaded with him to "say it soon, anyway, so that we can get it over."

Athill had been working to make up after their first serious disagreement. The "Shalinsky novel," titled *It's Harder to Be Anybody*, had met with categorical rejection from all the key people. "I am rather unhappy with the book," André Deutsch had written back in the spring, "and very much hope that you will agree to put it aside." If published, he declared, it will be sure to "slow down—if not stop altogether—your remarkable progress as a novelist in terms of prestige, and your somewhat slower progress in terms of money." Diana Athill had been more explicit: "The book is a satire," she wrote in a lengthy critique. "A satire on what? On everything in sight. Everyone, you are saying in effect, is stupid and grotesque, Jews and Gentiles alike." A stung Richler had, by his own admission, written Deutsch "a frisky, drunken letter" which he hoped his publisher hadn't taken the wrong way. "Well there, Andre," it began, "next time you want to tell me one of my books is stinky you might take more than a paragraph. You can't be that busy, can you?" By autumn, though, he was deciding that the material belonged "in my book of short stories in a form . . . that will use the best from the original story ['Shalinsky, and the Jewish Problem'] and the attempted novel." The story collection, originally titled *St. Urbain Street*, would now retain the abandoned novel's title, but still be all about "St. Urbain Street people."

Despite the holiday mood of their return to Canada, disappointments dogged Richler that spring and summer. In Rome he had learned that the producers of *No Love for Johnnie*, while calling his script "efficient," were handing the project to another writer—a script doctor—for the proverbial "fresh approach to the subject." It was "unlikely we shall be asking Mr. Richler to do any further work." His newfound affluence was also drawing the attention of the British taxman. "That goddamn cockney assistant of your accountant's is on to me again," an exasperated Ted Kotcheff, who was attempting to sort out his finances back in London, wrote in May. "He seems to think I'm an expert on your financial affairs: he's been on to me once a day ever since he got your papers." Those papers included receipts for income dating back two years and cancelled cheques to various individuals, including Jack Clayton and the plumber who "installed our ritz carlton"—their toilet—on Winchester Road. Kotcheff mentioned a hearing in June, which Richler, being in Canada, could not attend, and added, "Could you please communicate with your accountant how the hell you managed to live in the south of france during the writing of duddy kravitz?"

Those troubles culminated in an audit by Inland Revenue, and a bill for back taxes. But neither financial muddles, movie script woes, nor a failed short novel could dampen his mood on the eve of marriage and childbirth. He insisted that Kotcheff be his best man. "I don't want my kid born a bastard," he told him on the phone. "When are you coming?" Kotcheff had a film to finish shooting, and admitted, "it's a hell of a lot of moolah for four days." Still, "how many best friends does one have and how often does he get hitched to Florence?" he asked before flying over from London.

Getting hitched to Florence was what Mordecai did in Saint James the Apostle United Church, on St. Catherine Street, on July 27. No Richlers or Rosenbergs were invited, and Florence, whose mother had died in 1957, had recently lost her beloved father as well. With no rabbi willing to marry them, a United Church ceremony had to suffice. Weintraub and Kotcheff approached the minister to request certain conditions: citing the bride's late-stage pregnancy, that the ceremony be kept minimal; because the groom was Jewish, that the service avoid all religiosity. Their special pleading merely produced a lengthy service in the church vestibule, including a twenty-minute homily about the unbreakable bonds of marriage. Florence struggled with discomfort, especially in the heat; the fuming groom held his temper, at least until they were pronounced man and wife. Plans for a lobster dinner for husband, wife and best man the following evening were upset when Florence called the doctor to report pains, and was ordered to the hospital. She insisted Mordecai and Ted enjoy the meal without her, and spent the night in labour at Montreal General. Brian Moore's brother, Sean, worked there, and he borrowed a lab coat so that the new husband could visit his wife in the birthing room. Noah was born on July 29, and named after the character in *Son of a Smaller Hero*, with Ted Kotcheff enlisted as godfather. Daniel now had a baby brother, and the Richlers were a family of four.

III

THIS YEAR IN THE SALT MINES

The room was overcrowded and hot, and the mood tense from the start. "Am speaking at two synagogues here," he had joked before the event to André Deutsch. "This ought to help sales, too, but if I am stoned at either one of them I will hold you responsible." The occasion was his first reported public appearance in Canada, and both audience and venue—members of the city's Jewish Public Library in the new Beth Ora Synagogue in the suburb of Ville Saint-Laurent—made for a lively debut.

"Short, with long hair and the look of a sad dog, Mordecai Richler gives the impression of a shy uncommunicative individual," the *Montreal Monitor* noted on July 1, 1960. Luckily for him, he hadn't come alone. "Mr. Richler is married to a charming girl, a former model and Montrealer, whom he met and married in England." Unaware that the wedding was still a month off, and not remarking on her pregnancy, the reporter became the first of many to observe the positive effects of Florence's presence. "He seems quite relaxed with Mrs. Richler, every now and then whispers non-monosyllabic sentences into her ear and frequently smiles at her."

Wearing a yarmulke and reading from a prepared text, Richler launched straight in. Synagogues, he said, had become "religious drug stores," when they ought to be "above expediency and beyond the social pressures of wealth." A recent incident involving a trip to the opening of another temple with his Uncle Max had set him off. "I have seen the richest Jew in town cementing money into the corner of a synagogue," he said, of the practice of putting the names of donors on buildings. "It is hardly fitting for our children to be brought up in such an atmosphere of religion." As for bar mitzvahs, they were being "run like musical comedies," while money from affluent Jews better spent on education was going instead to building campaigns and community centres. His distemper with the materialistic tendencies and complacencies of Reform Judaism soaked through to the increasingly uneasy crowd. Here was the kind of synagogue where "Happy Bar-Mitzvah, Bernie!" had been shot; here were the kinds of North American Jews who left Duddy Kravitz seated on the steps outside with a bewildered old Galician immigrant telling him in Yiddish: "Some circus, isn't it?" About nouveau Judaism Richler had much to say, little of it good.

He took questions. Most constituted wounded attacks on his versions of local history, including his "dark" memories of Ste. Agathe and St. Urbain Street. "Why are you self-conscious about Jewish people living in areas together?" one man asked. "How can we be accepted?" another queried. "Why be accepted?" Richler answered. "You are an angry young man," a woman accused. "Not everybody can be angry." Another wondered why Duddy Kravitz couldn't have been called Tony instead. He didn't need to knock that one down. "Would it make you happier if he was Italian?" a supporter across the room shouted back at her. When the guest speaker did reply, it was mostly in monosyllables, according to the *Montreal Monitor*. Did he consider London his home? ". . . Um . . . a . . . I guess so." Did he enjoy public speaking? "No."

Stoned he was not, but neither was he embraced—nor heard correctly. The reporter admonished him for not being "too clear in his own mind what he wants," citing how he "glances backwards nostalgically at the old synagogue and its aura of mystery today lost, the old bearded rabbi transformed into a clean-shaven regular guy." Some months later, in the aftermath of more inflammatory comments in a *Maclean's* article titled "We Jews are

Almost as Bad as Gentiles" which amplified his complaints in the Beth Ora Synagogue, Richler summarized his sense of his own mind. "Anyone who writes seriously is a moralist. But moralists are critical, and, to a large degree, no-saying. What I know best is my own background and so to some I appear to be only critical of the Jews."

His emerging public image seemed evenly divided between the pleasure-loving and the profoundly moral, the iconoclastic and something rooted, if not in the tenets of Orthodox Judaism, then in the authority of the religion's oldest traditions of guidance and judgment. Audiences and readers, Jewish or otherwise, had a hard time recognizing, and then an even harder time accepting such contradictory impulses. Richler, not seeking their acceptance, driven by confrontation and biting humour, was already pressuring bland good taste and decorum, declaring himself without patience for those who couldn't abide a "Negro whoremonger, a contented adulterer, or a Jew who cheats on his income tax, buys a Jag with his ill-gotten gains, and is all the happier for it." Catapulted into this mood by his return to his hometown, he was also reverting to the mode that Joyce Weiner had scolded him for in the pre–*Duddy Kravitz* days: being overstimulated and reactive, opting to write about the latest thing to get him worked up.

So went his "year in the salt mines," as he described the sixteen-month stay in Montreal and Toronto. "I'm working bloody hard here," he told Diana Athill in October, "and life has been— and still is—hectic." In August the new father reported that baby Noah was "big, healthy, but noisy" and his parents naturally fatigued, a condition made worse by recently hosting both a "slam-bam party" and the "two Teds"—Kotcheff and Allan. "We miss London, and our friends there." And they were struggling with local prices. "Not only is it more pleasant over there," he said, dealing with the reality that his *Maclean's* fees stretched further when translated into sterling, "but it's fantastically expensive over here, goddam it."

Besides provoking Jews, he wrote a rollicking travelogue about the wrestling circuit and a report on a bodybuilding contest, along with a memoir titled "The Harsh Wonderland That Was St. Lawrence Main" for those Canadian-dollar fees. Our Man in London was now Our Man Back in Canada. That was good, as far as generating local controversy and sales went. Editors at the popular women's magazine *Chatelaine* ran a teaser next to an especially louche photo of the author-as-chain-smoker for his memoir "Why I Left Canada." "Eight years ago this well-known Canadian writer fell out of love with Canada and left. Now he returns. . . . And finds he hasn't really changed his mind."

His return did allow him to commence relationships with magazines in the United States and the U.K., first selling them on pieces about Canada. He reappeared in the coveted pages of the *New Statesman* with an essay titled "Canadian Outlook." "I come from a country where only two years ago there were no more than 50 English-language bookshops," it began, ripping into writers who hadn't followed him into exile "because bad taste and nationalism act in their interest." Though he detected "undercurrents of activity that were not there ten years ago," mentioning McClelland & Stewart as the "most intrepid" of the newly established local publishers, he still noticed the "scarcity of talent" and announced that "it is fanciful to talk of Canadian writing." Pieces sent back to London for the equally prestigious *Spectator* would include "Home Is Where Your Heart Aches," and a three-part series on nationalism and the arts in Canada in 1961 called "The Elected Squares." Indefatigable on the subject, Richler also made his longed-for debut in *Commentary* with the lengthy "Their Canada and Mine," a rich, detailed portrait of the old Jewish neighbourhood that touched on nearly every defining experience of his upbringing. "Canada, from the beginning, was second best," he wrote. "It made us nearly Americans." A kind of artistic statement, he would return to it and cannibalize it over and over. To Diana Athill he joked about the impact of finally publishing a piece in *Commentary*. "So I am now, as I told Brian, an in-Jew writer, I guess." Being an "in-Jew writer"—part of that New York intelligentsia-mafia of critics and authors—was important to a young Jewish writer hoping to make it big in America.

"A veritable yeshiva," he called the New York publishing scene, admiring how "Jewish writers seem to call each to each, editing, praising, slamming one another's books, plays, and cultural conference appearances."

Scribbling, scribbling, Richler went into overdrive in Montreal, churning out voluminous quantities. Not all of it pilloried Canada, but enough did to earn him a reputation as a bully, and someone establishing his career internationally by bashing his own country. He was a kind of horseman charging headlong through the culture, mowing down enemies at a gallop. He was also "spying on all the posh Jewish country clubs" in and around Montreal, and going to "Women's Clubs meetings" for *Maclean's*. Ostensibly, this was all towards the non-fiction book about Canada, the one that would twin with his new collection of stories set on St. Urbain Street.

Moses came over to the apartment one afternoon to meet his daughter-in-law and grandson. "Well, she's all right," he said in front of Florence. Then, in an aside to Mordecai: "How does she like being Jewish?" Coaxed into the nursery, he glanced into the bassinet and pronounced, "Babies are babies." Florence, still getting used to her husband's nature, now had his parent's reserve and quirky humour to negotiate as well. As his second shiksa wife in half a dozen years, she also had to deal with the disapproval of his clan. He took her to one family gathering where she watched generations of Richlers line up in front of a very aged, heavy-set woman seated in a chair: his bubbe Esther, now turned eighty-eight, who, though kinder to him than his ear-twisting great-grandmother had been, still believed that her late husband had banished Mordecai from his funeral. Birthing a male child straight away helped Florence's standing; so did the announcement early in 1961 that she was pregnant again, and the fact that Daniel, now four and with a Jewish father, was a bright, engaging boy. Most significantly, her beauty and charm influenced everyone who came into contact with her. In short, Florence was no Cathy Boudreau; she was the One, and her husband tolerated no further discussion about it. As his decision to return to Montreal to be wed and then not invite any of his family to the ceremony demonstrated, he was quite capable of being cut and dried about excluding them from his private life. Relations failed to get this at their peril.

Happily, Moses didn't need to be told to treat Florence as special. She was definitely "all right" as far as he was concerned, and he did not raise any of the thunderous objections to a mixed marriage that had so saddened and bemused his son back in 1955. Mordecai was getting along better with his father than he had since he was a boy. The grown-up child was finding much that was endearing in his parent, and after years of sharing Moses' odd comments and relaying his slant of mind to friends, and making use of those qualities in the character of Max Kravitz, he was discovering him anew.

Florence also now had Lily Rosenberg as a mother-in-law. Lily loved small children, and delighted equally in Noah and Daniel. Picking up his signals about Florence, or simply wishing to be agreeable, she treated her with respect, as she had Cathy. But it didn't take long for the daughter-in-law to remark on *her* odd manner. Unless asked a direct question, which she answered succinctly, Lily Rosenberg rarely engaged in conversation or looked people in the eye. She herself never asked questions or appeared curious about others. Florence remarked how her younger son was still the object of her smothering love—the same obsessive affection she had shown her own father, the late rabbi. But when she tried mentioning it, Richler, long accustomed to Lily's inwardness, was reluctant to discuss her in those terms.

He, in turn, was cool to Avrum during their stay, disapproving of what he understood to be his brother's dishonesty. Uncle Max remained a favourite, and had been the only relation to send a wedding gift (a fondue set). But even gentle, thoughtful Max fell out with him over the *Maclean's* piece, despite recalling Mordecai's embarrassment as a boy that his father had lacked the cash to get his name posted on the synagogue board of donors. Another favourite uncle, Israel, also cooled to him. Bernard, meanwhile, who had mailed cash to Europe, was once more aghast at

Mordecai's decision to intermarry. The varying familial estrangements, exacerbated by mutual feelings of being shunned and hurt, would persist for decades and remain largely unmediated, tensions amplified not only by his writings but by his increasing fame, itself tinged by a notoriety that many Richlers believed brought the clan no honour.

When not interviewing the photographer Yousuf Karsh or spying on Jewish country clubs, he was home with his wife and two small children, or meeting Bill Weintraub and *Gazette* sportswriter Dink Carroll for drinks at the Montreal Press Club. Getting to know Carroll, who had been covering the Canadiens team since he was a boy, was a thrill; even his gruff name evoked a manly sports world of cigars and whisky and fedora hats. But he was not seeking out fellow writers for companionship here in Montreal, such as Irving Layton and Leonard Cohen. Irving Layton, of de Bullion Street, former squire of his relative Suzanne Rosenberg and acolyte of A.M. Klein, was hard to miss. Sensual and attractive, with a huge appetite for life that drove his writing, he cultivated an outlandish persona. His poetry and manner alike were a shock to the Canadian system, as was his relentless self-promotion. Richler, who knew the poet well enough to say hello, and was often accused of the same crime of drawing attention to himself, nonetheless found his manner preposterous. He had less chance to form an opinion of one of Layton's more illustrious students, and the latest Montreal poet sensation—Leonard Cohen. Cohen, whose ancestor Rabbi Hirsch Cohen had battled Yudel Rosenberg for the kosher meat-blessing monopoly some four decades earlier, hailed from an affluent home adjacent to Murray Hill Park in Westmount, courtesy of his family's success as clothiers. Sexy and soulful, his baritone voice as powerful an instrument for poetry reading as for his songs, the twenty-six-year-old wore black turtlenecks and plucked a classical guitar. Cohen already had a book published, *Let Us Compare Mythologies*, and had used a Canada Council grant to move to London the previous December, arriving with his own Olivetti typewriter and his own raincoat shortly after Mordecai and Florence had left for Italy. He had worked that winter in Hampstead on a novel that would eventually be published under the title *Beautiful Losers* within a few blocks of Richler and Kotcheff's flat at 5 Winchester Road. But their first meeting would not be for a few years.

Being in Quebec that spring and summer meant the Richlers were present for the end of *la Grande noirceur*, the Great Darkness. Maurice Duplessis, whose regime had more or less encompassed Richler's life to date, had died the previous September. The society of censorious priests and mistreated workers, backroom deals among the Anglo elite and the French ruling class to maintain the status quo, was winding down. A deep social conservatism, primitive education and health services, the iron grip of the Catholic Church and an ingrained imbalance of wealth were all about to be challenged. As of June 22, 1960, with the election of the Liberal Party of Jean Lesage, a new Quebec was set to emerge. The transformation, astonishing for its rapidity and thoroughness, would eventually be accurately called *la Révolution tranquille*—the Quiet Revolution.

Richler arrived in Montreal in time to witness not only the passage of the province into modernity but an unprecedented fifth straight Stanley Cup for the Canadiens. To the Habs' victory in April was added a melancholy footnote in September: the retirement, after eighteen years, of the great Maurice Richard. "The Rocket" had been burning up and down the Forum ice since Mordy Richler first listened to games in the living room on St. Urbain Street. His suspension by the league back in March 1955, which had triggered a riot in the streets around the Forum and was believed by many to have kick-started populist Quebec nationalism, was an event he had missed from London. Still, Richard and *nos glorieux* belonged to Mordecai Richler as much as the Great Darkness of the Duplessis era. Much that had been bedrock about his hometown since he was a small child was suddenly cracking.

After so much activity and such proximity to his family, the move to Toronto in the autumn may have come as a relief. They went largely to widen professional contacts and to see if he and Florence could abide living there permanently. He knew the city only in passing, and contemplated it as a home without excitement. Ted Allan found them a furnished bungalow in an unassuming suburban neighbourhood northwest of the downtown. The home came with plastic over the couches and lampshades, and Florence ordered bed linens shipped from Montreal. "The house is fine," Richler reported to Bill Weintraub in November, "lots of room, and a fine basement rm for me, but we are far out, man. 20 minutes drive into town." The letter, encouraging him once more to join them for Christmas, mentioned various assignments underway, as well as prospects of a $500-per-month retainer for articles from his new friends at *Maclean's*. "As advance against future work," he explained of the arrangement, "while I finish my book."

He didn't specify which book. It wasn't *Duddy Kane's First Marriage*, as the second volume in the Kravitz trilogy was going to be titled. Nor was he referring to a third or fourth draft of *It's Harder to Be Anybody*, which André Deutsch and Diana Athill had so roundly rejected earlier in the fall and he had agreed to put aside. Though he was still working on the short-story collection set on St. Urbain Street, he was also writing a new novel, and a book of non-fiction.

"Haven't seen Jack McCl yet," he reported to Weintraub in November. "Will see him later this week." He had been quietly separating himself from William Collins & Sons in Toronto, who handled distribution for André Deutsch's titles in Canada. The charismatic Jack McClelland, who had first gone to work in his father's publishing firm, McClelland and Stewart, in 1946 after playing a distinguished role as a naval commander in the Battle of the Atlantic, was trying to lure him away from Collins. André Deutsch, operating under the old colonial understanding that Canada was an extension of Britain's market, imported their English editions into Canada. In most cases the financial arrangements were disadvantageous to the writer, and Richler resolved to stand on his own publishing feet in his home country. Jack McClelland was developing a publishing programme that would launch a main-stream Canadian literature. Flamboyant, brilliant and imagina-tive, the head of "M&S" was fast becoming godfather to a generation of writers—including those presumably suffering from the "paucity of talent" Richler had recently decried in the *New Statesman*. Regardless of the insults, or perhaps because of them, Jack McClelland loved a good argument—and even before *Duddy Kravitz* appeared, he had mailed a copy of the banned Nabokov novel *Lolita* to London with a note: "I hope you're not arrested because of it." Richler had returned the interest, even asking Collins to invite their rival to a belated Toronto launch of the novel at the Park Plaza Hotel, then the unofficial headquar-ters for the city's literary and media crowd, either in the cosy, smoky rooftop bar with its patio and views of the skyline, or in one of the plush rooms. When they failed to include Jack McClelland on their list of invitees, he slipped out of his own launch and met McClelland in the downstairs bar. He may have found an excuse—his latest favourite smoke, the slim Dutch cigar Schimmelpenninck, was available in the shop off the lobby—or he may not have bothered; Collins, whom he called "stinkers" in a letter, had ignored the glowing reviews and generous *Maclean's* excerpts, and ordered in from Deutsch only 750 copies of *Duddy Kravitz* for the Canadian market, many of which remained unsold.

It is easy to imagine the instantaneous bond between the charismatic McClelland, renowned for his colourful speech, undying support and loyalty to those he liked, and fondness for single malt whisky, and the similarly inclined Richler. The quick Park Plaza drink went well enough for him to verbally agree to jump to M&S with his next book. He also had, it turned out, a vital new friendship, of the kind he was gifted at: an abrupt, permanent blurring of professional and private boundaries, rooted in affection and respect, and fuelled by drinking and smoking, especially among men.

Not long after, he would inform his prospective new Canadian publisher of plans to inaugurate their professional relationship with the non-fiction work *Their Canada and Mine* (or "*Canada*

Paid Me," he punned of Levine's *Canada Made Me*.) "A warning," he wrote. "It reads less and less like a bk abt Canada, and more and more like an autobiog, with spleen." At the same time he would tell his father he had "just finished my novel yesterday, a short one this time," called, it seemed, *The Incomparable Atuk*. To paraphrase Steven Leacock, he was writing madly off in all directions.

Other friendships deepened too. Mordecai and Florence saw a now-divorced Ted Allan often; Ted loved the boys and adored Florence, and, like the "other" Ted—Ted Kotcheff—was happy to serve as her companion while her husband worked. Robert Fulford, then the literary editor of the *Toronto Daily Star*, was becoming a friend and booster. An autodidact with a fierce intelligence and sweeping curiosity, the intense, bespectacled Fulford was possibly his most sensitive reader. "Every piece of Richler prose contains something of his personality," he was soon to write, "[and] no matter what form it takes, it benefits from the sad, bitter and humorous approach which is peculiarly his." Bob Fulford would shortly be joining Peter Gzowski and Ken Lefolii at *Maclean's*. Another Toronto native, the boyish Gzowski, then twenty-seven, brought a private school education and unfinished university degree to his populist impulses as a writer and editor. Lefolii was about to take over as managing editor, under Blair Fraser, and then as editor-in-chief, where he would encourage the kind of cocky, assertive writing that was the specialty of Mordecai Richler. When, for instance, Gzowski commissioned a randy semi-fictional memoir from him called "Making it with the Chicks," the more staid editor Ralph Allen rejected it as being masturbatory. Lefolii waited until he was in charge and then ran the piece.

He did so even though Richler, writing in the *Spectator* about the Canadian cultural scene, declared *Maclean's,* then with a circulation of half a million, "an especially sad case." Or, again, like McClelland, Lefolii may have competitively redoubled his support precisely because Richler had trashed the magazine in print. These young editors, most still not thirty, with new families and new ambitions for Canadian journalism, seemed to be of the collective opinion that the abrasive Montrealer was exactly the breath of sharp air needed by their own publication in particular, and by the country in general. For this they would put up with his bite, and his often extravagant expense sheets. "Anyway," Gzowski joked in one letter, "why in hell *don't* you write a piece called "Why I Don't Like French Canadians"? Gzowski, in particular, already had a sure sense of the way the wind was rising in Canada—blowing the Anglo-English dust out of the corners.

Away from the *Maclean's* head offices on University Avenue the crew formed a social circle, wives and small children included. The hard drinking and the cynical banter in one of the Park Plaza bars or at living room cocktail parties helped persuade Richler that Toronto wasn't such a dreary place after all.

While in the city he ran into Cathy Boudreau's sister, Tess Taconis. He had remained friendly with Tess and her photographer husband, Kryn. Aware that her sister hadn't mentioned it to her ex, she informed him that Cathy had recently remarried to an Englishman, which meant he could stop payment on his alimony cheques. He also found out that Diana Athill had read Bill Weintraub's novel *Why Rock the Boat*, and liked it. "I am sure we will do it," she assured him. Another friend had a new book out with André Deutsch as well. Richler had enjoyed Brian Moore's *The Luck of Ginger Coffey*, but not as much as his earlier novels, and had told him the previous summer: "What the hell, this is only one man's opinion, and nobody is going to like all of anybody's books, and I hope it does bloody well." He meant both the criticism and the support; he wished, as always, the best for his friends.

Married with a small family now, and with rents and living expenses in an expensive city to negotiate, he had turned his attention to the business of securing his standing, and his friends, in Toronto. With Jack McClelland and the *Maclean's* crowd on side, only the CBC remained to be fully conquered. Robert Weaver was keen, including the story "The Summer My Grandmother Was Supposed to Die" in the anthology *Ten for Wednesday Night*, which he put together from fiction written for his radio programme. Slight but deeply felt, "The Summer My Grandmother . . ." is seen through the eyes of a St. Urbain Street boy who has grown up with an invalid grandmother in the back room. A hot summer in Montreal, and the old woman's gangrenous left leg needs several changes of dressing daily. "When we sat down to eat we could smell her," he remarks of meals in the adjacent kitchen. "God in heaven," his fierce mother says, "what's she holding on for?" His meek father is more polite. "It won't be long now . . . and she'll be better off, you know what I mean?"

Robert Weaver was among the guests who came to the Richlers' rented house for a Boxing Day party. Jack McClelland, Bob Fulford and Morley Callaghan, who had preceded Richler to Paris, where he famously floored Hemingway in a boxing bout, also made the trek out to Lawrence and Dufferin. Brian Moore, in town over the holidays, took them to dinner, and watched in astonishment when Richler had a restaurant phone brought to the table so he could make an expensive call to London. "You don't know what it's like to once have been poor," he explained. The St. Urbain Street kid was enjoying his new standing, and the gesture smacked of delight in being able to impress both his friend and his new wife.

But good parties and, soon enough, exposure on national television couldn't keep him rooted in any one place for long. It wasn't only that he and Florence were young and mobile, and so could avail themselves of opportunities; it was also the divided allegiances, the simultaneous pull of three cities, three cultures— London, New York, Montreal—that kept them in perpetual packing and unpacking mode.

———————

On May 23, 1962, long after the family had returned to England, the CBC advertised "two new CBC programs which should help Canadians to understand better the controversial young novelist, essayist and playwright, Mordecai Richler." The second programme was a radio play called "The Spare Room," set to air in June. The more interesting slot was for television, a one-hour episode of *Q for Quest* that would be "an unusual expedition into the circumstances and characters which make up Mr. Richler's past." Writing and narrating the script himself, he intermingled dramatizations of scenes from *Duddy Kravitz* and the story "It's Harder to Be Anybody" (from a collection "to be published soon") with on-camera reflections. "At a party in Montreal some months ago," he observed, "a man came up to me and said, 'When are you going to stop writing about St. Urbain Street and Outremont . . . and write something about Canada?'" About which he explained: "Of course, I consider the Jewish experience—my Jewish experience—as completely Canadian as, say, Morley Callaghan's or Hugh MacLennan's, and I suppose I will continue to write about St. Urbain for a long while yet, but, at the same time, I don't feel, as a Jew, very integrated into the Canadian way of life. Like most Jews in this country, I tend to think of myself as nearly-American." Canadian Jewish writers "are really regional American writers," and he was happy to declare, "I feel more at ease in New York than I do in Toronto." The idea of feeling allied to the United States, or wishing to be part of the larger-scale and more dynamic American literary scene, wasn't exclusive to either Mordecai Richler or Jewish Canadian authors; many artists, especially in the early and mid-century, had to think of themselves as members of a larger, trans-national community, simply to survive. But by the early 1960s Canadian cultural nationalism was making the expression of such ambivalences unfashionable, if not faintly treasonous to some. Just in time, it seemed, for him to weigh in on the sensitive matter. Canada, he said, cribbing from his own *Spectator* piece, was "here a professor, there a poet, and in between thousands of miles of wheat and indifference."

Scandalized reactions from the critical establishment aside, the full-throated expression of his singular personality was in lockstep with the struggle around him. One outsized artist and one undersized cultural industry were both looking to grow up, quickly. Like the cheering on of his hasty, uneven journalistic impulses by *Maclean's* and other publications, *Q for Quest* was part of a collective effort. Various editors and producers were willingly getting behind Mordecai Richler while he asserted his sad, bitter, humorous sensibility and bracing outsider values. No less important was the way they assisted him in thinking aloud, and in mapping out the terrain of his fictional village. Beginning in 1958, when Duddy Kravitz's Montreal came to him in an unsettling rush, he was indeed "paid," often well, "by Canada" to do what was essentially preparatory work for the major novels. The trouble was, he wasn't ready to write them yet, no matter how many times he announced the Duddy Kravitz trilogy or promised a St. Urbain Street story collection. Canada, or at least some of its new young cultural trendsetters, had done what they could to get their equally new young star out of the blocks. Now, back in London with his family and busy freelance career, it was up to him to write the books.

IV

TEL AVIV, LONDON, NEW YORK

"I saw Q for Quest last night," Ted Allan cheerfully reported from back in Toronto. "A very good performance from Mordecai, handsome and powerful in his individuality." Allan also conveyed the thoughts of his companion that evening: "He impressed me," she said. "Now when I read him it will be more disturbing." Allan ended the letter with an anxious question: "Has the grant come through yet?"

It had. Before boarding the ship back to England, Richler had tried finding out from the Guggenheim Foundation if he had been awarded a grant. He failed, but then received a radio call a day out of Southhampton from Bill Weintraub with the good news. Bill mentioned a condition: the winner had to be on American soil to receive the $5,500. The Guggenheim, awarded officially to allow for the completion of the Duddy Kravitz trilogy, brought status as well; among writers, the list of recipients reflected the brightest of North American talent, especially the up-and-coming. The money also made re-entry in London, including outfitting an apartment from scratch—"everything from carpets to kitchen hooks," he explained to his father—less fraught, though "we own nothing, except cutlery." He came into some film work in June, courtesy of Ted Kotcheff's insistence that his friend rewrite a comedy he had agreed to direct. Called *Tiara Tahiti* and set to star James Mason and John Mills, the script required a month of work, with time for whimsy. "I didn't have to come to

Tahiti," a character says. "I could have gone to Nassau again. The McClellands and Fulfords are there." To which her friend replies, "Who could put up with them again?"

The apartment at 11 Parkhill Road, Hampstead, was a marked improvement over the Winchester Road flat of two years before. An upper maisonette with a kitchen, living/dining room and study on the ground floor, and three bedrooms upstairs, it had central heating and all the mod cons. The study barely had space for a teak desk purchased by Richler, and which was covered with a cloth when guests visited, to act as a sideboard for serving drinks. Once Florence had done the unpacking and outfitting, buying everything at discount or on installment at John Lewis department store—a spree they decided could substitute for the wedding gifts they had not received—they anointed 11 Parkhill, which they considered their first real residence, with a small dinner party for director Jack Clayton and his new wife. Born Haya Harareet in Haifa, she hailed from Hollywood central casting. More exactly, Haya had been cast opposite Charlton Heston in the 1959 epic *Ben-Hur* as the young Jewess who converts to Christianity. Now twenty-seven, and already semi-retired from the movies, Haya Clayton had raven hair, dark features and an arresting fashion sense—simple Middle Eastern dresses with striking jewellery. She understood Florence Richler immediately: "It's as if you apologize for being beautiful," she told her. Haya Clayton was soon an important friend, a lifelong confidante who was protective of Florence, as many were, while recognizing her core strength, and who insisted she finally overcome her reluctance to spend money on clothes—she had worn the same outfits, mostly given to her as a model, for years—with the purchase of a cape. The Claytons became their closest London friends.

On July 29 the parents hosted a first birthday party for Noah. Their son was walking by September, the same month his older brother Daniel started elementary school. Even with an au pair, caring for two small boys while being pregnant made for long, exhausting days for their mother. Richler was already in the habit of slipping out in the late afternoon for a few drinks and not returning until dinner, occasionally with a friend in tow: Florence, a keen cook, was developing a reputation as someone whose table was worth being invited to. Soon, the more spacious new flat was readying for a fifth member. In early October Richler told his father that if the baby was a boy he would be called Jacob, if a girl, Emma. "It wd be nice if it's a girl," he said. He shared the outcome with Bill Weintraub: "Emma. 7lb, 12 onz, born on the 23rd," at Charing Cross Hospital. The father, as it happened, was having lunch with Brian Moore in a pub downstairs when Florence went into labour. Finding her alone in the room, he scoured the corridor in search of a doctor, returning with a Jamaican nurse who ended up doing the delivery. As with Ted Kotcheff and Noah, Moore was asked on the spot to be Emma's godfather. He accepted.

Amidst such happy bustle, the health of Moses Richler became a worry. He took ill in the summer and had a small cancer on his bladder removed. "Immediately I got your letter," Richler wrote on August 26, "I phoned the hospital in Montreal, but they could not connect me with your room. I finally got Max and he told me you were better." The letter included cash, along with an offer of further funding: "Enclosed, a cheque for $100. Let me know how you are and if you plan to take a rest. I hope," he added, speaking of Moses' second wife, "Sarah will insist on it." He also wrote to Brian Moore's brother, Sean, a doctor in Montreal, asking if he would check into his father's condition. "I was wondering," Moses Richler wrote in a touching letter once he had been discharged, "if an article could be made of my study at the Hospital, on the comical side, and of the odd characters." He had taken notes, which he offered to share. The elder Richler added a PS: "Av also came to see me at least twice daily and was in contact with the doctor at all times." The rift between the brothers appeared to weigh on their parent. The younger son, in turn, felt guilty for being so far away in his hour of need. The issue—being overseas, his ability to carry out his filial duties limited—would nag at him for years, and contribute to his blinkered views of both his father (favouring the positive) and his brother (high-lighting the negative), as well as his financial generosity. The last person some might have thought would behave like the "good Jewish son" displayed many of the qualities—and carried certain of the burdens.

Richler was no less busy professionally. "Another QUEST," he told his father of a new CBC assignment, "this one abt St Urbain St, will be done next season. Ditto a 90 minute radio piece about St. U. . . . " When not making TV, he was on it, appearing serious and very young. In the CBC programme *Close-Up* his friend Elaine Grand, partner of Reuben Ship, did the interview, perched non-chalantly on the arm of a chair, cigarette in hand, clearly a friend: "Onwards!" she exclaims after some of his more inflammatory comments. The smoking-filled half-hour was cut to twenty min-utes on air, along with the requisite shots of "Richler on the London streets, in pub, etc." Those expecting a blast from their Angry Young Man in Exile were not disappointed; he decried the provincialism of Canada and the mediocrity of Canadian politi-cians, and mused aloud once again on whether the country might not be better off joining its colossal southern neighbour. Later, even he wondered if he had gone overboard. But Robert Fulford, while assuring him he hadn't come across as obnoxious, congrat-ulated him on "saying all those awful things about Canada." Other awful things about Canada were being said by him in *Maclean's* and *Saturday Night*, where he debuted with a piece for the new editor there, his friend Kildare Dobbs. In the States, meanwhile, especially now that his agent Monica McCall was "getting me action," Richler was entertaining offers from glossy magazines like *Show*. In the smart, dry McCall, a senior figure in a senior agency—Graham Greene was another client—he had the kind of North American representation that he wanted, and had quietly argued with Joyce Weiner about for some time.

He was also happily planning for the occasion of Bill Weintraub's first novel. "Am mentioning your book to numerous producers here," he reported. "Can you afford to airmail me two extra copies? You never had an agent like me, you know." Weintraub, finally, was coming to London for Christmas. Richler had been coaxing him since the summer, including a note in August with a holiday already mapped. "Am planning a proper do . . . with goodies from Fortnum and other exotic points, Hope Kotcheff, black and back from Tahiti, you, Moores, will all be around the festive table. Come earlier, if you can." On one condition: "Bring smoked meat or don't come." And there was a complication to Weintraub's staying with them at 11 Parkhill: "Not getting much sleep here," he said, "what with babykins howling away." There were colds and flus to abide as well, and if the father wasn't doing much parenting beyond making funny faces on command or holding one child while Florence changed the "nappy" of another, he was around enough to catch those ailments. Richler may have been exempted, as per the societal norms of the times for men, from much actual caregiving, but he was happiest when snugly among his family.

Sleepless and harried but content, he was back in the swim of literary and film London. With *Tiara Tahiti* in the editing stage, and *No Love for Johnnie* soon in the theatres, his career as a screenwriter was on the rebound. "Din-dins at the Mirabelle," he told Weintraub, naming the film industry's favourite French restaurant in Mayfair. The importance of the dinner—producers for the Rank Corporation wanted to discuss adapting *A Choice of Enemies*—didn't stop him from misbehaving: "I disgraced myself by getting so drunk, toppling, and being carried off to the john by two flunkies," he confessed, exaggerating for comedic effect. The adaptation failed to come together but, in keeping with the ethos of the movie business in 1960s London, where much was tolerated and forgiven, he was given a contract for an original script by producer Betty Box and director Sydney Thomas, the same team who had hired a script doctor to fix *No Love for Johnnie*. "The film, in theory, will be shot in Montreal next winter," he told his father of the new project. "That means the 'exteriors' will be shot there and the 'interiors' back at Pinewood Studios here. It's a big job, really," he added. "I'm quite pleased."

Literary life was equally lively. "Mailer very hopped-up here," he wrote of the young American lion, lately involved in London fisticuffs with the poet Gregory Corso over a perceived anti-Semitic insult. "Ran into him at two parties." His mixed review of *Advertisements for Myself* appeared in the *Spectator* the week Norman Mailer was in town. Establishment publications and programmes wanted the smart, tough Canadian in their pages, or even on their screens: "Ken Tynan, of all people, of all things," he wrote of the critic's popular TV arts programme *Tempo*, "wanted to fly me to Vienna two wks ago to interview . . . John Huston." In British artistic circles, no figure burned more brightly than the flamboyant theatre critic and anti-censorship crusader Kenneth Tynan. Working for him would have provided a sure boost for a colonial like Mordecai Richler. Still, he passed on the offer to fly to Vienna to meet the great American director, citing the pressures of finishing his book. "I'm still having trouble with my book—books, rather—I move back and forth between one and the other." He sold a new story, "Some Grist for Mervyn's Mill," to the *Kenyon Review* in the United States, to *Town* in London and to the *Montrealer* in Canada. His longest, most accomplished story to date, it told of a pseudo-writer moving into the room that the grandmother in "The Summer My Grandmother Was Supposed to Die" had once occupied—the spare back room of a St. Urbain Street walk-up rented by a family quite like the Richlers, *circa* 1944. Mervyn's grand notions of himself as an artist are matched by the mother's romanticism about her late father, and the long-suffering father's quirks, including his curious puns. More mythologizing and village building, as well as further mockery, reminiscent of Hersh in *Duddy Kravitz*, of his own pompous youthful self.

Repackaging versions of the story "It's Harder to Be Anybody" no fewer than four times, including twice in Canada in the same year, reflected his capacity for hard work and his financial need. His entrepreneurial energy demonstrated an acute understanding—and a practicality unusual among writers—about the publishing business. On occasion, however, the re-packaging smacked of a cover for creative indecision, the case with "It's Harder to Be Anybody," already a failed novella and a story of wildly varying lengths, but still not a success on the page.

Though he had mentioned in October that he was writing a "comic novel . . . about a Canadian in Europe," it was a comic novel about an Eskimo in Toronto that he submitted in mid-December to Joyce Weiner. His agent and one-time confidante loved the manuscript—"the book is really terrific," she wrote on December 15, "it had me in stitches"—and thought it could be sent to publishers right away. Her enthusiasm may have been an attempt to boost their failing relationship. A lengthy letter, sent the same day as her praise of *The Incomparable Atuk*, as the short manuscript was being called, went over the grievances Richler had expressed in a meeting earlier in the week. She defended her ability to get him script work, puzzled over his annoyance that he seemed to be making all the industry contacts, not she, and took exception to his calling her an "un-commercial" literary agent and "not a show business person." In the end she granted that, while he might seek a separate London agent to handle his film projects, she would continue to blaze for her client "new literary trails as I have done these past ten years." She closed with high emotion and deepening resignation: "And, when your two other agents are roaring away in their Jags, maybe they will spare a passing wave for the "un-commercial agent, on whose efforts . . . they are so happily cashing in." Her enthusiasm notwithstanding, Richler withdrew *Atuk* to do more work on it. But he also made no move right away to acquire either a film agent or a different U.K. literary agent.

His busyness reached new heights. By Christmas 1961 he had three fiction manuscripts on the go, a non-fiction book about Canada evading completion, half a dozen outstanding magazine assignments for publications in London, New York and Toronto, the contract to write an original "Canadian" movie for Rank, verbal agreements to do two additional projects for Canadian TV and radio, along with trips to Israel for *Maclean's* and to the States for the Guggenheim. Plus the howling babykins, two small boys, their long-awaited house guest, Bill Weintraub, holiday dinner parties to host for friends, and still other parties to attend. And letters to write, with cheques enclosed, to both his parents. "George Drew invited me . . . us, rather . . . to his xmas party," he told his father. George Drew, a former premier of Ontario and now the Canadian high commissioner in London, was a name Moses Richler would have known. "Isn't that just ducky?"

There was also a wedding to attend. "Mo and Flo," as the invitation called them, witnessed the marriage of Ted Kotcheff to the lively London actress Sylvia Kay at a church in Ennismore Gardens. Richler was his best friend's best man, and the wedding party carried on late into the night at the White Elephant Club on Curzon Street in Soho. One of the newer private members' clubs, and especially popular with show business people, the White Elephant was where deals were made and anxious producers sat drinking until midnight, when first editions of the next morning's papers, containing reviews of their plays or movies, arrived. John Mortimer and screenwriter Frederic Raphael were members. The White Elephant had already admitted Ted Allan and Ted Kotcheff, and Richler would soon join as well. It was the kind of place, with interesting people to look at and gossip to overhear, that Florence preferred for drinks or dinner after a day with the children.

Richler was aware of how Florence graced his side in public, the classy companion to the unkempt author: "beauty and the beast" in the eyes of some of their bemused friends. More important, though, was her centrality to his productivity and happiness. If he had begun using the "cost" of keeping his wife in finery as a jokey excuse to squeeze higher fees and more work out of people—the opposite of the reality of her innate frugality, though true to his impulse to spend freely and sort out the balance sheet later—he was also working hard, in part to prove that he could be the provider he had so sweetly assured her he could be, back on the French Riviera. That Florence was a tireless homemaker, admired for her taste in all things, including decor, was a bonus for a man of limited discernment in these areas. That she was a devoted, adoring mother with a shared desire for a large family, and an acceptance that he should work those long days, and even go out for lunches and drinks, while she put in fourteen-hour shifts with the children, suited him well. Even better, where some wives might have balked at the pace he kept, and she certainly wasn't always happy with how much he drank (an awareness of the hazards of smoking didn't exist; Florence herself liked Gitanes), she was otherwise thrilled by the sight of him in full throttle, the passionate, driven man she had fallen in love with.

And he still couldn't quite believe his luck about that: her love for him, steadfast, unblinking and ongoing.

———————

"I envy you the Israel trip," Weintraub had joked back in the summer. "But take care. Chap I know, just back, says morals there lowest since Roman Empire and life one big sex orgy." On March 20, eleven days before his departure on his *Maclean's* assignment, Richler was enlisting Weintraub and a more recent Montreal friend, the Israeli immigrant Sonny Idelson, to help round up contacts and information about hotels. "I want the names of kibbutzim, any kibbutzim, where Montrealers have settled. I am particularly interested in the kibbutz settled by former members of Habonim, Montreal." More specifically, he wanted someone to track down his old Habonim comrade Earl Kruger, who would know how to reach them. His last-minute manners showed clear signs of fraying: "URGENT," the note declared. "On the phone, man. Don't have a drink first and grumble. Be friendly, be helpful, and your friends will be helpful too." The loyal, patient Weintraub came through. "Any night (except Friday, I presume), you will proceed to the Rothschild Institute Bowling Alley in Tel Aviv and there ask for a former poet named Elie Cohen of Montreal. Earl Kruger says he is now a bowling instructor and you know him from way back." Cohen, among others, could provide further advice from the ground.

It was all very eleventh-hour. But his treatment for the "Montreal film" was failing and, in a major setback, and the possible psychological cause of his rare complaints of writerly fatigue, the revised *The Incomparable Atuk* was not being embraced by editors. "I am absolutely convinced this is your worst book to date," Jack McClelland wrote. "Apart from stuffing it, let me know what you want us to do." André Deutsch, while liking the manuscript enough to accept it, and to write upbeat letters about the "brilliant little novel" to Richler's American publisher, was worried about the deeply Canadian content of the story, and the perennial issue of libel, which was then achieving nonsensical heights in Britain. "As you can see," Diana Athill wrote to Florence, enclosing the solicitor's report, "according to the lawyer almost everything in Atuk could be libellous." Sam Lawrence at Atlantic in New York, who had viewed *Duddy Kravitz* as the beginning of a long relationship, turned the book down flat, while still reserving the right to continue issuing its author's "serious work." Translated, as Richler himself put it, Lawrence was declaring *Atuk* "a bad local joke." He set off for Israel under the impression that he had lost a major publisher on the eve of his Guggenheim assault on America.

Touching down on April 1 at Lod airport, outside Tel Aviv, in a cabin full of passengers singing, clapping and weeping at having reached the Promised Land, was a deeply felt personal milestone as much as a professional assignment—one that he would revisit years later and write about again. More than a quarter-century since the four-year-old Muttle had nearly been whisked off to live in Palestine with his brother, mother and grandparents, and thirteen years since the teenager, once so committed to making aliyah in Eretz Yisrael, had opted instead to make a literary pilgrimage to Paris, he reached Israel.

But for a Montrealer trained in Europe and inclined towards the United States, what did the fourteen-year-old state represent? Richler was in reporter mode from the moment his shuttle bus ("Volkswagen") driver ("an Ethiopian Jew") from the airport asked him how he liked the place so far. He gave the same attention to the "youngsters with knitted *kippas* fastened to their heads with bobby pins" in the Allenby Road, and the restaurant featuring "wine-stained glasses" and "toothpicks in shot glasses," to conversations in bars and cafés, bowling alleys and nightclubs, and with art gallery owners and residents of a kibbutz near the Lebanese border and a village on the frontier with Jordan. He did unearth a few relatives, including an Orthodox cousin named Shmul, but avoided tracking down his former Habonim comrades, which he chalked up to his lingering sense that he had let them down. He conversed mostly with strangers, and his interview subjects ranged from patriots to naysayers, Jews to Arabs. Notably absent was any contact with government officials. His instincts lay with regular people; they were the voices he wanted to hear.

"Today he's in there," a cab driver told him as they drove past a prison block. "Who?" he asked. "The Eichmann," the driver replied. "The architect of the Holocaust," as Nazi fugitive Karl Adolf Eichmann had come to be known, had been captured by Israeli Mossad agents in Buenos Aires in 1960, where he had been working under a false name as a foreman at a Mercedes-Benz factory. Convicted in a Jerusalem court of crimes against humanity in December 1961, by the following April Eichmann was awaiting execution. He was hanged on May 31, weeks after Richler ended his tour.

Richler's own status as a Jew preoccupied him during his stay in Israel, which, while fascinating, was also characterized, as he admitted to Brian Moore, by "drinking too much at night; it is miserably lonely here." Even his name left Israelis wondering. "Do you really call yourself Mordecai in Canada?" a journalist asked, assuming he would only opt for such an ancient moniker as an act of defiance. "But it's my name," a baffled Richler answered. When he challenged Israeli assumptions about Arabs by suggesting that integrating an Arab in Israel was the same as integrating a Jew in Canada, a hotel manager replied, "No, sir. Never. You're always a Jew there." But what, he asked, did he have in common with a Yemenite Jew, for instance? "Jerusalem," the manager asserted. An academic he met, although a personal fan of Saul Bellow, Bernard Malamud and newcomer Philip Roth, confessed that Israelis didn't read these diasporic sorts. "The young think of them as ghetto writers," he said.

Richler wasn't enamoured with the communal lifestyle of the kibbutz, and found Jerusalem too steeped in religion. Cosmopolitan Tel Aviv suited him a little better but, truth be told, Canada or England suited him best. He was a Diaspora Jew, happy to live in places with loud clashes of peoples and cultures; perhaps even an assimilationist, since he found himself none too impressed with the notion, expressed repeatedly by Israelis across the country, that the new state was home to a new variety of Jew. He understood that they simply meant a Jew who, secure in his own homeland, had no need to pander to Gentiles, but he heard in the refrain a declaration that it was time for the Jews to kick around the Arabs. "The Arab settlements I visited in Israel were characterized by children with rickets, old men with trachoma, and ignorance and squalor everywhere."

"This Year in Jerusalem," as *Maclean's* titled the long three-part series, ran in August and September. "I can't remember when a piece of writing has been so highly complimented," Ken Lefolii would remark to his writer after the series appeared. "People I have never met or even heard of have called...." Peter Gzowski noted with delight that Richler, who had lately lost his standing as the worst anti-Semitic Canadian Jew to the critic and novelist David Lewis Stein, could now reclaim the crown. Question Israel's sense of its own unique identity? Wonder aloud if Jews weren't now treating stateless Arabs the way they had once been treated? Fighting words, guaranteed to light up the magazine switchboard and fill the mailbag with outrage.

———

On April 28, having flown back to London from Israel three days before to help Florence pack and ready the children for America, the family was on another jet across the Atlantic to New York. Beyond helping her with the children during a seven-hour flight, he had much to mull over. Brian Moore had arranged a house for them in the artists' colony of Amagansett, on the south shore of Long Island, ninety minutes from New York. Invitations had gone out to Montreal, Toronto and Manhattan for visitors, the invitees ranging from old friends to new business acquaintances, with even Moses and Sarah Richler encouraged to drive down to see their grandkids. They were anticipating a sociable, relaxing long summer away from the damp and rain of London. On their previous visit, as guests of the Moores, they'd met Philip Roth, two years younger than Richler, who had just won the National Book Award for his first collection of stories, *Goodbye, Columbus*, and the legendary *New Yorker* journalist A.J. Liebling, lover of boxing and horse racing. The explosive Norman Mailer, who had lately stabbed his now–second ex-wife at a party and pleaded guilty to aggravated assault; Left Bank alumnus and *Paris Review* co-founder Peter Matthiessen, at work on his novel *At Play in the Fields of the Lord*; and Joseph Heller, who a few months earlier had published his own first novel, the blackly comic, brilliant *Catch-22*, all summered in Amagansett. So did Willem de Kooning, then at the height of his powers as an abstract impressionist painter, and Arthur Miller and his glamorous wife, Marilyn Monroe. With its leafy streets, and bungalows on the beach or just off it, the village was an affordable place for writers to work, or simply hang out together. "The house is huge and, as they say, comfy," Richler duly reported.

Brian and Jackie Moore, who had wintered in London with their son, Michael, where Florence and Jackie had grown especially close, also planned to be on Long Island for the summer. Richler had just read the manuscript of his friend's new novel, *An Answer from Limbo*, while travelling in Israel. In his letter from the kibbutz confessing loneliness, he expressed "admiration for your new novel," along with certain reservations. Of a lesser note was the authenticity of some of the Yiddish expressions used by the one Jewish character; and of no consequence, he said, were any resemblances between that character—pushy, bragging novelist Max Bronstein—and himself. After all, "If I wrote a novel with lots of writers or wd-be writers in it I would be the best, most dedicated, talented boff in the book." But, semi-jokingly, he complained that Moore had beaten him to a great idea: someone collapsing in front of a TV. Because Moore had employed it in *An Answer from Limbo*, he couldn't use the image in the proposed third book of the Duddy Kravitz series—to be titled, as per his Guggenheim application, *The Bathtub*, and to have climaxed with the death of a beloved St. Urbain Street character by means grue-some but funny. "it all hinges on Max Kravitz, his father, getting into the bath with his portable tv set in sight, having a stroke, and sitting there through the weekend dying as he watches tv." Thanks to Moore, the idea was ruined. "Why do I hate you? Because now I can never use it."

The joke, like the entire letter, was strained, its jocular tone underwritten by stronger emotions. Fictional tensions between Moore's Jewish Max Bronstein and Irish Brendan Tierney, rooted in rivalry, status envy and strong personalities, mirrored reality. Richler's friendship with Brian Moore was important for a number of reasons, not least that he was his only equal as a novelist among his circle, a parity that only intensified the competition between them. It had never been a natural one, as with Ted Kotcheff, or even a clear mentoring, as with Ted Allan. Now the friendship was spiked by comments and innuendos—Moore had taken to calling him "The Bard," a term that had reached his ears—and by the lingering "wound" of the younger Richler beat-ing the older Moore, perhaps too gleefully, into print back in the early fifties. Both men were competitive and judgmental. Neither could brush off a slight. Moore's Northern Irish sensibility, at once courteous and appraising, polite and flinty, didn't always appreciate Richler's abrasive manners, or his profligacy with alcohol and money, especially when it came to him still not pick-ing up the cheque.

Then there was the matter of women and wives. In Montreal in 1960, informed by Brian that he'd been in town a few weeks earlier, when Mordecai was away but Florence in the apartment, Richler had asked why he hadn't called her. "She's too expensive,"

Moore had replied. He was joking that he might have had to take Florence to a fancy restaurant. But the implication—that the ambitious Richler had acquired himself a pricey "Perfect Writer's Wife," as Diana Athill once described the general phenomenon—was clear.

Equally unwelcome, if more accurate, was Brian Moore's refrain that journalism was a "dissipator of talent," an observation made in the presence of his wildly busy-with-journalism friend. The Irishman, who had lately won a Governor General's Award for *The Luck of Ginger Coffey*—a prize that had eluded *The Apprenticeship of Duddy Kravitz* two years earlier—had left Canada permanently for the United States, where he had begun to denounce the nation that had birthed him as a writer. While Mordecai Richler, of all people, could not have begrudged another commentator's scorn for the country, he wondered about Moore's vehemence. He also may have detected something that others had been remarking for some time: the respect he felt for Brian Moore was not being returned in kind.

All the same, Mordecai and Florence saw a great deal of Brian and Jackie in Amagansett, and for the most part those were happy days. Moore was a dutiful godfather to baby Emma, buying her gifts. Bill Weintraub came down from Montreal for a weekend and stayed for six weeks. Having met a woman at a party in the village one evening, Weintraub did not make it back to the house until the morning. He returned to find a painted sign in the window in Richler's handwriting: VACANCY. Two-year-old Noah especially took to Weintraub, and the two would walk off together along the beach to build sandcastles. Lily took the train down, and arrived in an ominous summer storm that her son, and his wife, delighted in as appropriate to her dour nature. But even Lily Rosenberg couldn't keep the sun from shining on Long Island. The routine—work in the morning and beach in the afternoon, dinners and parties in the evening—was reminiscent of their summers in southern France. He went shark fishing, catching two 300-pounders. On trips into New York to "check into Guggenheimville" and meet editors and publishers, there was also time for a Yankees game. The idyll needed more organizing now than it had in the easygoing days of Tourrettes, but still, with Phil Roth renting on the same street—"Baby Boy Roth," as Brian Moore called him—and screenwriter Josh Greenfeld as their house guest, along with weekend visits from various New York magazine and book editors, the village allowed for bohemian bonhomie. The condition—artist friends working and living side by side in a warm place—was one that Richler treasured. Stuck in London, Diana Athill sent a letter to him c/o Post Office, Amagansett, L.I. NY, containing her capsule summary of the experience. "Brian writes that summer is in full swing," she reported, "that Sam L. [Sam Lawrence] was hell, that P. Roth annoyed you all—I suppose somebody is being agreeable? Yes, of course—you all are."

By now, Richler had heard news that more than justified the Guggenheim sojourn in America. Once Sam Lawrence had rejected *Atuk*, Monica McCall had contacted Robert Gottlieb at Simon & Schuster. The gifted Gottlieb was a New York native with a degree from Columbia and two years' post-graduate at Cambridge, and a reputation, thanks in part to his nurturing of *Catch-22*, as the best young editor in New York. He had loved *Duddy Kravitz*. At thirty-one, wiry and alert, a bundle of energy and enthusiasms, he was the same age as the author, whose latest manuscript he quickly read and purchased. Once he had accepted *The Incomparable Atuk*, Gottlieb drove out to Amagansett to meet his new writer. The wry, rumpled Montrealer met the quick-minded, bespectacled New Yorker on the beach, and they became instant friends. It was the beginning of the longest and most rewarding professional relationship in Richler's life, a happy overlap of compatibility and talent with career. Gottlieb, an only child who sought to make his friends his family, invested personally in his authors, and was predisposed to intense, intimate friendships. He was soon editing and befriending Doris Lessing and Edna O'Brien as well. He would come to view Florence Richler as an intimate—or, better, as *the* intimate in the family, Mordecai not being someone who sought that kind of connection—a bond deepened by Florence's friendship with his soon-to-be second wife, actress Maria Tucci.

The introduction of Gottlieb and, four years later, the vibrant, fun-loving Tucci into their lives quickly came to serve another key purpose. In marrying Florence, Richler had known not only that she would require companionship and stimulation during his long workdays, but that his zero appetite for airing, let alone examining, emotional complexities would never provide her curious nature with the sustenance it required. He couldn't talk to her effectively or at any length about matters as fundamental as their relationship and, later, the development and well-being of their children. He couldn't, but Ted Allan and Ted Kotcheff could, and, indicative of his practicality and confidence, he gave these friends his implicit blessing to develop a rare connection with his wife, one that did not preclude discussing *his* character, right down to his foibles. Once Bob Gottlieb and Maria Tucci were added to the short list of trusted intimates, Florence had a network she could count on for conversation and also for advice, support and insight—often into her silent and singular husband.

V

FOR MY FATHER

Finally, it was ready. "ATUK announced here for the spring, ditto Canada," he wrote to his father from London in September 1962. "It is a rather savage satire on Canada, so be prepared for angry . . . maybe even infuriated reviews." Back in the flat on Parkhill Road in the fall and winter, the Amagansett tan fading quickly, they were busy.

Florence suppressed her exhaustion from so many unpackings to cook and host, including a dinner party for Carol and Terry Southern, where she could only smile in secret amusement at Southern's solicitude for his wife; at another dinner, before she had joined her husband in England, he had taken her aside and asked her to run away with him, assuring her that she was missing out on something good when she declined. He was in London for several months "working for and with S. Kubrick on Dr. Lovelace or Something" at Shepperton Studios, in Richler's offhand comment. *Dr. Strangelove* was the title of the film, as he well knew. "Haven't met S.K. yet," he admitted of the audacious young American director Stanley Kubrick, who had lately turned the shocking *Lolita* into a film starring James Mason. Kubrick too lived in London, but did not mix with expatriate artists—or anyone else.

Leonard Cohen happened to be back in London as well that spring, on Hampstead High Street. When the twenty-eight-year old wasn't writing poetry or revising his own novel for M&S, he too was exchanging letters with Jack McClelland and Robert Weaver, full of complaints about the English weather. But he and Richler, two young writers from the same city and with some of the same editors and mentors, and both deeply informed by the more intellectual and spiritual dimensions of Judaism, failed once again to meet. Cohen, in fact, translated his hatred of English rain into a plane ticket for Greece.

It was time to bring his parents to London. "As soon as we can fix exact dates I will send you one ticket," he wrote to his father and Sarah, "which, alas, is all I can afford." He promised to make arrangements for "show and theatre tickets," and to "have a poker game for you." Apologizing for not being able to offer them a bed in the apartment, he rented a room nearby, with assurances that Florence would provide meals. "There is a shul not far from here, I think," he remarked. "There are lots of Jewish people in our neighbourhood, Jewish stores, delicatessens, restaurants, etc." Clearly, he was "selling" London to Moses, who would have to obtain his first-ever passport. "I'd like you to have this sort of vacation for once," the good son Mordecai explained. On top of the expenses for the trip, he was sending those monthly remittances, called "gifts," for his father, the withdrawals now made automatically from his London bank. He was mailing Lily cheques as well, and she too was about to be brought to England at his strained expense. "Mom in March," he wrote. "Wow."

Richler loved sports, and was doing as much sportswriting as he could, his passions—hockey and boxing, baseball, snooker and fishing—all easily traceable to his childhood. *Maclean's*, pleased by the feedback for the Israel series, flew him to Stockholm to cover the 1963 hockey championships. He booked into the posh Hotel Continental but did most of his reporting of the Trail Smoke Eaters, a squad out of British Columbia sent to represent the nation, from either the bar in the hotel where the players were staying, or the rink, offering an affectionate and prescient portrait of Canadian amateurs being humbled by the Czechs, who "play with infinitely more elegance." Back home, he sat in the Load of Hay interviewing heavyweight boxer Henry

Cooper. Known as "Our 'Enry" by his adoring fans, the southpaw, a greengrocer by trade, had a fatal flaw: a left eyebrow prone to being too easily cut. It didn't keep him from knocking down a cocky Cassius Clay at Wembley Stadium in June that year. "Use your 'ammer, 'enry," Richler heard the crowd chant of the East Londoner's fearsome left hook. But a few minutes later, Clay, shortly to be reborn as Muhammad Ali, went to work on Cooper's bloody head until the referee stopped the match.

Literary scribblings at this time included reviews of everything from children's books to Norman Mailer's first and only collection of poems. Ron Bryden, the Trinidad-born, Canada-schooled *Spectator* editor and theatre critic, assigned him two novels together: John Braine's *Life at the Top*, the sequel to *Room at the Top*, which Jack Clayton had turned into an award-winning film script, doctored by Richler—and Penelope Mortimer's *The Pumpkin Eater*. The web of intersections revealed in this single assignment reveals much about the intimacy of literary London. Penelope Mortimer had provided a lift to *Duddy Kravitz* back in 1959, a boost comparable to the one performed by her husband, John, in steering a too-cheerful Florence Mann through her divorce court appearance; Jack Clayton was committed to making *The Pumpkin Eater*, having recently enlisted John Mortimer to help fix Truman Capote's script for his 1961 film *The Innocents*. Then there were the Ted Kotcheff connections. Fresh off shooting his first feature-length film, *Tiara Tahiti* (script-doctored by Mordecai Richler), Kotcheff would soon be angling to bring Braine's sequel to the big screen, and upon getting the directing assignment would hire his best friend, and lately best man, to write the script, this time for full credit. It was a tight, supportive web, and it made the work more enjoyable. It also produced three Jack Clayton projects—*Room at the Top, The Innocents* and *The Pumpkin Eater*—ranked among the finest films in postwar British cinema.

It was film work too, frustrating because it took him from fiction, that filled his bank account. British cinema remained a lively, profitable industry. A shift was slowly occurring away from

the acclaimed "Kitchen Sink Realism" of the British New Wave
to the sexier, more international era of the sixties—the first
James Bond film, *Dr. No,* starring Sean Connery, was the sleeper
success of 1962—with breakout hits like *Alfie* and *Georgy Girl*
about to mark a new openness, especially about sexuality, and
offer up a new kind of anti-hero, of the Michael Caine–Terence
Stamp variety. But movies of all sorts were still being produced
in the major studios at Shepperton and Pinewood (the great
Ealing Studios had recently been bought by the BBC), and there
was plenty of writing and directing work, including for those
Canadians who had washed ashore back in the 1950s and trained
in live TV. Earlier in the year, Richler had script-doctored for the
Box-Thomas team again, earning, after some pleading, a co-
credit for *The Wild and the Willing.* It told of a brutish young man
who, at loose among the middle classes at a provincial university, proves himself adept at seduction, including of a professor's
wife. "A real stinker, I'm afraid," he warned his father, though the
movie did birth several more stars: John Hurt, Samantha Eggar
and Ian McShane.

Following on *Room at the Top* and *No Love for Johnnie, The Wild
and the Willing* marked the third time the Montrealer—viewed, as
a Canadian, as closer to an overseas Brit than a genuine foreigner—had been called upon by the English movie industry to
reveal the class scaffolding still underpinning its "new" society.
Scripting *Life at the Top* the next year would mark the climax, and
conclusion, of this sideline.

The damaged friendship between Richler and another successful Canadian screenwriter in London, Stanley Mann, recovered
enough to resume being cordial and supportive, especially once
the extended Canadian Club scene shifted south of the Thames,
to the Putney area. Never again would they be real friends, but
Stanley was back on decent terms with Florence and his son.
Within a few years, Daniel, a boy of eight or nine, would see
enough of his birth parent to be stunned the day a schoolmate,
visiting the Richler house, wondered why he was calling his
"father" by the name of "Mordecai." Until that moment it had

never occurred to him that he had been instructed to refer to *this* "father"—Richler—by his first name because he had another one, the tall man named Stanley who was also his dad. No less curious, of course, was that Mordecai was his godfather as well.

"Very good news yesterday," Richler had written in early October. "My Box-Thomas job came through. Complete scripting this time, not a rewrite. A very pleasant thriller. Night of Wenceslas, by Lionel Davidson. Full of commie heavies in Prague," he told Weintraub, "State Police types. I call the most brutal one Gzowski." He and Peter Gzowski were writing back and forth that fall about his near-certain repatriation to Canada with his family. The destination was Toronto, especially now that the Lefolii-Fulford-Gzowski troika was in charge of *Maclean's*. The new editor, himself the father of three small children, weighed in happily. "Very good news for us here, of course, and I suspect you've come to the right man for advice." Robert Fulford, Kildare Dobbs, Brian Moore and Robert Weaver all had similar advice about Toronto living, and encouragement. The city seemed on the verge of acquiring Mordecai Richler as a resident.

London received Moses and Sarah Richler in early 1963. Richler took time off scriptwriting to show his father and stepmother the city in his small new Renault, taking them to the West End to see the comedy stage revue *Beyond the Fringe*, and to the White Elephant for dinner afterwards. "What did you think?" he asked Moses of the enormously influential revue written by and starring Peter Cook, Dudley Moore, Allan Bennett and Jonathan Miller, and a marked influence on 1960s British satire. "There was no chorus line," his father answered. Jack Clayton helped arrange a tour of Shepperton Studios, and other friends, including the Kotcheffs, had them to lunch or supper. The weather, unsurprisingly for January, wasn't co-operative—"London, filthy and cold . . . slushy"—and Moses' heath was frail. Later, Richler regretted not having taken his father to more things he liked: strip joints and risqué theatre reviews. But he was happy to host him and introduce him to his circle. Diana Athill, perceptive as always, got it right away. "Your father is splendid," she had written about an earlier meeting in Montreal. "It's sad to think that if he ever tries to claim that you owe a lot to him, he won't know how true that is. But every remark of his that you've ever quoted has been really monumental."

For her part, Florence thought her husband saw his parent through tinted glasses. She had sat with Moses one afternoon while he described in his usual guileless way his love of stamp collecting, and his innocence and lack of lived experience stayed with her. She felt that Moses Richler scarcely knew the world, or, perhaps, other people, including what made his son tick; and Mordecai himself didn't really know the man, having spent little time with him since he was a child. Even then, Moses had been an amiable but absent figure, always at the movies, evading his censorious wife. But just as his perspective on his father had been poisoned for years by his mother's relentless put-downs, and by his decision to ally himself with her in the divorce, so now those allegiances, and that perspective, had shifted. Moses Richler, he had decided, was the underdog, one of the losers, and it was to that figure that he vowed loyalty—in both art (as he liked to tell interviewers) and life.

"Next week I'm taking Daniel and Noah to the television studios to show them how a children's science fiction programme was done," he wrote not long afterwards, "to meet the monsters, just like you used to take me to the Hammond and Norton Circus." It mattered as well to him how Moses viewed Florence. Discussing the monthly sum he sent home, he went to great lengths to explain her involvement. "This $25 monthly was to go towards buying Florence a mini-car but she won't hear of it as long as you are in need. . . . this monthly help, for what it is worth, is Florence's gift as well as mine. And I'm passing this information on without Florence's knowledge," he added, "but only because I'd like you to know something more about her."

He had moved squarely to the defence of his father. "I'm sorry—very sorry to hear—you're strapped for money. And I'm bloody furious about Avrum, but of course I'm tired of saying that." His brother's behaviour, as he understood it, enraged him: "I'm really

put off with Av, and I do really think it's time he was of some real
help to you and my mother." He equally felt pain at Moses Richler's
lifelong slight at being kept on the margins of various Richler
businesses. "It must be very depressing for you that you're not a
partner in the transport biz," he wrote. He was increasingly
appalled that his father, now in his sixties, had to work overtime,
and that Sarah continued as a sales clerk in Eaton's. "Perhaps
now that you're assured of this 25 monthly, tax free, more overtime will no longer be necessary." He wanted desperately for his
parent a level of comfort and respect that was probably not available at this late stage. "You have really had quite enough in your
life and these should be good years for you."

Had Moses Richler suffered so much? That wasn't the point.
He was an old man now, sickly and vulnerable, and for his younger
boy that was unacceptable.

Lily Rosenberg's visit to London a couple of months later was
less celebratory or social. She had been twice before, and was
mostly there to visit her grandchildren. But she often stayed too
long, and was difficult, simultaneously smothering the children
and strangely inattentive and incurious—lost in her own head.
Florence, unlike her husband, couldn't vanish into a study for the
day to be free of her. They shared the apartment for hours, and
found each other—the pampered shiksa and beauty queen, to
Lily; the joyless woman and hard-to-please mother-in-law, to
Florence—difficult company. Florence, as a mother, was also
afraid of the dampening effect her very presence might have on
the children. Or even on their friends; once, bringing Lily to the
Claytons' country estate at Marlow, the adults watched in astonishment as she sat stiffly and silently for the entire afternoon.
But Florence had also been raised by a depressed mother and
knew how to abide this. Her husband, she accepted, would not
do much more than roll his eyes and flee the room. Nevertheless,
for vague reasons of filial responsibility, he was going to do right

by this parent as well, even going over her annual business accounts, which she xeroxed each tax season and mailed to England, checking income versus expenses, helping her balance her books—the sort of thing a spouse might do.

Lily sent, to put it mildly, exhaustingly mixed signals to him. "You say you are a difficult son," she wrote after one visit. "Well Muttel, on my trip before the last, you were not only difficult, you were cruel. I was ill for six months." Or else, after another spell in London: "I cannot tell you how much I enjoyed my trip, the entire visit was the most wonderful one, everything was perfect!" On the matter of her former family, the Richlers, she could turn vicious, grievances of a quarter-century ago suddenly come alive. "I was going to tell you how many of my relatives your father swindled out of their last dollar," she ranted in a letter that followed a tense phone conversation. "But better to leave it. I am weary and I do not see the necessity of trying to be 'right,' or justifying myself in any way." But she didn't leave it. "And how long is it since the Richlers called you the most terrible names," she asked him, "and now you are the one who adds lustre to their name, how can you be 'bad' as they said and so wonderful now." Such diatribes would often arrive accompanied by loving notes to the children and gifts. "Loads of love," she would sign off, a rote expression that caused her son to wince and his wife to further wonder about her husband's estranged, and strange, parents.

While waiting for *The Incomparable Atuk*, his first novel in four years, to appear, Richler worked hard to accumulate enough cash to buy a house in Toronto. To Bill Weintraub he vowed to have $15,000 in the bank by the autumn, for a down payment ($50,000 seemed a ballpark figure for such a residence, Bob Fulford estimated). But to get anywhere near that sum involved more than taking extra assignments with *Maclean's, Commentary* or the *Spectator*. So while he pressed for additional script work for radio as well—"I am sorry I can't give you an assignment for this," Bob Weaver apologized, "since I have three scripts of yours on hand already"—he had no choice but to focus again on writing for the movies. But he saw the Montreal thriller officially cancelled, watched another deal fall through, and spent too much time on the Prague thriller adaptation, which was supposed to start shooting in the fall. *Tiara Tahiti* finally came out to mostly poor reviews, and by summer he was "so badly in need of fresh monies" that "finances do not permit risky uprooting"—the move to Toronto was off. But he kept trying: in September he was reporting two more deals. One was "an original flick" to be done in partnership with Ted Kotcheff and Dirk Bogarde. He and Ted drove to Bogarde's country estate, where he got to ride in the handsome star's Rolls-Royce to discuss the idea: an updated, set-in-England satire based on a favourite novel of both men, Ivan Goncharov's *Oblomov,* a classic of nineteenth-century Russian literature. The other was a "big and lucrative film deal," yet to be finalized. By December 1963 the second option was the more likely: "The film is (this'll kill you) Life at the Top," he told Weintraub of the sequel to *Room at the Top.* "I'm to script and Ted Kotcheff is signing to direct."

And the payoff, besides some cheques, for a full year of chasing movie deals? His sixty-page script treatment for Bogarde, its running title *Sloth*, was dropped by the actor before any further money was spent. *Night of Wenceslas* got made under the title *Hot Enough for June*, but without, in the end, any writing credit for Richler, who after a dispute asked that his name be removed. Only *Life at the Top* looked likely to turn out decently.

It was a complicated time. Ted Allan was suing theatre director Joan Littlewood over money, and Richler himself had recently accompanied Ted Kotcheff on a tour of northern England, where Kotcheff had helped organize nights of People's Theatre, a programme championed by Littlewood, whose musical *Oh! What a Lovely War*, an unexpected West End hit, had emerged from exactly those kind of Left-minded workshops. That trip was much less fun than a theatrical outing with Florence, Elaine Grand and London-resident Philip Roth to see a Chichester production of Chekhov's *Uncle Vanya*, starring Laurence Olivier. The truth was, he thought the sight of amateur actors speechifying in unheated labour union halls farcical, self-serving gestures of solidarity by Leftist artists that glossed over the indifference of the "masses" to high art theatre, and said so. Kotcheff decided he was too cynical. But their dispute was companionable, the kind of passionate, lively argument, preferably over drinks and with no hard feelings afterwards, that both enjoyed. In the same way, Richler took in stride comments from Ted Solotaroff at *Commentary* about a review he had commissioned of him that was "too salty for us," especially given that the magazine had been "under a good deal of fire these days for being an offence in the eyes of the good respectable Jewish community."

Of all his magazine editors who were Jewish, Ted Solotaroff seemed the most kindred in spirit. Another graduate of Left Bank Paris, the acerbic essayist and editor, four times married and an old friend of Philip Roth, loved Richler's outrageousness, even when it caused him headaches. "It's a good job," he told him of another piece, "but I do want to go over it carefully and camou-flage some of its virulent anti-Semitism. You write like someone who has not yet been told that he is suffering from Jewish self-hatred." They joked back and forth about Jewish anxieties. "What are you doing having another child?" Solotaroff chided him on the birth of his second daughter, Martha, their fourth child, in 1964. "Unless of course you're concerned about the threat to the Jewish survival that is posed, as they say in certain magazines, by a failing birth-rate." A complaint followed: "It is therefore incumbent that we Jews. . . . We Jews. . . . We Jews. . . . Here the record always sticks."

Richler laughed like Solotaroff at the anxieties he saw preoccu-pying too many Jews. But he could be fierce—a horseman on behalf of his people when he felt it mattered. Sent by *Maclean's* to the Canadian air base in Baden-Soellingen in the Black Forest region of southern Germany, he deliberately courted impropriety with his article "The Social Side of the Cold War." Very much in the New Journalism mode of the era—frank, unmediated, driven by a strong personal perspective—it offered a powerful denuncia-tion of amnesia and complacency. He did more than mock the comfortable tedium of the lifestyles of the "good-natured, boyish" Canadian airmen stationed there. He slammed Canadians abroad for their obliviousness to where they were living, reporting on the military men and women who sang the praises of their hosts for being "so modern, so clean," and for having "the answer to living." With adults he named names, although with minors he avoided personal details. "Do you know what Dachau is?" he asked a fourteen-year-old who had been taken to the camp by his parents. "They used to punish people there," the boy answered. Pressing, Richler wondered if he knew why the Germans had killed so many Jews. "The Jews were against Hitler so he had to exterminate them," the teenager said with devastating candour.

Another conflict, while distasteful, planted the seed that eventually helped grow *St. Urbain's Horseman*. Florence was an old friend of director Silvio Narizzano, a fellow Montrealer and Mountaintop Theatre alumnus who had joined the Canadian exodus to England in the fifties to work in TV. Narizzano and his wife, Bea, remained part of the expatriate scene. He came under a legal cloud that summer of 1963 when he was accused with another man of indecent assault, rape and buggery. The victim was a Swedish au pair and the co-accused was a Londoner named Benjamin Franklin Levene. A navy deserter, the working-class Levene was known to police for a series of bomb hoaxes, one of which had shut down Victoria train station. At the trial the judge decided that Levene was a "pest," as the *News of the World* put it, and merited seven years in prison. Narizzano, an upstanding citizen, had made errors of judgment in the company he kept; he received a fine.

Richler attended the proceedings, either on his own or with Reuben Ship. Florence kept him company once or twice as well, and watched as he shifted from friend of the co-accused to cold-eyed reporter, taking mental notes on the already-emerging fault lines between hip and unhip, as well as the ageless class divisions underpinning the new Swinging London. Even the au pair victim was fast becoming a cliché of the era, especially with Elke Sommer, a stunning blonde German who had worked as a nanny, now a much-photographed starlet posing for *Playboy* and dating Peter Sellers. Mordecai and Florence would soon have one themselves: an attractive blonde German au pair named Monica who boasted of her father's learning to him.

The scandal circulated through the Canadian Club, prompting a query from Bill Weintraub in September: "Say, what's with Silvio? Was he framed? Does he still get work?" Narizzano did keep on working—he went on to direct the trendy 1965 hit *Georgy Girl*, starring Michael Redgrave's daughter Lynn, Alan Bates, and James Mason—and had no more business with Benjamin Levene. But a reporter who covered the trial received harassing postcards from the convicted rapist for years afterwards—as would Richler, once he, too, aroused Levene's ire.

The Canadian novelist Margaret Laurence had recently moved to the city with her two children after years in Africa and, more recently, a spell in Vancouver, planning to make a fresh start. Rumour had it that the restless Laurence had actually followed a lover across a continent and an ocean. He turned out to be George Lamming, Richler's former drinking and cavorting companion from his own early London days. The Barbadian novelist had lived in Canada for a period before also returning to England, which he would soon leave again to take up a teaching post at the University of the West Indies. Laurence, thirty-five, a passionate, generous-hearted woman with a major talent and a drinking problem, was completing the novel that ultimately became *The Stone Angel*. "I'd be grateful if you and Florence would have her over some evening and introduce her to a few people," Jack McClelland asked. "She's extremely intelligent and a lot of fun."

Though it didn't happen right away, they eventually included her in an autumn party at Parkhill Road. She met their children and various London literary sorts, including Penelope Mortimer. Lamming joined them, and got into a heated discussion with the playwright David Mercer. Upset that Mercer was flirting with an actress he was interested in, Lamming twisted his ear. When Mercer started yelling, Richler, generally more inclined to observe than intervene, sided with his friend and told the other man to go home. Margaret Laurence, apparently still besotted with the Barbadian, who had rebuffed her since her arrival in the city, became upset. Robert Weaver, in town on CBC business, had brought her to the Richlers, and the gentle producer ended up escorting a despairing Laurence back to her flat in nearby Heath Hurst Road. The next month Mordecai and Florence visited her in the house she had decided to rent in the countryside near High Wycombe, the beginning of her decade-long sojourn in rural England.

A more complex literary entanglement involved the novelist Jack Ludwig, then teaching at Bard College outside New York. Richler had met the Winnipegger before, including at Amagansett, and would shortly be seeing him socially, once Ludwig, whose childhood polio had left him with a limp and a seductive air of vulnerability, also relocated to London. At his request, Richler had provided a recommendation to the Guggenheim, one of two letters he had written to the foundation in 1962. (Norman Levine had also applied and asked for his support.) Then there was Ludwig's rollicking first novel, *Confusions.* It marked him as a fellow literary traveller, with its mix of social, sexual and satirical play on the exploits and encounters of an identity-seeking American Jew at Harvard. Ludwig's debt to his close friend and fellow Bard professor Saul Bellow was evident. A year later Bellow would publish *Herzog*, which contained a scantily fictionalized version of Ludwig's affair with his wife, rendered as the cuckolding of Moses Herzog by the charming, deceitful Valentine Gersbach. Rather than feeling any shame at the awkward life-art overlap, Ludwig began telling his students he had been the model for Gersbach, and declaring *Herzog* on a par with James Joyce's *Ulysses.*

The most significant writing done by Mordecai Richler in 1963 related, indirectly, to the Ludwig-Bellow connection. He adapted the English translation of Isaac Babel's play *Sunset* for television, retitling it *The Fall of Mendel Krick.* The play, written in the mid-1920s by the Russian and produced only a few times before being denounced, was based on his stories about the Jewish quarter of Odessa. Published in English in 1955 with a brilliant introduction by the renowned critic Lionel Trilling, *The Collected Stories of Isaac Babel* unfolded a bracing world of Eastern European Jewish experience. Trilling declared Isaac Babel a genius, and his "extinction," first in the form of self-willed silence and then in a labour camp in January 1940, the most significant event in the then-still-unfolding story of Soviet repression.

Whether describing his own adventures riding to war with Red Cossacks or detailing the codes among the criminals of Odessa, Babel's vision was a particular revelation, and thrill, to diasporic Jews. Trilling traced Babel's awareness of the complexity of his identity to seeing his father on his knees before a Cossack captain on a horse. His Jewishness, born of the vibrant minority culture of Odessa, was fraught and unresolved. Jews in North America or Western Europe who were wondering about their own roaring selves found affirmation in Babel's urgent characters, and a spiritual godfather in their wry, anguished author.

In New York in 1961, Richler had been introduced to Nathalie Babel, the author's exiled daughter, then a professor of French at Barnard College. The following year, after Ted Kotcheff sold the BBC on the idea of an adaptation of *Sunset*, they learned that the absence of any legal agreement between the Soviet Union and the West meant there was no mechanism to pay Babel's estate royalties for the material. Taken with Nathalie Babel's spirit, Richler demanded that she receive a fee for their use of her father's play instead. That settled, he wrote the script, sticking closely to the English translation. Babel's story of the anti-hero father-and-son underworld bosses Mendel and Benya Krick was wild: it is the Odessa ghetto, *circa* 1913, and patriarch Mendel Krick, a drunken womanizer who impregnates a young Russian girl, is about to be barred from the synagogue for bad behaviour. Undaunted, he sabotages a proposal of marriage for his own daughter. Ready to run off with the Russian girl and disinherit his family, Krick is stopped by the violent intervention of his sons. They beat the old man into submission, resurrect the wedding and get the rabbi to oversee the ceremony

It aired in the spring in the U.K., to decent ratings and reviews. However, the CBC wasn't interested in acquiring *The Fall of Mendel*

Krick from the BBC, one producer claiming a Jew would never strike his own father, and going so far as to question whether Mordecai Richler understood the race. When he recast Mendel Krick for radio on spec, hoping it might be more palatable to Canadian listeners, he met with the same indifference. Robert Weaver struggled to explain. "I have tried the script out on three producers, and for some reason cannot find anyone prepared to do it," he said. "I think there is just an unfortunate lack of sympathy and understanding for Isaac Babel." Babel wasn't for mainstream cultural Anglo-Saxon Canada *circa* 1963. He was for Lionel Trilling and Alfred Kazin, Saul Bellow and Philip Roth, Jack Ludwig and Norman Levine. He was for Mordecai Richler and his evolving sense of himself as, in no particular order, a Jew, a writer and a man.

Finally, more than a year after he had completed it, *The Incomparable Atuk* appeared in bookstores. At the insistence of Bob Gottlieb, the American edition was retitled *Stick Your Neck Out*. "For My Father," read the dedication. "ATUK comes out in Sept.," Richler told Weintraub in June, "and Simon & Schuster seem to be enthusiastic, hopeful, etc. They assure me they are planning boffo promos and adverts. Seems the gal who "made" Catch-22 is behind ATUK. Good." Early reports out of the United States were encouraging enough: a Columbia professor and *New Yorker* critic assured Gottlieb the novel was "outrageously funny . . . brilliant." *Saturday Review* described it as a free-ranging satire on the phony world of advertising and media, and *Commentary* called it amusing, with "a gallery of moral grotesques" for characters. In England, the *Spectator* thought the book had its moments, while his friend Ron Bryden, now at the *New Statesman*, expressed admiration for the parodies of Jewish obsessions and Canadian insecurities. The *Globe and Mail* applauded his moral purpose "to show the effects of total commercialization and exploitation of the arts and the media." But, painfully, the small but influential literary magazine *Tamarack Review* said it was scarcely more than "an amusing toy."

The brief, off-kilter *Atuk* tells the tale of a Baffin Bay Eskimo who comes to Toronto to be celebrated for his intrinsic nobility.

He is soon an entrepreneur, exploiting his transported family to produce tacky aboriginal artwork, and bedding a famous teenage swimmer. Surrounding him is a confederacy of condescending dunces, all spouting cultural nationalism while peddling their own cultural crap. Pulling most strings in Companytown Canada is the tycoon Buck Twentyman. Stereotypes are flung about like confetti: Jews have big noses; Eskimos are lazy and don't bathe; Chinese are good only for cheap labour; to Natives everyone else is "white"; and for a while Atuk proves himself trickster-clever at using these conventions to prosper, and evading being anyone's fool.

But heads eventually roll. First Atuk is "outed" as a cannibal and arrested—once, lost in the Barrens, he was obliged to eat a United States intelligence officer, for which he is abruptly elevated to the status of nationalist hero. Sprung from jail to appear on a Twentyman TV quiz show titled *Stick Your Neck Out*, he is fed an impossible question about the career of hockey legend Howie Morenz. For his wrong answer he pays with his actual head.

By Christmas, the verdict was in. "ATUK did not sell well in the USA" he admitted to Weintraub: "one-pager in New Republic (boffo); nice in SHOW and COMMENTARY; included among outstanding of year in New York Times and Trib, but no, repeat no sales."

Had this compressed, feral novel, a clever but glib exercise in kicking at the cultural pricks, been worth the cost of delaying, again and again, the proposed sequel to *Duddy Kravitz*? Joyce Weiner, still officially his British literary agent, no longer had the authority over her former "boy writer" to scold him for his tendency to chase the tail of his latest undigested experiences. If she had, she might have rehearsed an updated version of that old grievance, joining what was now a chorus of insiders and cheerleaders, among them Diana Athill and Jack McClelland, the Guggenheim committee and most critics, in singing a refrain over and over until it rang in his ears: *Write the next Duddy!*

VI

HILLCREST, KINGSTON HILL, SURREY

"Man, what happened?" Bill Weintraub asked on December 21, 1963. "A cryptic note from Brian, just received, says you were borne into your new house on a stretcher, and are in a plaster cast. Most disturbing, this." To which Richler replied, "Abt the cast, slipped discville again, but bad this time. Anyway I'm out of it now and tomorrow I'm to be measured for a surgical belt and I only have to wear that for a year." He had been bedridden for six weeks, unable to either work effectively or be much help with the renovations. But Weintraub's query could as easily have applied to the changes of heart that autumn. Instead of breaking the bank for a home in downtown Toronto, Mordecai and Florence had bought one in the village of Kingston Hill, near Wimbledon and Heathrow airport and half an hour's drive from Piccadilly. They wanted to raise the children in a proper home, and England suited them better for the moment, for both career and lifestyle. They explored some sites outside the city, including viewing a charming cottage once owned by Mary Shelley, author of *Frankenstein,* in a village close to where the Claytons lived. But it proved too cramped, and even Richler, who was not tall, bumped his head climbing the stairs.

The house in Kingston Hill had everything. "At the moment, the men are putting in central oil-fired heating (at a horrifying cost), re-wiring, etc," he told Weintraub. "It's a big house, but old, man, very old, and a lot has to be done to it. . . . Big gardens, lots of rooms." Set back on a wide property, the three-storey house had an office on the top floor, four bedrooms, a nineteen-foot drawing room and spacious kitchen, and a large enough back garden for the kids to play in and Florence to plant. There were schools nearby, both public and private, shops directly across the road, and a pleasant town centre a mile to the south. "Hillcrest," as it was called, cost Richler virtually all the money he had in the world. Still, once he wrote a cheque for a hefty down payment—assisted by a generous loan from Brian Moore, who had lately sold *Ginger Coffey* to the movies—the mortgage payments ended up about the same as the rent on Parkhill Road. There were all those upgrades to factor in, of course, along with furnishings. "Our house is enormous," he admitted, "and lots of fun, but, man, am I ever broke." Shortly, he would sign to script *Life at the Top* and his account would be replenished.

Neither the temporary cash deficit, the weeks of lost work nor the slipped discs could diminish the pride evident in letters to friends. Even the teasing jab from *Commentary* editor Ted Solotaroff, who wondered if he was becoming "one of those fox-hunting Jews," couldn't do it. The purchase of Hillcrest represented the end of a two-year march to put his movie money to good use. It also marked a level of success as a breadwinner. Being able to provide for his wife and children—four, soon enough; Florence was pregnant again by spring—was fundamental to his self-esteem. So, for that matter, was his ability to be the dutiful son and assist his parents financially. Now thirty-three, Richler was an old-fashioned man and an old-fashioned Jew, and the fact that he had been raised in a household where the father had failed to provide only intensified his drive. As for the notoriously precarious business of being a literary writer, he was evolving a hard line about what the "calling" exempted one from. The short answer was "nothing at all"; he would no more accept special pleading for himself than he would for Canada as a nation. Being a good artist, he would later say, was no harder than being a good cabinetmaker. In private, he would admit that he simply had to write; it was in his nature, the fuel that kept him going. But in public he declined to acknowledge the existence of an artistic temperament—even though, by any measure, he possessed one.

He was equally old-fashioned about money. For all their closeness, the Richlers did not discuss finances. He earned the income and managed it; she ran the household and raised the children, and was content. The dynamic would shift slightly in the years to come, with Florence's rising desire to generate modest earnings of her own, but his mantra would forever be that they enjoy themselves more—better restaurants and hotels, finer whiskies and champagnes—and she worry less about economizing. But he always strove to ensure his family a level of comfort through the travail of what he liked to call his small cottage industry: the shop upstairs, the living quarters below. He would tolerate nothing less for Florence and the kids.

Being the breadwinner in 1964 definitely meant more movies and journalism. But he was canny nonetheless, rejecting a novice filmmaker who proposed an elaborate scheme to bring *Duddy Kravitz* to the screen for a mere $5,000 fee. "I've got a large family and I'm hard and expensive," Richler informed the man, ending the exchange. By April, with his back on the mend, he was planning two trips, one for *Life at the Top* and another for the American magazine *Holiday*. Ron Bryden, now a friend to both Mordecai and Florence and hired away from the *New Statesman* by *Town*, asked him to be his film critic. The gig didn't last long—being bedridden meant he couldn't get to theatres—but he was managing regular pieces for *Maclean's* (most notably trashing a feel-good book by a popular Toronto rabbi) as well as for the *Spectator, New Statesman, Punch,* the *Manchester Guardian* and the *Sunday Times.* The quality of his output was variable but complaints from editors were rare. There were so few writers with his teeth and range and appetite.

An urbanite who could barely distinguish one flower from another, he claimed to be finding a way to relax after his long bouts in the office upstairs. "My big kick these days is gardening," he told Weintraub. "I'm out there most of the time digging in bonemeal, hop manure, planting flowering shrubs, and digging

a path. . . . When you come over, I'll see to it that you have fresh
roses in yr bedroom." Florence, aware of her husband's ability to
parrot what someone else had said—a journalist's short-term
memory trick, to demonstrate knowledge where little or none
existed—had delightedly observed him issuing instructions to a
gardener using her words, verbatim. In his surprising, casual references to bonemeal and manure, Bill Weintraub heard her voice.
"Writing is my hobby now," the city boy added primly.

By spring of that year the Richlers were settled into Hillcrest,
with a pregnant Florence happy in the garden and the children
in local prep schools. "Noah goes to school," he reported, "wears
a school cap and tie, and thinks some thgs are 'super.' Others
'horrid.'" After just one term, like many good socialists, as he
himself quipped, the parents had bailed and scraped together
the money to transfer eight-year-old Daniel and five-year-old
Noah to a posh private prep school called Gatehouse close by
Richmond Park, where their English accents grew still more
refined and Noah, being precocious, was advanced by a grade.
Once Emma, and later Martha, was ready for school, Leftist
injury was added to insult: the girls were enrolled, at their
mother's insistence, in Holy Cross, a Catholic school around
the corner from the house, complete with nuns in habits. The
girls loved the uniforms and the nuns; their father was bemused
by the religious crossbreeding inside his own home. Florence
liked to cook Jewish foods, and he was content to celebrate
select Jewish holidays, including Passover, when he read the
Haggadah aloud in English and the children participated, unless
Haya Clayton was there to read or sing it in Hebrew. Family
Seders often started out on text, so to speak, before his reserve
of memorized Hebrew dried up, and then switched to wider
discussions about Jewish history. Hanukkah, too, was fine by
him, though the eight-day candles were more likely to be lit if
Max Richler was in town, but not Rosh Hashanah, Sukkot, or
Yom Kippur. His passion for playing Father Christmas made for
festive December 25ths, and he was equally fond of hiding chocolate eggs at Easter.

Such a family in such a setting required a dog. Animal and bird lover Jack Clayton, who had already bought the Richler children their first pets—a pair of ringed doves—turned up at Hillcrest one day with an elegant golden retriever. But Shane, as the dog was dubbed, after the Alan Ladd movie, proved too large, knocking over the kids. He had to go. Next, it was Ted Allan's turn to add to the household, in his case a toy poodle. Mordecai and Florence didn't love the neurotic creature, but they did love Ted. It lasted a few months.

Richler and Ted Kotcheff spent several days in the northern industrial town of Bradford scouting out locations for the adaptation of *Life at the Top*—Richler had a draft of the script already complete—and plotting how to render its core Englishness on screen, as Jack Clayton had done with *Room at the Top* five years before. In nearby Leeds they explored the old working-class Jewish neighbourhood, already then largely Pakistani, and had a meal in the sole remaining kosher restaurant. His write-up of the venue for the *Sunday Times,* which he believed an affectionate poke at such throwbacks, with their ill-tempered waiters and wine-stained, breadcrumb-covered tablecloths, earned the paper the threat of a lawsuit. When he refused to retract he had to traipse back to Leeds with a *Times* solicitor and eat in the restaurant again. Finding no wine stains, the lawyer decided it could only come down to Richler's word against the proprietor's; a better settlement offer from the newspaper made the lawsuit go away.

More ill-tempered waiters and wine-stained tablecloths awaited him when he flew to New York to do a piece for *Holiday* on what remained of the summer resorts in the Catskills north of the city, known as the Borscht Belt. Ted Allan and his brother George kept him company, and for a hilarious week they circulated through the venerable resorts, including the "Disneyland with knishes" that was the legendary Grossinger's. Richler marvelled at the "unlovely spiky bunch" that were the hotel's largely lower- and middle-class clientele. Thinking of his father, and of Ste. Agathe and the Rosenberg Inn—thinking too of the Leeds restaurateur

who had misunderstood his affectionate digs—he used the
Borscht Belt to launch a passionate defence of the "most frequently fired at class of American Jews," with their sour stomachs and cancer scares, their "unmarriageable" daughters off to
join civil rights campaigns in Mississippi. Smart literary Jews of
the Bellow, Mailer, Kazin crowd might take shots at this generation, but not Richler. The thirty-three-year-old soon-to-be father
of four, lately bedridden with a bad back, was beyond feeling
superior to anyone—in either body or soul.

He had debuted in *Holiday* a year earlier with "Canadiana: One
Man's View," among his more strident censurings of his homeland. Any objection to a union of the country with the United
States on the basis of the loss of identity would be incorrect, he
stated, given the distinct identities of states such as Maine and
Texas. That set a number of readers off, with a great pianist and
a good poet, in particular, raising objections. "I had dinner last
night with Glenn Gould who is full of curiosity about you," an
editor at *Holiday* informed him. "He thinks you are a meany and
a bully. I assured him you were neither, but just felt Toronto was
improvable." But fellow Montrealer Irving Layton believed the
insult deserved public rebuke. Mordecai Richler, he wrote in a
letter to the editor, "has not lived in Canada for a decade and
apparently has no intention of returning to the country of his
birth. . . . Having cut his roots, and since he's no Joyce, his novels
have become progressively thinner and feebler—ephemeral
puffballs."

Richler, whose dislike of the showy poet ran deep, had already
heard from Irving Layton in the letters page of *Maclean's*. His
editor friends in Toronto had excised the more vituperative
remarks from print, most notably Layton's contention that he
was an establishment ass-kisser masquerading as surly rebel,
someone who had decided years ago that "it's smart and profitable to retail family skeletons and to caricature Jews." The personal attack stung. "Mr. Layton is swinging wildly again," he
retorted, accusing him of distorting his remarks about the differences between natural and cultural borders, adding, "This is

hardly the same as saying that I would like A.M. Klein, Adele Wiseman, or Leonard Cohen to take up residence in Texas." Then he pounced on a favourite theme—the nationalistic cultural project. "False cultural frontiers, art as a patriotic production, makes for hysteria."

Had he advocated dissolving Canada into the United States? In a 1965 review of George Grant's influential *Lament for a Nation*, he did come close. "Canada, Grant concludes, is a satellite," he wrote. "Yes, of course, but its independence . . . was always illusory." To be a Canadian "was to turn pinched backs on the most exciting events on the continent, and to be a party to one of the most foolish, unnecessary and artificial of frontiers." Whether he believed this or not—had a referendum to join the United States been held at this time in his life, he might well have voted in favour—the sentiment infuriated many. For Richler in angry, calculated offence mode, that was reason enough to express it.

A few months after the Layton dust-up, Bill Weintraub socialized on the island of Hydra with Leonard Cohen. "A nice guy, very bright, with a sense of humour," he reported. Unbeknownst to Weintraub, Cohen had told a journalist that, had he run into Mordecai Richler after the *Holiday* article appeared, he would have taken a swing at him. He was due back in Montreal in the autumn to launch his new book of poems at a party being arranged for him, Irving Layton and Earle Birney, to be hosted by Jack McClelland. Had Richler been in the city as well, and accepted his publisher's invitation to drink with the poets, the night might have ended with fisticuffs. Anglo Montreal boasted three of the more prominent young (youngish, in Layton's case) writers in Canada, two from the same high school, but woe to anyone who might think to organize a group reading. Trapped in the middle was their mutual publisher and friend, Jack McClelland. He had to use all his charms to step carefully in letters and conversations alike.

Nationalism of any kind and in any place was, and would remain, a problem for Richler. Nationalism in Quebec was about to become a huge one. He had piggybacked a trip to Canada onto the *Holiday*-financed travel to the Catskills. With *Maclean's* footing the bill for a stay in Montreal, he arrived for the Victoria Day holiday, booking into the Mount Royal Hotel, a favourite spot on account of the Press Club in its basement. He suspected the celebration of the birth of Queen Victoria would be lively, given the recent emergence of separatist sentiment in the province, complete with its own radical fringe. Known as the *Front de libération du Québec*, or FLQ, the group was already responsible for a year-long terrorist campaign that included planting bombs in Westmount mailboxes. A thousand police, some on horseback, were deployed to subdue a crowd of demonstrators in what was later dubbed by the francophone media *la Nuit de la matraque*, the Night of the Truncheon, and he witnessed the fracas and saw the flags being burned. Later, it was learned that a bomb had been planted on the Victoria Bridge. It failed to explode, but the FLQ had already bombed a railway line that the prime minister was scheduled to travel, and killed a sixty-five-year-old night watchman at an army recruitment centre.

Richler, who carried on to the northern Ontario town of Timmins for a brief book-promotion stop and then to Toronto to visit his friends at *Maclean's*, staying with the Lefoliis and drinking late with Bob Fulford, was still in the country on June 1 when the leaders of the cell were arrested. His expense account for the trip told the tale of the good times had by all concerned, including a faux bill of 69 cents for "gift for mine hosts, the Lefoliis, cokes with Casimir Gzowski's grandson, expert on separatist question, long night with R. Fulford, Bombay Bicycle Room expert."

Yet to come over the next half-dozen years were FLQ bombings of the stock exchange and mayor's residence, and riots at McGill University, along with multiple bank robberies to fund the terror campaign. But the incidents of spring 1964 were already plenty for him. This despite his confession, in the account of the Victoria Day protest he wrote for *Maclean's,* that on first learning of the agitations in Quebec from London he had expressed relief that, finally, something was happening in Canada. "The French, the English, the Jews . . . and What's Bugging Everybody" ran in

August in English and then again in November in the magazine's French edition. Its clumsy cutline—"This is a highly personal and utterly outspoken account of what it's like to come home to Canada in 1964 and feel for the first time the interesting but inflammatory new mood the rest of us are already beginning to take for granted"—hinted at both the unruly writing therein, and the editors' determination to assert little control over their pugilist. "The two cultures have never really merged, they've only lived side by side with extreme discomfort, and it seems unlikely that they will ever learn to share the same house," he wrote. Careening from empathy with the separatists to dismissals of Canada to satiric attacks on enemies, the piece read like the bedraggled late-night regrets of a writer who has grown weary of his own grinding views on a subject.

Soon afterwards, Richler told his editor at *Holiday* that he planned to take a break from writing about Canada. "I am glad you have taken the pledge for two years," replied the editor, who had lately dined with Glenn Gould. "You could easily get a reputation as a bully." Another reason for the moratorium related to changes inside *Maclean's*. Management, unimpressed with its innovative, maverick editorial staff, had forced Ken Lefolii's resignation, prompting Gzowski, Fulford, David Lewis Stein and several other younger editors to quit in protest. (Peter C. Newman had departed a couple of months earlier.) Aside from two minor pieces, Richler would not write again for *Maclean's* for seven years.

When much of the material, and almost none of the attitude, from "The French, the English, the Jews" resurfaced that autumn in "Letter from Canada" in *Encounter*, a third, possibly subconscious reason for his moratorium came to light. "Quebec Oui, Ottawa Non!" opened with a comparison of the Victoria Day demonstration he had just witnessed with the Rocket Richard riot of 1955, an incident he had not seen. He thoughtfully outlined the grievances of French Canada, and introduced British readers to key moments in Quebec's ongoing quiet revolution, taking special care to damn the Duplessis government. Key emerging figures were identified, from the "brilliant" separatist newcomer René

Lévesque to the federalist Pierre Elliott Trudeau, founder and
editor of *Cité Libre* and one of seven authors of the "Canadian
Manifesto," which, as Richler remarked with approval, appealed
for "social justice, a fairer distribution of wealth, and a revised
penal code, rather than more nationalistic heat." Even his forays
into the solitudes of St. Urbain Street had become more measured. "We fought them stereotype for stereotype," he wrote of
Jewish and French perceptions of each other.

————————

Earlier in the year he had traded testy letters with Diana Athill,
who had heard rumours that he had been showing partial manuscripts around town. "I have, of course, shown neither of the two
novels in progress to any other British publisher," he assured her
in February. The question of which novels were then "in progress"
still stood. One was the lingering and unsuccessful *It's Harder to
Be Anybody*. The other was something entirely fresh: an abandoned TV play about "one man's obsession with a no-good cousin
who is persistently crossing his path but whom he has never met,"
in the earliest stages of being reborn as a major work of fiction.
My Cousin, the Horseman had planned to open with a horseman
riding through Hyde Park, London, and to feature a main character, a Canadian journalist living in Swiss Cottage with his wife
and children, named either Meyer or, in another draft, Jacob
Hersh. (The cousin was variously Moe or Joey.) Scenes were
sketched involving Jacob reading a registered letter meant for his
mysterious cousin, and a distressed dress shop employee in
cahoots with a certain Harry—"a Londoner, class-bound, a small
failure"—to blackmail Jacob for his relation's bad behaviour.

   Though the play was never completed, and St*. Urbain's Horseman*
was years from coming clear in his imagination, the book's foundation was suddenly in evidence. What Richler already had,
besides the basic story of the expatriate Canadian and his shadowy cousin, were the textures he wished for Jake Hersh's life as
husband, father, son, friend and moviemaker. They were largely

drawn from his own life: everything from having his tax audit handled by the "god-damned cockney assistant" to a friend's being co-accused of a sex crime with a disreputable local, from purchasing a huge London house to being husband to a beautiful woman, hosting a Montreal-Jewish mother from Hell and employing a blonde German au pair, was going to be put to rich use. The same was true for the world of working for the movies, his dormant memories of his black-sheep Great-uncle Baruch, whose son Michael never felt welcome among the Richlers, and even the cab driver's passing mention of "The Eichmann" awaiting execution in a Jerusalem jail. Put to use, too, would be the image of the horseman, drawn either from Isaac Babel's famous remark that "When a Jew gets on a horse, he stops being a Jew" or from his own rabbi grandfather's sketches of horsemen—or both. All of which would make it logical for him to set the novel in the restless, frustrating year of 1963. And yet the key artistic discovery—the "right" reason for him to employ his own life in a novel—was still waiting to be made.

VII

LIKE *HERZOG*

He began work that summer. "All I can say about the novel," he told André Deutsch in October 1965, "is that it is set in London, it's more in the vein of DUDDY KRAVITZ, and should have its biggest potential market here." He also apologized for requesting an advance on the manuscript, pleading necessity. "Sorry if I come off tough on all this but I've got four kids—or almost four—and I don't like writing films." Just a few days before, he had shocked himself by turning down another movie offer: *The Blue Max*, the story of a young pilot in the German air force at the end of the First World War. "7000, plus six weeks in Africa," he explained to Bill Weintraub, "is the most I've ever turned down, and I have not been altogether sober since. . . . Trouble is," he continued, of sacrificing cash for fiction, "even as I sit down and 'type page one' it [the new novel] will already have cost me more than $20,000." On learning of the decision, Jack McClelland failed to soothe his conscience. "You are absolutely out of your mind," he wrote. "I think being a father has gone to your head and has probably addled your brains." Nightmares of film deals turned down—director Irvin Kershner, fresh off making *The Luck of Ginger Coffey*, asking if he would like to adapt Isaac Bashevis Singer's *The Magician of Lublin*; Stanley Donen offering a rewrite of a comedy-thriller set to star Gregory Peck and Sophia Loren—continued to haunt him.

He no longer consulted Joyce Weiner about movie business,

and finally dismissed her as his literary agent as well. This despite her recent success in selling the Hebrew rights to *Duddy Kravitz*, albeit for a modest fee. ("I should think you will be a riot in Israel," she predicted.) She seemed sanguine in her letter of October 19, 1964, acknowledging his decision and suggesting they "cut everything off as from today." They did, and he was shortly being represented by David Machin at A.P. Watt & Son, a distinguished London agency. Joyce Weiner, who had done so much for his early confidence and career alike, summoned the courtesy to congratulate him on the latest news out of Hillcrest: "I am truly delighted to hear about the new daughter."

Martha Richler was born on October 11, 1964, in the Catholic Hospital in Wimbledon, with Jack Clayton agreeing to be her godfather. For a third time, Richler managed to miss the blessed event; delivering quickly again, Florence had the baby in the hospital room with only a nurse, a Sister Camilla, on hand. The delighted father was also not-so-secretly relieved; though he rarely spoke of it, with each birth he expected a catastrophe, the world being what it was, and took a healthy child to be sign of his and Florence's enormous good luck.

He flew Lily over for three weeks. Florence, though apprehensive about the general effect her grim manner had on them all, knew that her mother-in-law loved the children and wanted to be near her son. There was more space in the new house, though London was a little removed, limiting trips out for reasons other than shopping. But Richler insisted on occasional romantic dinners. Sometimes they crossed the Thames to the White Elephant Club or a favourite Chelsea restaurant. Other nights they got no farther than Putney. Happily, a number of friends had moved into the lately fashionable neighbourhood along the South Bank. Ted Allan, back writing scripts for movies, had a place with a view of the river—once he paid to raise his living room floor by six inches. He lived near the vivacious Irish novelist Edna O'Brien, a London resident and fellow post-colonial since 1954, and someone the Richlers, both the parents and the children—O'Brien had two sons of similar ages to Daniel and Noah—were getting to know. Her sexually frank trilogy of novels about country girls had lately been banned and even burned in her homeland. Stanley Mann, newly remarried, bought a house on Putney Green, near his former flatmate Sean Connery. The "old" crowd, still up in Hampstead and Swiss Cottage—Diana Athill and the Kotcheffs, the actress Beryl Bainbridge, whose first novel was imminent, and the Irish-Jewish playwright Stanley Price—crossed the Thames for poker games and parties at the Richlers' in Kingston Hill or Ted Allan's in Putney. Stanley Price, for one, couldn't figure why he had bought in goyish Surrey.

One news item settled a small cloud over the conviviality. Diana Athill had visited Brian and Jackie Moore in Amagansett late in the summer. Franklin and Jean Russell were also among the guests. A native of Newfoundland, Franklin was a successful author of nature books; Jean, an actress from Nova Scotia with a quiet intelligence and effortless elegance, put some in mind of Florence Richler. Athill, observant of Jean's appeal and admiring a meal she cooked one evening for the group, noted as well that Jackie Moore, mother of a seven-year-old and never fussy about her appearance, had let herself go. The Moores and Russells were best friends, and had pooled resources to buy a farmhouse in New Jersey as a shared weekend destination. But in the fall Brian Moore and Jean Russell became lovers, literally running off together and dissolving the two marriages on the spot.

On learning the details, Richler contacted both Brian and Jackie, and wrote to Bill Weintraub: "I was really very surprised . . . it seemed the most solid of marriages." Thinking of them as friends in possible need, he noted that Moore was not impetuous. "If Brian *is* deeply in love then one needn't worry about him." Jackie, and their son, Michael, were more his—and Florence's—concern. "I've phoned Jackie and I have also written asking her and Mike to come over for xmas."

Jackie Moore didn't make it to England with her boy, and struggled for months after the breakup. But she had company. By early 1965 Weintraub's letters would be reporting her relationship with the very same Franklin Russell. From London, the

Richlers, recalling their own drama of seven years before, must have mused on how easily romantic entanglements could take on the air of French farce—"quadrilateral switcheroos," in Weintraub's witty phrasing. The Moores' divorce was not pleasant, but Brian was soon remarried to Jean, and Jackie to Franklin.

Other news from home concerned the health of Moses Richler. He had undergone another operation in November, his third in as many years, and though he was healing, and hailed from a long-living clan, there were intimations. More and more the responsible son, Richler sent a cheque for a new dressing gown—Moses thanked him and told him that, since he already had one, he would use the money to buy shirts instead. And Avrum, he reported happily, "is more regular with his payments now," and had visited his father twice the previous weekend, bringing his wife and kids. "Under separate cover I have sent CHANUKA GELDT for the children," he wrote. Moses and Lily had that in common: a steady barrage of Jewish religious calendars and gifts for the kids of their apostate son. "Yes, Max's chanuka gifts arrived," he told his father of his Uncle Max's offerings, "and now whenever Noah pulls his sword he says, I'm a Maccabee." Richler, who might easily have ignored the obligations of the Jewish calendar, replied with his own faithful transatlantic shipments: a bar mitzvah gift for Max's son, Hanukkah flowers for his ancient grandmother ("with a card from Mordecai, Florence, and children"), cheques for various relations for various weddings or birthdays or festivals. He also tried calling, not always easy, given the exorbitant rates and routine delays of several hours just to get a line. "Thanks for the EREV ROSH HASHANA call," Moses said of one effort.

A much-longed-for year of concentrated work on the Horseman novel was poised to begin. "Novelville" was what he called the psychic space needed to work near-exclusively on fiction. Excited by the new manuscript, he fought hard to keep it on top of the pile during the winter and spring of 1965, as he fended off film offers and most, if not all, magazine assignments. He had finished the "final final" rewrites of *Life at the Top* and a lengthy piece for *Vogue* on Gordon Craig, the octogenarian theatre magnate whose stories he had listened to over pastis in the Café Cresp in Tourrettes in the fifties. He had had fun too with a shameless self-advertisement for his London cabal published in *Maclean's*: "What's British Television Got? Canadians, All Over the Place." But he couldn't resist generating attention for friends and supporting other writers, and starting in January, he resurrected his and Norman Levine's idea for an anthology of Canadian writing. Aware of his distance from the scene back home—the sting of Irving Layton's remark lingered, perhaps—he wrote to those who could help. Soon he had Naïm Kattan, John Robert Colombo and George Woodcock as talent scouts offering up names, addresses, poems, even books, by writers who merited inclusion. Like his father, Richler enjoyed collecting things, storing newspaper clippings, articles and books away, to be pulled back out in a year or five years, or a decade. There was some pack rat and more scholar *manqué* in the impulse, and if any memories lingered of Yudel Rosenberg's study on Esplanade, when the infant Muttle had played on its floor, they would have been of a cluttered desk and bursting bookshelves—indications of not only a learned man but a busy one.

Novelville was being invaded by more than writing assignments. There was a new baby in Hillcrest, and a new au pair. There were bouts of flu, measles and chicken pox, tonsils out and babies not sleeping. And being a Canadian in London meant continuous visitors: Alex and Gloria Cherney, Sonny and Bella Idelson, and Percy Tannenbaum from the *Gazette* all passed through during the first eighteen months in the new house. At a minimum, they needed to be met for a meal and shown the sights; for a select few, a room was provided. (Those who brought smoked meat were more likely to receive the full welcome.) American editors and writers, some old friends from Paris or New York, others friends of friends, including a couple that Philip Roth sent his way, had to be entertained as well. He also hosted his Aunt Ruth, his mother's still striking sister, taking her to the White Elephant Club with Ted Kotcheff, the pair of them revelling in the one female Rosenberg/Richler with a hint of style. His Uncle Abraham Rosenberg, too, showed up in town, and Mordecai dutifully took the rabbi and his wife to dinner. ("He's really a very boring man, and I'm afraid I haven't seen the last of him," he reported to his father.) Finally, his cousin Lionel Albert, Ruth's son, now lived in London with his family, and the Richlers saw them occasionally.

Business dinners filled many evenings, and the commute made the nights longer. "Tonight we're going out with the Claytons and the Jean le Carrés," he told Bill Weintraub. "Jack is going to make his book." Ex-MI6 David Cornwell's fourth novel, *The Looking Glass War*—John Le Carré was his pen name—published that spring, was showing signs of matching its acclaimed predecessor, *The Spy Who Came in from the Cold*, about the "Great Game" of Cold War espionage. Richard Burton had starred in the film adaptation of that novel, directed by Martin Ritt, and Le Carré's brilliant career was taking off. The dinner was enjoyable, but there were strong reasons for Richler himself to be interested in working on *The Looking Glass War*. While not as accomplished, *A Choice of Enemies* had anticipated Le Carré's early novels, and the English author and the potential Canadian scriptwriter shared a vision of the dangerous absurdity of great, impersonal ideas. They also shared, like many artists of their generation, a nostalgia for the England of grey skies and grey overcoats, plain flats and plain lives. Moreover, *The Spy Who Came in from the Cold*, produced by Shepperton Studios and shot in Dublin, spoke to intellectuals who had been shaped by the McCarthy era. American director Martin Ritt had been blacklisted, and expatriate Sam Wanamaker, a victim of the hysteria and someone the Richlers knew socially, was cast as a ruthless German double agent.

A line from the film about how the names on lists of expendable agents and operatives were all of real people, with wives and children depending on them, echoed a sentiment Richler expressed to his son Daniel around the time he declined to script *The Blue Max*. The ten-year-old boy belonged to a war games society at his school. This was much to the displeasure of his father who, forgetful of his own re-enactments of Guadalcanal on St. Urbain Street, noted the resemblance between kids 'play' and General Montgomery's pushing of toy soldiers around a gaming table during battle preparations. To re-enact the second Battle of El Alamein, Daniel and Noah collected soldiers and tanks and made a battlefield with papier-mâché dunes and ridges. Emma's passion broadened out to collecting Napoleonics, painting the soldiers in oils and using her own hair for the horses' manes.

His remarks about Montgomery, duly ignored by his war-playing kids, weren't meant as any teaching moment. Another time, when Daniel launched into a plot summary of a movie, Richler cut him off: "I can hardly wait until you're grown up, so we can have a real conversation." The psychology of children did not interest him, including that of his own, and so like many authors, their minds forever preoccupied by their chosen obsessions, he switched off when subjects or stories had no appeal, or utility, to him. A question from Emma about why Judaism was referred to more often as a nationality than a religion initially produced a fatherly harrumph: "Nonsense," he said. Only when Daniel encouraged him to give a proper answer did he explain to his daughter why the heritage was cultural and geographical, as well as religious. Curious Emma, attempting to parse the family's makeup without the benefit of her distracted parent's wisdom, enrolled with her sister in a convent school, decided that the boys were probably Jewish, the girls not. As a small child, Martha found her dad a little intimidating.

In early summer Richler absconded from Novelville again to tussle with Norman Mailer in *Encounter*. It was his third piece in as many years on the American author, who remained a passing acquaintance, and the most damning. He had attended a reading by Mailer at the Mayfair Theatre in the West End. "A frightfully hip audience," one critic described the crowd, "that included people like Jonathan Miller, Ken Tynan, bevies of beautiful girls with long blonde hair . . . a sprinkling of Negroes, and all three sexes." Mailer himself was then in full glory as a mix of literary provocateur, huckster and unhinged alpha male, and Richler sought to bring him down to size. Agreeing with the majority of critics, he dismissed *An American Dream* as an "obviously appalling" novel. Mailer's fiction might be better, he decided, if he stopped behaving like a kid "brawling under an *Esquire* street lamp," a reference to a recent profile of him by James Baldwin, and acted instead like a man. What were real men doing? They were "sitting inside writing novels. Like *Herzog.*"

No need to inform discerning *Encounter* readers that Saul Bellow had published the year's most celebrated novel. Richler's three pieces on Mailer would soon be matched by the same number about the Chicago novelist for the *Spectator*, in barely eighteen months. He had already read *The Adventures of Augie March* and heard its inherent call of liberation to Jewish North American writers to quit supplying exotic and quaint immigrant tales and, instead, just be themselves on the page. His study of Bellow began with a January review of *Herzog* and continued with a piece on the early novel *The Victim* and coverage of his play *The Last Analysis.* Above all, it was *Herzog*, which he called "a song of praise, Chassidic in its intensity and delight in life," that started him thinking freshly about how, and even why, to incorporate autobiography into fiction. Bellow himself had made the case in *Encounter* the year before, arguing that the distractions of any American age shouldn't stop novelists from exploring the private self in their books. Only by tracking interior and exterior equally could the writer be truly engaged with his life and the times.

Bellow may have been the Jewish liberator, but he had had to work the idea through in his own novels before others could understand his larger point. With its autobiographical trajectory, including an account of its author's wandering eye and failed second marriage, its frank sexism and impolitic politics, *Herzog* marked the clearest expression of his ambition. To the surprise of many, the meandering days and careening thoughts of wayward academic Moses Herzog, closer to a kind of sensory, spiritual update of a life in progress than a conventional "story," became a bestseller.

But *The Incomparable Atuk* was hardly this kind of novel. Little of Richler's passionate complexity showed in it. The less successful *The Acrobats* and *Son of a Smaller Hero* had featured more of him in their pages, but the problem then had been that the "self" ready and willing to be transformed into fiction hadn't yet been formed. *The Apprenticeship of Duddy Kravitz* had offered something of the youngish Richler, at least in its vibrant bodily textures, but he hadn't followed it up. In the intervening six years he hadn't, aside from two short stories, written about St. Urbain Street or Montreal.

Herzog offered him a model, along with a challenge. Like his creator, Moses Herzog was the child of Russian Jews who had immigrated to Montreal at the turn of the century. Napoleon Street, a few streets down from St. Urbain and one generation earlier, was the starting point for Herzog's memories of a childhood in the ghetto, complete with references to early jobs with the CPR and a family junkyard, a gift wrapped in the Yiddish newspaper *Der Keneder Odler* and a father running booze into the States during Prohibition. Along with these details came the sounds of Yiddish mixing freely with English—"You're an *edel-mensch*," Herzog's aunt scolds, "Get your hands dirty? Not you. . . . "—and, more tentatively, with French: "Come here, little Moses, and sit on your old *tante*'s knee. What a dear little *yingele*." For Richler, reading in someone else's book about "his" declared fictional turf had to amount to a bracing slap, a call to do it better, or more deeply, or with the Faulknerian commitment he had outlined in letters back in 1959. Bellow was, by his estimate, the greatest living novelist in America. But he wasn't particularly funny. Nor was he grounding his vision of the human experience quite so much in the vagaries, generally unflattering, of the body. Richler was funny, and was coming steadily, via back braces and heart palpitations and a sick father, to that more compassionate vision. Bodily decrepitude, as both measurable, observable "reality" and metaphor for the absurdity of the human condition, was on his mind.

Notwithstanding Bellow's literary challenge to the novelists of his "American Age," Richler, although initially excited by the

"Horseman" story, became uncertain about it. Robert Weaver, noting that his friend sounded "a little gloomy," encouraged him by requesting an excerpt from the manuscript for *Tamarack Review*. Instead, in October he filled out an application for a Canada Council grant to give him "the time to complete a novel, ST. URBAIN'S HORSEMAN." The book, "long and complex, is set in Montreal, England and Israel. It has been several years in progress, and continues with several of the characters first introduced in THE APPRENTICESHIP OF DUDDY KRAVITZ (1959), though it is not the second volume in that projected trilogy." He claimed he had a first draft already done, aided by advances from all three of his English-language publishers. Letters of support were forwarded by Melvin Lasky of *Encounter*, Norman Podhoretz of *Commentary* and Philip Rahv of *Partisan Review*, Jack McClelland and Kingsley Amis. He requested $5,000 and was awarded $6,500.

But by the end of that same month, although he could offer Philip Rahv a chapter from the novel for use in his annual anthology, *Modern Occasions*—the first official sighting of *St. Urbain's Horseman*—he had put the work aside. "Am doing the screenplay for Jack Clayton's new pic," he explained. "THE LOOKING GLASS WAR. The whole screenplay. Columbia pix. Big BIG monies, too. Start tomorrow." By the following April, he vowed, he would be back at the manuscript, once more free from financial pressures. But he also mentioned in the same letter to Bill Weintraub that his "book of Can. essays" would be out the next summer. Switching projects in midstream, promising "finished" manuscripts that never appeared—these were signs that he was once again floundering.

The script for *The Looking Glass War* was pressing, with the shoot scheduled for the following spring. But other interesting assignments lured him away. Especially engaging was a TV interview with expatriate Canadian media baron Roy Thomson. His former *Maclean's* editor Ken Lefolii had taken a job as a producer with the daring new CBC newsmagazine *This Hour Has Seven Days*. Created and co-hosted by the young polymath Patrick Watson, the show was a natural fit for Richler. "Do you think this is your country or are you still Canadian?" he asked the much older Thomson in his London office. It was one of two dozen concise questions that Richler, demure in his one suit and tie, managed in ten minutes of television. Though a couple were cheeky—"You don't think it's stuffy?" he inquired of the British House of Lords, which the baron had joined at the cost of his Canadian citizenship—several more were incisive. "Do you feel that by accepting the title you access success on their terms?" He even probed the impact of extreme wealth and power on the baron's children. "Do you feel the sons of very successful men have special problems?" he asked. Surprisingly, Thomson gave a thoughtful answer. His son and heir, Ken, he granted, might find it hard.

Richler handled Thomson well. He could read men quickly, decide their character and proceed with a confidence that, in turn, marked him as worthy of respect. "I'm launched on a new career, *bubbele*," he joked with Bill Weintraub about *This Hour Has Seven Days*, ". . . and now they want more. Plenty more." It was true; Ken Lefolii thought the interview might be the beginning of a new sideline for his friend. Richler was invited back on the show a few months later to discuss the war in Vietnam, but the irreverently serious *This Hour Has Seven Days* was soon off the air. Still, his success with Lord Thomson was revealing. From early on he had shown the knack of doing a great number of things well. Not for nothing was the eighteenth-century giant of letters Dr. Johnson one of his lifelong models. Johnson, too, often found himself steered by financial necessity and over-whelmed by pleasing, sometimes distracting choices.

Life at the Top opened in London that same autumn. Ted Kotcheff and Richler had tried to convert the liabilities of the novel into cinematic attributes. But following up an epochal film like *Room at the Top* obliged something more than a "ten years later" resumption of the story of the social climber Joe Lampton, which was all that John Braine had provided. The *New York Times* commented that Braine's unwillingness to offer "any new exposures of the nature and resources" of Lampton had left the screen-writer without dramatic material. That proved to be the consensus opinion, a reality Richler noted nervously in a December letter, saying the film "cost a whacking amt of monies to make" and had "a good commercial—if not much of a critical—chance."

It would be nine years before the friends would again be sporting tuxedos at a premiere of a film they had worked on together. In the interim Richler had the biggest scripting assignment of his life to complete, and he knew that, by almost every measure—from quality of source material to choice of director—John Le Carré's *The Looking Glass War* was his best chance to really make it in the movies.

VIII

SITTING SHIVA

"We have a radio, piano, gramophone, television, phone, an electrolux cleaner," wrote Norman Levine in spring 1966 of his house above the seaside town of St. Ives, in Cornwall. "No need to take yr typewriter," he added, extolling the study as the finest room, "you can use this one." So that August, the Richlers and the Levines swapped homes for two weeks. For Mordecai and Florence, whose only vacation in years had been a weekend in Paris, the swap allowed for a holiday with the four children on the wild, beautiful west coast of England.

Norman Levine was a friend, albeit not a close one. Differences seemed greater than similarities between the two sons of Orthodox Canadian Jews in exile. Levine hadn't published a book since *Canada Made Me* eight years before. For his one-off excoriation of Canada, the Ottawa native had paid the price that Richler might have reasonably expected to have exacted from him for any number of books or articles. Unlike Richler, however, he had little aptitude or appetite for developing relationships and support networks to protect and bolster him; a quiet, rather precise, gentle man, he was not a natural hustler and fighter ready to defend and expand his turf. In St. Ives Levine developed friendships with the great painter Francis Bacon and other artists, and in the 1960s he wrote several of the short stories that would establish him as an austere master of the form. But his situation, financial and professional, would remain precarious throughout his life, and, as a father of five, he frequently borrowed money from friends to scrape by. Richler, who had his own young family to look after, sent him small sums.

The Levine cottage proved too rustic, and Cornwall too windy and cold: "next summer, the south of France," Richler grumbled afterwards. His mood wasn't helped by a harrowing recent ride on the roller-coaster movie business. He had put aside *St. Urbain's Horseman* to script *The Looking Glass War*, working closely with Jack Clayton. In the spring he reported that Clayton was pleased with the draft and the project was a "go"; by June, studio upheaval had abruptly crashed it—or "temporarily shelved" it. "Actually," he told Weintraub, "the trouble is Columbia is teetering. . . . Well, there is a chance Paramount will take over the project. Columbia wants to sell."

At least, he remarked, "am working on the novel, which is going slowly." Shortly before they set off on holiday, Richler complained to André Deutsch about some overdue cheques: "As I continue and continue with this long and bloody novel, I find myself increasingly short of brandy and cigar monies." The allusion to cigars hinted at another cause for turmoil; he had lately tried to quit smoking. "How is the book going and how is the non-smoking regime?" Brian Moore inquired. Not well: within a few months he would be telling friends that he had only managed to cut back on the number of cigars he enjoyed each day. By September Moore was commiserating with his latest jam-up with the novel—"Sorry to hear that you're again having trouble." Jack McClelland was less consoling: "What do you mean you're stuck on the novel for god's sake? Do you mean you are busy writing it? Or do you mean you are bogged down? It is high time it was finished."

Richler had meant bogged down. Still unable to see the big book clearly, and more and more inflamed by the times, he happily digressed into a "satiric novel" conceived almost a year earlier, when he assured the Canada Council that he would devote himself to *St. Urbain's Horseman*. This was none other than *It's Harder to Be Anybody*, the manuscript begun in 1959 as a story, abandoned in 1960 as the "Shalinsky novel," and reincarnated several times since. Unwilling to quit on the central conceit, he had resumed work on it the summer of 1965. Ostensibly, the conceit concerned a Gentile who can't convince people that he *isn't* Jewish. But the ruse, and his attachment to it, went deeper. The phrase was lifted from a popular Yiddish play by Sholom Aleichem. *It's Hard to Be a Jew* was first performed in Russia in 1911, and an amateur production in Montreal in 1949 was reviewed by student journalist Mordecai Richler. Born Sholom Rabinovich in Kiev, Sholom Aleichem was sacrosanct among Diaspora Jews for his preservation, in stories, novels and plays, of the already diminished, soon-to-vanish world of the shtetl. In *It's Hard to Be a Jew* a Russian, the son of a general, exchanges identities with a Jewish friend for a year. He lives with a family and falls in love with the daughter. The Jewish boy, in turn, experiences love among the Cossacks. Of late, Aleichem's work was reaching a wider audience; *Fiddler on the Roof*, a Broadway phenomenon of 1964, was loosely based on his stories of Tevye the Milkman.

Sholom Aleichem lived part of his adult life in Odessa. But his kinship with Isaac Babel ended there. Tevye the Milkman marked one kind of European Jew; Benya Krik, the underworld boss, another. Certain Jews in the New World, in particular younger intellectuals raised in the lee of the Holocaust, felt obliged to choose between them. Krik, in a sense, rode a horse boldly, and so had stopped being a quaint, harmless member of the Hebrew faith; Tevye sang and danced, lived and died in his cloistered village. For someone of Richler's disposition, the decision was easy.

In the aphoristic "It's hard to be a Jew," a common phrase among Old World Jewish people, he could gather nearly all the aspects of his faith that simultaneously irked and stirred, dismayed and attracted him. At his inaugural public appearance at the synagogue in Montreal, an audience member had asked why he couldn't write like Sholom Aleichem, instead of all the "garbage about your people." Certain letters from his father in the 1950s, most notably Moses Richler's denunciation of his proposed marriage to Cathy Boudreau on the premise that a Gentile wife,

or her family, would eventually blame the Jew for all their problems, had rung similar bells. Still further back had been Lily
Richler's stories about her rabbi father for the *Canadian Jewish
Review*. "Ah, it's hard to be a Jew!" women sighed on being told
that a chicken for Rosh Hashanah had too much fat, and so
couldn't be blessed as kosher. The saying implied the demands
made by Talmud rules and the burden of being the "chosen
people, hinting at a fatalism tinged by passivity. But it also contained an impassioned response to a world evidently, and often
violently, hostile to the Jews, as well as a higher sense of responsibility born of the faith's astringent and demanding traditions of
moral clarity and action. Historically, Judaism had brought the
concept of moral man to the fore, and while being a "good" observant Jew did not impress Richler much, being a moral one did,
even if it obliged standing apart, dwelling perpetually in a lonely
place. "There is more to Jewishness than observance," he would
later say, citing famous "Shabbas goys" like Franz Kafka and Saul
Bellow. "There is invention, imagination, a cherishing of the book,
reverence for scholarship, appetite for life, sensual appreciation,
and, above all, humanity, tolerance." If it was hard being that kind
of Jew, it was also the only kind Mordecai Richler wanted to be.
Letting go of the complex, rich satiric possibilities of the *It's Hard
to be a Jew/It's Harder to be Anybody* idea was no easier.

He explained to the frustrated Jack McClelland what had happened. "After many months of sweating over *St. Urbain's Horseman*
I got depressed and put it aside, which hurt, and suddenly got
started on a novel, a satire." The tale of the two books became a
formal competition when his Simon & Schuster editor, Bob
Gottlieb, visited in early November. Using the daring of his
American editor to encourage his Canadian publisher to be bold,
Richler relayed the sequence of events to McClelland. "Gottlieb
came over, and I showed him half of the satirical novel and he
had put up $2500 against St. Urbain [but he said] he would put
up $2500 against this one, provided he didn't think St. Urbain
was a loss, so I showed him 200 pages of St. Urbain and his
enthusiasm was boundless." A deal was struck on the

spot—spring delivery of the satiric novel, more money for *St. Urbain's Horseman* later in the year—and Richler, joking that "I count you a friend, which is costly," asked Jack McClelland to take the same risk: purchase two unfinished novels by a novelist who had been struggling of late to complete anything. "No vintage brandies, no roulette, less smoked salmon," he promised of 1967. Adding, "All I can tell about the new novel is that it is not set in Canada, but in Swinging London and is staggeringly filthy. As I rewrite, I blush. What a sewer I am." Unmentioned, for the moment, was that the "new" novel was actually a radical reconception of *It's Harder to Be Anybody*, updated in dishonour, so to speak, of Cool Britannia.

McClelland too had seen parts of the "older" manuscript—the Horseman novel. His interest piqued, he now agreed to a $500 advance for the filthy book. "Okay, so make your book sexy," he wrote back. "You can't shake me. We publish Leonard Cohen. We are dedicated to sex." When Richler still hadn't seen the cheque by December, he prodded his publisher: "Why, the kids asked me, aren't we getting gifts for Christmas like all other Jewish kids? Are we poor like Norman Levine?" The money arrived shortly thereafter.

The two-novel plan, long shot as it was, proved the spur that Richler required. At the time it was proposed—fall 1966—he had published one slim novel since *Duddy Kravitz* in 1959; over the next five years he would publish four books, including two novels. The satiric fiction, its eventual title *Cocksure,* would land him on the bestseller lists, win awards and acclaim, and be counted as an outrageous mirror held up to an outrageous age. Written out of his moral dismay, its satiric influences the same mash— Jonathan Swift and Franz Kafka, Evelyn Waugh and Joseph Heller—that had informed *The Incomparable Atuk*, it was a brilliant example of an artistic screed perfectly timed and timely, its relevance linked directly to the excesses it was addressing. The other project, while slower of impulse and more difficult to execute, attentive, as per the Saul Bellow dictum, to both the private life and the public times, would not only yield *St. Urbain's*

Horseman but reveal his own "pattern in the carpet," as Henry
James described it: the unique stitching to any imagination that
could be reworked in countless original ways.

———————

"I just visited your father and he is in excellent spirits," Max
Richler wrote to his nephew in October 1966. "The reason he
could not talk when you phoned was that he had a tube through
his nose—post-operation procedure." For a fourth time in less
than a decade, Moses Richler had gone under the knife, three of
the procedures for cancer. For a fourth time, his son had not been
in the country when illness struck.

From his home in England he was solicitous and generous, his
letters models of a filial respect that appear, at times, almost a
fantasy of the relationship he wished he'd had with his parent. In
his constant references to the friends he had introduced to Moses,
along with the barrage of books and articles, reviews of his work
and even mentions in London gossip columns that he sent across
the ocean, there may have been some pride in his own achieve-
ments, but far more was a desire to enliven his father's existence
via association. He took care to praise Moses for reading *Herzog*,
at his recommendation, adding with a wink that he should be
ashamed of also having enjoyed the erotic classic *Fanny Hill*.
Knowing of his father's infatuation with the movies, he made certain to drop celebrity names, in particular those he counted as
friends. "Sean Connery (James Bond) is going to direct one of
Ted Allan's plays in New York. Sean has to go to Japan first to
make a new James Bond film."

The painful undercurrent running through the letters was that
he lived on the far side of an ocean and had not been home in
three years. Worse, he had promised a visit in October, only to
have to cancel. "I'm short of funds at the moment," he confessed,
"and was on the verge of writing to say I wasn't coming when Max
phoned and told me you were in the hospital." He asked his
London doctor to call his father's doctor and go over his

condition, and announced a plan: a spring visit, when "you will be completely restored to health." (Moses was scheduled for radiation therapy in February.) He even proposed a father-son trip to New York, where they could attend rehearsals of Ted Allan's new musical. "We cd rent a car in New York and go to Grossinger's for the weekend," he wrote with real tenderness. "We could do all sorts of things together and I'd make sure you got sufficient rest." Tellingly, his anxieties extended to whether his parent was being accorded proper respect by his family. "I understand Av has been to the hospital? Has he brought the children around yet?" Or Moses' own siblings, the formidable Richler clan? "Am also pleased to hear that your brothers are treating you so well, which is, after all, as it should be, considering how kind you have always been to them." The family wounds of a quarter-century ago, felt both for himself and on behalf of his father, were unhealed.

"For the first time in months and months, my plans are settled," he assured him in November. "At least for six months ahead." He actually resolved to make two trips to Montreal, one for Moses, the other at the invitation of "Universal Writers," a pavilion at Expo 67, the much-anticipated world's fair to be held in the city from June through September 1967. Richler didn't quite know what a three-day appearance at Universal Writers would involve—"to show my cock at a congress at Dupont Audit," he speculated to Bill Weintraub—but they were paying his way over, plus a $200 honorarium. "All very useful," he wrote, "as after all this time novelizing I am short, baby."

Luckily, his energy ran high that winter. For the first time in a decade, he wasn't writing or even attempting to generate a movie or TV script; the suspension of activity around the once-so-promising Clayton-Richler collaboration on *The Looking Glass War* turned out to be permanent. Though Columbia did end up making the film, they did so with another director and a different script. It was a painful setback, but the weight off his shoulders benefited the fiction. By April, he was writing to McClelland with assurances that the satiric half of the plan was finished. "It's dirty, Jack," he declared in the buoyant tones of someone who has finally kept a major deadline. "Full of obscenities, comic obscenities, and I don't know if this is going to mean trouble for you in Canada." During the winter he had submitted ten pages of the manuscript to his old Paris acquaintance George Plimpton at the *Paris Review*. Plimpton declared it winner of the magazine's humour award. The prize? "Five hundred bucks or Jackie Kennedy."

Practically speaking, he had, as he never failed to point out to his editors, a large and growing family to feed. He would take all, or nearly all, the work they could provide, and he could write decently, if often hastily, about pretty much anything: books, movies, theatre, sports, politics or some combination thereof. But whether due to the security of the book deals or the freedom from scriptwriting, when not driving headlong to complete *Cocksure*, he now managed to produce some of the best journalism of his career for the "snob magazines," as he dubbed them. Two reviews and one essay stood out. The previous spring he had reviewed *Encyclopedia of Jews in Sports*. Tongue in cheek, he had declared the volume, largely aimed at the bar mitzvah boy, "a pioneering work" in countering the "oldest myth about the Jew—that he is a 'stranger to athletics,'" and called for further icon-smashing volumes on subjects ranging from "Jewish Drunks" to "High School Drop Outs," "Thugs from Noah to Today," and "Famous Jewish Homosexuals, Professional and Amateur, Throughout History." A companion review of the autobiography of the pitcher Sandy Koufax regressed into a memoir of his own boyhood infatuation with the Montreal Royals team, including its lone Jewish athlete, Herman Kitman. "Hey, Kermit," he quoted himself and his friends taunting the luckless player on Saturdays, "you *pipick*-head, you think it's right for you to strike out on *Shabbes*?" *Commentary* editor-in-chief Norman Podhoretz assured him that he was "sending it to the printer with little or no editing today." Podhoretz added a PS about the Jewish Koufax: he was 25–8 with twelve games left in the season.

Podhoretz was another apostate New York Jewish intellectual, admired or excoriated for repositioning himself away from the

inherited Left views of his upbringing to Barry Goldwater republicanism. Richler would review two of Podhoretz's own books in
the next couple of years. During the sixties, far from trying to
avoid reviewing friends or contacts, he used his influence to pen
notices about, among others, Terry Southern, Kildare Dobbs,
George Plimpton and Alfred Kazin. He had a huge appetite for
professional friendships. As well, given the ascendancy of Jewish
writers and Jewish-themed writing—"We need more gentile
novelists," he would soon be remarking, "they should be encouraged"—it would have been difficult to avoid any intersection. And
Richler wanted to intersect with his fellow scribes, to engage
with them and thus fulfill his own job description as a witness to
his age. What better way than by taking on the books and authors, ideas and currents, defining that era?

For Jewish kids on the eve of the Second World War, comic book
heroes had been morale-boosting fantasies. "They were invulner-
able" he wrote, "all-conquering, whereas we were puny, miserable and defeated." They were also more reliable than real-life
heroes; in 1939 and 1940, only Captain Marvel could stop the
Nazis from rampaging across Europe. In a compression of public
and personal, of the broad Jewish experience and his own specific upbringing, Richler expressed a notion familiar to Jews of
his generation: *Superman* and *The Flash* "were our golems." "The
Great Comic Book Heroes," first published in May 1967 in
Encounter, was an afternoon or two of work. But in his review of
Jules Feiffer's book about Captain Marvel, Superman, the Human
Torch, the Batman and Robin, et al., he either recovered or discovered the primacy of his own experience of being shaped—or
"warped" in his word—by those same heroes. Superman, he
pointed out, was the creation of Jewish boys, one a Toronto
native, and "there is no doubt, for instance, that *The Green Lantern*
has its origin in Hassidic mythology." *The Flash* marked a new
era, he believed: still Jewish, but Reform.

Mordecai Richler, *circa* Christmas 1966, was no superhero. He was a few weeks shy of thirty-six, overworked and under-exercised, a sufferer, thanks to sitting for hours on end at the typewriter, of the proverbial "bad back." He smoked and drank. Dieting efforts, overseen by Florence, were faring only so well with a man who, if at a restaurant with a friend who ordered a lean smoked meat sandwich, would ask, half-jokingly at best, if he could be served the extra fat. Now his teeth were failing him; four needed to come out, and a bridge put in. "My gums are bloody agony," he confessed to his father. "I am very tired these days," he admitted in February. That note to Montreal included a separate letter from Noah, thanking Moses for the gift of stamps. "Dear Grandfather or *zeyda*," the six-year-old had typed out on his father's machine. He mentioned that he had to write to Ted Kotcheff as well. "Martha is two," the boy clarified for his grandfather, whom he hadn't seen since he was a toddler, "I am six, Emma is five, and Daniel is ten."

Richler was in particular high spirits that winter, however, over the good news from Bill Weintraub. For years he had been worrying in letters and calls about his friend's battles with depression and alcohol, alternatively cajoling, scolding, and encouraging him to fight harder. The door to the Richler home was always open to Bill, who belonged to a small group who were *de facto* family, "real" uncles to the children, rather than the vast number of aunts and uncles back in Canada who remained largely hypothetical. Mordecai rarely mentioned his extended family to Florence or the children. They didn't know, for instance, that his Uncle Joe was in financial straits or his Uncle Harry, the former high-flyer, likely to declare bankruptcy. Even if they had been informed that his cousin Mike was in hospital or their step-grandmother's daughter was pregnant, they wouldn't have had much to say—they'd never met these people. Bill Weintraub, in contrast, the children knew and loved. His news from before Christmas was to be celebrated. Bill hadn't had a drink in six months, was in a new relationship, and had no fewer than three film projects underway, including a documentary about a messy divorce, which he was co-writing

with the former Jackie Moore. "A new life," Weintraub summarized, "a fine and new girlfriend. I feel better than I have in years."
He was adamant that Richler should get to Montreal for Expo,
itself part of the larger celebrations to mark Canada's centenary.
"It's very lively these days."

While Jackie Moore was working with Bill, Richler and her ex-
husband continued to exchange friendly letters, most of which
contained reports about the "madness, suits and nonsense," as
Moore put it, of his nasty divorce. The Irishman did some character scouting about the new American director of *The Looking
Glass War* to see if Richler's script might be salvaged, and in turn
sent sincere thanks to him for arranging a meeting with Jack
Clayton. Their professional lives, too, continued in parallel, with
new novels to struggle over and film projects to complain about.
Still, Moore now lived in Malibu and Richler in London, and they
were rarely in the same city together.

In April he flew to Montreal to see Moses. He commanded that
his host, Bill Weintraub, organize a party while he was there, and
had sent a guest list from London back in January. The list evidenced both his boundless energy for scripting plans and his
determination to maintain his friendships from afar. Among
those to be invited were "the Idelsons, Naïm Kattan & his missus,
Cherneys . . . Dink Caroll . . . Neil Comptons, Bob Fulfords (who
are being sent to Mtl, from April 1–Labour Day, Toronto Star
EXPO correspond.), my Uncle Max . . . Sean Moores, Adele
Wiseman, Frank Scotts." He also requested "a stage separatist,
some black power negroes, one faggot," declaring that all were
to be "cordially invited to what we London Swingers call a
THINGEE. . . . Right? Right. And thank you very much, baby," he
added.

His will was done, naturally, but he spent most of Passover with
his father. He also called his brother. Nearly all his information
about Avrum was being filtered through letters from his parents.
Under the impression that his sibling continued to shield his children from Moses, he demanded that he bring them to visit their
zeyda. Avrum, unaware of the perception that he was denying his

father access to his grandchildren, complied. Interestingly, there was no parallel discussion about Mordecai's children, who did not know their grandfather at all.

The brothers wound up celebrating a sombre Passover with their bedridden parent in his apartment on Walkley Avenue in N.D.G, dining on a Seder plate put together by Sarah. Moses could barely speak, and it fell to Avrum and Mordecai to pose the ritual questions from the Haggadah. "Write cheerful letters to your father," Sarah Richler asked her stepson on the eve of his flight back to England. He was returning less than two months later for Expo, planning to see more of Moses, but her letter to London in early May was not encouraging. "Dad, himself, is going down in health," she wrote of her husband. "There is a change in him every day."

On June 7 Bill Weintraub returned to his apartment to find a telegram. ARRIVING WEDNESDAY NOON FOR FATHERS FUNERAL. WLL CONTACT YOU ON ARRIVAL. MORDECAI.

The telegram was sent two days into a new war in the Middle East. Richler had parted ways with some fellow Jewish intellectuals the month before by declining to sign a second open letter (he had signed the first) organized by the World Jewish Congress and printed in the *Sunday Times*, calling for the British government to break an earlier Egyptian naval blockade of the Gulf of Aqaba. On June 5 Israel, convinced that Egypt's President Nasser was preparing to invade, had launched a pre-emptive attack. In a single day the country destroyed the air defences of Egypt and Syria. Jordan, in turn, attacked West Jerusalem. By June 10, however, Israel had delivered a humiliating defeat to its Arab enemies, all the more remarkable for its swiftness. It seized several new territories: the Gaza Strip and Sinai Peninsula from Egypt, the Golan Heights from Syria and the West Bank, including East Jerusalem, from Jordan.

Max Richler met his nephew at the airport on day three of the war, and remarked that he already had a bottle of whisky on the go. Richler tolerated flights better with alcohol, but he was also steeling himself for the traditional seven-day period of mourning, cloistered with his extended family. The family was expected to sit shiva together, in a house or apartment, symbolically struck so low by the loss that they would repose only on low chairs or the floor, all mirrors covered, seeking ways to heal through days filled with stories about the loved one, sustained by generous quantities of food supplied by friends.

For Richler, a week in the company of his aunts and uncles amounted to a Dante-like trial, all the more hellish for being stationary. He made a show of his discomfort, beginning at the funeral, where he refused to allow either his jacket or his tie to be cut by the rabbi, a mourning ritual. "This is an expensive jacket," he explained. During shiva in Moses' small apartment, he declined to put on the tefillin, and though he sat on the floor, he did so with a bottle of whisky in hand and little to say to the relations, who—with certain exceptions, Max Richler most notably— had condescended to his father all his life. Grandmother Richler, in turn, summarized her disgust with her grandson: "*Ehr drinkt, ehr pisht*"—"He drinks, he pisses," she said.

Richler must have done a lot of both over the seven days. But he also did a considerable amount of listening to his clan chatter among—they presumed—themselves. "Something of a family party," was how he later described the week to Diana Athill. "One day I'll tell you about it."

It was during shiva that Avrum asked him why he drank so much. "If I don't drink, I can't write," he answered. He meant the daily pressures, and the corresponding need for a liquid boost not in order to create but for release, and for relaxation afterwards. He didn't drink while working—he was meticulous about that—and while writing only unscrewed a bottle, or ordered a Scotch, once the day's business was done. Like most professional writers, he never found it easy to produce good sentences, whether for a knock-off newspaper piece or the opening scene of a cherished novel. The uncertainty that accompanied creating, crafting and producing works of fiction that he could be proud of was becoming an epic, daily struggle with doubt and anxiety. To keep at this, he was telling his brother, he had to drink.

If Avrum nourished any hopes that their father's death might initiate a reconciliation between them, he was soon disappointed. Richler, who held grudges, had a huge one against him, and not only because of the distortions their mother had spread about Avrum's treatment of her. His complaint against his older sibling, possibly not quite formed in his own mind, went much further back, to the goings-on inside 5257 St. Urbain Street in late winter 1944. But that conversation between them could not happen in June 1967, and Avrum Richler, then making a new life as an optometrist in St. John's, Newfoundland, said goodbye to Mordecai without knowing when they might meet again. Months later their Uncle Max, sensitive to the estrangement, made sure Mordecai was aware that Avrum was paying his portion of the funeral expenses. He also lauded Mordecai's generosity with Sarah Richler, whom he continued to support. "Your cheque arrived and you certainly have done more than your share," Max Richler noted.

Richler's kindness to his stepmother, Sarah, didn't earn him the one legacy he actually sought: the diaries his father had written in his private code. Family members, long dismissive of Moses' obsessive note taking, had lately started to wonder about the contents, a response suggesting some worry about the secrets within. Secrets or not, relations had good reason for not wanting Moses' son to see the diaries. *Son of a Smaller Hero* had created a profound breach of trust between the writer and his family. Richler had never apologized for that book, or for any of the short stories that drew directly on his childhood, or even for the tonal overlaps between fiction and life in *Duddy Kravitz*. Soon, there would be scenes in *St. Urbain's Horseman* of alarming similarity to the events of 1967. In this regard he wasn't to be trusted, a plain truth about many authors. Equally, writers who take no prisoners in their work can expect little or no mercy from those they assail, however indirectly or even unintentionally. He understood this, and once past actually wanting to expose hypocrisy and to out secrets, was still aware that his writing caused hurt among family members. That he kept on in this manner was a function both of his bruising art and nature alike.

Whatever her reasons, Sarah Richler denied her stepson access to the locked room where his father had stored his personal papers. But she did give him Moses' tallith. She also gave him a stack of love letters written by Lily to Julius Frankel, which Moses had discovered, alerting him to the farce of his marriage, and which he had held as bitter ransom for twenty-five years.

Lily Rosenberg was not invited to the funeral, nor was she invited to sit shiva.

IX

MINORITY MAN

"Suddenly," he wrote of Montreal in the magical summer of 1967, "all the ambitious building of twelve years, the high-rise apartments, the downtown skyscrapers, the slum clearance projects, the elegant new metro, the Place Ville Marie, the Place des Arts, the new network of express highways, the new hotels, have added up to another city." Expo, meant as a coming-out party for Canada, was underway when Richler returned in late June to appear at the Universal Pavilion, and then again three weeks later to write about the fair for the *New York Review of Books*.

He stayed with Bill Weintraub on the second visit, but did see his mother; it was their first time together since the death of her ex-husband. Bob Fulford, in the city working on a book about Expo, witnessed a farewell at the pavilion between Mordecai and Lily that suggested only a bare residual affection on the son's part. Florence joined him for the third sojourn, her own first appearance in her hometown in several years. Minus the children, they could socialize freely with friends, including meeting Magda Landau, the demure Polish émigrée and antique jewellery expert who had lately changed Bill Weintraub's life for the better. Richler confessed to being "overwhelmed by the difference" in Montreal; he liked what he saw, even the tepid Saint-Jean-Baptiste parade on June 23, an occasion in the past for nationalist flare-ups. "If only three years ago English-speaking Canadians were running scared," he noted, "then this summer, whenever the so-called 'Quiet Revolution' came up, it was as a joke." The essay, his second for the prestigious *NYROB,* seemed tired and distracted—like its author, still reeling from the loss of his father.

In November he made a fourth transatlantic crossing in eight months, ostensibly to gather materials and meet with writers for the anthology of Canadian writing, and to fullfil an assignment from Peter Gzowski to cover the Grey Cup football championship in Ottawa. But above all he came to attend a special wedding in Montreal: Bill Weintraub and Magda Landau were married by a rabbi on Sunday, November 26, with a party that evening at the home of their old friend Alex Cherney.

While in Ottawa he met up again with his friends Bernard and Sylvia Ostry. After a period as on-air host for the CBC, Bernard Ostry was shortly going to work for the new Liberal government. At their house Richler was introduced to Ostry's future boss, the then minister of justice, Pierre Elliott Trudeau. Plans for the dynamic, fiercely anti-separatist Trudeau were already in play, with many of Richler's friends, such as the Ostrys, in the vanguard of support for the man they felt could bring Canada into the modern world with style and intelligence. "Trudeau might *win*," Peter Gzowski would be telling him later that winter of the spectacular ascent of the charismatic Outremont native. "Jesus! Pierre Trudeau as prime minister!"

"NEWSWEEK, just out, smashing. LIFE, boffo. TIME, favourable, and still Best Read list. BOOK WORLD, zingy, lead review. BOOK WEEK, Chi., smash lead notice. NATION, come this Friday or next, page and a quarter lead, hotsy." In Canada, too, "FULFORD in Toronto Star, wowsy, CALLAGHAN in Tely, very favourable." The sexy satire Richler had promised his publishers was out and the news could not have been better. "Here, we are on Cloud-9, or COCKSURE-9." A month later, U.K. feedback was still more excited. "First Sunday enormous leads in Observer," he wrote, displaying his eagle eye for literary hierarchies, "Sunday Times, with big photos. Boffo in daily Times, comparing me to Swift the Dean. Boffo lead with pix in Guardian, also with the old Dean comparisons. Pretty good lead in New Statesman." All this, plus zingy sales in England, despite the usual Richler jam-up—being banned by the W.H. Smith chain for obscenity, an embargo that also cost *Cocksure* distribution in South Africa, New Zealand and Australia. "Smashing paperback sales to Bantam" meant a $15,000 advance for the paperback reprint; "Hollywood noises" yielded an early $35,000 option against $100,000 if the movie was made.

"Filmland is still driving me starker," he reported of the interest in adapting the book for the screen. "With long distance calls from Hollywood. With Mike Nichols on the phone to me from the Savoy. With Peter Hall taking me to lunch and telling me how badly he wants to do it. With Jack Lemmon's co. inviting me to drinks here today." He had drinks with Nichols, who was en route to Italy to scout locations for the movie adaptation of Joseph Heller's *Catch-22*, while awaiting further word from Hall, the gifted young theatre director. "Just teasing, promising, talking," he admitted of the flurry. Mike Nichols matched the terms offered by the winning bid—Filmways, a London production company, with Peter Hall set to direct—but lost out in the end because he couldn't promise to direct the movie himself. With Filmways, too, Richler got to write the screenplay. "I'm scripting, starting tomorrow," he said in July.

After the "heavy nervy drink time" of the waiting period came months of "feeling chipper." To pile it on, there was renewed interest in an option of *The Incomparable Atuk* by a New York stage producer, along with still another grant from a Canadian cultural agency. "And 4,000 dollar grant from Prov of QUEBEC," he told Weintraub. "Je souviens, baby. Je very souviens."

Cocksure, dedicated "For Jack and Haya," was wild satiric concoction. Told with enormous vitality, it enveloped the story of expatriate Gentile Canadian book editor Mortimer Griffin's trials with the Judaism forced upon him by the unsinkable Shalinsky in a surreal tale excoriating Hollywood and Swinging London. Griffin, a hapless everyman, is no match for the vulgarities of the liberated times. Nor can he stand up to Star Maker, the "aging undying" movie mogul who cannibalizes his stars and starlets to feed his immortality. Accused of being both a Jew and an anti-Semite, he loses everything, including his children and formerly prudish wife. She dissolves into the arms of his best friend, a reprobate artist named Ziggy Spicehandler, while he finishes up embroiled in a "romance" with an actress named Polly. Fantasy and farce: Polly is a Star Maker automaton, a puppet acting out "scenes" from a movie.

A more malignant figure than Buck Twentyman of *Atuk*, the character of Star Maker summarizes the era. No longer either male or female, due to the grafting of various body parts, Star Maker is primed biologically to do what a disgruntled employee suggests he do metaphorically: "Go fuck yourself." This ultimate act of autoeroticism is followed, still more outlandishly, by his getting pregnant from his own seed. Here, indeed, was Richler the avenging prophet, outlining an allegory of sin and damnation. Here, too, was the social critic snarling at snake oil salesmen of "cool" and self-serving exponents of political correctness, along with ripping at the very hipster Londoner now buying the novel in the hope of finding depravity, and thus a groovy reading experience.

Had he found his role as a modern "Swift the Dean," both fuelled and ruled by savage indignation? Novelist Anthony Burgess thought so. What may have been the most insightful review of *Cocksure* did not appear in print. Instead, sent an advance copy of the novel, Burgess—whose already iconic novel *A Clockwork Orange* had been accused of peddling the pornography of violence—replied with an effusive letter. "The whole point is, of course, that the book is a satire of those obscenities of thought, conduct and prejudice which a permissive society is so rapidly making available. . . . " As Burgess saw it, Richler had to be shocking: "The moral force of the satire would have been much diminished if he hadn't deliberately rubbed away at the sore of his own disgust." Calling the novel a "genuine work of literature," he said, "it's the sort of book I should like to have written myself, and I probably lack the moral courage." Moral courage was what compelled the other positive "review" that Richler treasured the most. Florence loved *Cocksure* from the start. She was proud of him for having written such a book.

Tony Godwin, editor-in-chief at Weidenfeld & Nicolson, now published Mordecai Richler in England. Like the split from Joyce Weiner, the parting from André Deutsch had been protracted. For years Richler had been complaining of the small advances and minimal publicity being offered by the perpetually cash-strapped firm. Diana Athill recognized the problem but could do little to persuade her boss to spend enough to keep him happy. Richler's dissatisfaction had long been tempered by his loyalty and friendship with Deutsch and, in particular, with Athill, and by the reality of his limited commercial success. But with a new novel finally ready, a new agent wishing to prove his worth and still more bills to pay, he had finally jumped.

As it happened, André Deutsch—feisty, honourable, a supporter of new talent—lost not only Mordecai Richler in the late 1960s; Brian Moore, Philip Roth, John Updike and V.S. Naipaul all sought better arrangements elsewhere.

Richler turned to Weidenfeld & Nicolson, itself a relatively new house, under another remarkable European Jewish figure, George Weidenfeld, and the Scottish Nigel Nicolson, son of Vita Sackville-West, Virginia Woolf's friend and lover, and Sir Harold Nicolson. They had very successfully published Nabokov's controversial novel *Lolita* and survived its trial for obscenity. For a second time, Richler ended up with one of the few London publishers run by a Jew. Their offer was far from exorbitant. "1250, as opposed to 450 Deutschland offer," he explained to Weintraub, a figure that included a small advance for an essay collection to be titled *Hunting Tigers Under Glass.* When he called this figure "smashing," he meant for "book money," not "movie money." Even £1,250 for a novel compared poorly with the £5,000 he was commanding for a script. He appreciated the differences between the industries, especially given his proudly "literary" credentials; writers who wrote those sorts of books—as opposed, say, to the Irving Stones and Herman Wouks of the blockbuster genre— could expect only so much from publishers. Movieland, in contrast, was where both high profits and low standards reigned, and he had no qualms about squeezing producers for every dollar or pound. Bill Weintraub was forever astounded by his aggressive bargaining. "I am agog at your sangfroid," he admitted during the white-knuckle negotiations for the film option.

The decision to go with Weidenfeld & Nicolson also related to its editor-in-chief. Mordecai and Florence had both taken to Tony Godwin, a charming, puckish figure much liked in publishing circles, who once described himself as "a hothouse degenerate Englishman." Godwin, then married to the photographer Fay Godwin and a close friend of Bob Gottlieb's, returned the affection. A shrewd and generous editor, he expressed a determination to advance Mordecai Richler's career. Such enthusiasm was welcome, especially for the not-to-all-tastes *Cocksure,* as was the news out of America that Gottlieb had been appointed publisher of Borzoi Books, an imprint at Alfred A. Knopf, early in 1968, and that by agreement he would be bringing his writers with him from Simon & Schuster. Gottlieb's wife, Maria Tucci, had finally met Florence not long before in Connecticut, and had overcome an advance warning from the adoring husband that the woman she was about to encounter was "very, very beautiful." Florence was beautiful, Tucci agreed, but more important, she was smart and kind. "Hugs and kisses to all Richlers," Gottlieb proclaimed with typical intimacy, "also to Godwins, O'Briens, Claytons; all Swinging London."

A new team was assembling around Richler, and the timing was perfect. The final piece of the jigsaw, and the cause of such instant and serious attention to *Cocksure* as a movie property, was film agent Bob Shapiro. Only twenty-nine when he arrived in London to represent the William Morris Agency, Shapiro fell in immediately with Jack Clayton. He was soon representing Clayton, along with Peter Sellers, Twiggy, Omar Sharif and Tony

Richardson. Canadians Ted Kotcheff and Christopher Plummer became clients as well. Clayton introduced him to Richler in the bar of Claridge's Hotel, and the two men took to each other at once, despite—or perhaps because of—the fact that the rumpled Richler first announced that he was distrustful of agents, and then, having ascertained that Shapiro had an expense account, ordered a bottle of whisky.

Bob Shapiro, in short, passed the test. Richler did that with new acquaintances, professional or private: tried them out for character size, favouring liveliness and mischief, hesitating before caution or rote correctness. His swift decisions tended to be final. If in, it was for good; if not, it probably wasn't going to happen. Florence disliked this tendency in her husband, especially the judgment that accompanied a failed test, while acknowledging that he usually got the person right.

She also never quite forgot her own early days as Stanley Mann's wife, feeling the silent probing and disapproval of Mort Richler at parties. As well, by now he was more certain than ever of whom he wanted to keep company with, to call friend. In his personal life this meant drinking, poker-playing, Florence-approving sorts, mostly male. The Richlers hosted small gatherings where close friends were treated to excellent food cooked by Florence, and the occasional proper party, where Sean Connery could be spotted in the kitchen with her, and Rod Steiger, lately winner of an Academy Award for *In the Heat of the Night*, might be seen sidling up to the red-headed Edna O'Brien on the couch. The gifted and amiable Canadian director Norman Jewison, who had directed Steiger's Oscar-winning role and would shortly be buying Sean Connery's house on Putney Heath to establish his London residency, might be there as well.

Friday night poker soirees still featured the two Teds, Jack and Haya Clayton, Alan Rakoff and Reuben Ship, along with fly-ins— director Mel Brooks and his wife, the acclaimed actress Anne Bancroft, or agent Gareth Wigan and the beautiful Natalie Wood. Between rounds Brooks shared anecdotes about shooting his latest movie, *The Producers*; Bancroft, who had starred in Jack

Clayton's *The Pumpkin Eater* and Mike Nichols' *The Graduate*, chatted and played with Emma and Noah. Nights out would involve the same people, whether a party at Ted Allan's where Richler might exchange sharp, not entirely genial banter with the original Broadway Tevye himself, Zero Mostel; or a dinner at Stanley Price's house in Hampstead with Philip Roth, where the men held a contest to see who could issue the longest, most inventive string of obscenities; or even occasional drinks with the irascible Kingsley Amis. Roth was a natural comrade, and a great talker; he was also, to Richler's disappointment, a teetotaller. There were boozy dinners at L'Étoile in Charlotte Street with visiting Brian and Jean Moore, or family lunches outside the city in Marlow, the country home of the Claytons, with its vast grounds and the coop where Jack Clayton kept carrier pigeons. The kids loved visiting Marlow.

Mordecai Richler's people, drawn largely from the book and movie worlds, were serious and smart, sharp and occasionally glamorous. He had every reason to be content with the life he and Florence had built for themselves in England. London in 1968 was alive with the new and the possible, with miniskirts on the streets and Julie Christie in the cinema. Moral outrage was fuelled by Pope Paul VI's encyclical *Humanae Vitae*, against contraception, by the deaths of Martin Luther King and Bobby Kennedy, by the Vietnam War, which sent thousands of students marching against the American Embassy and mounted police in Grosvenor Square. A broad spectrum of activities and lifestyles was available to the curious and extroverted Londoner: "Orgies? *Where?* I haven't been to one and nobody I know has been to one either," Richler grumbled. John Updike's spouse-swapping *Couples* may have been the scandal of the season, with Roth's libidinous *Portnoy's Complaint* getting ready to titillate the following spring, but for his generation sex meant something quite different from the new siren call of free love, even if his moral dismay at the hypersexualization of modern society had scarcely registered beneath the appearance of much libido in *Cocksure.* "They are handling Portnoy and Couples," he complained of the W.H. Smith chain's decision to ban the paperback as well, "but I'm too dirty for them. A distinction of sorts," he added ruefully. To add insult to injury, he would soon be lying next to Florence in bed while she giggled reading Roth's wicked book.

If the popsters of the middle years of the sixties had mildly irritated Richler, they had still been largely clean-shaven and nattily attired, with recognizable impulses. But the shift into the hippie ethos of the back end of the decade, druggy and long-haired and sitar-playing, not to mention "into" Mao and Che and every other liberation movement, represented a new kind of rebellion, or expression. He saw much of it as shallow, elitist and self-regarding, and a threat to genuine values, reserving special scorn for the sin of being trendy, which he called "modish foolery." The truth was, he had gotten on well with hardscrabble 1950s London and done okay with the emerging city of cool in the early 1960s. About the tail end of the decade he had less good to report.

An incident from 1966 with Mason Hoffenberg hadn't endeared the period to him. Though he had not seen his old Paris friend in years, he had heard from Terry Southern of Hoffenberg's worsening dependency on heroin. When the American showed up in London, he first hung out among the hipsters of Chelsea, many of whom gravitated to the flat of "it" girl Marianne Faithfull. She had become a pop star with "As Tears Go By," written by her then-boyfriend, Mick Jagger, and now had a heroin addiction of her own. Hoffenberg, then forty-four, must have struck the flower children as a scary ghost. He called Richler out of the blue and asked for his help. Over the years a number of friends, including Diana Athill, had witnessed his tenderness with Hoffenberg, a person he instinctively liked, despite his chronic disrepair. First he drove him to Hillcrest, asking the girls to vacate their room for the night. Hoffenberg arrived at the Richler house needing a fix, and Richler had trouble finding a vein in his bandaged, needle-scarred arms. In the kitchen Florence insisted on changing the bandages. Hoffenberg remained silent and withdrawn, and had no contact with the children. The next morning Richler tried to arrange a prescription for methadone for him, without success, and in the end he dropped him near Leicester Square where he could score.

Not long after, he wrote a touching and funny memoir about Paris in which he mentioned recently returning to the city for a lavish weekend with Florence at the Hotel George V. Different ghosts from the past loomed up, leaving him nervous and embarrassed. Here were the "unlucky or insufficiently talented," drinkers and junkies, rent-skippers and reprobates, still to be found "drifting from café to café, cruelly winded now, grubbiness no longer redeemed by youth, bald, twitchy, defensive, and embittered." The piece, titled "A Sense of the Ridiculous," was dedicated to Joe Dughi and Mason Hoffenberg.

His impatience with youth culture—he was now thirty-six—and the instant icons of Swinging London was deepening. "Their seriousness is often spurious and half-educated, and they are being critically oversold," he wrote of the era's defining films, reserving special scorn for Michelangelo Antonioni's *Blow-Up*, which he found "simplified and untrue" and about "attitudes, not people." "Joyless sexual connections" also struck him as a glib theme, though he was careful to clarify that nudity in movies "gives me a charge" and that he liked a good orgy scene. "What I do object to is the hot stuff going by another name."

In 1968 he published an extraordinary 7,000-word piece on James Bond for *Encounter*. Richler, who could bang out a column in an afternoon, spent weeks on "Bond," mindful of the attention it would command. The character, the films and Ian Fleming's thirteen novels were popular, a pleasing fantasy of postwar British prowess; a fantasy, he contended, that was meaningless unless "tacked to the canvas of diminishing England." Using a recent biography of Fleming, who had died three years earlier, along with a praising study of the Bond novels by Kingsley Amis, he attacked the author's bigotry towards Jews (among others), his woman-fearing "boyishly smutty" sexism, and the plain truth that he had been an "appalling writer" and an "insufferably self-satisfied boor." For the anti-Semitism charge, he summoned the

memory of John Buchan's *The Thirty-Nine Steps*. The 1915 espionage novel by the future governor general of Canada, Lord
Tweedsmuir, includes a gratuitous passage in which plots against
England are ascribed to a conspiracy straight from *The Protocols
of the Elders of Zion*. Richler laid out clearly the direct line from
Buchan to Ian Fleming, with the enemies of the no-longer "Great"
Britain—nasties needing to be taken care of by the "licensed to
kill" secret agent—forever resembling those conniving Jews. "My
boys are crazy about the James Bond movies," he wrote, keeping
to himself a visit to Pinewood Studios with Daniel and Emma to
watch the "hero" Sean Connery shoot a scene. "They identify with
007, as yet unaware that they have been cast as the villains in the
dramas." But his childhood in Canada had been no different. "As
a boy I was brought up to revere John Buchan," he wrote, citing
the governor general's visit to Baron Byng on Junior Red Cross
Prize Day. Told that Lord Tweedsmuir stood for the "ultimate
British virtues" of fair play and gentlemanly conduct, the Jewish
boys and girls of Baron Byng were not informed that he also happened to be "an ignorant, nasty-minded anti-Semite."

Hoping to stave off a spat with Kingsley Amis, who he knew
was about to publish the first after-Fleming Bond novel under a
pseudonym, he apologized to him in print for coming across as
an "entirely humourless left-wing nag, a Hampstead harpie." But
he then proceeded with a critique that, if not left-wing Hampstead,
certainly embraced what was shortly to be dubbed the "post-
colonial" perspective on the vanished Empire. "Little England's
increasingly humiliated status has spawned a blinkered romanticism on the left and the right." In denial about its "shrivelled
island" standing, the right wing, he wrote, maintained that "vir-
tuous Albion is beset by disruptive communists within and foreign devils and conspirators without."

It would have been hard to imagine the prickly Kingsley Amis
not taking offence. Hardly more than acquaintances, they never
really spoke again at all, and when Richler ran into the then-aged
novelist in a club a quarter-century later he was greeted with
silence and a glare. But others delighted in these calculated

offences. "I greatly enjoyed reading your article on James Bond,"
the poet and CBC producer Phyllis Webb wrote from Toronto,
"and read a few excerpts from it today to one of our producers."
She also reported that the same producer had entered the room
quoting a different Richler article, this one from the *New Statesman.*
"Maple Leaf Culture Time" probed the modest indicators of an
emerging state-sponsored culture. Included in its provocations
were digs at "the dizzying prospect" of a Canadian film industry
and a description of the governor general of Canada as the Queen's
"second-floor maid." Coming off the James Bond essay, the quip
was no coincidence.

Why, then, the pull back to that same country of middling culture with a second-floor maid as the representative of the head
of state? In "Bond" he had alluded to Norman Mailer's concept
of the "minority man" as someone who "grows up with a double-
image of himself, his own and society's." He was thinking of two
different environments: Daniel and Noah's London of the late
1960s, and his Montreal of three decades earlier. He had been a
"minority" in his own country, by virtue of being a Jew; his sons
and daughters were likewise a minority in the country where
they were being raised. Yet all but one of his children were
Londoners by birth, with two Canadian parents, only one of
whom was Jewish. Didn't that make Daniel, Noah, Emma and
Martha part Jewish, part Canadian and, perhaps above all else,
English by childhood and education? They made fun of his
Canadian accent, reminding him of his own discomfort with the
Yiddish-inflected speech of his parents. He, in turn, was bemused
by the posh English intonations of the offspring of a St. Urbain
Street boy. On which side of the Atlantic, exactly, would his chil-
dren be a minority? On which side did they truly belong?

X

SWISS FAMILY RICHLER

"I am flabbergasted, to put it mildly, at your news of the impending stork," Bill Weintraub wrote in February '68. "Have you thought of buying a farm and putting them to work? They could keep a good few acres under cultivation while you retire." It was true: Florence was pregnant again, due to give birth in August. Weintraub, already busy on behalf of his friend—"So Mort will be needing a manor," Richler had announced before Christmas of his decision to accept a one-year position at his alma mater, Sir George Williams—couldn't resist further wisecracks. "When I think of the impending arrival of the Swiss Family Richler I think the only thing I can do is knock off work <u>entirely</u> for a few months to make arrangements. The dockside bus," he added, "is de rigueur." The proud father, actual and prospective, joked back, "Hey, do you and Magda want to buy any readymade children? We've got boys, girls, big ones, little ones. Can send photos." The offer had come with two sighs for Weintraub's ears only. "Will be 37 this Saturday." As well: "So much to do before Aug. My God, my God."

Richler, who rarely complained of the workloads he took on, had cause to be anxious about the upcoming six months prior to the family's temporary repatriation. The notion, already headache-inducing in the fall of 1967 when he first began to push his professor friend Neil Compton to make the invitation a reality, must have taken on a new level of derangement once Florence became pregnant, with the baby due in the weeks preceding the proposed departure. She certainly thought so; her husband's homing instinct, reignited by the "new" Montreal he had discovered the previous year, was putting stress on their happy family life. He would take care of a thousand details, from transport to housing to schools, and would, as Bill Weintraub had predicted with amusement, call on his trusted lieutenant in Montreal for help. But Florence would be both preparing and shepherding the assembly of children, and giving birth to still another, on the eve of the shipwreck of the Swiss Family Richler. It was a lot to ask, even of the most devoted wife and mother.

"Your travel bill did send a bit of a shudder through the corridors of Sir George Williams," Compton admitted, "especially since the Canada Council is proving ungenerous about support." Richler, who had lately surprised his old professor by asking him for a piece for inclusion in the Penguin anthology, kept the pressure up, and the university did, in the end, pay for the family to be repatriated, with the Council coming through with matching funds. Weintraub, meanwhile, also asked to submit something for the book, went to work finding a house, a task made more difficult by Richler's insistence on a year in the Quebec countryside. The Laurentians, to be exact, the shtetl of his youth. In the family equation, rural isolation might not be the perfect setting for the mother and children. No matter: his reverie of a robust writerly existence amidst the hills and streams wasn't to be denied. After heroic efforts, including repeated drives to examine properties, on his own or with Sonny Idelson as co-inspector, Weintraub located what appeared a near-ideal place: a sprawling house in Vaudreuil, a half-hour west of the city "via the new Trans-Canada highway" and right on the Lake of Two Mountains. Richler was thrilled, and grateful. "Prodigious thanks. You have come through splendidly for us." Then he was onto Weintraub about the lease, and a list of contents, and a new car, and schools for the kids and so on.

A recharged Quebec awaited him. "*Vive le Québec libre!*" former French president Charles de Gaulle had called from a balcony of

Montreal's city hall in July, igniting wild jubilation among the separatists and fury inside the federal government, his host. With Expo 67 a happy memory, nationalist rhetoric and extremism were once more front and centre. "You could have had yourself a real top notch story had you been in Montreal the day before yesterday," his Uncle Max reported of the 1968 Saint-Jean-Baptiste parade disturbances. "Bottle throwing, rioting, [Premier Daniel] Johnson escaping while Trudeau stood his ground calmly, smiling— Mayor Drapeau making sure his wife was safe and then coming out again to stay with Trudeau." Here were some of the key players, including the new prime minister Pierre Trudeau (he was elected two days after the Saint-Jean-Baptiste parade, where he won the admiration of the nation for coolly facing down the rioters) and combative mayor Jean Drapeau, soon to be paramount in a constitutional crisis. Here, too, were the emerging divides underlying that crisis. "Canadians," Max Richler remarked approvingly of the politicians, "both of whom have proven themselves to be loyal."

By the end of July Mordecai and Florence were both feeling overwhelmed. "Febrile" was how he had described the late spring. There were the ongoing negotiations for the option of "Cocksore," as he called it ("Cuntwise" was how he envisioned a version for women), a scandalous book in the top ten bestsellers. ("My father read your father's book," Daniel was told by a school friend. "What did he think of it?" the twelve-year-old asked. "F-I-L-T-H-Y," the boy replied.) High summer in London had gone from feverish to panicked. It didn't help that Richler had risen from another week in bed with a bad back to host the visiting Moores for drinks. It didn't help either that Florence was four days overdue, "anxious and weary." "I cant tell you how hectic thgs are here," he admitted to Weintraub, "with baby still to come, house unrented, no packing done, script to be written, boring business meetings re tax etc etc etc." "Florence will have to go into hospital tonight to have the damn thg," he finally reported. "This is somewhat unpleasant, alas, but not serious." The "damn thg" was born Jacob Richler on August 2 in Kingston Hospital, with his father, flask of Scotch in pocket, once more scouring the corridors for a nurse. Mother and child both came through fine, and Bob Gottlieb agreed to be godfather.

Ready or not, Florence, four children, Lisa, their irascible but much-liked live-in help, and a babe in arms embarked on the *Empress of Canada* on August 23, complete with clothes and books, cutlery and kitchen utensils. Ted Allan joined them, good company on the seven-day crossing. Richler saw them off at the docks. At last, with the house rented, the option deal almost complete, and a hundred matters yet outstanding, he caught a plane the next afternoon.

————

Before he left, Richler had outlined with typical precision and optimism his vision of the work year ahead. Besides the freelance journalism, including a column for Fulford and regular contributions for Gzowski, and in addition to the Penguin anthology, which was now several months overdue, he would script *Cocksure* until December, with the prospect of the producer casting the film in October and Peter Hall directing it in January. Once that was wrapped up, he could then resume writing *St. Urbain's Horseman*, enjoying long work periods in his country house. With that finished by the following June, he would feel free to embark on another script, "an original for Jack Clayton." ("We are setting the deal up now.") Sir George Williams, which had paid for ship and plane tickets, and was splitting his $12,000 salary as visiting writer-in-residence with the Canada Council, did not factor into his calculations for how his time would be allotted. He had negotiated one day a week of teaching, with a single class of ten students and an office to receive aspiring writers and their manuscripts. To his students, Richler announced at the outset that it was impossible to teach writing and, anyway, talent was a rare commodity. Any who ventured near the office generally found no writer in residence. In letters he joked about subletting the space to a bookie.

Even so, school administrators didn't seem to consider their money wasted. Sir George Williams University (the change to "Concordia" was a few years away), anxious to assert its status next to the perpetually more senior and prestigious McGill, was paying Richler to be on site, doing whatever it was he did. In the space of a decade, Canadian writers and Canadian writing had gone from being academically non-existent, or at least out of the academy's vision, to status-conferring. Margaret Atwood, then known mostly as a poet, had taught Victorian and American literature at Sir George the year before; in the autumn Richler would visit the University of Toronto, whose writer-in-residence was Jack Ludwig, also lately of south London. Any reports of his lacklustre enthusiasm for his modest Sir George duties didn't leave a black mark; Carleton University in Ottawa offered him a similar position, starting in September 1969.

The house in Wildwood, near the town of Vaudreuil, had much to recommend it: a lakeside setting, woods close by for the kids, a third-floor office with manorial views for the author. But the residence, soon dubbed "Noah's Ark" by Bill Weintraub, was so filthy when Richler first saw it, a few days ahead of his family, that he debated backing out. Exhaustion, perhaps, as well as practical considerations—where else would he put five children and a nursing wife?—obliged him to swallow the disappointment. With her usual calm, Florence went about cleaning up, and enrolling the oldest children in local schools. Early October in the countryside at least reminded the Richlers of the glories of a Canadian autumn. But after two months of broken appliances, leaks in halls, mattresses with springs coming through, damp rot and—the final insult—bats flying around at night, the family fled the scene, the lease broken. "Mrs. Richler," he reported in his letter to the landlord, "who is up twice nightly to feed the baby, is afraid to walk to the toilet," while his six-year-old daughter (Emma) "sleeps with a sheet pulled over her head because she is in terror."

But two months in the Ark did forge several family legends. There was the day Daniel and Noah, who liked to ramble through the forest to an overpass above the highway, were apprehended by an irate driver whose windshield they had shattered with a pebble. As punishment, their father cleared out their bank accounts to pay for the damage. More happily, there was the night of an early winter blizzard when Richler, who had gone to the airport to collect his editor Tony Godwin, got trapped in the city. When the phone line went dead, followed by an electrical outage, it was time to find candles and gather around the fire. Daniel, his imagination already vivid, regaled his siblings with ghost stories.

New friends solved the crisis of where to move next. At a Montreal Alouettes football game Richler was introduced to Jon and Carmen Robinson. He was a hard-nosed, fun-loving lawyer, part of the crew putting together the city's nascent professional baseball team, to be called the Expos, on behalf of its majority owner, Charles Bronfman. She was a therapist, cultured and stylish. Both had upper-class Montreal Jewish roots, with Carmen, whose brother was the financier Bernard Zuckerman, raised in Outremont and Jon in Westmount. The Robinsons owned a home near the summit in Westmount, a short walk from the mansion of those same Bronfmans. Soon enough, Jon Robinson was assisting Richler with his troublesome taxes and providing access to the Expos during their inaugural season, and Carmen had become a lasting friend of Florence's. Couples friendships, with all four partners finding each other congenial, were a specialty of the Richlers.

Number 1 Malcolm Road, Westmount, which the Robinsons helped to find, cost nearly twice as much as the Wildwood house to rent, and the move obliged packing up again and locating new schools. But it was also a handsome brick residence in the most affluent neighbourhood in Canada. Malcolm Road hovered near the summit, a short walk to the Robinsons and, theoretically, the Bronfmans. For that matter, it was within walking distance of the mansion owned by Leo and Sandra Kolber. The bright, scrappy Kolber was still another graduate from the old neighbourhood who had made good: McGill-trained as a lawyer, he was president of CEMP, the holding company for the children of Sam Bronfman, and, as a kind of surrogate son to the the legendary patriarch

"Mr. Sam," privy to family secrets. She was a poet and aspiring actress. The Robinsons hosted a party that the Kolbers attended. Subsequently, Leo Kolber and Richler had a few lunches together, and one night the couples dined in a French restaurant before returning to the Kolbers for drinks, where he told the novelist that if there was anything he wanted, he could get it for him. Florence assured him that her husband wanted nothing more than a pleasant evening with them.

Richler was suddenly a man about town. The house was a long walk or a short cab ride from the Press Club and the bar at the Ritz-Carlton, the Forum for a hockey game or, infrequently, his mother's rooming house in lower Westmount for a visit. He was also suddenly closer to Anglo power than ever before. Nestled in the belly of Westmount was an interesting place to be during the winter of 1968–69. It was not, however, where Richler needed to be situated; the dormant *St. Urbain's Horseman,* a novel whose Montreal settings all belonged in the old neighbourhood, was struggling to reawaken.

"Nothing has given me a bigger charge than to witness the hysteria in Westmount," he reported in *Saturday Night* the following June, of the resurgence in separatist agitations, with the parallel decline in housing values in English neighbourhoods. For the "WASPS of Westmount, it is the time of rumour, plot theory and fear," with many an elite—"today's scapegoat," as Jews had been in his youth—"ready to run to Ontari-ari-ari-o." His glee came through clearly, though he claimed it was tempered by compassion because "our indigenous rich goys lack the talent or resilience to cope with this sort of trauma."

Back on his home turf, there seemed no end to the fights he could get into, spats stretching from sea to shining sea. One nasty exchange involved the Toronto novelist Austin Clarke. Writing for nervy editor Bob Fulford, and filing from Montreal, lent Richler's *Saturday Night* columns a particular zing. He criticized Clarke, "a seemingly ferocious West Indian novelist and broadcaster," for declaring that his skin colour had denied him both greater material success in Canada and appearances on television, including on the popular CBC show *Front Page Challenge*. Clarke, he wrote, while despising the term "negro novelist," had "played the aforementioned string shrewdly enough to make a small niche for himself as a minor-league Leroi Jones." His indignation sprang less out of a sense of social injustice than from "his own personal show biz disappointments," and he mocked Clarke's status as a "self-advertised black militant." While the plight of blacks in America and southern Africa were of immediate concern, Richler saw no reason to suffer "windy, arrogant fools gladly, regardless of race, colour or creed." The point was one he would make over and over in the next several months; it wasn't the issues or stances he objected to, it was the attitudes accompanying them.

Austin Clarke had emigrated from Barbados to Canada to study at the University of Toronto and was then teaching at Yale University in Connecticut. His early novels virtually pioneered the concept of multiculturalism in Canadian literature. His reply, made privately to Richler, gave as good as he had got:

> You are running out of ideas, and imagination, baby, if you have to peddle all that shit. . . . I was going to reply to your thing, but I decided that there was nothing to reply to. I was going to challenge you to a fight, (the pen is irrelevant in this case), and possibly kick your little arse, but again, I have this advantage over you, I am not running out of ideas, baby. You dig it? I was going to simply call you a literary bastard, but then again, it would be pointless. So what should I do with a bankrupt little Richler like you?

Saturday Night had requested no editorial softening of his assault on Austin Clarke. Fulford didn't like everything Richler wrote, rejecting one piece and deleting a joke about oral sex and false teeth in another, but he liked having the most outlandish Canadian author in his magazine. Peter Gzowski felt the same at *Star Weekly*, even after discovering that a book review he'd assigned to him had already appeared in a British publication. "I <u>know</u> we need you more than you need us," Gzowski wrote.

Admissions like that, or editors who published pieces as intemperate as the Clarke column, emboldened Richler to be still more aggressive and, on occasion, gratuitous. In Canada, at least, he was rarely asked to temper his remarks. Nor was he often held to account for things he had written that weren't true, let alone fair or appropriate. He did, however, pay a human cost in terms of relationships, often with fellow writers and sometimes ones that he admired, whom he offended or hurt, and who in turn never forgave him. That list would only grow longer as the years passed, and the volumes of honest, provocative, often courageous, but also occasionally sloppy journalism continued to appear.

Problematically for him, in Canada and elsewhere, culture and politics in 1968–69 was a mixed bag of causes and idealisms, grass-roots activism and middle-class trendy attitudes. The era celebrated black power and student power, women's lib and "fighting the man." Kids were dropping out and getting high, waving Mao's Little Red Book and cheering their rebel comrades in Paris. Things were cool or uncool and people were hip or square. Nehru jackets spoke to cool; black suits and slim ties to the decade past. Richler, stubbornly uncool by current measures, and forgetful of his own trend-chasing identity explorations two decades earlier, brought the elephant gun of his evolved moral, political and artistic sensibility to the mouse of the Age of Aquarius. It wasn't a fair fight.

University campuses were where he could be found, weapon loaded. He arrived at Simon Fraser University in Vancouver a week after a student sit-in against a freeze in the province's education budget. He didn't think much of their activism when the radicals, having been arrested, immediately demanded that any criminal records be expunged. Attending the screening of a student film followed by a discussion between the professor and his class that struck him as ridiculous and pandering, he said as much, first face to face, and then in *Saturday Night*. The academic who had invited him later rued the impulse in a letter. "Mordecai Richler has always been impervious to all the arts except his own," the professor wrote. He also rightly pointed out that the author had once been the twenty-five-year-old responsible for *Son of a Smaller Hero*—not exactly a work of mature craft.

Richler revisited the Simon Fraser fiasco in the pages of his own college paper, the *Georgian*. Today's militants, he informed the similarly disposed students of Sir George, were "know-nothing paper tigers" who were "resolutely, self-confidently illiterate." Where once radicals recognized each other by their attitudes towards the Moscow Trials or Spain, now the "choice of haberdashery" provided the bond. But they weren't solely to blame. Too many of their teachers were mediocrities, "sycophantic, inadequate, and in craven retreat, with only the rare untrendy scholar redeeming academe by taking a stand for classic values." As a sidebar, he denounced, without commenting on his own values, the very position he had just willingly taken up—writer-in-residence—calling it mischievous to provide "formal how-to-do-it classes" in creativity.

Early in 1969 a group of West Indian students at Sir George Williams, frustrated by the pace of an investigation into a professor accused of racism, occupied the faculty lounge with their supporters. "Pretty hysterical," was how Bob Weaver described the atmosphere on the day he visited the campus. Richler met with the protesters and heard them out, but came away thinking that they were imposing a "black problem" on the university out of "issue-envy with the country to the south of us." He was in Ottawa a few days later on assignment for *Holiday* when some 150 radicals stormed the computer centre, causing two million dollars in damage. He happened to be in the gallery of the House of Commons the following afternoon when former prime minister John Diefenbaker wondered aloud if, given the number of copies of *Quotations from Chairman Mao* found among the arrested, the government of Canada shouldn't reconsider its decision not to recognize the People's Republic of China.

He was back in Ottawa in May for the Governor General's Literary Awards. Literature couldn't escape trendy rebellion either. For his untrendy part, Richler might have been expected to remark either on the source of the awards—they were founded by John Buchan, Lord Tweedsmuir—or the setting for the ceremony: Rideau Hall, where the Queen's "second-floor maid" resided. But he received his first "GG" quietly and, perhaps, a little hypocritically. He hadn't won for *Cocksure*—Alice Munro was recognized for her debut collection, *Dance of the Happy Shades*—or for non-fiction, in honour of *Hunting Tigers Under Glass.* Instead, the jury gave him a special prize for both books. He took a seat in the hall in his suit and tie, with Munro to one side and two empty chairs to the other. They belonged to authors who had declined their $2,500 prizes. One was separatist Hubert Aquin, winner of the French-language fiction award for his novel *Prochain épisode.* The other, more surprisingly, was Leonard Cohen, a winner for poetry. Cohen had explained, "Much in me strives for this honor but the poems themselves forbid it absolutely." The Montreal *Star* ran a photo of Richler next to the vacant spots, an expression of mild unease on his face. Rising to accept his award, he shook hands with Roland Michener, whom he later described, for first British and then Canadian readers, as having "the manner of the *maître d'hôtel* in a palm court restaurant." "*Êtes-vous canadien?*" the governor general asked. Taken aback, he confirmed his nationality in French, and then listened while Michener congratulated him in neither of their first languages. "*Merci,*" Richler finally said, ending a conversation that did not tempt him to moderate his views of the office.

That same evening, Leonard Cohen turned up at a party given by Jack McClelland in a suite in the Château Laurier. Ushering him into the washroom, Richler, fearing that the poet, whom he barely knew, had separatist leanings like Hubert Aquin, asked why he had declined the award. When Cohen admitted he wasn't sure, he softened. "Any other answer and I would have punched you in the nose," he said. While disavowing being any kind of nationalist, he still couldn't abide a fellow Anglo-Montrealer supporting the emerging movement to break Canada apart.

Twenty-four Sussex Drive, official residence of the prime minister, was around the corner from Rideau Hall. Pierre Trudeau had

come to the awards ceremony, and he invited Mordecai and
Florence to slip away from the pomp for drinks at his place. "Do
you read reviews?" the prime minister asked the novelist. When
Richler admitted he did, Trudeau said he couldn't be bothered
with newspapers—or journalists. He found Trudeau "looking
oddly fragile" after a year in office, the "tiresome swinger's image"
put aside to reveal a man who, while "certainly arrogant, even
boyishly vain," was someone of stature.

Much of the age's literary foment, and Richler's misgivings
about the emerging state-sponsored culture, wound up reflected
in his anthology, completed in Montreal. His introduction to
Canadian Writing Today framed his ambivalence about engaging
in any project that might be mistaken for boosterism. There were
the familiar tales of growing up in the cultural barrens of 1940s
Montreal and later suffering (or was it instigating?) the "blistering quarrel between stay-at-home and expatriate writers." Making
indirect reference to his recent afternoon at Rideau Hall, he once
more derided the role of governor general as the Queen's maid,
"a divisive reminder of colonial dependence" rightly rejected by
the "new militant French Canadian writers." But even those militants in Quebec were benefiting from the rapid ascent of an affluent literary culture of mixed quality and vitality. "If once the arts
in Canada were neglected, today, such is our longing, they are
being rushed into shouldering significances not yet justified by
fulfilment."

Canadian Writing Today kept the original 1956 promise to focus
on younger writers. Most everyone was present—Marshall
McLuhan, he was careful to point out, had declined permission
to excerpt from one of his books—and the list was notable as
much for its inclusion of enemies, perceived or real, as of friends.
Work by Neil Compton, Naïm Kattan, Brian Moore, William
Weintraub, Robert Fulford, Norman Levine, Mavis Gallant, Jack
Ludwig and younger acquaintances such as Margaret Atwood,
Alice Munro and John Metcalf came as no surprise. (A travel piece
about Newfoundland by Franklin Russell, the nature writer now
married to the former Jackie Moore, likely raised eyebrows in

Malibu.) But he also welcomed poems by Irving Layton and Leonard Cohen and prose by Austin Clarke, so recently reviled, and the same Hubert Aquin who had declined to receive a GG. The anthology included Quebec writers in translation, with Marie-Claire Blais, Réjean Ducharme and Jacques Godbout the most prominent, and as its third selection, the essay "The Sorry Tale of French-Canadian Nationalism" by one Pierre Elliott Trudeau.

"A winter to try men's souls," he called it—a time of campus radicals and Westmount letter bombers—when Montreal was "seething," and the former Paris of North America now "seemingly suing for the office of Saigon." But in private he admitted that his sojourn at Sir George Williams had been "a year-long party," not as well spent as it could have been. He and Florence deepened existing friendships and made important new ones. They gave entertaining parties in their Westmount house, and attended others, including a notable one at Jack McClelland's home in Toronto. "One of these days I'm going to learn not to drink at my own party so I'll have some idea afterwards what took place," McClelland wrote in its wake. The Richler children, while perhaps still too young to wonder why they weren't meeting more aunts, uncles or cousins in Montreal, did get a feeling for their parents' hometown: its glorious fall and endless winter, the everyday presence of two spoken languages in uneasy partnership, the importance of hockey and smoked meat to their father's well-being.

It had been a good year for that, too. Led by the ageless Jean Béliveau, the Habs won the Stanley Cup again, their second in a row and twelfth since Mutty first started listening in on the RCA radio. With the ceremonial first pitch in Jarry Park on a frigid day in April 1969, an event he and Florence attended with the Robinsons, the Montreal Expos were born, and the teenager who once skipped school to watch Jackie Robinson had a new local team to cheer for, this time in the big leagues. Florence had reconnected with her sister Muriel Gilbert, also an Expos fan, who later became someone Richler could watch games with on television.

Though his teaching duties had ended in April, the family stayed on until early August. The kids had to finish school and, mindful that *Cocksure* had not sold particularly well in Canada, he agreed with McClelland's request that he stick around for the publication of *The Street*, a collection of mostly older stories, including "The Summer My Grandmother Was Supposed to Die." His year in Montreal had helped bring the stories and memoirs in the book into greater resolution. For once he had not needed to send Bill Weintraub off to confirm details about the old neighbourhood; a five-minute car ride over the mountain had brought him back into the setting, if not the world—the neighbourhood was now largely Greek—of *The Street*. The flight of city Jews to the suburbs aside, he could still buy bagels on St. Viateur and a "Special" at Wilensky's, now moved around the corner onto Fairmount, order a steak at Moishe's on St. Lawrence with affluent Jews or a smoked meat with regular folk at Schwartz's a few doors down. Some things had changed about The Main but many had not, and if the preface to *The Street* included a nostalgic lament for the "hairier, more earthy Montreal" of his childhood, the dense textures, kaleidoscopic eye and gritty idiom of the prose asserted the vibrant "reality" of a literary landscape, first discovered in *Duddy Kravitz*, and now being remapped in miniature. The sweet tone, not to mention the cover illustration of a boy in cap beside homey images of Jewish ghetto life, disarmed local reviewers. The Montreal *Star* surprised itself by calling the book "an exquisitely sensitive picture of a community's past and its country's past." The *Gazette*, too, admitting that while *The Street* was probably a "stopgap" between novels, "this humane, evocative book is a richly-rewarding treat."

The preface carried the title "Going Home Again," and *The Street* featured a no-less-sweet and soon-to-be-familiar dedication: For DANIEL, NOAH, EMMA, MARTHA and JACOB.

XI

REST, REST, PERTURBED SPIRIT

August in London, and it was rainy and cold. The Swiss Family Richlers arrived at Heathrow at 3:30 a.m., Ted Allan waiting for them in the terminal. Four trunks still had to clear customs, with six boxes of books in transit. Soon enough they were settled back into their lovely, rambling Surrey house, the kids re-enrolled in school and the kitchen restocked, the latest adventure in the ancestral home of their parents ended. Sad news had greeted their return: Bea Narizzano, long separated from Silvio, had taken seriously ill. She died within the week, and Mordecai and Florence attended first a "fast cremation," and then a meal hosted by Silvio and prepared by the director's boyfriend. "Such, Weintraub, is Swinging London," he reported of Narizzano's new sexual orientation.

The trunks and boxes finally arrived as well. Richler, who would later joke about the books he had hauled back and forth across the Atlantic without ever reading, might have made the same quip about those boxes, containing as they did "all my references for the novel I'm working on." He'd been "attempting" to finish it after five years, and finding most mornings sour and unyielding. "Frequently, I feel I've lost something somewhere, spontaneity maybe, or honest appetite." On those days he recited a mantra to himself: "Your father had to be out at six every morning, driving to the junkyard in the sub-zero dark, through Montreal blizzards. You work at home, never at your desk before

nine." But this was his "endless novel," and his "most expensive":
he had refused another movie script offer to make one more
push, sketching improbable schedules for its completion. Always
there was a book review to do instead, or a film he needed to
see; always there was reason for the low word count, including
days when he did not manage a paragraph. He tried changing
typewriters. He tried going from black to blue ribbons and light
typing paper to heavy. Would the book, begun "on the other side
of the moon," ever be done, he worried, and, if so, could it possibly have been worth the effort?

Shortly before he left for Canada, he had arranged to attend a
trial at the Old Bailey, taking more notes. Years had passed since
he had watched Silvio Narizzano and the nefarious Benjamin
Levene be convicted of sex crimes. Levene, in fact, was now out
of prison, continuing to harass those he believed had contributed
to his unfair punishment. Richler himself heard from the disgraced accountant from time to time via postcards and the occasional crank call; if nothing else, Levene wanted him to know
that he knew where he lived. Though he claimed not to be worried, Florence did not like the thought of someone being out
there who partially blamed her husband for his woes. Excerpts
from *St. Urbain's Horseman* published throughout the decade had
suggested that a similar trial would provide the novel its spine,
but missing was the moral and plot centrality of his low-life
accomplice, Harry Stein, to his main character, Jake Hersh. In
September 1969, it suddenly came together: Levene and the
"cockney tax accountant" who had made life so miserable for
Richler; the plight of the uncool and unattractive in Swinging
London; a Canadian director in Hampstead with a beautiful wife
and an impossible mother visiting from Montreal; comic book
golems and the agonizing and so-far-unsuccessful hunt for
another Nazi fugitive, Josef Mengele, the "Angel of Death" phys-
ician from Auschwitz; Isaac Babel and W.H. Auden, the permanent shadow of Dr. Johnson. As well, Saul Bellow's insistence
that "Jews stand apart from the general nihilism of the west," and
that the messy, unresolved life of any one man captured at any

one moment could speak to the broader age with greater feeling than the most sweeping social canvas or wildest satire.

St. Urbain's Horseman took off that autumn. "Working prodigiously hard," he admitted. In January, "things are progressing on schedule, even better," he told Michael Spencer at the Canadian Film Development Corporation, who had optioned *The Street* and hired him to write the screenplay, "in spite of a slipped disc recurrence." His thirty-ninth birthday—"Last year as a Now-generationer"—passed with typewriter keys clacking. There was no doubt that he was gathering his best head of fiction-writing steam since the frenzied period that birthed *Cocksure.*

But even a "novel-writing year," as he had designated 1970, had its detours. A trip back to Canada in February cost him several weeks. He had agreed to make appearances in four western cities, to be followed by a reading at the Temple Emanu-El, in Westmount (fee request: $250, plus Canadiens tickets). At the University of Calgary he was introduced to a packed room of three hundred plus. Putting out his slim cigar, he offered his usual disclaimer—"I am not a performer so I will read this"—and then delivered a lecture pieced together from recent essays. The rest of the western tour was blighted by bad weather. Before he left London, Richler had called the Edmonton bookseller and now-publisher, Mel Hurtig, whom he had met before, asking if he wanted to show a Montrealer the splendour of the Rockies. The gregarious Hurtig, also the son of Galician immigrants—his mother, born and raised in Odessa, could remember hiding under her bed when Cossacks on horseback rode through the ghetto streets looking for Jews—had long been drawn to Richler's writing and his sardonic personality. Freezing rain robbed the men of much sightseeing during their drive through the mountains. A glum evening dining in a near-empty Banff Springs Hotel, the bad food matched by a bad lounge singer, ended with Richler insulting the musician, whom Hurtig had invited to their table. In Jasper he declined any walks in the sleet, spending much of the day ensconced in a pool hall. Hurtig, who remarked on how hard he drank from mid-afternoon onwards, was a disappointed host. Later, he was among the many westerners appalled at how Richler then reported on the "campus vaudeville circuit" in *Maclean's.* The sour "Endure, Endure" made cracks about everything and every place west of Winnipeg, with special scorn reserved for Alberta. Hurtig, mentioned by name, even got blamed for somehow triggering his ill temper.

Back in Montreal, audience questions at the Shaar were the usual mix of curiosity and effrontery. Florence flew in soon after, and the Robinsons threw them a party. He may have been longing to return to *St.Urbain's Horseman,* a book he had been writing for too long in his head and not long enough in his study, but he knew how much she loved to travel. He and Florence continued on to New York to stay with the Gottliebs for a lively week, using the guest bedroom often occupied by another Canadian, the actress Kate Reid, whom they had first met on the set of *The Trouble with Benny* all those years ago and who had recently appeared with Maria Tucci in Chekhov's *Three Sisters* in Connecticut, a production they had seen.

Lily Rosenberg, flown over by her son, was minding the children in London, and presumably did not come upon the manuscript in progress, which contained scenes of a mother in London babysitting her grandchildren, going through her son's study. Her presence at Hillcrest contributed, accidentally this time, to the brothers' estrangement. Avrum Richler, now remarried with a new family, had asked Lily to babysit for him in St. John's while he and his wife went, coincidentally, to London. She had demurred, citing problems with her furnace, only to answer the phone at Mordecai's house in Surrey when Avrum, hoping to see his brother for the first time since sitting shiva for Moses, called. Mother and older son did not speak for three more years, and the siblings saw each other rarely.

In Montreal Richler made time for another assignment: an interview with former detective inspector Ben Greenberg. He had run into Greenberg, now retired from the police force and working security for the Expos, in spring 1969, and the city's former solitary Jewish police inspector agreed to share tales about the bad old days. The result, he warned Bill Weintraub in a letter after he filed the piece, could be trouble. "Big ugly Ben Greenberg is going to come round looking for me," he said. "He keeps three (3) guns, you know. A snubnose Jaguar and two (2) revolvers." He also offered a sneak preview of a typical Greenberg quote: "What would you do, I asked Ben, if anybody made trouble for you? I'd air-condition the bastard, he said." To his irritation, the profile was spiked by *Maclean's. Saturday Night* eventually risked being air conditioned by publishing "The Life and Times of Detective Inspector Ben Greenberg" in early 1971. An upset Greenberg threatened to both bomb and castrate Richler.

In the past, the interruptions might have dissipated his focus. But not now, with the end in sight. "Am HORSEMANing again," he reported. He had also promised Michael Spencer at the Film Board that, come April 1, he would begin writing the script for *The Street*, especially once the film corporation sent him a cheque. They mailed the money, and he further subdivided his work day. In summer he took time off to fly across the Channel to Paris with Noah. Father and son stayed in a Left Bank hotel with a crooked flight of stairs and ate coq au vin at Chez Allard. One evening they dined with Mavis Gallant, the boy witnessing his parent display the kind of solicitude reserved for only a few women not named Florence. Richler gave Noah a watch that had once belonged to Terry Southern.

On August 31, 1970, he typed the magic words to Weintraub: "After five years on and off, many starts (lots of them false) I've finally finished ST URBAINS HORSEMAN." He mentioned a length—170,000 words, around 550 manuscript pages—and vowed to attempt some trimming. "Man, I _am_ exhausted," he said. "And tense." Copies had already gone out to Tony Godwin at Weidenfeld & Nicolson, Gottlieb at Simon & Schuster, and Jack McClelland, and "now I sit, and I wait, recalling all the dull passages, all the flat chapters. Shit." But he was consoled already. "Florence has read the ms and thks it's the best thg I've ever done." Though she might have good reason to lie—anything less than full approval could trigger a flurry of vengeful criticisms of "her clothes, her cooking and the mess she was making of raising our children," he joked in an essay—he knew she wouldn't.

He didn't have to wait long. "It came yesterday," Bob Gottlieb wrote of the manuscript. He had stayed up all night to read the book, and was now ready to offer both general praise, calling it "much much better" than what he had read back in 1966, and specific comments about characters and scenes. "You've somehow un-jerkied it," he said of the complex first part, with its movements back and forth in time. The editor said he wouldn't be seeking any rewrites or doing much editing of *Horseman*. "And in case you didn't know, it's finished," he added. "Rest, rest, perturbed spirit." A few days later Nina Bourne, the Knopf advertising guru famous for her punchy copy and large, heavy-rimmed glasses half hiding her small face, who had followed Gottlieb from Simon & Schuster and whom Richler adored, visiting her whenever he dropped by the office, weighed in: "It's full of glories," she said.

To show how finished *St. Urbain's Horseman* was, his American agent sent the manuscript to the women's magazine *McCall's*. They bought a seventeen-page excerpt for $3,500, and were the first among the five publications that had purchased chunks of the novel in progress over the last half-decade to be certain they were reading the final version. Richler's anxieties abated: "The thing to remember, excerpt-wise, when writing a novel," he advised Weintraub, "is to include a chapter with a recipe. Dig?"

———

On October 10 and 11 the two friends crossed letters. Richler was inquiring if Bill could take another photo from the old neighbourhood for use on the cover of the British edition of *The Street,* due out after *St. Urbain's Horseman* appeared. Weintraub was alerting him to the astonishing events unfolding in his hometown. "No doubt you have been reading of the week's Separatist kidnappings," he wrote. "We watch TV today, stunned, as incredible terrorist communiqués are read hourly, a letter read from Pierre Laporte (kidnapped) to Bourassa, pleading for his life." Weintraub agreed to snap the requested shot of St. Urbain Street, but not right away. "What with the tense, edgy atmosphere of Montreal these days, I don't want to be poking around strange streets taking pictures of other people's houses." Hysteria ruled the city, he remarked, "a feeling—unjustified, in my view, but widely held—of imminent apocalypse."

That week—or two weeks—changed Quebec, and Canada, forever. On October 5 the British trade commissioner, James Cross, was kidnapped from his Montreal home by the FLQ. A communiqué demanded a swap for "political prisoners," and a national broadcast of the "FLQ Manifesto" on the CBC. The broadcast was granted; the release of prisoners was declined. Five days later, on the date that Richler wrote about the photo, Quebec's vice-premier, Pierre Laporte, was also abducted. The next day the CBC broadcast his letter from captivity, addressed to his boss, Premier Robert Bourassa. On October 13 Pierre Trudeau, when asked how far he would go to bring an end to the crisis, replied, "Just watch me." Two days later again, with prominent Quebecers, among them René Lévesque, head of the newly formed Parti Québécois, calling for negotiations with the terrorists, the government of Quebec requested the intervention of the Canadian army. Trudeau went on air on October 16 to announce that he was implementing the War Measures Act, suspending habeas corpus, and granting police and army a wide range of powers. Pierre Laporte was assassinated by the FLQ within twenty-four hours of the announcement, his body left in the trunk of a car outside Montreal. Cross's kidnappers promised to kill their hostage as well if they were discovered by police. They had reason to fear they would be found; hundreds of city homes and apartments were raided the first night of martial law, with three hundred initial arrests. Soldiers from four different units were soon spread across Montreal, protecting everything from the radio and TV tower atop Mount Royal—the FLQ had tried blowing it up before—to mansions in Westmount. Soldiers in camouflage roamed the grounds.

"I hope this doesn't sound hysterical to you," Weintraub added in his letter of October 23, with the War Measures Act into its second week, "but you'd have to be in Montreal to know what I mean." Instead, Richler was sitting in his living room watching the news out of Canada lead the BBC evening broadcast night after night, for the first time he could remember. Then on November 5 an evening phone call came in from an editor at *Life* magazine, when he was preparing fireworks in the garden for Guy Fawkes Day, asking that he fly to Montreal immediately and report on the situation. That was reason enough to get him back home.

Arriving a couple of days after the arrest of the FLQ cell that had murdered Laporte—Cross was still being held—he accepted some battlefield tour-guiding by Weintraub. They drove past consulates, public buildings and mansions under army protection. On his own Richler wandered Westmount, noting the "For Sale" signs as much as the police presence, and had lunch with an unnamed French-Canadian novelist in Outremont, who assured him that it was no longer a question of whether Quebec would separate, but how soon. "Our children no longer call themselves Canadian, but Québécois," he quoted him in *Life.* He moved on to Ottawa, where he interviewed Lester B. Pearson. The former prime minister was philosophical about the War Measures Act, saying, "We have never fought for our freedom," adding that an independent Quebec would almost certainly be more, not less, dependent on Canada. The current prime minister, who might have sent his regrets given the situation, invited Richler to lunch. Trudeau preferred to talk about Jean-Paul Sartre and Herbert Marcuse with his guest, but he did make a telling remark about the lack of vigour among French-Canadian intellectuals, who "tend to build castles in the sky." Richler emerged from the conversation worried that Trudeau could be "undone by his autocratic manner" and that Canada "had now either to knit together as a country or fragment, wasting like Ireland, Montreal filling Belfast's depressing office."

In his hometown again, he interviewed newspaper editors and senators, using either his own contacts or those of John Scott, editor of *Time Canada* and another new friend. Finally, he sat down to lunch with René Lévesque—"an authentic people's tribune"—in a restaurant in the city's French east end. The "chain-smoking, obviously high-strung" Lévesque, he later reported, was right to declare that Quebec simply wasn't a province like the others. "They had bona fide grievances, and in 1970 were still suffering unnecessary insults." It was Lévesque who recommended Nick Auf der Maur as someone to consult about the "real" situation. Richler did add the *Gazette* columnist and city councillor to his list of interview subjects for the piece, finding him in a bar in Mountain Street. The tall, mischievous Auf der Maur, who had been briefly detained himself, was drinking with Terry Mosher, the brilliant young cartoonist who, signing himself "Aislin," had made a first pass at caricaturing Richler for a piece the previous summer in the Montreal *Star*. The likeness wasn't great, but that night the expat met two more Montrealers whose flamboyant characters, and sense of fun, would forever endear them to him.

Richler even tracked down David Molson, who ran the hockey team for the family. He had Molson declaring that "of all the old WASP families in the province, ours has always been closest to the natives," citing a French maid as evidence of their commitment to raising their children to be bilingual. Molson later protested that the quote attributed to him about his family had been fabricated, and he took no less exception to how Richler had characterized the French couple employed in his house. His letter, pointing out that Mordecai Richler had left Canada in 1951, did not threaten a lawsuit.

If he did a disservice to David Molson's actual words—likely the case; the quotes made the Westmount burgher a caricature of Anglo smugness out of one of Richler's own novels—it may have been in the rough service of a larger point about the Quebec and Canada about to emerge from the crisis. Aside from his scorn for the FLQ, Richler took an open-minded interest in the various players and their perspectives. He had certainly never reported a magazine piece with the vigour of the *Life* assignment. Back in

London—Cross was released on December 3 in exchange for safe passage to Cuba for his kidnappers—he wrote the article in less-than-ideal circumstances. Florence was hospitalized for two weeks to tend to a nagging ailment, Jackie and Frank Russell, parties in the French bedroom farce of a few years earlier, had come to visit, and the *Life* piece had to be airmailed to New York. Once Florence had been brought home, he had to do the Christmas shopping. "I'm exhausted," he confessed, a not uncommon complaint from the Horseman years.

A year earlier, just four months after the Swiss Family Richler had returned to England, he had sent a package to Canada House in Trafalgar Square. Though he was beyond sending books and articles to people he wished to court, this was something else: with a contented-in-exile wife and five quasi-English children, he had still thought it worthwhile entreating the high commissioner, Charles Ritchie, with magazine clippings and a copy of *The Street*. The elegant Ritchie, then still the lover of the Irish novelist Elizabeth Bowen, understood the overture: "Don't hesitate to get in touch about the immigration business," he wrote.

Canada, in short, continued to call. For some successful expatriates, the October crisis, with its intimations of still greater upheaval, might have confirmed the wisdom of staying abroad. But for Richler, with his tough-mindedness and appetite for conflict, the near opposite held true: the events of late 1970 had outlined a slowly forming narrative for his still-too-barren, too-colonized homeland, one that he wanted to be part of— especially given the centrality of his cherished Montreal to the unfolding story. "The world," he noted in *Life*, "so long elsewhere, might at last pay Canada a visit.

"Hello, hello."

"But each day you sit vacant writing nothing but still a prisoner to the typewriter—
each day like that is a special kind of hell. Questions come to you making small
wounds. Why are you making this book? Does it matter? Do you believe in it? That's
when you get up and have a cigarette and/or a cup of coffee. Then, a short walk.
Then another cigarette. You pick up things. Books you can't concentrate on.
Newspapers you can't understand. So on. Out again. Up to wander around the
neighbourhood bookshops. So many books! Who—how—why are they written?? . . .
Once you go after a truth, you can only get so close. . . . There is no fame big enough
or money bribery enough to compensate for the pain that goes into the making of a
novel. (Even the mixed joy of publication is paltry, aspirins for cancer.) So why do I
write? . . . Nearest I can come to it is, 'I have to.'" Letter to William Weintraub, 1954.

The photograph of Florence, 9, which Richler carried with him, including to the hospital in his final days: "From the time Mordecai first saw this picture [of me] he always liked it. I don't know when he quite pinched it but I saw it in his office. When I said, 'What's that doing here?' he gave no explanation, just a wave of the hand, but I was secretly quite pleased that he liked it. It surprised me and I wondered—what was the attachment? And when I read *Solomon* I understood. And afterwards, he laughed and said, 'hmmmm, useful.' " Florence Richler.

Modelling photograph by Anthony Buckley for Florence Mann, 1958, after she moved to London with her husband Stanley Mann. The *Liverpool Echo*, describing her as a "tall, raven-haired beauty with enormous blue-black eyes fringed with thick black lashes," mentioned that she modelled for Christian Dior in London. "Being an actress would be much more stimulating than being a mannequin," Florence was quoted in what the interviewer heard as a "soft Canadian burr."

1959. A weekend in Stratford-on-Avon for the new lovers—they would marry the following July.

Summer, 1962. The new family in Amagansett: Daniel, Noah, baby Emma.

"Brian writes that summer is in full swing, that Sam L. was hell, that P. Roth annoyed you all—I suppose *somebody* is being agreeable? Yes, of course—you all are." Letter to Richler from Diana Athill, following reports from Brian Moore of the social life in the Long Island artist community, which included friends Philip Roth and publisher Sam Lawrence.

Florence with Emma, the constant washing for three small children hanging behind her in the Amagansett yard.

"Nancy retrieved the baby, nursed him, and sang him to sleep. . . . Until [she] reappeared, no longer in slacks, but dressed to kill, wearing her Schmucci-Pucci, if you don't mind, and smelling like a perfumery. Yankel's Princess." From *St. Urbain's Horseman*.

1958. It was good to be young and talented in London: Mordecai and Florence at far right, with Ted Kotcheff turned towards the camera, at the annual awards dinner for The Guild of Television Producers and Directors, The Dorchester, Park Lane. The woman to Ted's left is his girlfriend Verity Lambert, who helped forward Richler's divorce from his first wife by getting "caught" in bed with him, and later went on to fame as a TV producer.

The first spring in the back garden at Hillcrest, Kingston Hill, Surrey, with Noah and baby Martha. "It's a big house, but old . . . very old. . . . Big garden, lots of rooms. . . . Our house is enormous, and lots of fun, but, man, am I ever broke." Letter to William Weintraub, 1964.

In Hillcrest he had a proper office for the first time. On the desk: manual typewriter, pot of tea, and two, maybe three, book manuscripts on the go. ". . . Five years in a room with a novel-in-progress can be more than grueling. If getting up to it some mornings is a pleasure, it is, just as often, a punishment. A self-inflicted punishment. There have been false starts, wrong turns, and weeks with nothing to show except sharpened pencils and bookshelves rearranged. I have rewritten chapters ten times that in the end simply didn't belong and had to be cut. Ironically, even unforgivably, it usually seems to be those passages over which I have labored most arduously, nurtured in the hothouse, as it were, that never really spring to life, and the pages that came too quickly, with utterly suspect ease, that read most felicitously." From "Why I Write," *Shovelling Trouble*.

The smart, irreverent *Maclean's* crowd, 1964. From left: Peter Gzowski, Robert Fulford and editor-in-chief Ken Lefolii, with Sandy Ross peeking over Fulford's shoulder, celebrating their mass resignation from the magazine in protest against management interference in the editorial process. Three years earlier, Fulford had perceptively written of the young writer he admired: "Every piece of Richler prose contains something of his personality, [and] no matter what form it takes, it benefits from the sad, bitter and humorous approach which is peculiarly his." From *Q for Quest*, CBC Television, 1961.

"Licensed to kill": Daniel and Emma, in their school uniforms, on set with the family's friend Sean Connery, a.k.a. James Bond, at Pinewood Studios. Touching on the threads of anti-Semitism running through the popular novels of the thirties and later (including Ian Fleming's), Richler wrote: "My boys are crazy about the James Bond movies, they identify with 007, as yet unaware that they have been cast as the villains of the dramas." From "Bond," *Shovelling Trouble*.

Mordecai Richler, on the eve of uprooting the family in order to return permanently to the country that was his "place."

The Swiss Family Richler (as William Weintraub once called them) in 1968.
"We were neither of one place nor the other. We lived in between, English or
Canadian as suited." Noah Richler in *This Is My Country, What's Yours?* Clockwise
from top: Emma, Noah, Daniel, Jake, Martha.

PART IV

LOOK AT ME NOW

I

AN AFFIRMING FLAME

"Maybe it's taken you all your life to ride down St. Urbain Street," Brian Moore wrote on June 1, 1971, "but you're there man, you're there. Or, should I say, quoting the book and knowing that one never leaves home, 'presumed there'?"

A month later Bob Fulford would write: "Did I tell you that I've seen several signs *Horseman* is becoming a kind of Bible, a sort of reference point for discussions of Canadian identity in this period?" The *Saturday Night* editor mentioned two articles he'd received that opened with quotes from it, and noted that "in each case they were using Jake's point of view or Duddy's to explain some facet of the Canadian relationship to the world." Robertson Davies, whose novel *Leaven of Malice* had impressed a younger Mordecai, rose with solemnity to the occasion. "You are one of the writers we have to thank for delivering Canadian writing from a narrowness that plagued it for so long. After all, what is *not* Canadian? Long may you live and write to delight us and remind us of what a varied lot we are." Davies then added a sweet request: "Can we meet again some time when you are in Canada? The only time we met we had no chance to talk sincerely."

Richler relayed the good news to Bill Weintraub. "I'm No.1 bestseller in Canada, says Toronto Star, for 6th week. Go, go, Horseman." "It has done something like 8000 in Canada so far," he reported to his American agent, Monica McCall, adding: "Phoned Bob last week and he says HORSEMAN has sold 11,400

copies, as of Sept 20, which is wonderful. I'm very pleased indeed."
Only the English were resisting, in spite of "marvellous reviews."
"Never mind, you'll get the booker prize," Brian Moore predicted.
The Booker Prize, co-founded by Tom Maschler, the publisher of
Jonathan Cape, was then in its third year of rewarding the finest
novel published by a writer from the Commonwealth, and no less
a figure than Saul Bellow—ineligible for the prize, as an
American—had been announced as a juror for 1971. "Booker is a
Jew, Bellow is a Jew, Maschler is a Jew, Richler is a Jew. . . . WELL
KNOWN! FIXED!" Moore kidded of his chances that autumn.

The publication of the novel was a major affair in Canada.
Richler was without peer in galvanizing the media, even from
his home in England. With *Time Canada*, edited by his friend
John Scott, he couldn't have asked for more extensive or sympathetic coverage. Scott, a gentle Anglo-Montrealer who had
once strolled with him through his old neighbourhood and listened while he summoned rich, exact memories—the names of
shops long ago closed, signs once posted in windows—spared
no expense either in splashing *Horseman* across the pages of the
magazine, or in making sure its controversial author was cast
in a golden light. Aislin's second attempt at a caricature, dubbed
"fabulously fleshy" by one critic—he had yet to "get" the tall
forehead and chaotic hair, bulbous nose and inward gaze—
adorned the cover. In the view of the unnamed writer, "a literary and personal stock-taking" had resulted in a "rich, complex,
deftly controlled book," both "enormously funny" and "more
self-revealing" than anything Richler had done before. Bill
Weintraub and Brian Moore provided anecdotes about their
early days together, and Jack McClelland offered a testimonial
to a man "very tough and hard-spoken on the outside, who is
completely devoted and dedicated to his family." Bob Fulford
said, "Of all the people I know, he is the one who, above all else,
seems to care that his friends get on, that things work out for
them." *Time* even contacted his mother. Lily Rosenberg found
her son "so Jewish, so lovably Jewish. . . . My father once said
that Mordecai had a Talmud head. I always see the rabbi in him."

In a smart definition of his satirical impulses, Lily decided that part of his rabbinical function was to point out faults within his own community. "Because he loves them so much," she said. "Like a mother."

Detractors were found—Morley Callaghan questioning his willingness to "write you a piece about anything," and Irving Layton doubting that he had ever developed "the being within himself"—but they were outflanked. Then there was the photo of the author in his back garden in London. In the foreground stood the taciturn but contented father, refreshment in hand, next to his smiling wife, "a beautiful and intelligent former model from Montreal." They posed in front of a pond, with toddler Jake behind them filling a watering can and Martha brushing her brother's hair. Further back into the garden was Emma in profile, Noah tossing a soccer ball in collared shirt and tie, and lanky Daniel with a hand across his face. "Can a satirist be a nice guy?" ran the caption.

The Swiss Family Richler was put to equally good use in a ten-minute segment on CBC TV that same month. A camera, tracking its way to his third-floor office in Hillcrest, first scanned the staircase from the street to the front door. Perched on various ledges and stone steps were three of his progeny. Nine-year-old Emma in particular got into her part, sporting an expression, half scowl and half bemusement, not unlike one often worn by her father. ("Emma typewrites that she is going to be a writer!" Brian Moore noted. "I believe her.") Other scenes showed Richler dropping the uniformed boys off at school and walking alone in a park. Further footage offered him at his desk, typewriter on display, the office piled with books and files. Smoking, half-smiling at the anecdote about his children finding his accent amusing, he transmitted confidence and authority: the writer in his prime, prodigious in print and life equally, with a new book marking the status. For a Canadian author of the era, this was media prime time.

"Dear Forty Plus," Brian Moore addressed a letter that spring. Richler's original plan had been to persuade his publishers to release the book on January 27, 1971—forty years to the day since his birth. "Forty's the watershed," he had observed. "Every man's most melancholy birthday." His career hung in the balance: at forty the novelist ceased being of "shining promise, romantically unkempt in appearance, refreshingly blunt, even if a reckless drinker," and so could tip easily into being "slovenly and boorish, a well-known soak of promise demonstrably unfulfilled."

His birthday fears were in keeping with *Horseman*'s opening pages. Jake Hersh, thirty-seven, bolts awake from another nightmare: "He's come," he cries of the *Doktor*, Nazi war criminal Josef Mengele, rumoured to be alive and well in Paraguay. Though "St. Urbain's Horseman will take him by surprise," for the moment the menace feels urgent, and it sends Jake downstairs for a predawn gin and tonic and a cigar. His trials are many. A St. Urbain Street boy—he is the pompous would-be artist Hersh from *Duddy Kravitz*, and remains a friend of the now-wealthy entrepreneur—raised by Yiddish-speaking parents, he has English children who mock his Canadian twang. His mother is staying with them at present, making him and his gorgeous shiksa wife, Nancy, miserable. The dark cloud of the clingy, insecure Mrs. Hersh is only one of several chronic anxieties. Disinclined to look after himself, Jake is convinced after a 5:30 a.m. reading of a magazine article about an actor's battle with colon cancer that he has the disease as well. "Now Jake stood nude, legs spread wide apart and back to the hall mirror, bent over with his head bobbing between his knees, probing his ass hole for cancer nails." His worries shift to lung cancer, then to an airplane crash.

Still, rectal cancer or a fiery plane crash would be preferable to his current ordeal: being tried in the Old Bailey for rape, aiding and abetting sodomy, and possession of cannabis. The alleged victim is a German au pair and the co-accused is his accountant's assistant, Harry Stein, who pretended to be him in order to pick up the girl.

Stein is one of two shady personalities Jake finds irresistible. His cousin Joey, the Horseman, is either the Golem, the mythical defender of the Jews, fighting in Palestine and hunting the Auschwitz angel of death, or a petty criminal fleeing the various messes he has made. One of those apparent messes, involving a London woman and a saddle and whip, links Joey and Harry Stein, the self-pitying cockney Jew whose after-work habits include soft pornography and blackmail. He is drawn to Harry Stein, and nearly implodes his privileged life in order to play the Golem, or even simply the charming ne'er-do-well, by proxy. The result—after the humiliation of being put on trial—is a mere scolding for him but prison for Stein.

> For Florence,
> and my other editors,
> Bob Gottlieb and Tony Godwin

read the dedication at the front of his most accomplished and deeply felt book to date, a novel of Bellow-like density and public/private intersections, but with a bawdiness, humour and humanity unique to its author's own "pattern in the carpet." The final stanza of W.H. Auden's "September 1, 1939" stands as a fitting epigraph:

> Defenceless under the night
> Our world in stupor lies;
> Yet, dotted everywhere,
> Ironic points of light
> Flash out wherever the Just
> Exchange their messages:
> May I, composed like them
> Of Eros and of dust,
> Beleaguered by the same
> Negation and despair,
> Show an affirming flame.

———

Mordecai and Florence flew to Montreal on May 19 for the book launch. Burnt-out from the final push on *Horseman* the previous autumn, he had been struggling to get much done. He had completed the long-overdue script for *The Street,* and made most of his other deadlines. Late-winter news from Canada had included the sudden death of his old mentor—and nemesis—Nathan Cohen, at the age of forty-seven, and rumours that McClelland & Stewart was in financial trouble. His professor friend Neil Compton had suffered a terrible accident that left him in a wheelchair. He had lately heard as well from his former sister-in-law, Tess Taconis; his ex-wife, Cathy, her third marriage over and now a Buddhist nun living in Taiwan, had been diagnosed with breast cancer, and urgently required funds for an operation. He made out an international money order and mailed it to J. Hananda (her Buddhist name) c/o a temple in Taipei.

The *Gazette* sent a reporter to the Ritz to interview the returned literary lion. As if in the spirit of the intensely corporeal *Horseman,* she fixated on Richler's appearance and manner. In his "cheerfully rumpled" shirt and "skinny maroonish tie" hanging around his "unhappy askew collar," he brought to mind a "haggard journalist run down by too many deadlines." Noting the Chivas Regal he was mixing with black coffee and the "skinny little brown cigars that come in delicate yellow boxes of tin," she declared that the "legend among Canadian Literature enthusiasts" was deliberately "unconcerned, blasé even," an impression reinforced when he removed his loafers and put his feet on the sofa.

Back in Montreal in the early summer, he spent a few evenings with Leo Kolber, the Bronfman insider he had met in 1968. The powerful Kolber, who also sat on the board of the Hollywood studio MGM, had done Richler a good turn already, hosting him and Michael Spencer from the Canadian Film Development Corporation for a private lunch and advising on how to kick-start a film industry in Canada. Now he was about to do another, albeit unwittingly. Temporarily separated from his wife, Kolber found happy company with the novelist, listening while Richler admitted he couldn't understand men who cheated on their wives, and in turn fielding questions about the Bronfmans, in particular the ailing "Mr. Sam." Assuming they were off the record, and possibly flattered by Richler's attention—had he known him better, he might have recognized a writer's sly self-interest—the lawyer answered frankly. On the night of July 10 Richler happened to be in his house when the call came announcing the death, at age eighty, of Sam Bronfman. Preliminary funeral arrangements were made on the spot, including the quality of the casket ordered from Paperman's Funeral Home for the multi-millionaire, who would be lying in state at the Samuel Bronfman Centre for two days. Leo Kolber thought nothing of being unguarded, unaware that the rich material in the epic Bronfman story would exert an irresistible pull on the novelist.

Movie people flocked to make *St. Urbain's Horseman*. First in line was Norman Jewison, under contract with United Artists. The Toronto-born director was now in his own third year of London exile, and had become a friend. United Artists didn't share his interest in the new novel, but with all the buzz around Richler, Jewison was able to convince them to option an old one. "Meanwhile," Richler explained to Weintraub in July, "Jewison/U-A will buy ATUK, or option it rather, paying 3,500 down against 35,000, if and when the pix hits the floor." His young but astute movie agent, Bob Shapiro, drew up the contract, but the deal with Jewison was finalized face to face: "Jewison coming to din-dins next week." Shapiro returned from a trip to Hollywood later in the summer hopeful that either of two major industry forces—directors Stanley Kramer and John Schlesinger—would come in with an offer. But "general feeling seems to be it's a marvy bk, but no flick." In the end, Alan J. Pakula, whose latest movie, *Klute*, would win an Academy Award for Jane Fonda the following spring, paid for the chance to try his hand at *Horseman*. Shapiro negotiated a double deal for his client: money for the option, and to write the screenplay. Richler went to work on the script in the fall.

For once, "book" money could hold its head high against the sums available for writing movies. Bantam paid $30,000 for the paperback rights to the novel for the United States and Canada, by far his biggest literary payday. With M&S having sold 12,000 copies of the hardcover in Canada, and the unfolding U.K. numbers promising, *St. Urbain's Horseman* was raising him to a higher level of commercial exposure. Foreign sales to publishers in Portugal, Japan and France, while for much smaller sums, represented a similar new rung. *Cocksure* too had sold into Holland, Japan and Italy to date. The era of globalized publishing, with simultaneous (or near) publication in a dozen markets, was still years away, and very few writers expected anything other than irregular and unpredictable foreign sales. Even so, the status of being an "international author," with recognition across cultures and languages, was one that Richler aspired to. Being in London was a good start—as was acquiring, on the advice of Bob Gottlieb, a new British agent.

Deborah Rogers, who also represented Edna O'Brien and Philip Roth, had impeccable literary taste, along with a warm, quirky personality. Married to the composer Michael Berkeley, the redoubtable Rogers was soon a friend as well—of both Mordecai and Florence, as so often was the case. Having a similarly astute representative in Monica McCall in New York, and the more and more influential Bob Gottlieb as friend and editor at the eminent house of Alfred and Blanche Knopf, he was positioned to "break out" along the literary lines of a John Fowles or even a Saul Bellow. With *Horseman* he finally seemed to have the right book, once again, at the right time. Being shortlisted in late September for the Booker Prize, as Brian Moore had predicted, also boded well. Four of the six authors on the list hailed from outside the U.K.: Mordecai Richler, his old London friend Doris Lessing from Rhodesia, the Irishman Tom Kilroy and the Trinidad-born South Indian V.S. Naipaul. While at the time only Naipaul would likely have been designated a post-colonial, this breadth of representation was striking and, for the new prize, a groundbreaking embrace of the ever-widening English-language literary culture.

But it was at this moment, even as he stepped onto the international podium, that he began to turn back in earnest towards

Canada, in both his life and his work. "I have been brooding about the idea ever since," he told Davidson Dunton, the president of Carleton University in Ottawa, where he was seeking another writer-in-residence position to provide a salary and cover the costs of repatriating his family, "trying to settle the agonizing question of a return to Canada in my mind once and for all. I mean, returning on a permanent basis and that, after twenty years in Europe, fifteen in London, is a hellishly difficult decision to make."

With his mind still not entirely made up, he and Florence took the children to Ireland in August for their first extended family holiday since the house-swapping in Cornwall. They rented a house in the village of Roundstone in Connemara, a remote region of West Galway, and after a night in Killarney settled in for three weeks of wandering the heather and swimming in chilly Galway Bay. Richler brought his typewriter and, for the first week, they were joined by his editor Tony Godwin, as company for Florence during the workdays. To his own surprise, he ended up relaxing as well, drinking in the local pubs and fishing. A local girl, hired to help Florence, arrived barefoot.

Though the latest Irish "Troubles," rekindled in the summer of 1969, were largely confined to the North, a half-day's journey from West Galway, he mentioned the deteriorating situation in Belfast and Derry in a letter to Brian Moore. In the six months since the FLQ crisis in Quebec, Moore, who knew about those Troubles in his bones, drafted a "non-fiction novel" about Canada's brief flirtation with what he dubbed, impatiently, the "sour Mao dough of revolutionary cliché." *The Revolution Script* was already finished and ready to be published, with an excerpt due shortly in the *Sunday Times*, when Richler requested a copy to read. "In a plain brown wrapper, for Christsakes!" he kidded, not wishing to be confused for an Irish revolutionary on the lam.

By the end of the holiday he had made his decision: en route back to England, he typed two lengthy letters from a hotel room in the town of Kilkenny. "This is to formally accept your offer of July 16 in principle," he informed Davidson Dunton. "Yes, I'd like

to come to Carleton, effective from July 1, 1972, to June 30, 1974."
He outlined the terms, as he understood them, including salary,
job description, $3,000 to help relocate the family, and even offi-
cial titles, for tax purposes. With Bill Weintraub, naturally, he was
more emotional. "With many misgivings, much apprehension,
etc etc," he wrote. "Which is to say we are repatriating. Back to
the penal colony."

Though the move was still a year away, he already had an elaborate plan. It featured buying a house in Montreal while keeping
Hillcrest for a couple of years "as an escape channel," then selling the London house and buying "a farm somewhere, our
summer dacha." He had not told the children of the impending
move: "Will spring the decision on them at Xmas, not before."
Ambivalence still lurked beneath the surface. "The truth is, I
prefer living in London, but—but—I fear for my novels." Naming
expatriate friends, including Doris Lessing and the novelist Dan
Jacobson, he wondered if "the work has thinned by too long an
absence from roots. I do not wish to consume my forties writing
historical novels (Jacobson) or abt imag worlds (Doris.) So," he
concluded jokingly, "honouring my talent, I will return."

Bill Weintraub's own joking underlined his excitement. "We are
most delighted to hear that you have finally decided to follow
your forebears over from Europe . . . above all, it is the children
who will benefit. Many of our faith go to college here and there
are very few professions that are not open to us." He advised his
old friend not to schlep "that heavy old furniture across the
ocean"—it would be "an embarrassment to your children when
they start bringing their 'dates' home," and said that, should he
and Florence have any queries about Canada, "it is all explained
in one of the pamphlets you will get from the Immigration
Department." But he also promised to inquire about schools, a
question Richler began asking of many Montrealers that autumn.
No less a figure than Jules Léger, then the undersecretary of state
for Canada and another friend of the Ostrys, and eventually to
become the governor general, replied with suggestions for
schools for Daniel, Noah, Emma, Martha and even little Jake.

Léger's note, suggesting the Collège Français in Outremont for the older boys, related to another nascent Richler plan: to educate his English children in Canada's other official language. "Revenez vite au pays," Jules Léger wrote. "Il a besoin de talent, voire de génie."

With Florence, who had at least as much invested in the decision as he did, he was more circumspect. The previous December, even before *St. Urbain's Horseman* appeared, he had taken her to dinner in nearby Wimbledon, and over drinks mentioned that he thought he had to go back to Canada, for the sake of his fiction, and that he would set a date once he had made the arrangements. They had not spoken of the matter since, not even during those relaxing weeks in Ireland.

The possibility of returning home only seemed to increase his gleeful fighting mood, as Robert Fulford, thanking him for his latest *Saturday Night* column, recognized: "It'll no doubt result in the prosecution and eventual destruction of our magazine and my own imprisonment." He ripped into cultural nationalism and boosterism, his language unadorned, and naming names, whether remarking on Pierre Trudeau's love life in a piece about why 1971 had been a bad year for Jews ("our PM abandoned Barbra Streisand for a shiksa," he wrote of the prime minister's marriage to Margaret Sinclair, the twenty-two-year-old bride), or noting that while French Canadians felt their grievances deeply they were "happily far removed from being the white niggers of North America, as advertised." One of the named, the critic George Woodcock, replied offence for offence. "Alas, poor Mordecai! So pathetically pompous and inexpressibly dull in his prose as the candid critic, the Canadian Cato!" Another, the poet Al Purdy, held his tongue in public, but never forgot, or forgave, being mocked by Mordecai Richler in a national publication.

The columns were hardly consistent with his own fortieth birthday party regrets at his youthful callousness towards fellow authors. Had that mea culpa been sincere? He may have been beyond wanting to change, especially if it meant softening his disapproval of human folly. "I write out of a general disgust with things," he admitted to an interviewer—a stark philosophical stance. He was who he was, and had been so since he stood arguing with his homeroom teacher at Baron Byng each morning in 1947, or even earlier, as a fourteen-year-old who went out of his way to stroll past his grandfather's front porch on the Sabbath, smoking a cigarette and wearing no yarmulke. He was also committed to being a satiric novelist and social critic.

Satire was not a form appreciated or even fully understood by the majority of Canadians. An innately bruising and frequently impolite form of discourse, its moral nature was occasionally obscured by the appearance of self-interest, bile or bigotry. In England, Richler scarcely stood out from the unruly literary crowd, and in the United States he was, as he liked to say, enrolled in the rowdy "Jew-boy" literary yeshiva. In his own country, however, to which he was now proposing a permanent return, he was, if not anomalous, then singular.

He was back in Canada again in October, dutifully if unhappily supporting his publisher's efforts to sell his novel. After circuit stops in Calgary, Winnipeg, Toronto and Ottawa, he dropped by Montreal long enough to see Ted Allan. Then living outside the city, Allan was working on a screen adaptation of his biography of Dr. Norman Bethune, a project, and an obsession, now decades old, and still nearly another two decades away from fruition as a troubled movie starring Donald Sutherland. Lily Rosenberg, isolated from most of her son's friends, kept in contact with Allan, and had recently mailed the fifty-five-year-old a food parcel containing "gefulte fish, jams, verenikas, herring, etc etc etc," as Allan reported in a letter to Hillcrest. "I think of you often . . . and miss you badly," he added. If the sentiment seemed a little emotional for correspondence with Mordecai, it was because the letter was addressed to Florence. They shared the intimacy; the two men remained old friends, if no longer mentor-pupil. The kids, too, loved Ted Allan, an important part of their family. "But the big news is your return here," Allan wrote. "I wish it was sooner than Mordecai said." Interestingly, Florence had not yet discussed the "big news" herself with her husband;

and he had yet to officially inform her of the decision he had made months before.

In New York, where he proceeded for a final week promoting *St. Urbain's Horseman*, he stayed with the Gottliebs on East 48th Street and had lunch with his agent Monica McCall. "I think this post-HORSEMAN time might be a good one for me to see mag editors," he told her, "say New Yorker, Esquire, Playboy, etc, to see how interested they might be in my doing things from Canada." With McCall, a sardonic, funny Scotswoman with a large reputation but a smallish client list, he plotted to make inroads with American magazines of the less "snob," and therefore better-paying, variety. He was still in Manhattan when the Booker Prize, valued at £5,000, was announced. The date had conflicted with his reading tour, and the ceremony itself was not yet the glamorous literary event of later years. Putting V.S. Naipaul's *In a Free State*, a book composed of three lengthy stories, on the shortlist for a novel award had been controversial. Two of the judges—John Fowles and Saul Bellow—had wanted it disqualified, but Antonia Fraser, Philip Toynbee and chair John Gross had overruled them. Mordecai and Florence debated the issue in private with friends but assumed that the gifted, trailblazing Naipaul, a rising literary star, would win regardless. Bellow didn't help by announcing a full month before the award that the jury had decided to select the best writer, not the best book. John Fowles had already gone public with his support for *St. Urbain's Horseman*, and with Bellow and Gross on the jury, the book seemed well positioned. V.S. Naipaul's triumph still came as a deep disappointment to Richler, perhaps almost as much as the missed opportunity to finally meet his fellow Montrealer and literary role model. As it happened, Saul Bellow hadn't pushed for his novel about Babel and bootleggers, Yiddish-inflected English and snowy ghetto streets to win, preferring *Goshawk Squadron* by Derek Robinson, a masterly if now largely forgotten tale of the war in the skies in 1918.

Finally, in December, he suggested to Florence that they book a table at the same Wimbledon restaurant where he had first raised the likelihood of repatriation a year earlier. She knew at once her life was about to be forever changed:

> "So, you've decided to go back?" I asked him. "I've decided *we* are going back," he replied. "And if it's possible, I'd like to go by spring." We sparred for a while over the value of literary exile, with my citing Joyce's *Ulysses* as a book that benefited from its author living abroad permanently, and Mordecai countering that Doris's [Lessing] own Booker short-listed title, *Briefing for a Descent into Hell*, had been concerned with aliens and other worlds, and he didn't want to end writing something like that—so disconnected from who he was. We both laughed, but neither changed the other's mind. He asked me to give it a year or so in Canada, and then see. I asked that we not tell the children until Boxing Day, so that Christmas would not be upset. That Boxing Day at supper he announced that we were off on another family adventure. But the truth was, we left England without even a discussion—just a statement.

"Next Christmas in Canada?" Richler had written to Bill Weintraub. Now he could confirm it: "We sail for Montreal on the Pushkin, on June 21," he told his friend in January. "Daniel, who has exams, will follow by plane three wks later."

II

RETURN OF THE PRODIGAL . . . AGAIN

"Florence now in bed with a temp of 104.... Power cuts. Freezing. Christ!" That was Edinburgh in January, a brief family holiday in the Scottish capital—Florence had joined him on a speaking engagement, along with Martha and Emma—ruined. Lily, en route to her first-ever visit to Israel, much of her ticket paid for by her son, had babysat the boys at Hillcrest while the others suffered the Scottish winter. The U.K., enduring a recession and a beleaguered Labour government beset by endless strikes, including a year-long postal stoppage, was overall a dour, depressing place in 1971–72, but Richler did return from Edinburgh with a surprising new story in his head. One evening, the ailing Florence found herself overwhelmed with bedtime duties. When one of the girls, taking a bath upstairs, called out, she plopped four-year-old Jake in his lap with orders to entertain him. Not a physically expressive person, and raised by a mother who rarely touched her sons, Richler favoured tickling and roughhousing with his children, as well as the occasional kiss planted on the lips and tasting of cigar. Emma insisted on moulding his wild hair into horns, which he allowed, and anyone could take his hand in public, which the younger ones did.

He had been reading bedtime stories since doing so with Daniel in Rome in 1960, and had promised to one day write a book only for his family. To amuse Jake, he began unspooling a tale off the top of his head. It was about a boy who had to say everything twice because no one paid him any attention. "Jacob Two-Two" had four older siblings, Noah, Emma, "Marfa" and Daniel, a tomato-loving writer for a father, and a mother who was kind and mostly to be found in the kitchen of their house in London. Florence overheard enough that night to suggest that he write the yarn down. He did—the bare bones of what would become *Jacob Two-Two Meets the Hooded Fang*. ". . . have also written, of all things, a children's book," he told Weintraub in late winter. "Yessiree."

The flu that Florence brought back from Edinburgh dragged on for a month and then developed into hepatitis. Misdiagnosed as depression, the illness forced her to spend almost two months in bed or struggling with basic tasks. Other factors contributed. Her husband continued to crave his seven-hour, seven-day workweek in the office upstairs. That kind of single-mindedness was only possible if Florence adopted the same schedule and lifestyle in daily matters: eating when he wanted, keeping the children quiet until he was finished writing or even napping, inviting guests over only in the evenings. She had long understood and agreed to these terms, believing in his gift, and loving him. She also believed in the role of the writer's wife as respectable and fulfilling, a kind of partnership. As he pushed himself harder, with the endless Atlantic crossings of the 1960s and two, three, four and finally five children in tow, so he pushed her harder as well. Adding to her strain were the demands she placed on herself. From the time she was a teenager, Florence Wood, then Mann, then Richler, had been a model of composed, even regal beauty, and perfect manners. Perfection in appearance, in comportment, in domestic management—cuisine, housekeeping, hosting—was the only standard she would accept for herself. In addition, while strong and independent, she remained the adopted daughter of a depressed mother. She was naturally accommodating, and wanted to please.

Repatriation to Canada was neither her idea nor her desire. Nor did she think it was necessarily the best thing for the children. A return to Montreal would serve Mordecai's work, and perhaps his own well-being: his instinct to go home, it was clear to her, was powerful, a defining aspect of his character. Her own attachment to England, formed earlier and rooted in her adopted family's history, ran much deeper. It was cultural if non-artistic; unlike Richler, who admitted that for all his years in the capital he still did not know what an Englishman did at night, Florence had no professional need to "understand" their hosts nor any frustration at being a resident outsider. Her early trips to London as a young woman had shaped her, as well as the news that many of the extended Wood family had been killed in the war. For her, these deaths amounted to sacrifices for the next generation, of which she counted herself a member. London was where she established her adult identity and found in abundance the kind of culture and companionship she craved.

Now it was the city where Daniel, Emma, Martha and Jake had all been born, and to which Noah had been returned before he was a year old. The children were Londoners, with a lovely house and nice schools, and friends who saw them as one of their own. Florence was slowly revealing the city to them as well, and had already taken the girls out of class one afternoon to see Rudolf Nureyev dance with Margot Fonteyn, and all the children, minus Jake, to *The Threepenny Opera*, a play familiar to them because their father hummed the tunes, especially his favourites, "Pirate Jenny" and "Mack the Knife." She had imagined that, as they grew older, these activities would widen in scope; one could never experience all of London, never tire of its pleasures. But now this plan, too, was being overthrown, with the childhood and even the identities of the children also being subjected to the exigencies of his creative life.

It was under these circumstances that Richler came up with the delightful story of Jacob Two-Two. While not primarily intended as a homage to the family's about-to-vanish life in London, and certainly not meant as any kind of apology for being the author of its ending, the short novel that would eventually ensure that the curious name of Mordecai Richler was known to generations of Canadian children derived some of its warmth and heartfelt emotion from the impending loss of what was being described.

Confirmation of the strain the family was under came, oddly, from four high-school students out of suburban Montreal. They had flown to London to interview Mordecai Richler, described in the *Gazette* as the "little Jewish boy who made it big on the international novelist scene," for a school project. Arriving at Hillcrest two hours early on a Sunday, the students hid behind a grocery store until the appointed time. Daniel let them in, and although the author had "a sick wife to tend to, five children to cope with, housework to do, and meals to prepare," he spent ninety minutes talking with the intrepid literature lovers. One of the boys later described him as "very tired looking with the beginnings of a double chin," and Bob Fulford sent back word of the astonishing sight, passed along the media grapevine, of "His Lordship doing all the cooking, cleaning, etc." Not until mid-April could Richler report good news to Bill Weintraub. "Florence all but restored to health now, which is dandy. Can hardly wait to Canneswards on April 28. . . . F joins me," he added. "May 1 on Carlton terrace." The Carlton was the legendary hotel in the French Riviera town that served as headquarters for see-and-be-seen star parading and distribution deals during the Film Festival, and he would be there for *Life* magazine, all expenses paid. Jack McClelland was attending the festival as well, for part of the period. "My roomie, as it were," Richler explained.

McClelland would leave Cannes to collect Canada's largest literary prize on his behalf. Richler might not have won the more exciting and financially rewarding Booker Prize, but in early April he was given his second Governor General's Award, for *St. Urbain's Horseman*. The cheque for $2,500 had come with an offer of airfare to attend the ceremony on May 5, but he had no intention of vacating Cannes early to have another strange conversation with the governor general. Good financial news continued that spring, including a fat royalty cheque for American sales of the novel, the promise of a 150,000 paperback print run, handsome Canadian residuals from the enshrinement of *Duddy Kravitz* on so many university and high school courses, and progress, and general optimism, with the *Horseman* script. Alan Pakula "continues a very fine, calm fellow to work with," he told Weintraub. "Warners' interest in project very strong. But these are early days, early days. My first rough draft runs to 200pp. Christ!"

But all the enthusiasm and work, the lengthy memos and dozen drafts, would still come to nothing; within a year, the productive and brilliant Pakula would be releasing the drama *Love and Death and the Whole Damn Thing*, followed by the second and third films to accompany *Klute* in what would later be dubbed his "paranoia trilogy"—*The Parallax View* in 1974 and *All the President's Men* in 1976. Much as he may have loved the novel, and liked Richler's script, *Horseman* was out of step with the director's current concerns.

As expected, Cannes was plenty of fun, especially with the inflated rates for hotel and food, plus his bar tab, looked after by *Life*. His coveted room at the Carlton, booked for ten days, was well used. First Florence joined him, sitting on the terrace people-watching and attending movie premieres. McClelland arrived at the hotel when Richler was out and bribed a bellhop to let him into the room, only to find himself immediately expelled in favour of eleven-year-old Emma. Florence, having flown back to Heathrow just a few hours earlier, had put her daughter on a plane for the adventure of her young life. Left on the terrace with a fruit drink while her father worked, Emma got to have lunch with Groucho Marx. "Will you marry me?" the comedian, then in his eighties, asked her. When Emma replied that she was too young, Marx vowed to ask again in three weeks. Anthony Burgess joined them at the table for a while, and one afternoon Ted Kotcheff and Michael Spencer sat sketching out the budget they would need to make *Duddy Kravitz*. Kotcheff, whose own Cannes festival debut as a director the year before, the Australia-set *Wake in Fright*, had been a critical success, vowed to raise the sum in eighteen months.

Richler regaled Bill Weintraub with some of the "lower-depth" cinematic fare he attended. "VIRGIN WITCH, SEX OLYMPICS, HOMO VAMPIRE, MONA (in which a girl blows two guys simultaneously), BORDELLO, etc etc." Florence gamely accompanied him to one 10 a.m. showing of porn. Half the audience, she noted, were Japanese media. Though Richler came away feeling buoyant from the meeting with Kotcheff about *Duddy Kravitz*, he was brought down to earth by a Columbia studio executive who declined his offer to attend the Canadian film gala that evening. "Canadian films have got no want-to-see," the executive informed him.

Most plans, outside of his work, involved the children, whether it was taking Noah to Paris or Emma to Cannes. Richler was proud of his handsome brood. He tried to keep a clear line between his family life and writing life, but sometimes allowed it to blur. His lifelong claim to despise the celebrity author, and his antipathy to promoting himself and his work, never matched that of J.D. Salinger or Thomas Pynchon, who simply refused to take part. Even while agreeing to a family portrait in *Time* and permitting a CBC camera to sweep up his kid-laden front steps, he was telling interviewers that "it may be a mistake to meet the writer," and "whether a writer is a marvellously charming, agreeable, generous man or whether he beats his wife and tortures his children is beside the point. That's private. The books are what matter one way or the other, and the two should not be confused." While he was a man "charged with contradictions," as he admitted, and comfortable holding contradictory positions, he was also keenly aware of how celebrity could sell books. With five children, he believed that he didn't have the luxury to be so pure. He also enjoyed, if not the fame that eventually came his way, then the opportunities to encounter new people, and mix it up, that accompanied a high public profile. Always thinking about his fiction, he was more than receptive to fresh faces; he needed them to feed his imagination, provide material for his satiric eye. When a friend offered to set up a dinner party to allow Richler to meet a wealthy Jew who had just moved into upper Westmount, he agreed: "Serve him up," he said of the opportunity to observe and record.

Together, the Richlers were definitely engaged parents. A nation unto itself, the family made its own definitions of membership and rules regarding everything from lifestyle to religion, and even what constituted reality. (Noah, Daniel, Emma, Marfa and Jacob were, after all, becoming characters in a book.) For father and mother both, what they had built together—the marriage and family, home and friendships, the opportunities for shared experiences—was a project, necessarily self-conscious and willed. It was a vision of adult contentment born out of childhood experiences of the near opposite.

For the five children, their tightly connected, storytelling, loving, slightly eccentric world was "normal"—how parents behaved, how families functioned. So the morning in June 1972 when the kids came downstairs at Hillcrest and found two women with shaved heads and white caftan robes having breakfast was not exceptional. By then, at least, the older children could identify one of the nuns as their father's former wife. The profile in *Time* had mentioned Cathy Boudreau. "You didn't tell me you were married!" Noah had complained after reading about it in the magazine. "You never asked," his parent had replied.

The early morning appearance of the Buddhist nun Hananda and her friend had been unannounced, save for a 5:30 a.m. phone call from the airport. Richler sat in petrified silence for most of the breakfast while Florence made polite conversation. When he tried ending the encounter by announcing that he had business in the city, Cathy asked for a lift. Recognizing the look of agony on his face, Florence offered to accompany them as well.

The family's life in England was drawing to a close. "Return of the prodigal . . . again," ran the Montreal *Gazette* headline. While he made, as usual, no effort to flatter his homeland—neither Montreal nor Toronto was a "capital" in the sense that London was, he said—he did ensure that readers knew he was aware of the changes in Quebec. "My French is terrible," he admitted. "We never had to speak it on St. Urbain Street." But his children, he told the newspaper, would be receiving tutoring in French on their arrival in the summer, and attending French schools in the fall. "It's a big change in my life," he said. "I've gotten to feel very secure here."

A big change for him, and for Florence, and for their English-accented children, about to experience the French language and

Quebec language politics from the trenches. "Locally, Pierre Vallières, as you may have heard, has renounced terrorism and embraced Peaceful Separatism," Bill Weintraub informed him earlier in the year, referring to the militant author of *White Niggers of America.* "This will no doubt cause property values in Westmount to go up, I fear." Westmount was where the Richlers were bound, on a monthly rental basis to start. School arrangements were also close to set: "boys accepted at Stanislas, girls at Marie de France," he wrote. His friend Alex Cherney, who had a son at the school, helped place the boys in the elite Collège Stanislas in Outremont, and Cherney's daughter had been engaged from across the Atlantic to do summer tutoring. Daniel, sitting exams at the posh St. Paul's, where his classmates included the son of playwright Harold Pinter, would miss the early tutorials.

By mid-June the usual pre-departure chaos reigned. "Just a hurried note to say that we arrive Friday am June 30," he told Bill Weintraub, "if I manage to complete 208 chores before then." These included dealing with the Filipino au pair—recently hired to emigrate with them to the New World—quitting at the last minute, getting papers for the budgerigars and ring-necked doves, packing eighteen wooden crates, some with those well-travelled, still-unread books, and readying yet another Richler car to cross the Atlantic in the hold of a ship. He vowed to work on the *Horseman* script on the boat, made plans to meet Alan Pakula on Long Island in August and was thrilled by unexpected film news: "Now Joe Heller of all people wants to option Cocksure and write the screenplay. Catch-23."

The final twenty-four hours at Hillcrest veered from drama to farce. Bob Gottlieb consoled a distraught Florence on the phone the night before the *Alexander Pushkin* set sail, and Ted Kotcheff, miserable at losing his dearest London friends, drove to the house to help with the final packing. With the car loaded the morning of June 21, Kotcheff watched in the vestibule as Richler smashed a toaster to the ground for no evident reason, exclaiming, "I always hated that toaster!" Florence burst into tears. However, being exhausted and overwhelmed didn't keep the couple from hosting a farewell party in their cabin on the *Pushkin* at Southampton dock. Richler had bought a case of liquor for the occasion, gin, Scotch and cognac, and among those who raised a glass to their safe passage was Norman Jewison, who listened closely to Richler's arguments for returning to Canada.

A what-the-hell letter from Jack McClelland to the ship's captain, proclaiming Mordecai Richler an "international celebrity" deserving of the finest hospitality, failed to alter the reality of the *Alexander Pushkin* as a thoroughly Soviet vessel. Florence, forbidden alcohol for a year because of the hepatitis, had to sip a Georgian mineral water that smelled like disinfectant. Food was nearly inedible, with fresh fruits served unripened. The passengers, described as Germans "immense of thigh, broad of belly" who sprawled on the deck "like beached whales," left apples and pears outside their cabins in the hope of softening them. Jacob, then four, joined his father for early morning strolls, where both helped themselves to the not-so-forbidden fruit.

———————

While walking the decks or revising the script of *St. Urbain's Horseman*, Richler, by his own admission, "took to brooding about home." He had time to reflect on two distinct challenges that awaited him. The first concerned the Quebec he was about to declare his permanent address. In contrast to his earlier thoughts about returning, some dating back to the mid-fifties, his new plan had never involved either Toronto or New York, despite the former's rise as English Canada's literary centre or the latter's standing as the centre of American culture and a place he had once thought of as his natural home. Montreal it was, and Montreal it could only be. Now in his early forties, he had achieved the recognition that would allow him to live away from literary capitals, large or small, if he chose, and still be confident he would get calls for as many assignments as he wanted. Likewise, while the city would never attract as many casual social encounters—the Mel Brookses and Philip Roths who happened to be in town—he had close friends there. And for a writer, in particular one compelled to serve as witness to his times, Montreal's recent volatility was not a black mark. "Hello, hello," he had chimed in the *Life* piece on the October Crisis. His hometown, to him always more charged with appetite and comfortable with shaded human behaviour than elsewhere in Canada, now contained within its multiplicities even more outsized contradictions. The city had defined him; the prodigal son was ready to return.

The decision to send the children to school in French itself marked his recognition that the province had changed, that French Canadians were finally emerging from their long history as the priest-ridden, Duplessis-cowed majority. He was enthusiastic about the strong literary culture in Quebec, which he had tracked in his journalism for a decade. While his literary leanings were British by training and Jewish-American by disposition, he was open to making local friends. As was his wont, he had done the spadework, most notably reaching out and across the linguistic limitations of his poor French to include Quebec writers in his 1960s anthology, *Canadian Writing Today*. Friendships with Naïm Kattan and his Quebec publisher, Claude Hurtubise, drew him as well. From the deck of the *Pushkin*, he may have believed he would achieve modest fellowship with the other literary solitude.

The second challenge was his family. Re-entering the orbit of the Richler clan was a minor concern; aside from being approached by relations at public events, he could control whom he saw. (His Uncle Joe, fallen on hard times, would soon be driving a city cab. Richler would hesitate each time he flagged a car, hoping it wasn't him.) Avrum, out of contact since their father's death, lived a thousand miles away, in St. John's. "You must be as surprised to be hearing from me as I am to be writing you," Avrum had written on the occasion of *St. Urbain's Horseman*. He had praised the novel, in particular the shiva and Seder scenes— "it really brought back memories, some good, some bad"—and itemized his own recent activities: a new young daughter and pregnant wife, a busy professional life that combined running an optometry practice with doing a Ph.D. in the faculty of medicine.

"If you'd care to, I'd like to hear from you," he added. Richler replied, saying he might pay a visit to Newfoundland one day. (Two years later his brother would write, "Good God, you said, as you saw who this letter was from, is Av still alive?")

Lily was the worry. His mother, now in her late sixties, awaited them in lower Westmount. On one level, there was little fresh cause for concern. For years she had been paying annual or semi-annual visits to London, and Mordecai to Montreal. Both sides had played their part, with Lily, at least, pretending she was semi-welcome in her son's house, or stoking any embers of guilt he might have with jabs that made it clear she felt maltreated and hard done by. "I know you are both looking forward with suspense to my coming visit," she wrote once. "Thank your lucky stars it is only for three days." Or in 1970: "One of these days . . . I must write to you and tell you what I think of your attitude and contact towards me. I do not want to hurt you and I do not want you to change, one cannot force love, it does not matter anymore to me." Since her retirement Lily had travelled extensively, often with his financial support, including a trip to Israel to sort out the legacy of the land purchases by Rabbi Rosenberg. She had also gone to the Soviet Union to seek out her long-lost niece Suzanne Rosenberg, now living in the Moscow of the Brezhnev thaw. She regularly sent fawning notes to her grandchildren, along with gifts for them and for Florence, including a dollhouse that cost Mordecai a fortune in duty when he went to collect it, and was only too happy to carry out small tasks for him, of the sort Moses Richler had once performed. "I sent off the gifts for the Hurtig girls as soon as I received your letter," she wrote of one assignment, after he had stayed with the publisher and his family in Edmonton. The volatile Lily announced that she wanted to reunite her estranged sons, seemily oblivious of her earlier attempt to poison one against the other. "He is missing the best time with the children," she wrote of Avrum's divorce. "At times I want to shake and shake him and at times I ache for him. I never have him out of my mind."

Richler himself sent mixed signals back to his mother. Those paid visits to London, often for babysitting, suggested some tolerance of her presence. The same was true of his occasional request that she perform a favour, and his generally prompt, if guarded, replies to her letters. He still asked Bill Weintraub to help her out with her affairs, often related to finances or travel. ("You know he is so decent a man," she wrote of Weintraub. "A joy.") The expenses Richler took care of—dentist's fees or plane tickets to visit her rabbi brother in Savannah—and the monthly cheques he continued to mail prompted revealing expressions of her gratitude: "It's not so much the money," Lily wrote, "it is the knowledge that you are a real son, and Florence a real daughter." Like the toys-for-kisses exchanges she foisted upon the children, that kind of emotional quid pro quo, her only way of connecting with people, irked and embarrassed her son. So did her matronizing attitude towards Florence, a stance rooted in her insecurity around her daughter-in-law.

He gradually found himself being more attentive to his mother, yet feeling less and less affection for her. Such a dynamic is routine in unhappy parent-child relationships, but for a man who disliked appeasement as much as he did, and who insisted on making moral assessments of each relationship, the situation was dispiriting. Grim duty, bordering on stubbornness, prolonged loveless devotion. So did a belief that providing his children with even limited exposure to a difficult grandparent was better than no contact. Above all else, Richler felt the cumulative effect of Lily's lifelong pathology of mingling guilt and manipulation in her relationships. He abhorred hypocrisy, and discerned it clearly in her behaviour. He seems to have recognized less how his own upbringing had made him susceptible to this kind of compromised interaction. He would only have had to reread the manuscript of *The Rotten People* to be reminded of how furious, and helpless, that psychological and emotional miseducation had left him as a young adult. But the manuscript had lately gone missing, stored, along with other early writings, inside the trunk his father had lent him in 1951, which had served as a coffee table in Hampstead. He could always have glanced at the "publishable" version of this fury and hurt. But even *Son of a*

Smaller Hero, a book he would eventually seek to keep out of print, might have been too-painful reading—especially with one of the primary manipulators still alive and in his life. Another revealing text, *The Acrobats*, would be reprinted once more before Richler decided that it too should be prevented from finding new readers. And at its author's request, that final edition no longer carried the dedication "For My Mother."

His relationship with his surviving parent was essentially terrible, and had been for some time. Two factors had lately altered the dynamic for the worse. For all her denials in letters, the portrait of Mrs. Hersh in *Horseman* had been hurtful to her. There could be no refuting her as the source of the character; many of the lines spoken by Jakes's cloying, sour mother on the page had first been spoken aloud by Lily Rosenberg to her daughter-in-law or son. Then, in the fall of 1971, Lily, whose aspirations to be a writer dated back to her pre-war columns in the *Canadian Jewish Review*, mailed him a manuscript she warned was "the first instalment of my memoirs, or life history." Another kind of warning followed: "I just want you to know that you had better read it, and Florence too. If you don't, well mine son, I will start sending articles to the press telling them I am your mother." He did eventually read the "book"—an early version of the memoir she would send around to publishers a few years later—but assured Florence that she needn't bother. It was junk, he told her. Unpublishable.

The house the family rented for a month was on Wood Avenue in Westmount, a short walk from Lily Rosenberg's rooming house on Stayner Street. Even once he and Florence bought a home three-quarters of the way up the mountain, they were still in the same, albeit vast, neighbourhood. How would this proximity play out? Even if he vowed between gritted teeth to remain the dutiful son, he must have guessed that the ending could be neither far off nor happy.

III

EDGEHILL ROAD

"Even though we arrived on July 1, we are only barely settled in—but—but in that time we have bought and furnished a spiffy house, placed the kids in French schools, acquired household help of sorts. . . ." Since his return four months earlier, he admitted to André Deutsch in November, the days "have been, and remain, extremely hectic." But he was ready to start a final draft of *Jacob Two-Two Meets the Hooded Fang*, "my children's book," the reason for the letter to his former English publisher. It had been his own idea to approach Deutsch with the manuscript, a way both of reviving an appreciated relationship and not bothering Weidenfeld & Nicolson with a "lesser" project. He was especially aware of Diana Athill's lingering regrets that he had left them. So he instructed his new British agent, Deborah Rogers, to send it to Deutsch, and sure enough, they bought the book for a typically modest advance. "It will be fun to be a Deutschnik again, even if only a juv. one," Richler said.

Shovelling Trouble, his new book of essays, encountered no hesitations in Canada. His reputation for penning ferocious—and very funny—journalism ensured that McClelland & Stewart would do fine, and they commissioned Terry Mosher, alias Aislin, to draw another caricature. This time, Aislin made good use of the famous hair, high forehead and baleful eyes, and introduced the props that would soon be synonymous with the persona: a Scotch in one hand and a lit match in the other, a cigarillo awaiting ignition. On the back was an intense, moody photograph, also featuring a cigarillo between rough fingers. In 1972 only two Canadian authors, Pierre Berton and Farley Mowat, could sell books with, in effect, their faces. Now, with Aislin's cartoon, M&S was asserting, there was a third. "Mordecai Richler returns to Canada this fall," the jacket copy began.

Some of the pieces in *Shovelling Trouble* reached back to the early sixties, sitting happily beside recent provocations such as the "Maple Leaf Culture Time" and "Êtes-Vous Canadien?" which had so infuriated people. His Paris memoir, "A Sense of the Ridiculous," and "Bond" rank among his best essays. Towards the end of a take-down of pop guru Timothy Leary was a quiet declaration: "Furthermore, poverty brutalizes, which is why I remain a social-ist." A revealing declaration of another sort lay buried in a review of an "ostensibly boring, but inadvertently hilarious" book about the history of the Jewish community in Canada. Scolding a luck-less rabbi for skipping over all the interesting Jews in favour of bland community builders, he mentioned a few glaring oversights: Communist MP Fred Rose, "fabulous gambler" Harry Ship, and boxers Maxie Berger and Louis Alter. All of them Richler's own kind of Canadian Jew—outsized and shaded, full of appetite and energy. But the most egregious fault of the rabbi's compendium was the diminishment of the Bronfman family saga to a couple of tepid sentences, with no mention made of their wild-Jew behav-iour as bootleggers and empire builders, "thereby reducing a tale, the natural material of Isaac Babel, to absolutely nothing."

The collection came out two years later in the United States under the title *Notes on an Endangered Species*, with one addi-tion. In the interim Richler had converted a minor catastro-phe—the folding of *Life* magazine before his Film Festival piece ran—into a triumph, thanks to Monica McCall's sale of a rewrit-ten version to *Harper's*. Relieved of expectations to report movie star glamour, he produced "Notes on an Endangered Species," a hilarious, sympathetic portrait of bottom-feeding producers, mostly Jewish and many composites, gathered at Cannes to trade in porn and schlock.

The spiffy house the Richlers purchased at 218 Edgehill Road put him within a few blocks of that Babel-worthy tale of the Bronfmans. The four-bedroom home, with its terraced back garden and garage entered from the street below, was within walking distance of the Bronfman mansion, occupied until recently by Mr. Sam himself. As a neighbourhood, Westmount had much to recommend it. Homes offered degrees of elegance and extravagance, with those higher up the slope boasting spectacular views of the downtown and the St. Lawrence River, the Eastern Townships and even Vermont, visible to the south on clear days. There was an abundance of schools and few rivals to Murray Hill or Westmount Park for urban public spaces. Many friends lived there now, including the Weintraubs and Idelsons, Cherneys and Robinsons, and most of the key political and business figures in the English-speaking city retained Westmount addresses. Back in the summer Florence, assuming that the gravitational pull extended all the way to childhood, had asked if he wanted to look at houses over the mountain, in the old neighbourhood. Homes along Esplanade or Jeanne Mance were more affordable, and closer to the touchstones of his Montreal. The apartment at 5257 St. Urbain even had a FOR SALE sign on it, if he wanted to bring things full circle. He dismissed the idea with a laugh. Richler, who went for walks most evenings, could always drive over Mount Royal if he wanted to wander those streets. The kind of living and—it would soon be apparent— observing he wished to do involved different Montreal streets, and different Montreal houses.

Repeating the 1963 dare of buying a property he could not afford and then double-daring himself to continue to generate the income to make the mortgage payment each month, he took much of the money he had saved and made a down payment on the sort of residence more likely to be the address of, if not a distillery mogul, then a business executive. Housing prices had suffered from the vagaries of politics, but 218 Edgehill Road was still a considerable purchase. In Westmount psycho-geography, the street ran above The Boulevard, the east-west traffic corridor that marked the invisible line between the affluent middle tier and the wealthy crown of the hill. It included a basement for teens and a comfortable third-floor office from which to operate the Richler cottage industry—with those stunning views.

Location mattered. He was not above demonstrating success. He had the spouse, the family and the standing; he also wanted the address. He was returning to Montreal, the city of his upbringing among fellow poor Jews and scrappy early adulthood. And whether he was returning as the Canada-bashing, wannabe-American described by his detractors or as the accomplished novelist destined, as Diana Athill had predicted, to become the "grand old man of Canadian letters," a house in upper Westmount gave him pleasure. Now, too, he would mingle with, or perhaps bump up against, the small but powerful Anglo elite, and not as an interloper.

"He conquered the world," a biographer of the Bronfman family would soon be writing of Sam Bronfman's own social ambitions, "but never Westmount." True or not, the Bronfman patriarch's mansion on Summit Circle was nestled in the heart of besieged Anglo affluence and influence. Mordecai Richler was there as well, albeit as a watcher, and so, in a sense, were the characters he had "reared" on St. Urbain Street, the after-the-main-chance Duddys and Jakes, now middle-aged entrepreneurs and professionals, making a play for a stake in mostly lower and middle Westmount. If the deliriously wealthy Bronfmans couldn't penetrate the carapace of Anglo-Saxon self-regard, what luck would his cast of adult Jewish urchins stand? But of course the point, always, was the striving and hustle, the sexual, political and huge comedic energy generated by this territorial battle being waged by one social group on another, all within the context of the wider war being fought for the city, the province and the country. Good stuff, in short, and he wasted no time positioning himself to witness, record and render it from the best seat possible.

So that September, it was in the living room of Edgehill Road that he sat with his sons watching the Canada-Russia hockey series. "Henderson makes a wild stab for it and falls," announcer

Foster Hewitt breathlessly told the nation during the final moments of the eighth and deciding game. "Here's another shot. Right in front. They score!! Henderson has scored for Canada!" If twelve-year-old Noah Richler had any lingering doubts about his father's nationality, watching him watch hockey settled the matter. He had already begun taking the children to Expos baseball games at Jarry Park, and as the endless Montreal winter settled in he would be coming home with the occasional pair of Habs press tickets, courtesy of his journalist friend Dink Carroll. Lucky was the child invited to the Forum with his dad.

Back in the summer Richler had met with James Downey, the young chair of the English department at Carleton University, and worked out a schedule for his duties. He would teach a once-a-week class in creative writing to a maximum of twenty students, and then serve as a "resource" in a fourth-year course on literary theory to be co-taught by Downey. Each Monday morning he took the train to Ottawa to teach the unteachable. He stayed overnight in a university guest house, had dinner with Sylvia and Bernard Ostry, or was hosted by professors in the faculty lounge, in order to be a living resource in the theory class the next morning. A taxi awaited him, and by late afternoon he was back in Montreal.

He selected the seminar students himself. John Aylen, later a friend, made the cut one year; an undergraduate named Graydon Carter, eventually the editor of *Vanity Fair*, applied too late. Richler warned each candidate that their hopes for the experience would almost certainly be dashed. Writing, he explained, obliged natural talent, which could not be instructed or acquired. Once in the classroom, where students were normally expected to read their work aloud and critique each other, he demanded that they quit that nonsense and read the great books, including the *Concise OED* and Fowler's *Modern English Usage*, instead. He also helped them develop tough skins. Incapable, as always, of dispensing false encouragement or of abiding pretense, he chewed one young man out for writing "pretentious horseshit" and told a young woman more gently that, while her story showed

promise, it was many drafts away from being decent. Avoid clichés, he instructed, and write clear and simple prose. No run-on
sentences or florid metaphors. Don't moralize or try to be clever.
Beyond such nuggets of advice, he had little to say. He did brighten
at any writing that showed energy and spark, and, in one student's memory, gave everyone the same grade—B. On one occasion he brought his class to the faculty club for drinks, and on
another day he picked up the tab for pizza and beer.

With the fourth-year group he could feel less a "fraud," as he
called authors (including himself) who pretended to teach creative writing. James Downey and his co-instructor, Rob McDougall,
would draw him out, earning terse, smart remarks about literature and film, and once or twice he found a discussion about a
book or author interesting enough to volunteer a thought. But
mostly the professors left their "living writer" to sit in smoky
silence. In the faculty club he was less gentle with his remarks,
verbally sparring about the hot-button topics of the day: Canadian
cultural nationalism and Quebec. Neither being in a classroom
nor exchanging faculty repartee suited his temperament. Nor
was there any real correspondence between these activities and
his views on the business of writing and being a writer. A classmate from Baron Byng, Jack Wolofsky, also commuting from
Montreal to Ottawa on Monday mornings, often ran into Richler
on the train. Wolofsky kept him company in the dining car, where
pre-noon gin and tonics could be ordered. He required extra for-
tification to face those bright-eyed undergraduates, with their
excess of self-confidence and inadequate background in books.

James Downey recognized Richler's limitations as a teacher,
but believed his presence alone benefited the more perceptive
students. That presence—authoritative and serious, a "real"
writer in their midst—was being noted by others too in the emerging Canadian scene. Robert Weaver had assigned the novelist
Graeme Gibson, soon to become the partner of Margaret Atwood,
to conduct radio interviews with Canadian authors, and Gibson
met with Richler in the Montreal CBC building in the fall of 1972.
Tall and ruggedly handsome, three years younger and with three

novels published, Gibson was well aware that his subject had produced seven works of fiction and two collections of essays so far, along with hundreds of articles and several screenplays, publishing in London and New York. At the same time, like many nationalists, Gibson resented his incessant attacks on Canada, especially those in American and U.K. publications, where he appeared to be earning a good buck off the bashing. Gibson, who admired *The Acrobats* and *Son of a Smaller Hero* as much as the "funny" novels, believing their seriousness to be benchmarks for Canadian writers, was disappointed when their author rejected them as near juvenilia. But he came away from the encounter with a sense of Richler as a kind of stern adult among the giddy teenagers of Canadian literature: an accomplished professional who actually earned a living by his pen.

The Richler children, with their English accents and beginners' French, faced their own classroom challenges that autumn. Collège Stanislas, a private lycée catering mostly to Outremont residents and staffed by ardent Quebec nationalists, did not embrace Daniel and Noah. Besides being tossed into the deep end of French-language instruction, they had the schoolyard to negotiate, where it was less their accents than their status as English speakers that served as provocation. Being declared, if not self-identified, as Jews—their father, after all, was a high-profile one—also did not help. The teenagers fought back, sometimes using fists, although Daniel, swift with his words, preferred to charm his way. A little of that tension, and the reality of the deepening nationalist sentiment among many French Montrealers, came home with the boys each afternoon, and for the more intense Noah, the WASPS and Jewish teenagers of Westmount were scarcely friendlier territory.

After a year Daniel moved on to Marianopolis, a private CEGEP, and Noah transferred to a public school. Though he now spoke decent French, most courses at Westmount High were taught in English. Neither of the girls had ended up at the severe Marie de France. Instead, after a spell at the local elementary school, Roslyn, Emma happily committed to studying in French with the nuns at Villa Sainte-Marcelline, and Martha was sent to the private Miss Edgar's and Miss Cramp's, also in Westmount. Jake, only five, attended kindergarten at Roslyn, then was switched to Selwyn House, still another private school a steep walk down the hill from Edgehill Road. That year the Richlers put four children into private school, a remarkable financial commitment for anyone, especially a writer with uncertain income.

Their father, in short, was once more writing multiple tuition cheques, and not all arrived on time. Creative financing, often with the advice of his friend the economist Sylvia Ostry, and the assistance of Jon Robinson, remained a necessary part of his dare of being that full-time writer with a large family and a Westmount address. The Carleton job helped stabilize that line on his tax form, but he was often scrambling; annual tax day involved emptying out the contents of his desk drawers onto the living room floor. Fortified with a meal from Florence and a bottle of Scotch, the two friends would go about compiling expenses and deductions. Jon Robinson used all his imagination to keep him from paying much, if any, tax, and at midnight he would drop the form in a nearby mailbox, moments before the penalty deadline.

Noah learned something of his sense of money when he and Emma went to put their pocket money in a Westmount bank. Their father offered to flip a coin with each, double or nothing, and actually took Noah's cash when he lost the toss. Worse, little Emma lost as well, but he let her keep her money. Although a quirky lesson, the exercise was in keeping with his inclination to teach his children, often forcefully, the capricious nature of money and chance, just as he had made the boys pay for the car window they smashed and, when they jokingly called a strike on leaf raking at Hillcrest, denying them movie funds. Daniel, as the oldest, detected the method in his mischief. Noah, only twelve when his life savings were wiped out in a coin toss, saw only the injustice. A bright, moody adolescent with some of the same independence and rebelliousness his father had shown at that age, he may have been on the receiving end of extra attention, and censure —Mordecai had noted the resemblance between himself and his first-born, right down to the pitch of his voice and certain mannerisms. Back in England Noah had been part of a shoplifting ring at his school, obliging his parent to defend him before the headmaster and to administer, to the acute embarrassment of both, his only spanking of a child. Many years later, Jake would emerge as a dead ringer for young adult Mordecai, but with a personality closer to his mother's.

Westmount High was located on St. Catherine Street West, just a few blocks from Stayner Street. As Richler had feared, Lily assumed their return would signal her greater involvement in their lives. She even hinted that an invitation to move into Edgehill Road would not be refused. The offer never came, but during the early months he and Florence gamely put up with unannounced visits, often early in the morning. Florence, as always, abided her innuendos and her joylessness; Mordecai, increasingly, did not. He told her that his mother could only be an "insidious presence" in their lives. Still hoping to salvage the children's relationship with their grandmother, she began sending them down the hill to have Sunday dinner with her. These go-between visits were awkward for the kids—long bouts of watching television in her living room and poking forks into the kosher foods she served. Lily occasionally invited her relations to meet the much-discussed, rarely sighted children of her famous son, but if they were hoping to glimpse him as well, they were disappointed; he declined to collect his brood afterwards and rarely asked questions about the visits. Their grandmother, they noticed, never came to their house any longer, and soon was scarcely even mentioned. Emma, for one, wondered how it was that her father did not love his own mother.

In a sense, *Jacob Two-Two Meets the Hooded Fang* was his answer. The book was redrafted over the winter of 1972–73, until the story of the boy who has to say everything twice because no one will listen to him the first time was ready to show editors. Jacob's adventures on Slimer's Isle amidst wolverines and snakes and the Hooded Fang, a former wrestler notorious for his hatred of small children who say things twice, had as its launching point an innocent quest: to purchase two pounds of the tomatoes his father loved, and so prove his usefulness. "Who's my favourite child?" Richler liked to call out, generally from the living room couch that was his end-of-day spot for reading the newspaper and watching sports. This family joke worked on two levels. Officially, it meant that he wanted someone to lower the volume on the set so he could nap, or look up a phone number, or bring him tea with lemon. "Favourite children" put on their coats to collect the paper in the morning; lately, older ones had begun to bundle up in snowstorms to hike to delis to fetch latkes and smoked meat. But the kids understood that their father would never truly leverage affection or play one child off the other; that he would never subject them to the manipulation he and his brother had been exposed to, and scarred by. He might often be distracted, a silent presence at the dinner table, his mind in a world elsewhere; he might occasionally be a grumpy parent, shouting at them to turn their damn music down and once graffiti-ing over the faces of the musicians on an album cover with speech bubbles containing the words "We're loud—stupid—rich"; he might be forever anxious to get back to his office, back to work, and he was certainly happy to let Florence take care of the daily, grinding details of running a household. But he was in the house, always, and was supportive. Jacob Two-Two could be brave because he felt loved and, even when in peril, protected. The same held true for his rescuers, the Child Power team of Shapiro (Emma) and O'Toole (Noah). In an earlier draft of the book Jacob is rescued by "Child Power children" from all across England. In the final version, it is a brother-sister affair.

Jacob Two-Two has its scary side, and features the malicious grocer Mr. Cooper and nasty Justice Rough. Guards Master Fish and Mistress Fowl are none too nice either. As well, the story stars the supposedly horrid Hooded Fang, who does his evil best to trip Jacob into saying other numbers besides two. "Can you tell me how many suns there are?" is one trick question, to which the boy answers that, besides him, "my father has two. Daniel and Noah." But no character evinces any real darkness or malice. Neither does the prose, attuned to the cadences of a small boy, strike the faintest Roald Dahl note of unease. Small wonder the Hooded Fang turns out to be afraid of stepping on cracks in the prison courtyard, his pockets yielding jelly beans and bubble gum. "I want my mommy," he wails at the end. He does, and Jacob and his siblings certainly did want their parents, who were enriching and sheltering them in books and life alike. But Richler did not want his mother—and had not, for many difficult years.

"Do you really want to do this book?" Bob Gottlieb wrote in February, enclosing a negative assessment from Knopf's juvenile editor, along with his own cool reaction. "Have you really put your back into it? Speak!" But Pantheon Books, an imprint of Knopf, ended up publishing *Jacob Two-Two* in the United States, where it disproved the editors' judgment well enough to merit a second printing and be named an outstanding book of the year by the *New York Times.* With M&S in Canada and André Deutsch in the U.K., acceptance was immediate. Only some initial reservations over Jacob's age led Richler to advance him from four to six. In very little time, *Jacob Two-Two* became beloved among children— and ultimately a classic.

"I will be in London in April, and hope to see André then if only to explain to him any long words in children's ms that may give him trouble. . . . MiGod, I miss London." But then he delayed the trip until late summer because "after a very febrile year here, I am working my way into a new novel," adding in customary fashion, "but I will not be signing a British contract until I've been to London and thoroughly gone into yours and other offers." Earlier, though, he had mentioned another project, possibly hoping Deutsch might sign it up instead. "Florence will, I hope, soon be settling down to the cook book." For years friends had been suggesting to Florence that she collect her recipes. With the children a little older—Jake was now approaching two plus two plus two—she had been contemplating finding work out of the house. While the book idea didn't evolve, Tony Godwin, aware of her value as her husband's first editor, did hire her as an editor for Weidenfeld & Nicolson. She edited several manuscripts, and enjoyed the work—when she could get to it.

In Florence's mind, Richler had returned to Canada in no small part to ready himself to write authoritatively about a clan based on the Bronfmans. He had had his eye on them from the start, but needed to recharge; *St. Urbain's Horseman* had emptied his imaginative reservoir like none of the previous novels. He was still seeing Leo Kolber socially and still asking questions about the family. Sam's son Charles, now the boss, was interested enough in Mordecai Richler to include him and Florence in cocktail parties at his mansion on Summit Circle and, later, his cousin Edward provided him with hockey tickets and invited him to his son's bar mitzvah. He took the tickets, passed on the bar mitzvah. But when he wrote a television play for the CBC in which a character mentioned that Sam Bronfman had been buried in a $12,500 casket, Kolber decided he could only have acquired that tidbit from him on the night Mr. Sam died. He confronted him about the indiscretion, wondering how they could sustain a friendship if he had to guard his every word. A harsh exchange followed, ending contact between them, a breach made awkward by the occasions they found themselves at the same party. Kolber extended his anger to Florence, snubbing her at a concert.

Though she felt Leo Kolber should have known that Mordecai Richler, drawn to outlandish characters and on record as declaring the Bronfmans a tale worth telling, would be listening closely to his stories about them, Florence did empathize with some of those who felt hard done by her husband and then expected an apology. She knew exactly when "the writer would take over—no compassion, ice would fill his heart as he saw that person only as a character." She also knew well his limited capacity for expressing contrition:

Even if he accidentally decapitated your best friend, he was unable to say "I'm sorry." In his manner and posture, he would let a person rant and rave and he would watch and listen. There was no satisfaction whatsoever, not even an "I'm sorry you feel that way." In the end very few people argued with him because they knew they would not get a response. What they may not have known was that he had a foul temper which he realized early on he could not afford to lose. His silence was sometimes a way of containing it. Just being alive, and being himself, cost Mordecai friendships.

But for a man with such an appreciation of his friends, and with so many close, valuable ones, these breaches reveal more than a tough nature. Transgressions of friendship suggest that one feels exempt from the rules—or feels it necessary to be exempted, because of one's art. Richler knew that the hurt he caused his mother and family by his disclosures, the wounds inflicted on friends, while infrequent, could bring lasting damage, yet he proceeded, believing he had the "right"—or simply had no choice but—to use whatever came his way. "I have no imagination," he liked to say, paraphrasing Isaac Babel. He could have been paraphrasing a thousand other authors, too, on the pitiless practices of the trade.

———

In March 1973 Mordecai Richler delivered two public lectures at Carleton University, having first given shortened versions at the University of Toronto and York. He also dispensed the scolding to the Jewish youth group in Niagara Falls (provided in the Preface). In another passage from those unpublished remarks, he made a striking reference to his grandfather. "There was a boy here last night," he said that same afternoon, "who had the chutzpah to bring up my grandfather's name, the late rabbi Yudel Rosenberg, a rabbi, a Chassidic scholar and writer of some distinction. He brought up my zeyda's name, and flung it at me, as if I were somehow dishonouring it. Let him be assured, far from dishonouring it, we are of a piece, something which he recognized when I was still a child, selecting me for a special gift." For decades, he hadn't given much thought to his mother's comments that he and his grandfather were alike. But now, older and more aware of his own character, he was coming around to acknowledging that inheritance. A few years earlier his mother, responding to a question from him, had told him about Rabbi Rosenberg's untranslated golem stories. More recently he inquired again about the work, and wondered if she still had the actual Simchat Torah, the handiwork of the rabbi, that he had carried around the synagogue as a small boy. Like most rebbes, Yudel Rosenberg had been an astrologer as well, and Richler remembered one of his Kabbala-inspired illustrations of the zodiac from St. Urbain Street. She did have the drawing still, which she gave him, and he had it framed.

"Playing the Circuit" was how he titled his Carleton "stand-up act," and he cheerfully unloaded on the audience the full range of insults (tenure allows "academic deadwood to pile up"), judgments (student radicals are "know-nothing paper tigers"), further summary dismissals of the job he was being paid to do (teaching creative writing "is a case of sheltered children sheltering children") and plenty of familiar jokes (asked to name a favourite novel, students reply: "fiction or non-fiction?"). For this he received effusive thanks from the university president, and an extra cheque. "Your lectures were a resounding success," he told him. "They had wit, brilliance, and careful analysis, nicely clothed in good judgment."

That summer he received an invitation that promised to liberate him financially from the lecture circuit. The powerful Book-of-the-Month Club, headquartered in New York, had never hired a Canadian reader to help them select titles from north of the border. The club contacted Jack McClelland for names. Robertson Davies would have been an obvious choice, or the erudite young Margaret Atwood, now a published poet, novelist and critic. But McClelland, aware that Richler had a large family, and read widely and deeply, recommended him. In August the BOMC offered him the job, at $1,000 a month plus $500 for each review he wrote for their newsletter, and he began sifting through the boxes of manuscripts and books shipped to Edgehill Road each week.

He still had a second year at Carleton, which he resolved to complete. In what may have been the ultimate expression of his practicality as well as his willingness to test what people would pay for his name, he even proposed extending the contract with the university, at a higher annual fee. They passed on the opportunity.

IV

FILTHY, DISGUSTING FELLOW

The TV drama that had irked Leo Kolber, *The Bells of Hell,* proved no less irritating to Richler himself. The young producer George Jonas, a Hungarian émigré who later became a noted columnist and author, was given a dream assignment by the CBC: to commission one-hour teleplays from Canada's leading writers for a weekly drama programme titled *The Play's the Thing.* Some of the authors Jonas contacted, such as novelist W.O. Mitchell, were veterans of the medium, but others, notably Margaret Atwood and Alice Munro, were new to it. Remembering the CBC's rejection of his Isaac Babel play a decade before, Richler hesitated until Jonas promised him complete editorial freedom and choice of director. The script he produced—arresting, raw-nerved and uncompromising—followed the plight of Manny Berger, a Toronto lawyer anxious about everything from his wife's fidelity to his son's drug habits and his own mortality. Sex looms all around this "good" Jew, but he can no more avail himself of the liberated times than his father, who trains binoculars on neighbours' windows in the hope of glimpsing naked women, can escape an old man's lust. Caught on camera fleeing a Yonge Street massage parlour, Manny is scorned by his family and has a nervous breakdown.

Richler wanted Ted Kotcheff or Norman Jewison to direct. With neither available, the neophyte Jonas ended up making the film himself. Too busy to attend the rehearsals, Richler only saw a rough cut of the result, and learned that it had been shot in seven days, and for a pittance. Being stiff and amateurish didn't stop *The Bells of Hell* from attracting more notice than it could withstand. The head of CBC television, Thom Benson, citing inappropriate themes and hinting that the film might be offensive to Jews, withdrew it, in part because a Toronto rabbi complained that the script merited comparison to both the "ancient anti-Jewish blood libel" and "the more recent doctors' plot concocted [against Jews] in Moscow in 1953." Richler met with Benson, and was astonished when the executive speculated that the corporation might still try selling the production to the BBC in England—where, apparently, inappropriate themes and anti-Semitism were okay.

Allies Bob Fulford, now back at the Toronto *Star*, and Peter Gzowski, currently host of *This Country in the Morning* on CBC radio and an editor at the monthly magazine *Toronto Life*, led the protests. Fulford wrote an overgenerous piece calling *The Bells of Hell* the finest drama shown on the network in the new decade; Gzowski, who convinced *Toronto Life* to publish the script, invited Bob Fulford and George Jonas on air to discuss the controversy. "CBC decision dumb, dumb, dumb," ran one newspaper editorial. Like many critics, the editorial writer used the suppression of Richler's script to lambaste the corporation for its temerity and self-censorship. Under enormous media pressure, Thom Benson reversed himself. In so doing, he guaranteed a much larger audience for *The Bells of Hell*. Richler wryly summed up the outcome: "They should have just done nothing and only 12 people would have watched it," he told the *Gazette*.

This latest unhappy encounter with the CBC, while further fuel for his conviction that state-sponsored Canadian culture produced mediocrity, was easier to laugh off in the wake of a rare satisfying movie experience. In late September 1973 he had stood, along with some two hundred others, on a corner in his old neighbourhood waiting for a horse to follow his script directions. Fifteen years after Ted Kotcheff had promised he would make a movie of his book, and more than two years since their budget meeting on the Carlton terrace at Cannes, the first day of shooting *The Apprenticeship of Duddy Kravitz* was underway. Author, director, producer and lawyer were all on set. "EXTERIOR. DAY. ANOTHER STREET. MONTREAL. 1948," the directions noted of the cadets' march from Fletcher's Field up Esplanade. ". . . a MILKMAN'S HORSE has stopped to defecate." The horse needed another hour to do its business, during which time a bottle of cognac was passed among the nervous but highly entertained observers. The scene was finally shot, with Duddy, played by Richard Dreyfuss, grinning his way through the whole experience, and Ted Kotcheff assuring Richler that, when it came to inserting titles over the opening sequence, he would be sure to superimpose "From a Novel by Mordecai Richler" over the dung.

The day had almost not happened. Kotcheff had stopped by Montreal a few months earlier, and after a long dinner the friends had fallen into reminiscing about that old promise, and their cocky youthful selves. By night's end they had resolved to give the project a final push. Besides a budget shortfall, there was a problem with the commissioned script; it was, in Kotcheff's view, unusable. Richler had to agree to rewrite it for a bargain fee of $5,000. In return, the director vowed not to take another film until the new script was ready. It took an old classmate from Baron Byng, Gerry Schneider, to cut a cheque for $75,000 for production to finally begin. Even Dreyfuss, then an unknown actor, was a lucky last-minute hire. Kotcheff had been searching for months for a lead, and Richler himself, on holiday with Florence and the children in Nova Scotia, had scoured the billboards of summer stock theatres for his protagonist. Lynn Stalmaster, a legendary casting director, agreed to help out, and he steered Kotcheff to the twenty-five-year-old Dreyfuss, shortly to appear in George Lucas's *American Graffiti*. Dreyfuss had been offered another part, but once Kotcheff showed him the script, he signed on.

Haste, and budget overruns, which saw both director and writer signing cheques to cover extra expenses, didn't stop *Duddy Kravitz* from being a successful shoot. Though Richler later called the process nerve-racking and charged with crises and acrimony, he turned up on set many days, supervising rewrites and discussing shots with Kotcheff, and seemed delighted to be back in the old neighbourhood, amidst vintage cars and actors in period costume. The locals came out to watch. He greeted familiar faces from his past, and chatted with Moe Wilensky, whose soda shop hosted the scenes involving Max Kravitz and his friends. Noah visited the set with him once, and got to eat a Wilensky "Special" and drink a cherry cola. Richler was approached by strangers his age, or even younger, who were convinced that they had been the original model for Duddy. In all, some sixty locations were used, including Schwartz's on The Main and the bagelry on St. Viateur, along with a shot of the cross looming on the slope of Mount Royal. Muttle, Mutty, Mordy's Montreal, captured on celluloid.

Richard Dreyfuss proved exactly the actor for the role, and he incarnated the character with the appetite and complexity that his creator had always envisioned. Off hours, the two played poker at Edgehill Road, joined by Ted Kotcheff and Jon Robinson. Richler's lawyer was kept plenty busy during the filming, convincing a reluctant cantor to sing for an extra $100, and dealing with a threatened lawsuit from a woman who, on visiting her deceased husband in the cemetery, found the name "Kravitz" superimposed over her family moniker. Robinson never took a fee for any services he provided for his friend, but did ask a favour: a tiny part in the movie. His rabbi character spoke one line.

Once shooting was complete in November, Ted Kotcheff, who edited his own films, went to work, hoping to have a finished product for the following April. Richler wasted no time doing his part, publishing a chatty account of the making of *Duddy Kravitz* in *Weekend*, and later revising it for *New York Magazine* for the American release. He engaged in a little self-mythologizing, telling of how the set designer, inspecting Westmount houses for use in the scene between Duddy and Mr. Calder, had the door slammed on him by one irate resident: "Richler?" the owner said. "Filthy, disgusting fellow. Out!" Again he found himself the anointed "best chance" for a struggling cultural industry. "There is a feeling going around that Duddy Kravitz is going to be the

Big Movie," the Montreal *Gazette* reported, "the one that's going to open up the film industry here, that's going to make Canadians line up to see a home-grown product."

While waiting, Richler went travelling. Stuart Hodgson, commissioner of the Northwest Territories, extended an invitation to him, along with publisher Mel Hurtig, to visit the North. In March he flew to Edmonton and met up with Hurtig again, staying at his house. The two men remained friends despite their poor trip together the last time—if uneasy and increasingly unlikely ones. Now Richler alternately irritated and amused Hurtig with his smoking, drinking and put-downs of all things Canadian—the Edmontonian's cultural nationalism would have been an irresistible target—and then they set off together for Yellowknife. They were put up in a penthouse suite in the city's only high-rise, owned by the commissioner to house special visitors, and upon returning from outings would find the decanters of Scotch, gin and vodka refilled. Richler took note of the "ugly main street" and the restaurants serving "unspeakable food," but was still taken with frontier Yellowknife, especially its squalid bars full of bush pilots and miners with outrageous stories to tell, its Hudson's Bay Overproof Rum (a potent brew then only available in the NWT), and a plant along the shores of Great Slave Lake where "enterprising Indians net whitefish and pike" to be shipped to Chicago as gefilte fish.

He and Hurtig kept Hodgson company on a ten-day plane tour across the eastern Arctic. A young interpreter named John Amagoalik, later a key figure in establishing the new territory of Nunavut, was also on board, and the Fairchild F-27 was ably piloted by Ray Creery, who once set it down in a snowstorm, partially breaking through the ice and obliging a rescue by local Inuit. The travellers ate reindeer and drank overproof rum, attended community meetings in smoke-heavy halls and wandered a village in the bright light of an Arctic night. They also got to feel the sensation of minus-40 temperatures on exposed skin. Hodgson often had no official lodgings, such as the equally well-provisioned apartment in Frobisher Bay (now Iqaluit), so the men were billeted with families, including a schoolteacher on the eastern shore of Baffin Bay. According to Hurtig, Richler spent much of his time in the high Arctic badmouthing the Inuit for living in such harsh, inhospitable places, and being rude to those who hosted them. He also made sure to find a phone to call Florence at least once a day; whatever else he may have thought about him, Mel Hurtig admired his devotion to his wife. In the end, Richler, who definitely travelled better with Florence as company—and as an effective moderator of his behaviour and mediator with others—did cut his tour short by a few days, later inviting Ray Creery, who had a brother in Montreal, to visit. His friendship with Hurtig, however, was over.

The trip, difficult and exasperating as it may have been, awoke a primordial attraction in him to those northern landscapes, and to the kinds of people who washed up in towns like Yellowknife. It also provided first-hand knowledge of how to pilot a bush plane and slaughter a seal, and the contents of a humble Inuit home. Mel Hurtig didn't know Richler well enough to realize that neither his mood nor his drinking affected his observational powers, or his memory. Everything he had seen, heard and done during that initial experience of the North would be put to use.

———

The Apprenticeship of Duddy Kravitz, starring Richard Dreyfuss, Micheline Lanctôt, Jack Warden and Randy Quaid, was released on April 11, 1974. It was a lively film, true to the nervy, anti-heroic textures of the book, and if some of the haste and cost-cutting were evident in a few scenes, Kotcheff's sharp direction and Dreyfuss's vitality more than compensated. The premiere, a black-tie charity event—$100 per ticket—took place in the cavernous new Place des Arts complex in Montreal. The crowd ranged from Sam Bronfman's widow, Saidye, to Richler's buddies from the newspapers, to Florence and the children and even Lily, assigned a private escort for the night: Bill Weintraub, who volunteered to collect her and sit with her at a safe remove. The author dutifully donned a tuxedo for the occasion. In the lobby he had words with the Bronfman matriarch, a tart trade of insults, with Saidye Bronfman saying, "Well, Mordecai, you've come a long way for a St. Urbain Street boy," and Mordecai retorting, "And you've come a long way for a bootlegger's wife." Later, at a dinner with their friends John and Janet Scott, Florence took him to task for speaking to Saidye Bronfman—or any elderly person, to whom he normally accorded automatic respect—in such a manner.

The Place des Arts premiere offered a show of force by Montreal's English cultural community. Reviews were excellent, and the movie was soon attracting sold-out viewings around the country. Quebec had lately produced several major films, including Claude Jutra's *Mon Oncle Antoine* and *La Vraie Nature de Bernadette* by Gilles Carle, and saw cinema as helping define the pending "nation." *Duddy Kravitz* had no such intentions, but it did boost the less-evolved English-Canadian cinema. Its success also further empowered Anglo or, rather, Jewish Montreal to stake its own modest terrain. Years earlier, a local producer named Harry Gulkin had optioned the Ted Allan story "Lies My Father Told Me," an autobiographical account of an Orthodox boy in the ghetto of the 1920s. Allan had written the script, and in the summer of 1972 a film crew had taken over those same streets. Not until 1975, however, in the wake of *Duddy Kravitz*, would the charming *Lies My Father Told Me* be released. A year later Gulkin would once more seek a permit to film in the old neighbourhood, this time for his adaptation of *Jacob Two-Two Meets the Hooded Fang*. So would the Quebec separatist Claude Jutra, who in 1978 agreed to direct a TV version of Richler's story "Some Grist from Mervyn's Mill," to be titled *The Wordsmith*, again setting up lights and cameras in those blocks.

But politics in Quebec were becoming more divisive. In 1972 the Liberal government of Robert Bourassa passed Bill 22, the language law obliging children of immigrants to be enrolled in French schools. By then Bourassa was fighting for his political life against the surging Parti Québécois of the charismatic ex-journalist René Lévesque. Richler admired the street-smart,

chain-smoking Lévesque more than the stiff technocrat Bourassa.
As the politics of the day became all-engrossing, the Press Club
in the Mount Royal Hotel, with its long mahogany bar and red
leather furniture, was a popular destination for him, as for many,
particularly since women had been granted full membership in
1969. Other bars, like Au Cépage in Old Montreal and Woody's,
were favoured as well for their intimate, clubby feeling. Richler
met there most afternoons with Doris Giller from the *Star* and
Terry Mosher, Ian Mayer and Dink Carroll from the *Gazette*.
Carroll was the grizzled sports veteran, source of gossip and free
tickets; the Scotsman Mayer, a laconic, erudite man with a serious drinking problem, turned to him for counsel and cash, both
of which he provided. Nick Auf der Maur, lately co-editor of a
collection of essays on Quebec and separatism, was also coming
into the picture. He was roguishly charming, a superior drinker
and raconteur who knew everyone around town and whom
nearly everyone, in turn, wanted to know. At first he had struck
Richler as lightweight but, in an unusual reversal of an early judgment, he soon held his irreverence and eye for the absurd in high
regard, while upbraiding him for his slack journalism. They
became good friends and, eventually, co-conspirators.

Doris Giller was the rare woman at the table. Another product
of The Main—her parents had sent her to Commercial High
instead of Baron Byng, hoping to get her training as a secretary—
she was attractive, smart and high-spirited, able to smoke and
drink with the most hardened of male colleagues. Her new husband, it turned out, was none other than Jack Rabinovitch, Baron
Byng class of '47. Now the executive vice-president of Trizec, a
commercial property investment firm, Jack had not seen Mordy
Richler much since their days of playing hooky and shooting
pool together. The two couples became fast friends. Rabinovitch
was a semi-teetotaller, but Richler would meet him in the old
neighbourhood for steaks and smoked meat. The regulars,
including Doris Giller, were all English-speaking Montrealers.
Many French-speakers, especially in the media, were bilingual.
And yet, had anyone attempted to bring a French colleague into

the circle it might have caused friction. On the eve of the province's two-decade flirtation with separation, political divergences would have been an impediment. There were also temperamental differences. With his city buddies, Richler looked for wit, preferably caustic, and a healthy cynicism about everything from the latest grandiose schemes of Mayor Drapeau, whose Olympic Games, set to be held in August 1976, had converted swaths of Montreal into giant construction sites, to the pending move of the Expos from intimate Jarry Park to the cavernous Olympic Stadium. He wanted to feel comfortable and relaxed, not confronted or challenged.

Bill Weintraub, now happily remarried and a successful documentary filmmaker, was not part of this group. His relationship with Florence and the children remained close, and he would be the person Richler turned to first in real need. But Weintraub, a recovering alcoholic, no longer felt comfortable in the bars, and accepted his exclusion from this part of his life.

When the Baron Byng alumni proposed a twenty-fifth-year reunion to celebrate the class of 1948, they opted to ask class president Mordecai Richler, who had begun contributing to a bursary for needy students, to speak at the event. Florence wisely declined to witness her husband in old-school mode, so he asked Doris Giller to come along instead, and to bring her husband, notable graduate of the previous year. Jack Rabinovitch wondered aloud if the guest speaker could avoid "creating havoc" at the reunion. A group of singers had been engaged to perform, and Richler, following them to the stage, was more than unimpressed. "I'll be very brief," he told his former classmates. "Baron Byng turned out to be a lot more useful to me than it was for most of you. I think the notion of this reunion was a good idea, but I don't know who found those appalling, funny singers or what they had to do with us. Other than that," he added over the sound of hissing, "I'm very pleased to be here." By the time he sat back at the table he was in a fighting mood. "Do you want to go?" Rabinovitch asked. "Those guys aren't pushing me out of my school," he replied, and stayed for another hour.

Former classmates aside, his friendships in Montreal were easier fits than those he was developing with what Margaret Laurence had begun calling the "tribe" of Canadian writers. Living in England all those years had allowed him to befriend tribal members while having an excellent excuse to remain aloof from the politics, entanglements and petty jealousies implicit in belonging to any collective. Now ensconced in Canada as one of the highest-profile novelists in the country, he was being sought for support of various good writerly causes. Margaret Laurence herself, his rival for stature and a much-beloved individual, back from London and about to settle in the central Ontario village of Lakefield, complained to him about the pressures in a letter—"I refuse to give talks any more," she wrote, of the "circuit" that Richler described in *Maclean's*, "they kill me"—only to then play her part in pressuring him onto prize juries and into the newly formed Writers' Union of Canada. (He served on the juries but declined union membership.) Still, so forceful was the thrust of literary nationalism during the 1970s—everyone seemed to be preparing school texts and anthologies, organizing reading series and agitating with government and censors, critics and editors, for greater attention to Canadian material—that even Mordecai Richler, lone wolf and instinctive anti-nationalist, allowed himself to be pulled along. He joined a delegation of writers to Ottawa, headed by the bestselling Pierre Berton and Margaret Laurence, to protest the import of cheap foreign editions of their books into Canada, for which they received only half royalties. But far preferable was the company of Florence and family, friends and books. Or else the boys (and Doris Giller) at the bar(s), chatting about politics and sports, having a good laugh.

V

AN OLD JACKET, WORN AND TORN

Two years had now passed since the family had repatriated. With notions of a return to England banished—from Richler's mind, at least; the children remained a little perplexed, with thirteen-year-old Emma in particular pining for London—he was ready to enact phase two of the plan he had outlined to Bill Weintraub. In July 1974 the Richlers purchased the much-dreamed-about dacha in the countryside outside the city. New York friends Kay and Elliot Cattarulla were visiting, and they suggested a house-hunting outing together. On driving up to a large, white clapboard house perched above a lake, Mordecai and Florence were both enthralled. But the house and lake were not in the Laurentians, where poor French and Jews had once summered. Instead, they had gone looking in the formerly *Judenfrei* Eastern Townships, still the preserve of Anglo, and some French, affluence, in particular for the political classes. As with the purchase of the house on Edgehill Road, there were good reasons for choosing a property on Lake Memphremagog, near the hamlet of Austin. Doris Giller and Jack Rabinovitch had a place nearby, and several visits to them had confirmed the beauty of the gently rolling landscape. The house itself, with its elegant setting and stone porch overlooking a quiet northern arm of the long lake, its wide windows and four bedrooms, had everything they wanted, including a central second-floor space for an office for Richler and plenty of fairly level ground for a garden for Florence. It also had a dock, a boathouse and, perhaps most beguilingly, a wetland with a stream.

The presidents of the Liberal Party of Quebec and of the Montreal Alouettes football team had houses on the same unpaved road in from the highway. The Benedictine monastery of Saint-Benoît-du-Lac, a favourite retreat for Prime Minister Trudeau, was nearby, and across Lake Memphremagog was the estate of the then-elderly Wilder Penfield, the famous neurosurgeon. Other powerful Quebecers, some friends, some about to become so, also lived within a short drive. Friends and, as *Joshua Then and Now* would evidence by the end of the decade, subjects as well. Once Richler committed to Westmount, where the people he was now interested in writing about lived, the Townships became the logical site for a summer house.

"Still weak, still woozy, from too much booze," he wrote to his old friend Brian Moore in August 1974, about a recent trip to New York to promote *Duddy Kravitz*, where he had been chauffeured from interview to interview by Paramount publicity flacks and had by his own admission acquitted himself poorly as a spokesman for the movie. He shared the gossipy good news from "this place we bought on the lake," the purchase of which, he had already decided, had been a "splendid idea." As for the movie, he reported "a mill three" gross in Canada already, and two-block-long lineups to see it in New York despite his ineptness, plus distribution deals for half a dozen countries, including the U.K. Just as exciting for him was the spike in book sales: in Canada *The Apprenticeship of Duddy Kravitz* had sold 25,000 copies in the front half of 1974 alone. Better yet, he had a new contract with Ballantine for a first-ever U.S. paperback edition. Initial printing: 125,000. "Which, as you well know, is somewhat better than the original S. Lawrence sale of 1200," in 1959 at Atlantic Press.

The tone of the letter wasn't entirely breezy. The friends, as a group, had always had honest exchanges about their newly completed novels, and Brian Moore and Bill Weintraub had been direct with him in the past. Now he straightforwardly volunteered his dislike of Moore's latest novel, *The Great Victorian Collection*.

Moore had sent the manuscript to Bob Gottlieb for publication, and Richler, despite his private views, said he had "given Gottlieb shit for turning it down." But since Moore seemingly hadn't asked him to read the manuscript, how had he become familiar with it? "Jack McCl sent it to me," he admitted. On a happier note, he outlined plans for the "Canadian library" he was assembling for the Book-of-the-Month Club. "First two authors the inevitable Callaghan and MacLennan," he wrote, "but then, if they sell reasonably well, to be followed by Rob. Davies and B. Moore." As much as he wanted to please his friend, he was possibly irking him as well; once more it was the younger Mordecai who had the "power," courtesy of his new job with BOMC, and while he was not lording it over the older, proud Irishman, he might have guessed, based on experiences going back nearly two decades, that Moore would find it irritating. He could be oddly clumsy with him—or he was still competing. But the following year he would use his influence to ensure the selection of *The Great Victorian Collection* by both the book club and the jury of the Governor General's Award for Fiction.

He also advised Moore to sell his archives to the University of Calgary, as he had done. "Calgary is neck deep in oil monies," he explained. He divulged the terms he and Jon Robinson had negotiated—"50,000 cash over five years; 50,000 in tax certs"—so Moore could demand the same. "First, however, I went through letters, removing personal ones . . . putting some of these in a box not to be opened until 25 years after corress. has departed for Big Editor in the Sky." The archive sale helped finance the country house, as did cheques from *Playboy* and the *New York Times Magazine*. This was quality pay, and to wide readerships. His first piece with *Playboy*, then still a model of masculine literary cool, with stories by top-quality writers alongside pretty women wearing no clothes, ran in July. It was a short piece on wicked Arctic whisky, and led to his being assigned a feature on conspiracy theories that had him flying out to Los Angeles in the autumn and making his way north to Carmel to meet with the publisher of *Conspiracy Newsletter*. (She asked for his driver's licence, to make sure he was who he claimed to be.) To get to Carmel, Richler had to pass by Malibu, where the Moores lived in a spectacular house overlooking the ocean. He visited them, but that reunion, their first in years, was fraught, and a harbinger of the coolness to come; a request that Moore collect him at the airport, a one-hour drive, had been declined, and he turned up in a foul mood.

With two houses and multiple tuition cheques, he was "scribbling," as he called it, for quality magazines, as well as filing regular reviews for the *Book-of-the-Month Club News* and even accepting $300 for a 3,500-word essay for *American Libraries* about which Canadian books librarians should purchase "to help patrons develop an understanding of Canada today." The commission came with a request that he sprinkle twenty to twenty-five worthy titles, both fiction and non-fiction, throughout the text. Such a clumsy format, not to mention low pay for a high word count, hardly seemed worth his time. But Richler, who could and did say no to assignments, was keener than he cared to admit to be a literary power broker. He delivered a bright piece that began: "Canada's English-speaking writers are now a largely discontented, even fulminating, lot, the most militant bitterly anti-American, given to cultural paranoia." American librarians may have found the slant and tone somewhat baffling.

But his least likely commission involved the National Ballet of Canada. When the young Toronto dance journalist John Fraser criticized the company for a scheduling decision that involved touring the United States, he became an accidental hero of the easily aroused cultural nationalists. The ballet's response to Fraser's perceived attack was to hire Mordecai Richler to pen the lead article in their programme for the 1975–76 season. While not averse to ballet—he had attended the occasional performance as a young man—and an opera fan who hummed arias from *Rigoletto*, he was in no position to judge John Fraser's observations. Regardless, he conducted phone interviews with the company's founder, Celia Franca, and its current artistic director, and quizzed Florence about particulars. The opening sentence must have had ballet lovers scratching their heads at least as hard as those librarians: "In this country, where no hinge is more celebrated than Bobby Orr's knee, where the overriding myth evolves round the construction of a railroad, and the most sought-after masters of magic are plumbers or the managers of tax-fund shelters, ballet cannot be reckoned an integral part of the tradition." As for John Fraser, he was duly thrashed, his views declared "parochial and childish." The Richlers then travelled to Toronto for the season opening (ballet, not hockey), and Fraser, who had admired the novelist since reading *Cocksure* as a teenager, approached him in the lobby. "I am the unacceptable face of Canadian nationalism," he said. When Richler protested that his attack hadn't been "personal," the journalist showed the proper mettle by remarking that he too had done some hack work in his day. Richler laughed, and another friendship was born.

Large fees to amuse ballet patrons or small fees to confuse American librarians were all part of his determination to earn a more-than-decent living by his pen. A very proud man, he kept pace with friends who ran publishing houses and directed movies. (Later, they would head up Hollywood studios and own newspapers.) He also wanted the best for Florence, despite her own impulse to be moderate, and thought nothing of ordering the most expensive Scotch and cigars for himself. (Clothes were never a priority; when she insisted that he finally buy a new suit, he insisted she accompany him to Holt Renfrew to help him choose it, allotting five minutes for the transaction.) Those were, to an extent, the status assertions of someone raised poor, and the hallmarks of public achievement that he felt he had earned. In private, his pride about money centred on his success as a provider, able to keep his family in comfort and fund his children's education; able as well to assure himself that the promise he had made to Florence back in 1958, that she would want for nothing, was one he had kept—a boast she had found amusing, never suspecting it was other than the bravado of a courting lover. He was dead serious, old-fashioned, chivalrous, in his understanding of domestic roles and romantic love alike.

Assignments large or small, mainstream or eccentric, poured in from Canada and the United States. Notably absent, however, were publishing credits in newspapers or magazines out of London, once his journalistic bread and butter. By mid-decade he had already ceased having much profile in that market. He was simply gone from the scene, gone from drinks with editors and parties where newly installed editors could be met, and gone from the new force in literary career-making: BBC television, with its culture of smooth-talking literary heads. He was not concerned. The weakness of the British pound meant that fees, already low, translated into fractions of what he was being paid by Toronto and New York editors.

The sweet summer of 1974 was soured only by bitter exchanges with Lily Rosenberg. A year earlier Florence had bid on an antique fur coat at an auction, thinking it would suit her mother-in-law, whom she rarely saw anymore, and about whom her husband refused to speak. She had sent it to her as a gift. A chance encounter with Richler at a bank, and then a brief visit by him to Stayner Street in June, triggered two harsh letters from Lily to Edgehill Road. In the first, addressed to her son, she complained that he hadn't taken her to watch *Duddy Kravitz* being filmed, despite bringing his own children several times. "I begged you just tell me where the filming took place and I would go myself," she wrote. (She had in any case grilled the kids for details.) His obduracy was "the culmination of years of neglect, years when you could not even bear to sit near me." But now her eyes were open: "It finally got to me that I am a problem mother." As for his visit in June, she had assumed it would lead to an invitation to drive down to the Townships in the new family Peugeot wagon. "I ran out and shopped for things the children like," Lily wrote. "I made ready a few things and took out my bathing suit, and waited for your call to go and get into your new car and see your beautiful country house." The call never came. "I will never go to your country house," she vowed, "and I will never get into your new car. Never."

Claiming she had been deathly ill earlier in the year, and still lived "in terror of a stroke," she dismissed his financial support as irrelevant to their relationship. "Where is love," she wrote in a typing frenzy, "where is concern, where is sensitivity, where is understanding. Where is visiting," she added, "where is communication?" His neglect was contributing to her poor health. "I have to say this, you make me ill." She told Mordecai not to bother with his occasional "duty" phone calls and, summoning the biblical story of Joseph and his coat of many colours, told him she preferred to remember him "as a young man, and how wonderful you were, how devoted and thoughtful, and I thank you for that. What happened to you?" she said. "I don't know, and you know what, I no longer even care."

Pleading, scolding, emotional manipulation were nothing new. But then she wrote separately to Florence. In that note she returned a cheque for $500 that he had made out to her on June 30. Later she also sent back the fur coat, which she had already complained about in person. "And Florence saved for years to buy you a fur coat," she quoted her son telling her. No matter; Lily could never wear it again. "The fur coat you bought for me gave me much pleasure just because you purchased it," she told her daughter-in-law. "That did not eliminate the fact that it was an old jacket, worn and torn." She resumed berating Mordecai, calling him vindictive and cruel, and vowed to repay all the money—$3,000, by her estimate—he had sent over the years. A decade earlier she had written to him, "I always wonder what my grandchildren will be like when they are adults, what their careers will be, I may even be a great-grandmother one day. We'll see. It will be great to watch them develop." But the next time the children were sent down the hill for their awkward Sunday ritual with her, she slammed the door on them. Slammed the door on her relationship with her five grandchildren, and with her own child, her once-golden boy.

"I always wondered if I should write to thank you re: Book-of-the-Month Club," Margaret Laurence said to Richler after he recommended *The Diviners*. The BOMC, already the source of steady income and rising influence, had invited him to serve on its permanent New York jury, a salaried position at three times the monthly rate. His reputation and efforts, along with the push made by his New York agent, were resulting in commissions from the best magazines on the continent, save, perhaps, the elusive *New Yorker*, where Mavis Gallant, and a more recent acquaintance Alice Munro, were publishing fiction on a regular basis. An entry in a biographical dictionary sketched him, correctly, as an establishment figure: "Their present home is Westmount, a posh hillside district of Montreal. Richler is said to be warm and loyal to friends, rude to antipathetic strangers, and somewhat sardonic in press interviews. A quiet, intense man, he unwinds with poker and snooker." Even so, a new Mordecai Richler adult novel was clearly required. His British agent, Deborah Rogers, worried already by the time lapse between books, was anxious that he produce another major work. So were his other editors and his friends. *Gursky Was Here* was officially that work-in-progress. But the manuscript was already a slog, and he kept writing chunks of text, scrapping them and starting over. He was unsure of the tone or the focus: on Manny Berger, the middle-class social climber, or on the fearsome rise of the Gurskys all the way to the top? Flailing away at an unformed manuscript meant that he was not yet ready to write it.

Christmas 1974 was festive. Edna O'Brien was in Montreal and stayed with the Richlers, but minus her boys, Sasha and Carlos, with whom Daniel and Noah had once played in London. Ted Kotcheff was in the city as well. "Mordecai, that's a very potent drink," Kotcheff commented on his friend's bartending habits. "A potent drink for a potent man," he replied. Potent, yes, but also a portent, as he put it in a January 1975 letter to Brian Moore, who had been complaining about his ulcers: "I think of ulcers as minor stuff. Unfair, really, but such are my fears of the real thing." Fears of steady, irrevocable bodily decay, with the "real thing"—death—not so far up ahead, would fuel a more furious note to a Montreal producer a year later. "I am forty-six years old, my teeth are loose, I wear reading glasses. Cognac has begun to keep me awake, and I'm too old for pipe dreams at Ruby Foo's." Neil Compton, who had become wheelchair-bound, had died back in 1972, and Reuben Ship, his star much dimmed by failure and alcohol, had passed away in 1974. The roll call of the lost wasn't long, not yet, but it was already audible.

If he couldn't find his way into a new novel, he might still generate income with a commercial non-fiction project. He believed he had something. During that trip to the Arctic he had heard the story of Martin Hartwell, the bush pilot who had crashed his plane in November 1972 near Great Bear Lake, five hundred miles north of Edmonton. On board the Beechcraft were a pregnant Inuk woman and her nephew, a teenaged Inuit boy with appendicitis, and a British nurse named Judy Hill, who was escorting them to hospital in Yellowknife. Hill died on impact—the plane flew into a hillside in low cloud—and the Inuk woman succumbed to her injuries on the first day. For two weeks Hartwell, who had two broken ankles and a shattered knee, huddled with the boy in temperatures that dropped to minus thirty-five Fahrenheit. The boy died into the third week, but the pilot was found alive after thirty-one days. In the only interview he gave, Hartwell claimed he had survived on a diet of melted snow and lichens. An inquiry, headed by Judge William Morrow, later revealed that he had cannibalized the leg of the nurse to sustain himself.

Richler wasted no time in dubbing the tale "I Ate Nurse Judy" and pursuing the rights to tell Hartwell's version in a book. The pilot refused his overtures at first, only to later invite him to Yellowknife, where they agreed to terms over access and the sharing of royalties. By May he had a folder of Hartwell's private documents in his possession, and had verbally negotiated advances with M&S in Canada, Knopf in the United States and Macmillan in the U.K. Publishers fought for "I Ate Nurse Judy" less because of Mordecai Richler's reputation than because of the phenomenal interest generated by a newly published book titled *Alive!* In it, Piers Paul Read recounted a similar tale of harrowing survival and taboo practices involving a Uruguayan rugby team whose plane crashed in the Andes. Richler had rightly guessed that the Hartwell tale would be a hot property, at least for a while.

The project didn't make creative sense for him. He explained to Justice Morrow, soon a friend, that the book would be "a new departure." But, he added, "I have long been fascinated by the Martin Hartwell case, and the many things it tells us obliquely about Canada, the North, and well . . . people." He envisioned an ambitious schedule: "two weeks at home, two weeks North," venturing up to the Arctic once a month from February until the summer: "I will need quarters where I can tape, interview, bush pilots, old-timers, officials, etc etc." With a flight from Montreal to Yellowknife costing as much as a ticket to London, he had to generate financing: a piece on Yellowknife for *Travel & Leisure* (formerly *Holiday*), and "Harper's has definitely commissioned me to go along on your long April tour," he wrote to Justice Morrow, who had invited him to observe while he heard cases in communities in the Arctic. For March, he would travel to Yellowknife again, "researching a piece on bush pilots, probably for Esquire," and then to Ottawa to "enlist the help" of the RCMP and the Department of Indian Affairs. Clearly, he was taken with the North, and serious about the book.

So much so that he was willing to do much more of what he would actually have preferred to do much less: travel. The hustling required to put together the Hartwell project ran contrary to his nature—a hare's schedule for a tortoise's disposition. A naturally slow, meditative person, needing routine—the daily walk, the smoke in a bar—to carry on his perpetual inner dialogue with his novels, Richler took to assignments that involved the disruption and haste of travel with grim determination. Like public appearances, airplanes could be abided only with alcohol. Both were infinitely easier in the company of his wife.

Florence joined him for the first trip. In Yellowknife they stayed in a hotel suite built for a royal visit that never occurred, and watched at breakfast as ravens roamed the lawn. While they were in the suite, Michael Spencer called to say that Richler had been nominated for an Academy Award for his *Duddy Kravitz* screenplay. The next day the couple celebrated with a glass of champagne at 10,000 feet, courtesy of a quick trip farther west to Whitehorse in the Yukon. Bill and Genevieve Morrow shared the six-seater Navajo and supplied the Veuve Clicquot, along with the wide, open vistas of the beautiful but desolate landscape below. A few weeks later the Richlers were in California for the Academy Awards.

The drift of expatriates from London, where the movie scene had lately cooled, to Los Angeles, meant they now had plenty of friends in Hollywood. His film agent Bob Shapiro and Ted Kotcheff already called Beverly Hills home, and soon Stanley Mann and Jack and Haya Clayton would be in L.A. as well. Mordecai and Florence stayed with the Shapiros at first, moving later to the Beverly Wilshire hotel, and had breakfast with Ted Kotcheff in the Polo Lounge of the Beverly Hills hotel. Richler delighted, as always, in the crude vitality of the movie industry, in particular its marginal players, many of whom were Jews of similar background and appetite to himself. Ted Kotcheff was happy to feed him gossip, as was his old friend, screenwriter and fellow Oscar nominee Josh Greenfeld, whom he met for lunch. From the status-crushing mistake of showing up at a club in an ordinary car to the workings of an industry party, he couldn't hear enough about the devious, money- and ego-driven movie trade. If there had been an obvious subject for a Mordecai Richler non-fiction book in 1975, it would have been the cads and characters, illusions and pipe dreams of (as he later proclaimed in the *New York Times Magazine*) "O God! O Hollywood!"

Not only had he been nominated for an Academy Award; his screenplay had also been shortlisted by the Writers Guild of America. On the evening of the WG awards, the Richlers sat at a table with the Shapiros and Kotcheffs, waiting to hear if the presenter, Carl Foreman, a formerly blacklisted screenwriter and producer, would call his name. Except that Foreman wouldn't be calling him alone. The nomination for the *Duddy Kravitz* script was being shared by Mordecai Richler and Lionel Chetwynd. Chetwynd, seated at another table, was the Montreal-born

screenwriter whom Kotcheff had first commissioned to adapt
the novel. Richler's rewrite was extensive, but Chetwynd had
successfully petitioned for a share of profits and a co-credit.
Offended that a stranger should insist on recognition for an
adaptation of his own novel, which had not even been successful, he made no effort at civility. When Foreman did announce
their names, and each made a brief acceptance speech, Richler
told the crowd, "I've never seen this man before." His presumed
joke earned a laugh but later, when Chetwynd tried introducing
himself with a soothing apology for being lucky enough to share
the prize, he was rebuffed. "Be cordial to you?" Richler said.
"Don't flatter yourself."

At the Academy Awards, where *Duddy Kravitz* didn't win for
best adapted screenplay, it was the same: Lionel Chetwynd and
his wife in one row, Mordecai and Florence in the other. Chetwynd
claimed that he had been close enough to overhear Richler, who
he believed was drunk at both ceremonies and had decided to
play the role of artist as transgressor, being rude to actor Marty
Feldman and cursing Hollywood legend Lauren Bacall while
Florence sat by in mortified silence. As Florence recalled it, dismayed that he might have to mount the stage in front of a TV
audience and make a speech, he did drink heavily that evening.
But he had no contact at all with the still-beautiful Lauren Bacall,
and when Feldman, whom he knew from England, approached
to say hello, Chetwynd likely misread the usual blank stare he
fixed on people as a show of disrespect. It wasn't disrespect, as
such, although he could be hostile to strangers assuming they
had the right to interrupt him, even to express admiration for
his work, and he was capable of brushing off unwelcome
advances. Alcohol, too, affected his responses. Though Florence
very rarely saw his manner altered by drinking, others, including Mel Hurtig, thought that liquor turned him aggressive and
mean. And Florence had developed strategies to deal with his
moods. At a dinner party in London she had sensed him turning
belligerent and, excusing herself, had called the babysitter and
asked her to ring back in ten minutes. On getting the call she

apologized to their hosts, saying they had to excuse themselves for family reasons.

Workwise, he could scarcely afford the time for even a few luxurious, all-expenses-paid days in sunny California. The magazine commissions loomed, and the travel schedule he had outlined to Justice Morrow must have been exhausting to contemplate, let alone keep. He had his BOMC duties as well, the boxes of manuscripts and books piling up in Edgehill Road often obliging to him to prolong his days of work with hours of evening reading. As if that weren't literature enough, he had agreed to be a juror for the second year in a row for the Governor General's Award for Fiction. In 1974 Laurence's *The Diviners* had been the consensus selection, but there were grumbles in 1975, some centred on Richler's personal conflicts of interest, when the jury was persuaded to honour Brian Moore's *The Great Victorian Collection* over Robertson Davies' *World of Wonders* and Farley Mowat's *The Snow Walker*, a work of fiction that bore, curiously enough, similarities to the Martin Hartwell story.

Remarkably, he agreed to Canada Council literary chief Naïm Kattan's request that he sit for a third consecutive appointment the following spring, this time as chairman of all the prize juries, including the fiction group, composed of Alice Munro and Margaret Laurence. While that experience would not be much happier—Laurence browbeat fellow jurors so hard to select her friend Marian Engel's *Bear* as winner that she later apologized—the decision making was kept behind closed doors: no shortlist was announced. "You were splendid, calming, etc," Laurence wrote to him afterwards, "although you must have been mad as hell at me for my sermonizing." In addition, Richler also did promotion tours of New York, Detroit and Chicago for *Jacob Two-Two* and, on another occasion, of Washington, Baltimore and Boston for a belated American edition of *The Street*. Days of awkward interviews dissolved into evenings alone in hotel bars; not a recipe for contentment or productivity.

To add to all the work pressures, Mordecai and Florence were now the parents of teenage boys. Eighteen-year-old Daniel had a punk fashion sense, causing his father to call him a horse's ass, and was fronting a band called the Alpha Jerks. Though their lyrics rejected Quebec sovereignty, he still didn't like their music, and said as much. But father and eldest son rarely exchanged harsh words and, if anything, Daniel sought any reaction he could muster from his distracted, non-verbal parent. He took Daniel and Noah to Moishe's steakhouse one night and replied to their queries about what exactly he "did" as a writer: "I take the twenty-six letters of the alphabet, and I mix them up together." Daniel, briefly enrolled at McGill University—he dropped out after just two months of studying art history and classical flute—possessed his mother's warmth with his own charisma, and was shortly to launch a successful and highly public career in radio and TV. Noah, in contrast, bored at school—a school where *The Apprenticeship of Duddy Kravitz* was a set text, obliging him to write an essay on it—and cast from the same introspective mould as his father, began at the age of fifteen to show a more serious interest in drugs. While still underage, he drove their car into a bus, prompting a street-kid reaction from his father: "Did anyone see you?" he asked first. Noah and his friends also made mischief in Westmount Park, broke into girlfriends' houses, and happily rode bicycles while stoned through the artificial lake on Mount Royal.

That episode let to a charge of vandalism, and an appearance in a Montreal courtroom. After listening to the judge lecture Noah on good citizenship, Richler stood up to criticize the court for wasting money prosecuting harmless pranks. Such was the force of his argument that the judge granted his point. Noah too was impressed by his abrupt and concise fluency. No doubt his father was thinking of his own various youthful misdemeanours, from shoplifting to truancy, and how little they had been about an inadequate sense of citizenship. He was also calling for good sense and judgment in the presence of an externally mandated judge of behaviour and morals. In the case of his father, Noah learned that day, courage and impropriety, truth speaking and loyalty, honesty and belligerence could not be disentangled.

Not long after Richler had escorted one son to court in Montreal, he accompanied another to Toronto to appear on television. Being a "kiddy author," as he called it, set him on a different kind of literary circuit. In May 1975 M&S launched *Jacob Two-Two* with a "Child Power Popsicle Party" at a children's bookstore in Toronto. Jack McClelland took special delight in commanding him to attend this promotion. Kids, served Popsicles, could get their copies of the book signed by the author or the real star—eight-year-old Jacob. The father-son sales team was revived for the CBC show *90 Minutes Live*. Old friend Peter Gzowski was the host, and he addressed the live studio audience: "Would you please welcome Mordecai Richler and Jacob Richler." Out they came together, hand in hand, father in suit and tie and son in school uniform. Jacob, now nine, had a missing tooth and the residue of a British accent. He sat in the chair next to Gzowski's desk. His father, who lit a cigarillo, took the next seat, his more than usually wild hair begging for intervention. "It was in the nature of a promise to the children," he said of the story's origins. "Was there anything in the book that was true?" the host asked the boy. "Not really," Jake answered.

"There is nothing in talking to children that should be stressed any more than in talking to an adult," Richler explained in an article about the experience. "Honesty and goodwill should be the ideal in all communications." A child "doesn't expect you to lie to him or to cheat him. I try, as a parent of five children of my own and as a writer, not to abuse that innocence."

His appearance on Gzowski's show followed on another CBC television profile, in which he agreed to let the camera trail him through the familiar streets where his own childhood deceits had occurred, including the alleyway between St. Urbain and Clark, site of boxcar races and games of tag. Though he spoke about the old neighbourhood, he made no mention of any traumas— nor would he, ever, outside the pages of *Son of a Smaller Hero*. The source of much of that trauma, Lily Rosenberg, was not asked to babysit her grandchildren, or even look in on them, when Mordecai and Florence flew to California in the autumn.

Thanks to the success of *Duddy Kravitz*, director Ted Kotcheff had
been offered *Fun with Dick and Jane*, a satire of American middle-
class life set to star Jane Fonda and George Segal. The story of
an upwardly mobile couple who resort to crime after the husband
is let go from his aerospace job had satiric potential. But the
script was too serious, and Kotcheff insisted that his friend, now
with his own momentum thanks to the Writers Guild prize and
Academy Award nomination, be brought in to rewrite it. Richler
flew down by himself first, met Jane Fonda and named his terms:
$30,000 for three weeks of script-fixing, a suite at the Beverly
Wilshire, and $500 a week living expenses. Plus two first-class
tickets: one for him, another for Florence. They had fun in
Tinseltown, accompanying Jack and Haya Clayton to a party at
legendary agent Irving "Lefty" Lazar's Malibu mansion, where
lines of cocaine were wheeled out on a trolley by a servant, but
Richler ended up one of five writers who worked on the script.
Some Hollywood nastiness ensued about credits, leaving a now-
familiar bitter industry taste in his mouth.

Even before the estrangement from his mother, Mordecai and
Florence had raised their children with little conventional family
support: no grandparents to provide after-school relief or substitute for a weekend; no uncle or aunt who would take a surly teenager to a hockey game. They relied on themselves, their devoted
and loving friends, plus a series of au pairs and housekeepers.
That was demanding for both adults and children. But it also
made for an intense family dynamic, with each upset or rupture
or joy felt by everyone.

As for Lily Rosenberg, she was now just a figure sighted on
the streets of lower Westmount or bumped into at a bank. In the
late spring of 1976 she decided the best way to ensure that her
sons, neither of whom spoke to her any longer, heard her complaints was to record and send them separately made cassette
tapes. "I don't have two sons—I have two stones," was a typical
remark in the version she made for Avrum. In the course of a
two-hour monologue directed at Mordecai, she enumerated all
the wrongs she had suffered at the hands of everyone she had

ever met, loved or brought into the world. He listened to the screed in his office. Florence asked him about the tapes, and recalled his answer: "He told me I need not concern myself with the matter. Occasionally, but not often, he was that unequivocal, and I knew from the tone of his voice that he had decided on a course of action, and was not going to be dissuaded. And, yes, the conversation was that brief. 'I'll take care of it,' he said."

VI

DEAR MAW

August 4/76

Dear Maw:

I have of course listened to your tapes (O God, the wonders of this electronic age), shaking my head, angry here, incredulous there, but most often overcome with sadness at what you have done to yourself. Such accumulated bile. So much bitterness. All unavailing. And for the most part, self-imposed.

If your old age tastes of ashes, if you are wretched, lonely, worried about your health, money, I am sorry. I am very sorry. For, certainly, it is sad. But now that you are seventy can't you at last grasp that you have brought most of this on yourself. Will your life, such a ball of rage, inchoate rage, go forever unexamined? Who has ever denied you money? Not me. Not Florence. Until you stormed out of our lives, fulminating, a couple of years back, I had been sending you money for God knows how many years. Flying you over to London. Flying you to Florida. Buying you a colour tv set long before I could afford one myself, just as Florence saved to buy you a fur coat many years before she ever had one. I have always been a responsible son, both to you and my father, and I do not reproach myself on that count. I also sent my father money. I also flew him to London, though only once, alas, and for that I do reproach myself now.

A few words about my father, as he seems to be such a festering point with you, even after all these wasting years.

I never reproached you aloud, or in my own mind, for

divorcing him. I really don't know where you got this, among other screwy ideas. It was a bad marriage for you. It was not a good marriage for him. Clearly a divorce was the best solution. But neither do I apologize, nor am I ashamed, that as the years passed I came to regard my father with increasing affection. I enjoyed his company. He was fun to be with. And I like to think that in his last years, we gave each other pleasure. Certainly now that he's gone, I miss him. Even so, as you raised the point, I did not say kaddish for him for longer than a week. Yes, I loved him, but I am not an observant Jew. I don't say kaddish.

You really must stop brooding about my father and divorce of more than 30 years ago. If there is another world, which I doubt, I think the fears expressed on your tapes are imaginary: surely, your divorce will also be recognised there. If there is another world, I like to think of my old man sitting first row centre in the Gaiety Theatre of the heavens, watching Lili St. Cyr, untroubled by either his first or second wife. Or playing gin rummy, perhaps, and holding a winning hand for once. Don't, please, screw it up for him by telling him he has to get dressed and go to the theatre or a lecture. Leave him be, leave him be.

You might also stop brooding about and abusing the Richlers. After all, I'm a Richler myself. My wife and children also go by that name. Not that I fancy most of my aunts and uncles any more than I do the Rosenbergs. I see Max maybe twice a year. I haven't seen Louis in ages. And while it's true my grandfather Richler, never a buddy of mine, may have given less than honest weight on that old junk yard scale, to compare him to a Mafia don only gives me the giggles.

If you are jealous of my non-existent relationship with the Richlers, you also protest I have rejected the Rosenbergs. Oh dear oh dear. What Rosenbergs? The only one I was attached to was Israel, and when he was alive, I took Florence to meet him. Israel, Ruth and Lionel aside, I hardly ever knew any Rosenbergs, and I still can't tell one from another. I was, you must allow, brought up with the Richlers. We were young together. Hence, my

lingering fondness for them. As for the Rosenbergs, well now, I
don't recall ever hearing from any of them while I was making
do on one meal a day in Europe, trying to learn how to write. But
once my name became somewhat known, all at once, they came
out of the woodwork. Hello, hello. Montreal, Hamilton, Toronto,
New York, was suddenly filled with family. I am, believe me, not
resentful. I am amused. I also have no sense of Rosenberg family.
If the Rosenbergs were mentioned at all in our house when I was
a child, it was to hear you curse them. They were, you assured
me, vile. Book stealers. Printing plate smugglers. Liars, cheats.
Like, come to think of it, the Richlers. Like, come to think of it,
almost anybody you ever mentioned. My God, for a lady charged
with love, as you protest on the tapes, you certainly loathed a
considerable body of people.

Please don't Rosenberg me any Rosenbergs, or Richler me any
Richlers. I have a family. My family is Ted Allan. He is the grandparent of our children. He enjoys them, they adore him, and one
does not devour the other. My family is Jack and Haya, Kotcheff,
the Gottliebs, Nina Bourne, Jack McClelland . . . and more, many
more. . . .

And what about you and your family? From the tapes, I gather
that you and Ruth are not talking again. I hope you do appreciate that it is difficult for me to keep track of your turbulent relationship with your sister, among others. One year, she's odious,
the next you're travelling companions. I do note, however, that
you and Abraham are now on good terms. I'm pleased, for your
sake. But I remember that pompous, tiresome man very well, I
also recall his coarse and dim-witted wife, and hold them both in
small regard. O Hillel, O Akiba, look on this suburban rabbi, his
drawers stuffed with jewellery. My first and uncherished memory
of Abraham goes back to his actually locking me in a rat-filled
shed when I was barely Jake's age, so that he could get on with
his poker game. If we took them out to dinner in London, rest
assured it was for your sake, not the pleasure of their company.
I do not care to see him again. I certainly do not look to him for
moral instruction. He could not, if you recall, bring himself to

send his sick mother five dollars monthly. I have always sent you money and am certainly prepared to send you even more now.

Maw, you're perverse. You say I "abandoned" you. How? When? One morning as I was sitting in my garden, very hungover indeed, you came down the stairs, seething, and told me how much you hated me and how I had made your life miserable. O, good morning, sunshine. All because you had not been invited to the set of Duddy Kravitz. I did not want you on the set. I did not want anybody on the set, as I explained. Because the set was chaos. A crisis every day. Charged with acrimony. I only visited it grudgingly myself, because I had to.

In those days we also invited you to stay at the house when we went off together on a trip. We didn't do this because we couldn't afford a sitter. We did it because we thought you enjoyed it, it might yield an opportunity for you to develop a relationship with your grandchildren. But when I learned that you were complaining about it, churning, telling people you were being used, I immediately cut it out. Maw, you are so deeply embittered, so filled with discontent, there is no pleasing you. If we hadn't asked you to stay you would have been insulted: if we did, you complained to people when they called.

After your childish outburst over Duddy Kravitz, I went to your house, tried to reason with you, only to have my three hundred dollar cheque returned, with the suggestion it would be best if I did not come round again. You made it clear you did not want to see me and I have honoured your wishes. Now, typically, you complain that I don't come round. You can't sit in the garden, you are ashamed for my sake. You can't go out, I'm an embarrassment to you. You can't see your friends lest they ask what news have you of me. When did you go out before? What friend did you lose because of me? You didn't go out. You had no friends. And I am hardly the one to blame, if you have alienated everybody.

Furthermore, don't protect me, please. You may tell anybody you like that we do not see each other, but you might also add it was you who stormed out of the house. But I don't think it proper for you to grieve with suburban doctors, saying I abandoned you. I did not abandon you. You refused my help. That, to be fair, is your privilege. But please don't distort what happened.

Why haven't you seen or called the children? How dare you accuse Florence or the kids of also "abandoning" you. Mindless, hysterical nonsense. What are you talking about?

After our quarrel, I explained to the children you were angry with me, our relationship hadn't been good for years, but that was not any affair of theirs. It should not interfere with their relationship with their grandmother. And then you, as is your gift, ruined that too. You dumped on them. Instead of settling on a relationship with your grandchildren, you told little innocent Emma, a girl of 12, that her father was abnormal. So, naturally, you scared her off. You also scared the others off. The truth is you were never interested in them per se but only in the pleasure they could give you. The truth is if they used to visit your house on Sundays it was only because Florence being Florence used to insist on it.

And so, having shut the children out, you now say they've abandoned you.

Maw, your tapes reek of a chilling vanity, self-praise, self-deception, and distortion.

Item: I did not walk away from you at the bloody bank. I came up to you, asked you how you were getting on, and you glared back and swept off, as is your habit.

You also have the bad taste to suggest that I regret having been born a Jew. Oh, Maw, you are really not painfully bright. Or, God help us, perceptive.

You also accuse me of lying. My dear mother, if there's one thing you have given me (and do not flatter yourself, it is not my talent) it is an abiding hatred for the lies and liars. Shit, I was raised on your self-serving lies, pretensions, and social-climbing. I wouldn't have any of it in my house. My house is a good house. The parents don't deprecate each other to their children. The children love their parents. Not by divine right, please note, but because we are earning it. Nobody is entitled to love.

. . . . You tell me, on the tapes, how dignified, loving, intelligent, sensitive thinking, you are. Such a lady would be surrounded by troops of friends, loving children, adoring grandchildren. Such a lady wouldn't stoop to telling a 12-year-old girl her father is abnormal and, furthermore, shove an illiterate manuscript at her to read.

And no matter what you've heard, Jacob Two-Two has not been translated into French. I don't know what your friend is talking about.

Avrum is responsible for himself. My, God, he's 50 years old. I certainly don't blame myself for his deviousness. And, if once I started to become known, you began to favour me over him, it's because you're a snob.

I have not abandoned you. You have removed yourself, seething, from the scene because you feel insufficiently loved and would not settle for civility and maybe a better relationship with your grandchildren. But look here, I fully recognize my responsibilities. I wish you could manage a decent relationship with the children. But that, alas, is up to you, not me. If you wish to travel, I will provide you with air tickets. If you need money, I will send it. If you become ill, I will engage a nurse. I wish we could have a relationship that was at least cordial. If we can't have that, and you don't wish to see me, I can, if you like, arrange to have $200 monthly transferred to your account. Speak, and you may have it. But I have no remedy for the heart of your complaint, which seems to be that I loved my father more, as the years passed, and came to enjoy his company more than I did yours. Possibly, the fault isn't mine. Maybe he was more enjoyable.

Finally, if you take me for an imperfect son, you also never once understood me. Or what my work is about. Well then, at least take some satisfaction in that I am, after all, a happy man. I love my wife. I adore my children. I enjoy my work. My friends respect me, I respect them.

Among the distortions you feed on, there is, most offensive, perhaps, that dearly held picture of yourself as a self-sacrificing mother. Dignified, sensitive, loving, and, God help us, thinking.

In the evening of your life, abandoned by your fame-crazed son, you sit in your living room contemplating the books of Moses, lighting the sabbath candles. The last of the sagacious Rosenbergs. The Rabbi's God-fearing daughter.

Bullshit.

If, as you so readily quote, Moses enjoined us to honour our father and mother, I must point out there were some things Moses had not yet heard of.

When I was only 12 and had the misfortune to share a front bedroom with you, it did not strike you as undignified to consider your appetites first, your children later, which is to say, after you thought I was asleep you would take Frankel into your bed, the two of you humping together only 12 feet from a boy of 12. Another morning, I remember wakening to find your bed empty, and to discover you hiding, yes, hiding, beneath the bedcovers in Frankel's back bedroom . . . only to scoot into the shed when I left the room and then pretend that you had been there all the time, stoking the fire.

All things considered, I've not treated you badly all these years. And I repeat once more, I am willing to do all I can to ease your seventies. What I don't feel, however, I cannot simulate.

Best

Mordecai

VII

A GOOD HOUSE

"You can't be a Québécois, thirty-four, and intelligent, and not be a separatist," playwright Michel Tremblay told Richler shortly after René Lévesque and the Parti Québécois won a majority government on November 15, 1976. He was appearing on a TV programme with Tremblay and poet-turned-politician Gérald Godin, who had personally defeated no less than Liberal Party leader Robert Bourassa in a Montreal riding. Over drinks with the affable Godin afterwards, Richler, who continued to admire Lévesque, asked, "What is it you really want, a new marriage contract?" When the new politician answered in the affirmative, Richler wondered why, then, the Parti Québécois were seeking outright separation. He recommended they start negotiating with Ottawa instead, rather than risk a referendum, which he didn't believe they could win—at least, not if the choices were clearly stated. As always, he was not opposed either to French Quebecers achieving the respect and rank they deserved or to seeing the imperious WASP minority take it on the chin. Parti Québécois policies on education and social welfare suited his core beliefs as well; a house in upper Westmount and private schools for his children notwithstanding, he was, as he had recently reiterated, still a socialist, a believer in the responsibility of the state to ensure care and education for poor and working-class people. He certainly couldn't summon the fury of Charles Bronfman, who declared of the PQ, "those bastards are out to kill us," and threatened to move the Expos, which he majority-owned, out of the province.

But in private he was already concerned. He suggested early on that the PQ's language laws amounted to little more than "one form of intolerance displacing another," and within a few months of the election Camille Laurin, whom he later dubbed "the PQ minister of retribution," was recommending that English-speaking Quebecers cultivate better manners in keeping with their status. Nor was learning French going to solve the "problem" of being anglophone. "They could all be bilingual tomorrow morning," a PQ backbencher declared, "but this wouldn't change the fact that they think and live in English." Or that they ate in English. "I saw my nine-year-old being tossed in the unilingual slammer," Richler imagined, "having copped three years for eating alphabet soup whose letters were proved to be without accents *grave* or *aigu*."

He had actually been away from the country in the weeks surrounding the election. The year 1976 had been hectic, though not because of "I Ate Nurse Judy." The object of so much commercial ambition had been abandoned shortly after his return from Hollywood the previous spring. "No good will come of it," Richler told Noah of his reasons for not writing the book. Previously in his career, the dropping of a project had augured one of two things. Either he was ready to make a concerted push to complete a different book, or he was floundering. With his repeated announcements that *Gursky Was Here* was close to done, the former seemed the case. The reality was the latter. When the Montreal *Gazette* went snooping, including canvassing an anonymous friend, it got nowhere. "Who knows?" the friend said of the novel's story line. "He hasn't even told his wife, and he's been writing this one for years."

Dropping the story of Martin Hartwell didn't diminish his fascination with the North. In the April 1976 BOMC newsletter, the first to anoint him "Associate for Canada," he was asked for a feature piece on Canada. He chose to write about "our last frontier." Delivered in the mild tone expected of BOMC editorial board members, it nevertheless took on the controversy surrounding the proposed Mackenzie Valley Pipeline, a project that, while benefiting the "energy-hungry south," could threaten the "delicate balance of northern ecology." To help the club members across North America understand what was at stake, and to counter the widespread ignorance of northern culture and history, he recommended a batch of titles that he found "not only instructive, but immensely enjoyable," praising Farley Mowat's Top of the World trilogy about exploration of the far North, and early accounts by the explorers Samuel Hearne, Alexander Mackenzie and Sir John Franklin himself, before the "ill-fated" voyage of HMS *Erebus* and *Terror*. Two retellings of the Franklin tragedy, replete with their "harrowing tales of ice-locked ships—tiny, unbelievably vulnerable, by today's standards—wintering in the cruel Arctic seas sometimes for three years running, many of the men gradually succumbing to scurvy," were invaluable, and all these titles were now available in handsome new editions, thanks to "one of the most beautiful publishing ventures ever undertaken in this country, M.G. Hurtig's Canadian Reprint Series." The North, he warned club members, "becomes an addiction."

Before he set off for the Nice Film Festival to celebrate the launch of *Duddy Kravitz* dubbed into French, he himself finally encountered an icon of Quebec literature. Though her 1944 novel *The Tin Flute* had had a huge impact on many writers, including Mavis Gallant, and had certainly come to the notice of the adolescent Mordecai Richler, he had never met Gabrielle Roy. Jack McClelland, then about to publish her final novel in English translation, arranged a get-together in Montreal, and later heard back from Roy, whose fiction was being credited with helping trigger the kind of introspection among Québécois that had made the Quiet Revolution possible. "I found him, as you had said warmhearted," she wrote in her second language, "and what's more and which I did not expect in the least, sort of child-like, and even defenceless and vulnerable in a sense despite what is spoken of him." Richler, courteous to elderly people, was also respectful of writers he admired.

The family spent the summer on Lake Memphremagog. He bought a boat and took the boys fishing; Florence expanded her garden, and awoke one morning to find the asparagus miraculously grown, thanks to his "planting" supermarket stalks during the night. For the kids, the house and property were magic: diving off the dock and casting into the stream, exploring the long path out to the road. Evenings they spent as a family or with guests. "Isn't this a scene," Bob Gottlieb commented on entering the living room, where Mordecai and Florence sat quietly reading, along with all five children.

Their social network soon expanded, with nights of dinners in neighbours' houses or at restaurants tucked into nearby villages. Ted Allan showed up for a week and stayed for a month. He talked on the phone too much, passionate exchanges with friends and lovers, producers and analysts, leaving his host unable to make a call from his own house. He also left behind boxes of papers and personal belongings for safekeeping. But that was okay; he was Uncle Ted, "real" family. He would chat for hours with Florence in the kitchen or on the deck, taking in the view of Sargeant's Bay and the lake stretching away into the distance. Richler, in his office overhead on the second floor during working hours, or on the couch in the evening watching baseball, would contribute his usual minimal remarks, content that his old, sometimes frustrating friend was around to amuse the children and keep Florence happy.

Silence was his preferred mode of being among people, including his own family. A natural reticence, in conjunction with a head perpetually filled with characters, story, structure, left him often physically present at a dinner table but mentally elsewhere. The children were so accustomed to his quiet that they scarcely registered it—their father, a vivid absence. Florence, ever sensitive to how his mind functioned, knew at once when he was still "working," either further mulling over the day's output or simply making decisions about what was important to his creative life, what he *wished* to register of his surroundings, and what he did not. She learned not to take his withdrawals personally, as did, for the most part, the kids, who were practised early in the art of Not Disturbing Daddy. Others, of course, friends among them, never quite knew how to be with him in social situations. Ted Kotcheff, who had survived a week of near-silent drinking back in Tourrettes in the first days of their friendship, understood his singular, intense and surprisingly fragile artistic temperament better than most. "Life for Mordecai is painful," he told a journalist. "It's like walking on eyeballs."

Harry Gulkin, the producer who had optioned *Jacob Two-Two*, surprised many by generating enough money to go into production in July. Richler hadn't been involved in the screenplay; the American Theodore Flicker had written it. He was surprised to find out that twelve-year-old Martha had, with Florence's secret support, auditioned for, and won, the part of "Intrepid Shapiro," the character that represented her older sister, Emma, in the book. Acting in the film obliged Martha to travel back and forth from the Townships, her father doing most of the driving.

Living in the country didn't keep him from his beloved late-afternoon drinks routine. Within a few miles of the house were two bars, the Owl's Nest on Route 243 and the Thirsty Boot on the same road, where he began showing up at around four in the afternoon. Thinking nothing of drinking Macallans at the Ritz-Carlton Hotel bar on a Thursday with politicians and Westmount society ladies and then sipping a blended Scotch at the Boot on a Friday in a room shared with, as he called it, "other craftsmen (housepainters, self-taught carpenters, gravel pit operators)," he moved between city and country, elite and everyday. He did so with his usual unkempt appearance and taciturn manners, seeking no special treatment and often happily sitting smoking and drinking by himself. He was fond of his bar buddies and they of him, and he was soon delighting in the company of these new friends as much as the federal ministers and newspaper tycoons he would shortly be getting to know.

But the actual reason he had been out of the country and missed the provincial election related to a fateful call from Jack McClelland asking if he knew anyone who could provide a 10,000-word text for a coffee-table book of photos about Spain. The intuitive McClelland, who had a gift for subtly directing writers to the right material for their talent, was hoping he would take the job himself. Richler did agree to write the text, especially after McClelland offered a dollar a word plus travel expenses for him to visit Spain again for the first time in a quarter-century. He took the commission despite an already crowded fall schedule including a local assignment that he wouldn't dream of missing: covering the 1976 Canada Cup for *Weekend Magazine.* Enjoying a "privileged seat directly behind the communist bench" for a Russia-Sweden game at the Forum in September, he got to fulfill "a boyhood dream" by finally visiting the home dressing room after a game involving the Canadians. Unwilling to muscle his way into the media scrums surrounding players Phil Esposito and Bobby Orr, he retreated to a corner. Only after he had dodged repeated volleys of underwear and jockstraps did he realize he was standing next to the laundry bin.

But shortly before leaving for Spain, he and Florence learned some terrible news: Tony Godwin had died suddenly of heart failure in New York. Richler's renowned British editor, and friend to both, was just fifty-six, and into his second year of living and working in Manhattan. He too had visited Lake Memphremagog that summer, with his two sons. Miserable with the shock of it, they headed to New York for his memorial.

Florence accompanied him to Spain. With Lily no longer even on the margin of their lives—they had not spoken of her since he declared he would "take care of it" in late July, and Florence had neither asked to see, nor been offered, the letter—the kids were again looked after by the family housekeeper. Landing in the Spanish capital almost a year to the day after the death of Francisco Franco had initiated the country's return to parliamentary democracy, they checked into the Ritz. He noted at once that breakfast in the hotel's opulent dining room was three times what he had paid for a week's lodging in 1951. "Now Spain and I have both become middle class." From the start the trip—from the Valley of the Fallen down through Andalusia to Seville—made him quietly melancholy, wondering why "the journeys I once managed on spunk, depending on favourable winds, I now make on assignments, magazines footing the big bills which enable me to stay in hotels that used to be beyond the pale and dine in restaurants whose patrons I once despised, and possibly secretly envied, for their affluence." In this mood he met, often for expensive lunches, government officials who had, with the dictator dead and buried, happily gone over to the bourgeois side of life. Even Florence irritated him. Only twenty-four hours away from Montreal and she was already talking about the kids. She was also keeping her watch on Montreal time, the better, he complained, to fret over whether "it's time for Noah to get up, Jake to be home from school, Daniel to go to work, Emma to start her Latin, or Martha to leave for her Jr. Firefighter's class." "Let's forget about the kids for one night," he pleaded.

Richler had actually attended two funerals shortly before flying to Spain. His ninety-five-year-old grandmother, Esther Richler, had also passed away, and he went to the service and sat shiva with relatives one evening. "I hope this time you won't have to run," his sharp-tongued Uncle Bernard commented when he learned his nephew would be returning to Ibiza. The twenty-year-old's letter to his father, explaining that he was being expelled from the island due to his entanglements with the mysterious German colonel Mueller, had apparently circulated among the family. He realized that for all the intervening years he had been harbouring guilt and shame over the events the letter had relayed, bemoaning his lack of "poise or physical courage" in the face of the smear campaign. Now, though officially in the country to write a general essay, he was secretly there "in search of old friends on Ibiza, and in the hope of finding the colonel and expelling a nightmare" that had stayed with him since 1951. He even planned to confront the colonel.

As the plane landed on Ibiza, Florence watched her famously tough husband nearly dissolve with anxiety about what he might find. She knew how deeply he felt things; his sensitivity, the vulnerability he often displayed, if rarely put into words, never surprised her. The island had long ago ceased being isolated or rustic and, though not yet a rave-party destination, already boasted high-rise hotels and international tourist resorts. Disappointed, Richler wandered the town for two days seeking any familiar face and retelling already-familiar tales to her. A young man who resembled Juanito "Pus," the unofficial fisherman mayor who had made him welcome years before, directed him to his aged grandfather. The old Spaniard remembered Mauricio. The two sat in a café, Mordecai's questions about Mueller in his almost defunct Spanish baffling Juanito, until finally they confirmed that the colonel had died of cancer years before. No Mueller, no Rosita's bordello, no dockside cafés bustling with men drinking Fundador: the Ibiza he had known, and mythologized and aggrandized for so long, had vanished. If mainland Spain had set him to brooding over his complacent, middle-aged self, the island left him feeling foolish. It also made him homesick for his family and for Montreal. The country and its passions, the island and its characters, even the young Mordecai Richler who had made his rite of passage in those cafés and rooms, among those men, had only one chance left for survival: in the pages of a book.

What kind of book? was the question. He began debating it on the Air Iberia flight back across the Atlantic. Fuelled by regret, along with an abrupt desire to understand how Spain had shaped him and what had become of his youthful ardour, he sat down at his desk at Lake Memphremagog, where he was already spending more non-summer, non-weekend time than originally intended, and banged out a long travelogue-memoir for Jack McClelland. Florence read it and, thinking at once that the material was too personal, advised her husband to deploy most of it elsewhere. Heeding her advice, he submitted to M&S a shorter, more passable song of praise to the old town of Madrid and the Feria in Seville, spectacular Ronda and majestic Granada, with the bullfights triggering reflections on courage and a passage from *Don Quixote* flowing into a meditation on why Spanish genius was best evidenced in painting and architecture. His preface contained only a single, slightly cryptic hint of the effects that time had had on his imagination. "The more liberating the drunk," he wrote of that original epiphany at the fiesta in Valencia, "the greater the hangover."

He now went to work with alacrity. By the following summer the misfit text was a book-length memoir titled *Back to Ibiza.* It recounted those months on the island, his romance with the American he decided to call Pauline (instead of Helen), including their beach tryst watched and exposed, he always suspected, by Colonel Mueller himself, and his confrontations with the German who had come in his mind to embody the unrepentant Nazi, his date with justice delayed. In between were evocations of his apprenticeship in London and his horseman years as father and husband in Montreal. He described a 1951 photo of Pauline "snuggled into a black bikini, possibly the first to be seen on Ibiza, and I grinning foolishly beneath a broad-rimmed straw hat," and then gave a rare portrait of his one great love as she was their first day in Spain in November 1976, Florence "wearing a black wool dress . . . and a frothy wool scarf, looked absolutely lovely and was flushed with high spirits." He remembered Trafalgar Square in 1956, during the Suez Crisis rally, where the future lovers had first made their feelings known to each other, and vividly recalled his father's only visit to London. There were his friendships with Doris Lessing and the late Reuben Ship, once a mentor to him, whose final years had been sad. Nostalgia for his younger, more authentic self, and frank disclosures—"I miss my father, who died too early after a largely joyless life"—and curious self-accusations of being "a born coward," an "adaptable man," even a "cynical ideological drifter," ran through it. Fluid and instinctive, with the abrupt shifts in time and place that had distinguished *St. Urbain's Horseman*, the often startling *Back to Ibiza*, its self-portrait almost the opposite of his actual character, fell out of its author in dark spiritual night, raw and even unbidden.

But Florence wasn't sure a memoir was the right form for the preoccupations that Spain had brought to the surface. Neither was Bob Gottlieb, who advised him to go back to novel writing. With the two readers whose opinions mattered most in accord, he agreed. By the fall *Back to Ibiza*—a strange but vigorous short book—had been shelved.

Proof that there was a new Mordecai Richler novel in the works already existed. The January-February 1977 *Saturday Night* made much of "Manny Moves to Westmount," an excerpt from *Gursky Was Here*. Manny Berger, formerly of Toronto (and the teleplay *The Bells of Hell*), is buying his way into upper Westmount society by purchasing an "imposing grey stone house" well up a slope that has a "spectacular view of the city and the river below." Though the house faces south, it is exposed to "the wind blowing in from the Arctic, skimmed from the summit of the Barnes Ice Cap, itself a remnant of the Laurentian ice sheet, which had retreated from the city only 12,000 years" before. The fabulously wealthy Gurskys, former bootleggers turned distillers, live in splendour at the crown of the hill, with their lawyer and family trust fund manager Harvey Schwartz also dwelling in the clouds of the Montreal social hierarchy. Mr. Bernard, as the patriarch is commonly called, has already blessed the city with "a hospital, a theatre, a string quartet, and various university buildings," all of which are "boldly named after one departed Gursky or another." Only one ancestor is excluded from the orgy of self-mythologizing; nowhere is there evidence that "Solomon Gursky had also been here." Even the children of the black-sheep brother Solomon have been left out of the family businesses and sinecures. Among his offspring is the eccentric Henry, said to be "ensconced in Tuktoyaktuk, on the Beaufort Sea, a recluse doing anthropological work among the Eskimos, his theories crazed."

Funny and impudent, its high-profile character roster an audacious blur of life and fiction—few, in Anglo Montreal at least, would not have instantly connected "Mr. Bernard" with the late "Mr. Sam" and the Gurskys with the Bronfmans—"Manny Moves to Westmount" came out swinging. The Bronfmans themselves took note, and a story soon circulated that Richler's former acquaintance Leo Kolber had appeared in Jack McClelland's office with a casual, off-the-record warning not to publish *Gursky Was Here.* For McClelland, this was complicated; a decade earlier, in the wake of a losing year, he had agreed to an injection of funds by a silent-partner team made up of CEMP Investments, owned by the same Bronfmans, and the holding company of another wealthy Montreal family. Leo Kolber had done that deal at around the same time that his wife's book of poetry, *Bitter Sweet Lemons and Love,* at first rejected by M&S, was suddenly accepted. Richler, then just getting to know Leo, had needled Jack McClelland about Sandra Kolber's "ring-a-ding verses, namely, Me, Leo, and the Menopause." Subsequently, McClelland had commissioned a biography of Sam Bronfman, a book partially "bought" by the family's support—that is, paid for—only to have his biographer commit suicide while the manuscript was under consideration. (Richler's own friend, former *Time* editor John Scott, was hired to resume the biographical project, but then was dismissed before he wrote a word.) Richler himself heard nothing directly about his *Saturday Night* excerpt, except the silence of no further hockey tickets or invitations to bar mitzvahs and parties from the Bronfmans.

"Manny Moves to Westmount" reads like the sharp tip of a sprawling Mordecai Richler social comedy. But while he had already assembled maybe a third of the plot pieces of what would eventually fall into place as *Solomon Gursky Was Here*, he had generated no more than seventy-five pages of manuscript in five years. That was a fraction of what he needed. The novel was at the forefront of his thoughts and parts of it were mapped in his imagination, but not on the page. His own increasingly high standards for his fiction were partly to blame, and Jack McClelland would complain that he had "allowed himself too many damn distractions in the past"—without, notably, taking any blame for having personally dangled the distraction of Spain. But the more likely cause was his trip across the High Arctic in 1974, and his growing "addiction" to the North. As the references to Henry Gursky living on

the Beaufort Sea and those "winds from the Arctic" blowing over
Westmount suggested, the fictional landscape he had in mind was
suddenly much bigger than either Jewish Montreal, old neighbourhood or new, or even the vast, Isaac Babel–worthy story of
the Bronfmans/Gurskys. He wanted to incorporate this "other"
Canada into his narrative, and into his evolving vision of his native
land. As yet, he had no idea how to go about it.

He believed the North could also help sort his middle son out.
Hank Madison, the supreme court justice for the Yukon, had visited the Richlers the previous spring, and Noah had taken his
daughter on a canoe ride through the wetlands behind the house.
Shortly afterwards he was offered a summer job as a prospector's
assistant in Whitehorse. Richler, who recognized his intelligent
boy's awkward relationship with institutional learning, provided
him a dozen books for the long summer nights, by Koestler,
Stendhal, Dostoevsky, Lardner and Waugh. The seventeen-year-
old didn't get through them all, preferring a diet of fiction by
Graham Greene and Mordecai Richler, and followed the experience up with a year-long jaunt around Asia. ("Don't forget to write,"
his father told him. "Your mother will worry." Noah did write,
nearly every day.) He reappeared in Montreal with a shaven head
and an earring. Later, when his dependency on drugs briefly wors-
ened—a reality Florence kept from her husband for as long as she
could—Richler invited Noah, lately a waiter at Ben's Deli and student at Marianopolis College, to accompany him on a BOMC trip
to New York. In a hotel on Lexington Avenue, the father, breaking
a long silence, admitted he couldn't fathom his son's need to take
drugs. He relayed how painful it had been to watch Mason
Hoffenberg waste away, his talent squandered. "I've had a marvellous life," he told him. "I love my wife. I have wonderful children,
and I'm good at my work. Life for me is like . . . is like biting into
a piece of fresh fruit. A tomato. I don't know why you do it."

His father's rare display of deep emotion registered. Noah
soon kicked the habit and was accepted at McGill, where he
studied classics and went on to read Philosophy, Politics and
Economics at Balliol College, Oxford.

Far less dramatic parenting involved helping Jake build a make-shift nest out of a cardboard carton. The nine-year-old had begun his summer at the lake by rescuing a crow from a woodpile. He and his father drove into nearby Magog to buy an eyedropper, and began feeding the bird milk. While cautioning his boy that the bird might die, Richler realized that if it did, it would be the greatest loss Jacob had known so far in his happy life.

The Richler house was a good one, loving and functional. The parents were there for the children, and the kids themselves, while not immune from jealousies and rivalries, were each other's best friends and supports. As eldest, Daniel was the natural organizer and project mastermind; as youngest, Jake was fawned over, "everybody's toy." The intensity of Noah and Emma's relationship had been remarked by their father in *Jacob Two-Two,* and Martha, a radiant fair-haired child, had her own vivacious personality and her mother's sensitivity to art and design. All the Richler children adored their attentive, glamorous mother and revered their inattentive, unkempt father.

But when the kids, treated at school to warnings about the hazards of lung cancer, challenged one standard in the house— his heavy smoking of cigarettes, cigarillos and cigars, a habit that made the car into a perpetual smoking lounge—they got only so far. Together, they drew up a series of medical messages, illustrated with skulls, crossbones and bloody lungs, slipping them into every cigarette pack and matchbox they could find. His reaction went from amused to irritated over the course of a two-week campaign. "God dammit," he would say on finding another note. Florence, also still a smoker, finally suggested that the campaign wind down before it turned ugly. She quit smoking not long afterwards. He did not.

VIII

OH! CANADA!

At a cocktail party at Harvard University in Boston in the spring of 1978, things started to go badly between Mordecai Richler and the Quebec nationalists. A speaker in a lecture series titled "The Future of North America: Canada, the United States, and Quebec Nationalism," he shook hands with another featured guest, Premier René Lévesque, referring to him by his title. "You know my name, you bum," Lévesque snapped. The premier added that a man named Stéphane Venne was promising to punch Richler in the face. Provoked, as he later put it, into "being equally foolish," Richler replied, "I'm not so difficult to find. My name's in the phone book." That was true—Florence insisted on keeping their home number listed, even during the worst hostilities to come—and the two former passing acquaintances parted as presumptive enemies.

The source of Lévesque's fury, and Venne's readiness to fight, was "Oh! Canada! Lament for a Divided Country," the cover story in the December *Atlantic Monthly*. Written nearly a year after the election, his first published foray into the new Quebec of Lévesque and the Parti Québécois was for the most part an example of the even-handed journalism about Canada that he could, and occasionally did, produce, usually for editors in New York or London. Like its forebear, his 1963 *New Statesman* analysis of the Quebec emerging from the Great Darkness, "Oh! Canada!" was sympathetic to French ambitions and thoughtful about the risks of separation, though it gave no quarter to Bill 101, the language charter passed that summer that declared French the only language allowed on commercial signs in the province (with few exceptions). The piece had its instant critics, with the *Gazette* declaring it "smug, petty, peevish, and patronizing." Jack McClelland defended it: "The article did a helluva lot of good and gave a lot of people a clear understanding of what is going on for the first time. If you weren't such an anti-semitic bastard, the world would be your oyster." McClelland was referencing a small but catastrophic error. Repeating a mistake first made by McGill law professor Irwin Cotler, Richler had claimed that the PQ election theme song, *"Demain nous appartient"* ("Tomorrow Belongs to Us"), borrowed from a modern version of a Nazi youth anthem composed for the Broadway play, and later hit film, *Cabaret*. Stéphane Venne, a Québécois songwriter, had been its actual author, and he, among others, used the media to remind Richler, not unreasonably, of how easily misinformation repeated could acquire the rank of fact.

Worse, that had already happened to René Lévesque himself; on a lecture tour of the United States, hoping to gain sympathy and understanding among Americans for his cause, he had been scolded by the president of one university with a large Jewish population, who had been exposed to the misinformation about his party's theme song. The outcry inside Quebec wasn't helped by the certainty in some quarters that Richler did think separatists, if not all French Canadians, were anti-Semitic. His mockery of a PQ by-election candidate who used his platform as a radio talk-show host to declare that only a million Jews had died in the Holocaust was well placed; but the narrow-minded seized upon it as a tarnishing of the whole movement.

Richler had spoken at Harvard the previous autumn, at the behest of a young Canadian teaching there named David Staines. The gregarious Staines, later a professor at the University of Ottawa and editor of the New Canadian Library for M&S, had won Richler's affection by rescuing him from a dreary party being given in his honour at the Canadian consulate in Boston. Only wine was being offered by the consulate. The young academic wisely invited Mordecai and Florence back to his rooms for whisky and sports. A couple of days after the Richlers returned home, Staines received a call inviting him to visit the next time he was in Montreal.

Gaffes and heated exchanges notwithstanding, Richler believed that decency would dominate the debate inside Quebec. "There is tremendous civility in this city, and whatever the political tensions so far, the argument has been conducted in civil tones." He had declared René Lévesque and his new opponent, Quebec Liberal Party leader Claude Ryan, to be "people of tremendous good will" and "social democrats." But he began to worry that "a lot of strong feelings are going to surface and . . . this city is in for a bad time." The referendum on sovereignty, a little more than a year away, would likely mean hearing from "the rowdies on both sides." Almost two decades earlier, he had written about the yeshiva that was the disputatious world of Jewish letters in New York. Quebec might not be its match for literary firepower, but the debate, about politics and fair governance, language and identity, was as lively and, to his mind, as essential. Soon he was arguing with PQ minister Jacques Parizeau over dinner, courtesy of a party organized by Peter White, Brian Mulroney's future chief-of-staff, at his home in Knowlton in the Townships. That exchange grew heated enough for Florence to act as conciliator: "I think it's a matter of semantics," she told Parizeau of her husband's blunt remarks about sovereignty. Media mogul Conrad Black, scion of a wealthy Anglo-Montreal family and recently the author of a sympathetic biography of Maurice Duplessis, was at the dinner. Richler, who despised Duplessis, sparred energetically with Black too. With Jacques Parizeau, the conversation was not the start of another friendship; with the patrician Conrad Black, who also chummed around with Nick Auf der Maur, it was.

But some old friendships did not survive the passing of time. "Natasha, your god-daughter, is now 22," Nina Squires, formerly Lamming, wrote of her daughter's pending marriage. Richler, who had not seen or heard from George Lamming in years, was invited to the wedding in Port-of-Spain, Trinidad. Many years later he would run into George Lamming at the International Festival of Authors at Harbourfront in Toronto. But Lamming, who had forsaken literature in favour of radical black politics, made a point of snubbing his old London friend.

He had not spoken to his mother since sending her his agonized and angry letter the previous August. She, in turn, had not contacted him or his family. Around this time he received some bonds from her, which Lily, intent on keeping her vow of paying back the money her son had given her, had signed over to him. She asked Bill Weintraub to act as intermediary. Later, Weintraub received a lengthy typed letter from her about Mordecai. "He befouled me in a five-page letter that no human being with any figment of decency would so treat a fellow human being, let alone a mother." She also complained of his treatment of Avrum: "And he does not want to know his brother." Misery and self-pity were painfully intertwined. "He robbed me of my will to live, to enjoy my old age after years of struggle and deprivation." She cried that her second child "lacks compassion, has no humility and is full of callous brutality," but then collapsed again in pathos: "I used to listen to the door bell, hoping he would come by, every face I saw, seemed to me to be his." At the bottom, scrawled in a shaky hand, was an addendum: "Enclosed—copy of a letter when I still human. I have since degenerated."

Bill Weintraub decided it was best not to mention the letter to his friend. Unbeknownst to both him and Richler, Lily's only surviving friendship, with her sister Ruth, was also unravelling. Ruth was receiving similarly disordered letters, and on the outside of an envelope in which she kept them, she wrote, "Lily's poison lying pen. Her mind is twisting and sick." But neither Ruth's analysis of her sister's mental state, nor Lily's own heart-rending self-identification as subhuman, would correspond with the Lily Rosenberg who would emerge briefly, a few years later, as a vigorous and busy published author.

———

Now in his late forties, and looking and feeling every year of it, thanks to excess smoking and working and a deficit of exercise, Mordecai Richler still believed the ultimate job of a novelist was to produce one work that would last. He also worried that, after a certain stage, a writer might not have another big book in him. He had been in this spot ten years before, although he had been younger then, with the brief, puzzling *Atuk* and his "big book" about Joey the horseman showing no real direction. His solution then had been *Cocksure*, a brilliantly sharp, single-note tune, manageable for a writer who was a natural novelist capable of extraordinary concentration, and who could hold several novels at once in his head for years before committing them to paper. So it was hardly surprising that by the fall of 1977 he had a story entirely different from *Gursky* underway, born of his return to Spain and the abandoned memoir *Back to Ibiza*.

The tale of Joshua Shapiro, another streetwise Montreal Jew from the old neighbourhood—a celebrity sportswriter obsessed with the Spanish Civil War, now living in lower Westmount and married to a variation on the shiksa goddess, in this instance the passionate, unstable Pauline—was from the start going to follow the Saul Bellow model that had sprung *St. Urbain's Horseman* to life. A second instalment, in short, of the ongoing state of the author's soul. In addition, *Joshua*, as the manuscript was called from the outset, would widen the scope of *Duddy Kravitz* to reflect the dispersion of those ghetto Jews across the social and geographical strata of Montreal. The earlier novel, written in England, had been a largely instinctive comedic portrait of the rough-hewn denizens of "his" neighbourhood in his colonial-minded hometown. The new novel, written in Montreal, was going to be more self-aware in its ambitions. He intended to unfurl a canvas that would reveal the values and mores of a fractious, immature society as yet unsure of its native identity.

The characters would still be mostly his kind of Montrealers, but they would be more numerous and of more outlandish comedic design, and would also reside in Westmount or in the tony Townships, irritating the indigenous WASPS with their relentless energy and social climbing. He even planned to satirize William Lyon Mackenzie King, the eccentric, forever-serving prime minister from his childhood, whose startlingly revealing diaries had become available to the public starting in 1977. He trusted his friend Bernie Ostry, now a deputy minister in Pierre Trudeau's government, would supply incriminating tidbits about the subject of his Ph.D. thesis back in the fifties.

The story in his head was a sprawling, polyphonic novel. Of his two previous attempts on such a scale, the first had taken six years to complete and the second had stalled. With his BOMC duties and a new monthly column in *Maclean's*, the odds of his completing it in time to avoid going a full decade without publishing an adult novel were not good.

―――――

In a self-portrait for *Weekend* magazine, Richler sketched his routine in the early days of *Joshua*. "A Day in the Life" began for him at 8 a.m., an hour later than for Florence, with a leisurely breakfast and two papers, the *Gazette* and the *Globe and Mail*. Once the mail was read, by 9:15 or so, he was at his desk, drinking tea with lemon and smoking "little cigars." Many mornings he ended up making "phone calls and lists and schedules. Anything to avoid actually settling down to write." At midday he could honourably descend from his office to have a light lunch, pickled herring or tinned salmon, and enjoy a fifteen-minute nap. Then it was back upstairs for another easy or tough or anguished few hours. "I've spent a week on a page," he wrote, "and also written eight pages in a day." Revising a chapter was "much more enjoyable" than its first conception. More enjoyable still was quitting time, around 4 p.m., when he could walk down the hill—forty minutes in summer, longer in winter—to the Ritz or the Press Club, where friends awaited, and where he could "stop for an hour or so and have a talk and a drink." On his return to Edgehill Road the family would have a "very full meal" together, Florence cooking and the girls washing up, the conversation—carried on, presumably, around his silence—about everything from politics to school to the activities of old friends. The parents would then retire to the study for coffee, with the kids joining them to talk further. "I don't actually put on slippers," he joked. "I wear slippers all day."

The twenty-four months that produced the 500-page manuscript of *Joshua Then and Now*, while far from incident-free, were placid by comparison with earlier periods. But even so, a sustained creative run faced the challenge of his multi-tasking. He had his BOMC trips to New York, where his influence on the jury was growing. As the Canadian reader he had done full reviews of Lester Pearson's memoirs and Peter C. Newman's *The Canadian Establishment*, and supported fiction by Norman Levine and Marian Engel, and poetry by Irving Layton and Alden Nowlan. Now, with a full BOMC column at his disposal, he wrote about Atwood's *Lady Oracle* and Morley Callaghan's *Closer to the Sun*, Josh Greenfeld's memoir of his autistic son and a true-life crime book co-written by George Jonas and his wife, Barbara Amiel. Among the judges, he and novelist Wilfrid Sheed—the "young turks" of the panel, and soon good friends—tended to think alike, and would work to persuade the others. In 1977 he pushed hard for two quite different books: *Song of Solomon*, the third novel by the African-American Toni Morrison, and *The World According to Garp,* the inventive, outrageous fourth novel by a little-known New Hampshire writer named John Irving. Maria Tucci and Bob Gottlieb organized a dinner party not long after to introduce the future Nobel Prize–winning Toni Morrison to the Richlers.

A year later he devoted columns to two M&S titles: Pierre Berton's *The Wild Frontier*, a series of true-life tales about disastrous treks across Northern Canada, and Peter C. Newman's *Bronfman Dynasty*, the first full account of the distillery clan, undertaken in the wake of the sad fates of previous attempts at writing about the family. Newman's book provided something of great personal importance to Richler: it confirmed the dozens of stories he had learned over the years about Mr. Sam and the clan, only a few of which had originated with Leo Kolber. It also provided several more. (An earlier book, James H. Gray's *Booze:*

The Impact of Whisky on the Prairie West, gave him lots of tales as well.) But he also knew one or two things about what Newman had gone through to write his account, and what he himself might face. The manuscript of *Bronfman Dynasty* had been mysteriously leaked to Charles Bronfman, a breach possibly originating inside BOMC, where it had been sent for consideration, and the author had had to make dozens of corrections under threat of litigation. Earlier, too, Leo Kolber had reputedly kidded Newman in a letter, saying that he'd better be kind to the family in his book "Or I'll cut your balls off." Richler likely heard of that exchange via Jack McClelland.

In November 1978 he carved out ten days from his schedule to fly to Germany at the invitation of the Department of External Affairs to "peddle Canadian Culture" at seven universities in six different cities. Told that someone from the embassy would meet his plane in Frankfurt, he offered to help identify himself: "I could always wear the obligatory yellow armband." Diplomatically speaking, he was a curious choice, and he struggled to make nice with his hosts, especially before Florence joined him in Bonn. At "immensely civilized" dinner parties, he found himself staring at any guest over the age of fifty and wondering, "Where were you, my good man, on *Kristallnacht?* Where were you when your neighbours were screaming in the streets, blood flowing from their cracked heads?" He ended the piece he wrote about the experience, "A Jew in Germany," with a declaration of non-absolution for the war and the Holocaust. "The best that can be hoped for, I think, is possibly, just possibly, my children will forgive theirs."

A final distraction during the most intensive period of working on *Joshua* involved selling the Westmount house. Florence Wood had first left for London at age seventeen; Mordecai Richler had been nineteen when he opted for Europe instead of Israel. The Richler children, too, were out into the world sooner than some. Daniel, now a disc jockey with the Montreal station CHOM-FM, was living on St. Urbain Street, and Noah was studying at McGill. Emma, an undergraduate at Victoria College, University of Toronto—the clan flew to Toronto to celebrate her

eighteenth birthday—was home only for holidays, when family
life shifted to the Townships, and Martha would also be enrolled
at university before she turned eighteen. The Edgehill Road house
was no longer needed. They rented and eventually purchased an
apartment in the stately building known as the Chateau on
Sherbrooke Street, kitty-corner from the Ritz-Carlton and within
five minutes of the Press Club, Ben's Deli, and the bistro Le Mas
des Oliviers. A master bedroom for the parents, another for
Martha and Emma, and a small bedroom off the kitchen for Jake
left no space for a study. Richler took over the dining room, the
first time since Winchester Road in 1958 that he had no proper
office. But he was already finding Lake Memphremagog more
conducive to work, and was spending several days a week there,
often by himself. He also still owned the English house in Surrey,
which he rented out. Its value was soaring.

Not since the Richlers had lived on Parkhill Road in
Hampstead had favourite shops, restaurants and bars been
within a short walk. They were back in a city apartment in a
city neighbourhood.

He finished *Joshua Then and Now* in the Townships between
April and October. "Look at me now," Joshua Shapiro declares on
the opening page of his account of how he came, at age forty-
something, to be in a Montreal hospital, ribs cracked and a leg
broken, his brother-in-law dead and his wife gone missing.
Scandals haunt him, on account of these family troubles, and of
his having been "outed," thanks to an archive of forbidden love
letters he once fabricated on a lark with a novelist friend, also
now deceased. Joshua happened to be on the Spanish island of
Ibiza, where he had shamed himself a quarter-century earlier by
failing to confront a former Nazi propagandist, when the hapless
brother-in-law, Kevin Hornby, either a mastermind or a dupe in a
financial scandal, killed himself. That, in turn, caused Kevin's kid
sister (Joshua's wife, Pauline) to have a breakdown. Both hail
from a patrician Westmount clan, their father a senator; Joshua's
mother, in contrast, is a stripper—she provided rare entertainment at her son's bar mitzvah—and his father, Reuben, a boxer

turned muscle for the Jewish mob. Now the Shapiro clan are holed up in their country house on Lake Memphremagog, scene of summer frolics among the Anglo-Montreal elite, with Reuben and the senator, unlikely friends across the divide, watching over the wounded family.

Beleaguered and besieged, more and more caustic about the world's follies, Joshua Shapiro is also increasingly awed by his own good fortune as a father and husband. The highly sexed, highly strung Pauline, passionate gardener and self-doubting parent, moves him no less. His own "loopy mother," her stage name Esty Blossom, he might still find amusing, except that she tells reporters "she and her son were now estranged." Reuben Shapiro, erstwhile pugilist and Bible scholar—disavowing New Testament tales about "the guy on the stick," he crosses Talmudic wisdom with mobster world view to teach his teenaged son about "fucking and the Jewish tradition"—is one of a kind, raw and authentic. Bad luck that Esther Shapiro, "born into Outremont affluence, a Leventhal," married into "a family of thugs out of Odessa."

In addition to Reuben and Esther, the book crackles with blazing character creations. There is dark Jack Trimble, a faux-Englishman with authentic English class hatreds, and sex-besotted, alcoholic novelist Sidney Murdoch, a relic of roaring-fifties London. There is amoral Jane Trimble, a bundle of Westmount privilege and nastiness; Joshua's Uncle Bernard, a former businessman reduced to driving a cab and verbally abusing his nephew; and his gang of appetite-charged friends from the old neighbourhood. Finally, there are the Gurskys, lurking mostly off-page, and Duddy Kravitz, in another cameo while awaiting the resumption of the proposed trilogy that will chart his destiny.

Committed to an uncensored study of the heterosexual Jewish mid-century male, in *Joshua*, more than in any previous book, Mordecai Richler made brilliant, vivid humour of the "Jewy thundercloud" that his protagonist brought with him and the "Jewy network" of the New York media. But he responded to the powerful emerging trends of the 1970s—the most prominent being feminism and gay rights—with about the same sensitivity he had long applied to cultural nationalism. The triggering joke of *Joshua*, the love letters between Joshua and Sidney Murdoch, dated back to the café schemes among expatriate Americans in Paris. Fifties humour went unappreciated by some in 1980, especially the idea that an eyewitness account of the men kissing in a Hollywood hotel room (a non-sexual embrace by a distressed Joshua) would trigger a newsworthy scandal. The same held true for his mockery of the suspicious late-life feminism of Esther Shapiro. From Esty Blossom, star of porn flicks, Joshua's mother had lately "graduated to women's lib. The movement." In Ottawa to advocate for abortion on demand, Esther thrust herself and her placard in front of the TV cameras. SMELLY IT MAY BE, the placard read, BUT MY CUNT BELONGS TO ME.

Richler redrafted the book several times, having flirted with what would have been his debut first-person narration, and crafted certain sections over and over. But had he paused for breath between completing the manuscript and submitting it, he might have been perturbed not by bland passages or a growing list of stylistic tics but by the sound of too many echoes from *St. Urbain's Horseman*. With Diana Athill no longer his editor, Tony Godwin passed away, and Bob Gottlieb disinclined to provide detailed textual comments about books he thought were successful, such echoes were not then the subject of editorial discussion. *Joshua* is its own story, and the size and makeup of its social canvas are large and new and riotous. But it marks little advance in vision, unlike *Duddy Kravitz* and *Horseman*, and isn't like his stylistically daring satires of the sixties. "I love his book," one detractor quipped ungenerously. "I buy it every time he writes it."

Still, by autumn he had a highly entertaining novel to show his editors, and by Christmas all three publishers were commited to bringing the much-delayed, much-anticipated new Mordecai Richler novel out in the spring. For his part, he had to be, if not fully content with the book, then "grateful," as he told a journalist, to have pulled the novel he wished to write—more or less—out of his artistic hat. "I feel better when I wake up," he explained.

PART V

M.R. WAS HERE

I

A VERY COMPLEX MAN

"The vibrations are very good," Richler noted in April 1980, on the eve of the publication of *Joshua* "and it will probably have the largest print run I've ever had." He was right: M&S and Knopf each printed twenty thousand hardcover copies, with Macmillan settling on ten thousand for the U.K. market. The American edition came with a blurb from Joseph Heller. "It's wildly funny! It's full of people, full of plot, full of feeling. I think it's his best." The reviewers did not hold back either: "a richly comic satire in the best uninhibited Richler tradition"; "Complex in scope, outrageously comic, and tightly constructed... the crowning achievement of his career." *Maclean's*, speaking of their own columnist, said, "Richler is a *real* writer, which is rare, and even a *good* writer, which is rarer still. In fact, one is tempted to call him a *great* writer." In the United States the review in the *New York Times* lauded the sense of life he "crammed into his book so much in the way of gags, social satire, suspense, stinging dialogue, sports and political trivia, and flashbacks," but its partner notice in the *New York Times Book Review*, to which he was now a contributor, had a harsh criticism, especially for a writer who sought to define his own particular landscape in his work. "It's as if a rich and unusual body of fictional material had become a kind of prison for a writer who is condemned to repeat himself ever more vehemently and inflexibly." Within a few months M&S would be ordering a second and then a third printing of the novel.

The Canadian media lined up at his door, in city or country. A young freelance journalist named Sandra Martin, obliged to make her way to the house in Austin via public bus, arrived in the early afternoon. She remarked at once how Richler "hates being observed," and found him "shy, uncomfortable, polite, and taciturn," a "highly intelligent man with invisible yet ultra sophisticated antennae absorbing every nuance, every sound, for later processing." Their interview, repeatedly interrupted by his refilling his glass with vodka and grapefruit juice—at each refill, he would offer her one—was typically trying; he brushed aside personal questions with the "baleful stare of a recalcitrant bull wearily steaming up to defend his turf." But when she explained that she was reluctant to drink because she was pregnant, he spoke warmly about being a father, confessing his own fears for the health of each newborn. "How could we be so lucky again?" he said about his and Florence's anxieties. Sandra Martin's piece was one of the best about a novelist who produced works that "are in fact the charts of a very complex man."

He could be that way, especially with strangers: irritable and ill at ease, hating the public process, whether or not he appeared to court it at times, lashing out in defence of his private and imaginative space. He also knew his own worth. Invited to become an Officer of the Order of Canada, he replied that since Margaret Laurence, Hugh MacLennan and Gabrielle Roy had all been invested at the higher level of companion, being offered the lesser honour struck him more as "put-down than salute." When a TV interviewer kept asking bland questions that had been prepared by a producer, he scolded him for not formulating his own thoughts. At readings he could subject an audience to minutes of censorious silence if a question struck him as rude or banal— "You're just being a boor, aren't you?" he replied to one such questioner—and as a guest speaker before another group he insulted his host for taking too long with her introduction. At a party he infuriated a pulp fiction novelist by suggesting that if he really cared about literature he would stop writing. Even his friend Peter Gzowski, widely considered the most gifted interviewer on Canadian radio, said he had to brace himself before an on-air encounter, citing his stern intelligence.

The presence of Florence did not always guarantee improved behaviour. But she continued to try to alleviate his discomfort, a role she did not relish. From time to time she would even coach her husband on how not to look "like this great patriarchal figure who's going to terrify everybody." Mordecai would offer to force a smile on his face before stepping on stage or into a room; Florence would tell him that there was no need to go *that* far. His blank stare on greeting strangers—an inheritance, perhaps, of Lily's inwardness—she could do nothing to temper.

But there were equal numbers of stories of the courteous, kindly Richler who, besides adoring his wife and family and being an amusing, loyal friend, could be as solicitous of pregnant journalists and secretaries at publishing houses, and who worried about accidentally ignoring only vaguely remembered faces from the old neighbourhood. He had no small talk, and was a quick, confident reader of strangers, an enemy of sacred cows, a severe judge of the crime of being a phony. Peter Dale Scott, Frank Scott's son and the poet diplomat he had known in London in the fifties, ran into him decades later. "Why did you sell out?" Richler asked him almost immediately. Scott took it as an accusation that he had forsworn the risky vocation of artist for a career in External Affairs, but Richler could deliver mischief with the deadpan expression of one of the Borscht Belt comedians he adored. At a reading at Harbourfront in Toronto, he announced to the crowd that, having recently studied the language, he planned to read from the Albanian translation of his latest book that evening. "Just kidding," he had to assure the stunned audience. He also wasn't above switching shoes left outside hotel doors for polishing, or answering to another name in order to obtain a free limo ride back to a hotel. Even his public drinking, so often remarked by journalists, contained an element of legend building—Richler the boozer and smoker, unfettered and unapologetic—with the reality at home with friends and family a great deal more benign.

A complex man, and one who had his off-days. Accounts by those who knew him would remain consistently admiring and loving; accounts by those who stepped into his path, even with the best intentions, or simply failed his instant test of character, would remain mixed and sometimes angry or disappointed. One young fan who tried his luck in London that year was Nigel Horne, a reporter working for the *Evening Standard*. A friend employed by Richler's literary agent Deborah Rogers had smuggled him an advance copy of *Joshua Then and Now*, and when the author flew to England to promote the book, Horne decided to ambush him at his hotel. Standing in the lobby of the Dorchester, the personable Horne, recognizing the distinctive countenance, introduced himself with a comment about how much he had loved the novel. Richler told him that if that was the case he would buy him a whisky. They retired to the hotel bar.

Nigel Horne was also a working journalist, and Richler had sympathy for his fellows. He too was still picking up work, especially when the subject matter appealed to him. Just before *Joshua* appeared, he invited Brian Mulroney to lunch at the Ritz, on the expense account of the American magazine *Geo,* which had commissioned him to do another piece about Quebec. Mulroney, having failed in his 1976 bid for the Conservative Party leadership, was working in the private sector, but according to mutual friends he knew "where the horses were buried." Richler found the businessman-politician a worthy lunch partner: a bilingual small-town Quebecer who had risen by his own wiles; a natural-born flatterer and schmoozer who was also savvy and, indeed, free with indiscreet anecdotes. At the Ritz, Mulroney predicted a 60/40 victory for the "no"—the federalist—side in the upcoming referendum. When they met again for lunch later that year, at the Mount Royal Club, an institution that had once gone out of its way to refuse Sam Bronfman membership—later Charles Bronfman, his son, was granted entry along with, as Richler put it, "a number of toilet-trained French Canadians"—Mulroney arranged a private room where they could talk more freely.

Though he had encountered Pierre Elliott Trudeau occasionally, and had lately sparred with René Lévesque, Richler's acquaintance with Brian Mulroney inaugurated a new level of engagement with the Canadian political classes. (In England, he and Florence had attended dinner parties with politicians Michael Foot and Nye Bevan.) The Townships hosted many leading federal politicians—Quebec remained a breeding ground for the most sophisticated and best-positioned players on the national scene—and his instinct, as always, was to meet them at least once, preferably over cigars and Scotch, so that he could size each one up as a politician, and as a man. They, in turn, wanted to meet the notorious Mordecai Richler, despite his track record of not suffering the pompous or dishonest lightly. Encounters, via friends and contacts, almost fell into his lap; he rarely cultivated relationships. Rather, he enjoyed being welcomed into homes and clubs otherwise out of bounds for working-class Jews from St. Urbain Street, and the majority of Canadian novelists. His own imaginative domain was increasingly those places and people, if only to drop his déclassé protagonists into their midst, exposing one and all to satiric scrutiny. Any club that excluded Sam Bronfman was a club he wanted to infiltrate. All the better if he could do so at the invitation of an entertaining raconteur and stylish political operator, and with a snifter of cognac in hand.

Soon Richler would be reporting on the machinations that would bring Mulroney first to party and then to federal power, and by the end of the decade he would be breaking bread with both Conservative senators and Liberal cabinet ministers, along with various backroom power brokers, as well as being a censorious presence at political conventions of various stripes. A few of these people, including Liberal minister Don Johnston and Conservative senator John Lynch-Staunton, became lasting friends.

Brian Mulroney called the referendum perfectly. On May 20, Quebecers voted 59.6 percent "No" and 40.4 percent "Yes" to a 107-word question about whether the province should pursue a path to sovereignty. Trudeau, having "risen again like Lazarus" in February—voters had returned him to power with a majority government after almost a year out of office—was gracious in victory. He spoke of the collective cost of the referendum, "the broken friendships, the strained family relationships, the hurt pride." Lévesque, on stage after the loss, told the faithful (in both languages), "If I understand you correctly, you are saying, *À la prochaine*." For Richler, watching the coverage on television with Florence, the gaunt, hoarse-voiced Lévesque's gravely defiant response to the outcome was a stirring moment. He was reminded why he continued to like the people's tribune, despite their recent dispute. Lévesque was authentic, a man with a common touch and widespread sympathies. Had politics not come between them—and Richler, like many others, did not like the sound of "*à la prochaine*," especially after such a "silly, sneaky smart, or downright ugly" campaign—he might well have sought Lévesque as a drinking (and smoking) companion.

While Quebec voted to stay in Canada, the Canadiens, cruising towards their sixth straight Stanley Cup, suffered a shocking early exit from the playoffs. In early April Richler had travelled to Connecticut for the elimination round between Montreal and the expansion Hartford Whalers. He wasn't there to see the Habs; the magazine *Inside Sports* had commissioned him to cover the presumed final days of the epic career of Gordie Howe, then a fifty-two-year-old grandfather sharing the same ice as his two sons. The night before the game that would, it was widely assumed, eliminate Hartford, Richler played a few hands of poker at the team hotel with Habs coach Claude Ruel and the very same Toe Blake he had interviewed for the long-vanished *Herald*, sneaking into the Forum as a teenager. The next afternoon he took a taxi to the suburb where Howe lived. The interview was futile, with both men enduring long pauses, and about the only subject that seemed to interest the hockey great was his Amway products business. Howe offered him a ride back into the city. "I understand you write novels?" he finally asked.

Hockey and politics did not keep him from promoting the best-selling *Joshua Then and Now*. In the fall, however, the shortlists for the Governor General's Award in Canada and the Booker Prize in the U.K. revealed that he had no hope of getting any extra boost for the book. In England the Booker jury did select its first Canadian since Richler himself had been shortlisted back in 1971 (aside from Brian Moore in 1976, regarded as Irish on that side of the Atlantic), but it was Alice Munro's *The Beggar Maid* that was nominated, along with six other titles, and William Golding won for *Rites of Passage.* In Canada, where the "GGs" remained quirky, the jury shortlisted only three titles. Leon Rooke and Susan Musgrave lost out to the poet George Bowering for his historical novel *Burning Water.* Being Canadian, Richler wasn't eligible for either the Pulitzer or the National Book Awards in the United States. But two writers he much admired were being feted across the border: Philip Roth was shortlisted for the Pulitzer in 1980 for *The Ghost Writer* and the National Book Award celebrated *The World According to Garp.*

Joshua Then and Now continued to display allegiance to all three literary nations. It was a deeply Montreal novel that used London-learned satiric techniques in the service of an imperative born out of postwar New York Jewish creative ferment. It was also a "New World" comedy, a hilarious post-colonial take on Canada with a debt to Dickens and Waugh, Babel and the Talmud in about equal proportions. The social canvas Richler wanted to fill and the satiric battles he wished to fight—the alliances needing to be maintained and the balances kept—all these factors made for ongoing complexity. Such dynamics also obliged constant rethinking of what exactly "his" kind of novel should look like. Given the singularity of his voice, the process took time and exacted a toll, especially in a Canadian context. Richler wasn't simply unlike the majority of Canadian authors, including the group fast becoming dominant that had lately emerged out of Southern Ontario—Margaret Atwood and Alice Munro, Robertson Davies and Timothy Findley; he wasn't like them at all.

In September he was invited to show his high-profile "difference"—Robert Fulford aptly describing him as "the loyal opposition to the governing ideas of Canadian culture"—at a seminar on the future of the Canadian film industry in Toronto. He did not disappoint. Canadian filmmakers, he declared, were going about their business with "unbelievably bad taste larded with greed." There were exceptions, but "most of what we've produced here is embarrassing even in its intentions." The Canadian Film Development Corporation, which had paid him well for his *The Street* script and helped float *Duddy Kravitz*, should not be financing crap. As for the crap-movie producers themselves, they were nothing more than "snivelling little greasers." The greasers did not take kindly to his biting and irreverent remarks, especially given that they were delivered during the annual "Festival of Festivals," meant in part to showcase all the *good* things happening in Canadian movies. Robert Lantos, the thirty-one-year-old Hungarian-born producer who had scored a hit two years earlier with the erotic film *In Praise of Older Women*, attended the scolding. But he had reason to feel exempt, having already optioned *Joshua* for the movies.

In December Richler answered a letter from Avrum that contained an olive branch from his mother. "You say Maw might be inclined to heal the rift, if I apologize to her," he wrote. "But what am I to apologize for? She's the one who decided not to see me any more, and when I kept sending the kids around, scared them off, telling Emma I was crazy." He confessed to "feeling awfully sad about the whole affair," mostly because "she must be very lonely indeed and I am in a position to make her life easier financially." But he was glad that Avrum was keeping an eye on things. "And, to come clean," he continued, "you baffle me too. Last time you came to Montreal you phoned me in the country, you wanted to talk before the Byng reunion, but when I dropped my work to drive into town early you were no longer available. You didn't want to talk after all." The letter had opened with an emotive sigh: "Avrum, Avrum, what can I say?" The answer—nothing, for now— ensured a continuing distance between the siblings. Mordecai did promise again to visit Newfoundland, one of the few provinces he had not seen, and so finally meet Avrum's children, Dvorah and Jonathan.

Lily herself was soon heard from again. Her mode of communication was not a private letter or tape; it was an interview with "Leah" Rosenberg, published in the *Canadian Jewish News* in spring 1981. "I made a decision," she said of her famous son. "I want nothing from him—no money, no contact. I don't need it. I never read his books. Or see his films. I put him out of my life. . . . He knows I'm proud and strong. I don't think about him anymore. . . . I don't even know where he lives," she added untruthfully, "maybe in Montreal." And what was the occasion for these remarkable utterances by the seventy-seven-year-old, described as "busy, busy, with letters, phone calls, invitations, calls from reporters, critics, and readers"? As Lily explained, "My publisher sent him my book. But there was no reaction. Not even an acknowledgement."

But Richler had read some version of his mother's manuscript a full decade before—the "unpublishable" junk he told Florence she needn't bother with. By Lily's own account, she had only begun the memoir in 1974 and had spent years revising it, encouraged by "helpful editors" including Mel Hurtig, who thought the chaotic text was important. In the end Hurtig didn't offer to issue *The Errand Runner: Memoirs of a Rabbi's Daughter*, by "Leah" Rosenberg, but he did help her to hire a freelance editor who rendered the manuscript publishable. As far as Lily was concerned, John Wiley & Sons in Toronto bought the book on its own merits. "I never mentioned our connection," she told the *Canadian Jewish News*, "and made them promise not to mention it." The illogic of that remark seemed of a piece with the memoir itself. To "protect the reticent members" of her family, all names were changed: Moses Richler became "Aaron Wilensky," Avrum and Mordecai were "Ari" and "Moshe." This despite the inclusion of photographs. A photo taken at Ste. Agathe, *circa* 1944, was captioned "Leah" and "Moshe," with Lily and Mordecai clearly in the frame. The portrait of the Rosenberg clan taken on the occasion of the rebbe's seventieth birthday was also reproduced, with Lily's own siblings likewise assigned other names.

The Errand Runner tells of Lily/Leah's boundless love for her rabbi father, "a lion of a man, a king of Israel," crafting him as blameless in the misfortune of her arranged marriage to Aaron Wilensky and declaring herself his eternal "errand runner," or assistant. Forgetting her actual age when the marriage was arranged, she speaks of Aaron/Moses as a "truck driver" in his family's firm. "He was sexually vibrant," she confides. The memoir makes little of her own decision to end the marriage, and nothing of how she went about it; Julius Frankel is mentioned only indirectly, and in a context well away from 5257 St. Urbain where her younger son had witnessed her having sex with him. Much space is devoted to her beloved boys, until they become troublesome men. "Then enter intermarriage!" "I had long ago abandoned the hope of the rabbinate," she admits. "When Moshe declared he would follow a literary occupation, I was not surprised. We were after all a literary family." But her pride in Ari, a successful optometrist with a Ph.D., is equal. "Always when I am greeted with the exclamation 'I read about your famous son,' my retort is inevitably 'Which one?'"

Leah/Lily, still living in a four-room flat within her "former rooming house on a quiet little street in downtown Montreal," told the *Canadian Jewish News* of the "curious estrangement" with Mordecai (or "Mordechai," according to her). The breach had left her "disturbed and baffled." She suspected he was under the false impression that she had wanted to interfere in his life. "He lived a different life, with his family and his friends, and I began to feel I wasn't wanted." Now, though, as she "reaps the warm plaudits of friends and readers," Leah Rosenberg was revived. She was up at 5:30 every morning, "reading and typing, jotting memories of her struggling years, seeing people, answering fan mail and calls, and most times still clacking away at 2 or 3 into the following morning." And her new book? Tales of a rooming house. "It's so funny I'm laughing all the way to the typewriter."

Richler was slow to read *The Errand Runner*. In the end, he paged through it, without comment about its contents. Even after a decade of work, Leah Rosenberg's memoir remained a mess, and it had found a publisher because of who her son was, and in the hope of what it might say about him. On the second count, there had to be disappointment: *The Errand Runner* is devoid of insights, positive or negative, into the adult "Moshe" or "Mordechai," almost as if Lily was still waiting by her door in case he knocked. Its author bears almost no resemblance to the furious, fragile woman who wrote her sons those excoriating letters. What merit there is, aside from the hidden poignancy that underlies virtually every sentence, relates to what a review described as its "touching" quality: "touching in the naïveness with which Leah Rosenberg describes her willingness to be a slave to her Judaism, to be submissive to her father who deprived her of the higher learning she could obviously have enjoyed and mastered."

Richler certainly had strong views about his mother's book, but he said nothing. Once, he might have expressed them, glancingly and jokingly, in a quippy letter to Bill Weintraub or Brian Moore. That amounted to all the intimacy he sought with most people, except for Florence and, earlier, his parents. But he was no longer the letter writer he had once been. Living in Spain, France and England for the better part of twenty years had made him a garrulous correspondent. He was younger then, far from home and making fundamental decisions about his life; he had important things to say, and took the time to write them down. Back in Canada, with far less of urgent importance to relay or thrash out, as in the case of his arguments about religion with his father, he could simply pick up the phone or, better, arrange to meet for a drink. (Later, as the technology allowed, he would become a master of the funny short fax—the perfect medium for his wit.) Except for business notes to Deborah Rogers in London and the occasional letter to one of the Teds in California, he rarely corresponded any longer. There were obviously exceptions, of which his 1976 letter to Lily Rosenberg, a document he typed out, revised, typed out again, and then copied before mailing to her, was the most remarkable. His children were starting to scatter to New York, London and Toronto, and now provided other, if still infrequent occasions for him to write. In October he sent a birthday note to Emma, then studying in the south of France. The unwitting bearer of this paean to private happiness was also its subject.

October 20.81
Emma, dear, Happy Birthday!
For this birthday, your 20th, I am sending you (under separate cover) your mother. My beautiful and cherished wife. Please handle with care & affection & devotion, as she has always handled you.

Special Confidential Instructions for Mother-Gift-Care.
1. For the duration of her stay, please keep the Mother in a warm, clean, cheerful hotel. No flea-bag, please. The Mother tends to wilt in flea-bags.
2. For best results, it is recommended to keep the Mother dust-free and please remember to WATER AT LEAST ONCE A DAY. Preferably with dry white wine, vintage stuff.
3. You will find that nothing improves Mother-Disposition more than a regular ration of cheese, the smellier the better.
4. Walk the Mother regularly to improve her appetite.
5. You will find that she responds well to damp old churches and crumbling castles.

Faults to watch out for.
1. The Mother is inclined to save pennies, a failing that shd not be encouraged. Eat well, drink well. Spoil her. She deserves it.
2. The Mother suffers from a gardening obsession. Do not let her rake anybody else's leaves. Be firm on this point.

Useful hints.
No bus trip or excursion is too good for the Mother. Take her

to Arles. Take her everywhere. Do not let her protest that such-and-such a trip or tour costs too much. If she reacts violently, pop some cheese into her mouth. (Carry cheese with you at all times.)

Enjoy yourselves, both of you, I love you both.
Sincerely yours,

The Father

A month later, with The Mother safely returned, he did type a longish letter to Deborah Rogers. Once done with business matters, he summarized his domestic circumstance for his English agent, another professional contact whom he and Florence had come to think of, along with her composer husband, Michael Berkeley, as a close friend. The summary, delivered in accidental free verse, sang no less fully of his contentment, mingled with native melancholy at the way his settled life was playing out. First he mentioned an upcoming trip to London and then Paris in February, and Florence's own recent visit to Emma in Aix-en-Provence.

But these days this is a very quiet house.
Em's in France.
Marf's studying in NY state.
Daniel's in Toronto.
Noah lives around the corner but pops up usually when we
are sitting down to dinner.
Only Jake's at home.

II

MY FATHER'S LIFE

Big novels weren't the only kind Richler wanted to write. They were the kind of fiction that emptied him, as though he had to pour all of himself into each one and then wait to be filled back up. That took time and involved, as Florence observed, much silence, anxiety and brooding about whether he had anything more to say. No longer a writer of short stories, and without any ideas for a non-fiction book, he inaugurated the 1980s with a protracted phase of tending to his existing cultural properties. Some authors, drained by the writing experience or else anxious to leave the world of the last novel behind in favour of the next, happily hand their books over to others for adaptations for screen, stage or radio. Not Richler. He had learned early on that the residual income from a novel or even a short story could far surpass what he was originally paid for it. Even when the adaptations didn't turn out well, they still earned him additional income. (*The Wordsmith*, a kind of salvaging of his never-produced script for *The Street*, had finally aired on the CBC the previous September, sluggish and dull, despite the gifted Claude Jutra as director and the talented young actor Saul Rubinek as would-be novelist Mervyn Kaplansky.) Adapting his own work also allowed him to keep some control over it. Whether he was always the best person to translate his words to screen, in terms of producing a filmable script, was never discussed. He knew how to write movies, and certainly knew the material; who could do a better job?

Within a year of publishing *Joshua,* he was busy writing no fewer than three scripts based on the novel. The savvy young producer Robert Lantos, who had attended McGill and lived just behind the Chateau off Sherbrooke Street, and his business partner, fellow Montrealer Stephen J. Roth, had optioned the novel for $150,000, and they agreed to pay him the same amount again to write the script. They also struck a separate deal to simultaneously film a CBC television miniseries version. Richler decided to share that writing job with his old friend Ted Kotcheff. The involvement of the versatile Kotcheff, whose latest credit, the action film *Rambo: First Blood*, starring Sylvester Stallone, had bumped his fee into the million-per-film range, gave *Joshua* an international credibility boost. At around the same time, the CBC commissioned a five-hour radio version of the novel. That meant two hours on the big screen, three and a half on the small, plus a full five on radio. If the relative speed of the writing of *Joshua* meant he had lived with his cast of characters for only two years, he was now back with them for another, possibly longer spell. *Horseman* hadn't recycled as easily—a stalled film, no radio adaptation—but *Jacob Two-Two* had already been made into a movie, a dramatic reading and a play. The director, Stephen Katz, who had done the inaugural *Jacob Two-Two* at the Young People's Theatre in Toronto in 1981, would oversee the radio version of *Joshua.*

But Richler was also willing to work for little or nothing on another residual project. Eighteen months earlier, the Montreal impresario Sam Gesser had approached him with an exciting idea: a full-scale musical based on *Duddy Kravitz.* He was delighted. Though never a big fan of plays, he loved musicals, especially the rowdier ones that brought to mind the burlesques his father had taken him to as a teenager. In an extreme example of his sliding scale, he sold the option to the affable, much-liked producer and fellow St. Urbain Street boy for $1, knowing that Gesser was about to incur huge costs in the high-risks game of mounting musical theatre. Then Richler, perhaps not wanting the spectre of another Lionel Chetwynd, signed on to do the libretto on spec. To write the music and lyrics, Gesser hired and paid the respected

Broadway team of Mike Stoller and Jerry Lieber, responsible for songs like Elvis Presley's "Jailhouse Rock" and Peggy Lee's "Is That All There Is?" He also convinced director and choreographer Brian Macdonald, whose production of Gilbert and Sullivan's *The Mikado* had been a hit at the Stratford Festival in southern Ontario, to direct. Stratford, in fact, mentioned *Duddy Kravitz* the musical as a possible feature of its 1980 season. That proved to be wildly premature. But by 1983 there was confident talk that it might first open in Berlin, and then premiere in Canada in Edmonton the following April before touring North America.

"Technically speaking, as I used to brag at college, I'm a bastard." If Lily Rosenberg read the August 1982 issue of *Esquire*, she may well have described her son as one. There it was, in glossy, wide-circulation print; the angry story of his childhood and youth, and her affair with the unnamed "refugee in the spare bedroom." *Esquire* had asked him to write a piece about his father, and after many drafts he broke a fifteen-year silence about Moses Richler to deliver an electrifying, intensely felt memorial. "After the funeral," it began, "I was given my father's *talis*, his prayer shawl, and (oh my God) a file containing all the letters I had written to him while I was living abroad, as well as carbon copies he had kept of the letters he had sent to me." From that point on, "My Father's Life" simulated the variety of funeral eulogy that has mourners squirming and praying it will soon be over.

He reported his "horrendously embarrassing" demands for money and his recognition that, as a rebellious boy, "I embarrassed him." But the more painful revelations were of Lily's ritual humiliations of her husband, often in front of his sons, and the reality that nearly everyone condescended to him, including the elegant German-Jewish boarder who sang opera arias in the tub. Then, finally, came the inevitable: "After his marriage to my mother blew apart, he moved into a rented room. Stunned, humiliated. St. Urbain's cuckold." "I'm returning your mother's love letters to her," he quoted his stepmother, Sarah. "The ones he found that time. You know, from the refugee."

"Vengeance was mine," Richler wrote in "My Father's Life," of telling his father back in 1942 or 1943 that he had witnessed his grandfather Shmarya Richler cheat a customer at the scrapyard. Vengeance, or retribution, drove the essay as well. He had to know he was behaving cruelly towards his mother, but for her to respond to his "Dear Maw" letter with a book as dishonest as *The Errand Runner* obliged a public correction, for the simple value of speaking the truth.

But, typically, he also spared neither the father he had come to love, nor himself. Moses Richler had been afraid of his own father, his wife, even his younger son, who ate bacon and took streetcars on the Sabbath. "But nobody was ever afraid of Moses Isaac Richler," that son wrote. "He was far too gentle. . . . I was charged with appetite, my father had none." Moses was a man who "never talked to me about anything. Not his own boyhood. His feelings. Or his dreams." A man who never got to "see Paris. Never read Yeats. Never stayed out with the boys drinking too much." Also, who didn't seem to enjoy being with his own family— not "my mother, my brother, me." But then the unexpected happened: "My father became my son," he wrote, of supporting him financially. "On visits home, I took him to restaurants. I bought him treats." And Moses, showing his own empathy, would fill soda bottles with Scotch whisky for his boy at family gatherings. "There'll be nothing for you to drink there," he would explain, "and I know you." But Mordecai Richler knew himself too, and he wondered if Moses, rather than being passive and sweet-natured, had actually been a coward. Echoing the striking self-lacerations in the unpublished *Back to Ibiza*—evidence of how dark his moods could occasionally get—he called himself out for his failings. "Like me, who would travel miles to avoid a quarrel. Who tends to remember slights—recording them in my mind's eye—transmogrifying them—finally publishing them in a code more accessible than my father's. Making them the stuff of fiction." In the closing paragraph he admitted he had committed another crime:

waiting too long to fly back to Canada to take Moses to the Catskills to see Grossinger's resort and New York for a couple of shows. "The next time I flew to Montreal it was to bury him."

———————

That July, Richler welcomed the *Globe and Mail* to Lake Memphremagog. Officially, the occasion was the radio adaptation of *Joshua*, set for the fall. Though careful to show him sipping Rémy-Martin and smoking a Schimmelpenninck on the patio of his "summer residence," the journalist, arriving with more an agenda than an assignment, was most interested in resurrecting the 1970s debates about his antinationalist journalism. A professor of English at Carleton was quoted as saying that "he kicked Canada in the groin" and that, when he taught one of his novels, "I make it very clear that Richler is an Americanized Canadian, that he's not writing from the same kind of stance as most other Canadian novelists; he is, after all, on the board of directors for *America's* Book-of-the-Month Club." To this apparent zinger, Richler was allowed to respond. "I don't think in categories, but I am a Canadian. There are a lot of foolish people out there and I'm not running for office. . . . I didn't come into this world licensed, and there's no reason anyone has to applaud." State-sponsored mediocrity aside, he wanted it made clear that he believed Canada had many excellent writers: "Alice Munro, Mavis Gallant, Margaret Atwood, Margaret Laurence and Robertson Davies are just a few."

Anglo-Canadians weren't the only ones who felt pricked. *Le Devoir* ran an opinion piece that summer titled "*Le Dénigreur venu du froid.*" "The Disparager Who Came in from the Cold" chastised the "Anglo-Montreal novelist" for engaging in his favourite pastime the previous weekend in the *New York Times*: "poking at the pride of Montrealers." Richler's short piece, for the sports section, had decried the decline of local teams and mocked the PQ for obliging baseball fans by law to order a *hambourgeois* instead of a hamburger in a ballpark, the unpopular Olympic Stadium (the "Big O"). Lévesque's deputy minister used a lecture at Harvard to denounce what he saw as this Quebec-bashing. The United States would "know us better," Jacques-Yvan Morin asserted, were it not that "the person transmitting the message from Quebec may have a particular axe to grind," and that the article "by Mr. Mordecai Richler, contained a measure of venom against Quebec with which it would be difficult to compete." In reply, Richler called Morin a "silly bugger," pointing out that by repeating his jibes in such a prestigious setting he had granted them, and their author, fresh voice.

His own unwillingness to forget was becoming, if not greater— his constancy of character, from childhood through to middle years, astounded everyone who knew him for long—then more pronounced. The undertones of anti-Semitism worried him a great deal; he pointed out that the Jewish population of Quebec had been reduced by fifteen thousand, the "first to pack their bags" being "young university graduates, most of them bilingual, not all of them fleeing their mothers." That same year the nation-alist Saint-Jean-Baptiste Society began to lobby for a proper monument for "one of its philosophical progenitors," the Abbé Lionel Groulx. Groulx, who had died in 1962, had already appeared on a stamp, and had a Montreal subway station named after him. For Richler, this was plenty for an openly anti-Semitic, fascist-leaning cleric who once wrote of the Jew, "We must also con-sider his innate passion for money. A passion often monstrous and one that removes all scruples from him." Then, in 1982, Francis Simard—one of the FLQ members who kidnapped and murdered Pierre Laporte, for which he had spent a decade a prison—resurfaced with a memoir. At a press conference hosted by the Saint-Jean-Baptiste Society, Simard called the execution of Laporte "a decision of sincerity and conviction" that, once taken, was done with humane swiftness. Richler, busy clipping articles and storing them in folders, was tracking the history that some Quebecers were deciding to forget.

———

That October he took a break from Quebec. "We are going to Africa—yes, Africa—(me, on assignment for Signature mag)—on safari—yes—and en route we will fly to London and be there for five days," Richler wrote to his agent Deborah Rogers. *Signature*, a glossy magazine out of Los Angeles, was offering to send him and Florence on a luxury safari through the Great Rift Valley and the Masai Mara game reserve. He had run into André Deutsch in the Knopf offices in New York a few months before, and accepted his old publisher's invitation to stay with him in Fulham. He and Florence had dinner one evening with Deutsch, his wife, and his first editor, Diana Athill. While in London he had met up with Alan Maclean, his editor at Macmillan and the younger brother of the Soviet spy Donald Maclean, for drinks. With Maclean about to leave his position, Richler was thinking of changing publishers again, on the advice of Bob Gottlieb. But he did discuss his newest "between novels project" with him—an anthology of modern humour.

Mordecai and Florence landed in Nairobi. They were joined by their safari partners: Bob Shapiro and his wife Sandi, and Ted Kotcheff and his new spouse, Laifun Chung. At Richler's request, Bob Shapiro had brought a recording of wild animal calls put together by the Warner Brothers sound department. On their first night in camp, he played the tape outside the Richler tent, causing Florence some alarm. Other nights the disturbances were real; especially surprising were the baboons urinating on the canvas to assert territorial claims. Cooks prepared meals and crews made and unmade the camp each evening and morning. For eleven days, guides drove the couples from site to site, where they spotted giraffes, waterbuck, elephants, wildebeests, a pride of lions, cheetahs and leopards, hippos and crocodiles. "It's the same everywhere," he said to Florence as they watched hyenas tearing into the corpse of a fresh kill, a remark closer to his view of human nature than most of what he had ventured in glossy print. "Gazelles, gazelles," he wrote in *Signature*, attempting a nature-induced swoon, "breaking into a trot and, if alarmed, literally flying across the flat open country." "Safari" benefited only once from a dry Richler observation that the whole place was basically "a meat rack." It was otherwise bland stuff, the writer on vacation as well.

Only that wasn't quite the case. Even in the company of good friends, Richler still hated flying and still hated the commotion of travel. The trips were mostly for Florence, whose inclusion he often built into the deals he made, and who thrilled to each new experience. Her delight, in turn, pleased him perhaps more than anything else, and made these "work holidays" endurable.

"I think I've got leprosy," he joked with Deborah Rogers upon his return. "Or maybe Bubonic plague. Certainly I have come home with a skin ailment." He complained of waking up at 4:30 a.m. and being ready for dinner and bed by mid-afternoon. "This is ridiculous, this jet lag business." But the Richlers would be back in England in the spring, for a literary festival, and then off on another paid trip. Down the Nile, perhaps. "Depends on Signature mag," he explained, "my travel agent without equal."

In the meantime, he was busy "working non-stop on the anthol. and the essays right now." *The Best of Modern Humour* had already been purchased by Knopf in the States and M&S in Canada. It would also be a BOMC book, under the stewardship of chairman Al Silverman, ensuring exposure and sales. Club jurors could not submit their own books for consideration, but editing an anthology was different. He already had a prospective list of sixty or so contributors, and was promising a 5,000-word introduction. In the same letter he asked his British editor "What about the Monty Python group? Have they published anything?"

By the following summer the book was finished (without Monty Python). "It had to make me laugh, sometimes at seven o'clock in the morning, before my first cup of coffee, which may have been playing dirty pool," he wrote of his criterion for selecting a story or excerpt. The anthology includes some classics—from P.G. Wodehouse and Damon Runyon, Groucho Marx and Evelyn Waugh—along with a selection from literary icons: Saul Bellow and Joseph Heller, Eudora Welty and John Cheever. The work of friends such as Terry Southern and Philip Roth, Wilfrid Sheed and John Mortimer, Art Buchwald and Beryl Bainbridge gave the book a good modern slant, alongside many New York, and *New Yorker*, staples: Woody Allen and Fran Lebowitz, Calvin Trillin and Russell Baker. His two decades in England resulted in the inclusion of the then-neglected great Flann O'Brien and the less and less funny V.S. Naipaul; and from Canada exactly two countrymen—Stephen Leacock, who had died in 1944, and Bruce McCall, who lived in the States and published in the *New Yorker*. Leacock, at least, was the lead selection. Ted Allan, who had also published the occasional humour piece in the *New Yorker*, was sore at being excluded. For Allan it was second time unlucky; though Richler's earlier anthology, *Canadian Writing Today*, had been littered with the work of friends, nothing by him had been featured there either.

In New York, Art Cooper, the newly installed editor of *GQ*, decided he wanted Richler's own version of funny in his magazine. Cooper had once made a casual list of the five best contemporary comic novels, with Joseph Heller. He had named *Catch-22*, but Heller had insisted that Mordecai Richler's *Cocksure* be at the top. Heller might have listed *Joshua Then and Now* as well, if only for the outrageous Old Testament blasphemies from Reuben Shapiro, which seemed of a piece with the novel he was then completing: *God Knows,* the purported deathbed memoirs of King David. For *The Best of Modern Humour*, Richler had opted to excerpt from Heller's more recent *Good as Gold*. With Roth he went for the shock-value jugular, excerpting with the author's encouragement the notorious "Whacking Off" chapter from *Portnoy's Complaint*. Though it had been years since they had seen one another, exchanging only the occasional letter in between, the book provided an excuse for a reunion. Philip Roth, then in a relationship with the actress Claire Bloom, invited the Richlers to dinner in London in spring 1983, when they passed back through the city after another *Signature* assignment in France. He offered to put them up for the night, and later insisted they stop by his other home, outside Kent, Connecticut, next time they drove down to New York.

Wilfrid Sheed, Richler's conspiratorial companion in book selection for BOMC, had first suggested his fellow juror to Art Cooper for the *GQ* gig. The personable Cooper was immediately struck by Richler's appearance; the author, he thought, with his "large Old Testament head, a shaggy, greying mane and the bemused mien of a man who suddenly discovers his socks don't match," personified the "central-casting" image of a writer. Willing to overlook signs that he didn't read *GQ* regularly—Richler was surprised to learn it wasn't a quarterly, as the title suggested—Cooper began the ritual of hosting monthly literary lunches at the Four Seasons for him and Wilfrid Sheed. He couldn't always attend himself, and sometimes sent a junior editor to the legendary power-lunching venue at Park and East 52nd to keep the literary lions company—and take care of the cheque. Adam Gopnik, then in his late twenties, had himself grown up in an apartment in the Chateau on Sherbrooke Street, one of three children of American academics who had taken positions at McGill. Aware as a boy of his famous neighbour, and greatly influenced as a young writer by Richler's work and presence, Gopnik was intimidated to find himself seated at a table with him. He was also awed by how well the older writers talked, and how heartily they lunched.

Wilfrid Sheed, lover of baseball and boxing, Tin Pan Alley and books, was ideal company. Over the course of two or three hours, Gopnik would watch as tables of other magazine and book editors with other writers came and went, their salads and mineral waters half-finished, while his charges, feasting on starters and meaty mains and moving from vodkas to wine to cognacs, held their old-school ground. Gopnik was later hired as an editor by Bob Gottlieb at Knopf, when Richler introduced him.

New opportunities emerged from the monthly BOMC trips to Manhattan, where he met more people and could discuss ideas for pieces. Like assembling an anthology of humour, this was time away from fiction writing, which he had not done since the burst that had produced *Joshua* five years earlier. But New York itself was a lure; he and Florence loved the city, loved staying

with the Gottliebs on East 48th Street and going to favourite restaurants. Expatriate Canadian Lorne Michaels, executive producer of the iconic variety show *Saturday Night Live*, became a
friend, and the Richlers later attended his wedding on Long
Island. Richler even talked about moving to Manhattan, now
that the children were grown up. It helped that he was a comfortable insider, respected and appreciated by a generation of
editors and writers, and that both the yeshiva of the 1960s and
the "Jewy media" of the 1970s and '80s remained sympathetic
cultural forces in the city.

In 1987 he would be one of two Canadians included in
Congregation: Contemporary Writers Read the Jewish Bible, a who's-
who of Jewish novelists, poets and dramatists, including Harold
Bloom, Elie Wiesel, Isaac Bashevis Singer, Cynthia Ozick,
Francine Prose and Gordon Lish. Assigned Deuteronomy, the
book of the Pentateuch telling of the death of Moses, Richler was
in Reuben Shapiro mode: "Certainly our forefathers, gathered in
Moab, this side of Jordan, were a loutish lot, a bunch of good ol'
boys, much given to carousing, wenching, pilfering, fighting and
sacking cities."

Unbeknownst to his Canadian critics, he was known among
his fellow club jurors and New York media in general as an advocate for his homeland, despite the fact that his efforts at convincing, say, the *Times* to pay greater attention to the goings-on in
Quebec or Canada usually met with indifference and time-worn
cracks about the boring neighbour to the north. He also continued to champion Canadian titles for the club, pushing, for example, *The Chinese*, by the *Globe and Mail*'s recent China bureau chief,
John Fraser, as a main selection in late 1981. Friends were rarely
far from his mind. In 1984 he called Bob Shapiro about *Empire of
the Sun*, a manuscript he had just read by J.G. Ballard. Florence
read it too and encouraged him to make the call. Known mostly
for his science fiction, J.G. Ballard had produced a powerful, realistic novel based on his own childhood in the tumult of 1930s
Shanghai. Richler saw its potential as a film right away, even
hoping it might be a project for Jack Clayton, and suggested that

Shapiro inquire about the option. *Empire of the Sun*, directed by Steven Spielberg, was the eventual outcome.

Home Sweet Home, his new collection of essays on Canadian themes, was now ready, with Knopf and M&S set to publish the hardcover in the spring. In the U.K. he had officially ended his brief relationship with Macmillan and moved to the publishing house of Chatto & Windus. But he had not told André Deutsch, who had lately published *Jacob Two-Two,* and put the Richlers up in London, that he wouldn't be getting the next novel. He had asked his agent to break the news. "I've had a letter from Andre D.," he said to Deborah Rogers, "asking about my novel. Obviously, you have been remiss. Or cowardly. Or both. And have not told The Deutsch that I've gone to Chatto." He even jokingly warned her that he would be blaming her so as to make the whole thing easier. "And so . . . I've written to Andre, saying . . . taking your advice, against my better judgement, I have come to terms with Carmen."

Carmen Callil, the feisty Australian director at Chatto, had lately migrated from the House of Virago, publisher of women writers overlooked in a largely male publishing industry, and a key force in the rise and visibility of feminism in England. On paper, the outspoken Callil was not a likely editor to court Mordecai Richler, whom she had first met in the 1960s in the John Snow pub in Soho, then popular with the literary crowd. But Callil had loved *Cocksure* and *Horseman,* and liked him. Deborah Rogers, her close friend, could happily tell him, "Carmen seems to be enormously chuffed that you are on their list, which is gratifying." The pre-sale of the novel in the U.K. was largely due to his desire to see *Home Sweet Home* published there; Chatto would only do the essays if they knew they would later get the novel as well. In Canada, he was able to use the interest of the forceful young editor-in-chief of Penguin Canada, Cynthia Good, to get a separate deal for the paperback edition of the essays without yet committing *Gursky Was Here.* ("$16,000 for essays?" Deborah Rogers asked incredulously from London.) As always, he negotiated his own Canadian deals: he had no need for a local agent, where he could effectively represent himself.

Of course, neither Carmen Callil nor Deborah Rogers, two of
the canniest women in British publishing, had any real idea that
the novel in question still consisted of little more than those same
seventy-five manuscript pages from 1977. Neither had been
involved with Richler during his last bout of publishing agony, the
long birth of *Horseman*. Not that he was obscuring his schedule, or
promising *Gursky* anytime soon. "Off to LA on Friday to meet with
Kotcheff and turn in final final JOSHUA revisions," he had reported
in late February. "They are supposed to begin shooting in July.
From there its NY, and then fabled Edmonton, rehearsal and opening of DUDDY." On April 21 Ted Kotcheff wrote, "Up to page 60
thereabouts. I think the script is quite marvellous—the impossible
love story between two extreme opposites. Then suddenly, the
movie loses its central thrust and its POV [point of view] and
becomes a series of expositional scenes about worthless people."
True to their long friendship, the director did not spare the feelings of his screenwriter, telling him that he had to rethink Acts II
and III, especially the incessant and, to Kotcheff, tiresome attacks
on those worthless Westmount types. Then he dismissed his substantial requests as trifles. "Well, Mordecai," he wrote, "shouldn't
take much to run these changes through the old Underwood."
Richler would keep on revising the script, now three years and a
dozen drafts old, right until the eve of the first day of shooting.

Musical theatre, however, was a bizarre new experience for
him. He knew it was a "very different world from what I am used
to" when one of the songwriters for *Duddy Kravitz* asked him,
"You know Duddy the best. Do you think of him as a baritone or
a tenor?" A reporter attending a press conference announcing
the musical wondered if it might end up another *Yentl*, Isaac
Bashevis Singer's play about a girl pretending to be a boy to study
Torah at a yeshiva, and recently a successful movie starring
Barbra Streisand. "Duddy is not a transvestite," Richler replied,
adding laconically, "I'm really doing this musical because I've
always wanted to spend March in Edmonton." To his surprise, by
early 1984 producer Sam Gesser had put together a $1.4 million
production budget. He'd had the help of Doug Cohen, whom

Richler had first met on their transatlantic crossing in 1950, and of the Edmonton theatre producer Joe Shoctor, the son of a Galician scrap metal dealer who had settled in Alberta. Shoctor, co-founder of the city's Citadel Theatre, made *Duddy Kravitz* part of its 1983–84 subscription season, in advance of a hoped-for tour of nine Canadian cities, and then Broadway. Gesser had his Lieber and Stoller songs and his Richler book, as well as a young Broadway star, Lonny Price, ready to play Duddy. The world premiere was set for April 7.

The month proved a disaster. Richler, away from Florence and Jake for about twenty-seven days too long for his own good, was kept a virtual prisoner in an anonymous hotel room for hours on end, hammering out revisions to the struggling *Duddy Kravitz* musical, while dealing with the vexing *Joshua* script. He'd then wander to the Citadel Theatre only to hear director Brian Macdonald complain about another scene that wasn't working. Evenings, he smoked and drank in the hotel bar, often alone— his closest friend in Edmonton, Mel Hurtig, was a friend no longer. As with Richard Dreyfuss ten years earlier, he got on well with Lonny Price, his young "stage" Duddy, but even the actor, lately of a Stephen Sondheim musical, had reservations about several of the songs he was expected to perform. Over two and a half hours the cast belted out "More, More, More," a showstopper depicting dinner at a Jewish summer resort, and "On Your Toes," delivered by the crippled underworld boss "The Boy Wonder," who danced on his crutches. "You Breathe Out, I Breathe In," sung by Yvette, aspired to be a tender, chart-topping, ballad, while the play's keynote, "Friends," was meant to reaffirm Duddy and Virgil as unlikely amigos. This despite Richler's insistence that the ending, where Duddy forges Virgil's name on a cheque to buy the final parcel of land, thus betraying him and Yvette, survive from the novel. The producers badly wanted him not to forge the cheque, and to be rewarded with the girl: a happy ending, to meet musical audience expectations.

The notion of a quiet debut for *Duddy Kravitz* in Alberta, with weeks to work out the kinks before the national media took notice, had been naïve; if Mordecai Richler was involved in a project, it was national news. Media flew in for the April 7 premiere, and flew back out unimpressed. *Maclean's* was kindest, liking Macdonald's dance choreography and Price's portrayal of Duddy, as well as the first-act renderings of "an extended Yiddish musical joke bursting with the jaunty rhythms" of Stoller and Lieber, and "the salty idiom of Montreal's St. Urbain Street," courtesy of Richler. Much needed to be done—the show's creators, the critic admitted, were "long on talent and short on experience with musicals"—but now, with the pressure of the "premature opening" eased, "Macdonald and Richler can concentrate on making *Duddy* fulfil its abundant promise." Others, including the *Edmonton Journal*, saw less to redeem, and once Brian Macdonald, having stayed an extra two weeks to fix what he could, returned to Stratford, the play was left to float or sink.

Sam Gesser poured more money into it, hiring another director to retool the show for its next stop, Ottawa. Richler remained loyal, to both the production and the producer, dutifully appearing in the capital in June, where, if possible, things only got worse. Booked into the 2,250-seat National Arts Centre, the play sold only a quarter of the tickets and received additional bad reviews. Admitting he had "gambled and lost" as much as a million dollars of his own money, Gesser shut *Duddy Kravitz* down after four nights, cancelling the rest of the tour and any thoughts of Broadway. Blame was spread evenly: a too-elaborate story and a terrible set; a score that was at least four decent songs short of working. "Richler wrote a great book," Sam Gesser told a newspaper, "the music just wasn't there." Richler in turn tried to absorb more of the blame. "The cast was splendid," he said. "The rest of us let them down."

———

A bruising experience like *Duddy Kravitz* would have sent many writers scurrying back to their quiet offices and solitary book projects. But Richler careened from a failed musical to the set of the movie of *Joshua Then and Now*, finally ready to start shooting in July. Robert Lantos and Stephen Roth had raised a respectable budget of nine million dollars. Twentieth Century Fox contributed some in exchange for distribution rights in the States, but the bulk of the cash belonged to the government-funded Telefilm Canada. That meant casting rules. Told he could now have only two Americans in the leads—with *The Apprenticeship of Duddy Kravitz*, six non-Canadians had been cast in key parts—Ted Kotcheff, having failed to woo Dustin Hoffman, opted for James Woods as Joshua and, with Richler's emphatic approval, Alan Arkin as Reuben. He had the sexy Cybill Shepherd, then seemingly on the brink of stardom, ready to play Pauline, but no amount of begging, including a personal appearance in front of Telefilm executives in Ottawa, would win him this exemption. The Quebec actress Gabrielle Lazure was cast instead. Her beauty was patrician, like a WASP princess, but she spoke English with a French accent, hardly right for the daughter of a senator from Westmount. Regardless, and regardless that his script still wasn't right—"There's no climax," the director complained; "Ted, I'm written out," the screenwriter replied, "I've got nothing more to give"—shooting began near Brockville, Ontario, with the St. Lawrence Seaway doubling for Lake Memphremagog and Mordecai and Florence looking on. Among the crew of seventy was twenty-two-year-old Emma, interested in becoming an actor and given a job as one of Kotcheff's assistants. It was a large undertaking: there were 120 speaking parts, and 1,500 more actors were cast as extras over the four-month shoot, with much of the filming done in Westmount and the old Jewish neighbourhood, as well as several days in London.

That filming went about as well as the play rehearsal in Edmonton. The original bad idea of shooting for both feature film and TV, obliging Richler to produce a 150-page script for one and 180 pages for another, got worse when actors were asked to do scenes twice, with different dialogue, and Ted Kotcheff tried to keep two movies in his head. He struggled to get the performances he wanted and had frequent run-ins with his beleaguered producers. Richler, on set for rewrites, sided with his friend and, as per their long custom as the "talent," spent the budget freely and sometimes, in the view of Robert Lantos, frivolously, insisting among other things that they purchase a dozen $600 brandy snifters for a scene in a posh club. Lantos, though, still liked both men, especially Mordecai, with whom he occasionally had drinks, their houses being close by. With the film over budget, Kotcheff and Lantos had to fly down to Hollywood with forty-five minutes of footage to avoid losing control of it to the studio. Alan Arkin delivered as Reuben, but James Woods, a gifted actor, seemed aloof from his character. Worse, Lazure's accent required that she be dubbed, and the love story lacked the climax Kotcheff had kept asking Richler for. Even so, *Joshua Then and Now* was selected for the official competition at the 1985 Cannes Film Festival—the first Canadian film to be so chosen in more than a decade.

Like most successful literary novels, *Joshua* translated problematically to the screen for the same reason it worked so well on the page: the interiority, intimate and engrossing, of its narrative voice. And even Richler could not provide the film with his own abrasive, funny authorial self. Compounding the difficulty were the regular time-shifts—from 1940s Jewish ghetto to 1950s London to 1970s Montreal—so essential to his storytelling, but so awkward, for a variety of reasons, in a script. As with *St. Urbain's Horseman*, he had written a novel all the better for being harder to film.

He was "written out," at least where movies and musicals were concerned. But there was one good-news story for the year. On June 24 Richler sent a note to André Deutsch. "Enclosed, a couple of reviews of JACOB TWO TWO, which really went very well indeed." Unhappy with the original stage adaptation of *Jacob Two-Two*, he had decided to write his own script, work he squeezed into the winter of 1983–84. Director Peter Moss, soon to be a regular collaborator, put together an impressive team to remount the play at Toronto's Young People's Theatre. Dennis Lee, acclaimed author of both the classic long poem *Civil Elegies* for adults, and the wildly popular rhymes for children, *Alligator Pie*, provided the lyrics; composer Philip Balsam put them to Motown-influenced music. "A feast of witty words and singable music," in the estimation of the Toronto *Star*. "It's a delightful 90-minute musical fantasy," the *Globe and Mail* pronounced, "and a faithful rendering of an equally delightful children's book." "It now seems all but definite," Richler told the British publisher of the book, "that it will play at the Old Vic next Easter. I will keep you informed."

III

ONE'S INTENTIONS ARE ALWAYS MUCH GRANDER

"We are well, and had a fine Christmas," he wrote to Deborah Rogers on January 27, 1985, "as I hope you did. And, oh yes, I am now actually finally resolutely at work on my N–V–L. However, I have found this so exhausting, we are off to Morocco on Friday, one week at the fabled La Mamounia Hotel in Marrakech." He could joke about his manic schedule, but there was little to indicate that he had done much work yet on *Gursky Was Here*, and a great deal to suggest that he was weary. Now in his mid-fifties, he continued to operate his one-man cottage industry. While retaining two literary agents—Rogers in London and now Lynn Nesbit in the United States—and with a companion who was his most trusted editor, he remained his own staff and boss. Coming off a four-year stretch of attending to the plays, movies and musicals that his fiction had birthed, there could be no doubt that his will was as fierce as ever, and his work ethic as committed.

But there was reason to wonder about the way he was treating himself. As he had admitted to his brother almost two decades before, alcohol in part fuelled the engine that kept him going at his impossible pace. At the end of each long workday, it took the edge off, dulling worries about deadline pressures and financial concerns. Smoking, too, had been intrinsic to his productivity since his first days on Ibiza. At twenty, he was a young man energized by appetite; at forty, creaks and groans appeared, charted unflinchingly in *Horseman* and *Joshua*. Now, with fifty creeping towards sixty, his stamina was a concern.

Since its inception a dozen years earlier, the shape of *Gursky Was Here*, still largely in his imagination, had evolved from expansive to epic: multiple plot strands spanning centuries and continents would shortly bind together everything from Inuit mythology to the Franklin Expedition, prairie bootlegger lore to tales of the nineteenth-century English demimonde. Though a four-generation family saga formed the narrative spine, the Gursky clan would end up as only part of a huge cast. The research, some of it completed—those trips to the North and the abandoned Martin Hartwell project, the reading he had done on the explorers and adventurers—had to be integrated, a challenge for someone who had previously dismissed "research" in a novel as a dubious concept. *Gursky* promised to demand more of his talent and determination than anything he had yet attempted, and the newness of many of the settings and preoccupations placed the work so far outside his comfort zone that he knew it was unlikely he could replicate the two-year creative explosion that had produced *Joshua Then and Now*. So far, the novel had proven elusive and frustrating, possibly beyond him. But Florence, who had read only the four thousand words published in 1977 in *Saturday Night* offered encouragement during a rare conversation about his work, reminding him of the winding road that had once carried him from the unsuccessful Shalinsky story and novel to *Cocksure*. "Please get on with it," she said.

What he did know about the *Gursky* manuscript was that the exceptional Moses Berger, rather than his commonplace brother Manny, should be the focus (somewhere between 1977 and 1985 Manny disappeared completely) and that the spirit of Solomon Gursky, trickster and magician, so dissatified with the limitations of one life and identity that he created multiple lives and identities for himself, must animate the narrative. Once he had awarded Solomon Gursky pride of place in the title, he felt he "actually finally resolutely" had a novel worth struggling to complete.

He and Florence still fled the Montreal winter in January—a working holiday, naturally, for *GQ*. "Landing in Casablanca," he wrote, "I resisted the impulse to bark 'Round up the usual suspects.'" In Marrakech they settled into La Mamounia, a former palace adjacent to a park, and awoke to the muezzin's call to prayer, and breakfast on a balcony overlooking orange trees. Provided with a driver-guide, they climbed up into the Atlas Mountains, a white-knuckle ride on a "one-lane road falling away to steep sheer cliffs," where they ate pigeon pie and a tajine of lamb with olives and lemons. But after four days of "spicy exotic fare," he admitted, "the stuff of my dreams was now poached eggs on toast or maybe a tuna salad."

Cannes for the premiere of *Joshua Then and Now*, however, was not going to be another paid holiday. The festival extended an invitation to the director and two stars of movies that were selected for competition, sending Kotcheff to France but not Richler. Robert Lantos and Stephen Roth, as producers, would be there at their own expense, to sell the film. He voiced his objection in the *Gazette*. "I'm grateful that the producers, between making such soft-porn blockbusters as 'Heavenly Bodies' and 'Bedroom Eyes,' were able to take time off from their busy schedules to travel first-class to Cannes with their wives." Considering that he was agitating to take time off in order to travel first-class to Cannes with *his* wife, the pot did seem to be calling the kettle black. *Joshua* received a standing ovation at Cannes, but reviews were mixed and the film did poorly at the box office, with the TV version faring no better. Attending the opening at the Toronto Film Festival in September, Richler told a journalist that "nothing ever comes out the way you envisioned. One's intentions are always much grander."

That autumn he got into a larger public spat, calling down the wrath of a province upon his head. While in Edmonton the previous spring for the musical, he had profiled Canada's hockey superstar Wayne Gretzky for the *New York Times Sports Magazine*. The piece appeared in late September 1985, to coincide with the new NHL season—the Oilers were now fresh off their second of four straight Stanley Cups—and it managed to offend most of Alberta. Richler had done only a brief interview with the twenty-four-year-old, at a suburban restaurant located, as he noted, "between welding shops and cinder-block strip joints and used-car lots," but he concluded that Gretzky was "curiously bland" and "incapable of genuine wit or irreverence." Though a big fan of TV soap operas, the athlete never bothered with fiction, having no time, as he explained, "to read stories that aren't real." After dismissing him on these grounds, Richler let rip on Edmonton itself. It was, he declared, "the boiler room" of Canada, with no decent restaurants and "nothing to delight the eye" aside from the "grim religious zealots" who "loom on street corners, speaking in tongues, and intrepid hookers in miniskirts" rapping on the "windows of cars that have stopped for traffic." The locals, he added, were a "truly admirable lot," if only for suffering "an abominable climate as well as isolation from the cities of light."

The *Edmonton Sun* launched an amusing counter-assault by publishing his home phone number in Montreal and encouraging readers to give him a call. More earnestly, Mel Hurtig, never shy about attacking his former friend, used the letters page to declare him a "rude little wimp" and "the perfect obsequious colonial." To the list of Richler crimes he added the scarcity of Canadians in *The Best of Modern Humour* and—unfairly—the under-representation of Canadian selections by the BOMC. Richler did not even try to defend himself, offering only faux contrition: "Edmonton, Edmonton, I apologize. Ever since the article appeared, I have suffered a crisis of conscience, haunted by the damage I may have done. In my nightmares, I see those tens of thousands of tourists who were bound for Edmonton in January, eager to gawk at its architectural marvels and stroll down its elegant boulevards and dine in its fabled restaurants, cancelling out because of the lies I had written." Montreal friends and allies got in on the fun. A *Gazette* sports column titled "Hey, Edmonton: grow up, please" noted that "naughty Mordecai Richler is in trouble." An Aislin cartoon offered a mug shot of the author with

"Write-in CANDIDATE FOR PREMIER OF ALBERTA," beneath a ballot box marked with an X.

Edmontonians had a point. Richler had written another piece in the *New York Times Sports Magazine* the year before, a profile of baseball legend Pete Rose. He had flown to Cincinnati, where Rose was player-manager, and eaten a breakfast of steak, eggs and home fries in his subject's suburban mansion. The athlete, while not yet disgraced by the gambling scandal that would damage his legacy, had already left his first wife and children for a former cheerleader, now pregnant. (She cooked the breakfast.) He also drove a Porsche. Richler may have found his character, if not shallow, then certainly clichéd; he may also have noted the modest charms of the Ohio city. But he hadn't spent a winter month in Cincinnati labouring over a musical that local critics then trashed. And Pete Rose, while verging on scandalous, had a colourful appetite—for steak and cheerleaders, at least—that he found engaging. In other words—unlike boring Wayne Gretzky, great though he was on the ice, this athlete wasn't a WASP Canadian, a group that Richler never grew weary of trashing in print.

"Hey, we're doing a story on Montreal—get me Mordecai Richler," the *Gazette* society columnist Tommy Schnurmacher complained sarcastically when *Vogue*, of all magazines, ran an eighteen-page spread on Canada, with Richler contributing a piece on Montreal. Citing his opening sentence, which declared that the city had been "on a bad roll ever since Nov 15, 1976" (the election of the PQ), Schnurmacher sighed in regret at still another tossed-off rant about the rise of "the intrepid language police or tongue troopers." Frustration with both his high profile as a commentator on Canada abroad, and the nature of his assaults, was at a peak.

All of which made the critical and commercial reception of the aptly named *Home Sweet Home* remarkable. A collection of Richler's journalism about Canada, it contained his fierce eulogy "My Father's Life," and "North of Sixty," his piece on bush pilots, along with most of his lowest antinationalist blows. From the snarls at frozen cheerleaders at Grey Cups and tongue-tied governors general, to the October Crisis "issue-envy" screed, to his abrasive book tours of prairie towns, and right up to the Quebec articles that had got him called a bum by René Lévesque, it was a collection that became a national bestseller in English Canada and was greeted by critics with praise along the lines of "entertainingly vicious," "wonderfully bittersweet," his "wit, irony and imagery" shining through the "perceptive and thoroughly hilarious" prose. On the cover was a caricature, originally from the *New York Review of Books*, depicting him naked, wild-haired and inwardly gazing, an upside-down maple leaf covering his privates.

The relationship between Richler and English Canada was as complex as ever. But it was also solid: an engagement, albeit fractious and occasionally marred by name-calling, about the fundamental issue of building a society that was civil and cultured. If the engagement was largely of his making, if at times he simply could not resist picking a street fight, he also accepted harsh, sometimes fair, sometimes unfair criticism of his writing and himself as part of the cost of forcing his satiric outrage on his country's citizenry.

But as the next few years would prove, French Quebec had never been interested in this kind of relationship, and saw no reason to accept his terms for what constituted a rational, intelligent way of living in the city he really did believe was his home sweet home.

———

"For Jack McClelland," read the dedication, "without whose encouragement this book might never have been written." That was a joke; McClelland, no fan of chronically unprofitable collections of essays, hadn't particularly wanted to publish *Home Sweet Home*. But the dedication also honoured what was now his longest continuous publishing relationship. It was a friendship that, while never as intimate as those he enjoyed with Bob Gottlieb or the late Tony Godwin, was grounded in genuine affection and

mutual respect. The great Jack McClelland's career was in its twilight, a fading out accelerated by chronic financial woes at M&S.
The situation reached crisis point in 1985, prompting McClelland
to sell his family firm to Toronto real estate developer Avie
Bennett, although he agreed to stay on as a consultant, with CBC
broadcaster and writer Adrienne Clarkson briefly replacing him
as publisher. In early 1986 Richler decided he was ready to sign
a contract for *Gursky Was Here.* At $50,000, the advance offered
by M&S was not unreasonable, given that both *Horseman* and
Joshua had turned a profit. As well, there was suddenly big money
in the Canadian publishing air, something new; the agent Lucinda
Vardey had garnered a million-dollar advance for a client not
long before, and Peter C. Newman, represented by Toronto entertainment lawyer Michael Levine, had recently procured a half-
million-dollar advance for a proposed multi-volume history of
the Hudson's Bay Company. Avie Bennett, who had long revered
Richler's work, had no problem with the figure. Not long after,
however, Jack McClelland, uncomfortable with his nebulous new
role, resigned outright, causing Richler to waver. To his surprise,
McClelland himself told him in private that he could do much
better with his novel elsewhere: upwards of $300,000 at auction.
An open auction wasn't Richler's style—he valued personal relationships too much to be sold to the highest bidder—but he took
note of the new market realities.

He decided to meet the shrewd Jewish real estate mogul who
wanted into the unprofitable book trade. Avie Bennett, innocent
of Richler's method of character judgment but knowing how
important Florence's assessment might be, made what she recognized immediately as an error: he invited the Richlers to dinner
at Il Posto restaurant in Yorkville. Her husband, she knew, preferred to make such decisions one-on-one, preferably in a publisher's office. The evening went poorly. Richler, drinking heavily
and grunting most answers, struck Bennett and his wife, Beverly,
as rude. Florence did her usual best to compensate, but her
charms went only so far. As well, it was transmitted to the Richlers
that Beverly Bennett might try her hand as an editorial reader for

M&S, suggesting to him that Canada's most esteemed publishing house was a bauble purchased by a wealthy man for his book-loving wife. Not long afterwards, Richler took Bob Gottlieb's advice again and called Cynthia Good, the vivacious thirty-three-year-old editor-in-chief at Penguin who had, wisely it turned out, paid handsomely for the paperback rights to his essay collection. Sensing that she might have a chance to sign Richler, Good drove from Toronto to Lake Memphremagog to meet him. She won over both Mordecai and Florence, and he returned the advance to M&S, signing instead with Penguin for $80,000. Adrienne Clarkson and Avie Bennett had a legal case for keeping *Gursky Was Here*, but resolved to let it go. As a reward, he provided the firm with a substantial consolation prize: a new Jacob Two-Two novel. With *Jacob Two-Two Meets the Hooded Fang* now enshrined, dog-eared and Kool-Aid–stained, on a hundred thousand bookshelves across Canada, and the musical version a near-annual sold-out production at the Young People's Theatre, a sequel was happy news. He drafted *Jacob Two-Two and the Dinosaur* in the country, looking out over the beautiful, placid lake where his children had once swum.

He continued to travel to New York on BOMC business—early in 1987 he convinced fellow jurors to make Alice Munro's *The Beggar Maid* a main selection—and flew to London and Paris, mostly for pleasure, or to northern Quebec and New Brunswick for fishing, a pastime he was finding more and more agreeable, in small part for the fish, in larger part for the company of friends, and Jake, whom he sometimes took with him. One trip back to England involved finally selling the house in Surrey. He did well on the transaction and, with BOMC now paying him $45,000 a year, told Daniel that, even if he quit writing, he and Florence could live comfortably. A prudent investor, often on the advice of his Uncle Max, he was cautious about playing the stock market. When global stock prices plummeted on "Black Monday" in October 1987, he could congratulate himself for not having succumbed to the greed and foolishness that cost so many investors their life savings.

Some of the Surrey money went into a new addition to the country house: a cedar and glass snooker room. Florence did all the preparation, assuring him that the addition was of a master bedroom, and then surprising him one day with the delivery of a full-sized snooker table. Roger George, a.k.a. Sweet Pea, a local housepainter and general fix-it man, had been doing odd jobs for Florence for years, and had become friends with her and Jake, taking them on excursions around the Townships to abandoned mines and hidden waterfalls. With Sweet Pea on the property for much of the summer, a friendship now emerged between the Townships local and the Montreal writer. His first sighting of the scrappy Roger George, brawling in the parking lot of a bar, endeared the man to him at once, and they were soon drinking together at the Owl's Nest, where Richler, as a regular player, had his name taped on one of the pinball machines, granting priority access. They also went fishing for cold-water lake trout in Northern Quebec, taking Jake along. George, whose roots in the area traced back to the mid-nineteenth century, knew pretty much everybody and their business, legal or otherwise. When some weekend houses in the vicinity were broken into, but not the Richlers', it became clear that Mordecai was drinking with the right guys. He couldn't have been more pleased.

Once the room was finished, with its views of lake and woods and Florence's garden, it hosted not only a snooker table but a 1960s Coca-Cola machine, framed sheets of snooker rules and regulations, a stuffed deer head with human eyes cut out from a fashion magazine, Moses Richler's old engraved chisel, and reproductions of drawings of two Georgian-era boxers. The family began to host a tournament every Boxing Day, for house guests and local buddies. Sweet Pea described Richler as a sneaky rather than superior player; his children called him "Captain Hook" in honour of his ability to "snooker" his opponents. He won most tournaments (only Daniel was a better player) and loved replicating those pool halls of his youth. On workdays Florence would register his imminent arrival in the kitchen for lunch by the sound of him potting a few balls first.

As Florence and Mordecai spent longer periods in the country, Jake Richler, now almost twenty, stayed alone in the condo on

Sherbrooke Street. Their youngest child had gone through the usual male Richler ups and downs at school, and after finishing CEGEP, or junior college, he had taken a job as a cub reporter with a free newspaper. Like all his brothers and sisters, Jake was very close to his mother. But he also had an easygoing relationship with his father, often accompanying him to the bar at the end of the day and sitting with his friends, where his physical resemblance to Richler as a young man caused amusement. His being the youngest, and the last at home, definitely contributed to their relationship; so did his warm, relaxed temperament, and his sense of humour, very much his own but also—as Mordecai and Florence both remarked—so like his father's.

Richler was instinctively suspicious of education as a delaying tactic, advising that "as soon as you have wings, use them." Having left McGill after less than a semester, Daniel, for instance, was now making a national name for himself as a cultural commentator on the CBC and, soon, as writer and host of the literary show *Imprint*. Noah worked for the BBC in London as a radio documentarian. Emma, striking in appearance and with a quiet gift for comedy, was launching her career as an actress at the Stratford Theatre Festival in southern Ontario. Only Martha, who had studied art history and who looked so much like Florence, and had her analytical intelligence, showed signs of wanting a career in academia. ("We're not the scholarship types," Richler once consoled Noah after he was turned down for a Rhodes.) Having taken degrees from Harvard and then Columbia, Martha announced an interest in doing a Ph.D. On hearing this, her father pulled out book after book by art historians and announced, "Look, he didn't have a Ph.D."

What Jake couldn't be in 1986, of course, was two times two plus two plus two, the age assigned to Jacob in the sequel his father was writing. In *Jacob Two-Two and the Dinosaur*, the eight-year-old's parents return from a safari in Africa with a lizard. The family live in Canada now, both in Montreal and in a country house, and Jacob has brothers who put up *Sports Illustrated* swimsuit posters and listen to David Bowie, and sisters who paint their fingernails pink and swoon over Robert Redford. Poor Jacob remains just a kid who says everything twice. When the nation's Slick Willie of a prime minister, Perry Pleaser, finds out about Dippy the dinosaur, he decides that slaying the creature will boost his popularity. Jacob defends his friend against the perfidious PM. In the end, having deposited Dippy safely in the mountains of British Columbia, Jacob must endure the further lies of the fibber prime minister, who claims he rescued the boy from the dragon.

Jokes abound—Perry Pleaser sounds a lot like then Prime Minister Brian Mulroney—but for every gag that rings true to kids, every exchange of family banter, another sounds forced, distant from the imaginative space occupied by children. Missing as well is the heartfelt paean to the joys, then fresh to its author, of being part of a happy family, which had provided the underlying music of the first book. The moment that produced *Jacob Two-Two Meets the Hooded Fang* had passed, like those magical years of the Swiss Family Richler. Nevertheless, "For Daniel, Noah, Emma, Marfa and Jacob," the dedication read once again.

"Interrupted my endless novel to do my second Jacob Two-Two book, JACOB TWO-TWO AND THE DINOSAUR," he wrote to André Deutsch, to whom he owed the manuscript, in February 1986, "and didn't want to write until I had finished it, and Florence had pronounced. . . . I have finished it. Florence likes it!" His relief was twofold: at completing the story, and at doing so despite a flaring up of an old health issue. "I've been knocked flat by a recurrence of my old disc problem, but am now in the hands of a Chinese maker of magic, who will either cripple or cure me."

Although lacking the effortless charm of the original *Jacob Two-Two*, the sequel sold well and Peter Moss at the Young People's Theatre wasted little time commissioning a stage adaptation. Kids loved the book, and the play as well.

But Richler's popularity in French Quebec was no greater than it ever had been when the publishers of a new edition of *L'Apprentissage de Duddy Kravitz* asked him to sign copies at a book fair in Montreal. He waited at the booth for ten minutes after his presence was announced before someone stopped by. The man, who had spotted another smoker, asked for a light.

By the time Jake Richler began joining his father at Woody's for a late afternoon drink, the "Canadian political carnival" was approaching its big-tent era. His circle of city drinking pals had evolved. It had also suffered the loss of its only female member; Doris Giller relocated to Toronto in 1985 with her husband, Jack Rabinovitch, whose business had shifted to Ontario. Old-timers Terry Mosher (Aislin) and Hubie Bauch from the *Gazette*, along with the political gadfly and columnist Nick Auf der Maur, had lately been joined by the lawyer Richard Holden and business-man John Aylen, a former student of Richler's at Carleton, and, less often, by Conrad Black. It was a band of merry pranksters, smart and informed, and their increasing collective ire and dis-dain with local politics was translating into public gesture.

At the very end of 1986 the Quebec Court of Appeal ruled that the PQ's ban on languages other than French on commercial signs was a violation of rights protected by the charters of both Canada and Quebec. Premier Robert Bourassa, unexpectedly back in power after defeating the PQ in 1985, decided to test "intimidating nationalist winds" by taking the matter further, to the Supreme Court of Canada. But when that court also threw out the law, he evoked a clause that exempted his government from complying. Richler's exasperation approached exploding point. In such antag-onism towards other-language minorities he saw a sure path towards the diminishment of Montreal as a city and Quebec as a civil society. Attacks against Hasidic Jews in Outremont, a fire in an English-language school in Quebec City, an attempt to burn down the headquarters of an Anglo rights group called Alliance Quebec—these were disturbing and uncivil acts and, worse still, recognizable from his childhood in the shadow of fascism. Assertions by nationalists with regard to the French language sounded to him like assertions of racial exclusivity and bully threats. "René Lévesque was not an anti-Semite," he would remark. "Neither is Jacques Parizeau. All the same, Jews who have been Quebecers for generations understand only too well that when thousands of flag-waving nationalists march through the streets roaring 'Le Québec aux Québécois!' they do not have in mind anybody named Ginsburg. Or MacGregor, come to think of it."

Or Richler. By late 1987, only one of his children still called the province home. Like many anglophone Quebecers, the Richlers now saw their grown and moved-away children and, eventually, their grandchildren, on holidays. Although little more than a minor demographic trend to a large number of Quebecers, the voluntary exile of young English-speakers represented another kind of diminishment for many families in Montreal.

On November 1, 1987, René Lévesque died of a heart attack. He was just sixty-five and had been out of politics for two years. Richler had once presumed him to be a kindred spirit, but they had parted company fiercely, and with Lévesque as well he had become more and more exasperated. So much so that when he wrote his "in memoriam" to the former premier, his words spoke to his own hardened feelings about Quebec's separatist impulse, now into its fourth decade and far from played out. Lévesque, he said, had been charismatic and "vulnerable," but also dishonest. Had the former premier "chosen to hang me . . . even as he tightened the rope around my neck, he would have complained about how humiliating it was for him to spring the trapdoor." He did not join the hundred thousand Montrealers who lined the streets for the funeral.

He didn't need to leave his living room to become embroiled in another controversy. A CBC television crew visited the Chateau on November 18 to interview him about his views on economics in relation to culture. That autumn there was no more incendiary issue in Canadian political life than the question of a free trade agreement with the United States, and its effects on the economy and culture of Canada. The previous day he had driven to Ottawa to appear before a House of Commons committee, where he spoke in favour of free trade. He had been invited by Conservative friends seeking the imprimatur of a major artist who didn't feel culturally threatened. His sentiments were genuine, but many believed his action allowed the Conservatives to turn him into a poster boy for the party. (Though they never discussed it, Florence assumed he voted Liberal in Canada and Labour in the U.K.) Aside from joking that if supporting free trade meant he wouldn't have to drink Ontario wines, all the better—"There is only so much I am prepared to drink for my country"—he was reasonably measured. But in arguing that Canadian culture did not need special protection from the United States, he did appear almost to wish the death of the embattled, still fledgling Canadian film industry, and he wasn't interested in automatically supporting Canadian-owned publishing companies who received grants from the Canada Council. Referring to international publishers, he noted that "foreign-owned cultural imperialists" took greater risks in issuing first novels than did the likes of Mel Hurtig, a so-called Captain Canada.

That was unfair—Hurtig's publishing programme was all non-fiction—but the broader moral position was one he had held from early days: protectionism was for the mediocre. Books, films, wines, should succeed or fail on the basis of their quality, not their label. Whether his maverick stance on culture, a reflection of an instinctive dislike of being told by anyone what he should sip, read or view, really helped the Conservative cause was debatable. But it did achieve the near impossible: it made many Canadian writers and cultural figures even angrier with him. Given that Margaret Atwood, now possibly both the most successful Canadian novelist internationally and the de facto spokesperson for cultural nationalism, had appeared before the same committee, voicing her anti–free-trade position, Mordecai Richler had never seemed more isolated. But when an MP from Alberta, hoping for a sound bite, pressed him to admit that Mulroney's government was ruling the country splendidly, he snapped back. The prime minister, he pointed out, had opposed free trade just four years before. Nor was he trusted by regular people.

Now he was on television from a chair in his living room, with Florence listening quietly from the kitchen, debating the issue on *The Journal* with the playwright and journalist Rick Salutin, who was speaking from Toronto, along with Barbara Frum, the host of the newsmagazine show. Salutin saw free trade as completing the absorption of Canada into "the ethos of the United States"—"the country is at stake," he said—and accused him of having done a separate "deal" with the Conservatives and agreeing to be the government's answer to Margaret Atwood. "I'm not playing any role," Richler replied. "I'm just expressing my views on this matter." As for Canada being absorbed into the ethos of America, that, he contended, had been happening "for as long as I can remember." Hair combed and manner authoritative, he returned to a core assertion: real writers and artists, driven by their obsessions, would keep on producing, no matter what the cultural playing field. The performance, though brief, was impressive, especially for someone uncomfortable in front of the camera. The image of Richler smoking, disagreeing, his views unapologetic and entirely his own—a kind of literary elder statesman, minus any state—would stand in Canadian minds for the next two years. That was how long he would be perceived to be "away" while completing his seemingly endless novel.

How far along was he now? Enough to type out a title page on a 400-page manuscript and mark "Dec 15/87" in the top corner.

SOLOMON GURSKY WAS HERE
A Novel
By Mordecai Richler

IV

THE GURSKY FAMILY TREE

1. Gideon begat Ephraim

"Scout's honor," he wrote to Carmen Callil at Chatto & Windus on March 5, 1988, "I will deliver the fat filthy novel this autumn." This despite evidence that he was still sorting out the tectonics that would eventually need to settle into the book's narrative continents. *Gursky*, well into a second draft, involved seven generations of the booze-empire clan, and had eight sections of between four and nine chapters each. Aware of the potential for reader confusion, Richler offered to provide an Old Testament–like lineage, with one Gursky begetting another. His editors preferred a family tree, to be affixed at the front, complete with dates: from the adolescent adventures of Ephraim Gursky (1817–1910) in England all the way to the event-filled adolescence of his great-great-great-nephew Isaac Gursky (b. 1961) in the Canadian Arctic and New York. They settled on using both.

The 400-page draft already displayed the two epigraphs that would appear in the final book. First was Solomon Gursky himself, quoted as saying, "Gerald Murphy got it wrong—living twice, maybe three times, is the best revenge." He was followed by Sir Hyman Kaplansky paraphrasing literary critic Cyril Connolly's remark that had meant so much to the young Mordecai Richler: "Cyril once observed that the only reason for writing was to create a masterpiece. But if you haven't got it in you to make a great

work of art there is another option—you can become one." From
the start, his mischief was layered. The use of remarks by his own
characters as epigraphs marked a departure from the usual cita-
tions from W.H. Auden. That both of these quotes explored the
notion of living multiple lives, and of transforming those multiplicities into works of art, was equally provocative: *Solomon Gursky
Was Here* had aspirations to be that very art. With the reader's
eventual discovery that Gursky and Kaplansky are one and the
same, the mischief widens into commentary about the nature of
novels themselves. Fair warning was being given at the start
about this unfolding trickster's story, and the ambitions of the
author for his massive and already surprising ninth fiction.

Four books underpinned the architecture of *Gursky*, with the
same sly determination. The Old Testament, *The Newgate
Calendar*, *The Quest for Corvo* by A.J.A. Symons and Peter C.
Newman's *Bronfman Dynasty* go unmentioned in the novel, aside
from a passing allusion to Symons's little-known 1934 study of
the biographical form. In a note Richler acknowledges the texts
that he "dug deeply into" for information about the Franklin
Expedition and Prohibition, nineteenth-century London and
Haida mythology, without referring to those four. To mention the
Old Testament would have been like acknowledging that he had
used a dictionary. *The Newgate Calendar*, an anthology of historical broadsheets and chapbooks recounting tales of the more
lurid denizens of London's notorious Newgate Prison, had been
his occasional bedtime reading for twenty years. It had helped
conjure Ephraim Gursky's backstory; according to Moses Berger
he is even listed in the prison rolls. But another book about crime
and punishment in England, *The Victorian Underworld*, was a more
direct source for descriptions of Cheapside and Newgate prison.

The Quest for Corvo, which he had first read as a teenager and
had alluded to in *Horseman*, was put to brilliant use. William Rolfe,
an eccentric, mysterious, shape-shifting English nineteenth-
century writer and painter, and failed aspirant to the priesthood,
was the "Corvo" in question. Rolfe styled himself Baron Corvo
and kept a stuffed raven on his work desk—*corvo* being Italian for

"raven." Solomon Gursky, his own death faked, first re-emerges with the same name: Baron Corvo. Later he calls himself Mr. Corbeau, French for "raven," and even later, Herr Dr. Otto Raven. The playful declension of these various ravens was Richler; his inspiration was Rolfe, via Symons's *Quest*.

Not mentioning Peter C. Newman's biography of the Bronfman dynasty was strategic. The risk of taking on the Bronfmans remained unchanged. He was already rehearsing a disclaimer about any Gursky/Bronfman linkages that he would repeat over and over when the book appeared—"I will not have five years of my life reduced to gossip"—and was bracing to keep his fiction free, both imaginatively and legally, from the clutches of being dubbed a *roman à clef*. He had already received early warning that the family might take exception, as they had previously, after a reading from the manuscript at Harbourfront had brought expressions of interest from Seagram's lawyers. To credit *Bronfman Dynasty* would be to welcome the comparison between life and art, and swing open the door to litigation. It also wouldn't have been an accurate reflection of his actual sources for family lore, including books he had read, current and former friends he had spoken with, and the legacy of growing up in Jewish Montreal during the heyday of "Mr. Sam" as the richest, meanest, smartest, most philanthropic—i.e., the most talked about in barbershops and around gin rummy tables—of their kind.

"Nobody on Lake Memphremagog knew where he had come from," the first line of the first full draft read, "except that one morning—during the record cold spell of 1851—a big menacing black bird, the likes of which they had never seen before, soared above the crude mill town of Magog, swooping again and again." In the end, the final part of the sentence appeared unchanged from the opening: "One morning—during the record cold spell of 1851—a big menacing black bird. . . ."

2. Ephraim begat Aaron

"For the past year my wife and I have been rooted in our country cottage," Richler wrote in a journal he kept for the American quarterly *Antaeus*, "where I continue to struggle with a long and convoluted novel." In May 1988 he and Florence decided to redo the kitchen. For the job he retained Sweet Pea and a man named Buzz, another crony from the Owl's Nest. Supposed to take six weeks, the noise and disruption lasted well into the summer. Florence went to Italy with some friends. Richler attempted to bond with the lanky Buzz. Believing he was deaf, he asked if he should write things down. "Well I'm afraid he don't read too good," Sweet Pea replied. "TRY SHOUTING." (Buzz was, in fact, quite shy.) In *Gursky* there would be scenes involving amiable Townships locals called Strawberry and Legion Hall, their speech equally rough-hewn. Richler also bought Florence an expensive imported Aga cooker to allow for still better gourmet meals, especially for guests. Even so, his "soul foods" weren't available at the lake. "Pickled herring. Rye bread. Smoked meat." Locally there was little. "The nearby town of Magog," he noted, "also lacks a decent butcher or fishmonger."

From the opening chapter of Part I, set in and around Magog in the year 1851, with locals coming under the spell of the mysterious "Brother Ephraim," *Gursky* began its yo-yo movements through time. Chapter 2 introduces Moses Berger, in his cabin in the Townships. His age and disposition—fifty-something, apostate Jewish, caustic, whisky-drinking and Monte Cristo smoking— might have initially cast Berger as the "update" of Joshua Shapiro and Jake Hersh; that is, the author stand-in, representing him in his most recent evolution. But differences soon become pronounced, not the least being Moses' background as the son of the poet and Gursky speech writer L.B. Berger, and his alcoholism. Unlike any previous boozing Richler narrator, Moses goes on regular benders and checks into rehab. He is also single and childless, unable to sustain a relationship or be a sexual partner. Even more distressing, Moses Berger can't complete the project—a biography of Solomon Gursky—that has been his one and only adult preoccupation.

Early scenes involve writing unlike anything Richler had

attempted. "Ephraim tucked his grandson under the buffalo robes, laid his rifle within reach, and cracked his whip high, urging the dogs," runs one sentence detailing the boy Solomon's flight to the shores of the Polar Sea with his ancient grandfather. "The first being made by the Great Being was a failure, he was imperfect, and therefore was cast aside and called *kub-la-na* or *kod-lu-na*, which means white man." The depths of research, the sharp, exacting description—of carving a caribou, of melting honey and coating a knife blade to slice a wolf's tongue—placed new demands on someone previously inclined to write about his own place and time, and to prefer settings that he had personally experienced. For a writer who liked to cite Babel's remark that he had no imagination, his vividly rendered scenes in underworld Victorian London and aboard one of Franklin's ships, among the Inuit and out on the early twentieth-century prairies, demanded an unprecedented degree of imaginative engagement. *Gursky* was expansive enough to include familiar milieux—the "Caboose" bar in the Townships, the Mandrake and Bale of Hay in 1950s London, a Montreal rooming house and an inn in Ste. Agathe—but now these were secondary settings, sources of neither the novel's deepest colours nor its richest narratives.

It also told the most outrageous Jewish joke of his career. By smuggling the young Ephraim Gursky onto Franklin's 1845 expedition, and having him survive the disaster thanks to the kosher foods he has brought along, Richler insinuated the diasporic Jewish experience and sensibility into the most unlikely of national narrative myths. He then proposed that Ephraim found a cult of his own devising—and, often enough, his own seed—among the Inuit. "I am Ephraim, the Lord thy God," he tells them, "and thou shalt have no other gods before me." The "CHURCH OF THE MILLENARIANS, Founder Brother Ephraim" leaves a cryptic legacy of Inuit wearing tallith and observing Yom Kippur. There is also Ephraim's tragic flaw: his providing for "all contingencies save that of the Arctic adherent": the church members who, insisting on remaining celibate and fasting from sundown to sunrise of the holy day, find themselves in a place where the sun stays below the horizon for several months on end. Many starve, and die devout. Others seek "satisfaction among the unclean."

But even in that spring of 1988 Richler still had doubts—expressed, as always, half-jokingly. "Given the opportunity I could shaft it right now with a more scathing review than any I'm likely to see when I finish it. I've always suspected that every novelist writes one too many, and now that I'm fifty-seven all those luminous brain cells I once counted on seem extinguished by Remy Martin or Glenlivet. I wonder if my turn has come."

3. Aaron begat Bernard, Solomon & Morrie

"As you know, I haven't seen maw in years but I do get hit with menacing embittered letters from her (each one registered) from time to time, and I shd do something about seeing her." He had heard from his brother out of the blue—"Naturally, I was more than a little surprised, but also pleased, to hear from you again after so many years"—and remembered having drinks with Avrum's son Michael from his first marriage. He expressed regret that his sibling's second marriage was also ending in divorce. As for seeing Lily, Richler was determined to finish his novel first, and that wouldn't happen until "November at the earliest. My God," he added, "is she really 84? What does she live on? Is she pressed for funds? I would certainly like to know."

Having summarized what the children were doing and explained his own work, he once more promised Avrum that he would get to Newfoundland, still the only Canadian province he had yet to visit, and hoped that, when his brother was next in Montreal, he might visit him . . . "and that would be nice (and about time)," he added by hand. He again supplied him with his phone number in the country. Avrum was sixty-two, Mordecai fifty-seven, and the two brothers were increasingly uneasy with their estrangement, its nature still unclear, knowing that precious time was passing. But, aside from attending a funeral together, neither was yet able to make a move.

He worked long, light-filled days through the summer. His

upstairs office, overlooking the bay through wide windows, evidenced the dimensions of the project underway. It was dominated by his plain wooden desk. On the desk, his bulky Smith-Corona typewriter, a white notepad beside it, an ashtray brimming with cigar butts and a tea tray sticky with lemon pips; behind it, a curved shelf piled high with books open face down and newspaper clippings, notes about calls to make and matters to look up. Shelves stuffed with books lined the three remaining walls. With two bedrooms, formerly belonging to the kids but lately mostly used by guests, running off the large space, anyone sleeping late awoke to the hushed clack of electronic keys. The machine beeped with each spelling error; he never figured out how to shut the function off. He didn't mind the openness of the office, liked being within hailing distance of Florence downstairs, or anyone who might pass through to the bedrooms.

Much of his energy now was focused on the "Bernard, Solomon & Morrie" generation of Gurskys, both their coming of age as Jewish emigrants on the prairies and intrepid bootleggers during the Prohibition era, and their decades as super-rich Westmount distillers. From Solomon's fateful winning poker hand, which launches the family fortunes, to the murder of a Gursky loyalist (the bullet likely directed at Solomon on orders from his own brother Bernard), through to the trial of all three Gurskys during the 1930s, huge scene follows huge scene, as he splits the tale into fragments. A supporting cast for the outlandish and profane Mr. Bernard and the trickster Solomon, even for the mild, simpering Morrie, has to be created. Enter the sycophant family lawyer Harvey Schwartz, a survivor from the "Manny Moves to Westmount" excerpt, and long ago identified in a newspaper as being modelled on Leo Kolber, right down to the poet wife with book titles like *Hugs, Pain, and Chocolate Chip Cookies*; the mysterious WASP beauty, Diana McClure, Solomon's love interest, she of the "one eye brown and one blue" portrait; and Bert Smith, the woeful customs agent and lifelong Gursky enemy living in a rooming house in lowest Westmount, overseen by the snooping Mrs. Jenkins.

With two dozen more characters, and three or four more sub-plots, the hydra-headed narrative expanded by the week. Most of the notes that he made during the summer were concerned, not surprisingly, with the chronology and arrangement of the eight parts; even a novelist this gifted at narrative time-shifts had to be struggling to manage so many, often through such intuitive leaps. There are indications that he originally thought to include still more plots and stories than appeared in the final version. "Dentistry history" he noted as one strand. He also listed "Zundel/teacher," a reference to Ernst Zundel, the Albertan teacher then on trial for teaching Holocaust denial, and "Welcome to the world of AIDS." The manuscript, "fat, filthy," already topped 200,000 words.

Something else positioned on his office desk in the country house factored into *Gursky.* Florence had a framed hand-coloured photo of herself as a child of nine, her hair in ringlets and a bow. She recalled how it went missing one day from her bedside collection, reappearing on his desk upstairs. Only much later it became apparent that he liked to keep the photograph near him, both as his keepsake and, earlier, as the source of Solomon Gursky's obsession with his photo of his beloved.

From the time Mordecai first saw this picture—it was in the country—he always liked it. I don't know when he quite pinched it but I saw it in his office. When I said, "What's that doing here?" he dismissed it and gave no explanation, just a wave of the hand, but I was secretly quite pleased that he liked it. It surprised me and I wondered—what was the attachment? And when I read *Solomon* I understood. And afterwards, he laughed and said, "hmmmm, useful."

4. Bernard begat Lionel, Anita & Nathan

In early September Richler went fishing. In *Gursky,* Moses Berger runs into an obnoxious fourth-generation Gursky at a fishing camp called Larry's Gulch in Restigouche in New Brunswick, where the men bet a thousand dollars on who can catch the most salmon. Richler had fished with Jake at a Restigouche camp, as well as elsewhere in the province. On this occasion, though, he was fulfilling "a long-cherished dream" of fishing for salmon in the Scottish islands of Shetland and Orkney, for *GQ*. Florence joined him, along with Bob and Sandi Shapiro, helping him overcome his usual dislike of flying, along with "one more cognac." The fishing expedition turned out to be dismal but an excuse for a funny account bolstered by lame jokes about Scottish weather and accents and "obsequious wine stewards" in $200-a-night hotels. As always, these scribblings served as a break, and as a chance to pick up details he might use in the book. Back safely in Canada, he pushed for a Christmas completion of the manuscript.

Before leaving for Scotland he received some bad news. The Book-of-the-Month Club was moving to new corporate ownership, and three of the five judges were to be let go. His friend and jury chairman, Al Silverman, had wielded the axe, and besides losing his salary, Richler was incensed that he had described the firings as "evolutionary." "The man is weak," he told his friend, the also-dismissed Wilfrid Sheed—an irreversible character pronouncement. Neither was he too pleased that eighty-five-year-old Clifford Fadiman had been retained over him, nor that he had to sign a two-year gag order before receiving the severance package, which included a full year's pay. The long-term effect of the loss of those regular funded visits to New York, where he could meet his writing friends and see his editors, would prove considerable; by the late 1990s his profile in the United States would be diminished, despite the publication of two more well-regarded novels. In the short term, he had extra time to finish *Gursky*.

"What he wanted, above all," Moses admits to himself, "was for the old man to love him. For the old man to look upon him as a son." Moses Berger's contest with Barney Gursky at the fishing lodge typifies his relationship with the sprawling clan. Some Gurskys, like Solomon's daughter Clara, he becomes romantically involved with; others, like Mr. Bernard, he stalks as a would-be biographer. In the case of Solomon/Sir Hyman, the relationship is that of a largely absent father to a largely awe-struck son. Many character portraits in *Gursky* crackle with satiric malice. For Harvey Schwartz, Bert Smith and the wild Jew Bernard Gursky, Richler wrote with his knives drawn, but the sharpest blade was reserved for L.B. Berger, pompous minor poet and unsupportive natural father of the talented Moses. For sabotag-ing his son's chance to publish in the *New Yorker* alone—L.B., himself rejected by the magazine, hides an acceptance letter for a short story written by Moses—the elder Berger receives all his creator's scorn.

Compounding this crime are the literary sins of self-pity and inflated self-regard, and the larger artistic sin of "selling out" by writing speeches for rich, ignorant booze barons. Poet, novelist, lawyer and would-be politician A.M. Klein, the one-time Baron Byng student who became a pillar of the Montreal Jewish estab-lishment, had also been a long-time speech writer for Sam Bronfman. Klein, seventeen years in the grave and silent for the last twenty years of his life, was being steadily rehabilitated by a generation of academics convinced of his poetic importance. For Richler to model L.B. Berger so closely on him, and then portray Berger with such hostility, struck some as vindictive and others as revealing. Moses Berger's wilful debunking of the diasporic variety of Jewish suffering and self-definition—a stance embodied in his decision to stand up in a theatre showing an emotionally manipulative version of the Anne Frank story and shout to a stage full of Nazis searching an Amsterdam apartment, "Look in the attic! She's hiding in the attic!"—may have been a clue to his, and his creator's, distaste for what he saw as the self-serving artistic weakness embodied by Klein. But that still didn't account for the portrait of L.B. Berger. While previous novels had offered an array of father-son relationships, *Gursky* made an actual theme of the distinction between a spiritual and a blood parent. Richler, raised "in private" by a gentle but weak father, and reared "in public" on the vanities and, in his view, hypocrisies of the local high-profile figure A.M. Klein, seemed to be sketching in print the ideal spiritual parent. For him, that father crossed the Trickster with the Golem, the Jewish Superman of comic books with the Horseman of Isaac Babel.

Moses Berger launches his life as a drinker on the slights and psychic burdens of being the son of L.B. The ravages of alcoholism in Moses' character and destiny mark *Gursky*, and if Richler's daily late-afternoon sojourns in the Thirsty Boot on Highway 243 with Sweet Pea and Buzz weren't in his thoughts, or his friendship with the alcoholic Ian Mayer, who would shortly succumb to lung cancer, then his Thursday visits with friends at Woody's on Crescent Street, where the ebullient Nick Auf der Maur was fighting the bottle, may well have been. Wilfrid Sheed was also struggling. Richler himself was widely viewed as a heavy drinker, in no small part due to his need for alcohol to cope with any contact with the media and any appearances, where a few Scotches were likely to make him funny and witty—the way he was in private, and wished to be in public. His natural reticence ran deep, for all his hundreds of readings, lectures and book signings over the decades, and he may have suffered a kind of phobia, requiring liquor as a prop. In the private domain, however, his drinking was not out of the ordinary, beginning with a glass in the late afternoon, and family and friends rarely remarked any alteration to his mood because of it. He maintained a successful and busy career, a rich and functioning personal life and a strong sexual appetite. He was not, in short, like Moses Berger, a character born of observing friends in the throes of the disease of alcoholism, and perhaps pondering a "what if?" question about himself.

5. Solomon begat Henry & Lucy

By December 1988 he had a novel to show Florence. As was the custom, she read the 800-page manuscript in virtually a single epic sitting, staying up through the night and brushing off his anxious interruptions to check her reactions. She recalled:

I remember finishing *Solomon Gursky Was Here* at three-thirty in the morning, and he would come in periodically, and I would say with a gesture, "Just go away—I'll let you know when I'm finished." He'd turn around and go back to bed, not sleep; he would be waiting. I remember telling him, "Look this applies too much pressure, so either I wait and read it when you're out of the house or. . . ." He accepted that. It was very touching after such a long time to continue to have that relationship and to be trusted on that level.

Florence pronounced *Gursky* wonderful, his best book. But she also suggested that a set piece, only marginally attached to a larger plot, be cut. "The Dental Academy Awards Night" recounted a "documentary" concerning a dentist named Overbite who crosses the United States on a skateboard to raise funds for a "Dental Anti-Defamation League." Her forceful request for this edit, as well as a few other trimmings, led to a rare altercation. Richler, who was off to New York for one of his last BOMC meetings, left the house without the usual shows of affection, and was cold on the phone that evening from the brownstone of Bob Gottlieb and Maria Tucci. But later she received a call from Gottlieb himself. He too, after reading the enormous book in typically swift order—he had sent his exhausted, on-edge author to the movies to avoid any interruptions—had sat down with him. Gottlieb, independent of Florence's judgment, recommended excising the same material from the manuscript. A sheepish Richler called his wife to issue a rare apology. He ended up taking another two months to trim twenty thousand words at the behest of his crack editorial team. "FOR FLORENCE," the dedication already read.

He did some manuscript reading of his own around this time. For years he had been advising his children not to follow in his footsteps. "I don't want five little Mordecais running around," he told Daniel. "Choose your own profession." So far, however, his two oldest children, raised in a magical and slightly cloistered world of books and movies and the passionate, lively, entertaining people who made them, had been unable to resist. Besides publishing journalism in some of the same magazines as his father, Noah was working on a novel in London. Daniel had abandoned his secure, high-profile job with the CBC—a decision Richler approved of, on principle—to finish his own first fiction. He had done so despite his father's specific warnings about the difficulty of earning a living as an author. When Daniel asked him to look at an early draft of his book, he agreed. He was typically terse, suggesting only that the manuscript was too long and wordy, but he did help his son find an agent—Jack McClelland, then attempting to reinvent himself. The high-spirited, language-besotted *Kicking Tomorrow* was purchased by M&S. In the tradition of novels by Richler men, it too was dedicated to Florence. Noah didn't ultimately publish his novel, but the emergence of the next generation of Richlers in the Canadian media was underway.

One especially wild plot in *Gursky* that neither Florence nor Bob Gottlieb objected to concerns the ghastly fate of Henry Gursky. The only son of Solomon, devoutly Orthodox and committed to keeping the faith with Ephraim's long-ago project, lives in a settlement called Tulugaqtitut, Northwest Territories, with his native wife, Nialie, and their son, Isaac. Henry embarrasses his boy, whom he is pressing to study at the yeshiva of the Hasidic Lubavitcher Rebbe in Brooklyn, by purchasing his own three-masted, Franklin-like ship, in anticipation of the pending coming of the Jewish messiah, the Moshiach. (The ship, dubbed Crazy Henry's Ark, is immediately locked in ice.) The gentle, slightly mad Gursky's own day of reckoning arrives when he, his son and a native boy attempt to cross the Barrens by dogsled. At last, in the final fifty pages of *Gursky*, Richler was able to make use of the story of pilot Martin Hartwell. Isaac Gursky alone survives twenty-three days of extreme cold and, he later claims, attacks by ravens. "Isaac survived by slicing chunks out of Henry's thighs," a bush pilot informs Moses. Soon the denizens of the local bar have concocted a parody of Robert

Service that underscores the novel's wonderfully complex, and
occasionally lethal, father-son relationships.

> There are strange things done 'neath the
> Midnight Sun,
> But the thing that made us quail
> Was the night the Jew
> In want of stew
> Braised his father in a pail.

6. Morrie begat Barney & Charna

"I am delighted by your response to GURSKY," Richler wrote to
Carmen Callil on May 17, 1989. "Sonny phoned yesterday, equally
enthusiastic. Now I am waiting for someone to tell me the truth."
Sonny Mehta, not Bob Gottlieb, was now officially his editor at
Knopf; Gottlieb had resigned from Knopf in late 1987 to take over
as editor of the *New Yorker*, leaving the unfinished *Gursky* to his
successor, a rising Indo-British industry star brought in from
Picador in London to run Knopf. Before he left, Gottlieb arranged
for Mehta to shepherd a few of his final book projects through,
including his friend Mordecai Richler's novel. Mehta had come
of age in the "Revenge of the Empire" era of British publishing,
with Salman Rushdie, Kazuo Ishiguro and Timothy Mo leading
the charge in crafting intricate, subversive narratives, so it was
not surprising that he gravitated to the energetic polyphonies of
Gursky. And "Viking-Penguin, Toronto, will publish here first
week of November," Richler told Callil, "so I must get revisions
done pronto. The editor there, Cynthia Good, is in close contact
with Dr. Gottlieb, the magazine editor."

Good did offer a few editorial suggestions, including questioning a scene where Sir Hyman serves blood-filled matzos to Gentile
guests at his London mansion. Richler let it stand. Most of the
revisions he did accept were done at the behest of the Chatto
editor who had been put in charge of his work. Alison Samuel
had joined Chatto only three years before, but she was already

highly respected as the young editor of the South African novelist J.M. Coetzee. Samuel suggested he amend spots where his
language was too cute, and agitated for a rethink of the character of Isaac Gursky. In the story the adolescent drifts down to New
York in the wake of the tragedy of his father, the word "cannibal"
following him like a curse. She was right. Richler, determined to
chart the devolution of the later generations of the Gursky clan,
had made Isaac too hideous, especially for a boy of fifteen.
Ephraim, Solomon and even the odious Bernard were engaging
precisely *for* their roaring ambitions and appetites, whereas the
younger ones lacked such fire. In the end the "final" Gursky sorts
himself out and, after a nasty power struggle among various offspring, emerges as co-director of the family booze empire.

"Hope the revisions, substitute pages etc you've got are the
final final final ones," he wrote to Alison Samuel in mid-July,
adding—his sense of loyalty always unwavering—"after consultation with Bob Gottlieb." He then responded to the usual British
publishing concern about libel. "Relax," he told her, "I have had
lengthy talks with Toronto lawyer who anticipates no difficulties,
but has asked for certain small changes, which I've made."
Samuel's worries were directed at the devastating character
sketches and fabricated diary/book entries of British literary and
theatre personalities in the scenes in *Gursky* depicting Sir
Hyman's dealings with the postwar British elite. A few years earlier, the Canadian novelist Timothy Findley had found no British
takers for his acclaimed bestselling novel *Famous Last Words*, due
to fears of legal fallout from his portrayals of the Duke and
Duchess of Windsor. Richler, suspecting his British editor might
not even be aware of the more pronounced libel concern in
Canada, explained it to her. "My concern here was the Bronfmans
(Seagram), the billionaire bootlegging family that came out of
the west to Montreal. But Sam, who bears certain resemblances
to Mr. Bernard, is dead, and Solomon, Morrie, etc, Ephraim,
Isaac, etc, are total inventions."

Unbeknownst to him, the Bronfmans had already got their
hands on the manuscript. As with Newman's *Bronfman Dynasty*

twelve years earlier, the clan had managed to obtain a copy well in advance of publication. In Newman's case, the early exposure had led to his being required to make hundreds of changes. Michael Levine, the lawyer and literary agent, was also a Bronfman cousin who advised Charles Bronfman's charitable foundation, and the family asked him to read the novel. Levine sent in a twelve-page report pointing out all the places in *Gursky* where the author, clearly lifting stories and characters from real life, had libelled the family. But then he recommended that they do nothing. Besides remarking that the book was superb, he suggested that taking action would put the Bronfmans, more than Mordecai Richler, on trial.

The matter might have ended there had Richler, learning of the lawyer's recommendation, not agreed to meet him for breakfast at the Four Seasons Hotel in Toronto. They got along at once—Levine was a storyteller and knew everybody—and Richler, showing his usual psychological adeptness with men, ended the meeting by asking the lawyer to represent *him*. "All my life I've wanted a Bronfman lawyer," he told the startled and flattered Michael Levine. As luck would have it, a *Globe and Mail* journalist was in the restaurant, and next day the paper reported a meeting between the *Gursky* author and the Bronfman lawyer. Levine had to then field a call from Leo Kolber, still distressed by what he believed was Richler's betrayal all those years before, and assuage any Bronfman worries that he had gone over to the dark side. Levine, a self-described "Jew lite" and "fifth-generation Torontonian pseudo-wasp," amused Richler. He could dance a fine line, keeping all his clients happy at once, even when they were directly at odds with each other, and was renowned as a tenacious and loyal advocate on behalf of those he represented. Richler didn't want a literary agent or need anyone's help arranging book deals for Canada, but he did invite Levine to work as his entertainment lawyer on his film properties. Another friendship was born.

The "sequestering" period needed to put together the Gursky family tree was nearly complete. Richler was even ready to discuss the novel and submit to interviews. In one, in "a Bishop Street bar, smoking his distinctive Schimmelpenninck cigars, drinking Glenlivet scotch, joking with regulars," he admitted, "I put the pressure on myself" by taking so long between books, and confessed that it "has a very large cast." Richler was "out from under" the novel, ready once more to discuss politics, both national and local, and to speak his mind forcefully. Of Canada as a nation: "I don't think it's ever really come together except as a holding company of some kind." On the city of Ottawa: "Had Montreal remained the capital of this country, instead of a silly little cow town, you would never have had this whole Quebec problem." And of the Quebec problem: "It's endlessly childish. Whichever side of the argument you are on. Grown men arguing about the size of lettering on signs and whether they can be inside or outside! It's so wasteful, parochial and degrading."

Released from the solitude and silence of novel writing, he was even ready to attend a July conference in Saskatoon on the art of humour. He had made enemies in the west, and perhaps wanted to show, if not remorse, then a willingness to reconcile. Writing about the early Gursky years in Manitoba and Saskatchewan had also warmed him to the vast landscapes and tough, no-nonsense citizens. Whatever the reasons, he found himself on stage with the writer Brian Fawcett and a comedian named Sheila Gostick, talking about what makes for funny. But he should have known better; like most funny people, he hesitated to analyze the gift, and ended up a sour, unaccommodating panellist, willing only to exchange sharp disagreements with Fawcett. He did redeem himself with the audience by reading from a humorous essay. He also met two local authors and admirers. The novelist and academic David Carpenter, who collected him at the airport, had written an afterword to the Canadian Library edition of *Duddy Kravitz*; the shy young novelist Guy Vanderhaeghe had done the same for *St. Urbain's Horseman*, but he initially balked at bringing a courtesy bottle of Scotch to Richler's hotel room, fearing his notorious bark. David Carpenter persuaded Vanderhaeghe that Mordecai Richler had been asking to meet *him*, and that, in private, he was a different person. Richler got on with both men, and became friends with Vanderhaeghe.

7. Henry begat Isaac

Solomon Gursky Was Here was launched at the International Festival of Authors in Toronto in October 1989. In addition to giving a reading, Richler participated, alongside Margaret Atwood and the renowned economist John Kenneth Galbraith, in a tribute to Robertson Davies. It was his second year in a row paying tribute to an elder, having agreed in 1988 to salute Morley Callaghan on the same stage. He complimented the stylish Davies for not only being a master of magic but looking like one, in contrast with most writers, who resemble "drug dealers, school mistresses who have been discharged for moral turpitude, card sharpers, barmaids or shoplifters." At a dinner before the event, seated next to the very tall, elegant Galbraith, he deferred to another intimidating Anglo-Saxon. "You're not going to smoke that thing around me, are you?" Galbraith asked, referring to the cigar he was about to light up. "Oh no sir, no sir," Richler replied, butting out. The moment was a foretaste of another impending battle in the new decade: the growing intolerance of public smoking.

"A big, risky marriage of extravagant comic myth and compelling realism," cried *Maclean's*, and a "stunning triumph of the imagination." In Alberta, critics declared it "a masterpiece of complexity and intelligence" and "a superb work, a rowdy, roistering *tour de force*." The *Vancouver Sun* observed "Richler's maturity of style," and even his old sparring partner George Woodcock granted that it was an "admirably sustained novel . . . an impressive balance of comedy and pathos that no writers achieve early and few achieve at all." By February alone, *Gurksy* would have sold 38,000 copies in hardcover in Canada, with another 20,000 printed once it was named a Canadian Book-of-the-Month Club selection— some consolation for his being terminated as a juror. "So far the reviews have been mostly grand," he informed Deborah Rogers.

The purest insight into *Solomon Gursky Was Here* came from a ten-minute CBC TV segment that aired on the evening newscast *The National*. Rex Murphy, forewarned by colleagues that talking to Richler would be bruising, travelled to the Townships ready for a hostile interview. He found him polite and courteous. It didn't hurt that Murphy, the erudite, maverick Newfoundland commentator and critic, passionate about literature and well read, brought the force of his own powerful reading of the novel to the encounter. By devoting years of work to *Gursky*, a book with "epic appetite," Murphy told Canadians, "Richler has done something large here." CBC viewers, many catching sight of the author for the first time since the debate about free trade, received his thoughtful answers. "I took a lot of risks," he said. "You start off with dreams of perfection. It never ends up that way." But it was notable how much Mordecai Richler had aged during the intervening twenty-four months. He appeared ragged and puffy, his hair gone grey and his voice rasped with fatigue. Penguin, while careful to run each media request by him—he refused about half, mostly those for very small outlets—had nevertheless subjected him to close to fifty TV, radio and print interviews, many of them lengthy. He had done his part; once he agreed to a media encounter, he kept his word and, more often than not, was generous, if also still testy with bad or rude interviewers, and not above walking out of unpleasant encounters.

The cameras hinted at the mental and physical effort he had expended in order to lift *Gursky* over a decade to its present level. It had begun as a jumble of too many stories and characters spread across too much narrative, with the thematic ambitions threatening to overtax a structure he had to perpetually redesign, leaving him much of the time unsure that his opus wasn't a colossal miscalculation. His greatest book, the one he had been born to write—though possible only after decades of lived experience, literary training and deepening wisdom about human affairs—had been the hardest to get right. Though he would never have said it, *Gursky* was also both his contribution to Canadian literature, and his challenge to it—to be bigger, bolder, funnier, more profane and outrageous and full of teeming life. This was his testament, his declaration that "M.R. Was Here"; it was the novel he hoped would outlast him. But if either its inherent complexities, its pressuring of the stamina and taste of most readers, or simply its strangeness—strange to Canadian writing, strange even to his own canon—meant that *Gursky* would be a slow, tough sell, so be it.

The final page, in fact, spoke to the elusiveness of not only Richler's aspirations but those of any artist who seeks to remake the world, fresh and original, in fiction. Like Jake Hirsh with his eternal Horseman, Moses Berger—his own work and life a hopeless muddle—watches as a small airplane is transformed into a "big menacing black bird, the likes of which hadn't been seen over Lake Memphremagog since the record cold spell of 1851." What else could it be but the raven, with its eternal "unquenchable itch to meddle and provoke things, to play tricks on the world and its creatures?"

In conversation with the young poet Margaret Atwood, Montreal, 1968, who would later compare Richler as a satirist to George Orwell. Atwood's husband, the writer Graeme Gibson, said: "The thing for me was how thoroughly he was a writer. He was always doing it. It was the forties, fifties idea of the writer, with the drink, the manual typewriter, and pounding it out. . . . There was something Calvinist about his approach to writing. He'd say that you don't deserve the good times if you're not there in the bad times. You had to work every day."

1971, at the launch of *St. Urbain's Horseman* in Montreal, with Jack McClelland. "I think he really loved him," Florence Richler said of her husband's publisher and friend. Richler wrote of the struggles of Canadian literature two decades earlier: "Changes were in the wind. The audacious Jack McClelland, back from the war, had just inherited the reins at McClelland and Stewart, and the admirable Robert Weaver was beginning to establish himself at the CBC. Between the two of them, they contrived to sponsor writers who would yank Canlit into the twentieth century, but we had no way of knowing that yet." From Richler's afterword to *The Moslem Wife and Other Stories* by Mavis Gallant.

The Dad with Jacob, 7, in his Selwyn House school uniform, and Martha, 11, carrying the new bestseller.

"Once there was a boy called Jacob Two-Two. He was two plus two plus two years old. He had two ears and two eyes and two arms and two feet and two shoes. He also had two older sisters, Emma and Marfa, and two older brothers, Daniel and Noah. And they all lived in a rambling old house on Kingston Hill in England."
From *Jacob Two-Two Meets the Hooded Fang.*

"Kiddy author" with his readers, reading from *Jacob Two-Two* in Westmount Library, Montreal, 1975.

"There is nothing in talking to children that should be stressed any more than in talking to an adult. Honesty and goodwill should be the ideal in all communications. [A child] doesn't expect you to lie to him or to cheat him. I try, as a parent of five children of my own and as a writer, not to abuse that innocence."

Making the movie: Richler visiting Wilensky's, now on Clark Street, during filming of *The Apprenticeship of Duddy Kravitz*, fall 1973.

Terry Mosher, a.k.a. Aislin, became Mordecai Richler's unofficial caricaturist. Though not his first attempt, this 1973 cartoon shows the great Montreal cartoonist finally "getting" his subject: the hair, the features, the props—cigarillo and Scotch. Three dozen more caricatures would follow.

"Researching" *Gursky*: with Mel Hurtig in the High Arctic in March 1974. The North, he wrote, "becomes an addiction." "Our Last Frontier," BOMC newsletter, April 1976.

The Esteemed Gentlemen: The Book-of-the-Month Club, with their first "Associate for Canada," early 1980s. Fellow jurors: Al Silverman, David W. McCullough, Clifton Fadiman, Wilfrid Sheed and Mordecai. Books columnist William French of the *Globe and Mail* wrote of the BOMC board that its decisions played "no small part in the shaping of cultural tastes and attitudes in North America." Richler's influential position in New York allowed him to champion Canadian writers to an American audience, including Margaret Atwood and Alice Munro. He also fought hard for Toni Morrison's *Song of Solomon* and the young John Irving's *The World According to Garp*. The effect of a BOMC Selection or a Main Selection had considerable effect on an author's standing and finances.

"No matter how long I continue to live abroad, I do feel forever rooted in Montreal's St. Urbain Street. That was my time, my place, and I have elected myself to get it right." From "Why I Write," *Shovelling Trouble*.
Back in the old neighbourhood: Richler poses on the second-floor landing of 5257 St. Urbain Street, circa 1979.

"He was very conscious of time. He was almost always rushed. 'I must get back to work. I must get back to work.' It was a constant refrain." Martha Richler.
Richler, at his rolltop work desk, in the apartment in the Chateau, Sherbrooke Street, 1980s.

"Working eight hours a day, six days a week." Richler on the light-filled office landing in the "dacha" overlooking Lake Memphremagog. "This is home to me. . . . We have had several homes but we bought this in 1975 and have lived here longer than anywhere. I can work better out here. We go into town once a week, have lunch, see friends and our son Jake, buy food and come home."

"Mordecai's dream was always to have a place in the country." Florence Richler. Out together on Lake Memphremagog. "In the early morning hours, before anybody else in the cottage had risen, he watched the lake's sole surviving loon wheeling over the water, diving for sunfish and smelts. . . . In the evening, there were the robins feeding on water spiders. He couldn't see Susy and Teddy on the dock below—even if he strained, they were beyond his line of vision—but he could hear Susy squealing each time Teddy hooked a perch, and he blessed them." From *Joshua Then and Now*.

"Under that corrugated surface lay a very, very deep feeling man. . . . Life for Mordecai was painful [at times] like walking on eyeballs. But nobody ever loved me the way Mordecai loved me. He was capable of great feeling. That was a side of Mordecai that few people saw." Ted Kotcheff, the Richlers' lifelong friend, on safari in Kenya in 1984. "This, you might think, is how things were in the Garden of Eden. But, on closer examination, it is most certainly not a peaceable kingdom. Put more plainly, it's a meat rack . . ." From "Safari," *Belling the Cat*.

Among the Lions: Richler honoured with his peers at the "Literary Lions Evening" at the New York Public Library, November 9, 1989. From left to right, front row: Edward Albee, Tess Gallagher, Amy Clampitt, Bharati Mukherjee, Eve Merriam, William Zinsser. Second row: Mordecai Richler, Avery Corman, Carl Bernstein, Elmore Leonard, Joseph Mitchell, Hunter S. Thompson. Top row: William Arrowsmith, Lucille Clifton, Jay McInerney, Garry Wills, Robert Giroux, Kate Simon, Nat Hentoff. "Like any serious writer, I want to write one novel that will last, something that will make me remembered after death, and so I'm compelled to keep trying." From "Why I Write," *Shovelling Trouble*.

A tough critic: Daniel Richler, as host of the TV Ontario book programme, *Imprint*, debates his father's presentation of women and literary bullying. "Well, I'm a very old-fashioned man." Mordecai Richler to Daniel Richler on air, fall 1990.

PART VI

HANG IN OLD FRIEND

I

BACK ON THE MAP

A publicist at Chatto & Windus received a few tips from her colleague across the Atlantic at Penguin Canada about how to handle Mordecai Richler during his upcoming *Gursky* promotion tour in the U.K. She summarized the conversation for Alison Samuel:

a) He drinks a lot

b) He will cost us a lot of money in glenfiddich/glenlivet

c) He drinks a worrying amount before readings/interviews, but he doesn't get noticeably drunk so don't panic

d) He does sometimes get a bit bad tempered when he's had a few

e) He doesn't like to be talked to much—i.e. if going on a long journey he likes to sit quietly, not chit-chat (v. sensible)

f) She puts all of the above down to the fact that he's really rather shy, and she thinks he is basically a truly wonderful person, etc.

So nothing we didn't already know, really.

The tolerant British had clearly seen worse among their eclectic and distinguished authors, but Canadians still appeared to have problems with outsized personalities. In certain nationalist literary circles, at least, it seemed the crimes of Mordecai Richler required ongoing punishment. In February, a three-book shortlist for the Governor General's Literary Award for Fiction was announced, with *Gursky* not on it. Outrage at the exclusion was expressed in public by the Harbourfront Festival director, Greg Gatenby, and the internationally esteemed critic Alberto Manguel, and in private by Robertson Davies. Manguel also mailed a postcard to the Townships: "Can one apologize for the awful stupidity of the G.G. jurors even though one has nothing to do with the set-up?" he wrote. "Of all the *#!!**!! fools!!" Richler himself questioned the exclusion of Leon Rooke's explosive novel *A Good Baby,* and said, "I was on a Governor General's Award committee, with Alice Munro and Margaret Laurence, and we had no scores to settle, and we weren't consumed by envy." Paul Quarrington's *Whale Music* was named the winner that March.

Concern inside Chatto that Mordecai Richler could prove a difficult author may have been triggered by his responses to the regular "Author Questionnaire" designed to provide direction to the media. *How long have you been at work on this book?* met with the reply "Too long. Say, five years." To the query *How did the idea for your book originate?* he replied, "Are you kidding me?" *In your opinion, what is the market for your book?* merited "Vast." *Do you mind being interviewed on radio or TV?* "Yes, but I'll do it if it isn't too silly." His British publisher got off easy compared to the Dutch translator of *Gursky*, who mailed five pages of textual queries. In ascending order of impatience: *What does "Sally of County Clare" mean?* "A girl called Sally who comes from County Clare." To a query about Camelot: "Look it up, for Christ's sake!" To *What is "the Corgi"?* "I'll give you a hint. 'Woof, woof, woof!'" To the translator's bafflement at one colloquialism: "Oh, come on. Do you really understand English?"

But on the whole, loving the wheeling and dealing, and sensing momentum for *Gursky* even before it appeared in England, Richler was happy to be out and about. His career was moving once more. In the U.K. Deborah Rogers was currently negotiating a deal that would involve new editions of earlier books as well. "GURSKY for them OK," he wrote of the offer from Vintage

U.K., "so long as they re-release—as a minimum—COCKSURE and ST URBAINS HORSEMAN, or—as a max—ditto DUDDY and JOSHUA." He wound up accepting £15,000 for the paperback of *Gursky*, plus new editions of *Duddy* and *Horseman*.

In London in March after a week's holiday in Portugal with Florence, he offered to make himself available. "I have no idea where we are going to stay yet," he told Alison Samuel, "but I am available for Telegraph Mag, and anybody else important, anytime." He had reasons for expecting attention from the *Daily Telegraph*. The conservative paper was now owned by his occasional dinner and drinks companion, the media baron (if not yet Lord) Conrad Black. Its weekend magazine, moreover, was being edited by the young journalist admirer who had risked introducing himself in a hotel lobby nine years before. Sure enough, Nigel Horne commissioned a profile of him to run when the novel appeared in June. Being in London also allowed Richler to better explain his various book projects. He hand-delivered his latest collection of essays to Deborah Rogers, hoping Chatto would publish it as well. Feeling generative after the long haul with *Gursky,* he wanted Chatto to publish the collection along with his new anthology. *Writers on World War II*, which he had been slowly assembling for three years, using his own library and memories of books and articles he had read as far back as the war itself, was now finally on track, thanks in part to his assistant: daughter Martha, her own career as an artist and author still in embryo, who dutifully visited libraries to locate material.

He was also bracing himself to write his article on Quebec for the *New Yorker*. The commission, the most substantial of his career, had come about in a manner unique to the magazine. Calling Bob Gottlieb to explain the idea—with a close friend as editor-in-chief, there would be no need to pass any editorial gates—he was told on the spot to go ahead and write about the province's sign laws at whatever length, and in whatever time frame, he thought correct. No fee was discussed, as per the *New Yorker* custom of considering money, and even word count, unworthy subjects; once the piece was edited, he would be paid a fee commensurate with the final length. Though not quite ready to start the assignment, he delivered a remarkable speech on a related topic in Toronto. Asked to participate in a benefit for the Harbourfront Reading Series organized by Greg Gatenby and moderated by Peter Gzowski, Richler used the pulpit to denounce the Meech Lake Constitutional Accord. The accord, negotiated in 1987 by Prime Minister Brian Mulroney, was intended to persuade Quebec to endorse the 1982 Canadian Constitution and increase support within the province for remaining in Canada. To that end, it recommended that the province be recognized as a "distinct society" and be granted a constitutional veto. Saying yes to Meech Lake, Richler told the crowd of four hundred, was akin to saying yes to separatism. His lecture, powerfully, passionately argued and, for him, notably devoid of jokes, earned a standing ovation from an audience packed with heads of arts organizations, publishers and editors, as well as provincial politicians and business elites. It was a calculated use of his influence as a public figure to galvanize opinion.

He was determined. When he had said a few years earlier that he had gone public with his views on free trade simply to express his opinion, he had meant it. Free trade itself was not a make-or-break issue for him, but Quebec's language laws, and the apparent drift towards sovereignty, were fundamental. He was about to employ lecterns, TV and radio appearances, the pages of newspapers and magazines, even the shelves of bookshops, in the fight, not of his literary life, but of his life as a citizen and ardent Montrealer. In tone and content the speech in Toronto announced his battle plan.

Woody's Pub became a "safe house" for the irreverent hometown crowd. He might have to travel to Toronto to rally national opinion makers, and make use of contacts in New York to place articles in the *New York Times* and the *New Yorker*, but stirring up trouble in Quebec required little more than a ten-minute walk from their apartment in the Chateau. On days when he was in the city he showed up at the bar by five, had two or three cocktails and called Florence at six-thirty to confirm the dinner hour.

On warm afternoons he and his friends sat on the outdoor patio; otherwise, they huddled on stools near the counter. While not the ringleader—Nick Auf der Maur wore that crown—Richler brought the authority of his nature, and his wider fame. Smoking and drinking, reading newspapers and arguing about their contents, they concocted hilarious schemes and pranks such as the "Twice As Much Society," a group that would lobby for a law obliging people to speak French twice as loudly as they did English. Or they drafted letters to Premier Bourassa insisting that his recently announced bill to reward new births with cash—the "fertility payola"—include only ethnically pure French-speaking Quebecers, lest "garlicky Allophones, driven by avarice, take to polluting the province with racially impure families of a dozen kids or more."

From Woody's, Richler even helped found a political party to champion English rights in the wake of the premier's invoking his veto to preserve Bill 178, the amended version of the original language law 101, against constitutional challenges. Called, on his recommendation, the Equality Party—hotter heads had wanted "Liberty" or "Freedom"—the party had obtained the requisite number of signatures in spring 1989 to be officially designated. He then recruited the "ostensibly affable but often acerbic" Montreal lawyer Richard Holden to stand for election in Westmount. The corpulent, amusing Holden, still another outlandish, hard-drinking maverick, and a former friend of Brian Mulroney's, had run twice for federal office as a Conservative. He won his seat this time, narrowly, and no less a figure than Mordecai Richler campaigned door to door to help woo voters.

Once Woody's went out of business, Holden joined Richler, Auf der Maur and the rest in Grumpy's Bar, four doors down on Bishop Street. Their crowd required "a watering hole that was well lit, cashed personal checks, did not blast its patrons with rock music, and employed a barmaid who never acknowledged to phone callers that you had even been in that afternoon, never mind that you stood there now, unless you agreed to it with a nod." Aislin commemorated the change of headquarters with a

1991 *Gazette* cartoon showing Nick Auf der Maur heading into Grumpy's for the "Unhappy Hour 12–12." A sign on the sidewalk railing advertised, "Tonight! Every nite! Every afternoon too! THE WORLD (as we know it) ANGLOPHONIE CONFERENCE." The brilliant and now sober Aislin, interested in simultaneously observing and immortalizing his friends, had one cartoon of his boulevardier pals rejected for being *too* pitiless an observation of their habits: riffing off an article about an experiment to cure alcoholism using a weed, a process which had revealed that hamsters possessed huge capacities for liquor, the cartoon depicted Auf der Maur (recognizable by his hat) and three other hamsters at a counter, riotously drunk.

Outside the bar, Richler's fears that Quebec had not distanced itself as much as it believed from its anti-Semitic past were being confirmed by events and remarks. Whether it was the "folk hero" owner of a tabloid newspaper quoted rebuking his staff for writing positively about Jews, or vandals spray-painting swastikas on the walls of an Outremont yeshiva, the evidence disturbed him. In the bar, on a stool with the daily papers, or at the country house with scissors and a clippings file, Richler was bracing to start the *New Yorker* assignment. The longer he waited, it seemed, the stronger his case became, with almost daily news of troubling fresh comment and incident. A confrontation, loud and ugly, was becoming inevitable.

In April, Florence and he flew to New York to promote *Gursky*. He gave a Canadian Consulate–sponsored reading, sharing the podium with his Quebec playwright acquaintance Michel Tremblay and his new Saskatoon friend Guy Vanderhaeghe, and juggled more media interviews. Between engagements he and Florence managed drinks at Sardi's and dinner at Elaine's, New York's most fashionable restaurant. There they ran into a bloated and distracted Terry Southern, with whom he had spent such easy, wild times in France, and who, charming and handsome, had once made a pass at Florence. Southern's career had soared so high in the 1960s, in the wake of the epochal *Dr. Strangelove* script and film, that his descent in the 1970s and '80s had struck many as free fall, as he was dragged down by financial woes and a dearth of new projects, and battled stomach cancer. They chatted about the death of Mason Hoffenberg in 1986, and went their separate ways. Terry Southern too would be dead within a few years.

American reviews were respectable, although Richler had been forewarned by Bob Gottlieb that the novelist Francine Prose in the *New York Times Book Review* was going to give the book a hard time. She had problems with certain of the characters, or caricatures, in particular of the "Eskimos"—"Though being Jewish apparently enables Mr. Richler to feel on safe ground with outrageous Jewish jokes," she noted, "he is, so to speak, on much thinner ice here"—and joined a growing chorus of reviewers, often though not always women, impatient with his female characters. The *Wall Street Journal* said the book "brims with enthusiasm for life at its most absurd" and in *New York*, in whose pages he had appeared as a reviewer, the critic and editor Rhoda Koenig wrote, "Pushy, pushy, pushy—Mordecai Richler's Jews, in *Solomon Gursky Was Here*, are everywhere." Amidst acclaim for the "enormous iceberg of a plot" and the author's "talent for mimicry" lay the same objection. Richler, she noted, "is less comfortable with fully fleshed characters, women in particular. A persistent note of sourness undermines his satire."

Later that year, he heard again about his failings with female characters from his own son. Daniel Richler, now the host of the literary TV show *Imprint*, which he had stamped with his own distinct, witty intelligence, agreed to interview the ferocious, often monosyllabic Mordecai Richler on air, and though he had no intention of firing Oedipal barbs, he did ask questions others might not dare. "There are descriptions of women that permeate *Solomon Gursky Was Here*," he said, "where what you describe first is, as it were, that which arrives first: the bosomy ladies in various permutations." When Richler protested, his oldest child explained that "in the modern feminist sensibility people find that objectionable. I think they find it kind of old-fashioned." "Well, I'm a very old-fashioned man," his parent replied. He had been trading in comedic grotesques since *The Incomparable Atuk*, but questions concerning his portrayal of women were fair. They echoed similar observations made about *Joshua*, and it was true, and correct, that the changing times were no longer cutting "old-fashioned" male writers the slack they had once enjoyed. Equally true was that the public objections of certain critics were seconded by the private hesitations of Florence, the presumed model for the idealized shiksa beauties of the major novels. She believed that he could push himself to grant women more of the complexity, and vividness, of his male creations.

Daniel, while nervous about taking his father on, even playfully, addressed one of the other "raps" against him: his tendency in his non-fiction to apply lethal satiric firepower to easy targets. He went after him for pillorying "the innocent victims of your contempt" in reviews (often for *GQ*) in reviews of books produced by, say, Patti Reagan and Shirley MacLaine. "There's no doubt that it's hilarious," he said of those reviews, "but sometimes one feels that you're not picking on people your own size." Outmanoeuvred, his bemused parent conceded this point too: "Well, maybe I am a bit of a bully."

"He pulled out all my bad reviews!" Richler told Florence in the hotel afterwards, with his interrogator present. He was enormously proud of Daniel, as he was of all their children.

Only a small percentage of the essays in *Broadsides: Reviews and Opinions* showed him picking on someone not his own size. The insightful preface to Deuteronomy was included, along with a fine introduction to a new edition of *All Quiet on the Western Front*. The selection demonstrated the changing direction of his career. If the credits in his debut collection, *Shooting Tigers under Glass,* had represented a who's who of places to publish in 1960s England, *Broadsides* offered a similar front rank of American print media: *Playboy, GQ, New York Magazine, New York Times Book Review*. Canada was represented by only two small pieces from the *Gazette,* a situation that the recent hiring of John Fraser at *Saturday Night,* a magazine now also owned by Conrad Black, was about to emphatically correct. (Richler had just published a raw-knuckled piece on the New Democratic Party convention with

Saturday Night, its insults spread widely, but too late for inclusion in the book.) There were no credits from British magazines or newspapers. Still, Vintage published *Broadsides*, along with the paperback of *Gursky* and the reissues. All were retailed in book-shops around the U.K. in a stand-alone bookcase—an expensive marketing commitment and a marker of a novelist of stature, with a major new release, and the backlist, on display together.

In early June the Richlers were in London again. They stayed with the Claytons in Marlow the first night before moving to André Deutsch's home in Fulham for a week—still friends, despite all. The *Telegraph Weekend Magazine* profile arranged by Nigel Horne greeted their arrival, and it couldn't have been more auspicious. "Hanging Out with Moses" called *Gursky* "big, bold and swarming with eccentric characters" and its author "one of those novelists whose sales and, indeed, public esteem have never matched their talent." The effect was aided by a contact sheet's worth of close-up, unsparing photos of him, hair bedev-illed and glasses perched low. The *Telegraph Weekend Magazine* led off a successful week of publicity in London and the best reviews to date—none of which took exception to the book's treatment of its women. Carmen Callil hosted a lively party at her house in Notting Hill Gate, attended by many old friends from the publishing and television worlds. The couple left England buoyant with the reception and the rumoured prospects that *Gursky* might find a spot on the Booker shortlist that autumn. "I know how hard everyone worked," Deborah Rogers wrote to Callil later in the month, "and I am so very grateful as I believe—and I think Mordecai feels too—that he is really back on the map." Chaotic as her London office always was, with manu-scripts, contracts and cushions vying for space on chairs and floors, and for all the genuine affection and respect she had for her clients and many of the publishers she worked with, Deborah Rogers was not London's leading literary agent at the time with-out reason: she used the warmth of the moment to emphasize that the wait for another Mordecai Richler novel would not be so long—"he truly promises that the next one will be with us soon"—and began negotiations for it, delivering a signed contract to him in December.

The good feeling about *Gursky* was confirmed when the book won the Commonwealth Writers' Prize. That meant a trip to Sydney at the end of October and an audience with the Queen in early November. At Buckingham Palace he and Florence received an etiquette lesson from a chamberlain, and then were shown into a room where the Queen sat. She asked if their children watched too much television, and reported on having met both Brian Mulroney and—with greater avidity—Pierre Trudeau. The audience, scripted at five minutes, lasted fifteen, with Richler, reasonably well turned out in a suit and tie, giving his usual concise, eloquent answers. Australia and New Zealand, meanwhile, had amounted to a nearly three-week trip for the couple, with long spells in Sydney and Auckland, bookended by the most exhausting flights of their lives. Mid-September, and the announcement of the shortlist for the Booker Prize brought the best news of all. Six novels, including *Gursky*, were selected. Two competitors were friends: Brian Moore for *Lies of Silence* and the funny, brilliant Beryl Bainbridge, whom he saw for drinks whenever he was in town and who was shortly to become close to Emma, for *An Awfully Big Adventure*. They joined John McGahern's *Amongst Women*, Penelope Fitzgerald's *The Gate of Angels* and another Chatto & Windus book, A.S. Byatt's *Possession*. It was a powerful list, although some of the critics dubbed it geriatric, the average author age being sixty-one. (At fifty-four, Byatt was the youngest.) Betting on the Bookers was now popular, and oddsmakers had made Moore, on his third nomination, the frontrunner, followed by McGahern. Richler, who did not phone or write his old friend with congratulations, did see the odds shift slightly in his favour. By the eve of the awards he had gone from seven to one, a long shot, to eleven to four, with more money being bet on *Gursky* than on any other novel.

Still, by halfway through the black-tie dinner, with him slouched uncomfortably in his tuxedo and Florence smiling and bravely charming their table of guests, it was apparent from the direction the TV cameras were aiming—at the table reserved for Antonia Byatt—that he wasn't going to beat those odds. Noah, seated elsewhere, glanced at his parents when *Possession* was called, and noticed the looks they exchanged: supportive and loving. It neither helped nor hurt that the senior juror, Sir Denis Forman, took Richler aside to express his admiration of *Gursky*, a view sadly not fully shared by his jury, three of four of whom were women and had apparently voiced complaints similar to those of the New York critics. With the failure to win went the best chance for the novel to take its place in the canon of Canadian literature or for Richler to attain certain international appeal. Chance plays a role in the fate of any book, and chance did not favour *Gursky* that night in London.

For Brian Moore, too, the 1990 Booker outcome must have been bitter. The two former friends could manage only a handshake and banalities, none of the words either consoling or cheering. Their friendship, uneasy and competitive from the start, had gone sour as far back as Moore's remarriage in the late 1960s, with neither stubborn, proud man willing to admit it for decades. Now it was officially defunct.

The Booker disappointment aside, Richler still felt, as he reported to Deborah Rogers in the new year, that he was "back on the map" in England, and took an assignment with the *Telegraph Weekend Magazine*—reporting on his and Florence's trip to Australia in the autumn—and completed the radio script for *Jacob Two-Two* for the BBC. All this despite being "awfully behind because of the hospital week and then 14 days of waiting for all the bloody test results." The hospital stay, in late November, had been necessitated by a tumour on his bladder. It had proven both benign, and a wake-up call. "As Florence told you, I've been reprieved. However, I've had such a scare that I've cut out smoking, and it's driving me crazy." He and Florence were back in London still one more time in January, to see Emma, who had decided to live there, perform in *Morte D'Arthur* at the Lyric Theatre in Hammersmith.

Not smoking drove him crazy for about eighteen months, with occasional relapses. Work suffered—he had been puffing and

typing since he was sixteen—and though he received encouragement from his family and friends, including colleagues at Penguin
Canada, who launched their own office campaign against cigarettes by tacking a photo of their star author with the caption IF
HE CAN QUIT SMOKING, SO CAN YOU to a bulletin board, the
effort was doomed. Thinking he might smoke fewer, he switched
from the ultra-thin Schimmelpenninck to the thicker Davidoff
demi-tasse, and tried not to light up his first one until after lunch.

While in London to see Emma onstage, he met Nigel Horne for
lunch at the Savoy. Horne asked him to write another piece.
Agreeing, he suggested a fee several times the industry norm.
Horne was taken aback. "Conrad's a rich man," Richler explained
of the *Telegraph*'s proprietor. The young editor tried to keep pace
with his guest; whiskies before the roast beef meal and double
cognacs afterwards. The bill topped £200, the largest total he had
ever tried to expense. Horne must have blanched, for Richler
decided on the spot that he owed Conrad Black the same amount
from a bet they had made in Montreal on a hockey game. He wrote
a cheque and asked Horne to drop it off in Black's office on Canary
Wharf. The young editor did so and received his boss's surprised
but bemused approval of the hire, and a lesson in the cost of doing
business with Mordecai Richler. "He's a great writer," Black said.

Horne hired him a few more times during his five years as
editor. When he lost his job at the *Telegraph*, he expected, given
the mercenary norm of most writer-editor relationships, not to
hear from Richler again until he had obtained a new position of
power. Instead, one of the first calls he received was from Canada,
and it included an open invitation to visit him and Florence in
Montreal. When Horne did finally make it to the country house
in 1994, he found himself surrounded by other guests, often young
editors out of New York or Toronto, some friends of the children,
some of Richler's own acquaintance, all being made welcome. His
loyalty to old friends—Ted Allan and Ted Kotcheff, Bill Weintraub,
the Ostrys in Ottawa and Rabinovitches in Toronto—was matched
by a receptivity to forming new friendships, both professional and
personal (and with luck, the usual quick dissolve between the

two). Guy Vanderhaeghe, who had won the Governor General's Award in 1982 for *Man Descending* and was achieving greater recognition as a novelist, was the recipient of the sure signs of Richler affection: a "good word" put in on his behalf with publishers and editors internationally, and brief, jokey faxes. David Staines, who had rescued him from the dreary party in Boston some years before and was now at the University of Ottawa, visited him at the lake, or at the Press Club in Ottawa. Likewise, in an interesting dimension of their marriage, he and Florence maintained an unusually large number of "couple friendships," complementing each other and perhaps accommodating each other's varying tastes. Even when there was a divorce, as with the Robinsons, Florence remained close to Carmen, attending opera and theatre with her, and Richler occasionally saw Jon, who still helped with his taxes.

One exception was Jack McClelland. In the spring of 1991 McClelland was set to receive an achievement award from the Toronto Arts Council for his outstanding contribution to publishing in Canada. Richler agreed months ahead of time to present it to him, only to realize closer to the date that he had double-booked, and would be in California on a lecture tour. McClelland was irate and questioned his excuse. Stung, Richler suggested he call him in San Francisco on the day as proof. He wondered why his old friend, once inclined to make light of such baubles, would take a "Rotary award" so seriously. But he was not thinking of McClelland's state in the wake of losing his company, or of the fact that he was now floundering as a literary agent, disregarded by those who had once lionized him. The friendship didn't recover from the mix-up, and McClelland later found an excuse not to attend Martha's wedding.

Much of the winter had been devoted to wrapping up work on the anthology *Writers on World War II*, which Martha continued to assist with, despite a slow recovery from a ruptured appendix. They rescheduled a Paris trip as a result until October, and Richler confessed to friends that he and Florence had a larger lifestyle plan underway: to spend several months a year in

London—away from "the endless winters here." The anthology, his third effort, was close to his heart. The opening pages were almost a private *Bildungsroman* disguised as a foreword, given over to his childhood awakening to the war, and his early adult wanderings in postwar Europe. The first selection, W.H. Auden's "September 1, 1939," was perfect—a personal homage to an enduring influence. Beyond Auden lay many other essential literary influences, from Orwell to Waugh to Norman Lewis, Sartre and de Beauvoir to Gide and Céline. First Martha and then Carmen Callil encouraged him to think more widely about the war's participants, especially women, leading to the inclusion of work by Japanese writers Yukio Mishima and Shusaku Endo, as well as German witnesses to the implosion of their country, and the Russian diarist Marie Vassiltchikov on life in wartime Berlin. He also found space for friends: Doris Lessing, Wilfrid Sheed, Brian Moore, and Canadians Farley Mowat, Joy Kogawa and Czech transplant Josef Škvorecký. Highlighting Elie Wiesel and Primo Levi on the Holocaust was obvious, but the two excerpts from *Hasidic Tales of the Holocaust* by Yaffa Eliach were less expected, and no less powerful.

By June, with *Writers on World War II* wrapped up, he was in Manhattan having drinks with Sonny Mehta at Knopf. "This September," he wrote soon after to Deborah Rogers, "the New Yorker will be running approx. 20,000 words of mine abt Quebec . . . its hilarious sign laws . . . etc etc. I am expanding this into a short book—50,000 to 60,000 words—that I will deliver at the end of July or mid-August. Sonny will publish it in Feb at Knopf and Viking will do it here." He faxed her his handwritten two-page outline for *The Language of Signs*, as it was then titled, which he had already sent to Knopf and Penguin, and which promised to take "a close look at the western world's goofiest and most unnecessary political crisis." "Time is of the essence," he told his agent. A national referendum on the latest constitutional accord was set for fall 1992, and he wanted *The Language of Signs* out by April, at the latest. "Can Carmen manage that? Or do her pub plans for WWII anthol. [coming in February] complicate matters?" Adding, "Please assure Carmen, after she has absorbed the ding-a-ling news, that I will get back to my novel as soon as this is done…. But I do feel deeply abt things here, and nothing embarrasses Quebecers more than to be ridiculed abroad."

In a letter early in the summer he had reported a direct lightning strike that had left the cottage without electricity. "We both glow in the dark." He was about to be hit by two more lightning strikes. "Inside/Outside," as the *New Yorker* piece was called, was due on the stands in late September, and the retitled *Oh Canada! Oh Quebec!*, a manuscript banged out on his electric typewriter in the course of a few months at the lake, was set for publication in March 1992. He faxed or mailed sections to Cynthia Good at Penguin as he wrote them; she responded, mostly with requests for more information and elaboration. Both the essay and the book would cause jolts even a natural-born agitator could not have braced for.

THINGS ARE BAD ENOUGH WITHOUT NASTINESS FROM MORDECAI RICHLER

I n mid-September, with the manuscript nearly complete and a copy of the *New Yorker* containing his 32-page article on Quebec's sign laws in his pocket, Richler flew to Saskatchewan to appear at a fundraiser for the Writer's Guild. He had paid his own way out and was staying with Guy and Margaret Vanderhaeghe. The magazine was hitting newsstands across the country by the time he took the stage in Saskatoon. Throughout Quebec, the *New Yorker* was already virtually sold out.

He heard just before the event that trouble was brewing. Florence phoned to report that, thanks to their long practice of keeping their number listed, she was picking up the receiver not only to the calls of concerned friends but to the threatening remarks of strangers, delivered in French. At dinner with the Vanderhaeghes he mentioned that recently a Montreal cabbie, noticing him on the sidewalk, had shouted out of his car, "That's him! The Jew!" Concerned for Florence, he abandoned plans to go fishing and flew home the next morning.

"Inside/Outside" was an instant scandal. The Montreal *Gazette* had obtained an advance copy, and its thoughtful features writer, Mark Abley, began expansively. "For English-speaking Montrealers, he's our sardonic laureate, our homegrown hero. Even when he exposes our foibles and absurdities, we secretly relish the sting of his wit." In his "survey of recent Quebec history, retold for out-siders and with a devastating use of details," Richler was operating from a stance of "weary resignation" about everything from venal politicians and silly sign laws to the "thorny question of anti-Semitism." Abley's major objection was that "Inside/ Outside" was a joyless exercise, in contrast to Richler's fiction. His text, expanded for national coverage in the *Globe and Mail* without his approval, emphasized both the prestige and influence of the *New Yorker*, "probably the foremost cultural magazine in the English-speaking world," and repeated the rumour of Richler's fee—$40,000 U.S.—which first surfaced in the French newspaper *La Presse*. Richler himself, on air with a CBC journalist, disputed the figure, saying only that it was too high. If so, it wasn't by much; the magazine routinely paid in the $2-per-word range.

The brickbats came fast and hard. A provincial politician wanted him arrested for treason. A prominent elderly Quebecer, Michel Bélanger, dismissed him as an outsider: "He isn't part of the family," he told the media. In *La Presse* he was derided first as a hater of French Quebecers and then, in an editorial with accompanying cartoon, as someone whose prose was a "show of bad faith, of contempt and morbid introspection." In *Le Devoir*, the intelligent, fiery editor-in-chief, Lise Bissonnette, herself a novelist, penned an editorial on September 18 titled "The View from Woody's Pub," first reproducing (in translation) Mel Hurtig's old complaints of his one-time friend as lazy, vulgar, an obsequious colonialist, with the jibe that he "adores this kind of hysterical attention." Declining to note the attention Richler paid in "Inside/ Outside" to the record of anti-Semitism in the pages of a bygone *Le Devoir*, she accused him of writing a racist tract himself. "Imagine for a moment that a famous white writer, living in Chicago, proposed to write for the *New Yorker* a 'satire' of the same style on the black society in the midst of which he lives, that he treats it time and again as a 'tribe,' that he expresses shock that women there formerly reproduced like 'sows'; would the editors agree to touch it?"

The "sow" reference in particular, given out of context—Richler was in fact remarking on the "punishing level of reproduction" expected of French-Canadian women on account of the Church's

Revanche du berceau policy—was paraded as an insult to Quebec's female population. No amount of reiteration on his part that he felt the same way about the huge families produced by other Orthodox communities—the Jews, for instance—would make this charge go away.

The English-language media were scarcely happier. Unlike the features writer, Mark Abley, the *Gazette*'s in-house separatist, Ed Bantey, called it "abusive and inflammatory" and "objectively, if not legally, hate propaganda." In the *Globe and Mail*, Quebec columnist Lysiane Gagnon decried the appearance of "Inside/Outside" in broader societal terms: given that Montreal, beset by high unemployment and boarded-up businesses, rotating strikes and a disastrous sports stadium that had lately shed a 50-ton beam, was in "dire straits," Richler should not have delivered such a "devastating" article, especially given his conclusion that the city's decline would not stop. "Things Are Bad Enough without Nastiness from Mordecai Richler," the newspaper titled her complaint. Two days later its Quebec correspondent, Ray Conlogue, wrote that "every two or three years Mordecai Richler mounts the lucrative podium of a well-known magazine to deliver himself of a thunderbolt directed against the province of Quebec." A rare moment of levity occurred when Richler, being interviewed in his living room for the dinner-hour news by the local CBC anchor Denis Trudeau, responded to the question about his friend Richard Holden's denunciation of "Inside/Outside" by observing that nothing Holden said after mid-afternoon should be taken seriously. When Trudeau then inquired if Richler was, in effect, also inclined to issue public remarks while drunk, he issued a flat no. A few moments later he pointedly transferred his glass of Scotch from one hand to the other, on camera.

Articles, opinion pieces and countless letters filled newspapers in Quebec and other parts of Canada. Some defended him for the specifics of his arguments or simply for his right to be provocative. Others attacked him on all fronts, even for his high praise of Pierre Trudeau. No single article published by any Canadian had ever achieved such instant notoriety—or impact.

A nastier TV encounter took place in his apartment in the Chateau. He had agreed to an interview with Radio-Canada, to be conducted in English on September 20. The reporter, Madeleine Poulin, ambushed him outside the building a few minutes ahead of the appointed hour. Offended, he insisted the camera be turned off and then, once the crew were inside the apartment, having filmed him opening the door to them, vowed to provide only three minutes of material. Otherwise, he said, he would be misquoted. "Is it your style or a way of getting attention," Poulin began, "or do you really despise everything you set your eyes upon in Canada, including the French in Quebec?" Seated again in his living-room chair, he denied that he hated any thing or place, including the province. "This is my home, and I enjoy it here." For fifteen minutes he defended himself against the charge that he was a vengeful, out-of-touch curmudgeon who neither understood nor liked French Quebecers. "Why did you do it?" Poulin asked repeatedly, as though grilling a murder suspect. The interview turned still more hostile on the subject of Richler's refusal to be interviewed in French. He read the language, he explained, and had sent his children to French schools, but no, he was unwilling to speak it in public. "It's a lack of interest," Poulin accused. To which he snapped, "Let's say [my French is] better than your Hebrew." He apologized. She did not.

The following Saturday he returned fire in the *Gazette*, addressing his critics by name, and refuting them point by point. "I seem to have read again and again that I called francophone grandmothers sows," he wrote. "This is not true." Mocking Lise Bissonnette, who would, he felt certain, prefer a late-afternoon yogurt to a drinking session with friends (an allusion to her implying that he did too much of his thinking out of a bottle), he noted that she had published her editorial without referring to his charge that "Le Devoir was burdened by a long and disgraceful history of anti-Semitism." He corrected Ray Conlogue's *Globe and Mail* comment about his repeated "thunderbolts" against Quebec, saying he had fired them only twice before—in the *Atlantic* in 1977 and again in 1984—and divulged the contents of

Conlogue's phone conversation with a *New Yorker* editor, in which he called Richler "a disaffected, English-speaking Jewish writer, outside the mainstream [of Quebec]." (The editor had written the remarks down and passed them along.) He reiterated his commitment to Montreal and Canada, and made clear the realities, for someone of his stature, of dedicating so much time to Quebec. "In the past six months, while I have been working on my book about Quebec, I turned down several film offers that would have earned me many times the return I can expect from a book of no more than parochial interest."

Later interviewed again by the *Gazette,* Richler warned that the *New Yorker* article had been just "the nice part" of it. But he also added soberly, "I'm not pleased by the anger. I wish it had provoked intelligent, instead of shrill, response."

"Inside/Outside" did provoke more angry than intelligent reactions, but it mattered a great deal that it was Mordecai Richler who penned those twenty thousand careful, sometimes plodding words about Quebec's language and sign laws. Aware of the scrutiny he would receive, he had been on his best behaviour with the *New Yorker*, laying out his arguments, opting for facts over quips, not going for funny. But he could say almost nothing that wouldn't be interpreted as nasty; his motives could only be, in the eyes of many French Quebecers, dark and self-serving. Québécois, by and large, did not read his fiction, and did not understand or appreciate his sensibility. Living in a different language and largely part of a different culture, they remained oblivious, in literary terms, to the satiric tradition he was writing from. Some thought that he wasn't really speaking to them since he was writing in English—and, in this case, for an American publication. While the *New Yorker* piece was designed for maximum humiliation of the separatist agenda, it was done for the rest of Canada, by way—like his speech in Toronto—of galvanizing the country. It was one maverick's very strong opinion and view, but it was also politics, and he was playing hard.

In the *Gazette* Richler raised a disturbing spectre with regard to the attention his fee with the *New Yorker* had drawn. He cited a speech by Claude Ryan delivered in the late 1960s. "Whenever a French Canadian wants to pass a severe judgement on one of his compatriots," Ryan told an audience, "he will often be heard to say, 'He's a bad Jew'—meaning that he made a fast dollar at the expense of his compatriots, either in the practice of his profession, or the conduct of his business." Ryan was speaking of a slightly older Quebec, which many people acknowledged had been anti-Semitic, as much of the rest of Canada had been. An accusation underlay the citation, and it was incendiary: some Quebecers believed he was vilifying them because he was a Jew, and Jews, disloyal and money-obsessed, would do anything for a quick buck. Interestingly, no one picked up on the innuendo, even though he repeated it, for good measure, in the postscript to *Oh Canada! Oh Quebec!*

Mordecai Richler, while definitely a street fighter, was not a likely warrior on behalf of any larger community. *Will no one soothe our fevered brows?* the popular local comedy musical duo, Bowser and Blue, asked in their annual review. *Will no one even try? / "I'll do my best," replied / Brave Sir Mordecai.* Once, entering Ben's Deli late at night with Florence, he was given a standing ovation by diners who saw him as their champion. That he found amusing. More than once, passing strangers entreated him to "Give those frogs hell!" That he found offensive. An unexpected letter that he received in early October hinted at the shift in local Jewish perceptions of the notorious "self-hating Jew." "Dear Mordecai (Mutty), If the PQ keep bringing up the 'Je me Souviens' bit that goes back to Wolfe and Montcalm," wrote his aunt Anne, of the province's "motto" imprinted on license plates, "we have every right to 'Je me Souviens' about what took place in the 20s–30s–40s." His father's sister, whom he had probably seen a half a dozen times in forty years, extended a collective thumbs-up to her nephew. "I want you to know that in this instance we all heartily agree with what you had to say."

His emerging role as a kind of accidental local horseman, riding into battle for his own reasons—a commitment to Montreal and Quebec, a belief in fairness and civility—while being perceived as

either a sour agent of majority community destruction or a
minority community hero, had a primal hold on his imagination.
It was Yudel Rosenberg's stick drawings of Jewish Cossacks, and
tales of golems sprung to life to save imperilled Jews, back in
psychological play with his grandson a half-century later.
Reviewing a biography of mobster Meyer Lansky, he wrote of the
hoodlums of New York as "the most colourfully named bunch of
bandits this side of the Newgate Calendar," shifting from references to the murder of a local Jewish mobster on Esplanade
Street when he was three years old to the film presentations of
"Tough Jews" such as Dustin Hoffman as Dutch Schultz, and
Warren Beatty as Bugsy Siegel. So rich and raucous was this history "that what is called for to complete the story of our American
Jewish heritage is a writer the stature of Isaac Babel." That
December, when *Playboy* invited him to file a lengthy appreciation of Woody Allen, both his movies and writings, he made a
feeling connection between himself and the self-deprecating New
Yorker. Allen too had to endure accusations of being a self-hating
Jew throughout his career, as well as such questions as: "Do you
believe in Jewish comedy, born from fear, aggressiveness, exag-
geration, self-defence?" The filmmaker was also, in Richler's
view, "a disciple—filtered through S.J. Perelman, mind you—of
the twelfth-century philosopher Maimonides, author of *The Guide
to the Perplexed*." Hearing an echo of Maimonides in the themes
of Woody Allen's *Crimes and Misdemeanors* allowed him to share
with *Playboy* readers the passage in *The Guide* that had been his
mantra since he was a young adult poring over the book in southern France. "Men frequently think that the evils of the world are
more numerous than the good things.... Not only common people
make this mistake, but even many who believe that they are
wise." Tough Jews and mean streets, Maimonides and Babel,
arced back to the earliest and most enduring preoccupations
of the now sixty-one-year-old.

Richler's *bona fides* as his own brand of tough guy were on view
for Jack Rabinovitch one evening that winter. Rabinovitch, having
checked into the Ritz-Carlton, poked his head into the Maritime

Bar. He spotted his friend there, scowling into his Scotch. Motioning across the room to where Bernard Landry, the former PQ cabinet minister, sat with a group, Richler indicated that Rabinovitch had to join him for a drink. Landry was someone he held in particularly low esteem; judging by an earlier exchange between the men in the same venue, the feeling was mutual. "I hate you," Richler reported Landry saying, "you're a racist"; to which, startled, he had replied, "Landry, you're nothing but a country bumpkin." "I'm not leaving before he does," Richler now said. "He's not about to push me out of my favourite bar." Though Rabinovitch was hungry, he wound up sitting with him for hours. Only when Landry had departed would Richler release his friend.

Who could outstare the other and not blink? Who would ultimately back down? In a way, it was the kind of confrontation Richler had lost when he fled the irate Colonel Mueller on Ibiza in June 1951. That one "defeat" had haunted him his entire adult life. There was little or no chance he would be the first to leave any room again.

———————

Around the time of his imbroglio with Quebec, Richler's troubles were compounded by a summons to appear in a law court in London. The summons, accusing him and his former publisher Weidenfeld & Nicolson of character defamation, marked the nadir of a nasty quarter-century-long dispute with the convicted rapist Benjamin Levene. The disgraced Londoner had been sentenced to six years for his assault on a Swedish au pair girl; his fellow accused was the Canadian director (and Richler's friend) Sylvio Narizzano, who had been let off with a scolding. Levene had begun his campaign of epistolary revenge on those he viewed as responsible for his imprisonment as far back as the mid-1960s. Once *St. Urbain's Horseman* appeared, Levene, aware that he had been transformed into Harry Stein in the book, redoubled his harassment of Mordecai Richler with a string of demented and strange notes and cards. These letters tracked him from the house in Kingston, Surrey, to Edgehill Road in Canada, despite Levene's faulty addressing of envelopes— "Morticia Richler, Labor Zionist international 'Auther' Sherboune st West, Montreal," presumably thanks to Richler's high profile. For twenty more years after Levene was released he mailed these eccentric, faintly menacing missives. Canadian law enforcement, aware of the harassment, even contacted Richler once, asking if he wanted to press charges. He declined.

One Levene note, scribbled on a Catholic Mass card, was marked "harry Stein died at the infamous hands of jake & friends 1963—resurrected 1968," a reference both to Richler basing Harry Stein on him in the novel, and to his own release from prison in 1968. Others were straightforwardly threatening: "Richler, you shit, your expensive under-wear, Dirty Yid—I am enjoying all this you created me, so live with Harry Stein et all. The fucking world is going to know about all of us...that piece of educated dogshit silvio naratzano —how long did it take you 'sons of jewish whores' to work out the book...." Even Florence was not spared his venom. Another postcard, addressed to "Lady Richler" and beginning "My Dear Rifka," included the lines "I regret to tell you that your husband is a close friend of VICIOUS homosexuals from earlier times...that your husband is a disgrace, even to Jews."

The absurd summons went nowhere, and Levene was never heard from again. But his persistence was telling; Richler had gotten the dark heart of Benjamin Levene, the London Jew, in the Harry Stein character perfectly. Such a shadowy campaign was exactly what the disgraced bookkeeper from *St. Urbain's Horseman* would have inflicted on his enemies. Some writers might have taken this unsettling example of the potential consequences of using real-life models in fiction as a sign not to do it again, but Richler was, as the Gursky-Bronfman and even the Harry Schwartz–Leo Kolber connections attested, unrepentant about the practice. He was a very tough-minded artist, and man—as Quebec nationalists were now discovering.

———

Round Two of Mordecai Richler versus the Separatists (and many others) resumed in early March. *Oh Canada! Oh Quebec! Requiem for a Divided Country* was published by Penguin in an original trade paper edition deliberately priced to sell at an accessible $14.99. Sell it did, moving forty thousand copies in the first weeks and then reprinting three times in six months. For once, Richler's famous countenance, used to retail books in Canada for decades, wasn't featured anywhere on the jacket. Instead, Penguin mocked up a stop sign with "*Arrêt*" (Stop) spray-painted out and "101" scrawled below. A hefty support network within *Oh Canada!* also revealed that this was no ordinary Richler release: a postscript followed by an appendix, extensive endnotes and a selected bibliography. "Actually Carmen shd. be proud," he had written to Deborah Rogers the previous summer, as part of his plan to convince Chatto to get on board his crusade. "This will be a real book with footnotes and a bibliography just like grownups write." The dedication—"For Daniel and Jill, Noah, Emma, Marfa, and Jacob"—a grouping previously the preserve of the Jacob Two-Two series, also underlined his reasons for writing the book. "Jill" was the new addition—the creative TV producer Jill Offman, whom Daniel had married in 1991.

Two weeks before publication, Richler travelled to Toronto to be interviewed for CBC's *The National* newscast. Having refused, as usual, to succumb to either a makeup artist or a comb, he sat across from his friend Barbara Frum declaring the situation "the most unnecessary of quarrels." From a city where the two cultures "once enriched each other" to one stuck in a "quagmire of tribalism," much of it fuelled by "narrow, parochial, nationalist politicians," Montreal, he said, had been much diminished. Some 250,000 English-speakers had fled the province since 1976. Though he believed in self-definition, and so would support, sadly, a legitimate vote for independence, he refused to grant the same legitimacy to any vote for the vague "sovereignty-association" status being proposed by the PQ. "I fear a referendum will be close," he said. "If 50/51/52 percent want to stay in Canada, it could be a very acrimonious situation." He reminded Frum of the charges of historic anti-Semitism—"French Canadians supported the Vichy regime," and that *Le Devoir* of that period had been "interchangeable with *Der Stürmer*," the notorious Nazi newspaper— and wondered why he continued to be identified as a "Jewish writer," whereas no one would think to speak of Michel Tremblay as a "Catholic writer" or Alice Munro as a "Protestant" one. His *New Yorker* chronicle of the sign laws had embarrassed Quebecers? So be it. "It should embarrass them," he said. "I wasn't ridiculing the people; I was ridiculing the law." Moreover, he pointed out, "independence is a bourgeois conceit; it would be at a cost to workers and farmers."

Cogent and sharp, the interview served notice of just how prepared he was to defend himself again. The worried expression on his face in the final seconds might have been read as concern for what lay ahead. But there was a more specific reason: Barbara Frum, the feisty, intelligent, much-loved national broadcaster, was in the late stages of her struggle with leukemia, and had barely managed the fifteen minutes. He had asked her off-camera if she was okay and offered to reschedule but, determined to the last, she got through it. Sixteen days later, back in Toronto for a full publicity tour, he greeted his Penguin publicist, Karen Cossar, in the hotel lobby one morning, distraught at the news that Barbara Frum had died during the night. Requesting a few minutes alone, he took himself away for a walk in the surrounding streets.

By then, *Oh Canada! Oh Quebec!*, still a week short of being released, was already being called "hate propaganda" in Parliament. A Bloc Québécois MP had risen in the House of Commons to request the book be banned under a section of the Criminal Code that allowed prosecution of a publication that might incite public hatred. In the view of MP Pierrette Venne, *Oh Canada!* was doing that very thing, via serialized excerpts in the Montreal *Gazette*. Richler derided Venne as "not very bright." *Le Devoir* then took fierce editorial exception to its 1930s incarnation being equated with a Nazi publication. Bypassing the media's responsibility to freedom of expression, Lise Bissonnette criticized the CBC for giving Richler a platform to express his views, and declared, "there are no words to express the disgust and the anger we feel...this defamation broadcast across Canada casts its shadow on all who are today associated with *Le Devoir*." But the newspaper did not hesitate to use its own platform—one follow-up article called on English Canadians to collectively denounce Richler—nor stint on wild statements, most egregiously in a piece later in the month that accused *Oh Canada!* of similarities to Hitler's *Mein Kampf.*

On it went: name-calling and denunciation, occasionally with insight, mostly ad hominem. On the new CBC network, Newsworld, in the most heated exchange of the "campaign" of 1992, the bilingual journalist Jean-François Lisée got into a near shouting match with Richler over his admission in *Oh Canada!* that he had incorrectly equated the PQ theme song to a Nazi melody in his 1977 *Atlantic* article, confessing there to the "embarrassing gaffe" without, as always, apologizing for it. "Lévesque was besieged with charges of anti-Semitism because of you," Lisée said, recalling the American university that cancelled its invitation to the premier after the piece appeared. Later, Lisée spoke on Radio-Canada about his reasons for treating Richler so roughly on English television. "The contempt he has for Quebecers, and for the facts, that trickles from every page, hurt me, as a Quebecer. . . . Here in Quebec we know that he exaggerates, but someone has to say it to English Canadians." "Do we need a strategy to deal with the influence of Mordecai Richler in the United States?" the Radio-Canada host asked Lisée. "Yes," he answered.

Interviews and audiences were largely respectful, although a reading at the National Library in Ottawa turned ugly for a while. Many, whether they agreed with his hard line or not, were relieved, even grateful, that he had brought the debate into the open; it was, after all, a discussion not just about the future of Quebec— the nation itself was at stake. So he didn't cancel scheduled events, despite the threats and the likelihood of friction, and accepted most requests. He faced down hostile critics throughout

Quebec. Once, when he was crossing Sherbrooke Street with Florence, a driver stuck his head out of his car window and shouted at them, "*Quelle horreur!*" Abusive letters arrived in the Chateau mail slot, which he sometimes read aloud to her and Jake. Threatening or obscene phone messages filled the answering machine as well—"Go back to Germany—they know how to treat their Jews there" was one—with Jake, alone in the apartment for much of the week, occasionally picking up the call to engage the critic in fluent French. The youngest Richler was now a bartender in an Old Montreal spot popular with journalists from *La Presse*, and had to listen while an editor at the paper suggested he get his father to come down to the bar. "I'll reinvent the Holocaust for him," the man said. In the Townships, the Richler house in its quiet spot at the end of the secluded lane was defaced by a swastika and piles of excrement. His friends at the Owl's Nest insisted on lending him a rifle, which he kept under the bed. He had no idea how to fire it.

Attacks, insults, even threats, only made him more resolved. "Angry Richler won't let up on Quebec," ran a headline. But he admitted to wishing he had spent the past year writing fiction instead of wrangling with his province, and in private told friends that he was becoming exhausted by the fracas.

He made a quick trip to France to promote the translation of *Gursky,* and then flew to Belfast to give a previously cancelled lecture. "He won't get back to the unfinished novel for another few weeks," a journalist reported there, "but he is already thinking about it." *Barney's Version* was still two years away but his anxiety about the "next novel" was part of a general uneasiness about mortality, time running out. "Increasingly, you worry," he said of the capacity to keep generating fresh ideas. "It's like a baseball pitcher who might come up with a sore arm next season. You keep hoping you can throw red-hot, but who knows. . . ."

Letters about *Oh Canada!* did arrive as well from well-wishers like Timothy Findley and Robertson Davies. Not many, though; in a note back to Findley, he wrote: "You have no idea how lonely your letter was." His sense of being isolated, shared only with close friends, wasn't helped by the way the Montreal newspapers stretched their coverage of the controversy to sell papers. Richler, who continued to read three or four newspapers a day in both languages—the *Globe* and *Gazette, La Presse* and the *New York Times*—saw his own face almost daily in one publication or another. Determined to refute erroneous allegations, especially those concerning factual accuracy, he had to pore over the articles, many bristling with invective. He also felt obliged to answer them, again (and again): in *Maclean's* and *Saturday Night*, and in the *Wall Street Journal* on July 1, Canada Day.

He wasn't too weary to assist the publicity efforts of Chatto, who were publishing *Oh Canada!* in the U.K. very much as a favour, by agreeing to be the writer and on-air host of a BBC television documentary about the situation in the fall. "There was a feeling at the BBC that something should be done about the Canadian constitutional breakdown," the segment's producer told the *Globe and Mail*, "and a feeling that something should be done with Mordecai." When a French-Canadian observer hypothesized that the BBC wouldn't hire Yasser Arafat to make a film about Israel, the producer disagreed. "That's when things become interesting," he said. The titles assigned to U.K. reviews of the book served his agitprop campaign well. "The Paranoia of the French-Canadians" in the *Sunday Telegraph* (by noted historian Paul Johnson) vied with "Quebec's Tainted Separatist Dream" in the *Guardian* and "Tongue-Troopers Bitten" in *The Independent.* The more limited U.S. coverage included a *New York Times Book Review* titled "The Idiocy du Jour," and *Kirkus Reviews* noted that *Oh Canada!* revealed "even intellectual Francophones [to be] as blinkered and narrow-minded as peasants in a Marcel Pagnol comedy." The book didn't sell many copies in either country, but the point was made. "Nothing hurts the nationalists here more than ridicule abroad," he told the *Financial Post*, "and I'm happy to oblige."

In Quebec itself, only a tiny French publisher, Éditions Baluc, dared brave a translation of the disgraceful tract. It didn't appear until the fall, too late to benefit from the fracas. But the French publication of *Gursky* in the same spring as *Oh Canada!* was unfortunate for the novel. Or not. "Normally, the translation of a novel by Mordecai Richler would pass almost without notice in Quebec," *Le Devoir* literary critic Odile Tremblay wrote. She went on to praise much about this obscure local author's "dense and abundant" novel, including its prose, which has the force of "an avalanche." But despite high praise in France and in the English-speaking world, only a few "specialists" knew him in Montreal. "The most celebrated of English-Canadian authors is not a prophet in his own country. But obviously, this year everything has changed."

———————

Richler's battle against what he saw as unjust and destructive in the Quebec political climate had been lonely, and many others, made of less tough stuff, would have wilted. Fighting it over a two-year period, and in the sixty-first and sixty-second years of his life, left him drained. His friend John Scott believed the deterioration of Montreal affected his temperament; his expressions of caring deeply for the city, and the fate of the province, were sincere, as was his sense of permanent loss. Shocks, too, of the inevitable sort—illnesses, downturns, deaths—were registering more acutely with him, and perhaps contributing to an autumnal mood. When Bob Gottlieb was let go from the *New Yorker*, replaced by the *Vanity Fair* editor Tina Brown, he quite typically commiserated with his friend and concealed his feelings with a joke: "I've always wanted to open a deli, maybe in Miami," he faxed Gottlieb, "but what has held me back all these years is the need of a partner I could trust at the cash register. What do you think?" But with the death of Barbara Frum, and the news that Jack Rabinovitch's beloved wife, Doris Giller, had been diagnosed with cancer, there was no humour to be found, or even many words. While a few critics had picked out a low note of sadness in the high-spirited *Gursky,* the philosophical melancholy of Barney Panofsky, whose code of living was that "life is fundamentally absurd and no one really understands anyone else," was beginning to form in his mind during this tumultuous period.

He had written *Oh Canada! Oh Quebec!* for a reason, and could claim a huge success in the terms by which he mostly defined it: as a provocation and call to action; as an act of radical, dissenting citizenry. But he was also wondering if he had best spent his time and energy on it. The book, expanding marginally on the arguments of the *New Yorker* piece, contained some arresting passages, but it was far from his best work, and not only because of the haste of its composition. Relying on his newspaper clippings and the insights gleaned at Woody's, and counting as always on his vivid engagement with his childhood, he had done much hard thinking but less real reporting. His stationary position left a 281-page book reading like an expanded magazine piece, despite its power and the impact it had on public affairs in English Canada. He never discussed those weaknesses, but he did, in a sense, acknowledge the truth of the criticisms by spending the end of the summer and early autumn of 1992 planning a trip that would involve him in a different kind of "look backwards," and much careful reporting. And though he intended to produce only another major article, in the end he generated a better book instead. He and Florence were going to Israel.

III

THE GOLEM

On the eve of his dismissal from the *New Yorker*, Bob Gottlieb had commissioned a piece from Richler about the fate of those Montreal Habonim comrades who had made aliyah to Israel when the state first came into being. He would find and interview long-ago friends like Ezra Lifshitz and Sol and Fayge Cohen, and tell their stories. During his only other visit, in 1962, he had avoided seeking out those comrades, sheepish about his own failure to commit to Eretz Yisrael. The *New Yorker* commission covered costs, and the Israeli government offered to provide accommodation for a month in a state guest house in Jerusalem. Once *GQ* agreed to a piece on Egypt—allowing him to build in a week in Cairo and down the Nile—he had the most extensive work holiday he had yet created, and one he knew that Florence would love. They timed the travel, starting with a few days in Germany, to occur after a momentous event— the marriage of Martha to Alfred Wise, who worked in advertising, in September, with the reception held at the country house. But they made sure to be out of the country for another: the national referendum on the Charlottetown Accord at the end of October 1992. After his long year in the front lines of the Quebec political battle, being half a world away on the day when Canadians voted on whether to approve the latest package of constitutional amendments, born out of the failure of Meech Lake, was a fine idea. He didn't support the Charlottetown Accord either, and had already made his position public. Besides, he needed to turn his thoughts elsewhere.

To that end, in Montreal he once again bought gruff, amiable Sonny Idelson lunch—just as he had in 1962. The Idelsons, since immigrating to Canada in the 1950s, continued to spend a month each winter in Tel Aviv. The men met at Moishe's steakhouse, where Richler, doing preliminary research, kibitzed with a waiter from the neighbourhood about the boys and girls of their era who had gotten involved in Habonim and Hashomer Hatzair. Talking to Sonny about Israeli politics braced him for the month ahead, in a land where the subject battered and bruised its citizens in a manner inconceivable to even the most fervent Canadian or Quebec nationalist. His own positions on Middle East complexities had been thoroughly thought out and long set. When Moses Berger dubbed Ariel Sharon a "self-satisfied thug" in *Gursky*, he was speaking for his creator, who had elsewhere called the war-mongering Israeli leader "a Jewish fascist." Jerusalem, he believed, should be an international city, and the Middle East should encompass an Arab state for Palestinians and an Israel along the lines envisioned by the recently elected prime minister Yitzhak Rabinh, whose emerging "land for peace" policy appeared a way forward.

Both Joey Hersh in *Horseman* and Solomon Gursky had earned mythopoetic status by running guns and weapons into an earlier, more innocent version of the state. Youthful romanticism aside—Richler's about Israel, the country's about itself—the nation he was returning to now was much changed from 1962, though not, as he wished, towards a more secular conception. Chances were good that he would end up liking this Israel still less, and feel a deeper estrangement from its project, but he set off buoyed by the undertaking and in open-minded good spirits.

His first hour on Israeli soil provided a potent metaphor. Conrad Black, who now owned the *Jerusalem Post* as well as the *Daily Telegraph* and *Saturday Night*, had sent an employee to meet the Richlers at the airport and drive them to the guest house thirty miles away. Richler was attracted to Conrad Black's larger-than-life, buccaneering character, and Black to his, and the two men had kept in touch after the newspaper mogul moved to England. In London in April for a week to work on the BBC documentary, the Richlers had attended an election-night *Daily Telegraph* party at the Savoy. The Conservatives, under John Major, had won a surprising majority government. Mordecai and Florence had been chatting with their host at the entranceway when Margaret Thatcher, who had resigned back in 1990 in the hope that her successor could repair the party's reputation before an election, appeared beside them. "We've done it! We've done it!" the Iron Lady told Conrad Black.

In the confusion at the airport in Jerusalem, neither Richler nor the driver remembered to put his new electric typewriter in the trunk of the vehicle. By the time they realized the mistake and called to ask about a black case left at curbside, the type-writer had been blown up by security forces. Though Black offered to replace the machine, Richler was content—it was a better anecdote if he swallowed the loss himself.

The Mishkenot Sha'ananim guest house, perched on a hill in West Jerusalem, was an elegant base for an autumn stay. From their suite balcony he and Florence had views of the Tower of David and the old city walls, with the Judean desert beyond. The Jaffa Gate was a short walk away, as were many attractions. They arrived during Sukkot, the seven-day thanksgiving festival he remembered from his childhood, and were soon observing the complexities of life in Jerusalem up close. The *Globe and Mail* bureau chief Patrick Martin and his wife, Bronwyn Drainie, lived nearby and offered to show them the city and country; Paul Workman, a CBC reporter whose own apartment was in the German Colony, fifteen minutes away on foot, arranged visits for Richler to refugee camps, and interviews with politicians. They dined with the Workmans, and with Drainie and Martin, and were invited on most other evenings to social events or private dinners.

One night Bronwyn Drainie thought she detected disappointment in Florence at being excluded from reporter-related outings, and set herself to keep her company. The women toured a Palestinian refugee camp and wandered the old city; another day, they visited the Rockefeller Museum in East Jerusalem, and met up with their husbands at the top of the Via Dolorosa. Richler arrived out of breath—he couldn't take more than a few steep steps without stopping—and they paused to watch priests re-enact the stages of the cross, shouldering an actual wooden cross. Most members of the procession, he noted, were in gold golf shirts and baseball caps—North American Christian tourists. "I spent my whole life trying to avoid people like this," he told Drainie. "What the hell am I doing here?" They followed the procession for four stages before veering off in search of a drink. That wasn't much easier than climbing the Via Dolorosa; much of Jerusalem, being a Muslim town, remained dry. By evening they found themselves at a Catholic hostel for pilgrims outside the gate, which served decent wines. Another night they dined in the American Colony Hotel in East Jerusalem, a neighbourhood most Jews avoided after dark. Bronwyn Drainie, seated next to Richler, abandoned the hope of conversation; he was, she realized, too busy watching everyone and everything, taking mental notes.

Different doors opened for different reasons. Paul Workman escorted him to a Palestinian camp, and then he was driven on to meet a hardline politician from the West Bank settlement movement. He made his own way to encounters with former Habonim comrades, some of whom he hadn't seen since 1948. He hired a taxi to the kibbutz in the Negev where Ezra Lifshitz, his former group leader, still lived, and found him content with his hard, non-materialistic life. En route he chatted with a Moroccan driver with slangy English. The driver asked what kind of car he drove. "A Ferrari 250 GT Berlinetta," he replied, kidding. "Sure. What else," the cabbie said. "So what do you make of the poor Jews here in Israel?" He had dinner with Gdalyah Wiseman, whom he had last seen in 1947, at his modest home in the Haifa Hills. Wiseman, who had been training to be an engineer at McGill, had ended up fighting in the wars; he had never dreamed he would be "serving in the army until I was fifty-eight years old." Other expatriate Montrealers relayed similar stories of sacrifice, and dreams tempered, if not abandoned. Israeli officials, persuaded by the stature of the *New Yorker*—he was not shy about explaining whom he was on assignment for—also granted him interviews. Then there were extended family relations scattered throughout the country, most still devoutly Orthodox and politically conservative. In 1962 he had encountered one such Richler relation, the locksmith Shmul Shimshoni. Now he sought out Shmul's sister Shaindel, whom he used to play with on St. Urbain Street. She lived with her husband in a town outside Tel Aviv. "What do you remember of me back then?" she asked.

He remembered that conversation with these Richlers had often faltered back then, though less so with Shaindel's son, the journalist Sam Orbaum. In 1989 Richler had received an invitation from Jerusalem: "I could not resist including you, of whom I am very proud, on my wedding list," Sam Orbaum wrote. After explaining who exactly he was—"your first cousin, once removed"—Orbaum mentioned that he was a columnist at the *Jerusalem Post*. "If you ever visit Israel, please contact me." As a boy in Montreal, keen to become a writer, Orbaum had been told by the family to "make the world forget Mordecai." Now, finally sitting down with his idol, adult to adult, he realized he had to make an impression. When Richler began spouting what he considered clichés about Palestine and the peace process, he challenged him on the inconsistencies, including the apparent irony of his demand for a two-state solution in Israel while insisting on a unified Canada. They got into an argument, with Richler, having run out of smokes, forced to borrow his cigarettes. Orbaum produced a lively profile that appeared in the *Post* in early November. "There was a time when only the Jews of Montreal were outraged by Mordecai Richler," he began. "Now everyone is."

On the morning after the Charlottetown Accord referendum, Mordecai and Florence had breakfast at Bronwyn Drainie and Patrick Martin's apartment, where they pored over the results. He was pleased by the outcome, especially the rejection of the accord inside Quebec. Canada must have seemed far away at that moment, and impossibly innocent by world standards of calamity and disorder. Two weeks earlier they had read news of an earthquake in Egypt that had killed 340 people and injured thousands. Following that, a terrorist group had ambushed a tourist bus, killing an English nurse, while another extremist had stabbed three Russian tourists. Jews weren't being targeted directly, but had reasons to be especially cautious. "What do you think?" Florence asked him, wondering whether to cancel the next stage of their trip and her dream of a Nile cruise. He answered with a joke about wiping the doorposts of their hotel rooms with the blood of a lamb. They carried on to Egypt, saw Cairo and the pyramids and then flew to Luxor. Before boarding the ship, Richler checked for bullet holes, but after a visit to the Temple of Luxor they rode down the Nile as far as the Aswan islands, passing along shores of sugar-cane, date and banana plantations. A few days after they left Egypt, they read that tourist authorities had suspended Nile excursions, citing fundamentalist violence against tourists.

He wrote the adventure up for *GQ* in April while working simultaneously on Gottlieb's *New Yorker* assignment. But another essay by another Richler delighted him more than either. Invited to contribute to a British anthology called *Fatherhood*, Noah opened his memoir with a paragraph about standing as a small boy at a urinal next to his father. "I guess I came up to about his thigh, my scrotum barely descended. . . ." As small boys do, he examined his father's "mammoth sausage weighing heavily in his hand, the urine falling noisily. . . . I thought: I'll never be that big." From that to confessions of teenage lust and rage and drug use, to admissions of son-of-a-big-man anxieties—"My psychological history is easy to figure; I loved my Mom, but wanted to do good for Pa"—to a touching closing paragraph on the connection between father and son, the essay had authenticity and rawness and good writing in the right Richler measure. Noah even quoted his father on the rigours of wooing women: "It takes a little work, you know," he had told him after asking a rare question about Noah's romantic life. "I mean I didn't get your mother just like *that*." In a letter to his son, Richler said he was "both flattered and moved" by the piece. He then corrected him on a point of accuracy about their first father-son trip together. Noah remembered going to Paris when he was ten; Richler recalled a business trip to Bath when his then eight-year-old asked if he could come along. "I looked at mummy and mummy looked at me, both of us amused, and I said why not? Especially after you promised I cd have a drink whenever I wanted one, you wd wait for me outside the pub like a good boy." He added a wish for the upcoming holiday: "Let's have a grand Christmas and thank you for the essay." Along with Daniel's novel *Kicking Tomorrow*, a bestseller in Canada in 1991, that made two published Richler children. So far.

But Quebec, he soon found out, hadn't stopped thinking about him while he was away in the Middle East. On his return, he learned that a new book on the history of Jews in the province had excised all mention of his name for fear of offending francophones. Defending himself in the *Globe and Mail* in an article headed "My Life as a Racist," he referred to an editorial cartoon that had run in *La Presse* in the wake of the BBC documentary he had written and narrated. "Mordecai Richler is known, so he is credible—the BBC," ran the headnote, a reference to the producer's remark from the previous summer. Below a drawing of a "wise old coot sipping coffee" was the line "Hitler was also well known." Both the Canadian Jewish Congress and the B'nai Brith (neither big fans of his) condemned the cartoon, leading *La Presse* to issue a semi-apology. On and on it went: Richler being denounced, called names; Richler correcting the mistakes, reasserting his positions, including, if not above all, his stance as a both proud and happy Quebecer. "I speak for a party of one," he kept pointing out.

By April the *New Yorker* article on Israel was overlong and still unfinished. It now went well beyond telling those Habonim tales, to blending general reportage, political commentary, autobiography, with a nod towards the defining influence of Jewish legend on his own intellectual formation. It was, in short, a book.

"For the past five, exhausting months," he wrote to his supportive English publisher, Carmen Callil, "I have been working on a book about my Jewish adventures, which may lose me whatever Jewish establishment readers I have left. I hope to be done by September, maybe sooner." Sending the piece to the *New Yorker* in May and apologizing for its condition, he more or less invited the magazine to reject it. They did.

In the letter to Carmen Callil, he confirmed a plan that had been in the works almost since their repatriation in 1972: "I expect to break last week in June for a week in London if only to inspect our spiffy new flat," he wrote. "Florence might fly over a week earlier. In any event, we fully intend to come over November 1 or so for a five-month stay." Negotiating those endless Quebec winters had grown tedious. Hazardous, too, most notably on the day in the country when he slipped on ice on the driveway. "How do you feel about going back to London and finding a place for us?" he said on re-entering the house, bruised. At once, a very happy Florence knew that they had spent their last winter in Canada. She flew over immediately, and in four days had found a place off Sloane Square in the elegant neighbourhood of Chelsea. Though she called with a plan to courier some photos to him, Richler said he didn't need to see it; if she liked the apartment, he would too.

But a sad event brought them to Toronto at the end of April to support Jack Rabinovitch. Doris Giller, born five days before and three blocks away from Mordecai Richler in January 1931, had succumbed to lung cancer at the age of sixty-two. She had begun her career as a secretary for a supermarket chain, and by dint of determination, her generous personality and warm humour, had risen to be that rare thing at the time—a female reporter in a man's world, and an editor at three of the country's daily newspapers. She was admired and loved by Mordecai and Florence, as by many, and her early death was a terrible blow.

———

"Mordecai Richler has generously agreed to put his head on the block to raise funds," the programme read, complete with an Aislin caricature of the author, apple stuffed in mouth, asking, "ROAST? ME? Le Maître?" After the sorrow of Doris Giller's death, it was a much happier event that brought notable Torontonians up to Montreal: a roast held in the Oval Room of the Ritz-Carlton Hotel on May 10 to benefit a nascent literary festival. The organizers sold all 370 tickets to the cocktail reception and dinner. Among the "cooks" were old and new friends: Peter Gzowski, John Fraser and Ted Allan from Toronto, Bill Weintraub, Senator John Lynch-Staunton and Don Johnston from Montreal, along with the comedy duo Bowser and Blue, who performed "Brave Sir Mordecai." A "surprise" speaker turned out to be Jake, who got the biggest laughs with tales of his technology-impaired father's recent slow awakening to the pleasures of the fax machine. Disgruntled minority jokes abounded—"Public speaking in English," Bill Weintraub noted, "is still permitted in Montreal—indoors"—and two intrepid French Quebecers risked calumny: *Le Devoir*'s news director Benoît Aubin and the TV journalist Francine Pelletier, both speaking in English. At the podium the roastee, thanking the francophones for crossing tribal lines, admitted that he had been expecting them to be, like the relative size of French signs, two-thirds larger than everyone else.

That same month Richler, when not sprawled on the couch watching the Canadiens win the Stanley Cup again after an unacceptable seven-year drought, was also busy agitating and irritating. Brian Mulroney had announced his resignation as prime minister for June. *Saturday Night* commissioned a farewell commentary, and he obliged with a scurrilous rip. Opening with a wild reference to the bygone days of Mulroney and Richard Holden enjoying boozy four-hour lunches in Montreal—men "so engaged can do no harm to the body politic"—he ridiculed Holden for his now-infamous quitting of the Equality Party to join the Parti Québécois: "he abandoned his WASP and Jewish drinking companions *de souche* and joined both AA and the PQ." Brian Mulroney, he declared, had also "overpaid for swearing off the

sauce," as sobriety alone could have propelled the prime minister into the arms of the "dozy" Ronald Reagan and the Bushes—
"inarticulate 'out of the loop' George and the menacingly sweet
'Bar.'" It was the opening salvo of a relentlessly sustained attack
on all things Mulroney, including the "dunderheads and bottom-
feeders" he attracted to his first cabinet, as well as on the man
himself, though less for his dealings with Quebec than for his
pork-barrel politics and tolerance of corruption. One sentence
launched many a scandalized dinner conversation in English
Canada that summer: "In office, Brian Mulroney lied regularly,
even when it wasn't necessary, just to keep in shape."

The piece caused a stir inside *Saturday Night*. It was set to
appear in print much as he had submitted it, but its existence
was leaked to Mulroney. The prime minister—his resignation
took effect on June 24—called *Saturday Night* owner Conrad Black
asking if the article was especially hostile and, if it was, could it
be softened? Black, who later said he never considered showing
it to Mulroney, read it himself and, calling the PM back, told him
that, while he certainly wouldn't like Mordecai Richler's take on
things, the piece wasn't defamatory, and was entertaining.
Mulroney said that was fine and never mentioned it again, and
what was surely the most intemperate, take-no-prisoners farewell to a Canadian politician ever published appeared to a roar
of shock and amusement.

For his part, on June 11 Richler showed up at the Conservative
National Convention in Ottawa, where some of the surviving
dunderheads and bottom-feeders no doubt affixed him with their
best Bernard Landry stares. Later, revising the essay for his next
collection, *Belling the Cat*, he added a section on the convention,
and the doomed new leader, Kim Campbell. As for the now-
legendary sentence about lying, it was expanded. "All politicians
lie," the final version read, "but few as often, or as mellifluously,
as did Sincerely Yours, Brian Mulroney, who lied even when it
wasn't necessary, just to keep in shape, his voice, a dead give-
away, sinking into his Guccis whenever he was about to deliver
one of his whoppers."

Some wondered if Mordecai Richler could go a day without a confrontation, on paper or in person. In reality, most days passed quietly that summer of 1993, as he worked on the Israel book in the Townships. In August a still-grieving Jack Rabinovitch met him at Grumpy's in Montreal for drinks. He had resolved to create a literary prize in memory of his late wife. Jack was not a literary man, but Doris Giller had been a passionate reader; would Mordecai advise him? He agreed on the spot to serve as a juror for the first couple of years of the Giller Prize, as Jack wanted to call it. Appreciating the need for credibility, he recommended that Rabinovitch ask Alice Munro, as a writer of the highest reputation, and David Staines, as someone with academically sound credentials, to do the same. The following January he flew home from London expressly to attend a press conference at the Four Seasons Hotel in Toronto announcing the new prize, its value— $25,000—a guarantee of attention. "My late wife was a fun person," Jack Rabinovitch told the CBC. "Mordecai and I come from a fun background and so it seemed like a natural thing to do."

This Year in Jerusalem was on the fall 1994 list of the fairly new house of Knopf Canada, founded two years earlier by Louise Dennys, who had been invited by Sonny Mehta to create the first "Knopf" outside of the United States. Richler, while liking Cynthia Good at Penguin personally, had never developed the professional rapport with her that he had hoped for. With Bob Gottlieb now a friend rather than an editor, and Jack McClelland once a friend but not an editor—and now sadly not even a friend—he had gone from having intense relationships with all three of his English-language publishers to being particularly close to none. Gottlieb's nebulous current standing, in fact, partially forced the move. Following his custom of the last thirty years, Richler sent him the manuscript of the new book for feedback. The move appeared to upset both Sonny Mehta and the senior editor Jon Segal, obliging him to ask his agent, Lynn Nesbit—Monica McCall had long since retired—to smooth things over. "Please explain to Sonny that I had no idea I had inadvertently wandered into a free-fire zone between himself and Bob, and, furthermore, than I had offended Jon Segal," he told Nesbit, a poised and widely connected New Yorker. He went on to express hope that the decision he'd made earlier to leave Penguin in Canada would help heal any wounds. "I hope Sonny is pleased that I have moved this ms to Knopf Canada and will also see that they get to do my new novel."

Louise Dennys, lately of the independent Lester & Orpen Dennys, was a gifted literary editor. A niece—and the editor by then—of the novelist Graham Greene, the English-born Dennys had shown an affinity for both Canadian and international writing from early in her career, being the first to publish Josef Škvorecký in his adopted country, discovering young writers like Yann Martel, publishing Quebec writers in translation and bringing international authors such as Alberto Manguel, John Irving, Ian McEwan and Kazuo Ishiguro to the attention of Canadians. Dennys, also Brian Moore's Canadian publisher, knew Richler slightly—while at her small independent house of L&OD she'd had the chutzpah, as he saw it, to pitch him the idea of collecting his sports pieces—but was still surprised when he called her out of the blue, asking if she would like to publish him as well. He, it turned out, appreciated her and her former partner Malcolm Lester's willingness to translate Quebec writers, and to take chances on titles like Irving Abella's *None Is Too Many*, a book that had forced Canadians to fully confront the government's anti-Semitism during the Second World War. He didn't mind, either, that in her youth Dennys had been a blackjack croupier at the Penthouse Club in London.

One reason for her surprise at his call was the common knowledge that Richler had already accepted an advance from Penguin for a new novel. But as was his wont, he had simply informed Cynthia Good that he was changing his mind and breaking the contract. In a fax typed out in London in early 1994, one possibly never sent—the text was unusually littered with typos—he wrote that they had had a good and profitable ride together and, the decision being nothing personal, he hoped to have a drink with her in Toronto in June. "I will return my 50,000 dollar advance against the novel within a month," he added. He did return it, and later suggested a consolation project for Penguin, a book about literary feuds that he never got around to putting together. Instead, he signed with Knopf for *This Year in Jerusalem* and then, neither side wasting any time solidifying the relationship, agreed in July to publish two more books.

The second contract, witnessed by Roger George, a.k.a. Sweet Pea, called for $170,000 advance against future royalties from the sale of both a new collection of essays, tentatively titled *Celebrations* and valued at $20,000, to be delivered that same autumn, and then, for January 1996, *Untitled Novel: A Sequel to The Apprenticeship of Duddy Kravitz*. Nor did he ask Louise Dennys to pay him more for the novel than Penguin had offered. He pegged it as being worth $150,000, the same figure Penguin had agreed to pay him overall, based on sales of *Gursky*. Fair was fair to him; he was an open and direct businessman, never seeking to maximize advances, disliking the idea of not earning out. Dennys soon learned that her famous client, now under contract for several years—indeed, he would remain with her for the rest of his life—liked to tell her how much he wanted for a book, against potential earnings, and when he thought it should be published. She listened closely. He suggested a print run of ten thousand copies for *This Year in Jerusalem*; Dennys bet him a bottle of Glenlivet that they could sell twelve thousand. Six months later, she and her husband, Ric Young, drove the bottle to the Townships, when invited to stay there by Mordecai and Florence. Out of the publishing relationship another friendship was born—and a friendship again between the couples, a distinct, enduring pattern to his married life.

Louise Dennys soon discovered the established practices of his working life too: his habit, for instance, of changing directions on projects and missing deadlines. *Celebrations*, due out in 1995, would end up as *Belling the Cat*, published in 1998. "Untitled Novel," supposed to be the long-delayed sequel to *Duddy Kravitz*, set for fall 1996, would emerge as *Barney's Version*, released in September 1997 with no more than a couple of very funny cameo spots for the still-incorrigible Duddy. Cynthia Good was hurt, professionally and personally, by his decision. But there was no use arguing with him, and any doubts she may have had about the sincerity of his insistence that they remain friends were put aside when he called her to meet for drinks or breakfast. Years later, when her plan to visit the Townships was rocked by the dissolution of her marriage, he demanded she come regardless, believing he and Florence could help lift her spirits. That too was a lifelong practice: to keep up contacts with those he liked, even in the wake of a dispute or parting of ways; to perpetually widen his professional network, because he both wanted to know everything that was going on and—silent though he might sometimes choose to be—sought good company and good talk over a good meal, especially one cooked by Florence.

He did most of the hard work on *This Year in Jerusalem* in the new flat in London. A traditional leasehold, the three-bedroom apartment at 25 Sloane Court West was a handsome Georgian walk-up, with a kitchen facing the front and a large sitting room looking onto a garden reserved for residents. Up the stairs were the bedrooms and a tiny study. Their first winter back in England after twenty years was a great pleasure. Emma, living over in Camden Town, helped settle her parents in their home. Noah, at the BBC and also in London, did the same. Back among old friends—the Claytons and the Deutsches, Deborah Rogers and Michael Berkeley, set designer Tim O'Brien from the TV drama days, and Diana Athill—the couple hosted dinners at the flat and dined out in favourite restaurants, some dating back to the happy, chaotic days of the 1960s and early '70s. Canadian friends like the Don Johnstons and Michael Levine, "my entertainment lawyer," as he introduced him, would visit. The suddenly high-profile presence in the English capital of Conrad Black and his new wife, the conservative journalist Barbara Amiel (who had earlier dated Richler's old publisher George Weidenfeld), meant invitations to *Daily Telegraph* parties, along with more intimate lunches with the media baron. Florence could attend all the galleries, theatres and concert halls she craved, and he got to rediscover the pleasures of reading the "quality" British newspapers while sipping a single malt and smoking a cigar in a pub. He started off subscribing to no fewer than five morning papers, eventually settling on the *Guardian* and *Daily Telegraph*; afternoons he would walk out to buy the *Herald Tribune*, for the hockey scores—just as he had in Hampstead in 1958. He missed the *Listener*, now defunct, but read both old standbys—the *Spectator* and *Economist*—and newer finds: the *Literary Review* and the "twee" *Oldie*.

Those old media standbys, like those cherished friends and classic restaurants, made it clear even before he began filing the occasional piece on London that his relationship with the city was both nostalgic and "of the era" that had formed him as a writer and a man. The recent literary sensation *London Fields*, by Martin Amis, son of Kingsley, and the film *My Beautiful Laundrette*, by screenwriter and novelist Hanif Kureishi, were two examples of the later twentieth-century city as rendered by artists: decaying and undone, multicultural and sexually diverse, with "Little England" mostly dead and gone. But Richler as a writer was not engaged with this London, or even much interested in it. The city he would incarnate in his fiction for a final time, glancingly, in *Barney's Version*, would belong to the era of the World's End pub and the Mandrake Club, Brixton squats and bottle parties in Hampstead.

Towards the end of his work on *This Year in Jerusalem* he made a quietly momentous decision. In Israel he'd had lunch with his "religious cousin" Benjy, last reported in *Maclean's* in 1962 asking a shopkeeper if the bottle of cognac Richler wanted to buy was kosher. Three decades later, Benjy Richler was assistant director of the Institute of Microfilmed Hebrew Manuscripts at the Jewish National and University Library. They discussed his work microfilming the writings of medieval Jewish scribes, including Maimonides. He featured the lunch, focusing on the importance of books and bookbinding in preserving Hebrew history and culture, otherwise prone to everything from natural loss to mass burnings during the Crusades, in medieval Paris and Italy, and in Nazi Germany. "Before my cousin went loping off toward King David Street," he wrote, "he left me two gifts." One was a scholarly work by Benjy Richler himself, inscribed "To Mottl, from Benjy." The other was a recently issued Hebrew edition of the "puckish tall tales" about the Maharal of Prague and the Golem. It too was written by a member of his family: Yudel Rosenberg.

Richler, who could no longer remember any of the Hebrew he had learned, asked Sonny Idelson to translate his grandfather's stories. He then inserted one into his own book. Chapter Twenty-One of *This Year in Jerusalem*, a work otherwise entirely by Mordecai Richler, opened like this:

HOW THE MAHARAL OF PRAGUE, WITH THE AID OF THE GOLEM, FOILED A PLOT BY THE EVIL PRIEST TADISCH TO CONVERT A BEAUTIFUL GIRL TO CHRISTIANITY

By Rabbi Yudel Rosenberg

In the city of Prague, there was a wealthy and influential vintner named Berger. . . .

The tale, presented without explanation, aside from a footnote crediting "Sonny Iddelson" with the translation from *The Golem of Prague and Other Tales of Wonder*, was framed by private significances. At the end of Chapter Twenty was the scene where Benjy Richler handed his cousin his own scholarly work, along with the collection by their forebear. Chapter Twenty-Two then opened with the sentence "Monday, October 19, was Simchat Torah, the eighth day of Sukkot"—resurrecting the memory of the terrified nine-year-old parading the heavy Sefer Torah scrolls around the synagogue to the accompaniment of singing and clapping. As he explained it, "Dropping one is a sin—in my case, a sin compounded by the fact that the Sefer Torah I was given the honour of carrying had been the work of my grandfather

Rabbi Yudel Rosenberg, who was also a scribe, a *sofer*." But otherwise Chapter Twenty-One simply recounted, in Rosenberg's words, the story of Yossele, the Golem, called upon to rescue a fallible "daughter of Israel" who, falling in love with a Christian duke, allows herself to be imprisoned in a church cloister by Christians. Rendered invisible, the Golem slips into the cloister and, awakening the daughter, hides her in a giant sack. The clay creature then returns the girl to her parents. Romantic drama ensues, with the daughter being presumed dead and her grieving fiancé withdrawing from the world to study Torah and convert to Judaism. The ending is happy and just, with the lovers—now both of the Jewish faith—reunited, and an evil priest getting his comeuppance.

The chapter could be a plea for religious tolerance drawn from Orthodox Jewish lore. Or a nod to the Superman/saviour fantasy of twentieth-century diasporic Jewish life. Above all, it seems a largely private reference, in keeping with his furious defence of himself in Niagara Falls in 1973 as the boy with the "special gift" in his grandfather's eyes. His childhood pride in that grandfather-as-writer had come full circle, alongside a pride in the continuum of the Richler clan as writers, operating now from locales all over Europe and North America, be they Orthodox or apostate or, in the case of his own children, a generation of purely secular Jews. While less flashy than Ephraim Gursky being smuggled on board the Franklin Expedition or, soon to come, the identification of Barney Panofsky as a "wild Jew" out of Isaac Babel, the Golem story was an assertion by Richler of his sense of the unfolding, evolving Jewish identity—his own and, if they wished to embrace these markers of belonging, that of others.

"For Ezra Lifshitz, Sol and Fayge Cohen, My Cousin Benjy, and the Others Who Made Aliyah," read the dedication. "My cousin" Sam Orbaum, "drafted as my researcher," was thanked in the acknowledgements. "Will send you . . . copies of THIS YEAR IN JERUSALEM as soon as available," Richler wrote to Orbaum in May 1994. "A long excerpt has already appeared in London Daily

Telegraph magazine, another in TLS, and other excerpts will be run in Saturday Night and American Spectator." The Knopf Canada hardcover edition, scheduled for September, put the author firmly back on the front jacket.

IV

RICHLER CALLS IT

Shortly before the September 1994 provincial election in Quebec, which saw the Parti Québécois returned to power under Jacques Parizeau, with the promise of another referendum in the new year, Richler wrote to Emma in London. He admitted to being "up against it here, many thgs to be done before we Londonwards on Nov. 5." "Madness," he called the pace of a pending reading tour to promote *This Year in Jerusalem*, with stops in Vancouver, Calgary, Washington, New York and Boston, as well as three separate visits to Toronto. One night in Toronto, he and Florence had dinner at Louise Dennys and Ric Young's Spadina Road apartment, with the director David Cronenberg and his wife. Cronenberg, English Canada's most original filmmaker, was an old friend of the couple, and Ric Young, as a joke, asked a chef friend to prepare a "Toronto smoked meat sandwich" to outdo the best in Montreal for their star guest. In his letter to his daughter, still a struggling actress, Richler promised to advocate on Emma's behalf with Cronenberg, "slip in how talented you are . . . and deserving of a long over-due break." Dennys, already close enough to the family to be rooting for the kids, hoped the dinner might land the talented Emma that break as well.

In Vancouver, Richler was unexpectedly approached at an event by Cathy Boudreau. They went for a drink afterwards. He hadn't seen his ex-wife in years, and found himself sitting across the table from a still gregarious, sharp-tongued seventy-two-year-old. Cathy was living in the city, and though no longer a Buddhist nun, remained involved in a spiritual life. She told him about her latest guru and they talked together about old times in London.

He was still travelling, despite his dislike of so much movement, and meeting new people, despite an impatience with boring company and a tendency to show it. His appetite for fresh assignments was no less robust. Since completing the book in the spring his essay and article writing had been progressing at full steam: a smaller, less incendiary piece on Quebec for the *New Yorker* and an essay on Saul Bellow for the *National Review*, his regular columns for *Saturday Night*, including a denunciation of the acclaimed Steven Spielberg film titled "Why I Hate Schindler's List," which garnered him as much riotous feedback as his Mulroney takedown. Richler continued his usual literature-lite columns for *GQ* as well, along with a travel assignment for Art Cooper, this time minus Florence, that saw him flying south from London to the massive and controversial Sun City resort complex in South Africa on the eve of the nation's first general election since the dismantling of apartheid had begun in 1990. As a show of respect he also edited and wrote an afterword for a New Canadian Library selection of Mavis Gallant's stories, calling her in Paris to solicit her views on which stories to use. He ended up doing this work for free after betting M&S owner Avie Bennett, now a friend despite their rocky start with *Gursky*—Bennett was also part owner of the Expos, and they went to baseball games together, often after a steak at Moishe's—double or nothing on the meagre $300 fee, and losing.

That summer he and Florence took a couple of days to fly to Nova Scotia, where they boarded a tiny prop plane to carry on to Sable Island, a sandbar about 110 miles off the coast. The trip was organized by Don and Heather Johnston, and included Pierre Trudeau. The agreeable Johnston, knowing that Richler had had occasional dealings with Trudeau during his time in office, and that both admired each other's strong political stances, had brought them together for a meal in an Italian restaurant in the spring. Though equally quiet, inclined more to listen than to speak, they had gotten on well enough for Johnston to suggest a trip to the remote island, famous for its rare wild ponies and marine life as well as its shipwrecks. Florence was thrilled by the idea. Packing a picnic, the five guests spent a happy day on the otherworldly spit of sand. At the island weather station an employee, one of five year-round residents of Sable, unexpectedly pulled out a copy of *Gursky* for signing by the author. The same request wasn't made of Trudeau, who had lately published his memoirs. Don Johnston was used to not being the automatic centre of attention, but Pierre Trudeau, he noted with bemusement, was not.

But before the Richlers could "Londonwards on Nov. 5," Richler had to help ensure that the Giller Prize debuted in a manner befitting the memory of Doris Giller. As chair of the jury, he had added to his workload that spring, summer and fall by reading seventy Canadian novels, narrowing the list, alongside fellow jurors Alice Munro and David Staines, to five. The jurors and the shortlisted writers all stayed at the Four Seasons Hotel in Toronto, courtesy of Jack Rabinovitch. At the black-tie dinner in the ballroom, Richler was funny and relaxed at the podium. It was a glittering event that permanently altered the landscape of Canadian literature, adding Booker-like drama and prestige—and, very importantly, sales for the lucky author. The gifted M.G. Vassanji—a diasporic Indian raised in East Africa who had travelled to Australia with Richler in 1990 to collect his own regional Commonwealth Writers' Prize—now received a $25,000 cheque from him for his novel *The Book of Secrets*. The night was a roaring success, and Rabinovitch's ambition—to create an award that would command attention for novels and writers, and an event that would bring a more relaxed Montreal style to the Toronto literary scene—was realized.

From the Giller ceremony it was directly across the Atlantic to begin a second winter in London in the flat on Sloane Court West. The site of his first interview was the Groucho Club, on Dean Street in Soho, which had been founded in the mid-1980s as an alternative to the traditional "gentleman's club" by a group of irreverent London publishers including Graham C. Greene, Liz Calder and Carmen Callil, all from Richler's publishing house. The club, named for the comedian who once asked eleven-year-old Emma Richler to marry him, and who swore he would never belong to any club that would have him, was the perfect venue to encounter, in the opinion of the *Scotland on Sunday* journalist, the "cantankerous iconoclast" and "scabrous wit." Richler, naturally, turned out to be neither. The profile sketched a courteous and friendly literary tribal elder whose raspy voice sounded as if "his vocal cords had been sanded with a matchbox." Saying he had tried to quit smoking once, after "they found a spot on one of my lungs in 1991," he admitted to being jolted by that brush with mortality. "Jeez, that scared me, the tubes, the tests." Over glasses of Macallan and a burger with fries, Richler, more at ease with a British journalist than he had been in recent years with anyone in the Canadian media, granted that it was "a bugger. Those little betrayals of the body." He told of a Vancouver woman who had kindly said, when she asked him to sign her copy of *This Year in Jerusalem*, that she hoped he might live long enough to return to her city. "I pray she wasn't a clairvoyant," he said.

"Have just finished new Jacob cutie-pie book: JACOB TWO-TWO'S FIRST SPY CASE," he had written before leaving for England. "In London, on with the novel. . . ." The third Jacob Two-Two had been still another summer project, and he took the completed manuscript to England to make revisions. But the winter of 1994–95 marked the real start of the novel that he had sold to Carmen Callil in late 1990, and more recently to Cynthia Good and then to Louise Dennys. The Knopf Canada contract, signed just five months earlier, had signalled the resurrection of Duddy Kravitz as his subject matter in his descripton of the project, but by the time he sat down to start he had an entirely different story, and a largely different cast of characters, sketched out on the white pad of paper he kept next to his typewriter. Noah, hoping his father might write a novel that expanded on the preoccupations of *This Year in Jerusalem*, found himself instead keeping him company one afternoon in London's West End while he searched theatre bookshops for titles about tap dancing and vaudeville.

He was excited; his ideas for the novel offered several fresh challenges. To begin with, he was determined to tell the tale of his new protagonist, Barney Panofsky, in the first person. Few of the critics who had complained that his writing was reductively autobiographical had noted that he had yet to employ that form of narration, sometimes associated with self-regarding fiction. After nine novels and a dozen stories, he wanted to unfold his latest narrative through the "I" of a single unreliable perspective. He was also determined to create strong female characters. *Barney Like the Player Piano*, as he told Dennys he was thinking of calling it, would have three key women, and they would provide the story with its actual structure: Barney's "book," his version of events, would be bannered by the section headings "Clara," "The Second Mrs. Panofsky" and "Miriam." The women would, each in turn, hold sway over the most reprobate and unashamedly old-fashioned man Richler had ever created.

While the new novel didn't aspire to the structural sophistication of *Gursky*, it was trying one other thing new. Moses Berger had been writing the definitive biography of Solomon Gursky. That work, though, was never shown, and he remained simply a character in a book who said he was writing a book. In contrast, *Barney Like the Player Piano* was going to *be* Barney Panofsky's memoir of his "wasted life," told while he was slowly succumbing to Alzheimer's, an unravelling he would have to chart through his use of language itself in the story. Still more of a challenge would be the twist at the end: Barney's loss of narrative control, due to the creep of the disease. Richler was outlining a novel about a memoir, a work to which fancy literary terms, the sort he might have once been inclined to mock—post-structural, self-reflexive—could be applied.

He was also going to be using a storytelling technique, its existence recently confirmed by Sonny Idelson's translation, employed by his own grandfather to justify his fanciful, politically purposeful reinventions of the Golem stories during the era of czarist

pogroms and marauding Cossacks. Yudel Rosenberg claimed he
had found the sixteenth-century tales in a dusty old library and
merely transcribed them. They were "Rosenberg's Version."

At the same time, Richler wanted to infuse the new novel
with the criminal trials and suicides that had kept the pages
turning in *Horseman* and *Joshua. Gursky* had forgone those story
pleasures, or partially buried them beneath layers of technical
dazzle, and it remained, five years into the world, more admired
than enjoyed. Richler wanted his novels to entertain; *Barney*, a
return to the mode of author/pilgrim's progress, its anti-hero
about the same age and disposition as his creator, could count
on that symmetry to propel the comedy and misadventure. But
the book would also introduce a flashier technique into the mix:
a mystery revealed in the final pages. He didn't only want a disappearance and trial. He wanted the engaging presumption of
murder, of crime unresolved and punishment deferred.

In short, the sixty-four-year-old wanted a lot from his as-yet-
unwritten tenth work of fiction. To meet the deadline with Knopf
Canada, he had to deliver something in twelve months. That
seemed unlikely, as Louise Dennys herself knew. She had imposed
the impossible time frame as a spur, despite being aware of how
fundamental his sideline engagements with politics and journalism were to feeding his satiric gift.

London, too, was as distracting as ever. It was a sociable place
to spend the winter, though they suffered a major loss late in
February—Jack Clayton died at the age of seventy-four, his brilliant career as a film director having been curtailed by a stroke.
His death cast a long shadow. They had last seen him the year
before, when Florence hosted a dinner party for him and Haya
at the flat. Mordecai and Florence were becoming accustomed to
the passing of friends. "I remember a golden evening in London
when it was simply wonderful to be alive and in the company of
loved ones," he said at the memorial. He was recalling a dinner
twenty years earlier, with the Claytons, at Bob and Sandi Shapiro's
flat, followed by rounds of poker and, at 4 a.m., a cab ride to the
London cinema telecast of the Ali-Frazier fight in New York,

ending with breakfast at sunrise at the Connaught Hotel. "My irreplaceable friend Jack was a man of quality," he said. "But he was also a troubled spirit, given to brooding, far too vulnerable to criticism."

"London Then and Now," a nostalgic piece for *GQ*, marked the end, after some two hundred columns, of his regular arrangement with editor Art Cooper. But that summer saw another Richler in the magazine. This time it was Jacob, debuting with a piece commissioned by Cooper about his father. "Just the other night," the youngest Richler began, "in a downtown-Montreal bar, a thickly bearded stranger approached me, acting on a hot tip. 'So,' he said, 'I heard you're Mordecai Richler's son. What's it like having such a famous father?'" He had also recently published a memoir about washing dishes in the Ritz-Carlton Hotel in *Saturday Night*, where he was about to graduate from intern to junior editor under new editor Ken Whyte. His father knew what the bounds were with his children; he could help, but they would not thank him if he meddled too far. But he was pleased for Jake and that summer wrote to Dan Colson, the chief operating officer of the *Telegraph*, owned, like *Saturday Night*, by Conrad Black. "Please convey the following to Conrad and Barbara. Now that our youngest son, Jacob, toils for Saturday Night for something like $1.75 an hour . . . and oldest son, Daniel, is now writing a piece for them, and soon maybe Noah (a BBC radio producer), and I do a monthly column, I think Hollinger ought to do the decent thing and change the title of the mag to RICHLER'S MONTHLY NEWSLETTER or some such." He once told a journalist, "Having a famous father can sometimes open a door for children. After the door has been opened, it's up to them."

That was also the year Martha, having recently finished a guide to the National Gallery of Art in Washington that would eventually sell hundreds of thousands of copies, began her career as a political cartoonist in London, filing a strip in the *Express* as "Marf," her childhood nickname. Her satiric eye, while gentler than her father's, identified her as a Richler, even though she chose to keep the family name out of her professional life.

With Daniel, Noah, Jake and Martha all in print, only Emma, still an actress, remained unpublished. But even she had been working, with his guidance, on a handbook about wine. He had written to Louise Dennys of her ambition, noting that his eldest daughter had skill as a writer, and was an oenophile. One afternoon at the house in the country, after reading what Emma had written so far, the two women sat and talked about it on the dock. Dennys soon realized that Emma had the instinct, imagination and language to be a novelist; she suspected that writing about wine was a tentative first step into the crowded and intimidating waters of being a scribbling Richler.

With Jacob at *Saturday Night*, his father could indulge his fancy for mischief, designed for maximum group amusement, usually at the end of long days of work. While eloquent, Mordecai Richler was not verbally dextrous, and didn't like talking on the phone. The written word was his natural vehicle for humour, sharp or soft, scathing or benign, and short faxes allowed him to share his wit, as well as his boyish love of pranks, with friends. These transmissions were definitely for all eyes:

TO: JACOB RICHLER, ESQ
PRIVATE AND CONFIDENTIAL EYES ONLY

Dear Jacob,
Thanks for all the stamps (half price is a good deal), but as they will only do for Canadian postage, in future, please send them to my Montreal address, marked HOLD FOR ARRIVAL. Yes, I am interested in those office computers, but I find the price you suggest rather steep, seeing as they are second-hand and surely no longer "state-of-the-art." Re Ken Whyte's desk: I can't make an offer until you advise me of dimensions, number of drawers, etc. But I have no interest in the coffee-maker. Sorry about that.

Your ever-helpful
DAD

PS: I wouldn't worry about what could just be a harmless rash, but, yes, I do think it would be considerate to wear gloves at the office until you've checked it out.

Or to *Saturday Night*'s former editor John Fraser, who now held the distinguished position of Master of Massey College, University of Toronto.

FAX TO: JOHN FRASER a.k.a. MASSEY MASTER
PRIVATE AND CONFIDENTIAL
NO PEEKING

Dear Master Fraser,
I am grateful for your offer of the job of Massey's writer-in-rez, however, I am troubled by your demand that I kick back 20 percent of my salary to you in cash. Is this a time-honoured Massey tradition, or one of your innovations? Like demanding photographs of any personhood of the feminine gender who submitted an article to Saturday Night.

I would also like to acknowledge receipt of those three Massey computers, and once I have disposed of this lot, I will forward the usual cheque.

Meanwhile, I would like more details—and a price list—for the wines available from Massey's fabled cellars.

Best wishes,
Mordecai

There was still fun to be had in the business. "The Three-Cognac Lunch, and Other Tips on How to Get Ahead in Magazines" ran in the June issue of *Saturday Night*. (Ken Whyte, the laconic, quietly daring young editor, wanted him in the magazine all the time.) It offered a summary of his career as a journalist, complete with a photo of himself at a poker table, a bottle of Rémy Martin in play. Lively stories abounded—"forty years of scribble scribble and I've been sued only once," he wrote, remembering the irate Jewish restaurant owner in Leeds—as did tales of freelance bravado, whether it was snagging assignments that would allow him and Florence to travel at someone else's expense, or awards to "four star" editors based on their willingness to pick up monster cheques for meals. But the piece was above all else a paean to a literary mode of living, a way of life, nervy and unscripted, boozy and impecunious, nearing its end; "I fear I belong to the last generation of novelists who could supplement their incomes, earning life-sustaining cigar and cognac money, by scribbling for the mags."

"The Three-Cognac Lunch" showed vivid recall of details from decades past, even for Richler. One reason may have been the interviews he had agreed to give about his early days with a potential biographer. Michael Coren, a journalist and radio and television host based in Toronto, had published biographies of C.S. Lewis, Sir Arthur Conan Doyle, H.G. Wells and G.K. Chesterton. He was a friend of Daniel's, and he wrote asking him to consider the project. "Some words of warning from an older writer to a younger one," Richler replied, saying he would think it over. "You had better think it over too because I don't see this as a very profitable enterprise." He agreed a week later but with a condition: "You are not to reveal that I am a cross-dresser, elected Queen Esther in the last cross-dressing annual Purim Ball at the Holy Blossom temple in Toronto." Coren soon abandoned the project, finding Richler's friends guarded and wearying of the Montreal Jewish experience. Two years later, his host from Israel, Bronwyn Drainie, proposed the same idea. Richler met her for a drink before a Giller ceremony but admitted to being increasingly uncomfortable with the notion. A few months later he ducked the possibility with a note saying that "it would be way too difficult to make this happen."

June brought more sad news. Ted Allan, their close and great friend, passed away at the age of eighty-one. As with Jack

Clayton, his death was grieved by parents and children alike. For Florence, the complex, passionate Allan had been a treasured confidant; for Mordecai, an early mentor and even father figure. The age difference between himself and some of his most important early friends—Ted Allan, Jack Clayton, Brian Moore—was taking its toll.

But bright notes sounded too for the family. Nigel Horne, the former editor of the *Telegraph Weekend Magazine*, who had had the temerity years before to step in front of the literary lion in the Dorchester hotel, entered their lives fully that summer. Within a few months of the invitation to the Townships, their younger daughter and the journalist were living together. Horne wrote a letter to Richler professing his love for Martha. By way of endorsement, he simply told his prospective son-in-law that the couple were henceforth expected for family holidays. The same welcome was soon extended to the Toronto fashion journalist Leanne Delap, who began dating Jacob in 1996.

Jacob Two-Two's First Spy Case, published in the fall, wasn't only funnier than its predecessor. While he was still unable to recapture the magical Swiss Family Richler atmosphere *circa* 1971, the novel felt more buoyant, less a labour of business than an expression of ongoing love for the dynamics of the series: the large happy family never grown up or old; the two times two times two boy Jacob and those often-named siblings—Daniel, Noah, Emma and Marfa. The story involved Jacob's travails under the new regime at his private school, called "Privilege House." The cast—nasty principal I.M. Greedyguts and ghastly caterer Perfectly Loathsome Leo Louse, eccentric spy X. Barnaby Dinglebat—supplied the adult grotesques. He invented a few new tricks to keep his young readers engaged, such as a chapter written backwards that required a mirror in order to read it. He also allowed in a little more of himself and of his real relationship with his real Jacob, mentioning how the boy had often kept the father company on after-work walks, and considered him a pal. But he paid homage not only to Jake but to his whole gang of long-ago kids, now adults with wives, husbands, careers, and soon babies of their own. One passage in particular, revisiting the "favourite child" routine, sounded a familiar family note from a quarter-century ago: "I am burdened with five kids," their father wrote, "four of them ungrateful, lazy beyond compare, each one capable of eating through a basket of peaches in an hour, ordering the most expensive dish on the menu if I take them out to dinner, always forgetting to give me phone messages, and—the worse offence of all—*failing to laugh at my jokes.* However, my four stinkers aside, I am also blessed with one child who is totally lovable. Obliging. Respectful. Eager to help at all times. But who is it?"

His fans, mostly under the age of ten, lined up eagerly in the bookshops for signed copies, but the adult world was in tumult again as the October 30 referendum drew close. "I think the referendum is going to be okay," he told a journalist while signing in a Toronto shop. "My poll is 57 for the no and 43 for the yes." Closer to the vote he talked to the Toronto *Star* book critic Philip Marchand a little about the Jacob Two-Two series, and a lot more about the campaign, now in its final countdown. Marchand, declaring him "one of the most politically and socially committed writers in Canada," emphasized his loyalty to "the rough-edged, partially corrupt, but basically tolerant and easy-going" Montreal of his childhood as a key to appreciating his adult commitment to city and country alike. "For the PQ to try to win it by subterfuge is shocking," Richler said, noting that large numbers of Quebecers had been convinced they could vote for sovereignty and still send politicians to Ottawa. As the days passed, acknowledging the effectiveness of the separatist leader Lucien Bouchard, he revised his earlier prediction, fearing the best they could hope for now was a 55–45 victory. "I just don't want them trampling on any flags," he said of the potential fallout in English Canada. But his hopes were dwindling rapidly; a few days later, he decided it might come as close as a 52–48 count in favour of no. He feared now a further erosion of the province's Jewish population. "We'll be left with the poor and the old," he said.

On the day itself he and Florence voted early, then drove down to the Townships. Part of the afternoon he spent with the young journalist Guy Lawson, on assignment with *Harper's*, following the coverage on television. He now truly feared the worst, he admitted, including the prospect of violence accompanying a split decision. That evening he and Florence, with muted relief, watched the No side win by a fraction—50.4 versus 49.6—and then the inflammatory concession speech by Jacques Parizeau at the Palais des Congrès, where the premier angrily declared the loss the result of "*l'argent et le vote ethnique*"—"money and the ethnic vote." Two weeks later Richler stepped onto the same stage to deliver the keynote address before fifteen hundred teachers from the province's Protestant, Catholic and Jewish associations, opening with "Good evening, fellow ethnics." The two dozen teachers who boycotted the speech outside the convention centre could not dampen his spirits, and he could not hide his relief at the outcome. "This is still a good neighbourhood," he said of Canada, "worth preserving, so long as it remains intact."

Years of being pilloried in Quebec, called a bigot and enemy of the people, had done colossal damage to his reputation in the province. If his name hadn't been turned into an actual epithet in certain nationalist circles, or a term used to scare children, it was certainly rarely mentioned in praise or even with respect. So thorough was the vilification campaign that an Egyptian-born academic, Nadia Khouri, published a pro-Richler book-length essay analyzing the hostility—*Qui a peur de Mordecai Richler?* (*Who's Afraid of Mordecai Richler?*) He lost friends, too, in his campaign against the sovereignty movement and the language laws; even the moderate Naïm Kattan could not forgive his attacks on André Laurendeau in *Oh Canada! Oh Quebec!* Early in the new year an official at the Canadian embassy in Paris assembled a list of a hundred leading English-Canadian writers to be celebrated in France, and intentionally omitted Richler so as not to offend Quebecers. (A few fellow writers, including Mavis Gallant and Alberto Manguel, who had previously expressed outrage at *Gursky* being ignored for the Governor General's Award, withdrew from that event to protest his exclusion.) He was paying for his outspoken ways. But he was not going to stop doing what he did—his amiable lecture to the teachers' association was as close as he would get to extending any olive branch—and the "relationship" between Richler and French Quebec was fated to deteriorate further.

With the tumultuous year of 1995 nearly behind them, it was off to London for the Richlers, and continued work on *Barney Like the Player Piano*. Despite the distress of the referendum, a bullet-form letter to Emma, their flat-minder and housewarmer, was all high spirits and enthusiasm for the work at hand, and a longing to be surrounded again by the necessary tools of his productive craft. The list, signed "Rex," a family nickname for him, read in part:

Please visit Harrods tobacconists and acquire four (4) packs of Davidoff's Demi-Tass to ensure my good humour on arrival. Other good humour needs:
One (1) bottle Macallans 12 year old gargle.
Drop in on woggy newsagent, and please order the following, beginning Sunday a.m., Nov 18:
Observer, Sunday Telegraph, and Independent
Daily Times and Guardian
Weekly Spectator and Economist
Private Eye.

Mmmn. Cherry tomatoes. Plenty.

See you Sunday am. And Ms Marf, I hope.

Sincerely yours,
Rex

V

KEEP FIGHTING. DON'T DESPAIR

Now an early riser, Richler was often at his desk by eight o'clock, typing steadily until lunch. Afternoons, after a nap, allowed for another couple of hours of writing or rewriting. Away from the regular crew at Ziggy's or three-hour lunches in New York, his workdays stretched longer than they had in recent years. Evenings, too, grew shorter, with dinner guests at Sloane Court occasionally surprised when their hosts said goodnight well before eleven.

As spring 1996 came around, the paperback of *This Year in Jerusalem* did occasion a few interviews and appearances, one for the *Jewish Chronicle*. Readers of the British weekly, which awarded book prizes each year, had twice singled him out as best novelist. But even at sixty-five, he still had a living parent, "the Jewish mother, assertive, domineering, querulous," who had taken "the ultimate revenge by publishing her own book." She had not been forgotten, although in the interview Richler, admitting that he didn't "get on too well" with his mother, did not volunteer that he hadn't seen her since 1976, or that she had been battling Alzheimer's for at least a decade, a situation Avrum and his third wife, Eve, had been experiencing first-hand since they had gener-ously taken her in several years earlier, in St. John's. The family's unhappiness became public when a CBC crew, preparing a docu-mentary on him for the *Life and Times* series, did what he had still not managed: they flew to Newfoundland to talk to his brother.

Interviewed on a rocky perch outside town, Avrum, a bespectacled seventy-year-old who, aside from sharing his gravelly voice, bore little resemblance to his famous sibling, asked Mordecai on national television to please contact him. Good drama, the scene also marked a new level of intrusiveness by the media into the private lives of those they decided were celebrities.

Earlier—on February 7, two weeks after his sixty-fifth birthday—Richler gave a public reading from *Barney Like the Player Piano*. Ferdinand Mount, the editor of the *Times Literary Supplement*, was an occasional dinner guest at the Richler flat. The *TLS* held a prestigious reading series at the Queen Elizabeth Hall in the South Bank Complex, and Mount invited him to read with Edna O'Brien and Amy Tan. Tan, author of the global phenomenon *The Joy Luck Club*, was the big draw, with the *Independent*, for instance, announcing the other two writers on the "Fiction International" bill to be the Irish novelist O'Brien and "Mordechai" Richler. His old friend O'Brien went first, charming the crowd of nine hundred; she was followed by Richler—who, according to Nigel Horne, seated in the audience with Martha, Emma, Noah and Florence—shuffled onstage to a smattering of applause. Dressed in his usual corduroy, pants slung low and hair in revolt, he began reading in his clipped, deadpan voice. The laughter, starting out low, grew in force, obliging him to wait a few times before proceeding, and to his surprise and delight he won a long ovation at the end.

Afterwards, he and Florence took the family to dinner at Orso's in Covent Garden. By now it was nearly ten o'clock, and he had been drinking Scotch, as he did to boost himself before public events, since the late afternoon. He also had not eaten since lunch—another consequence of nerves. He excused himself to go to the washroom. A few minutes later Emma, having noticed his pallor, asked Nigel to check on him. He found his father-in-law on the lavatory floor, being sick. He helped him clean up, and walked him back to the table. Thirty years earlier, when Richler had drunk himself silly at a London business dinner with movie people, it had produced a funny if rueful letter to Bill Weintraub.

The incident in Covent Garden had to register differently. He was a pensioner now, and couldn't drink and smoke and push himself as in the old days. His body—at the South Bank he had won the crowd with frank descriptions of Barney Panofsky's struggles to urinate at night and remember the names of objects—was aging, and required better care.

————————

Back in Montreal in the spring, Richler was despondent at the physical effects of the referendum on the city. They had come home in time for a farewell dinner for their long-time friends Don and Heather Johnston at the Mount Royal Club in late May, having stopped in Toronto first to fete Johnston's new appointment as secretary-general of the OECD in Paris. Among the guests at the exclusive Montreal club, still largely the domain of old Westmount wealth and corporate lawyers, were Prime Minister Jean Chrétien, whom he had lately mocked for being unable to "speak either language adequately," and Pierre Trudeau. Asked by Don Johnston to say a few words, a tuxedoed, cigar-in-hand Richler opened drily with "Prime Minister, Madame Chrétien, this isn't one of my usual hangouts." He then mixed cracks about mad cow disease with distress at what he saw in his beloved city that spring: "I have never encountered so many depressed people, or seen so many shops on Sherbrooke Street, Crescent, Mountain, and elsewhere that were *à louer, à vendre*, or simply boarded up."

Once among his pranksters at his usual hangout, Winnie's Bar, their privacy guarded by the fierce, plain-speaking bartender Margo MacGillivray, he plotted more mischief. Mischief with a difference, specific to both those boarded-up shops and the lingering smell of Jacques Parizeau's ugly contention that "money and the ethnic vote"—that is, immigrants, Anglos and federal support—had cost "real" Quebecers their chance to form a nation. With René Lévesque, Richler had been somewhat tempered by his respect for the man; with Parizeau, that was not a problem.

In late June he called a press conference in the bar to announce the formation of the "Impure Wool Society" and the "Prix Parizeau," an award to be given for a novel or short-story collection published by an "impure" Quebec writer. "I'm obviously ridiculing Mr. Parizeau and what he stands for, which I find highly objectionable." The old term "pure wool," or *pure laine*, described a Quebecer who could claim unmixed French-Canadian ancestry. A cheque for $3,000 and a signed Aislin cartoon, he promised, would be handed out to the writer, whose sole credential had to be the *lack* of what one journalist called "full francophoniness." Financial backers, their arms gently twisted, included Michael Levine, Moses Znaimer and Avie Bennett. The "Impure Wool Society" sounded like the "William Lyon Mackenzie King Memorial Society" from *Joshua*; the "Prix Parizeau," with its mockery of the provincialism, if not bigotry, of elements within the nationalist movement, was of a spirit with Moses Berger's vocal denunciation of a clammy play about Anne Frank in *Gursky*. He was also lifting some of the outrageous acts of political satire from his books and playing them out in his life. In the essay "My Father's Life," written twenty years earlier, Richler had accused himself of hiding behind fiction to settle scores, of being a kind of coward. Whatever one thought of the abrasive sixty-something political satirist, there could be no denying his courage in sticking his neck out, over and over, regardless of how many people lined up for the chance to lower the guillotine.

The media responded to the prize with earnest lack of humour. When he wasn't being taken to the Quebec Human Rights Commission by an old ultranationalist enemy (once the subject of his published mockery), Gilles Rhéaume, for creating an award that was "hateful, contemptuous and racist," he was mixing it up in the *Gazette* with journalist Mark Abley. Abley pointed out the contradictions in the Prix Parizeau, not the least being that a writer such as Yann Martel, a native French-speaking Montrealer with deep Quebec roots, who wrote in English and was already admired for his stories and first novel, was ineligible. Richler, declaring the journalist to be suffering from the malady of political correctness, agreed that Martel couldn't win. "Life is no bowl of cherries." Later, he noted how unfair it was that he had himself been deemed ineligible for the Miss Italia pageant in Toronto, never mind the racy photo he had included in his application. The debate with Abley petered out, the Human Rights Commission declared the complaint premature and wrote to him explaining why they had decided not to go ahead—a document he framed to hang in the Townships alongside his Governor General's Award and invitation to Buckingham Palace. The Prix Parizeau awarded cash and caricature to impure books for two autumns running, with John Aylen and Bill Weintraub doing the judging. Their task was not onerous; a few publishers got into the spirit of the award but many did not, although Véhicule Press, the distinguished local publisher of the winner of the second and final prize, a story collection by the poet David Manicom, rose to the occasion by featuring the accolade in its catalogue. Richler himself got to use the forum of the annual "ceremony" to denounce further absurdities, such as recent seizures by language police officers of specialty Passover products that had not been labelled in French. "Matzogate," he called the tempest.

In a speech given at the University of Waterloo a few years later, with political life in Montreal and Quebec becalmed, and the city—and the economy—emerging from the effects of the latest cliff-edge flirtation with sovereignty, Mordecai Richler put his own satiric battles in good, sane context. "I manned the barricades, so to speak, for the legal right to munch unilingually labelled kosher matzos in Quebec for more than 60 days a year. I also protected the right of a pet-shop parrot to be unilingually English. As a consequence, nice people still stop me on the street and thank me for taking a stand. It's embarrassing, for my stand, such as it is, hardly qualifies me as a latter-day Spartacus or Tom Paine or Rosa Luxemburg."

Such extracurricular activities could prove fatally distracting to some writers, especially during the push to complete a book. As ever, though, Richler thrived on the sport of it. In the case of *Barney*, now being drafted at full speed—"We are delaying our

departure to our winter quarters in London until Dec 1," he wrote
to Conrad Black, "so that I can first finish another of my too-long,
overcomplicated novels"—the positive friction created by his
engagements with local politics was being matched by the stim-
ulus of an all-pervasive mortality. He wasn't simply crafting the
character of Barney's friend, the indulgent film-producer Hymie
Mintzbaum, out of the manic charms of the recently deceased
Ted Allan, or modelling some of Bernard "Boogie" Moscovitch's
dark talent and addictions on the late Mason Hoffenberg; he himself was paralleling Barney Panofsky's sense of the steady advance
of death, using real time and real-life anxieties. Barney does more
than just check the obituary pages for "enemies I have outlasted
and icons no longer among the quick." He does so in the very
same years that Richler was writing him into existence. "Nineteen
ninety-five got off to a bad start for boozers," he would write early
in the novel. "Peter Cook and a raging Colonel John Osborne
both gone." In those same years, Barney was sending prank letters to former friends and strangers similar to the faxes Richler
sent to *his* friends; later, the author would take to signing his
name backwards on the occasional letter, in homage to the mov-
ingly scrawled note from a decrepit Hymie Mintzbaum, his ability to write scrambled by a stroke—

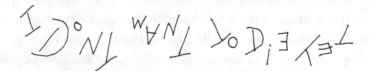

Once deciphered, it would read: I Don't Want to Die Yet. He even
used his own handwriting in the final book.

Congruencies, overlaps, a macabre dance of life and art, life
and death, lay behind the coursing energy of *Barney Like the Player
Piano*. Within a few months of the Richlers' return to England in
early December, two additional encounters with mortality would
occur just in time, so to speak, to further colour the project, and
shake its creator—but to the benefit of the novel, which would
soon be acclaimed as his most expressive and emotional.

――――――

On December 3 Mordecai Richler appeared on the CBC Newsworld show *Pamela Wallin Live*. It was normally taped in Toronto, but Wallin and her crew had flown to London for a week. Another guest on her programme that evening was Michael Ignatieff. It was Richler's first encounter with the forty-nine-year-old writer and documentary maker. They had many friends in common, among them former NDP leader Bob Rae, John Fraser at Massey College and lawyer Michael Levine, who had become Ignatieff's literary agent, and within a couple of years Mordecai and Florence would be seeing Ignatieff and his new wife, Zsuzsanna Zsohar, for dinners in their flat in East London. As always, Richler was curious to meet people of interest and import. As always, too, he moved easily along the political spectrum, caring little for formal party or ideological affiliations. (Ignatieff, while years away from entering Canadian politics, was known as a hawkish Liberal.) Richler's approach to friendship mirrored his own political values: better to be interesting and lively and true to your complex self than merely, blandly consistent to a party line.

For the same reason and at the same time, he enjoyed the company of Conrad Black, who was at a far remove politically from Michael Ignatieff, attending Black and Amiel's annual Christmas parties in their spectacular London home. Black had shown him friendship, and Richler found him good company: arguing with a man or woman of intelligence was always more appealing to him than sharing their political colours. When later asked by a CBC crew making a documentary to comment about the acquisitive media baron, he neither praised nor damned him. "I don't think [Black] should be dismissed out of hand," he simply said, noting the steady extinction of individual newspaper owners in Canada. Privately he tried to persuade Black to "blindside all those tiresome Canada-Firsters who have greeted your takeover of Southams like the second coming of Vlad the Impaler" by hiring "some young spark to edit a *Weekly Southam's Book Review* that could be inserted in all the Southam papers, as well as being

sold in bookshops like the New York Times Book Review." (It
didn't happen.) Black, of course, did own *Saturday Night*, where
Jake worked for cheap and his father for good pay as a columnist, and he now also controlled the *Gazette*, whose conciliatory
approach to Quebec nationalism under previous ownership (and
editorship) was fast being supplanted by a more aggressive
stance, and which would open its doors to him. Richler had been
pursued for years by *Gazette* editor and Ziggy's habitué Ashok
Chandwani to write a weekly column on Quebec. Now he negotiated with Conrad Black directly, over lunch at Canary Wharf,
demanding a steep fee for each 800-word column, and then
cheerfully threatening to spread the rumour among mutual
friends that "Conrad couldn't afford me." Black was taken aback.
He stood up and said he had to leave the table for a few minutes
to think about it. When he sat down again, he agreed to pay an
unprecedented (and much gossiped about) $2,000 per column.
Starting that spring of 1997, Richler began launching attacks on
favourite targets—Quebec nationalists, the language laws, Brian
Mulroney—from the amplified pulpit of a newspaper chain with
thirty-three dailies and three million readers. The Sunday *Gazette*
circulation went up by 6,000 almost immediately.

All the children, along with their spouses or companions, joined
their parents for the Christmas holiday, Emma riding the bus
from Camden Town, others flying across the ocean. (Noah, on
assignment for the BBC, returned from Pakistan just in time.) But
the mood was tempered by news about Nick Auf der Maur.
Shortly before the holidays the beloved fifty-four-year-old journalist and boulevardier used his *Gazette* column to announce the
discovery of a malignant tumour in his neck. It turned out to be
carcinoma and required immediate radiation, with the survival
rate pegged at 50–50. In January Auf der Maur, who smoked two
packs of Gitanes a day, began treatments. "I know it's debilitat-
ing," Richler wrote to him on January 20, "maybe even awful, but

hang in, old friend, because we're betting on you here." He recounted his own cancer scare of five years earlier, and how "the chances of recurrence were 50–50, but I'm still here to tell the tale." He added hugs from Florence and encouragement: "Keep fighting. Don't despair." Every couple of days, the encouraging faxes were sent.

Conrad Black instructed the *Gazette* to continue paying Nick Auf der Maur his column fee during his treatment. Richler remained a determined, funny cheerleader, cracking wise about Auf der Maur's recent eleventh-hour visits to the Catholic church—"You'd better cover home plate as well, and send a note to the Lubovitcher Rebbe in Crown Heights, Brooklyn"—and making as light as possible of reality. "John Aylen reports your original tumour was the size of a communion wafer, but I prefer to thk it was more like a matzoh ball." In one note, where he mentioned his recent sixty-sixth birthday, celebrated with Martha, Emma and Noah, he joked at Jacob's expense: "Jake forgot to call to pay tribute, and so I am obliged to rewrite the will." In another: "I hope to attend your 66th, even if I have to be rolled in drooling in wheelchair." Fax after fax ends with: "Hang in there."

It was nearly the exact wording that the stroke-affected Hymie would send to Barney when he was finally committed to the King David Nursing Home: HANG IN OLD FRIEND.

Meanwhile, "my dubiously titled novel," as he called *Barney Like the Player Piano* in a letter to his agent Deborah Rogers in mid-January, was nearing completion. "Chatto will publish in September, ditto Knopf/Canada, and Bob will do it in Jan 98." The manuscript had gone out in December to Louise Dennys in Toronto, Alison Samuel at Chatto and "Bob" in New York. Bob Gottlieb, out of the *New Yorker*, was now back at his former publishing house of Knopf as an editor-at-large, working mostly from home. Gottlieb, loving the book, made only his usual few tweaks. Dennys, equally thrilled with it, sent back a marked-up manuscript and thirty pages of notes, followed by phone conversations over the next few months. Among her suggestions was that he balance Barney Panofsky's unreformed views of women with evidence of those qualities that would make him appealing to the three who had, in fact, married him. For Dennys, *Barney* was foremost a great love story, as well as a passionate, enraged cry against "the dying of the light," and the protagonist's flaws had to be big enough to cause the dissolution of the one marriage that had brought him happiness. She also recommended he pull back once or twice before a couple of his most gratuitously offensive remarks. Alison Samuel supported her in questioning his handling of the "reveal" ending that unravelled the mystery of Boogie Moscovitch's disappearance. Richler consulted Gottlieb, who suggested a completely different ending, but Richler wrote to Dennys, now his primary editor, explaining that he was going to stick to his own version. He would take grief from friends and admirers alike for the improbability of this twist in an otherwise deeply probable novel.

In mid-January he thought he had three weeks of work left on the manuscript. But he paid attention to his editors' comments, and on March 1 he reported, "I've been working like a fiend on novel revisions just finished yesterday." Remarks about the book being another "overcomplicated novel" failed to hide the excitement and even surprise in his letters; *Barney* was proving to be a profoundly different writing experience from *Gursky* or *Horseman*. Then Florence, reading the final draft and pronouncing it wonderful, came up with a superior title: *Barney's Version*.

The couple had another reason for celebration. Martha and Nigel were married on March 7, the reception, highlighted by wedding cake and bagels, held at the Sloane Court flat. "I make a point of attending all my daughter's weddings," he began his remarks. After a quick trip home to give a lecture in Calgary, he further revised the manuscript into April.

Its technical and structural challenges notwithstanding, *Barney's Version* was written with a surety that arced back to the six-month-long creative free fall that had produced *Duddy Kravitz*. The novel, while simpler in design than *Gursky*, brimmed equally with characters and incident. Barney's tale, shifting time periods in his usual manner, bringing vividly to life the Paris of 1950–51 and the Montreal of fall 1995, simulated both an old man's instinctive "speak memory" approach to revisiting his past, and his tendency to shift wildly and circle over events. His "version" is just that: a single perspective. Hence the brilliance of Florence's new title. *Barney's Version,* which abandons Richler's favoured technique of multiple points of view, had to belong to Barney Panofsky only, one man's take on himself and his life and times. Until, that is, his son Michael, a lurking presence throughout in the punctilious footnotes he provides to his father's text, steps in to complete the story after the rising waters of Alzheimer's have drowned his most precious possession: his raw identity.

But even in the darkening shadow of the disease, Barney Panofsky does not fade away. He is as much himself on page 403, his final day as a fully sentient being, as he was on page one. By ending his portion of the novel with the same preoccupations— his love of his family and his ceaseless anxiety for their safety and happiness, the "unjust world" everyone must negotiate, his own failings and limitations—Richler issues his loudest, most poignant declaration of the stuff that best defines human beings: relationships, passion, defiance. That and the body, ever more decrepit and failing. So abundant are the references to the lot we face at the edge of the abyss—from dentures to bowels to incontinence, diets to pills and medications—that they give a kind of physicality to the prose.

Being in the *Herzog* mode of charting a life in situ, the novel could make easy use of autobiographical fragments. "I was Barney Panofsky when I was writing it," Richler said of the process, "but not before and not after." The wedding reception scene at the Ritz, where Barney, betrothed to the Second Mrs. Panofsky, is instantly besotted with Miriam Greenberg, "absolutely exquisite" with "long hair black as a raven's wing, striking blue eyes, ivory skin," is Richler's admission that he fell in love with Florence at the wedding party thrown for him and Cathy Boudreau, and a personal portrait of Florence Mann at the time, right down to the "layered blue chiffon cocktail dress" worn by Miriam in the novel and, often, by the future Mrs. Richler in life. Barney's apartment in Montreal is modelled on the apartment in the Chateau, including the rolltop desk where he has trouble writing. His late-night calls to his children, all of whom live outside Quebec, or their concerned calls to him, are born of his close relationship with his own physically distant offspring. Among Barney's reprobate habits, besides smoking cigars and drinking Scotch in excess, is his conjuring of his old, possibly imagined love affair with a teacher to summon sexual desire. And if Mrs. Ogilvy is more a boy's fantasy than Evelyn Sacks was in reality, a passing remark by Michael Panofsky in his afterword—that his father boasted of sleeping with his teacher when he was fourteen—certainly anchors it in Richler's world. Boulevardiers in the novel, most notably the heavy-boozing *Gazette* journalist Zack Keeler and the nefarious lawyer John Hughes-McNoughton, sound similar chords from his circle of friends, and their watering hole, Dink's, could easily be replaced by Woody's or Winnie's, Grumpy's or, most recently, Ziggy's. Barney's father, Detective-Inspector Izzy Panofsky, far closer in temperament to the "imagined" Reuben Shapiro than Moses Richler, delivers hilarious lines of dialogue straight from the mouth of Ben Greenberg, the Jewish Montreal cop Richler had infuriated with his profile in *Saturday Night*. And Barney's son Saul, living for a period in radical squalor on St. Urbain Street and mixing it up in the manner of the student revolutionaries who trashed Sir George Williams while Richler was writer-in-residence, borrows from both Noah and Daniel's coming-of-age disaffections.

"Your father," Irv Nussbaum tells Michael Panofsky in the novel's final pages, "was one of your real wild Jews. A *bonditt*. A *mazik*. A devil. I could have sworn he was out of Odessa." *Barney's Version* shows the results of Mordecai Richler's sustained thinking in

adulthood about the nature of his Jewish identity. The likes of
Barney Panofsky, he implies—a *sui generis* Jewish identity specific
to a period and a culture—can't be transferred. With their aging,
disintegrating bodies go their singular, fierce dispositions.

It was this clear-eyed, joyous, tough-minded book that he
brought back to Knopf Canada for final copy edits in the spring.
Before their departure, he and Florence stayed up late watching
the landslide victory of Tony Blair and the Labour Party over the
Conservatives in early May. Then the patriarch issued instructions to Jake similar to those he gave to Emma when they prepared to leave for England each autumn. In this case, to be a
"favourite child," Jake had first to drive from Toronto to Montreal,
and outfit *two* residences in advance. "If you weren't an ungrateful, selfish, spoilt rotten snotnose you would Montrealwards on
Friday May 8. Get Aylen to help you pick up Saab on Saturday
morning, and then meet your ageing, loving, ever-providing parents at Mirabel. . . . You do what you think best, my son," he added
nonchalantly, threatening again to leave Jake's share of the estate
to the Humane Society. Jake, accustomed to the banter and enormously fond of his parents, as were his brothers and sisters, did
as asked, calling Sweet Pea to recharge the car battery, provision-
ing the Chateau apartment and booking a table at Le Mas des
Oliviers for lunch one day and Moishe's for dinner on another.

Having lately asked Nick Auf der Maur to check a few facts for
the novel, Richler invited him to a steak dinner with Florence,
Jake and John Aylen. Auf der Maur, still thinner and weaker, had
aged a decade in a winter, but remained his lively, funny self.
Aware of the financial stress that being off work so long was causing him, even with the *Gazette* still sending a weekly cheque,
Richler made inquiries of other newspapers on behalf of his sick
friend, asking them to hire Auf der Maur or even simply use his
copy. Later in the summer, after Auf der Maur went through surgery on his throat and neck, he helped organize a fundraiser at
Ziggy's to pay for an upgrade to a private room. They raised
$4,500, with Conrad Black contributing from London and Richler
quietly buying most of the raffle tickets himself.

On his return from England the good, generous friend and former good, generous son might have made a short trip to a cemetery in Côte-des-Neiges. Back in March Richler had received a long-expected call from his sibling. "Muttle, we're orphans," Avrum said. "Oh, she died," Mordecai replied. When his brother asked if he was planning to fly back from London for the funeral in Montreal—Lily's body was being transported from St. John's—he answered, "Are you kidding?" He requested few details and, after he told Florence the news, let her know that he wished to say and hear no more about his mother.

So it ended between parent and child: after a long, bitter silence, a still deeper and longer quiet settled in. For unlike with Moses, eulogized in "My Father's Life," no similar consideration would be given to Lily Rosenberg's equally difficult, largely unfulfilled time on earth. Maybe a quarter-century earlier, when he was finding her behaviour tolerable enough to summon the comedic Mrs. Hersh in *Horseman*, he might have found empathetic words. But after he returned with his family to Montreal in 1972, and to her volatile mix of wrath, unpredictability and possible mental illness . . . ? Even a haunting overlap—Richler writing about Alzheimer's while his parent experienced it—did not merit remark, and perhaps he was not fully aware of that sorrowful connection. Avrum, Eve and Avrum's grown children, along with a scattering of Rosenbergs and Richlers, saw Lily Rosenberg to her resting place in the Baron de Hirsch Cemetery, close to the mausoleum housing Yudel and Sarah-Gittel Rosenberg but closer, ironically, to the grave of Moses Richler. But Mordecai did not pay his respects to the memory of his mother—then or ever.

For Florence, read the dedication to *Barney's Version*, and below that single line, *and in memory of four absent friends: Jack Clayton, Ted Allan, Tony Godwin, and Ian Mayer*. Mortality had coloured the writing of the book from its earliest stages to its final revisions; fair enough that of the five names listed, only one was still among, as Barney puts it, "the quick." "There's just one trip around the block and you'd better have as good a time as possible without hurting anyone else," Richler told a journalist. "But beyond that, that's it." A proudly upright, rather phallic cigar, the smoke drifting lazily, adorned the Canadian jacket, with the author in full on the back, his direct gaze and craggy essence captured.

In June, a few months prior to publication, Louise Dennys pulled an excerpt from *Barney's Version* to run in *Saturday Night*. The editor, Ken Whyte, who had become a good friend of Mordecai's, had the idea of charging Absolut Vodka a fee in exchange for laying out a page of the excerpt in the shape of a vodka bottle sporting "Absolut Mordecai" in block letters, and "Presented by Absolut Vodka" on the title page. To convince the distiller, he showed them the text. Absolut asked that a reference in the excerpt to Johnnie Walker Black be changed to their brand, and that an allusion to Boogie Moscovitch "sucking some substance into his nose with a straw" be deleted. Richler, presented with the plan, was amused by the idea but not about changing his text. He wanted to support Ken Whyte, a risk-taking editor of the old school, and the venerable magazine he had so long written for, which was, as always, struggling to survive. In the end, he sent Whyte a fax about altering the unsponsored reference to Johnnie Walker: either Absolut live with the reference being reduced simply to "Scotch" or he would add a line denouncing vodka as leading to "blindness, impotence, and cancer." The reference to cocaine also had to stay.

The association of the excerpt with Absolut Vodka became a matter of controversy. The accusation was that Richler had personally benefited financially. Given his criticisms of blurring the line between art and commerce, some dating back to the 1950s, and his unforgiving stance on A.M. Klein's employment as speech writer and poet laureate for Sam Bronfman, the "Absolut Mordecai" pitch smacked to some of saying one thing while doing another. But the excerpt did not achieve placement because of Absolut's patronage—it had already been taken by the magazine before that—and the distiller paid *Saturday Night* for its ad placement, in the usual way. But being called a hypocrite stung

him more than most of the epithets hurled by Quebec nationalists. He was angered by the automatic supposition of guilt, but
he was still able to be funny about it. "I do have my principles,"
he told the *Globe and Mail.* "Had Ken Whyte come up with a sponsor for my novel excerpt who was a yogurt or crunchy granola
maker, I would have said absolutely no."

That same month he tangled again with Quebec. He used a language slot in the *New York Times Book Review* to remind any
Americans who might have allowed the contretemps over the
province's language laws to fade from their thoughts, that notwithstanding Quebec had given Canada "our most talented playwright, Michel Tremblay; that internationally renowned maker of
theatrical magic, Robert Lepage; the films of Denys Arcand . . .
and the Cirque de Soleil"; that despite such accomplishments,
signs, surely of a secure, prospering culture, "some *pure laine*
Québécois still regard the language of the impure woollies as a
desecration of their streets." Evoking "Matzogate" in the *New York
Times* compelled TV host Morley Safer, an old acquaintance from
London, with a crew from the popular CBS show *60 Minutes*—by
far the biggest American media outlet to date, and therefore
the most embarrassing to Quebec—to Montreal to see what all
the silliness was about, and then to share their findings, complete with an interview with Richler, with twenty million
Americans. Relations between him and the nationalists, it
turned out, *could* get worse.

A confident Louise Dennys, recognizing the tenderness and
depth of feeling in *Barney's Version* and its huge, unflinching
embrace of mortality and loss, in a novel as funny as anything he
had written, ignored her writer's prediction that she would soon
be owing him another bottle of single malt and ordered a huge
first printing of eighty thousand copies for September. Richler
could feel good about her optimism, at least, during the summer
of waiting, in contrast to his emerging foreboding about how the
book would be published in England and the United States. "I'm
a worried man," he wrote to Deborah Rogers in July, "charged—
maybe overcharged—with pre-publication jitters re England."

When someone at Chatto questioned flying him over for publicity, he wondered if he was obsolescent. "Maybe BBC, book pages, are no longer interested in an old fart like me, and I will just have to live with that." He asked his agent to check Chatto's publicity plans for the novel, or were they just going to "drop it on London and see if it floats." In the autumn, similar jitters about the U.S. market surfaced in angry letters to Knopf in New York about review copies. "Hey, I've got a better idea," he scolded a publicist, about their tardiness in sending *Barney's Version* to key people in advance of publication in January. "Why don't you wait until my fucking novel is remaindered and send out copies then?"

His worries proved unjustified. Chatto did fly him over for a week at the end of September—he paid for an extra ticket for Florence—and while the publicity schedule was modest, the acclaim was stellar. (The *TLS* dissented, finding Barney Panofsky "hard to take.") One review stood out. The highly regarded critic and writer Alberto Manguel, who had always watched Richler's work appreciatively, stepped forward in the *Sunday Times*. Praising the "deep, dark business" of mortality below the novel's comedy, Manguel wrote, "Richler fashions a marvel . . . like Dr. Johnson at his insulting best, Barney at the top of his form is unsurpassed. . . . Richler has written a Lear for our selfish, penny-pinching times, a Lear uncluttered by divided kingdoms and quarrelling daughters. Even the fool is dispensed with—Barney is his own fool, 'a very foolish, fond old man, smelling of mortality.'" The *Spectator* acknowledged that "Richler is the funniest novelist at present at work in the English language." Four major British papers put *Barney's Version* on their best-of-year lists. Most reassuring was the insistence of the *Daily Telegraph* that the "moving, funny, combative, sometimes tasteless" novel had been shamefully overlooked by the Booker Prize committee for 1997. "What more could Booker judges and commentators—or anybody else—want from a novel?" The Booker for 1997 went to Arundhati Roy's *The God of Small Things.*

In the United States, too, he received glowing reviews to only marginal effect. Joseph Heller called the novel "joyful and exciting from beginning to end" and John Updike took it on thoughtfully in the *New Yorker.* Updike, more than forgiving— Barney, after all, extolling the modest values of his writing style, boasts that "I rein in my metaphors, unlike John Updike"—aptly described it as "a rollicking novel laden with rue," and provided a stirring final paragraph: "What entertains and affects us in *Barney's Version* is the headlong, spendthrift passage of a life, redeemed from oblivion in the unbridled telling. The edge of the grave makes a lively point of vantage."

But in Canada, things could hardly have gone better. Knopf Canada brought the book out with guns blazing, and his publicist, Sharon Klein, asked if he would submit to a cross-country reading tour. The *New Criterion* requested that he keep a diary. "Peddler's Diary" covered the month, from mid-September to mid-October, that he spent on tour, with one week in England and the rest in Canada. Misadventures—the cancellation of a BBC interview with Melvyn Bragg, a combative lunch with the *Globe and Mail* journalist Jan Wong—were played for laughs. Jan Wong, whose "Lunch with" column was notorious for being deliberately abrasive, went for the jugular. "At 66, he has a bulbous red nose, glowering eyes and grey hair that flops over his forehead like a damp mop," she wrote. "His melon-shaped belly bulges over his chinos." Noting that he "could care less that the smoke from his Davidoff cigarillo, which he puffs throughout his clam chowder, might bother others," she probed his reputation as a grump and a drinker. Richler played along, saying, "I'm a very agreeable fellow" and "Nothing you've read about me is true" and "I don't drink nearly as much as people think. But I enjoy the reputation." Amused and exasperated by the end in equal measures, he ended their encounter with a quip: "My next appointment isn't for 25 minutes. We could go somewhere and shoot up drugs." He wrote a version of the lunch himself in "Peddler's Diary," recounting how Jan Wong had said that she and her Jewish husband "have a *seder* every Friday night." "That must be a Jewish-Chinese custom," Richler observed. "We manage it only once a year. On Passover." The tribulations of public readings were entertainingly relayed, including an event at Convocation Hall, University of Toronto. At that book-signing a woman told him, "I read your last novel, *Solomon Gursky Was Here.* It took me two years. WHAT A STRUGGLE!"

Sharon Klein found her author warm and agreeable. She respected his dislike of chit-chat and his ease with long silences, though he enjoyed doing post-mortems with her about interviews, and could be highly critical. Klein quietly noted how often even seasoned journalists, flustered by his stature, tried to out-funny Mordecai Richler. When she called asking if he would do a literary breakfast at the Ritz-Carlton in Montreal, along with the great figure skater Toller Cranston, who had published his memoirs, he declined to share a bill with a skater, snapping, "Do I have to wear a tutu?" Five minutes later, after a conversation with Florence, who appreciated Cranston's artistry, he called her back to agree. Later, when Knopf was sold to the German company Bertelsmann, he faxed Klein and company president David Kent, both of whom were Jewish, gleefully suggesting they pack their bags and clear out of the building before it was too late.

Few Canadian readers experienced any difficulties with *Barney's Version.* The novel climbed swiftly to the top of bestseller lists and perched there throughout the autumn. Newspapers and magazines competed to lavish praise on it: "an embarrassment of riches," "beautifully written." While the Governor General's fiction jury didn't agree, the Giller did, naming *Barney's Version* one of five finalists, with a jury of Peter Gzowski, Mavis Gallant and Bonnie Burnard making the selections. The Richlers sat at Jack Rabinovitch's table, Mordecai as ever uncomfortable in his "penguin suit," Florence as ever dazzling, with Jake and Noah on hand. Louise Dennys and Ric Young were at the table as well. The crowd at the Four Seasons ballroom, now an annual hand-picked gathering of four hundred media, agents, publishers and writers, stood for a prolonged standing ovation when his name was called. "The award I've coveted since the age of twelve, the Cy Young award, continues to elude me," he said, referring to the prize given annually to the best pitchers in major-league baseball. He paid tribute to Florence, calling her his first and most exacting editor, and to his friend Jack Rabinovitch.

"Oh, I won a prize here," he wrote to Deborah Rogers on the eve of their return to the U.K. "The Giller. $25,000 Canadian." Not long afterwards, he also happily admitted defeat to his Toronto editor, who had bet him that they would sell more than sixty thousand copies. When dining or having a drink with his publishers, Richler expected them to pay—his hand rarely strayed towards the bill—but this time, he and Florence took Louise Dennys and Ric Young to dinner at Bistro 990 on Bay Street, and picked up the cheque.

PART VII

PHILEMON
AND BAUCIS

I

BOYISHLY PROUD

"I once dared to hope," Barney Panofsky admits, "that Miriam and I, into our nineties, would expire simultaneously, like Philemon and Baucis. Then a beneficial Zeus, with a gentle stroke of his caduceus, would transmogrify us into two trees, whose branches would fondle each other in winter, our leaves intermingling in the spring." Mordecai Richler was not given to using classical mythology in his work, and wouldn't have now had the story not been a favourite of Florence's. She loved Ovid's *Metamorphoses*, and in the case of the myth of the elderly lovers hoping to die together and be entwined for eternity, the older Babylonian version, with its mention of mulberry trees, pleased her the most. He nestled the unexpected reference into *Barney's Version* for his wife, speaking once more in a manner more private than public of his undying love for the woman he had been wed to for thirty-eight years, and been infatuated with since their initial encounter six years earlier still.

His devotion had been unwavering. Tales abounded of courtesies shown by Mordecai to Florence, often remembered by friends and strangers for their unselfconscious chivalry: kneeling on a sidewalk to fix a broken heel, lambasting a waiter for failing to attend to her first. Equally evident was the ongoing physical attraction, and desire for intimacy, between them. Now pensioners, the Richlers continued to walk along streets arm in arm or hand in hand, and routinely retreated at parties and social functions to whisper intimately, as though in the thrall of new love. Nor was he any less needy of her than he had been four decades earlier. Their children traded amused accounts of his obsessive calling home when on the road, or his reluctance to travel at all without Florence, especially on assignment, when she would know enough about French wines for him to ask the right questions, or could describe the flowers and plants in a Marrakech park. He also rarely left any of their apartments or houses, even for a walk, without leaving behind a note, always pithy, often funny.

As for seeing the pyramids and the Wailing Wall, dining in Michelin-approved restaurants and staying in five-star hotels, Richler only enjoyed such activities fully in her company. He had promised to show her the world back in 1959. What he had really meant, which she had intuited, was that he wanted to discover the world with her, and her alone. Over and over, in ways spoken and unspoken, he demonstrated eternal gratitude to his spouse for producing and raising a family he could still scarcely believe was his own, and he never ceased being the young man who had wanted to display, and even quietly boast of, having wooed, won and made happy a beautiful woman. More than that: Richler had known from the start that Florence Mann, née Wood, should be, had to be, Florence Richler, not because of her physical beauty but for the quality of her mind and her kindly nature. There had never been any other woman for him, and if Lily Rosenberg had made any single fatal error in dealing with her adult son, it had been failing to understand that fierce fact.

But a critical moment in *Barney's Version* posed a question about sexual fidelity. Barney Panofsky loses his Baucis in part because of a one-night stand fuelled by alcohol and male vanity, and devoid of meaning or even pleasure. His ardour for Miriam remains undying, as does his emotional and spiritual constancy to her. Regardless, he is alone at the end of the novel, and so faces the long, darkening corridor of Alzheimer's without his heart's desire. Miriam doesn't leave him only because of the affair, but that outcome imbues the novel with poignancy and, as Alberto Manguel noted, a tragic dimension without precedent in his other books. On handing the manuscript of *Barney's Version* to Florence to read, evidently concerned she might make a link between art and life, he had issued what was, for him, a rare disclaimer: "Incidentally," he said, "I have never had an affair since we met. But I cannot keep writing just about you."

Pre-marriage, he had been sexually aggressive and active. With Cathy Boudreau, he had strayed. During his second, far more substantial union he had become a well-known writer who spent, as he readily admitted, many nights away from his family, drinking in exactly those kinds of hotel bars where a sodden Barney encounters, and allows himself to be seduced by, a young actress. Rumours about Mordecai Richler being involved in extramarital affairs were few, and only delivered in whispers; but they were audible. While his novels were emphatically not mirrors of his life, like most novelists he relied on his own emotional state at the time of composition to steer the emotional trajectory of the story. *Barney's Version* is a little darker, a little more reflective and, for sure, regretful. It may also be a meditation on the vulnerability and tragic nature of romantic relationships, arguing, perhaps, for not judging harshly about things that ultimately matter little— if at all. Barney's twin declarations of his only real priorities— "Miriam, Miriam, my heart's desire" and "My children, my children"—certainly echoed those of his creator.

As a father, Richler was now speaking more openly in public about his children's careers. The previous autumn he had agreed to be interviewed with Martha for a British magazine. The youngest Richler daughter described her parent as "a deeply honest, unpretentious man" who nevertheless required such quiet for his profession that his children had learned to go off and "do their own quiet things too," perhaps unconsciously being directed into adult lives in the arts. He, in turn, called Martha "the happiest of children" and "a woman with a great imagination." Then, from the patriarch: "For Martha, as with all my children, I wish only happiness and the possibility to do something she really enjoys." "Marf," as she signed her cartoons, admitted that she had been slow to show him a children's book she was working on, both because "he prefers to see things when they're done" and on account of his tendency to be a "judgemental father." This stood in contrast with Florence, "a much softer, more sympathetic, natural teacher." Show him her writing she did, though, following the tracks blazed by Daniel, Noah and Jake. Within a year or so Emma too would complete the absorption of the Richler children in those "quiet things" by asking both her parents to read a short story she had written about a large, quirky family, told through the eyes of the oldest daughter. He would embrace her effort with genuine appreciation, as well as the usual pride.

Accompanying the article were photos showing him puffing away on a Romeo y Julieta while Martha looked on. He still smoked cigars and cigarillos, and still expected to be permitted the pleasure in venues far more contentious than a photographer's studio. While the anti-smoking movement hadn't yet won the war outright, it was steadily winning most battles, from smoking sections in restaurants to smoky bars. This was leading to increasingly regular run-ins with either laws or people who believed refraining from smoking in public should be a courtesy naturally extended. On a talk show he took exception to a Harvard professor who claimed he was allergic to cigar smoke. "What, do you break out in spots?" he asked testily. At a lunch in his honour at Canada House in London he was asked, repeatedly, to extinguish his cigar during the meal, given the new government regulations. When he threatened to walk out, he was told only that his absence would be regretted. In restaurants, in contrast, even those now declared smoke-free, he lit up and, forever the pugilistic street kid, waited to see what would happen. When a waiter in Toronto whose manner suggested he might be gay reported the objections of fellow diners, Richler snapped, "I don't tell you what to put in your mouth." Indulging him about alcohol was one thing—Timothy Findley, who loved his "gorgeous sense of mischief," on another programme with Richler, nevertheless watched in astonishment as he asked a producer to go and find a bottle of cognac on a Sunday morning—but indulging his vigorous *other* habit, for him so connected over time to writing that it had become needful, was something else.

The Richlers welcomed the new year in Paris with Don and Heather Johnston and in the south of France with Martha and Nigel, who were renting a house there. He had more than the Giller and Canadian sales, or the reviews in the U.K., to celebrate: "Film rights sold," he reported to Deborah Rogers. "I will do the script." The charming Robert Lantos, himself fond of slim cigars and whisky, had recently produced a film of Brian Moore's, *Black Robe*. He remained a huge admirer of Mordecai Richler, both the man and the fiction, and believed their earlier movie collaboration, *Joshua Then and Now*, had been given a hard time. Alerted to *Barney's Version*, he read it in manuscript and made a pre-emptive bid to buy the rights outright—Norman Jewison was also interested—rather than simply purchasing an option. Paying a larger figure than the $300,000 for the rights and screenplay of *Joshua,* Lantos was agreeable to resurrecting the original arrangement: Richler scripting, Ted Kotcheff directing. That suited Kotcheff as well; from the moment he read his friend's book, he too knew it was a film he badly wanted to make.

Michael Levine, his entertainment lawyer in Toronto, had also resold the film rights to *Jacob Two-Two Meets the Hooded Fang*, and TV rights for all three books to Nelvana, who developed an animated series for YTV, a cable network devoted to programming for children. The film, a CBC production directed by George Bloomfield, had a cast that included Gary Busey as the Hooded Fang and Miranda Richardson as Miss Fowl. Filming was scheduled for the summer in Toronto, and Richler, once coveted for the role of a prophet in *The Last Temptation of Christ*, was again asked to appear onscreen, this time for three seconds of glory. With German and French sales of *Barney's Version* confirmed by Deborah Rogers, and the announcement in March that the novel had, like *Gursky*, won the regional Commonwealth Writers' Prize for Canada and the Caribbean, the momentum, in certain markets at least, looked set to continue. Earlier, Louise Dennys had put the novel in the hands of her Italian friend Roberto Calasso, the legendary publisher of Adelphi, insisting that he read it. An acclaimed novelist himself, Calasso is renowned for publishing some of the finest writers in the world, and for making literary novels bestsellers. Adelphi made an offer as well.

Richler was still in England when the miserable news came that Nick Auf der Maur, to whom he had resumed sending cheering faxes, had succumbed to cancer after his sixteen-month battle. Despite fighting a brain tumour, the larger-than-life fellow prankster had resumed drinking after his earlier bout, still filing the occasional *Gazette* column into February. His life was celebrated at Saint Patrick's Basilica on April 13. Jake, who had grown up listening to his father and Auf der Maur exchanging jokes and banter in Ziggy's Bar, delivered two eulogies—his own and his father's. He also contributed a piece to *Nick: A Montreal Life*, already in the planning stages in the weeks before his passing, which was published that same fall. Friends, including Terry Mosher (Aislin), Conrad Black and Brian Mulroney, wrote or drew memorials, and Richler provided an introduction. "Nick was a cherished friend," he wrote. "An original," the greatest of praise. The project, organized, appropriately enough, in Ziggy's, ended up a celebration and eulogy for more than Nick Auf der Maur; his and Richler's crowd, hard-drinking and heavy-smoking, were in their twilight.

Jake, in his own "bio note" in the book, added that his first son, Maximilian Niklaus, was born a few days before Nick's death. "My lovely Florence a bubba," Richler joked with Louise Dennys. Florence became a grandmother twice over in April: Jill Offman and Daniel had a baby girl, called Poppy, later in the month.

That spring *Barney's Version* was named winner of the Stephen Leacock Medal for Humour, and Richler was declared the 1998 "Canadian of the Year" by the Canadian Club. He returned to Montreal, but a few days before his scheduled trip to collect both accolades—a sold-out luncheon in Toronto for five hundred on June 8 and a ceremony in Orillia, Ontario, home of Stephen Leacock, the following weekend—he fell ill. An operation to remove a cancerous kidney was scheduled for June 9. Reporters, reaching him in his room at the Montreal General Hospital, were told by the patient, "It's not a life-threatening operation. It's done pretty often and I'll just have a difficult week." Other reports followed, of hate mail being sent to the hospital, and his publicist, Sharon Klein, was alarmed enough by the attention to call for calm. "Everything is greatly exaggerated," she said. "People have gone nutso over this." Noah flew in from London to be with his father, whose convalescence was not aided by the depressing, dilapidated room. The police suggested moving him—for safety, not comfort—but the patient suggested they instead arrest the letter senders. Morphine kept him wobbly much of the week, his thoughts flitting in and out of coherence, and he even ignored the Stanley Cup playoffs on TV. "But can you imagine," he was lucid enough to joke with his son, "hockey in June?" He also amused the nurses. "No, I won't," he told one who tried putting an oxygen mask over his face, "it's an anti-Semitic machine." This rallying humour cheered Florence and the family; she called close friends to report his spiritedness. Jake, who had lately moved back to Montreal with his new family, helped out as well.

The phone rang constantly. Notes from friends arrived, including one from Brian Moore in California. Richler wept reading it, mulling over their "foolishly aborted friendship." Recovery was slow—suffering from chronic obstructive pulmonary disease, he had difficultly catching his breath—and the summer passed quietly, mostly at the lake. He quit smoking again, and cut back on the alcohol. After the first scare in 1993, Florence had requested that a friend, psychologist and Westmount resident Carmen Robinson, ask her daughter, an oncologist, to read him the riot act about the statistical realities of continuing to smoke. It had done no good.

"I'm OK," Richler wrote later in the summer to a friend. "Mended. But now I look on my five kids with calculating eyes. I think of them as a standby kidney bank, walking around with live spares." Even those well aware of his toughness and determination were impressed; not only did he manage notes to friends during his recovery but by filing before the operation, he didn't miss a deadline for *Saturday Night* or a single weekly appearance in the Southam chain. Nor did being sick keep him from helping friends in similar circumstances. Sweet Pea George remained a regular drinking companion and fix-it guy around the country house, and Richler had happily climbed into his dilapidated truck for long rides to go fishing, even once requesting that he collect him at the Ritz-Carlton in the vehicle. When Sweet Pea was put on a long waiting list for a back operation, Richler made some calls on his behalf, landing him an appointment at the Jewish General the following week. "No Jewish jokes," he advised.

Luckily for him, a larger project, assembling the collection *Belling the Cat*, had been completed just before the operation. The collection, which he had originally wanted to call *Bye Bye Mulroney and Other Celebrations*, went ahead as a fall release from Knopf Canada to coincide with the paperback edition of *Barney's Version*. The pugilistic and now-expanded Mulroney send-off stood prominent, as did his offending profile of the young Wayne Gretzky. Alongside travel pieces on Egypt, Kenya, South Africa, Morocco and Germany were essays on subjects from Woody Allen to Saul Bellow, Sam Bronfman to Mark Twain. He also lightly reworked his *Saturday Night* memoir about the magazine trade as an introduction, moving the sentence about the end days of a certain literary sensibility to the top. By opening *Belling the Cat* with the assertion "I fear I belong to the last generation of novelists who could supplement their incomes . . ." Richler was making two points. First, he was still around as a journalist, a "scribbler," still vigorous and involved at the age of sixty-seven. Secondly, as the list of twenty-odd magazines gone missing since he had begun his career attested, with the *Weekender* and *Tamarack Review* possibly the most lamented, it wasn't only old writers who were dying off. *In Memory of Nick Auf der Maur, 1942–1998*, the dedication read.

Richler and Bill Weintraub were having lunch in Le Mas des Oliviers one day, seated at the table near the wine racks at the back, which was Mordecai and Florence's favourite—he liked being able to observe the room, see who was coming and going, usually without being detected—when the same Brian Mulroney, back practising law and living in Westmount, sat down with a large group towards the front. When it came time to leave, Weintraub, aware that Richler hadn't crossed paths with the former prime minister since pillorying him in *Saturday Night,* asked if he wanted to slip out through the kitchen. "No damn way," he said. As they neared the table, Mulroney stood to greet them. Weintraub, half expecting fisticuffs, sensed Richler stiffen. But instead of a fight, Brian Mulroney wanted a handshake. Ever the politician, he put his arm around his fiercest critic and, turning to his group, smoothly introduced the famous Mordecai Richler as a friend.

A couple of years later Richler would be reporting, in a fax to John Fraser at Massey College, his most recent contact with Brian Mulroney.

Oh, I also had a couple of phone calls from de PM. Mulroney. First time his office called we had just arrived at our dacha in Townships.

Ring, ring.

"Hello."

"I have a call for Mr. Richler from the Prime Minister," said an officious operator.

"Of which country?" I asked.

Which failed to earn me even a chuckle.

"This is prime Richler," claimed the *Ottawa Citizen* of *Belling the Cat,* "clear-eyed, intolerant of lies and deception, disrespectful of sacred cows." But the collection, his funniest, most vigorous and most perceptive since *Hunting Tigers Under Glass* three decades earlier, didn't find publication internationally; parochialism was entering the world of publishing, and in light of the modest sales of *Barney's Version* in England and the U.S. his publishers would not take on a book of essays. He needed to have kept a higher profile in those markets, or had a breakout success with one of his novels.

But in Canada he was now Mordecai, the most recognized literary figure in the country. On October 27 a new national newspaper, owned by Conrad Black and edited by Ken Whyte, was launched. In a statement of intent, Whyte spoke of the "astonishing array of literary talent" that he had assembled for the *National Post*, with Mordecai Richler the biggest name. Whyte had called to ask him to write for him, and after further negotiations with Black, in which his fee was upped again, he became the most successful content "sell" in the publication. A repatriated Noah Richler as book editor and a back-in-Toronto Jake Richler as food critic were hired as well. Whyte also announced conservative columnists Mark Steyn and Linda Frum in that initial roster, which left little doubt about the paper's ideological leanings. A handful of major Canadian authors declined to write for the *National Post* because of its politics, but Richler had no such qualms, believing in Ken Whyte's ability to produce a newspaper of quality. The attraction for him was not its political bent. As always, it was personal: he liked Whyte and knew that neither he nor Conrad Black would interfere with his copy. Others saw his prominence in the *National Post*, in conjunction with his usual mockery of the excesses of the Left and political correctness, as an indication that he had succumbed to creeping conservatism. Such an accusation overlooked his never-ending attacks on Mulroney, and remarks of the order that, had the Reform Party won the 1997 federal election, they would have declared Hitler's birthday a national holiday. Even the successful attempt to "unite the Right," a movement nurtured in the editorial pages of the *National Post*, occasioned near-libellous scorn by Richler, often only a page or two away in the same edition.

He was right not to worry about the paper questioning his content. Whyte, who had once allowed an editor at *Saturday Night* to change one of Richler's pieces without consulting him— "This doesn't sound like me," he had complained—ran the columns virtually untouched. Richler was forever his own man, contrarian and cynical, scolding and judgmental, the cat that could never be belled.

Happily back in London that winter with Florence, and with the girls a cab ride or two away across the city, he worked on the script of *Barney's Version*. He also accepted an advance from M&S for a fourth Jacob Two-Two book, *How Jacob Two-Two Saved the Stanley Cup for Montreal*, which never got much beyond a hand-written list of what he planned for the story and several attempts at a first chapter. Dated "April 17/99," one opening relays how Jacob Two-Two, his eternal eight-year-old, "lives in a rambling old house in Montreal, Canada, where his father had to be the city's number one hockey fan, feeling good when the Montreal Habitants won a game and sour when they didn't." Roles were outlined for returning characters Shapiro and O'Toole, Butch "Madman" Kowalski, Miss Sour Pickle and Mr. Dinglebat, as well as new creations: "those notorious criminals The Catholic Kosher Two—namely, Euclid LaFontaine and Shloime Ginsberg," and goalie "Frank 'The Stopper' McBride" and his wife "Brumhilde." Other notes promised an exploration of "goalies—strange birds" and "hockey policeman sitting in corner," as well as reminders to himself to emphasize "snowball blizzards" and a team titled "The Montreal Snowballs." But the manuscript never proceeded past page five.

He had "mended," as he told his friend, and for a period tried to eat better, drink less and take longer walks. He had kept to his latest non-smoking regime for almost a year, although on hugging him each evening after he returned from the bar, Florence could count whether he had succumbed by one or two Davidoffs in the company of friends and Scotch. Predictably, not smoking at the typewriter during the workday had come at a cost: 800-word newspaper columns he could manage; anything more substantial was a challenge. In early January his endurance was put to a melancholy test. Brian Moore passed away in Malibu, and the new editor at *Saturday Night*, Paul Tough, asked him to reminisce about his friend in his column. It was an emotional undertaking. "In the past," he told Tough and associate editor Dianna Symonds, in a January 18 fax, "I have always agreed to trims/cuts to make my observer column fit the page, but this time I must insist on your running this overlength tribute without cuts."

"On Monday, January 11," the eulogy began, "I came home from one of my long afternoon walks and Florence said, 'I'm afraid I've got bad news. Brian Moore died last night.'" Telling for the first time the tale of their brushing up against each other at the 1990 Booker ceremony, each too "boyishly proud" to exchange more than pleasantries, he spoke of being "the closest of friends for years" with Moore, who once upon a time had taught Daniel how to ride a bike on Long Island, and had served diligently as Emma's godfather. "The pleasures of his company were immense," he said. He did not detail their falling-out; it was not what counted at that moment. But it was still hard to say exactly what had happened; the drift apart had occurred over a long period, and gone unexamined by both of them. The friendship had simply ebbed and been allowed to die, neither side feeling quite strongly enough to fight for it. Of the literary fate of Brian Moore's thirty novels, he deferred judgment. "Time alone will settle that, and time is an unreliable bitch."

Richler's winter of work in London was also interrupted by a trip home with Florence to deliver a lecture at the University of Waterloo—"Canadian Conundrums," a fairly gentle look back over a half-century of engagement with his homeland, including the recent *"opéra bouffe"* in Quebec that had had him manning the barricades—and a stop in Toronto to have drinks with his obliging *Saturday Night* editors at a favourite old watering hole, the Rooftop Bar at the Park Plaza, where he had been exchanging banter and gossip with literary and media friends for forty years, and where Barney Panofsky, nervously awaiting his first lunch with the lovely Miriam, begins to order black coffee to combat a hangover, only "on impulse . . . ordered a Bloody Mary instead."

Come May, he returned to Montreal for the summer and fall with a completed draft of the script for *Barney's Version*. Robert Lantos pronounced himself happy with it—Ted Kotcheff had also read it, and provided notes—and there was talk of a $25-million budget, with shooting the following year in Paris and Montreal.

In June, York University awarded him an honorary doctorate, his first such accolade. Avie Bennett, then chancellor of the suburban Toronto university, made sure there was a paper cup of Scotch on stage during convocation for Richler's sipping pleasure. The former scourge of academics was courteous and friendly, shaking hands with everyone who dared approach him.

That spring the book *The Modern Library: The 200 Best Novels Since 1950* included *St. Urbain's Horseman* as one of their selections. Irish novelist Colm Tóibín had compiled the list with Carmen Callil, Richler's former publisher, as his co-editor. The list highlighted an emerging aspect of Richler's now half-century-old publishing career. Whether it was a 1998 *Quill & Quire* list of "most interesting, important and influential" Canadian books, which placed *Duddy Kravitz* near the top, or Anthony Burgess's faith in the brilliance of *Cocksure*, or the recent acclaim for *Barney's Version* as his crowning achievement, or the small but tenacious group, Florence Richler prominent among them, who believed the hard-won *Solomon Gursky Was Here* to be his masterpiece, the fact was that three, four, even five different novels, written over a span of four decades, competed for pride of place. The overall effect would ultimately confirm the dimensions of the achievement. But it diminished, perhaps, the impact of any individual book on the Canadian scene, where scholarly attention—as opposed to a public that bought 200,000 copies of *Barney's Version*—had shifted away from his work. By late spring 1999, with no new novel or even non-fiction on the go, he agreed to terms with Knopf Canada to produce a *Selected Essays 1960–2000*, which by its very nature would not involve much new material. His health was well short of the level needed to embark on another major work. Time would, of course, settle that—but time was, or could be, an unreliable bitch.

His best, most sustained piece of writing for the year harked back to his earliest awakenings as an Orthodox Jew, and drew on all the learning and thinking of his apostate adulthood. Grove Press in New York was issuing a series of twelve books of the Old Testament, each slim volume featuring an introduction by a prominent author, including Doris Lessing, or, in the case of Bono, leader singer for U2, a global celebrity. Assigned the Book of Job, Richler sought to do no less than pull down the entire temple of Judeo-Christian belief in a just God and justice on earth. "Mighty, capricious, vengeful, cruel, a jealous God, Jehovah can also be seen as a prankster, the first in a long line of dark Jewish humorists, extending to Frank Kafka in our day." Defining Jehovah's "testing" of Job as a "celestial hee-haw," he meditated on the famous lament: "Wherefore doth the way of the wicked prosper?" From the Book of Job itself to the Spanish Inquisition to pogroms in Russia, the path of the ultimate expression of evil was clear. "In those small-bean days," he said of being a Jew in Czarist Russia, "the innocent still had names, not a tattoo of numbers." He told a story from *Hasidic Tales of the Holocaust*, the collection he had featured in *Writers on World War II*. About to be put to death by the Nazis, a Ukrainian Hasid used his final moments on earth to recite a prayer in three languages, in which he blessed the Lord for not making him a heathen. "Then he walked to the edge of the pit, already filled with bodies, and was shot in the back of the head." Compelling evidence, in his mind, for a rethink of the whole "chosen people" blessing from Jehovah. "Enough is enough. As we enter into the new millennium, possibly he might consider favouring others with his love."

A singular dimension to the Richler family had become more pronounced in the winter he drafted the essay on Job. The decision of the parents to spend five or six months a year in London had been in keeping with the trajectory of their children's complicated identities. At any given moment Mordecai and Florence could locate an equal number of their offspring in London and Toronto. The girls ended up favouring England, like their mother, and by the end of the millennium it appeared that both Emma and Martha, both born and early schooled in England, their accents British, were confirmed Londoners. The boys, in contrast, thanks in part to recent opportunities at the *National Post*, were now residents of Toronto. Of the three, only Daniel, a teenager by the time he came to live in Montreal,

spoke with a mild English accent. Noah and Jake were sounding more and more Canadian. With the Richlers' two new
grandchildren also to be found in Toronto, the balance had
lately tipped. As for Montreal—the only city, perhaps that
ultimately mattered to him—the parents lived there alone now,
and for just part of the year.

Summer saw him purchasing a new car, a Jaguar, and
repeating an old mistake. Invited by the Humber School of
Writing to be an instructor at their summer seminar, and now
keen to find excuses for him and Florence to be in Toronto, he
accepted, despite unchanged views on teaching "creative writing." Put up at the Park Plaza for a week, all meals, drinks and
travel paid for, and soon supplied with an every-other-day bottle
of Scotch by school staff to keep him from raiding the mini-bar,
he nonetheless arrived at class the first morning and, ignoring
college regulations, lit a cigar and read the newspaper. For ten
minutes he smoked in silence, his back to the anxious students.
When the programme director, Joe Kertes, stopped by, he suggested an exercise: looking at writing samples. "What a good
idea," Richler said. He also informed the assembled that no good
novelist had ever emerged from a writing school. When he was
challenged—J.D. Salinger and Flannery O'Connor, for instance—
he conceded the point. The point, but not the principle: happier
smoking and chatting with Timothy Findley outside the building, and getting to meet Carol Shields, who had won the Pulitzer
Prize for *The Stone Diaries*, and the young novelist and poet Anne
Michaels, he didn't add much to the Humber School. But
Florence got to visit her children and grandchildren, and he was
able to confirm to himself just how unsuited he was to the classroom. He invited Joe Kertes to breakfast at the end of the week,
by way of thanks, but then hardly said a word.

He was, it turned out, orchestrating a longer stay in the city
that same autumn. He explained the arrangement to Conrad
Black. "We won't be returning to London until later December
as—through the good offices of John Fraser—I have agreed to be
the, um, Distinguished Visitor at Trinity College, U of T, from

early September through December. This will enable us to spend
more time with three children, now resident in Toronto, and our
two new grandchildren. Maybe we can get together in Toronto
this autumn or winter." But he was still in Montreal in September
when Richard Dreyfuss flew there as part of the film festival. The
movie star told the *Gazette* he was in town to promote a film and
to "consider doing another of Mordecai Richler's movies." This
was news to Richler, until he received a call from the mercurial
actor suggesting lunch. Unsure he was up to a solo meeting, he
importuned Michael Levine to fly to Montreal, and then booked
a table at Le Mas. Appearing with his wife and an assistant,
Dreyfuss pitched the idea of Richler writing a sequel to *Duddy
Kravitz*, with him playing his character in late middle years. He
then took his leave before the check arrived. Mumbling about
"unemployed actors," Richler insisted on paying the bill, and so
"owning" the anecdote.

II

TWO *ALTER KOCKERS*

To celebrate Florence's seventieth birthday in October, Richler plotted a surprise party. The couple were now installed for three months in a guest apartment in Trinity College. One of the founding colleges at the University of Toronto, the brick and stone Trinity stands as an elegant New World version of Oxbridge, complete with chapel and leafy quadrangle. John Fraser also provided him with an office at Massey, a literal New World conception of an English graduate residence. It was a block away, obliging Richler to break the pattern of forty years and "go to work" each morning. They made a joke of the commute, with Florence handing him his leather briefcase and wishing him a good day. (Actually, he returned for lunch.) Massey had a bar that opened towards the end of the afternoon, and with John and Elizabeth Fraser on site—the master lived in a house within the college—along with Fraser's administrative assistant, Anna Luengo, whom he knew from her time at *Saturday Night* and liked so much, he had a pleasant work environment. Fraser hosted dinners for the Richlers, including an evening when he confessed his regrets over his estrangement from poet Al Purdy to Professor Sam Solecki—Purdy, he told Solecki, using his term of high praise, was "an original"—and Florence spent time with her daughters-in-law and grandchildren. There were soon three: Poppy and Max, along with Simone, born to Leanne Delap and Jake in October. Old friend Jack Rabinovitch lived a

short cab ride away, as did Avie Bennett and Peter Gzowski, Ric
Young and Louise Dennys, Ken Whyte and Michael Levine. The
Richlers were invited to parties by plenty of newer friends too,
including co-founder of Roots Canada Michael Budman and his
wife, Diane Bald, and he had a "power breakfast," as he wrote to
Louise Dennys, with Heather Reisman, the entrepreneurial
founder of the new Indigo book chain.

Above all, he got to see plenty of his three sons. Noah even
called with offers of work in the book pages of the *National Post*.
His father declined some but accepted others, including his final
engagement the following spring with "the Jewish liberator."
"Saul Bellow is still capable of dazzling us," he wrote of *Ravelstein*,
published when the Nobel Prize winner was eighty-four—"when
I, for one, should I be among the quick, will be grateful if I can
still spell my name"—and he praised the master for "talents undiminished" a staggering fifty-four years after his debut in 1944.

Walking along Hoskin Avenue from apartment to office, or
smoking on a bench in the beautiful modern quadrangle of
Massey College—he found his office dingy—Mordecai Richler
would have struck awed students and university faculty as the
Great Man of Letters. But in his private pantheon, such acclaim
was reserved for very few: Isaac Babel and Franz Kafka, Samuel
Johnson and Maimonides. Saul Bellow, too, whom though he
would never have admitted it, he likely expected, jokes aside, to
outlive. He was, after all, only sixty-eight.

Preparing for Florence's party distracted Richler from the reality that he wasn't getting much work done in Toronto. Pulling off
a party for fifty, many coming from out of town, required concentration for him. John Fraser pitched in, along with Jack
Rabinovitch, who would be hosting the event at his house in
Rosedale. Haya Clayton flew from London and the Kotcheffs from
L.A. New York sent up Bob Gottlieb and Maria Tucci, accompanied by his other good friend from Knopf, the marketing copy-
writer Nina Bourne. A major contingent flew or drove from
Montreal, among them the Weintraubs and Lynch-Stauntons,
with the Scotts travelling from the Townships. David Staines

came from Ottawa; Bernard and Sylvia Ostry, now retired in Toronto, had only a few blocks to travel. Locals included the Levines and Whytes, Gzowskis and Bob Weaver, Michael Ondaatje and Linda Spalding, and Ric Young. The boys were there, though neither Emma nor Martha could fly in, and Louise Dennys, in Frankfurt for the annual Book Fair, a commitment organized six months previously, could only telephone her good wishes.

The morning of her birthday he left for "the office" without acknowledging the date. At lunch, when Florence was expecting an invitation to dinner at least, he was again silent. When he finally mentioned going out for a meal later in the afternoon, he said he wanted to keep it casual—no reservations—but suggested stopping by Jack Rabinovitch's house on Roxborough Street for a drink first. When she was presented with a living room of their closest friends, Florence's surprise was genuine. Behind her stood her husband, who nearly collapsed in relief at having pulled it off. Once Christopher Plummer showed up unexpectedly, the party kicked in as a proper Montreal night in Toronto.

Later that same evening, back at Trinity College, he opened a bottle of champagne and gave his wife a bracelet he had purchased at Tiffany's. Florence was so moved by his gesture that she waited until breakfast the next morning to ask him to return it. The extravagance was not them, and never had been.

Another bottle of champagne was opened in another Canadian city the following month. Richler had agreed to a reading tour of Atlantic Canada that would finally bring him to that elusive tenth province. Originally, he scheduled only one night in St. John's. Avrum and his wife, Eve, attended his reading, and then invited him and Florence to their house for a later supper. For the brothers, the evening marked just their fourth encounter since the summer of 1967; for the wives, it was a first meeting. (Avrum had seen a little of Florence in the 1960s.) Persuaded by the genial conversation with his sibling—he had been fearing a tense, awkward time of it—Richler called Avrum the following morning, saying that they had decided to stay an extra day. Avrum invited them to dinner at Bianca's, one of the city's finest restaurants, and towards the end of the meal Mordecai ordered a bottle of champagne to celebrate their reunion. He then asked his brother to join him in a sealed smoking room, out of earshot of Florence. Lighting a cigar, he launched into the real reason he had extended their stay: to address the "family secret." First he asked Avrum if he had found a letter from him to Lily among her belongings. "You didn't find a letter?" he asked twice. When his brother confirmed that he had not read the fatal letter of 1976, presumably destroyed by their mother, with its long final paragraph of revelation and accusation, he delivered the news he thought his sibling needed to hear with a bluntness that was likely purposeful. "I saw them fucking," he said. Avrum did not know what he was talking about. He explained: Lily and Frankel having sex in the bed next to him in 1944, when he was not quite thirteen and was hoping, as a boy might, that someone would come and "fix" his broken family.

His big brother had been away in Kingston in the winter of 1943–44. What role had the adolescent Mordecai assigned to his return? That skinny, timid eighteen-year-old Avrum would expel the "pretender" father and restore Moses to his rightful place? Instead, Avrum, upon reappearing in Montreal, had accepted the new regime, focusing on his own well-being and career, and leaving Mutty to fend for himself. Had a half-century of fitful, uneasy contact between the siblings—a lifetime, really, now largely spent—been the result of that one unforgettable incident? Richler, who said no more about it that night in St. John's, may have been trying to explain things; if not to apologize, then to make amends and bring the whole sorry narrative to an end in the only manner left—by speaking of it. He had not written directly about what had happened. He had once told his daughter Martha that he didn't believe in psychological explanations for adult behaviours, didn't believe any adult could be helpless, never mind a victim of his or her upbringing. Barney Panofsky, meriting comparisons to King Lear and willing to confess his seduction at the same age by a schoolteacher, had no stomach for either this kind of psychological self-examination, or a tragic vision of life. "O Lord, Please Spare Us This Psychobilge" ran the title of one of Richler's *National Post* columns. For Mordecai Richler, as for so many men of his generation, there were no excuses; there were actions and consequences. There was being true to yourself.

The brothers embraced that night. Avrum sensed that his sibling was ill, and frailer than he admitted; he wondered if he would see him again. But the following spring they had a final dinner at Moishe's on The Main. The restaurant was two blocks from their old high school, lately converted into the headquarters for a charity, and about half a mile from their old apartment at 5257 St. Urbain. Unfortunately for Avrum, he brought along one of his sons, who had never met his famous uncle. Richler was displeased, and left his brother the impression that, had they been alone, he would have spoken more about the incidents that had so shaped them both back in 1944. That conversation never happened.

Though he got an apartment, an office and a stipend, Richler had no official duties at the University of Toronto. Still, when the school was tardy in paying him for his services, he sent John Fraser another playful "open" fax.

My Dear Concierge,
In my misspent, impecunious youth I sometimes had to work for shady fringe film producers. I was never sure they would pay me and, if they did, that their cheques wouldn't bounce. With hindsight, I now grasp these were gentlemen of the old school compared to the begowned swindlers of the U. of T. I want my vigorish and I want it now.

Your grieving creditor,
Mordecai

But he did give a couple of public readings in Toronto, in packed auditoriums. One, a favour to Michael Levine's daughter, had him appearing before a roomful of private-school teenagers. He read from *Barney's Version* and, never too old to savour the pleasures of shock value, treated the girls of Bishop Strachan School to the passage featuring Izzy Panofsky's death, shortly after ejaculating, on a massage parlour table. His driver that day, courtesy of the cagey Levine, was a young actor named David Julian Hirsh, who the lawyer-agent thought would be perfect as Jake Hersh in the still-unmade film adaptation of *St. Urbain's Horseman.*

But Richler was more engaged by his rewrite of the *Barney's Version* script for Robert Lantos, who was paying him $50,000 for it. Lantos, first thrilled with the original draft, had thought it through and asked for a thorough revision. Richler sent the producer the new script early in 2000. The good news was the choice of director: "Kotcheff phoned last night to say Lantos has hired him to direct Barney's Version," he wrote to Levine. "The truth is I'm pleased." Calling his old friend "an immensely talented man" who had "sinned in recent years, doing hack work"— Kotcheff's recent movies had been ordinary fare—he envisioned them making an excellent team again. "We understand each other, work well together, and we shd both do well by Barney." But things remained unsettled enough, even with Ted Kotcheff supposedly on board, for him to joke with Deborah Rogers in the same month that "finally, money is in place, some 18-million Canadian, and now all we need is a director and a cast."

The new year, and new millennium, occasioned a burst of book-length energy. Richler, once more smoking heavily, and either attempting to hide the fact from Florence—on being told by Martha that his hair stank of cigarillo, he swore to her that next time he would "wear a hat"—or else driving her nearly to tears by puffing on a cigar throughout dinner, was also once more generating large-scale ideas. "Last autumn in N.Y.," he wrote to his agent in London, "I was invited to lunch by Nick and Tony Lyons, a charming father and son team who run a small publishing house . . . that brings out elegant 15,000 word books on sport by novelists . . . and I agreed," he continued sheepishly, "for a modest advance, to do 15,000 word[er] on snooker for them." He then broke the bad news, at least for Deborah Rogers: "However, as this is hardly compelling stuff for USA, I gave them permission to handle world rights, including Canada and U.K. It was foolish, maybe, but I was totally charmed by them. So I have interrupted my novel-in-progress to pronounce on snooker." The *New Yorker* had already agreed to publish a 4,000-word excerpt in the summer.

What novel in progress? On Feb 4, 2000, he faxed Louise Dennys from London. "Now that I'm at last novelizing, as they say in Hollywood, I'm prepared to sign a contract with Knopf Canada, but with no one else at the moment." As usual, he dictated the terms: ". . . same as they were for Barney's Version: if memory serves," he said, "50,000 on signature, 50,000 on delivery and 50,000 on pub." She agreed at once, grateful that with *Barney's Version* earning out, as he knew well, at over $400,000 in royalties so far, he could have asked for much more. Nor did his editor have any reason to doubt his ability to produce another novel. The timing—around two years after the publication of the last one—was about right, and any loss of resilience or stamina was not in public evidence. In consultation with him, Dennys assigned a submission date for "untitled novel by MR, 400 book length pages," and was glad to pay the advance on signing. If he delivered on time, she could release the new Mordecai Richler novel that autumn or early in 2003. She also bought *On Snooker* from the Lyonses for 2001 publication, so with the essay collection scheduled for 2002, Knopf Canada would have three more titles by the author in their catalogue, and Richler could lay claim to opening the new century with a demonstration of energy befitting a writer half his age.

He was living life strenuously still, writing while fulfilling other freelance scribbling duties. He was also available for speeches. His fees were flexible—from free to over $10,000—but "look here," he wrote from London to his speech agent about a lecture in Regina, "I'm an old fart of 69 next week. I can't squeeze in all that flying, and lecture, in such a short time frame." He did all the flying anyway, and even squeezed in a long dinner with Guy

Vanderhaeghe and Saskatchewan's premier, Roy Romanow. But
he was never for hire for just anyone, and balked when one potential client, the technology giant IBM, requested a pre-interview:
"This is irritating. Fucking insulting. I will not audition for IBM
or anybody." On his way back from Regina he spent a couple of
days in Toronto, where he enjoyed a "hungover, um, power breakfast," with Louise Dennys, and later admitted that the trip to
Canada had been "truly exhausting." In a note to his Knopf Canada
editor he joked about a title for the new novel—STOCKWELL
DAY WAS MY CATAMITE, a reference to the new leader of the
Reform Party—and asked her to add a clause to his contract stat-
ing that, should she leave the company, he would have the option
of returning the advance and making other arrangements. She
phoned to thank him for his confidence in her, but explained that
Random House did not allow such clauses in their contracts,
assuring him of the company's long-term commitment to his
work. He was serious about that; relationships, as always, mattered more than publishers, but he accepted her response. "Best
to my Meatloaf Mate," he added, referring to Ric, who was also
Jewish, and with whom Richler liked to eat meatloaf at the Four
Seasons Hotel, revelling in a four-star establishment keeping
such a homey dish on its menu.

He couldn't resist adding another flight, for himself and
Florence, for a "three-day stay in a grand villa Jack Rabinovitch
has rented for the month" in the village of St. Paul de Vence, with
its nostalgic echoes of winters past in the Alpes-Maritimes, and
then another again for a much-delayed fishing junket to Iceland.
His bad back laid him low in early April, recovering just in time
for him to catch a flight to Edinburgh to meet the snooker champion Stephen Hendry. Another fishing trip, to Labrador with Ric
Young, had to be postponed.

February had seen him seated in the Sloane Court flat for "one
hundred hours of white-knuckle TV spread over seventeen days"
watching Stephen Hendry, the player he intended to make the
focus of *On Snooker*, in the World Snooker Championship. To survive the ordeal required a daily "ten pack of Davidoff's Demi-tasse

cigarillos, a plentiful supply of cashews, a bowl of cherry tomatoes, a bottle of the Macallan. . . ." He happily trailed the professional snooker tour to Birmingham and Ireland. In Goff, County
Kildare, he found himself falling back on tried-and-true methods
of reportage: setting up in a hotel bar or hospitality suite, where
he could meet people and absorb stories and information. On
one day of reporting, the nearly seventy-year-old was "already
smashed" by late afternoon. Not long after, he boarded a train to
Sheffield to attend another competition, and booked an interview in the hotel bar with the Canadian snooker player Cliff "The
Grinder" Thornton, who forgot about the appointment. Richler
retired to his room "much the worse for too many single malts."

Smoking, drinking, writing: for Mordecai Richler, this was how
a book came into being. He went about the task into the spring
and summer of 2000. "Promised New Yorker delivery of 4000
word piece by May 10, to run in their August sports issue," he told
Nick Lyons. "Fully expect to deliver your snooker ms by September
2000, not likely before then." There was no sign of quitting, in his
character or his work habits.

That summer he turned his thoughts to one man he singularly
admired. He proposed to Dianna Symonds, the latest editor of the
"new dazzling" *Saturday Night*, that he expand another commission—a piece for a book of writings about Pierre Trudeau—into
a longer reflection for the magazine on his thirty-year-plus relationship with the retired prime minister. "I first met Pierre Trudeau
back in November, 1967," he wrote in "The Man behind the Mania,"
of the lunch in Ottawa hosted by his friends Bernard and Sylvia
Ostry, then an influential couple in the capital. Relating half a
dozen more encounters, including a strange meal in the presence
of Maggie Trudeau during the dissolution of that marriage, and
saying only that "we usually lunch in Montreal once a year," he
notably didn't quote any private conversations. For someone
occasionally accused by important friends of making unapproved
use of private remarks in his column—"You never said it was off-
the-record," Richler had snapped at John Lynch-Staunton after a
tale told over drinks showed up in the *National Post*—such

discretion was surprising. But Pierre Trudeau wasn't anyone else; like, perhaps, John Kenneth Galbraith, he was that rarest of creatures—a man Mordecai Richler naturally deferred to. "We are not intimates, or even friends, but merely acquaintances," he said, with similar deference. The piece radiated the kind of respect for a Canadian public figure that he was famous for *not* evidencing in his writings. The only time "we exchanged harsh words," he admitted, was that Sussex Drive lunch during the October Crisis. Had the prime minister really needed to impose the War Measures Act? he asked. A buzzer, alerting an irritated Trudeau to leave for question period in parliament, kept the exchange between the two Montrealers from growing more heated.

"The Man behind the Mania" ran as the cover story for the September 22 issue of *Saturday Night.* The timing couldn't have been more fortunate for the magazine; Pierre Trudeau died six days later. His body lay in state on Parliament Hill for two days before being transferred by train to Montreal's city hall, men, women and children lining the tracks between the cities to pay tribute. On October 3 a state funeral was held at Notre-Dame Basilica, with three thousand gathering in and around the church and millions watching on live television. The public outpouring had no equal in Canadian history.

A sense of passing time was in the air. Between requests for prefaces and offers of honorary degrees, the summer and fall of 2000 saw Richler being celebrated in a manner befitting his stature, and that perhaps reflected an emerging concern that he too might not be around much longer. In his commencement speech at McGill, where he received an honorary degree, he slagged the university for its former quotas that limited Jews, while also making fun of his meagre high-school average, which would have failed to gain him entry even as a Gentile. While in Sherbrooke for the Bishop's University commencement, he debated a scheme he had been pondering for a while: purchasing the *Sherbrooke Record* from Hollinger. "Can you provide me with a price tag, please, for taking this loser off your hands?" he wrote to Hollinger lawyer Peter Atkinson. Jack Rabinovitch was among "my Gang of Five," he said, who would boost the local money-loser by "introducing a topless page three girl and other sophisticated features." Rabinovitch, a reluctant gang member—using his usual whip of humour, authority and cajoling, Richler could get his way with most people about most things—counselled against the deal.

Dr. Richler, in turn, was now celebrating those dearest to him. For a seventieth birthday party for Jack Rabinovitch that he and Florence couldn't attend, he sent a fax to be read aloud. Using the Yiddish for "old fart," he opened with a joke: "Two alter kockers had sat in silence on their favourite bench for hours, lost in thought. Finally, one gave a long and languid 'Oy!' The other replied, 'You're telling *me*?'" Continuing in Barney Panofsky mode, he reported how it seemed only yesterday that he and Jack were comparing notes about pretty girls at Baron Byng. "Now we compare notes on how many times we got up to piss last night." How, he wondered, had "either of us got from there to here." At the end of the month Noah's new companion, the publisher Sarah MacLachlan, threw a party for his fortieth birthday. Once again, Richler provided a speech. "Within an hour of his birth," father wrote of son, "enchanted nurses, faces pressed against the glass of the babypen, were sighing with longing."

Later in the autumn, after years of helping celebrate Robertson Davies, Mavis Gallant and Brian Moore, he duly accepted the inevitable Greg Gatenby–orchestrated Harbourfront celebration of his life and work. John Fraser, Guy Vanderhaeghe, Ted Kotcheff and Bernard Ostry were joined on stage by the novelist Barbara Gowdy and the Canadian-American journalist and novelist Robert MacNeil. Fraser told of the "fax wars" between him and Richler; Kotcheff recalled the nights he sat watch in his car outside Florence's flat in North London, lest the young lovers be caught red-handed and her divorce be challenged. Montreal-born MacNeil, better known as an American television news anchor now, passed along humorist Calvin Trillin's contention that Mordecai Richler was the funniest Canadian, and then made a case for him as "a Saul Bellow, who stayed Canadian." For his part, Richler told the audience dryly: "It seems like only the day before yesterday that I had my tonsils removed on the dining-room table of our cold-water flat on St. Urbain Street, or became known as an ill-mannered, disreputable young novelist. I can cope with removal of my tonsils, and I can cope with disapproval. But being recognized as a likeable old fart of seventy years requires some adjustment." Midway through the evening, Gatenby announced that the guest of honour's glass of Scotch had gone missing. It was soon returned.

Adjustment was something he could not easily make. By now he was back to smoking and drinking—and, not incidentally, writing—at his near-usual levels. Florence, weary from her efforts to get him to moderate, asked Noah to intervene. He had tried before to scarcely any greater effect, some of their conversations dating far enough back to end up in *Barney's Version*, and after his father was released from hospital in 1998 he had lit a cigar on the terrace of the country house in front of his wife and son. Noah read the message clearly; he couldn't—wouldn't—change his ways. And when Richler made a point of asking Martha and Emma to bring him the maximum allowed number of Davidoff cigarillos from London whenever they visited, they knew equally clearly that refusing, or even doing the deed under protest, would not be looked upon kindly. He would host, feed, support any and all of his family, any time. In exchange, he expected them not to moralize with him. Even Florence, often nearly reduced to tears when he lit up, failed to get through to him, and by summer 2000 she had largely abandoned the fight. Turning to various friends for counsel, including Bob Gottlieb and Maria Tucci, with whom she spoke freely and intimately about her five children and husband, she sought to be reconciled to his wonderfully steadfast but also stubborn, silent nature. Noah, at least, had been mentally preparing for his death since the operation, if not earlier. Emma too looked on with concern, staying now with her parents while she completed revisions on her first novel. "This is a scribblers' factory," Richler wrote to Louise Dennys in August, "Emma hard at it in one room, me in another."

She and Ric Young visited the house that month as well. The visit, mostly personal, did have a professional dimension: in 2001 Knopf Canada would be publishing books by *père et fille*. Dennys and Emma spent time together, sitting on the dock again and discussing the manuscript. "Please advise Deb that all of our children are writers," he kidded with an employee at Deborah Rogers, "so I wd like her to negotiate a Family Package with a publisher. FIVE RICHLERS FOR THE PRICE OF FOUR. A ONCE IN A LIFETIME OFFER. ACT NOW."

In August he watched in perplexity as Conrad Black unexpectedly sold the *National Post* to rival CanWest, run by the Winnipeg tycoon Izzy Asper. He had heard rumours of a merger, but admitted he couldn't fathom why Black had lost faith in his own newspaper empire's bold, if so far money-bleeding, flagship. "It's not a great show of confidence," he said to the *Globe and Mail.* In private, he worried to Michael Levine about the future of the *National Post*'s editor, Ken Whyte, whom Levine represented. "If it's of any help," he faxed his lawyer on August 14, "please assure Izzy Asper that I think Ken is a fine fellow and a first-rate editor, and that the Post is lucky to have him." But, having sparred with Izzy Asper over Israel in the past, he added, "Mum's the word, if you think this endorsement could cost him his job." Whyte stayed on as editor.

In New York he met Tony Lyons, who was to publish *On Snooker* in the States, in order to secure a few more months to finish the manuscript, and negotiated with him for a collection of his sports pieces. "Your terms suit me fine. However, in sending me a contract please note I do want not any monies until January 2001. Tax problems this year." Between the most recent instalment of the *Barney's Version* script fee and the signing advance for the new novel, along with the now nearly $2,600 weekly invoice for his newspaper column, Richler had managed one of his most lucrative twelve-month periods ever. A third tax-deductible gift of his papers to the archive at the University of Calgary, hastily assembled in the autumn, helped with the "problem." No longer paying cash for material, the university provided a tax receipt of around $75,000. At sixty-nine he remained a good provider, which was important to him, and, though still more spender than saver, smart about money.

At the bottom of the note to Lyons was a mention that the contract for the new collection should be sent to him directly. "I'm leaving Janklow & Nesbit," he said of his American agent, Lynn Nesbit, feeling that she had done little to advance his career in the States, and rarely contacted him. Richler, who was still supposed to be compiling the essay collection for Knopf Canada— "warn me of how thin or fat a collection you can manage," he asked Dennys—admitted he had overbooked his autumn. "I'm going bonkers here," he wrote of the schedule. "P.S.," he told her, "New Yorker will now run excerpt in late Sept or early Oct." That didn't happen either.

Two other bits of news from the autumn were more cheering. Michael Levine, anxious to get any film project off the ground, had lately asked him how he felt about a TV miniseries based on *St. Urbain's Horseman*. "St. U's Horseman okay for TV," he wrote back, "especially with Ted Kotcheff." Near Christmas he received a note from the Director of Honours, Order of Canada, informing him that, indeed, having declined the lesser category a quarter-century earlier, he was finally being appointed a Companion of the Order of Canada. "Yes, I am honoured and do accept the appointment," he replied, and agreed to attend the ceremony at Rideau Hall the following spring, once returned from England.

Possibly the happiest night he spent that autumn wasn't the Harbourfront tribute, or Jack Rabinovitch's Giller gala event, which he and Florence attended, as usual. It was a small dinner set up by Bill Weintraub with Jackie Kahane. Richler had not seen the young comedian he'd met and observed in the summer of 1948 at the Manor House Hotel in Ste. Agathe, and who had helped him conceptualize the Cuckoo Kaplan character in *Duddy Kravitz*, in decades. The Baron Byng alumnus had gone on to a long career, including regular appearances on the *Ed Sullivan Show* and years as the unlikely warm-up act for Elvis Presley. (Kahane delivered the eulogy at Presley's funeral.) Now eighty, battling cancer and Parkinson's, the comedian and raconteur still performed live. Back in his hometown, Kahane agreed to have dinner with the Richlers and Weintraub at the Montefiore Club, on Guy Street. For three hours the Borscht-Belt graduate regaled the table with tales and jokes. Richler, who rarely lasted an hour at such dinners, was mesmerized; Florence had never seen him so content. Jackie Kahane died the following spring.

Earlier in the year Richler had complained to Deborah Rogers about the slowness of translations of *Barney's Version.* "Oh, cd your foreign rights mavens please find out when, if ever, Italian, German and Spanish publishers intend to bring out BARNEY." The German edition came out shortly thereafter—"even if one searches, fiction of this calibre comes up less than once a year," the Swiss magazine *Die Weltwoche* pronounced—but the Italian edition wouldn't be ready until the fall. Once they were back in London for Christmas, however, word of ecstatic early reviews reached them and, more surprisingly, of brisk sales; after a slow start, the book was taking off in Italy in the most astonishing way. "Barney's Version is boffo in Italy," he wrote his cousin Lionel Albert at the beginning of February, "and my Italian publisher has invited us to Italy, Naples and Rome, Feb 15–22. We did once live in Rome for six months, but we have never been to Naples or Capri, so shd be fun." But before Italy he had to complete *On Snooker*, now due to be published in the late summer. He sent the manuscript by courier to New York and Toronto on the second of January. "Florence found a number of repetitions in the ms," he kidded Dennys, "but I have left them in, for the moment, just to establish how skilful an editor you really are." Nick Lyons was especially happy with the book—"am much relieved by your kind words about ON SNOOKER," Richler wrote back—but Dennys was still on holiday, leading him to chide her for not responding more quickly.

He seemed in excellent spirits in early 2001. Not necessarily in great health; in January he declined an invitation from an American university by saying, "due to health reasons, I must cancel all engagements for at least six months, possibly longer," while simultaneously agreeing to give a lecture in Oxford. Excited about the coming trip to Italy, he was buoyed about his ability to still produce work and, perhaps, still be funny. Dennys and Ric Young were off to Israel shortly, and he advised them on hotels and restaurants. "Ric," he counselled, "don't allow Louise to pray at Wailing Wall, lest young haredim attack her with baseball bats. You can make a good impression in hassidic quarters if Louise walks ten paces behind you at all times. Her shaven head and wig," he added, "wd also go down well." Florence in the meantime was making her own plans. Returning the favour, she sprang a seventieth birthday party on him at the London flat, a mini-surprise nearly ruined the night before, when three of the "star" guests from Canada—Rabinovitch, Levine and Avie Bennett—ran into the couple at the Ivy restaurant. The kids also flew over, and Florence cooked a meal for the gathering. Levine brought good news; some frantic deal making resulted in the lawyer being able to present his client at the party with a cheque for $50,000 for the option for the TV version of *St. Urbain's Horseman*, a flourish that embarrassed the recipient. Of reaching three score and ten— better, he acknowledged, than many of his crowd—he announced that it was now "overtime." He didn't need to explain to the assembled that the full playoff hockey term was "sudden death overtime"—next goal wins.

He was keeping his usual close watch over business matters, whether correcting Knopf Canada's accounting department about a royalty percentage for *On Snooker* or arranging for *Saturday Night* to purchase a 5,000-word excerpt, at a rate more or less of his own deciding. He wasn't always at his sharpest—in a note to Deborah Rogers he suggested she try selling the snooker book, only to have to admit he had forgotten that he had given world rights to the Lyonses—but he was still fully engaged on his own behalf and, occasionally, on behalf of his children. In February he intervened to ensure Emma's smooth debut in *Saturday Night*. Dianna Symonds had bought one of the linked stories in *Sister Crazy*, which Knopf Canada was about to release, and was discussing a profile with them. When the Toronto *Star* scooped it with what Richler called a "grudging, mindless little piece" about Emma, he heard, second-hand, that Symonds might be reconsidering publication of the story. A fax to the editor settled it, and his daughter ended up on the cover. *National Post* subscribers encountered four Richlers inside that weekend edition: columnist father, fiction writer daughter, and two sons minding their regular beats.

He delighted in *Sister Crazy*; the originality of the voice is evident on every page. It is Emma Richler's own voice, too, warm and intimate, emotionally acute and honest. Two dimensions of *Sister Crazy* could have easily upset him, given his impatience with ascribing psychological underlays to human behaviour. The connected stories trace parallel themes via the narrator, middle-child Jemima Weiss, or "Jem": how an extraordinary childhood can leave an adult adrift. Emma's own struggles with depression were well known to her parents—Mordecai and Florence had worried about her for years—and the children in the Swiss Family Richler, now in their thirties and forties, were naturally experiencing their fair share of grown-up problems. *Sister Crazy* is a love song to one family's singularity. Just as Mordecai Richler had written the Jacob Two-Two books out of love for "Daniel, Noah, Emma, Marfa and Jacob," along with their perfect mother and endearing father, so had Emma Richler created her Weiss children—Ben, Jude, Jem, Harriet and Gus—with their gorgeous, sweet mother and stern, gentle patriarch. *Sister Crazy* ensured that the wonderments and mysteries of a certain family dynamic would endure, never mind that the children were off living ordinarily complicated adult lives, or that the father had cancer. That was life, inevitable and relentless; this was art, ordered and, possibly, lasting.

A man of letters to the end, his faith in literature undiminished, Richler had long identified the game—writing one book that might survive—and the odds. He knew the odds for himself, of course, upping the stakes with his own final books, taking more time and more risks; now, with Emma for sure in the RICHLER FAMILY PACKAGE he had joked about, there was someone else to lay down a claim and, perhaps, beat those odds. "For

My Mother and My Father, and For Bob Gottlieb," read the dedication in Emma Richler's first book.

"For Max, Poppy, and Simone," ran the dedication at the front
of her father's final book. By dedicating *On Snooker* to his grandchildren, Richler was likewise laying claim to a continuation of
those mysteries, that dynamic. But quietly, privately, he had also
begun reaching out in recent years to the family he had often not
wanted any part of: the vast Richler clan, still mostly of Montreal.
As with Avrum, he sought neither forgiveness nor apology from
his relations. He wished to demonstrate that, contrary to all they
might have heard and believed, he had not shed his skin; that he
remained as much Muttle, Mutty, Mordy as the feared, impossible Mordecai. Max Richler and Lionel Albert, along with Lionel's
mother, Ruth, until her death in 1984, had always had small roles
in his adult life. Likewise, his nephew Howard Richler, himself a
writer, had been hosted by Mordecai and Florence in London as
a young man, and kept in touch. When Howard Richler lost first
his wife in a terrible accident, and then his father, Richler's
cousin Louis, he wrote sympathetically, "Howard, you have
passed through the fires recently, haven't you?" Remembering
"Louie" as a "cherished cousin who was especially kind to me as
a kid," he suggested they meet in May "for a drink," and that
Howard bring along his mother, Phyllis. And when invited to the
bar mitzvah of the grandson of his Uncle David, the Duddy of childhood games and fights sixty years earlier, he surprised everyone by showing up. Joking with his cousin Hertzi Richler, the
father of the bar mitzvah boy, about the arrival of the Moshiach,
or messiah, he agreed to don the tefillin if Hertzi would down
two double Scotches. When Hertzi did so, he dutifully put on the
phylacteries, a scene captured by relatives on video. Hertzi then
reminded him that he remembered attending a Seder at Moses
Richler's house as a small boy, and how Mordecai had refused to
wear the tefillin. "Your father has been waiting all this time for
you to do this," he said.

On Snooker: The Game and the Characters Who Play It, a decent
piece of reportage, is enlivened at the start by a familiar sketch

of his Montreal childhood and early adult years in Paris. Though Richler centres the reminiscences around pool halls, he also gives unexpected voice to his mother. Literally: Lily Rosenberg, largely silent in his work since Mrs. Hersh in *St. Urbain's Horseman*, appears twice in direct quotations. In one, she is complaining about being held back in the ladies' auxiliary of their synagogue because of her poor marriage; "But your father is a junk dealer, he comes home he sits down to supper in his Penman's under-wear, what if somebody nice rang the doorbell, I ask you?" In the other, she confesses her anxieties about where her teenage son Mordy has been: "I'm sitting here afraid to use the phone in case you've been run over by a car or got into another fight with those French kids, rickets is too good for them, and Bessie is waiting for me to call her with my marble cake recipe, as if she won't ruin it no matter what I tell her." When, covering his tracks, he blames "that anti-Semite, Mr. Hoover" for making him stay after class, Lily says the teacher should be "reported to the author-ities." To which he replies, "Things will only get worse if we make trouble."

His own teenage voice doesn't quite ring true, but the voice of the mother does. And if it reflects the way his mother spoke and thought, she hardly seems the bitter woman of later life, letters and accounts. Possibly Richler was summoning for posterity an earlier, gentler memory. Or else, with Lily Rosenberg safely in the Baron de Hirsch Cemetery, he could transform her into a kind of irritating if still-endearing Jewish mother.

"Dear Special Victim," Richler wrote to Ted Kotcheff three days before they flew to Naples, kidding his old friend over his new job as executive producer of the TV series *Law & Order: Special Victims Unit*. "Bad night. Wakened at 2:30 a.m., eureka! I owe Kotcheff $175 US for cigarillos. Got up, peed, figured oh well my credit is good." He went on to describe the London weather— "Nasty winter here. Rain, rain, every day"—and outline their trip.

"We haven't been to Rome since Florence and I skedaddled there together and you came over for month-long weekend stay. Them, them, were the days, what?"

Once Adelphi had bought *Barney's Version*, a certain degree of exposure was guaranteed for it, given the publishing house's reputation. Still, *La Versione di Barney* was an unexpected bestseller—thirty thousand copies in hardcover, Richler soon reported. Backed by the support of the conservative newspaper *Il Foglio,* which decided that the novel, in the words of the editor, was "a complete modern theology of love and wisdom," as well as a licence-granting mechanism for any male feeling too long suppressed by women, Richler found himself being feted like a movie celebrity. Flying in to a book fair in Naples for three days, he and Florence carried on to Rome and then Venice. He did interviews on stage and in bookshops, and in Rome passed by window displays of *La Versione di Barney*, including author photographs, that left him as pleased, if not as giddy, as at those first sightings of *The Acrobats* in London shops in 1954. An unlikely candidate for the ranks of globally famous literary writers, in the mode of a Toni Morrison or Michael Ondaatje, he had never enjoyed particularly strong sales in any foreign-language markets, going back to the success of the early first novel. But in Italy, where Barney Panofsky's irreverent masculinity was entertaining, and his passion for his wife invigorating, the novel's exuberance generated not only those boffo sales but, shortly, a slang term: *Barneyano*, meaning a man who is politically incorrect and unapologetic. *Il Foglio* even launched a regular column called, after the journalist's first name, "Andrea's Version," in which the writer skewered, in the name of *Barneyano*, everything from the political left to feminists, while another newspaper declared *La Versione di Barney* the best novel of the year. Adelphi snapped up *On Snooker* and the three Jacob Two-Two books, and invited the Richlers back for a fall tour. "We were pursued everywhere for splashy interviews in newspapers, TV and radio," Richler reported with amusement to Deborah Rogers. A month later the news out of Italy was even better: "BARNEY has now gone into 4th impression in Italy:

40,000 now in print. I daresay I'm the biggest thingee to hit the European boot since the late, great Mussolini of blessed memory."

Nearly a year had now passed since he had signed the contract with Knopf Canada for "Untitled Novel, 350–400 pages." In the fall he had asked Noah to order him some books online, and Florence to keep an eye out for articles on certain subjects. But he wasn't ready to commit a word to manuscript until his return from Italy in late February, saying as much to Ken Whyte, and adding, with a familiar note of self-doubt, "Now for the next novel. Hell, who knows if I can handle one again."

III

OVERTIME

March, 2001. He'd had a notion for an eleventh novel as far back as fall 1999. Starting then, he had asked Florence to help find and clip newspaper articles of an unusually dark hue. "More Body Parts Found in Toronto Park" was a headline from December 9, 1999, that interested him. The same was true for "Affair with Youth Led to Axe Killing," from a February 2000 edition of the *Daily Telegraph*, which opened with the line "A father beheaded his neighbour with an axe after she gave birth to his teenage son's baby, Birmingham crown court was told yesterday." On March 27 he was fascinated enough by a *Times* piece about a man who killed a transsexual married to his daughter, and then "tied the body in chains and padlocks and weighed it down with dumbbells before pushing it out to sea on an airbed at Covehithe, Suffolk" to add it to the file. Florence knew better than to ask his reasons, but she had noted his deepening fascination with plastic surgery in recent years. An old friend who had had a facelift had approached him at a hotel, and he hadn't recognized her at first. Another time, greeting the wife of a prominent film agent—a woman straining to look half her age through successive cosmetic procedures—Florence observed him kissing the waxy cheeks with clinical attention. Her suspicions were confirmed when he asked if she would ever consider having work done. She said no, and when he added, questioningly, "Why alter yourself?" she was fairly certain that he was indeed "novelizing," as he had told Louise Dennys. But then *On Snooker* came along, costing him nearly a year.

As well, in the autumn of 2000 he had asked Noah to order *Making the Body Beautiful: A Cultural History of Aesthetic Surgery* and *Venus Envy: A History of Cosmetic Surgery*, books that seemed on topic with that waxy kiss. *Without Sanctuary: Lynching Photography in America* and *The Perfect Heresy*, a study of the Cathars, a Gnostic Christian sect in medieval France brutally suppressed by the Catholic Church, may have related to the grisly articles about violent crimes involving real or perceived sexual deviance. By the following March, he was writing lightly altered versions of those articles bannered with the heading "Ezra's Journal." Another entry was a transcribed excerpt from the historian Josephus, whom Richler had long considered an equal to Maimonides, if a less pronounced influence. Reading *The Jewish Wars* as a young adult had assured him that nothing was new under the sun, and that man was capable of any and all horrors (a passing remark made on safari in Kenya about the hyenas had struck a Josephus-like note in Florence's mind). Now he wanted to use Josephus in the new novel. Drawing from a section in *The Jewish Wars* called "Horrors of the Siege," he transcribed a brief account of how Syrian deserters, trying to hide their money by swallowing coins, would be cut open by Roman soldiers who "pulled the filthy money out of their bowels." On separate pages he also typed out advertisements of the "found humour" variety he liked to collect. One was reworked several times:

INFERTILITY NITE
DON'T BLAME YOUR WIFE OR DAMN YOUR HUSBAND
CUM TO THE BALLPARK HA, HA, HA!
12 RUMANIAN BABIES
TO BE GIVEN AWAY FREE
TO LUCKY TICKET HOLDERS
WEIGHING FROM 7 TO 11 LBS EACH
ABSOLUTELY NO RETURNS

More substantially, he drafted a scene involving a character named Marv who visits the Garber brothers, Hymie and Morrie, proprietors of Fantasy Holidays ("Your Dreams Realized"). The company, which had "tripled in value since its 1999 IPO," offered "accountants, dentists, bankers and brokers" a chance to live out their fantasies. Using his week in Sun City on assignment for *GQ*, Richler envisioned theme camps in the wilds of British Columbia where the affluent could play cowboys, with "high noon shootouts" and bronco-busting, alongside after-hours fun "with the Frontier Girls in the Last Chance and Pussy Galore Saloons." Women, mostly "imported from liberated Russia," were "on offer for take-home use, including marriage." Other Garber brother ventures included sports camps where the clientele could suit up against "former major league pros," and gladiator camps "enlivened by orgies in Nero's Palace, where strategically placed booths accounted for a nice turnover in Viagra tablets." Marv's pitch concerns something that Jews enjoying a "guilt trip" will "fork out plenty for." "Our people will love it," he says. "So will the anti-Semites. You reel in both those groups and there's hardly anybody left out there." But the brothers fear an intervention by the Anti-Defamation League. Once, Morrie reports, he took his wife to the Shakespeare festival at Stratford to see that play about the "Jewish insurance agent in Italy," and ran into protests. "Shit," Hymie adds, "a Jewish guy gets sued for feeling up his secretary and what do their lawyers say? Remember the six million." The conversation turns to rabbis who publish "kosher sex books" and claim "there's nothing wrong with making a video of yourself shtupping your wife." After further discussion, Marv demands a decision. "The best I can offer you is that we will fly it past a focus group," Morrie says. To which the entrepreneur replies, "Like hell you will. I want you to know I've mailed myself this idea in a registered letter. Dated. Unopened. You want to fuck with me I'm going to New Age Tours." And the fantasy holiday idea he is selling to the brothers? It is never clarified, and the 1,000-word scene, which exists in multiple versions, ends there.

Another fragment concerns a conversation between a father and son about the boy's prospective bride. "Molly graduated cum laude from McGill," the son says. "Her Master's Thesis, on 'Misogyny & the Heterosexualist in the Novels of Saul Bellow, Bernard Malamud, and Philip Roth,' won a gold medal." The girl's parents are notable as well: the father a lawyer with an honorary doctorate from Ben Gurion University, and the mother a painter who has shown on Greene Avenue in Westmount, and once sold a portrait to a Gursky brother.

A final story fragment involves a book publishing deal for a novel written by an older writer widely presumed to be washed up. "He'll never deliver, they said," a boastful editor notes. "He's past it. Now I'm cock of the walk. We're not only talking sales here, possibly a matter of indifference to an artist of your stature, but Booker Prize. Congratulations." He also got far enough into the manuscript—in his head, if not yet on the page—to jot down one of his content lists, signposts for how the story would unfold. He envisioned: *what's her bloodtype? / weight-watchers "That's cheating!" / brothel / L.A. / poker game "I acquiesce" / UFO / Gay Pride Night / Romanian Baby Night / Bernie re train wreck / plastic surgeon / $50,000 womb / "youthalize" / Aztecs / Conquistadors / Josephus / Queen Elizabeth bk.*

Taken together, and considering that he had promised Louise Dennys a substantial manuscript, all this suggests that the seventy-year-old was embarking on a novel that crossed the plot riot of *Gursky* with the satirical savagery, or even phantasmagoria, of *Cocksure.* How it all fit together—Marv and the Garber brothers, the late-career writer with a potential Booker winner, the father and daughter with Gursky links, the disturbing contents of "Ezra's Journal," including "The Horrors of the Siege" from Josephus, those plastic surgery books and queries, the sale of Romanian babies and the "$50,000 womb," let alone the Conquistadors and Aztecs and Cathars and photos of lynch-ings—was something Richler was still working on in early April. It looked to be years of work; he certainly would not be making his Janaury 2002 deadline. If any overarching theme can be discerned, it may have related to his remark to Florence: "Why alter yourself?" Transformations, disfigurations, violations, acts of wanton violence; all kinds of defilements upon the body, upsets to the natural order of life and death, birth and aging, appeared to be—in these jottings, cuttings and notes—at the forefront of his mind. Montreal, Westmount, Jewish energy and insecurity seemed certain, as always, to run like a river through the whole, and the humour promised to be as outrageous and morally fierce as anything he had produced.

As yet, the novel had no title.

———

April 10, 2001. At the "Oldie of the Year" luncheon, Richler was seated at a table opposite his old friend Beryl Bainbridge. He liked the *Oldie*, which offered a mix of short pieces, columns and reviews of mostly "senior," mostly British writers. In an issue from the previous summer, Richler's musings on gay rights had shared space with a review of the letters of Kingsley Amis and a novel by Malcolm Bradbury, as well as personal ads for residential homes for the elderly, a penile vacuum pump, and a dating offer by "Bucks, widow, 60, happy, healthy, and hopeful." He liked the *Oldie*'s busy social calendar almost as much. Its monthly luncheons, with guest speakers and a start time of "12 noon for drinks," or its larger annual banquet, both taking place at the venerable Simpson's-in-the-Strand restaurant, represented the kind of relaxed, self-amused London literary culture that he appreciated. For all his grumbling about Cool Britannia, his love of this aspect of the city, and his pleasure in being able to participate in it, remained strong. Enjoying a long lunch with a fellow veteran novelist had much to recommend it.

That day, however, he found he couldn't keep his meal down. Embarrassed, he left the hall. Beryl Bainbridge followed him, and a doctor who happened to be in attendance sat with him in the foyer, asking questions about his previous bout with cancer. A cab was called, and he returned to the flat in Sloane Court.

Florence quickly took him to a private hospital, where a young doctor wondered if he had an ulcer. An appointment was made for tests the following morning.

In a letter to his insurance broker two days later, Richler explained what happened next: "My stomach was pumped and it was suggested that I could be in serious trouble with a growth." He was monitored overnight, and told he required a biopsy. It being Easter weekend, medical attention threatened to be slow. He asked if returning home to Canada for treatment might be advisable. Florence booked the next available flight, on the sixteenth. While waiting, Richler managed to send several business faxes, informing Louise Dennys they would be in Montreal sooner than expected and confirming an autumn engagement in Vancouver. He also received visitors. Bob Gottlieb happened to be in town, and he and Deborah Rogers came by the flat for coffee. "Whaddaya know about this chemo?" he asked them. Frail, unable to mask his worry, he struck Rogers as gravely ill. Emma, then on the eve of a publicity tour in support of *Sister Crazy*—he had advised her to enjoy room service and, at the end of the day, go to the movies instead of a bar—saw her father on his final weekend in London. So did Nigel and Martha.

In Montreal, he typed out a list of questions for his consultation. Besides queries about hair loss and whether he should consider marijuana for the pain, he asked if he ought to cancel obligations—". . . lectures . . . publishers contracts." He also wondered about his energy level during chemo. Could he stay in the country house between treatments? Would they know soon if he was responding? Plus this: "my prospects ... based on yr experience." He started treatments at the end of April, with the notion of being finished by Christmas. Six to eight hard months, but then a family reunion for the holidays and a better 2002. Richler even asked the doctor if he had another book in him—once he had his strength back. On the same piece of paper, he jotted down the list of ailments he was facing. They were formidable: nodules found in his lungs, transitional cell carcinoma that had metastasized to his abdomen and chest.

He filed all four newspaper columns for April, and even managed 800 words for the May 5 edition of the *National Post.* That
piece, titled "Don't Look to Writers for Morality Lessons," warned
literature lovers not to expect much inspiration from the lives of
the authors themselves. "Too many celebrity writers," Richler
reported, "were outrageous liars, philanderers, drunks, druggies,
unsuitable babysitters, plagiarists, psychopaths, parasites, cow-
ards, indifferent dads or moms and bad credit risks." Coleridge,
Byron, Eliot, Pound, Dylan Thomas—"a notorious schnorrer"
(sponger)—Edmund Wilson, Faulkner, Fitzgerald, Auden,
Isherwood, even goodly George Orwell, lately alleged to have
been a snitch, all had "dismal track records." And Mordecai
Richler himself? Any such linkages went unremarked. Neither
did he mention his precarious health. But he did end the piece
on a distinct note of elegy. "There are, I think, two ways of looking at the work of writers to whom we are forever indebted. There
is that poem of Stephen Spender's that begins, 'I think continu-
ally of those who were truly great,' and concludes, 20 lines later,
'Born of the sun they travelled a short while towards the sun /
and left the vivid air signed with their honour.' Then there's a far
more modern disposition, cited by J. Lesley Fitton in his *The
Discovery of the Greek Bronze Age*: 'We perhaps live in an age when
worms are too prone to creep round the feet of great men to see
if they are made of clay.'"

————

May 8, 2001. Informed officially that the cancer was inoperable—
all treatments would be palliative—Richler was given between
one and three years to live. Florence wondered about telling the
children. "No need," he said, the decision final. Unable to manage
the columns—the piece of the previous weekend would be his
final published words—he was confined to the couch in the
Chateau when Emma, touring Canada with her book, stopped by
for a visit. Though he made jokes about his breathing apparatus
for her amusement, he was too sick to attend her reading that

night—and worried he would only draw attention to himself. Noah and Sarah MacLachlan were planning a dinner for Emma in their house in the Toronto neighbourhood of Cabbagetown a few days later, and he insisted on being there. He and Florence took the train and stayed with Jake, Leanne and their children. Louise Dennys and Ric Young saw him at the dinner and noticed how much weight he had lost. But Florence said he actually felt better, and that evening he seemed in good spirits. While in the city he made a point of visiting friends: Avie Bennett, Bernie and Sylvie Ostry, Jack Rabinovitch. With Rabinovitch, he drank a vodka and grapefruit juice through a straw. "Forget it, don't bug me," he said of his oldest friend's looks of concern. Back in Montreal he tried having drinks with the dwindled crowd at Ziggy's, even bringing along the racing cap he planned to wear when his hair fell out. He still wanted to be funny, and still was. But he couldn't stay long.

Starting in May, Richler began cancelling existing appointments and turning down others. "I'm suffering from a rather serious health problem and must cancel all my engagements for the rest of the year," he told his speech agent on May 23. "Sorry about this." He also requested discretion. "Please do not release any news of my problem to the intrusive press." He did the same with a lecture he was supposed to give at Bishop's University—"I have been struck with a serious, but not immediately life-threatening problem"—and apologized to Lyons Press for being slow to answer a fax. "These damn chemo treatments have left me very low on energy, to say the least," he reported on June 4. He was still able to bill *Saturday Night* for the excerpt from *On Snooker*, and wasn't ruling out a speaking engagement for early 2002, for which his fee would be $12,000. Neither was he quite willing to cancel the follow-up visit to Italy planned for September, where *La Versione di Barney* had now sold 70,000 in hardcover. On June 18 Richler wrote to his Italian publisher, "At the moment, we intend to fly overnight on Sept 4, arriving on Sept 5th, staying through the 9th." On the same day he also faxed his translator, Giulia Arborio Mella, mentioning an offer from another Italian publisher for *A Choice of Enemies.* He turned it down "rather than

muddy the waters" with Adelphi, and then added, "I'm willing to
see anything from DUDDY KRAVITZ onwards published in Italy,
but I was still learning my craft when I did those earlier novels."
Clearly, he had hopes for the fall; "I am amazed," he told Mella of
the Italian sales of his novel.

But earlier that same week he informed a new prospective
biographer, Reinhold Kramer, "As Bill Weintraub may have told
you, I am now one month into a six-month chemotherapy treatment, hoping to beat the rap." To the journalist Clive Everton he
said the same: "suffering from malignant tumours," he was
"hoping to beat the rap." With Louise Dennys he kicked around
titles for the collection of his sports pieces, which Knopf Canada
had decided to publish right away in the new year, in lieu of the
postponed essay collection; Dennys, knowing now how ill he
was, privately hoped that working on the sports collection would
provide a distraction for him from the treatments. On June 18
Richler suggested *Scenes from the Sporting Life* or *Dispatches from
the Sporting Life* as titles. "Choose," he told his editor, and she
picked the latter. He also mentioned that the CBC had bought
rights to turn both *Barney's Version* and *St. Urbain's Horseman* into
radio dramas, and asked her to send him two Knopf Canada
books on her list—Martin Amis's recent collection of essays, and
the "new Kapuscinski"—for pleasure reading. "In haste, much
love," he signed off.

Late in May, Richler managed one other significant outing. He
still had eight aunts and uncles extant among his long-living
paternal clan. Uncle Max, only a decade his senior, called to
inform him that his Aunt Celia, second-oldest of the fourteen
children of Shmarya and Molly, had died. Celia Hershcovich,
Orthodox and observant, had been no fan of her nephew; she
had, as a matter of fact, been among his more vocal critics from
the start. (Israeli journalist Sam Orbaum, her grandson, had
taken delight in tossing his name out at his grandmother, to
watch her fume.) Richler, in turn, had disliked his father's disapproving younger sister as far back as he could remember.
Thinking of that connection with Moses, or simply wanting to do

what he had done with Avrum and David Richler—be reconciled, if possible, without apology or explanation—he stunned
his extended family by showing up to the second day of shiva.
A nephew he did like, Meyer Richler, offered to take him, making
sure to bring along an extra yarmulke and a bottle of whisky. On
arriving in the apartment, Richler slipped the cap on his head
and sat in a corner. He had told Max he was worried people
wouldn't appreciate his presence. It appeared he was even bracing
for a repeat of the last Richler family shiva he attended for his
own father, when he had sat on the floor drinking from a bottle,
being ignored or scowled at, returning the coolness in kind.
Instead, his elderly aunts and uncles, nieces and nephews, some
of whom had not spoken to him at all since 1967 and not spoken
nicely to him for decades before that, gathered around his chair.

They shook his hand and made awkward but warm conversation. A few, Max included, embraced him. Aside from Max and
Meyer, none of these relatives had met his children, or even, with
the odd exception, Florence. Nor would they on that day; as he
had been doing for years, Richler was reconnecting with his
estranged family on his own, leaving his wife, sons and daughters
out of it. Not all the clan were impressed by his effort, including
his Uncle Bernard, a central figure in his early life. But for the most
part, Richlers were pleased to lay eyes on the famous—perhaps
notorious—Mordecai again, and said so, praising his accomplishments and even admitting that he had made the family proud.
Some thought he looked unwell, or at least ill at ease, and Richler
elected to inform only Max, in private, that he was fighting cancer
again. Curiously, Max came away with the impression that the
cancer was in his throat, not kidney—an indication, possibly, of
his overall discomfort. "He's a sick man," Meyer Richler informed
the clan as he was leaving.

In early June Martha flew home from London for a week. One
of Richler's lungs had collapsed and filled with liquid, leaving him
with a persistent cough. Martha noted that her father, though
sometimes too ill to go to the market after a chemo treatment,
was making lists and arrangements—preparing, perhaps, for his

family once he was gone. On June 6, unbeknownst to Florence or Martha, he managed to handwrite an addendum to his will, which he put into a brown envelope and later took to the hospital. He wrote it despite telling Daniel that he thought he had four years yet to live, at the outside, and for sure was set for the next one or two. Informed that it would soon be impossible to purchase ribbons for his Smith-Corona, the two of them went shopping together to buy all the store's remaining stock.

Florence was now his caregiver as well. She was paralyzed, not allowing herself to believe the end might be near. But in the most private of places—their bedroom—she saw a terrible omen. Every night for forty-one years the couple had slept, if not entwined, then with some kind of contact—back to back, even just their feet. But one evening, touching him gently on his waist, she asked, "Is this uncomfortable?" It was; he was in too much pain to be touched, even by her.

The final two friends to see him alive were Bill Weintraub and Don Johnston. Weintraub had volunteered to relieve Florence by taking him for a walk. They didn't get far, and sat on a bench on Sherbrooke near the Chateau, absorbing the early summer sun and bustling street life. From the bench Richler could see, or intimate, many of the touchstones of his life and work: the Ritz across the road and the main building of Concordia looming behind the Fine Arts Museum; Westmount a mile or so due west and McGill a few blocks to the east; Mount Royal rising up behind the entire downtown and Jeanne Mance Park, formerly Fletcher's Field, at the bottom of its eastern slope. But one morning when Weintraub came by the apartment, he was in too much discomfort to leave his spot on the couch. Florence, who had just brought him back from a chemo treatment, thought they might have to return again to the hospital. He rested that day, and Jake, home for a long weekend, drove his father and mother down to the summer house in the Townships for the Saint-Jean-Baptiste weekend. Don Johnston, in Canada from Paris, came by on the Saturday. He and Richler chatted for an hour in the kitchen. They also discussed getting together again soon, and Johnston departed with no sense that his friend was near death. But Jake, dismayed by his weight loss, lack of appetite, and chemo-induced nausea and naps, noticed that he had rallied for the visit. The next day he was far worse, and they returned to the city. Needing to be back in Toronto, Jake left with two disquieting memories. One was of his father's unusually tidy office in the country house, suggesting that work, once the fuel that drove his each and every day, had all of a sudden receded. The second was the way he squeezed his hand in farewell: too lingering, too plaintive. On the day Martha was to fly out, he told her he had a craving for sorbet. Martha ran out to a shop to buy some—his stomach, she and Florence reasoned, must have been burning—but he could manage only a spoonful. In the doorway he hugged his youngest daughter, squeezing his eyes shut to block the tears. When Martha called him from the airport, her mother reported that she'd forgotten her toothbrush. "Maybe she'll come back for it," she heard her father say.

Did he know he would not be lasting a month, let alone four years? Though he said nothing to Florence, she discerned signs of worry and deepening frailty. On the Monday it was decided he had to be admitted to hospital. He packed an overnight bag, filling the leather case with books, papers related to his medical condition, toiletries and clothes, plus his beloved framed photo of Florence as a child. He did not ask that the slight manuscript of the new novel be included. She was unaware the book even existed, in however rudimentary a form, or that Knopf Canada had already paid an advance for it. In the turmoil of his flight from London in April, he had neglected to bring the material home to Canada. He may have forgotten it; or he may have assumed he wouldn't be writing fiction again until the following winter, once he had beaten this latest rap.

They took a cab to the Montreal General. The short ride, along Sherbrooke and up Côte-des-Neiges, provided his final glimpses of his beloved hometown, beyond what would be visible from a hospital room window.

———————

July 2, 2001. A week in hospital had culminated in an operation
on the Friday to put a stent in his stomach. The first days had
had their moments of levity, despite the once-again gloomy quarters at the Montreal General: calls from friends, with whom he
generally dissembled, chatting about hockey or some other subject, including Ted Kotcheff, who was booked to fly up to Montreal
on July 4, and intimate conversations with Florence. He had even
felt well enough to reject with a joke the smoked meat that Noah,
who had driven from Toronto, brought him, on the grounds that,
since it wasn't from Schwartz's, he didn't want to risk going to
heaven with an inferior taste on his lips. On the Thursday night
Noah had his own version of the exchange experienced by Martha
and Jake; while he sat by his father's bed, encouraging him to
keep his strength up, the two men traded rare verbal expressions
of love. The next afternoon, the son fumed at finding him abandoned in a corridor without a blanket, awaiting the procedure.
But after the operation Richler kidded with the doctor, requesting a plate of chopped liver. By Saturday morning, the patient
had recovered enough to request a cigar. Florence had earlier
cornered a doctor to ask, in the absence of a firm diagnosis, what
was killing her husband. The doctor replied by miming a smoker
raising a cigarette to his lips. Now, aware that he was failing, she
could not think why she should deny him this oldest and, it
turned out, most lethal of his pleasures. She remembered:

> Noah was in hospital with me and he wanted so much to get
> Mordecai out of that room and allow him to see something dif-
> ferent. It was Noah at his most tender-hearted and thoughtful.
> He was told he could have a wheelchair. He took Mordecai
> down to the waiting room in the wheelchair but it was occu-
> pied and so he came back and we decided we'll take him out-
> side. So it was very difficult for Mordecai because people stare,
> naturally, and recognize him. Nevertheless, he managed to sit
> upright—but to look down when people stared—and Noah

took him down in the lift to where there is a lovely reading area, and then outside, and there he gave Mordecai a cigar and he just relished it. He managed to take two puffs and that was it. And then storm clouds gathered and torrential rains came and we both chuckled and took refuge.

Their laugh was private, a shared memory of the sort that a long-married couple can evoke without words and mutually enjoy. Florence recalled the memory, which involved, somewhat surprisingly, Lily Rosenberg:

One of the reasons there was this painful and lovely moment was because many many years ago when we rented the house in Amagansett, Lily came to visit, and Mordecai was to collect her at the train station which was a stone's throw from our place. It was a glorious morning and I was outside with the children. He came down from work to eat and she was arriving at about tea time. But at around 4 p.m. there was a horrendous storm, and Mordecai so enjoyed this because his mother was arriving and it was SO appropriate.

That night Richler suffered some kind of severe attack, its nature then unknown. Noah and Florence had returned to the apartment for dinner, only to receive a call from the hospital. He survived the night and once again rallied on the Sunday, asking her to return to take his overnight bag back to their apartment. There had been a rash of thefts of patients' belongings from their rooms, and he didn't want to lose its contents. He also asked her to bring him a few more things: a change of clothes, copies of the *Economist* and the *New Yorker*, and two books to read: Philip Roth's *The Dying Animal* and *Loving*, by Henry Green.

When I came back home from hospital to get the two books he requested, he also wanted his shaving kit. He was being moved to a new room across the hall. It was slightly larger and pink— yes, not very appropriate—but I thought it was fresh and clean and so I asked if he could be moved there and so he was wheeled across and I thought it remarkable that he sent me back to the flat for these two books and his shaving kit. This is a man who would have loved never to have to shave and here he was asking for the shaving kit, wasn't that wonderful. It seemed to me that meant he was feeling better but, in fact, upon later reflection, I realise he was preparing to die and he didn't want to be unshaven.

But in order to survive you have to tell yourself other reasons. . . . He wanted the *New Yorker* and the newspapers and I wanted to bring him some homemade chicken soup. I took it and put it in a very small cup so he wouldn't be overwhelmed and I was told there was a microwave at the end of the hall and before going, I put his newspapers on his tray and his shaving kit in his bathroom, and he did manage to drink two tablespoons of soup.

Noah left for Toronto on Sunday, under the impression his father had stabilized. Back in London in April, the first doctor, examining a CT scan, had thought he had detected an ulcer. In Montreal they hadn't found anything. As it happened, there may have been an ulcer, and the Friday operation on his stomach may have caused it to hemorrhage. An emergency operation was scheduled for Tuesday morning. Emma, calling from England earlier in the day, got him to laugh by relaying a classic first-time author's tale of reading to an audience of five. Richler also had a brief conversation with Guy and Marg Vanderhaeghe in Saskatoon, in which he managed a joke about Saskatchewan. Florence sat with him that evening.

At about 8:30 I went over to him to freshen up the bed. He had been mostly dozing and I kept telling myself that his requests were a good thing. But when I got close to him I felt an extreme weariness, an inability to speak, he talked little in hospital anyway, but. . . . There was a fluorescent light above his bed and I asked wasn't it too strong, shouldn't I turn it down a bit and there was a slight nod so I did that and I said to him,

I'll just sit in the chair and he shook his head but I said, No, that's what I want to do every day and every night.

I was about to dim the lights and make him more comfortable, when he stretched . . . he stretched out his right arm with great difficulty and touched my waist and said, "My beauty," which he never said to me in the whole time we were together. He didn't use words like that. There were gestures, obviously, but he never used words like that. I lowered the bed, dimmed the lights and sat in the chair and those were the last words he said to me.

I stayed until about midnight and then came home.

She was not in the apartment for long; in her absence he hemorrhaged again.

The phone rang about 3:30 and it was his doctor asking me if I could come to intensive care. I called the children and had to wait for them to get back to me about getting on planes. . . .

Early in the morning on July 3, Florence found herself alone with her husband. She remembered their final hours together.

Finally I was let into his room and parted the curtains in the intensive care room and there he was, looking so calm except that he had this huge stomach . . . so I sat down and began stroking his arm and did that for some time and it felt . . . warm . . . and then the nurse came in and asked if I wanted a glass of water and I said Yes, thank you, and I just kept stroking his arm waiting for him to wake up and then my eyes looked at all the tubes and . . . I saw one with about five inches of very red blood and following the tubing down towards him and realizing it wasn't attached to him, and then seeing nothing was attached to him anymore. I think until that moment I hadn't realized that he was dead and so I sat there, I suppose it is a state of shock that I should stroke his arm for hours, really non-stop, until the children arrived.

EPILOGUE

T ed Kotcheff reached Montreal in time to serve as a pall-
bearer at the funeral. He shared the duty with Bob Gottlieb,
also up from New York, Guy Vanderhaeghe from Saskatoon,
Jack Rabinovitch, Michael Levine, and Avie Bennett from Toronto,
along with Bill Weintraub and John Aylen. All the children and
their companions had arrived twenty-four hours before. The
family, along with Jack Rabinovitch and Bernie Ostry, went to
Paperman's Funeral Home, the same firm that had buried his
grandfather in 1935, to discuss the service. Florence, overcome
with grief and yet unaware of the addendum to his will, guessed
he would wish the simplest one imaginable, and certainly
wouldn't care to have it overseen by a rabbi. From Paperman's,
Noah called his Uncle Max to ask about finding a cantor. Max
Richler said he was one himself, and offered to say Kaddish, the
mourners' prayer. Examining the coffins, Florence was similarly
certain her husband would want the most modest available: a
pine coffin, without even the white satin lining.

Avrum Richler had flown in from Newfoundland. Extended
family, learning of the death in the media, tried, sometimes without success, to attend the service. Paperman's Funeral Home had
relocated long ago from St. Urbain Street to Jean Talon Boulevard,
near the Decarie Expressway. On the morning of the funeral, the
family and a few close friends gathered with the body beforehand
in a private parlour, the casket open. Richler had been laid out,

as Daniel described it, "in the same clothes he wore to work each morning." The casket was then closed and moved into the main chamber, where musicians performed Bach while the guests were being seated. Though Max Richler oversaw the simple memorial service, it was the children who spoke, each in turn, by their birth order. Daniel told the story of shopping for paper and typewriter ribbons three weeks earlier with his father, who said wryly of his pre-digital purchases, "I'm yesterday's man." He talked of his "energy, optimism and singular sense of purpose," and how his novels were "monumental love letters to Florence and stern advice to the rest of us." Noah too said his father's "greatest accomplishment was the house he built with Florence," and that "he loved every civilizing lesson he learned from my mother." Confirming his moral clarity and uncompromising nature, Noah called him a "greatly moral and unbelievably consistent man." Emma went next, telling of his dozen phone calls a day to her when Florence was absent. Imitating his clipped speech, she relayed his account of the "hot-dog omelette" he had made for himself two nights running, because "if you eat the same food you don't need to wash the pan." On the eve of his wife's return, wanting to please her, he shopped frantically for "quail eggs, smoked salmon, champagne and bouquets of white flowers." Martha read the poem "he so loved," Dylan Thomas's "Do Not Go Gentle into That Good Night," choking on the lines "And you, my father, there on the sad height / Curse, bless me now with your fierce tears, I pray." She stopped, bent over, and Emma quickly returned to the podium to stand beside her. An arm around her sister, she finished reciting the poem for her. When she finished, Martha recovered herself. In a brief, sudden display of overwhelming emotion she lifted her head, and exclaimed, "I just want to say Fuck You to all cancer." Finally, Jacob rose and spoke of how his father had been "looking forward to August, when the field tomatoes would be ripe," to the reading tour of Italy in September with Florence, and to a planned family Christmas in Toronto. "It was his failure to write a truly great novel, one that would endure, that got him out of bed each

morning," Jacob said. But "Mordecai was a better father and husband than a novelist, and it is the father and husband that we
can't live without. . . . He was a giant of a man who let us down
only once: when he left us without knowing how to cope without
him."

Emma had ended her remarks with an evocation of the Richlers
in mourning: "But I do feel blessed. I watched my family preparing for this yesterday, all of them better than I, some talking on
two telephones at once, filling me with awe and fascination, and
immense gratitude for this ferocious energy and robust devotion
which I wanted my daddy to see, as he would have been well
chuffed, although perhaps not surprised, because he made this
thing with my mother, this is his family, we are here."

The family had chosen a plot on Rose Hill, Mount Royal, with a
clear view of the Plateau and, beyond, to the east end of Montreal.
Jeanne Mance Park, Esplanade, the former YMHA, Baron Byng,
St. Urbain, The Main—his world lay directly below him. Once the
service was complete, the procession made its way behind the
mountain and up the slope. Max Richler said Kaddish for his
nephew under a warm July sun, and then the mourners dis-
persed. The Richlers hosted a wake at the Chateau for close
friends and family.

That evening, while the children and a few of the guests were
having a drink at Ziggy's Bar, Florence found the brown envelope
in his overnight bag. It contained the addendum to his will, composed back on June 6 and written out in his surprisingly vigorous handwriting. In summary, the document read:

Austin, Que
June 6/2001

Addendum to my will:

To Whom it May Concern:

I am now weeks into what promises to be an exhausting 6 months of chemo ~~therapy~~ therapy. Naturally, I am hoping for the ~~best~~, but there are no guarantees.

In the event I suffer an unanticipated side effect (a stroke, whatever?), ~~I hereby~~ and doctors adjudge me incapable of making decisions, I hereby grant my wife Florence power of attorney to make all decisions, financial or otherwise, on our behalf. I trust Florence completely.

I wish to be buried in the Mount Royal Cemetery, in Montreal, providing an adjoining plot is reserved for Florence, so that eventually we may lie beside each other in death, as we did so happily in life.

No rabbi, priest of minister is to speak at my graveside, but, for Tradition's sake, I would like our children to say Kaddish at my graveside.

I have not worked this hard for so long, so that Florence should deny herself anything.

That is it for now.

Mordecai Richler

The addendum went on to make clear his desire to be buried in the cheapest coffin available, and tidied up matters relating to his unfinished book projects and financial affairs.

———————

Public tributes filled the Canadian media for weeks. Margaret Atwood called him a "grumpy, scathing Diogenes"; Peter Gzowski said he would miss most "that voice over in the corner crying nonsense, pointing out the foibles and being outrageous and warm in many ways too." In the Canadian edition of *Time* Robert Gottlieb noted that "everybody's Mordecai Richler was different": at home he was "cherished as a literary treasure and resented as a national gadfly"; in England he was part of the crowd of young writers who gathered in the decade after the Second World War, and "interpreted their home countries to England, and vice versa"; while in the States he was a "master comic novelist." Art Cooper used his column in *GQ* to declare that "the world lost one of its finest writers of fiction, and I lost a dear friend." "He Made Montreal Cool," the column proclaimed. "Canada is back to bland again," his cousin Sam Orbaum wrote in the *Jerusalem Post*, "Mordecai Richler is dead." In *Maclean's*, Benoît Aubin, one of the two francophone journalists to roast him at the Ritz in 1993, put his passing in the context of Quebec-Canada relations. Noting how the death consumed the opening minutes of the CBC's *The National* in English, Aubin remarked that it had ranked third in the lineup of items in French. In Montreal the *Gazette* gave half its front page to the story, where *La Presse* consigned it to a few lines. Prime Minister Chrétien paid personal tribute to Richler; in Quebec the premier left the business of polite eulogy to the minister of culture. "English-Canadians had lost a hero," Aubin wrote, "French-Canadians had lost a villain."

In September 2001, the prominent Québécois filmmaker Jacques Godbout, writing in the *New York Times Magazine,* used the occasion of the debut of a new international arts festival in Quebec, titled "Quebec Fall," both to call him the province's greatest writer and to deride his memory. "Richler is no longer with us," Godbout wrote. "Let us hope that this 'Quebec Fall' will allow us to bury, as we did his ashes in Montreal last summer, the prejudices that he kept alive." The author and former McGill professor Witold Rybczynski replied, "Richler was always a thorn in the side of Quebec nationalists and separatists, because of his mordant wit and biting sarcasm, because he commanded a large audience and because, I suspect, he wrote uncomfortable truths." Both Godbout's article and Rybczynski's letter, appearing in the wake of the September 11 attacks in New York and Washington, went largely unnoticed. But the battle would continue.

On Snooker was published three weeks after his death. In America the book's modest success was unassisted by that long-discussed *New Yorker* excerpt. Richler never got that final credit in the magazine that had been the Holy Grail for writers since he was a teenager in those same Montreal pool halls. A few weeks later Louise Dennys sat down to write a letter to Florence in her capacity as her husband's literary executor, that would provide her with a full overview and understanding of the state of various projects. She explained that *Dispatches from the Sporting Life* was slated for publication in late spring 2002, but she wasn't sure about the proposed *Selected Essays 1960–2000*. "Do you know if he had begun to select material?" Another item was the novel. "Oh lord," Dennys wrote, "this is hard even to contemplate, let alone write about." She mentioned being "thrilled to hear he was working on it last January," but also aware that "much intervened, including the screenplay [of *Barney's Version*]. We did not communicate about it any more than that. I am rather assuming it had not gone far."

Knopf Canada sought an appropriate way to honour his memory, and with Jack Rabinovitch decided to commission an original typeface. It would first be used for the publication of *Dispatches from the Sporting Life*. A page at the back of the book entitled "A Note about the Type" states, "RICHLER is a completely original face, full of personality in the details, yet smooth in the composite effect." It is the first typeface known to be designed specifically for a single author's work.

On Snooker employs a whimsical photo Mordecai himself had discovered of the Queen Mother playing snooker. The jacket image for *Dispatches* reflects the personal nature of this last book, and the personal nature of the man too. The small snapshot shows him, sporty in waders and boots, on the front steps of a fishing lodge. One arm is around his journalist friend Bobby Stewart, and the other around Jacob, aged fourteen. On the back jacket is a shot taken by Bob Shapiro of Richler in the same outfit, cigarillo in hand, walking away from the camera.

On December 19, 2001, Florence Richler accepted the insignia of the Companion of Canada on behalf of her late husband. The honour was presented by his (briefly) former publisher Adrienne Clarkson, now the Governor General. Florence has left the insignia on the dining table in the Chateau apartment, next to the place setting that she continues to keep for him. Throughout the winter of 2001–02 she consulted on a memorial stone for the gravesite.

At the reception after the funeral, Robert Lantos had renewed his promise to make a film of *Barney's Version*. Years would go by, during which a new screenplay would be commissioned, before filming on the $28-million project would begin in Montreal. Paul Giamatti would play Barney, and Dustin Hoffman, sought so many years earlier to incarnate first Jake Hersh and then Joshua Shapiro, would take the role of Izzy Panofsky. The British actress Minnie Driver would play "The Second Mrs. Panofsky," and Lantos, determined to honour both his late friend and his final novel, would spend extra in order that the ongoing renovations of the Ritz-Carlton Hotel, then being converted into a condo-hotel complex, be completed in time to film the wedding scene in the ballroom. *Barney's Version*, directed by Richard Lewis and produced by Lantos in a co-production with the Italian company Three Amigos, was shown at the Toronto International Film Festival in September 2010.

Michael Levine's determination to bring *St. Urbain's Horseman* to the small screen also eventually paid off. In 2007 the CBC aired a four-hour adaptation of the novel. The director, Peter Moss, had been behind the staging of the Jacob Two-Two novels at the Young People's Theatre in Toronto, and had directed Emma Richler at Stratford. In the role of Jake Hersh was David Julian Hirsh, the young actor who had served for a day as Richler's driver back in 1999. The animated *Jacob Two-Two* series had made it to air as well, in 2003, running for sixty-five episodes. It was syndicated worldwide, including in China, where the animated version of the father, now speaking Mandarin, bore a striking resemblance to the original, right down to the bifocals and unruly hair.

Another kind of memorial for Mordecai Richler was created by his friends and admirers in 2002. Michael Levine organized a public celebration at the National Theatre in Montreal a year after his death, where friends, including Ted Kotcheff and Bob Gottlieb, Louise Dennys and Guy Vanderhaeghe, spoke, and Habs great Jean Béliveau, who had gone fishing once with Richler, read from one of his sports pieces. When Ken Whyte's tenure at the *National Post* ended after nearly two years of drastic budget cuts, he took a position at the McGill Institute for the Study of Canada. There, he helped organize a full conference on Richler. The event had sessions with titles like "A Canadian Jew Abroad," and cocktail parties in snooker rooms, with smoked meat from Schwartz's. The ongoing marvel of *La Versione di Barney* was also feted; by then, the novel had sold 300,000 copies in Italy. In the intervening year *Saturday Night* magazine had folded, after more than a century, and several more literary icons, including Timothy Findley, Carol Shields and Peter Gzowski, had passed away. Not long afterwards, Richard Holden would be dead as well. Three years later, an embattled Conrad Black, his newspaper empire vanished, would be sent to prison in Florida. Michael Posner's memoir of Richler, *The Last Honest Man*, capturing the memories, anecdotes and impressions of those who knew him well, appeared in 2006. In 2008 scholar Reinhold Kramer published *Mordecai Richler: Leaving St. Urbain.* The following year, novelist M.G. Vassanji, commissioned by

Penguin as part of their Extraordinary Canadians series, published a short biography of him.

Inside the Richler family as well, books continued to appear. Emma Richler's second novel, *Feed My Dear Dogs*, won acclaim in 2005, and was followed in 2006 by Noah Richler's intrepid non-fiction exploration of Canadian writing, *This Is My Country, What's Yours?* Promoting a French translation of his book in Quebec in 2008, Noah was attacked in a radio interview by a venerable Québécois novelist for the "sins" of his father— unforgotten, and certainly unforgiven. Martha Richler, active as a political cartoonist, illustrator and fashion designer, is working on a graphic novel, while Jacob Richler's book on Canadian chefs is slated for 2011. Noah continues to live in Toronto, with Sarah MacLachlan and their two daughters, as does Jake, now remarried. In 2006 Daniel Richler furthered the patterns of the Richler clan by moving with his wife and daughter to London, joining his two sisters there. Florence, who finally sold the London flat in 2008, lives in the Chateau on Sherbrooke Street. The house in the Townships, rented out through the year, is still used by the Richlers for two weeks in August, the siblings and their mother gathering there together.

"We were neither of one place nor the other," Noah Richler wrote of his brothers and sisters. "We lived in between, English or Canadian as suited." He also remarked on the true "nation" of Mordecai and Florence Richler: "What my parents had was each other. Cousins, aunts, uncles—even countries—did not come into it." Astute as that was, had Noah Richler wished, he could have written a separate and equally rich study of one Canadian writer's passionate engagement with one very particular geography. But as eloquent as any book on the subject of Mordecai Richler and Montreal could ever be is the tombstone monument eventually placed by Florence on the grave on the east slope of Rose Hill, Mount Royal. RICHLER, the pink granite tomb reads. Below that, on the right: MORDECAI 1931–2001; on the left, FLORENCE 1929–, the space for the date still empty. Above the names is a carving of a stack of books. Along the bottom is part of the addendum that Richler had scribbled in his final weeks when he requested a single burial plot for himself and his wife:

> *So that eventually we may lie beside each other in death,*
> *as we did so happily in life.*

Across from the stone, Florence Richler has had a bench installed, and a mulberry tree planted.

"We are not living through tragedy but farce," Richler scathingly declared. Here he poses for a *Saturday Night* photo shoot in May 1992, during the height of his battle with Quebec nationalism, after the "measured article I published in the *New Yorker* last autumn, a chronicle of the bizarre events that culminated in Bill 178 (the prohibition in Quebec of outdoor commercial signs using English), unleashed a storm."

"The truth is Canada is a cloud-cuckoo-land, an insufferably rich country governed by idiots, its self-made problems offering comic relief to the ills of the real world out there, where famine and racial strife and vandals in office are the unhappy rule." From *Barney's Version*.

Nick auf der Maur.
"Nick was a cherished friend.
An original." Mordecai, in
the introduction to *Nick:
A Montreal Life.*

"My irreplaceable friend Jack was a man of quality. . . ." The renowned film director
Jack Clayton, with his beloved pigeons.

Among friends at the cottage, early 1990s: Mordecai, Ted Allan, Noah, Bernie Ostry, share a joke, a bowl of favourite tomatoes to hand.

Asleep on the flight back after a happy excursion to Sable Island: Pierre Trudeau with Elizabeth Dickson, and Mordecai and Florence in the back.
"It was Bernie and Sylvia Ostry . . . who astutely judged Trudeau, then minister of justice, the most fascinating man in Ottawa and arranged for me to meet him for dinner at their house. I took to Trudeau immediately, amazed that we had such an unlikely politician enduring our nation's capital. . . . My political judgment infallible, I concluded he could never be elected prime minister. He was impaired by wit. Compromised by irony. Disqualified by an inability to suffer fools." From "The Man Behind the Mania," *Saturday Night*, Sept. 23, 2000.

Two old friends at a Giller Prize gala. Jack Rabinovitch, a friend from high school, came back into Mordecai's life in the 1970s. In honour of Jack's late wife, Doris Giller, he advised him on the creation of Canada's top literary prize.

Diana Athill, Mordecai's first editor when he was a young writer, wrote in her memoir *Stet: An Editor's Life*: "When I finished reading *Barney's Version* I felt nothing but delight at his having so triumphantly outlived his first publishing house; and I am happy . . . remembering that I once said to him 'You are going to end up as a Grand Old Man of Canadian Literature.' That is exactly what he did, if it were possible for a Grand Old Man to be wholly without pomposity."

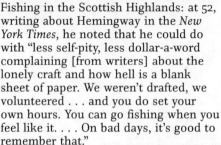

Fishing in the Scottish Highlands: at 52, writing about Hemingway in the *New York Times*, he noted that he could do with "less self-pity, less dollar-a-word complaining [from writers] about the lonely craft and how hell is a blank sheet of paper. We weren't drafted, we volunteered . . . and you do set your own hours. You can go fishing when you feel like it. . . . On bad days, it's good to remember that."

"The working stiffs who were my late-afternoon good companions at the Owl's Nest [the model for the Caboose in *Gursky*], an unassuming watering hole perched on cinder blocks on Highway 242: Dipstick, Sweet Pea, Coz and Buzz." Some of the companions in 1981, from left to right, back row: Bob Jameson the bartender, Alan Levoy, Roger "Sweet Pea" George (the model for Strawberry in *Gursky*, he witnessed Mordecai Richler's contract for *Barney's Version*). Front row: Mordecai, Jake, Dipstick (Larry Eldridge).

Mordecai and Avrum Richler, with Florence and Eve. At Bianca's restaurant in St. John's, the two brothers see each other for only the fourth time in forty years.

Fax to Nick Auf der Maur
from Mordecai Richler

Feb 11

Shalom, Chaver Auf der Maur:

Every time my fax goes ping ping, I rush upstairs anticipating
good news...big offers...from New York or even Toronto, and what I
get, instead, is another state-of-Auf-der-Maur's health bulletin.
From McKenna, Lynch-Staunton, John Aylen, or Jake. However, I
won't be impressed until I hear Princess has stopped to coo at your
bedside. But re-reading all those detailed reports (no word about
your bowel movements. are you regular? Big pieces? runny? I'm
longing to know), I gather you've lost some 20 pounds. Nick, you
lucky devil, you've struck gold. Forget all those best-selling
diet books (Calories Don't Count, Eat Fat, Grow Slim, etc et etc),
you've got the winner and shd be able to sign a contract worth
kazillions:

     CATCH CANCER AND GROW SLIM
       Fast fast results

     By Nicolas Auf der Maur

Hang in there.

Princess Di

Mordecai

Fax to Nick Auf der Maur
from Mordecai Richler

Feb 6

CONFIDENTIAL

EYES ONLY

Dear Nikita,

The buzz, the buzz. Big Normie Mailer has a new novel coming
in the spring. A life of Jesus. Written in the first person in,
wait for it, Elizabethan Engish. Wish I'd thought of that.
I hear, through the Winnie grapevine, that you've been to
an R.C. church. You'd better cover home plate as well, and send
a note to the Lubovitcher Rebbe in Crown Heights, Brooklyn.
Something else. The Wailing Wall in Jerusalem now has a fax
number, and, for a nominal fee, they will slip your memo to
Jehovah into a crack between the stones. Replies have to be
pre-paid. Don't mention Irving Steinberg's name.

       Best,

Fax to Louise Dennys
from Mordecai Richler

Feb 4 2000

Dear Louise:

Now that I'm at last novelizing, as they say in Hollywood,
I'm prepared to sign a contract with Knopf Canada, but with
nobody else for the moment...

Terms the same as they were for Barney's Version: if
memory serves, 50,000 on signature, 50,000 on delivery and
50,000 on pub. Please dont fax me a 132 page contract,
send it airmail at yr convenience. It should help me with my
meatloaf budget.

Delighted you will be welcoming Nigel and Martha. Many
thanks.

Best to my meatloafer buddy.

       Hugs,

Mordecai

Daniel, Emma, Noah, Jacob and Martha with their mother, on Rose Hill, Mount Royal, July 5, 2001.

> "And you, my father, there on the sad height,
> Curse, bless me now with your fierce tears, I pray."

From Dylan Thomas's "Do Not Go Gentle into That Good Night," recited by Martha Richler at the funeral of her father.

Courtesy of Emma Richler. Not to be reproduced.

BIBLIOGRAPHIC ESSAYS

Mordecai: The Life and Times uses neither footnotes nor endnotes. For readers interested in my primary research sources, or curious about some of the background, I've included here a short bibliographic essay for each section. More extensive notes, arranged by line and page, can be found on the website www.charlesforan.com. A full bibliography and index, and a complete list of the people I interviewed for the book are also available there.

PROLOGUE

I discovered Mordecai Richler's blistering 1973 speech to a Jewish student conference among his papers from the London flat. Curiously, the lecture, typed out in a fury after the reception the night before, was not included in any of the four donations he made over a thirty-year period to the Mordecai Richler archive in the Special Collections, University of Calgary. Instead, it travelled from his desk in Canada to his desk in London sometime in the 1990s. It is possible that he misplaced the document, rediscovered it after decades, and was considering whether to use it in some form in a column or essay.

A note about the archive. Like his father, Richler kept everything: drafts of articles and books; business correspondence; letters from friends and family, admirers and stalkers; clippings from newspapers and magazines; and receipts. (One folder contains a receipt for $40 for the coat Moses Richler bought his son in 1950.) Tens of thousands of documents, including many letters, may be examined by anyone who visits the Special Collections reading room. Another thousand or so letters, however, were placed in a restricted archive that Richler intended, as he explained in a letter to Brian Moore, to keep closed to inspection until twenty-five years after his death. That archive, composed largely of correspondence to and from Lily Rosenberg and Moses Richler, included the 1976 letter to his mother that is reproduced in Part IV. In 2008 the restricted archive was briefly opened, allowing me to examine and use—with the permission of the Richler Estate—that material.

Despite its size, the Mordecai Richler archive at the University of Calgary is notably lacking in two traditional sources for information about a subject. One is diaries, journals or extensive notes about works-in-progress, beyond an early diary he kept in Europe and the bare-bones jottings that filled the notepads next to his typewriter. The other is juvenilia: report cards and letters to parents, sketches and teenage stories, perhaps the comic book he wrote and drew with his brother, Avrum. The Mordecai Richler archive has a few notes signed "Mutty" and a couple of samples of "Mordy's" teenage story efforts, but nothing else of this sort. Avrum Richler, who hosted their mother in St. John's during her final years, attests to the fact that little juvenilia survived their childhoods. He speculates that Lily Rosenberg destroyed the material, out of bitterness.

PART I: MUTTLE, MUTTY, MORDY

Whenever possible, I have built this portrait of Richler's Montreal childhood using details drawn from his published writings. As admirers of his work know, those details are voluminous and richly sketched; his ardour for that urban village, that city, was boundless. Additional sources include interviews with family and friends, as well as other Montreal Jews who grew up in the "old" neighbourhood. These include, to name just three, Jack Wolofsky, whose family owned the Yiddish newspaper, and whom Richler punched in Grade 9; Lily Shatsky, another Talmud Torah student from the "wrong side" of Park Avenue, and among the St. Urbain urchins with whom Mordy shared the news that his grandmother had just died; and Jack Rabinovitch, who remembers the streets of his, and his friend's, childhood with no less acuity.

For information about the Richler and Rosenberg clans, I relied on the memories of Avrum Richler and Max Richler, among others. Two additional sources need to be acknowledged. Concordia professor of Judaic Studies Ira Robinson, the foremost authority on the life of Yudel Rosenberg and someone who knew Lily Rosenberg, has published widely on the rebbe and the era. His *Rabbis and Their Community* (2007) was particularly helpful, as was Professor Robinson himself. Lily/Leah Rosenberg's memoir, *The Errand Runner* (1981), was important to Part I as well. None of the thoughts I ascribe to her are speculation. They are, rather, how she characterized her father and mother, husband and sons—generally in no uncertain terms. While Richler's mother is not to be trusted on names, and is suspect on selected personal relationships—specifically, her affair with Julius Frankel—the consensus among family is that her memoir otherwise expresses the "truth" of her feelings about her long, troubled life.

That said, none of the accusations levelled in *The Errand Runner* of dishonesty among her husband's clan, in particular the business dealings of her father-in-law, Shmarya Richler, can be confirmed (although Mordecai and Avrum believed them, and witnessed apparent instances). These accusations remain a sore point for Richler family members, including several of Mordecai's own aunts and uncles still alive in 2010. Some never forgave him for offering a fictional version of his grandfather's cheating in *Son of a Smaller Hero*. No less incendiary among the Richlers has been the contention that Shmarya Richler struck his grandchildren. Richler first made the accusation in a 1999 interview with the *Globe and Mail*, to the dismay, once again, of his family. The strength of their denials, recorded by Michael Posner in *The Last Honest Man* (2004), startled even Avrum Richler, who had never witnessed his grandfather being violent, and he wondered if his brother had got this wrong. But Avrum, like everyone else, attests to a core quality of his character; whatever his other flaws, Mordecai Richler did not fabricate.

On the subject of uncertainty: in an interview with Evelyn Sacks, then eighty-seven, she repeated to me her claim that she and Mordecai Richler had been friends only, albeit close ones. She also characterized him in terms that suggested the friendship had been a defining experience in her own life, as it was in his. Her assertions were made in response to Michael Posner's speculations that she had had an affair with the teenager, one repeated by Reinhold Kramer in his biography with the caveat that the relationship may have stopped short of sex.

Both Posner and Kramer based their conjectures on the contents of *The Rotten People*, the unpublished novel Richler wrote in 1950–51. Evelyn Sacks, a spirited, funny woman, admitted that she possesses letters from Mordecai Richler, written during his early years in Europe, but has declined to share their contents. She did, however, recount a warm reunion she had with her former pupil almost a half-century later, when Richler took her and Lily Shatsky to the Ritz-Carlton for a drink.

Also on the matter of fabrications: Part I contains the only partial biographical "invention" in *Mordecai*. Better, I present one event in these pages with more narrative authority than memories allow. This involves Yudel Rosenberg retelling the Golem stories to his grandsons. As I point out in Chapter 2, Muttle was only four when his *zeyda* passed away, and was left with a scattering of dim, if still essential memories of this important figure. Avrum, being nine, recalled his grandfather more clearly, including those storytelling sessions in the apartment on Esplanade or during summer walks in the Laurentians. But Avrum does not remember any particular tales about the Golem. My reasons for emphasizing those Jewish superhero stories are twofold. First, they would have been natural choices for a Hasidic rabbi to tell his grandchildren: lively and action-oriented, with an edifying orthodox lesson. Second, the more Richler became interested in his grandfather, starting in earnest when he was in his thirties, the more his own fiction began to feature some variation on the Jewish saviour motif: Joey in *St. Urbain's Horseman* and Solomon in *Solomon Gursky Was Here*. Could the partial origin of this thematic obsession lie in those tales, delivered by no less an authority than their modern literary "inventor"—that is, Rabbi Yudel Rosenberg? I think so.

On the subject of names: Yiddish-derived nicknames, especially private diminutives for children, may be spelled variously. "Muttle," for instance, is also fine as "Muttel" or "Mottel"; "Mutty" is more frequently written out as "Mutti." (I opt for "Mutty" because Richler signed letters to his father using that form.) Avrum, too, whom I call "Voomy," after his mother's spelling, was also referred to by his mother as "Vroomie." The complexity and fluidity of Yiddish spellings can be a challenge. For that reason, all spellings in *Mordecai* are based on the *Canadian Oxford Dictionary*.

Two more books, and one poet, need to be flagged in the context of Montreal's historic solitudes. Irving Layton's memoir, *Waiting for the*

Messiah, offers a rich portrait of the Jewish ghetto in the 1930s and '40s. Interviewed later in life, Layton recalled his experiences of intercommunity exchanges, fisticuffs unrelated to either conscription or the fascism of Adrien Arcand. "The strongest memory I have is of clashes," Layton said. "Around Easter, during the death and resurrection of Jesus Christ, something seemed to happen to the gentiles. They took it as a cue to come and beat up the Jews. . . . So, without fail, every Easter they would descend . . . with bottles and bricks, and we'd be waiting for them on the roofs, like an army, with sticks and stones, with anything." Michel Tremblay's magical 1978 novel, *The Fat Woman Next Door Is Pregnant* (*La grosse femme d'à côté est enceinte*), offers its own perspective on the phenomenon of parallel lives on the Plateau. Transpiring in a single spring day in 1942 in a cluster of working-class streets so close to where Mordy Richler was being raised that the family's Shabbas goy could have been the child of one of the characters, the story is a Richlerian exercise in sensory detail and nostalgia. Early on, a woman remarks on the complexity, for her and her kind, of riding the tram down The Main. "But when the streetcar turned down Saint-Laurent, heading south, suddenly they'd calm down and sink back into the straw seats; all of them, without exception, owed money to the Jews on Saint-Laurent, especially to the merchants who sold furniture and clothes; and for them, the long street separating rue Mont-Royal and rue Sainte-Catherine was a very sensitive one to cross." Interestingly, the ardently nationalist Tremblay, while never a friend, remained on good terms with Richler. Florence and Mordecai often dined in the same French restaurant in downtown Montreal frequented by the great playwright, and the two writers would stop and chat.

A note about Montreal street and place names: the city is a palimpsest, a historic, political and linguistic competition for space. For Michel Tremblay, the street that caused his women to sink back into their seats in 1942 was called Saint-Laurent; for eleven-year-old Mordecai Richler, living two blocks over on St. Urbain, the ghetto's principal thoroughfare was known as St. Lawrence or The Main. If Mont-Royal to young Tremblay was Mount Royal to young Richler, that was little more than a difference of French/English spellings. More telling of the Montreal experience of the last half-century has been the legislated renaming of Fletcher's Field as Jeanne-Mance Park (or Park

Jeanne-Mance) and Dorchester Boulevard as René Lévesque Boulevard
(or Boulevard René Lévesque)—to name just two. As my biography
wishes to be equally rooted in the city's rich, layered soil, I have opted
to use the English names for streets and places, as Richler did in his
work, and in his life.

Finally, the poetry of A.M. Klein. Here is a small sampling from his
wondrous 1932 poem "Autobiographical," outlining his own orthodox
Jewish childhood.

> Hazelnut games, and games in the synagogue—
> The burrs, the Haman rattle,
> The Torah dance on Simchas Torah night.

As well:

> My father pickabacking me to bed
> To tell tall tales about the Baal Shem Tov—
> Letting me curl his beard.

PART II: APPRENTICE

While Paris certainly was a moveable feast for expatriates for much of
the twentieth century, it wasn't so clearly framed for Mordecai Richler
in the fall of 1950; neither Morley Callaghan's *That Summer in Paris* (1963)
nor Ernest Hemingway's *A Moveable Feast* (1964) had yet appeared. He
could read plenty of other books about the city or, even better, simply be
there, alongside legions of wide-eyed artistes (where, for instance, he
heard versions of the legendary Callaghan-Hemingway fist fight before any
book account of it). And Papa, who had drafted parts of *The Sun Also Rises*
in the cafés of Montparnasse three decades earlier, still kept his literary
progeny spiritual company in Paris, where the young Mordecai "devoured"
him, along with Malraux, Céline, Sartre and Camus, "determined to be a
real literary man."

"A room that is good and clean and true," wrote Bill Weintraub to Richler,
evoking in affectionate parody Papa's classic story "A Clean, Well-Lighted
Place." That letter can be found in *Getting Started* (2001), Weintraub's
charming memoir in letters and prose of the early years of his great

friendships with Richler, Brian Moore and Mavis Gallant. While Gallant's legendary Paris diaries have yet to be fully published, enough of her memories have appeared to render the period vivid. Here she is, for instance, in her own small room in Paris in the autumn of 1950, playing on a well-known theme of the Canadian Abroad, in England or Northern Europe, encountering a cold unlike anything experienced in their chilly homeland. "If I am working my hands get numb," she explained to Bill Weintraub, "and I have to soak them in warm water. I can now understand why the French never sleep alone. They aren't any sexier than any other race, but it's the only way of keeping warm."

William Weintraub's other book about the era, *City Unique* (1996), is an exceptionally lively account of the roaring Montreal of his and Richler's youth, and I relied on it for my own portrait of that city. Merrily Weisbord's *The Strangest Dream* (1983) deserves a mention for its rich outlining of how, as Richler put it of his 1950s London friends, people "bet their lives on politics" in the Jewish Montreal of the Depression and war eras as well. While many accounts exist of the Left expatriate scene in postwar London, and more and more scholars are writing about the "first wave" of post-colonial writing that took root there, few explore these dynamic trends from a Canadian perspective. For this reason, I am grateful to John Clement Ball's *Imagining London: Postcolonial Fiction and the Transnational Metropolis* (2004) for its insights, including those about the young Mort Richler. Diana Athill's *Stet* (2001) offers an endearing portrait of the Mordecai Richler and Brian Moore she first met then, as does Doris Lessing's memoir *Walking in the Shade* (1997). As I point out, Lessing's seminal novel *The Golden Notebook* (1962) sketches the same kinds of expats, found arguing, chattering and deceiving in *A Choice of Enemies*.

More generally, Part II seems the right place to begin acknowledging other books about Mordecai Richler. Michael Posner's stellar oral biography, *The Last Honest Man*, was an invaluable resource, as was Michael himself. Professor Reinhold Kramer's admirable *Mordecai Richler: Leaving St. Urbain* (2008) has been consulted throughout, and M.G. Vassanji's contribution to the Extraordinary Canadians series, *Mordecai Richler* (2009), is particularly strong on his childhood and early years in Europe. Joel Yanofsky's *Mordecai & Me* (2003), a quirky, intelligent memoir, explores Richler in the context of both Anglo Montreal and literary obsession; and though the nature of my project did not permit extensive writing about the novels themselves, I did read with interest Ada Craniford's *Mordecai Richler: A Life in Ten Novels* (2005). If this list of recently published titles suggests his work remains vital to the academy, that impression would be incorrect. Craniford aside, little scholarship has been devoted to Richler's fiction in recent years, an absence all the more striking given that his two greatest novels may also have been his last: *Solomon Gursky Was Here* and *Barney's Version.* Why scholars, most obviously Canadian ones, have shifted their attention elsewhere is a matter in need of discussion. (Richler's delight in pricking the academy, earning himself few friends and allies there, probably didn't help.) It is, unfortunately, a large subject, extending well beyond the merits of his books into the murky realms of culture wars and academic trends.

On a related matter—the spirited revival of A.M. Klein by Canadian scholars—I am in debt to Zailig Pollock for his *A.M. Klein: The Story of the Poet* (1994). Usher Caplan's biography *Like One That Dreamed: A Portrait of A.M. Klein (1982) was likewise helpful.*

PART III: HORSEMAN

Saul Bellow looms as large over this section of the biography as he did over mid-twentieth-century American literature. "I am an American, Chicago-born," *The Adventures of Augie March* famously opens, "and go at things as I have taught myself, free style, and will make the record of my own way: first to knock, first admitted; sometimes an innocent knock, sometimes a not so innocent." Congruencies abound between Richler and the iconic American novelist, beginning with their childhoods: Bellow was born in 1915 in Lachine, Quebec, to Russian-Jewish immigrant parents, and raised on Coloniale, a few streets over from St. Urbain. His father was a bootlegger, and they relocated to Chicago, possibly under threat of violence, when he was nine. Richler's upbringing didn't quite produce the American strut of Bellow's resonant "free style"; no Canadian, even one as *sui generis* as Mordecai Richler, can comfortably issue such a clarion song to, and of, the Walt Whitman "self." But he otherwise embraced much of Bellow's project, and certainly upheld his commitment to books that were other kinds of songs "of praise, Chassidic in . . . intensity and delight in life," as he wrote of *Herzog*. Reinhold Kramer is very good on this connection, and I am grateful to him for alerting me to how Bellow's conception of the novel inflected Richler's evolution as an artist.

Alfred Kazin has a cameo in Part III. In 1959 the great critic published the essay "The Alone Generation," about the failure of most modern literature to engage honestly with the times. The problem, Kazin believed, was one of disposition: too many books of, in effect, too little intensity and delight. One paragraph from his essay could stand as a defence of the hard-shelled *The Apprenticeship of Duddy Kravitz*. "I am tired of reading for compassion instead of pleasure," Kazin wrote. "In novel after novel, I am presented with people who are so soft, so wheedling, so importunate, that the actions in which they are involved are too indecisive to be interesting or to develop those implications which are the life-blood of narrative."

A word about Canadian writers in 1960s London. As he did with his fractious crowd in Canada, Jack McClelland kept up a correspondence with many of the principals, including Richler, Norman Levine, Brian Moore (his one year there), Leonard Cohen and Margaret Laurence. *Imagining Canadian Literature: The Selected Letters of Jack McClelland* (1998), edited by Sam Solecki, brings the publisher to bright life, and shows him trying to moderate Richler's habit of reviewing his fellow scribes, often with bite: "It's an open invitation to other critics and novelists to slander the hell out of your next book when it appears," McClelland wrote. James King has published biographies of both McClelland and Laurence. In the latter, Laurence's relationship with the Barbadian novelist George Lamming is outlined. According to King in *The Life of Margaret Laurence* (1998), their involvement was serious enough to torment her for years, including during the period she lived in London when she met the Richlers and attended a party at their flat in Hampstead. Another biographer, however, makes no mention of the affair.

Laurence's *The Stone Angel* was revised in London; Leonard Cohen wrote as much of *Beautiful Losers* in Montreal and Greece as he did in the English capital. Still, with the addition of *Duddy Kravitz*, a book

written in London and southern France, it becomes clear that three of
the landmarks of Canadian literature—fictions rooted in Montreal and
Manawaka, Manitoba—were partially or wholly realized abroad. While
viewing Canadian literature as an essentially post-colonial project
remains controversial, it is hard to argue with this evidence.

PART IV: LOOK AT ME NOW

Three more biographies proved important to me at this midpoint of
Richler's life. Lee Hill's *A Grand Guy: The Art and Life of Terry Southern*
(2001), Denis Sampson's *Brian Moore: The Chameleon Novelist* (1998) and
Elaine Kalman Naves' *Robert Weaver: Godfather of Canadian Literature*
(2008) all provided insights into these friends. Robert Fulford's memoir
Best Seat in the House (1998) was helpful in mapping out the literary and
journalism scenes in the 1960s and '70s, as was Bob himself, generous
with his time and his lively memories of *Maclean's*.

A word about the August 1976 letter from Mordecai to his mother in
Chapter 6. Apart from correcting spelling errors and deleting two brief
sentences referencing individuals not otherwise in the book, I have here
reprinted it in its original form. If ever a document required no gloss,
it is this forceful assertion of a son's grievance, and an unhappiness that
enduringly infected his life. Richler never showed the letter to anyone
aside from its intended recipient. He drafted a version, corrected it,
typed it out again, and then sent it to his mother, keeping one copy for
himself. Florence never saw it, or even knew it existed, and neither did
Avrum Richler, who had no idea what his brother was asking during
their reunion in 1999 when he took him aside to talk about the horrifying scene he recalled witnessing.

Richler placed the letter in the restricted section of the archives, for
some future biographer to find. Under the circumstances, I felt I could
only respect his pain and his anger by offering the document unvar-
nished and unannotated, a single chapter unto itself. I am eternally
grateful to Florence Richler for granting permission to use the letter in
all its ragged glory.

Lily Rosenberg's trips to the Soviet Union in the 1970s to visit relatives marked the tail end of a fascinating subplot in Richler's life as a
Rosenberg. In Part III, I mention that poet Irving Layton had once dated

a relation. Her name was Suzanne Rosenberg, and her mother, Helen, was the wife of Lily's half-brother, Benjamin Rosenberg. He lived and died in Europe—specifically, he was killed fighting with the Reds during the October Revolution—and his Polish widow and daughter, fleeing the newly established Soviet Union, attempted to rebuild their lives in Canada in the 1920s. Although the teenage Suzanne was soon a favourite of Yudel Rosenberg, her fiery Bolshevik mother was not. Tired of failing to rouse the masses in Depression-era Montreal, Helen Rosenberg eventually repatriated herself and her children. In so doing, she voluntarily re-entered the century's greatest social catastrophe. A predictably nightmarish tale ensued, complete with gulags and disappearances, all of it outlined in Suzanne Rosenberg's striking 1988 memoir, *A Soviet Odyssey*. While Richler probably read her book, he never found use in his fiction for this material. In keeping with his understanding of his role as a writer, he had little use, in fact, for historical, family-related material that preceded his own lifespan. "Where are we from?" young Joshua Shapiro asks his father in *Joshua Then and Now*. "Some shitty little village in Poland," Reuben replies.

In the relative scarcity of recent scholarly writing about Mordecai Richler, one essay stands out. Though just five pages long, Adam Gopnik's introduction to *Mordecai Richler Was Here* (2006), an attractively packaged selection of his prose, teems with fresh observations and trenchant insights. Gopnik's identification of Richler's larger subject as a novelist—his "Big Theme" (which he admits Richler would have rejected as pretentious)—as "the transformation of a post-colonial culture in a post-modern age," started me thinking differently about his work. I am thankful to Adam Gopnik for opening this unexpected door to understanding Mordecai Richler.

PART V: M.R. WAS HERE / PART VI: HANG IN OLD FRIEND
Unsurprisingly, the more recent the past, the less likely it has been recorded in books. As a result, I've relied heavily on the memories of friends and colleagues, as well as his family, to construct Richler's final decades. These years are also where I can contribute modestly through my experiences as a Montreal writer during the 1990s, and someone who met my subject a few times. In 1993 John Fraser, editor of *Saturday*

Night, where I was a contributing editor, invited me to the roast at the Ritz. Aside from shaking Richler's hand in the Maritime Bar, I had no contact with him that evening. Florence sat on one side of him at the head table, Bill Weintraub on the other. To my younger eyes, the event was that rarest of Canadian occurrences: an unselfconscious, unapologetic celebration of large character and larger literary accomplishment. I was glad to be there.

Two years later I attended the launch of *Qui a peur de Mordecai Richler?* (*Who's Afraid of Mordecai Richler?*) (1995), Nadia Khouri's account of his tussles with Quebec nationalism, at a French-language bookshop in downtown Montreal. Richler, who had learned of the book's existence only a few weeks earlier, showed up in support of Khouri, and stood for long periods by himself, observing the room. I reintroduced myself, and we chatted about Esther Delisle, the Quebec academic whose research into the anti-Semitism of Lionel Groulx and Depression-era *Le Devoir* had been incorporated into *Oh Canada! Oh Quebec!* (I had written a piece about Delisle for *Saturday Night*, and earlier talked about her with Richler by phone.) As was his habit with nearly all younger writers, Richler now volunteered kind words about the article, as well as general support. "Things were a lot easier when I started out," he said.

Peter C. Newman's *Bronfman Dynasty* (1978) is important to understanding the obsession that produced *Solomon Gursky Was Here*, and I am grateful to Michael Levine and John Scott for helping me sort out the intricacies of both the Bronfman family and the legion of would-be biographers. (Any outstanding errors remain mine alone.) I consulted *Ego and Ink* (2004), Chris Cobb's fine book on the rise of the *National Post*, and John Fraser and Conrad Black were generous with their stories. Finally, I'd be remiss if I didn't acknowledge the quiet influence, both then and now, of Aislin's brilliant cartoons of the Quebec of the era, and its players, including the boulevardiers—Nick Auf der Maur, Richard Holden, Hubie Bauch, John Aylen—whom he so loved to draw, and liked so much as people. No more acidic, attentive or deeply felt record of what transpired in the province in the 1980s and '90s exists than the "collected" Terry Mosher art of the period—except, arguably, for the writings of his friend Mordecai Richler.

PART VII: PHILEMON AND BAUCIS / EPILOGUE

It may seem strange to evoke members of Richler's extended family, from whom he was largely disaffected, in his final years. I was naturally interested in the memories of Max Richler, Avrum Richler, and Myer and Diane Richler, about the 1930s and '40s, but I was also very keen to learn about Richler's efforts to reconnect with his clan in his last months, gestures that everyone found remarkable and moving.

Finally, it was Florence Richler who explained to me the meaning behind the tender story of Philemon and Baucis—I had overlooked the reference in *Barney's Version*—and Florence who allowed me to go through the boxes from the London flat, where I found the fragments of his final novel. It was Florence too who suggested I might want to include selected paragraphs from the addendum to his will, especially if that most intimate of documents could be reproduced in his actual handwriting. Daniel, Noah, Emma, Martha and Jacob Richler kindly permitted me to reprint their powerful, then-private remarks from the funeral, and Louise Dennys and Ric Young, present at that final event, served as guides through it.

Among the dozens of letters of condolence sent to Florence Richler and the family, the July 24, 2001, letter from novelist Timothy Findley was especially thoughtful and poignant. "He had the guts," Findley wrote of Mordecai Richler, "—in every aspect of his life—to do what a person forever regrets not doing himself. He was a champion of the doing of things. For him, it was a basic truth, talk is cheap."

ACKNOWLEDGEMENTS

Among the many people owed thanks for their help, advice and encouragement in the writing of this biography, a few must first be singled out.

From start to finish, Florence Richler was generous, honest, frank, critical and hugely insightful about her husband, his work and their life together. As executor of the Richler Estate, she also granted me unrestricted access to all materials, including letters, manuscripts and even medical records not yet part of the public archive. Steadfast in her insistence that the book be unauthorized, a "warts and all" portrait of her beloved husband, Florence extended these courtesies without hesitation, just as she gave over hundreds of hours to conversations in Montreal, London and Toronto. Her reading of the manuscript was likewise done for reasons of accuracy and to ensure a richness of detail unavailable to any other biographer, and was once again offered without conditions. So, with all humility, I acknowledge that any outstanding mistakes of apprehension and fact are mine alone, and despite her extraordinary contributions. These few sentences cannot possibly express my gratitude to Florence.

My heartfelt gratitude as well to those closest to Mordecai Richler, who gave their time and effort to the public task of biography, when personal inclination was surely to remain private: Daniel Richler, Noah Richler, Emma Richler, Martha Richler and Jacob Richler, so helpful in so many ways; and to his close friends, kind to me out of memory of him: Ted Kotcheff, Jack Rabinovitch, Bill Weintraub and Robert Gottlieb. I would also like to thank Avrum Richler, whose assistance brought clarity to Mordecai Richler's early life and his relationship with his mother.

Mary Ladky has been supportive in ways she is both aware of, and likely could not identify. My particular debt to her is ongoing, to be repaid over the longest period negotiable. The same holds true for our daughters, Anna Foran and Claire Foran. Thanks also to Anna for her assistance in reading.

Louise Dennys, my publisher at the Knopf Random Canada Publishing Group, supported the book from its inception and was its passionate, engaged and patient editor through to its final hours. I could not have asked for a finer or more rigorous editorial guide.

My special thanks also to the following: James Lahey and Guy Lawson, my *consiglieri* in Toronto and New York, respectively; Mark Abley and Yann Martel for reading the entire manuscript in its earliest, even more alarming form; David Staines, Zailig Pollock, Bryan Demchinsky and Michael Peterman, for reading sections; John Fraser, for his wisdom; Michael Levine, for his advice; Jackie Kaiser, my agent, for her support; Michael Posner, for his book, and his enthusiasm; Pym Buitenhuis, for her diligence; Linda Gaboriau and Hervé de Fontenay, Denis and Gay Sampson, David Homel and Marie-Louise Gay, for their kind hosting in Montreal.

My thanks as well to those who contributed generously of their memories and insights:

In Montreal and environs: Pearl and Michael Adams, Cotton Aimers, Stan Asher, John Aylen, Hubie Bauch, Jerry Brown, Alex Cherney, Peter and Martha Duffield, Pat Duggan at the Montreal *Gazette* library, Sheila Fischman and Don Winkler, Roger George, the late Stan Gesser, Harry Gulkin, Shannon Hodge at the Jewish Public Library, Sonny Idelson, Don and Heather Johnston, Naïm Kattan, John Lynch-Staunton, Emile and Nicole Martel, Terry Mosher, Peter Moss, Howard Richler, Max Richler, Myer and Diane Richler, Honore Robertson, Carmen Robinson, Ira Robinson, Jon Robinson, Dr. Harry Rosen, Evelyn Sacks, John Scott, Lily Shatsky, Magda Weintraub, Merrily Weisbord and Arnie Gelbart, Jack, Judah and Sandy Wolofsky, and Joel Yanofsky.

In Toronto: Ken Alexander, Margaret Atwood, Conrad Black, Daniel Baird, Randy Boyagoda, Adrienne Clarkson, Karen Cossar, Kildare

Dobbs, Bronwyn Drainie, Linda Frum, Robert Fulford, Greg Gatenby, Graeme Gibson, Cynthia Good, Michael Ignatieff, Joe Kertes, Mark Kingwell, Martin Knelman, Katerie Lanthier, Robert Lantos, Martin Levin, Anna Luengo, David Macfarlane, Sarah MacLachlan, Sandra Martin, Alice Munro, Sylvia Ostry, Jackie Park, Anna Porter, Maxine Quigley, Neil Richler, Peter Dale Scott, Robin Sears, Antanas Sileika, Sam Solecki, Mary Stinson and Paul McIntyre at the CBC, Rosemary Sullivan, and Moses Znaimer. In Peterborough: Jonathan Bordo, Tony Jeffery, Norman Jewison, Orm and Barb Mitchell, Trent graduate students Anthony Donnelly and Ewa Krynski. In Guelph: Cathy Boudreau, Tess Taconis. In St. John's: Noreen Golfman, Lisa Moore, Eve Richler. In Saskatoon: David Carpenter, Guy Vanderhaeghe. In Ottawa: John Metcalf, Landon Pearson. In Edmonton: Mel Hurtig. In Calgary: Adrian Kelly, Robert Majzels, Victor Ramraj, Aritha van Herk; and of course to Apollonia Steele and Marlys Chevrefils at the Special Collections, University of Calgary archives.

In London: Diana Athill, Carmen Callil, Haya Clayton, David Cornwell, the late Clive Exton, Nigel Horne, Verity Lambert, the late John Mortimer, Ferdinand Mount, Deborah Rogers, Alison Samuel.

In New York: the late Nina Bourne, Adam Gopnik, Maya Kaimal, Maria Mottola and John Loonam, Paul Tough, Maria Tucci. In California: Stanley Mann, Jean Moore, Robert Shapiro.

In Paris: Mavis Gallant.

To the wonderful publishing team at Knopf Canada, who unstintingly gave of their expertise and dedication: Nina Ber, Barney Gilmore, Gena Gorrell, Carla Kean, Sharon Klein, Amanda Lewis, Michelle MacAleese, Jane McWhinney, Deirdre Molina.

And sincere thanks to the following for permission to use their photographs: Florence Richler, Jacob Richler, Martha Richler, Emma Richler, Noah Richler, Daniel Richler, Avrum Richler, Bill Weintraub, Lionel Albert, Margaret Atwood, Robert Fulford, Arthur Mackenzie Peers, Terry Mosher, Joe King, Joy von Tiedemann, Robert Shapiro, Sarah Snowbell, Mary Hilliard, and E. Kaye Fulton. Also to Bowser and Blue, for permission to quote the ballad of "Sir Mordecai."

PHOTO CREDITS

INSERT ONE

Page i (top) courtesy of Avrum Richler; (bottom) © Sarah Snowbell, courtesy of the Richler family

Page ii Courtesy of Lionel Albert

Page iii (top) © Special Collections, University of Calgary archives; (middle) courtesy of Claire Achman; (bottom) Courtesy of Avrum Richler

Page iv Courtesy of Avrum Richler

Page v (top, left) Courtesy of Avrum Richler; (top, right) © Special Collections, University of Calgary archives; (bottom) © Studio Kashton, Canadian Jewish Congress Charities Committee National Archives

Pages vi–vii Map © Sydney Berne. Map and caption reproduced from Joe King's *From the Ghetto to the Main: The Story of the Jews of Montreal* (Montreal: Montreal Jewish Publication Society, 2001).

Page viii © Glay Sperling/National Archives of Canada

INSERT TWO

Page i (top) © Roger Viollet/Getty Images; (bottom) Courtesy of Avrum Richler

Page ii Courtesy of the Richler family

Page iii (top) Courtesy of Avrum Richler; (bottom) Courtesy of the
Richler family

Page iv (top) © David Bier, courtesy of the Richler family; (bottom)
photographer unknown

Page v Courtesy of Avrum Richler

Page vi © Arthur Mackenzie Peers, Special Collections, University of
Calgary archives

Page vii Courtesy of the Richler family

Page viii (top) Courtesy of the Richler family; (bottom) Courtesy of
William Weintraub

INSERT THREE

Page i Courtesy of the Richler family

Page ii (top) Courtesy of the Richler family; (middle) © Anthony
Buckley, courtesy of the Richler family; (bottom) Courtesy of the
Richler family

Page iii Courtesy of William Weintraub

Page iv Courtesy of the Richler family

Page v Courtesy of the Richler family

Page vi (top) Courtesy of Robert Fulford; (bottom) Courtesy of the
Richler family.

Page vii © Fay Godwin—renowned photographer and the wife of
Tony Godwin, Richler's editor and friend. Courtesy of the Richler
family

Page viii Courtesy of the Richler family

INSERT FOUR

Page i (top) Courtesy of Margaret Atwood; (bottom) Courtesy of the
Richler family

Page ii (top and bottom) © Steve Jensen, *The Gazette* (Montreal) 1975.
Courtesy of the Richler family

Page iii (top) Courtesy of the Richler family; (bottom) © Aislin,
Montreal, *The Gazette*

Page iv Courtesy of the Richler family

Page v (top) © George Cree, *The Gazette* (Montreal); courtesy of the

Richler family; (bottom) Courtesy of the Richler family

Page vi (top) © Joy von Tiedemann; (bottom) Courtesy of the Richler family

Page vii (top) Courtesy of the Richler family; (bottom) © Mary Hilliard, courtesy of the Richler family

Page viii © TV Ontario, courtesy of the Richler family

INSERT FIVE

Page i © Jim Allen

Page ii (top) © Garth Pritchard, *The Gazette* © 1976; (bottom) Courtesy of the Richler family

Page iii (top) Courtesy of the Richler family; (bottom) © E. Kaye Fulton, courtesy of the Richler family

Page iv © Peter Redman/*National Post*

Page v (top left) Robert Shapiro; (top right) Courtesy of the Richler family; (bottom) Courtesy of Avrum Richler

Page vi Courtesy of the Richler family

Page vii © Christinne Muschi/*National Post*, courtesy of the Richler family

Page viii (top) Courtesy of the Richler family; (bottom) Courtesy of Emma Richler. Not for reproduction without permission

PERMISSIONS ON QUOTED TEXTS

The author has made every effort to locate and contact all the holders of copy-written material reproduced in this book, and expresses grateful acknowledgement for permission to reproduce from the following previously published material and sources:

The Richler Estate

Athill, Diana. *Stet: An Editor's Life* (London: Granta Books, 2001).

Eaton, Nicole & Hilary Weston, *At Home in Canada*. Photographs by Joy von Tiedemann (Toronto: Viking, 1995).

King, Joe. *From the Ghetto to the Main: The Story of the Jews of Montreal* (Montreal: Montreal Jewish Publication Society, 2001).

Posner, Michael, ed. *The Last Honest Man: Mordecai Richler: An Oral Biography* (Toronto: McClelland & Stewart, 2005).

"September 1, 1939," © 1940 & renewed 1968 by W.H. Auden, from COLLECTED POEMS OF W.H. AUDEN. Used by permission of Random House, Inc.

SELECTED INDEX

Note to the reader: Throughout this index the abbreviation F is used to signify Florence Richler and the abbreviation M is used to signify Mordecai Richler.

CHARLES FORAN is the author of eight previous books, including the novels *Carolan's Farewell* and *House on Fire*, and the award-winning non-fiction work *The Last House of Ulster*. Born and raised in Toronto, he holds degrees from the University of Toronto and University College Dublin, and has taught at universities in China, Hong Kong and Canada. A former resident of Montreal, where he was a columnist for the Montreal *Gazette* and reported on Quebec for *Saturday Night* magazine, he currently resides with his family in Peterborough, Ontario. Of his most recent book, the essay collection *Join the Revolution, Comrade*, one critic wrote: "Foran takes seriously his role as a writer who's alert and engaged with the world" (*Quill & Quire*). He has made documentaries for CBC Radio and is a contributing reviewer for the *Globe and Mail*. Visit his website: www.charlesforan.com.

ABOUT THE TYPE

The Richler typeface was commissioned in memory of Mordecai Richler and created by Canadian type designer Nick Shinn. It is an original face, full of personality in the details, yet smooth in the composite effect. Up close, each letter is a study in thematic style, with a subtle, firmly crafted, slightly offbeat quality that mocks both artful pretension and mindless conformity.

Richler is an open, evenly spaced book face designed for sustained reading at text size, in the mass. At display size—for titling and signage—it is animated by fine details, which are derived from the seminal influence of the broad pen on the classic types.

Taking its cue from the ingenious postmodern tour de force that is *Barney's Version*, the Richler typeface fuses present-day structure with traditional skill: its metrics (especially the mechanical rhythm of vertical strokes) are derived from the "technical" sans serifs that are the dominant trend in contemporary typography.